POLES AND JEWS

A Call for Myth Reconstruction

Jews of Poland

Series Editor
Antony Polonsky (Brandeis University)

Other Titles in this Series

Bolesław Prus and the Jews
Agnieszka Friedrich
Translated by Ben Koschalka

Palestine for the Third Time
Ksawery Pruszyński
Translated and with an introduction by Wiesiek Powaga

Blooming Spaces: The Collected Poetry, Prose, Critical Writing, and Letters of Debora Vogel
Debora Vogel
Edited by Anastasiya Lyubas

Macht Arbeit Frei?: German Economic Policy and Forced Labor of Jews in the General Government, 1939–1943
Witold W. Medykowski

New Directions in the History of the Jews in the Polish Lands
Edited by Antony Polonsky, Hanna Węgrzynek and Andrzej Żbikowski

Warsaw is My Country: The Story of Krystyna Bierzynska, 1928–1945
Beth Holmgren

For the Good of the Nation: Institutions for Jewish Children in Interwar Poland. A Documentary History
Edited and Translated by Sean Martin

POLES AND JEWS
A Call for Myth Reconstruction

Jennifer Stark-Blumenthal

ACADEMIC STUDIES PRESS
BOSTON
2025

Library of Congress Cataloging-in-Publication Data

Names: Stark-Blumenthal, Jennifer, 1965- author.
Title: Poles and Jews: a call for myth reconstruction / Jennifer Stark-Blumenthal.
Description: Boston: Academic Studies Press, 2024. | Series: Jews of Poland | Includes bibliographical references and index.
Identifiers: LCCN 2023048244 (print) | LCCN 2023048245 (ebook) | ISBN 9798887194097 (hardback) | ISBN 9798887194103 (adobe pdf) | ISBN 9798887194110 (epub)
Subjects: LCSH: Jews--Poland--History. | Jews--United States--Attitudes. | Polish people--Public opinion. | Antisemitism--Poland--History. | Poland--Ethnic relations.
Classification: LCC DS134.53 .S73 2024 (print) | LCC DS134.53 (ebook) | DDC 943.8/004924--dc23/eng/20231206
LC record available at https://lccn.loc.gov/2023048244
LC ebook record available at https://lccn.loc.gov/2023048245

Copyright © Academic Studies Press, 2024

ISBN 9798887194097 (hardback)
ISBN 9798897830657 (paperback)
ISBN 9798887194103 (adobe pdf)
ISBN 9798887194110 (epub)

Book design by PHi Business Solutions
Cover design by Ivan Grave
On the cover: "Sunflowers" by Kaja Maliszkiewicz, courtesy of the author.

Published by Academic Studies Press
1007 Chestnut Street
Newton, MA 02464

press@academicstudiespress.com
www.academicstudiespress.com

Contents

Acknowledgments	viii
List of Abbreviations	xi
Introduction	xiii
1. Myth and Reconstruction	1
2. Polish Feudalism and Its Middleman Minority	25
3. Tolerance and Resentment	46
4. Reform and Tradition	61
5. The 1830 Uprising and Its Consequences	82
6. Fraternity and Skepticism	98
7. Modernity and Fear	114
8. Migration and Nationalism	141
9. Destruction and Rebirth	169
10. Offense and Defense	198
11. Instability and Identity	224
12. Instability and Violence	256
13. Genocide and the Poles	272
14. Genocide and the Jews	315
15. Communism and the Jews	356
16. Party Strife and Anti-*Zionism*	399
17. Solidarity and the Church	423
18. Jewish Self-Discovery and Community Building	450
19. Myth and Its Reconstruction	477
20. Myth Reconstruction and the Backlash in Poland	507
21. Shifting Perspectives	537
Conclusion	551
Bibliography	565
Maps	589
Index	599

To my husband, Jeff
For initiating the conversation and supporting me in maintaining it,

To our friends, Kaja, Julia, and Magda
For responding and participating,

And to our children, Daniel, Jonah, and Lilly,
For taking this journey with all of us.

Acknowledgments

I could never have completed this project without the pivotal help provided by numerous individuals during the interview, research, and writing phases. My dear friends Julia and Kaja Maliszkiewicz, and Magda Olczak-Lipska not only organized our family's 2005 visit to Poland but also housed me in 2007 and accompanied me on interviews to film and translate. I could not have managed that latter trip without their devoted help. Beata and Przemek Maliszkiewicz welcomed my family to their home in 2005 and introduced us to Jewish Poland. My conversations with them are part of the foundation of this book.

Deborah Lipstadt kindly met with me to discuss methodology, noting the importance of being present in the same space with interviewees. By following that advice, I connected interpersonally with the interviewee, who in turn introduced me to more people to interview. For example, Beata Maliszkiewicz introduced me to her friend Barbara Weigl, who in turn connected me with Anna Lanota, a former activist in the Warsaw Ghetto. Maria Eleonora Olczak, who hosted us in 2005, introduced me to Michał Samet and Michał Rucki, Jewish communal leaders in Gdańsk. In preparation for my first interview trip, Guy Billauer, from the American Jewish Committee, introduced me to numerous Jews and Christians involved in restoring Jewish memory and rebuilding Jewish life in Poland. Jacek Olejnik acquainted me with those Poles then building the Polin Museum of the History of Polish Jews as well as graduate students engrossed in Jewish history and culture. Danuta, Ewa, and Henryk Reinert hosted me for a lovely evening while Marek, Ludmiła, and Emil Jeżowski and Józefina Wardanga invited me to dinner during both research trips, sharing their thoughts for hours. David and Marylou Bush provided a warm home during a research trip in New York City.

While I learned a tremendous amount from texts, meeting face-to-face with interviewees was the highlight of this project. I will remain forever grateful to the following people who gave of their time and trusted me with their thoughts: Polish Jewish community leaders Konstanty Gebert, Stanisław Krajewski, Rabbi Michael Schudrich, Rabbi Maciej Pawlak, Rabbi Yitzhak Rappaport, Rabbi Burt Shuman, Gosia Szymańska, Jan Gebert, Marek Jeżowski, Emil Jeżowski, Józefina and Adam Wardanga, Adam Szic, Tadeusz Woleński, Krzysztof Izdebski, and Joe Smoczyński; Polish Jewish students Jan Kirschenbaum, Alec Matuszewski,

Adam Mozdzyński, and Leon and Sarah Mazur; non-Jewish Polish allies of Jews, Jacek Olejnik, Ambassador Maciej Kozlowski, Robert Szuchta, Andrzej Folwarczny, Stanisław Obirek, Anna Szic, and Sebastian Rejak; American and Polish, Jewish and non-Jewish academicians Antony Polonsky, Krystyna Person, Marcin Wodziński, Annamaria Orla-Bukowska, Joanna Fikus, Zygmunt Stępiński, Kamila Dąbrowska, and Artur Markowski; Polish Christian lay people Krystyna Krupska-Wysocka, Beata Maliszkiewicz, Barbara Weigl, Przemek Maliszkiewicz, Michał Lorenc, Julia Maliszkiewicz, Kaja Maliszkiewicz, Magda Olczak, Bartek Olczak, Maria Eleonora Olczak, Martha Pech, Ewa, Henryk and Danuta Reinert; Warsaw Ghetto activist Anna Lanota and survivor Rubin Shafran; American Jewish leaders of and participants on trips to Poland Rabbi David Steinhardt, Leora Tec, Bernard Weiss, Yuval Caspi, Daniela Friedman, and Sam Durham.

Textual research and writing were formidable challenges. Dr. Jerry Legge, then history professor at the University of Georgia, was my first reader and an important source of encouragement. Antony Polonsky, who I met with several years after beginning this venture, not only showed interest in this project, but provided years of steady and patient guidance. He has always been quick to answer questions, share sources, and read drafts. He has altered my life and I remain indebted to him for his kindness. He opened doors, introducing me to numerous scholars in the field, who in turn, have provided help with understanding the past. Theodore Weeks, Glenn Dynner, and Artur Markowski answered questions, while Jerzy Tomaszewski and Marcin Wodziński also read early chapter drafts and directed me to additional source material.

Bonnie Wallace offered advice and constant support, helping me to find the courage I needed to meet this taxing endeavor. Sarah Swartz edited very early chapter drafts. Janice Harper not only helped me find my voice and tone, but also discussed important concepts with me. I would not have had the wherewithal to complete this project to the best of my abilities without her critical guidance.

Alessandra Ansani and Kira Nemirowsky at Academic Studies Press patiently walked me through the various phases of the publishing process. Kira also gained permissions for maps, which had proven beyond my grasp. As a copy editor, Stuart Allan worked through this beast of a project, sorting out numerous grammatical questions, and making sense of my footnotes. Eljas Koski organized the index, with sharp, detailed attention.

Leora Tec and Jurek Lubiński kindly and meticulously edited the spelling of Polish names and places.

Several friends have supported this endeavor. Lou Feldstein often sent me articles dealing with Poland; Amy Kaplan and Laura Levine, showed immense interest in each teeny, tiny step forward during a two decade period.

I am grateful to my parents' Arthur and Andrea Stark for helping Jeff with our young children when I took my first interview trip. They and my mother-in-law Sandra Schuster have been a great source of encouragement.

My children Daniel, Jonah, and Lilly, have grown up alongside this project. Their belief that I could complete it helped get me to the finish line. While Jonah and Lilly also transcribed many interviews (Daniel offered, but I knew he did not have the time), Julia, Ariel, and Himay's enthusiasm added fuel to this team.

I am most grateful to have been blessed with a partner who has been by my side throughout this journey. This book would not have come to fruition without Jeff's consistent intellectual, emotional, and financial support. Jeff urged me on, believing I could push through the hundreds of hurdles to realize my dream. Thank you Jeff for seeing that I could succeed.

While so many have helped move this project forward, in the end I am responsible for my perspectives culled from interviews, documents, and texts. Any mistakes found herein remain mine alone.

Jennifer Stark-Blumenthal
Atlanta, Georgia

List of Abbreviations

AJC	American Jewish Committee
AL	People's Army – Armia Ludowa
AK	Home Army – Armia Krajowa
Bezpieca	Ministry of Public Security
	Ministerstwo Bezpieczeństwa Publicznego
	Also known as MB and MBP
CKŻP	Central Committee of Jews in Poland
	Centralny Komitet Żydów w Polsce
FOP	Front for the Rebirth of Poland – Front Odrodzenia Polski
JEC	Joint Emergency Committee on European Jewish Affairs
JOINT	American Jewish Joint Distribution Committee
KOR	Workers' Defense Committee – Komitet Obrony Robotników
KRN	National Council of the Homeland – Krajowa Rada Narodowa
MB	Ministry of Public Security
MBP	Ministerstwo Bezpieczeństwa Publicznego
	Also known as Bezpieka
MKS	Interfactory Strike Committee
	Międzyzakladowy Komitet Strajkowy
MOL	March of the Living
MSW	Ministry of Security Matters
	Ministerstwo Spraw Wewnętrznych
NKVD	Soviet Security Service/Soviet Secret Police
NOWA	Independent Publishing House – Niezależna Oficyna Wydawnicza
NSZ	National Armed Forces – Narodowe Siły Zbrojne
OZN	Camp of National Unity – Obóz Zjednoczenia Narodowego
PKWN	Polish Committee of National Liberation
	Polski Komitet Wyzwolenia Narodowego
PO	Civic Platform – Platforma Obywatelska
POP	Basic Party Organization – Podstawowa Organizacja Partyjna
PiS	Law and Justice – Prawo i Sprawiedliwość
PPR	Polish Workers' Party – Polska Partia Robotnicza
PPS	Polish Socialist Party – Polska Partia Socjalistyczna
PRL	Polish People's Republic – Polska Rzeczpospolita Ludowa

PSL	Polish Peasant Party – Polskie Stronnictwo Ludowe
PZPR	Polish United Workers' Party – Polska Zjednoczona Partia Robotnicza
SB	Security Service – Służba Bezpieczeństwa
SLD	Democratic Left Union – Sojusz Lewicy Demokratycznej
TRJN	Provisional Government of National Unity Tymczasowy Rząd Jedności Narodowej
TSKŻ	Jewish Social and Cultural Association Towarzystwo Społeczno-Kulturalne Żydów w Polsce
WiN	Freedom and Independence Association Zrzeszenie Wolnośc i Niezawisłość
ZBoWiD	Union of Fighters for Freedom and Democracy Związek Bojowników o Wolnośc i Demokrację
ZOOM	All-Poland Jewish Youth Organization Żydowska Ogólnopolska Organizacja Młodzieżowa
ŻUL	Jewish Flying University – Żydowski Uniwersytet Latający

A Note on Place Names

Name changes of geographical locations, such as cities and towns, breed confusion for readers investigating the past. Those writing about Central and Eastern Europe, need be cognizant of such tumult wrought by shifting borders and corresponding language replacements. In this text, for any place names which have widely accepted English forms, I have used them. Thus, Warsaw, not Warszawa; Vilna, not Vilnius or Wilno, though Wilno is oft designated on official maps. However, in keeping with modern convention, I employ Kraków, not Cracow. A particularly difficult case arises with the Galician city that boasts four variants: the Polish Lwów, the German Lemberg, the Russian Lvov, and the Ukrainian Lviv. Here, I employ Lviv, though Lwów is shown on the maps if official at the time.

Introduction

Until 2004, I viewed myself as an open-minded, progressive person who refrained from stereotyping groups of people. I based any negative views of people on knowledge that I believed was rooted in *history*. That summer, however, I learned that discrimination had actually played a fundamental role throughout my life: I realized that I had been raised to view Poles as an enemy, not only by parents and grandparents, but also by rabbis and teachers. Postgraduate work in Jewish studies had not altered this prejudice, but only cemented it. That year, I stood on an intellectual precipice. Do I hold true to what I *know*, or do I risk questioning that knowledge and destabilizing parts of my identity?

Our current times underscore the need for the personal re-examination of one's knowledge of the Other. The global rise in ethno-nationalism and authoritarianism, COVID-19, and the unprovoked Russian invasion of Ukraine force us to question why we maintain hostile views of the Other. Concerning Poles and Jews specifically, our current global crises have only solidified the need for Poles and Jews to reevaluate the knowledge each holds of Other and Self.

An American Jew

A Jewish woman, I am third generation American-born. My ancestors hail from the Russian Empire. My mother's family arrived from Kyiv, now Ukraine's capital. My paternal great-grandparents traveled here from Poswol (Pasvalys), Lithuania. After landing on American shores, both sides maintained ties to the Old World through language, religious practice, family, and culture. Yet, concurrently, they each strove to become American. While they conversed in Yiddish at home, *most* learned enough English to speak it in public. They sent their children to public schools dressed in modern American clothes and considered religion a private matter.

I was raised primarily in the south suburbs of Chicago as a Conservative Jew. My identity meant that I felt superior around Reform Jews and insecure around Orthodox Jews. No doubt this singular internal response to the Other Jew mirrored the contentious antagonism felt across the American Jewish population in general. American Jews argued over ritual, politics, and assimilation. Our one central unifying force was the Holocaust—the Jewish genocide orchestrated by Nazi Germany during World War II.

My Jewish identity was stamped by growing up in the seventies, that time when formal Jewish educators, parents, and grandparents finally struggled more openly with the Holocaust.[1] Together with so many Jews of my generation, I am a product of post-Holocaust angst. Many teachers presented "being Jewish" through the lens of that tragedy. The lessons they taught often differed, but the starting place usually remained the same. My Jewish identity transformed into knowing that had I been there, I too would have been forced to bear the weight of the yellow star. For me, to be Jewish was to identify with the Holocaust's victims, to feel their suffering as my own.

Many in my generation grew to make decisions about religious and cultural affiliation based on this premise. Photographs of starving children on ghetto streets and mounds of corpses in camps urged us on a quest for Jewish survival. This knowledge and imagery united us as Jews and often informed our relationships. My future husband and I bonded over our shared desire to travel to Poland. Though we thought of it as desolate and cold, we longed to visit that place. We wanted to feel the past, to walk the streets of our ancestors, to imagine their heartache as they were torn from their homes, to envision their daily struggle for survival in the "Polish death camps."[2] We craved a journey to Poland so that we could effectively mourn our people's history. We both thought of this as the ultimate experience of our Jewish identity. We would journey into death to confirm that we were alive. We would raise up the past to ground the future.

---

1 The American Jewish community and general American populace did not know how to speak about the Holocaust in the immediate postwar years. In 1961, Israel televised the trial of Adolf Eichmann and brought in Holocaust survivors to give testimony. This public forum encouraged survivors worldwide to discuss their own experiences and permitted people to wrestle with the Holocaust as a reality. See Michael Rothberg, *Multidirectional Memory: Remembering the Holocaust in the Age of Decolonization* (Stanford: Stanford University Press, 2009), 176.

2 I want to make it clear that the Nazi death camps were not "Polish camps." Too often people refer to Nazi death camps as "Polish" due to their location within Poland's geographical borders. As I will discuss later, this mistake has had grave ramifications.

Camp Barney Medintz, 2004

Fast-forward twenty years: Jeff and I are married and have three children. Working to create a rich Jewish family life, we welcomed Jewish summer camp into our children's experience. In 2004, I accompanied Jeff to Camp Barney Medintz, located in northern Georgia, where he had volunteered as the physician for a week. One late afternoon, Jeff noticed three young women sitting at a picnic table, all wearing white aprons and bandanas covering their hair. Clearly, they were kitchen staff. Often isolated from the rest of camp culture, kitchen workers usually existed on the lowest rung of the camp's social ladder. Others in camp had a propensity to ignore them. I am most grateful that on this evening Jeff did not. Rather, hearing them speak in Polish, his curiosity compelled him to introduce himself.

Much to Jeff's surprise, he learned that these three young women were classical musicians on summer break from their respective universities in Poland. They were working at Camp Barney to earn tuition for the following semester. With an invitation to hear their music, that evening we began a journey into an impactful friendship. Deeply kind and respectful, they were at that incredible point of launching their lives, determining who they would become. After training in classical music for more than a decade, all three were pursuing other educational endeavors. Kaja was completing her fine arts degree, while Magda planned for law school. Kaja's sister, Julia, was studying performing arts in Denmark. Unlike most overseas staff who planned on traveling after camp ended, these young women hoped to find jobs and an affordable apartment in Atlanta. We offered them our guest room, refrigerator, and help in finding work.

Interestingly, until our last day at camp, both Jeff and I naively assumed that our new friends were Jewish. How odd it was, though, for us to believe that these women were Jewish given that we believed simultaneously (and erroneously) that no Jews currently lived in Poland, that "land of destruction." Apparently, we had preferred such cognitive dissonance rather than accepting that Christian Poles would be willing to work at a Jewish camp, let alone serve Jewish children. For according to everything we had heard in our own community, *all* Christian Poles were antisemites.

Once we realized our mistaken assumption, panic set in: How should we respond to their Polish Catholic origins? Do we close the door out of fear, and thereby relinquish a possible friendship? And what exactly did we fear? Certainly, they already knew of our Jewish identity. They were willing to trust us. Why could we not trust them? Emotion had jerked us into the past and hurled menacing questions at us. How did their relatives treat Jews during the war? What might their grandparents have done to "ours?" Are the "sins of the fathers" passed down to their children? Thankfully, reason reemerged and steadied our course. It forced us to remember their music and our meaningful conversations, and to see these three Polish women as individuals. It allowed us to open our door and home to them. While we had successfully disassociated our new friends from the stereotypes we held of their people, the more profound challenge would be to wrestle precisely with that deeply rooted negative perception of Poles as a whole.

Atlanta, Georgia

Nearly every evening after dinner, we four women—three emotionally charged by their twenties, one bracing for middle age—gathered around the table to delve into the personal: boyfriends, fiancé, husband, family, and the future. However, we cautiously evaded the taboo subject of Polish-Jewish relations. To protect our burgeoning friendship, we all avoided that area which threatened it most: perceptions of the past. And yet, resonating from beneath our guises was the sense that if we did not deal with these difficult matters sooner or later, then we would miss our unique opportunity to truly understand each other and ourselves.

In the third week of their stay, the subject of Polish-Jewish relations during World War II came up, and even then it was only in an isolated private conversation initiated courageously by Julia, then just eighteen. Standing in my narrow kitchen galley, both of us leaning against opposite counters for support, Julia bravely raised the topic of the stereotypes many Americans harbor about Polish people. She had been taught to regard Poles as fiercely brave, heroic in battle, and intensely patriotic; she saw her country as one filled with cultural and intellectual dynamism. Having to confront the American stereotype of the "ignorant, lazy, low-class Pole" shocked her. She had heard about this attitude; but experiencing it raised a visceral reaction. This anti-Polish bigotry was what I knew so well. In this moment of truth, I trembled from fear and embarrassment. I acknowledged our cruel generalizations about her people and the pain Poles feel from it. Haltingly, we then moved on to the belief among American Jews that most Poles were complicit in Hitler's destruction of European Jewry. And me? Well, though I tried to hide it from her, I was one of those American Jews, riding the bandwagon of blame and learned hatred.

Although Julia alone engaged with me over some of this harsh terrain, I knew that a barrier had been broken for all of us. It did not take long before the five of us, including Jeff, were able to discuss their families' histories during the war, as well as their views on the status of Jews in contemporary Poland. In the evening's calm, I first learned of their great-aunt who had hidden a three-year-old Jewish girl during the war, of their uncle's Jewish roots, and of a nation's youth awakening to the richness Jews had once brought to Polish culture. They claimed that many young Poles hungered for a connection to a Jewish heritage, grabbing at any shred of evidence they might have Jewish ancestors. According to Kaja, to testify to one's Jewish roots had become quite fashionable in 2004 Warsaw.

Listening to my new friends, I could not stave off my inner cynicism: *This can't be—they must be making up these stories to retain our confidence and friendship.* I could take everything else at face value. But I simply could not accept on hearsay that Poles were saviors of Jews during the Holocaust and that young Poles longed for Jewish roots! While I shared how odd it was for me to hear this information, I kept my deeper disbelief guarded.

Poland, 2005

It would not take long to discover the veracity of our new friends' stories. Thankful that we had welcomed their children into our home and taken care of them, Kaja and Julia's parents invited us to be their guests in Poland. Not only would we stay in their home, but their father, Przemek, insisted on being our tour guide for a full week. Having spoken of visiting Poland since we first dated, Jeff and I jumped at this opportunity. In March 2005, only seven months since our Polish friends' stay in Atlanta, we embarked on a once-in-a-lifetime opportunity to understand the Other. Would I be faced with a different reality in Poland than I had been taught? This trip would help me to ascertain whether these three women had acted as renegades by working at a Jewish summer camp or were typical young Poles.

Our friends took it upon themselves to arrange our itinerary. Neither Jeff nor I made many requests concerning our agenda, aside from visiting his grandfather's hometown of Gdańsk and the usual Holocaust tourist destinations, including the Warsaw Ghetto, Kazimierz, and Auschwitz. Kaja asked if we might be interested in attending Shabbat services. Yes, *if there really is a service to attend.* Would we want to have Shabbat dinner with the congregation? Yes, *if a congregation truly does exist.* Jews live in Poland today, they insisted. Well, I would see it with my own eyes.

Having arrived in Poland on a Friday afternoon, we readied for a Shabbat service. After twenty minutes of European road negotiations,[3] we found ourselves at the curb of Jewish alternative life in suburban Warsaw: Beit Warszawa. Formed officially in 1995 as a liberal alternative to the Orthodox Nożyk Synagogue, Beit Warszawa expanded in 1999 into a Jewish cultural association. In this new synagogue, more than seventy-five Jews had gathered for a lecture, Friday evening services, and Shabbat dinner! My jaw dropped. In Poland Jews were forming a new community—praying, learning, and celebrating Jewish life together. This revelation confounded me. My friends had been correct. What other truths of theirs were factual? How, I wondered, would this discovery affect my self-understanding?

Meeting Kaja's and Julia's father for the first time reinforced this sweltering conflict. Przemek presented a very different image of Poland than that with which I was raised. Given our short stay, I knew we did not have time to tiptoe around taboo subjects. If I wanted answers, I would have to be direct and ask the questions. Bracing myself, I asked him about relations between Poles and Jews. This then forty-nine-year-old university-educated Catholic Pole declared unequivocally that there had never been antisemitism in Poland!

Based on my own knowledge, such a position was unfathomable. It screamed of political revisionism. Holding my anger at bay, we continued our dialogue. Przemek did recognize that there had been tensions between Poles and Jews during the interwar period, 1918 to 1939. However, couching said conflict within an economic framework allowed him to dismiss antisemitism as the central factor dividing Poles and Jews.

I challenged his position that antisemitism did not exist in Poland, by raising what I recognized as an observable contradiction: "What about the 'Polish' death camps?" A kind and gentle man, Przemek's expression morphed into anger, frustration, and pain. He made it quite clear that Poles neither designed nor operated Auschwitz. He underscored that 250,000 Poles were killed in *that* Nazi death camp. (Current research puts the number of Poles killed in Auschwitz at roughly seventy-five thousand. But the point remains the same.)[4] Indeed, the Nazis first imprisoned Polish intellectuals at Auschwitz. These were Nazi death camps in which Poles, too, suffered and died. Ashamed to admit it,

---

3   Given that neither Kaja nor Magda owned a car, and that public transportation eats away at time, our friends involved their and their parents' friends in driving us.

4   Jonathan Webber, "Personal Reflections on Auschwitz Today," in *Auschwitz: A History in Photographs*, comp. and ed. Teresa Świebocka (Oświęcim: The Auschwitz-Birkenau State Museum, 2004), 287.

before this day I had not been concerned with or aware of what happened to the Poles when the Nazis stormed across their borders. I had been consumed only with my own people's tragedy and torment. The phrase "Polish death camps" outraged my Polish friend because it signified my misunderstandings of World War II and the Holocaust. It equated Poles with Nazis in the oppression of Jews while simultaneously denying the Poles' own victimization.

I left Poland muddled by new perspectives. Przemek's viewpoint on Polish antisemitism deeply disturbed me in that it challenged my understanding of basic Jewish *knowledge*. I was stunned by his stated truth, so convincingly did he present it. I had already been proven wrong about Jewish life in contemporary Poland. Could I be wrong also about Jewish life in Poland's past? Wrenching questions tormented me: (1) Why is my truth so different from his? (2) Is there something in his truth I need to learn and incorporate into my own? (3) Could my truth be partially constructed out of falsehoods and misrepresentations? So began a steady questioning of the education I had received at home, at my Conservative Hebrew school, in college classes, and graduate school, as well as through books and films. What struck me is that while at Brandeis as a Near Eastern and Judaic studies major with a concentration in Holocaust studies and later at the Jewish Theological Seminary, I had not heard Przemek's understanding expressed. Was I listening to the wrong people? Was I reading the wrong books, or subconsciously willfully ignoring part of their messages? My internalized truth wrestled with that presented by my Polish friends. The question for me quickly became: "Who is right?"

Poland, 2007 and 2019

To further grasp modern relations between Poles and Jews, I revisited Poland for two weeks in November 2007. Hosted by Kaja, Julia, Magda, Beata, and Przemek, I interviewed roughly forty individuals engaged in the rebirth of Poland's Jewish communities. There I met with government officials, Jewish religious leaders, and former priests. I spoke with well-known Jewish community representatives. I listened to Polish graduate students engaged with Jewish history, Polish and Jewish educators, Poles working on developing the new POLIN Museum of the History of Polish Jews, Jewish university student leaders, participants in Christian-Jewish dialogue, as well as Poles who had recently discovered their family's hidden Jewish roots. Among those I interviewed were Polish Christians working to support the Jewish community, which was then in self-discovery mode. This short, intense period further opened my eyes. I observed

Christian and Jewish Poles working together to foster greater understanding of both Judaism and the role Jews played in Polish history. I also witnessed their mutual support in reestablishing Jewish communities, especially in larger cities such as Warsaw and Kraków. This whole experience—from Camp Barney's worn footpaths to Poland's cobblestoned streets—informed my desire to write this book.

Over the course of time this book has changed. I began in 2007 with the narrow goal of raising American Jews' broader understanding of Poland, its people, and its renewed positive relationship with the Jewish past and present. I sought to bring context to different historical situations that occurred prior to the twentieth century, that period through which American Jews typecast the Polish past. In so doing, I hoped to help American Jews discard the readily grasped anti-Polish stereotypes that linger at our lips. While that vision remains a grounding principle of this book, I realized the need to broaden my approach.

Poles are not a monolith. With time, a more traditional Polish perspective has asserted greater control in politics and popular thinking, outpacing the liberal Polish agenda I first encountered in 2005. As often happens when cultures experience dramatic change, a backlash ensued. Traditionalists have assaulted the liberal Polish awakening due to fears of losing cultural control and political power. Traditionalists have made a power grab by reasserting their view of Polish patriotism.

Traditionally, Poles have fashioned Polish patriotism into a belief that all Poles are good and heroic. Concurrently, Polish patriotism identifies with the pain of Poland's particular past by embracing the role of most victimized nation. In its post-World War II communist incarnation, after roughly six million Jews were murdered, the Polish nationalist leadership maintained this most victimized image by ignoring the Jews' specific tragedy.

This neat understanding of Self would fall into question when the post-1989 Third Polish Republic welcomed in an era of change—openness to liberal Western cultural, political, and educational influences. Now Poles not only had to deal with Western acknowledgment and commemoration of the Jewish genocide, but in 2000 Jan Gross would force them to question Polish participation in the Jews' demise. In his book *Neighbors*, Gross details the Polish Christian murder of Jews in Jedwabne. As such, he damaged the Pole's proud self-image of resistance to the Nazis. To the country's credit, an open debate took place in Poland. It spawned numerous and consequential academic investigations into the Polish victimization of Jews during World War II. This ability of the Poles to look honestly at their past is an important part of the story that I present here.

The 2003 opening of the Polish Center for Holocaust Research (Centrum Badań nad Zagładą Żydów) is an outgrowth of this open debate. The center's agenda is to "contribute to the fight against prejudice, xenophobia and anti-Semitism, and to aid in the creation of an open society."[5] To build an open society necessitates peering into the dark past to discover uncomfortable truths. The center has waded into the muddy terrain with a specific focus on Polish attitudes and behavior towards the Jews during the Holocaust. Delving into previously untapped Polish archives, its members have opened inquiries into neglected topics, such as Polish and Jewish collaboration with the Nazis, Polish blackmail of Jews, Polish denouncers of Poles who aided Jews, as well as the role of the Polish "Blue" Police in the murder of the Jews.

In particular, researchers at the center have examined the Polish response in the provinces to Jewish refugees during the last phase of the Holocaust, that period after the German's final liquidation of the ghettos. In these smaller towns, ghettos were porous, and Jews were able to escape them. One historian, Andrzej Żbikowski, estimates that roughly three hundred thousand Jews escaped into the countryside during the final liquidation period.[6] Though perhaps too high of a figure, the center's question remains: How did Poles receive these Jewish refugees? Their research has uncovered that less than fifty thousand of those Jews seeking shelter survived. This low survival rate was due to a conflagration of animus and fear. Prewar relations between Poles and Jews in parts of the provinces had not been close. This lack of connection infused with Polish localized nationalist politics carried over to the wartime era. Researchers discovered that local Poles participated in the Nazi's hunt for the Jews and many betrayed fellow Christian Poles who helped these runaway Jews. Additionally, the center has questioned the heroism of some units within the Polish Home Army, which it revealed had also murdered Jews escaping the Nazis. Their research sheds light on the dark past, light which the current nationalist government endeavors to block.

Through its research, publications, seminars, and its Warsaw Ghetto data base that has cataloged and translated previously unknown documents, the Polish Center for Holocaust Research has greatly impacted the debate over

---

5 Polish Center for Holocaust Research, accessed May 3, 2021, https://www.holocaust research.pl.
6 Author's email correspondence with Antony Polonsky, who suggests that the estimated number of three hundred thousand Jewish escapees is probably too high.

Polish identity. It underscores the contradiction between the accepted national narrative of Polish aid to the Jews with documentation of Poles' victimization of Jews. Its members have continued to ask who the Poles were vis-à-vis the Jews. The center's members have expanded the singular shock of Jedwabne by revealing its repetition throughout locales in the broader region, as well as by expounding on various iterations of Polish antisemitism. That the center has deepened the public debate and continuously challenges the easy image of the good heroic Pole angers those who believe, need, and cling to that positive cultural cliché.

Changing Times: The Ethno-Nationalist Backlash

The fallout from Jedwabne and the center's later revelations left a large segment of Poles deflated. They were ripe to receive a glowing version of past Polish heroism and a renewed commemoration to Polish victimization. Conservative nationalist politicians latched onto this culture clash by nurturing the fear that once again Poles are under attack, this time through character defamation. Polish traditionalists reasserted their prideful self-image. They have elevated historians who offer apologetic perspectives to counter self-critical Polish historians regarding two central themes: the Poles' betrayal of and violence against Jews during World War II; and the number and motivation of those Poles who risked their lives to rescue Jews. This battle for the memory of the Polish past has widened the initial Jedwabne polarization. Concurrently, with its renewed cultural and political power, right-wing Polish nationalists have resolved to stifle, stall, and silence Other voices that portray Poles in a negative light, especially during World War II and the Holocaust. Thus, they passed the so-called "Holocaust Law" which the right-wing recently invoked to bring libel charges against two historians from the Polish Center for Holocaust Research, Barbara Engelking and Jan Grabowski.

While Polish nationalism has fed off the fury and fear that traditionalists raised in response to the Jedwabne fall from grace, there is no doubt that it is part of the global resurgence of nationalism and populism that has gained ground by stoking people's anger and fear concerning economic downturns, security threats, and loss of sovereignty. In Britain, it birthed Brexit, the UK's break from the European Union. In North America, it placed Donald Trump in the White House and permitted his cult of personality to launch an insurrection after his 2021 election loss. In Israel, under Bibi Netanyahu, it sidelined peace talks with the Palestinians and championed the annexation of settlements.⁷ Poland's current nationalist iteration is part of this global phenomenon.

Due to this grand shift, a fundamental change in the conversation about majority-minority relations has occurred globally, with glowing affirmations describing the majority. American nationalists willfully ignore the government's former and current mistreatment of Black and Brown people. Polish ethnonationalists willfully ignore or misrepresent current research in order to portray an exaggerated and distorted positive image of Polish-Jewish relations during World War II. To unite their respective political bases, campaigns in both countries have emphasized fear of incursion by brown refugees, whether from South America or Syria. As in the US and other countries, Poland's population has become deeply polarized over its nationalist and populist direction.

Changing Times: The Russian Invasion of Ukraine

On February 24, 2022, Vladimir Putin imposed a new world era when, without provocation, he ordered Russian troops to invade neighboring Ukraine. In that moment, he forced the world to confront the consequences of surging authoritarianism. In this stark and explosive struggle between Ukraine's developing democracy and Putin's entrenched despotism, Putin has waged an assault not only on that land and its people, but also by proxy on the West and its democratic values. Europe has not experienced this great a physical and political threat since World War II. Ukraine's young democracy had threatened Putin's plan to restore Russian influence on former Soviet bloc nations—Ukraine, Poland, Romania, Bulgaria, and other countries. Historian Yohanan Petrovsky-Shtern has warned that,

> Ukrainians today, of different origins and of different ethnicities, are defending your and my values. That is, they are defending the democratic world. That is something that we have to understand. The failure of Ukraine will be the failure of all of us. The failure of the European Union. The failure of the United Nations.⁸

---

7 Steve Hendrix, "As Israel's Longest-Serving Leader, Netanyahu Transformed His Country—and Left It More Divided Than Ever," *Washington Post*, June 12, 2021, https://www.washingtonpost.com/world/middle_east/israel-prime-minister-benjamin-netanyahu-legacy/2021/06/13/aa9b2d7e-c9e8-11eb-8708-64991f2acf28_story.html.

8 Nachi Weinstein, "With Yohanan Petrovsky-Shtern Discussing Russia's War Against Ukraine: The Stakes for the Jews," Seforimchatter, season 3, episode 37, MP3 audio, 45:01, February 27, 2022, https://seforimchatter.buzzsprout.com/1218638/10149479.

Through his scorched earth tactics, Putin projects what he is willing to do to enlarge his sphere of influence while becoming Russia's twenty-first-century Peter the Great.

Putin has courted widespread condemnation due to his disregard for international law and his barbaric destruction of Ukrainian civilians, whether in homes, hospitals, or hideouts. In their response, NATO allies have been straddling a narrow fence. While they have rallied quickly around Ukraine, bringing broad sweeping sanctions against Russia[9] and sending military aid to Volodymyr Zelenskiy's volunteer-bolstered army, NATO remains reluctant to join in the actual battle to save non-NATO Ukraine. Ever wary of Russia's vast nuclear arsenal, NATO seeks to prevent a third world war, which some fear has already begun.

How does this tragedy affect our understanding of Polish-Jewish relations, this book's topic? Responding to the Russian war against Ukraine, Poles have revealed an aspect of the Polish people that many in the West have not seen, whether due to stereotyping or lack of investigation. Compassion. Kindness. Heroism. As of May 7, 2022, more than 5.7 million Ukrainians have fled Putin's brutality. Mostly women and children (as men between eighteen and sixty must remain to defend the country), more than three million have made their way into Poland. Poland's economic growth and its prewar (2022) Ukrainian population of some 16% (due to longstanding patterns of labor migration) attracted refugees to find safety in the neighboring country. Facing its biggest humanitarian crisis since the Second World War, Poland has responded with a wonderfully genuine desire to help. As in Moldova, Romania, Slovakia, and to an extent Hungary, ordinary people have stepped up to offer clothing, medical supplies, warm food, transportation, and even housing. But in Poland the situation is more intense, given the sheer numbers of refugees crossing its borders. After just five weeks into the war, in Warsaw alone the number of Ukrainian refugees exceeded 10% of the city's population of 1.8 million.[10] Indeed, this humanitarian crisis has placed Poland on the frontline of a battle between good and evil, with Poles transforming into heroes before our eyes.

---

9   Norman Eisen, Aaron Klein, Mario Picon, Robin J. Lewis, Lilly Blumenthal, Scott Johnston, and Charlie Loudon, Brookings Sanctions Tracker, March 22, 2022, https://www.brookings.edu/research/the-brookings-sanctions-tracker/.
10 Fernanda Pires, "Poland's welcome of Ukrainian refugees comes with challenges," University of Michigan News, MP3 audio, 3:10, March 14, 2022, https://global.umich.edu/newsroom/polands-welcome-of-ukrainian-refugees-comes-with-challenges/.

Most Polish civil institutions have taken up the task of caring for the refugees. This is striking given the anti-refugee rhetoric in 2014 and 2015 when, as an EU member state, Donald Tusk's center-right Civic Platform (Platforma Obywatelska, PO) agreed to take in several thousand refugees from North Africa and the Middle East. During the election cycle, the right-wing Law and Justice Party (Prawo i Sprawiedliwość, PiS) greatly exaggerated the situation by spreading fear that the refugees would "flood" Poland with alien values and diseases. As a result, PiS ascended to power with 38% of the vote. There is no doubt that race and religion played a key role. There is no doubt that race and religion also played a key role when Poland recently closed its border with Belarus, lest brown Syrian Muslim refugees cross it.[11]

True, these Ukrainian refugees are different. They are mostly white. But this white population is multi-ethnic. Though the majority is Eastern Orthodox, between ninety-five and ninety-eight thousand of the refugees are Catholics, Georgians, Tatars, and Jews. Poles and Ukrainians have a long history. For centuries they inhabited the same land, which at times led to violence and resentment. In 1943 Ukrainian nationalists implemented ethnic cleansing policies, killing Polish inhabitants of Volhynia. They sought to create a "nationally pure space" in Western Ukraine by murdering between fifty thousand to sixty thousand Volhynian Poles. Throughout the duration of World War II, it is estimated that Ukrainian nationalists killed between seventy thousand and one hundred thousand Poles in Western Ukraine.[12] In the twenty-first century, Poles and Ukrainians have worked to restore good relations. Yet the Volhynian massacre "still carries potent political currency in relations between Poland and Ukraine."[13] Thus, that tens of thousands of Poles are working tirelessly to welcome Ukrainian refugees is meaningful. Not only are they demonstrating to the world the heroic side of Poland, which Poles hold dear and American Jews tend to ignore, but they have also demonstrated a desire to move beyond stereotyped generalizations in order to help a victim of a common enemy. For Poles know that Putin's goals do not end with Ukraine.

In response to the rise of authoritarianism in Poland, the global pandemic, and Russia's war on the West, my goals have necessarily transformed. I have augmented my initial focus on American Jews' misperceptions of the Polish past and Polish-Jewish relations with Poles' own misrepresentations of them.

---

11 Ibid.
12 Jared McBride, "Peasants into Perpetrators: The OUN-UPA and the Ethnic Cleansing of Volhynia, 1943–1944," *Slavic Review* 75, no. 3 (Fall 2016): 639.
13 Ibid.: 632.

What I have found is that at times both sides have failed to understand the Other not only because of a lack of knowledge, but also due to a willingness to trample over the Other to elevate the Self. To support my analysis, I provide readers with a synthesis of current research on Polish-Jewish relations coupled with a variety of Polish Christian, Polish Jewish, and American Jewish perspectives gleaned through interviews I conducted in 2007 and 2019. Having finally emerged at the end of this project, I now have a better grasp of Przemek's intense belief in his truth and the missing pieces from my own version. What I posit is a new construction by which to understand this long and complex relationship.

Reassessment and Reconstruction

The process of academic reassessment began in the 1980s when a few scholars stepped outside of their cultural boxes to encounter Polish-Jewish relations anew. Polish activists and intellectuals challenged their communist government's historiography, subjecting commonly held assumptions of the past to detached scholarly inquiry. In response, some Jewish Holocaust historians allowed themselves to open doors to a broader, more complex understanding of World War II. They began to challenge their own positions of contempt for Poland and its people.

Conferences on Polish-Jewish relations convened, with American, European, and Polish attendees. Creating meaningful dialogue, they built new relationships and developed deeper understanding. An early contributor to this process, the Polish scholar Jerzy Tomaszewski, underscored the importance of these meetings: although "[t]he beginnings were difficult . . . my impression was that at least there was a group of Jewish scholars in the USA who were not so different from me and some of my friends in Warsaw."[14]

In 1984, Antony Polonsky organized the First International Conference on Polish-Jewish Studies, held in Oxford, England. Over the years, the conference facilitated the introduction of Jewish history and culture into the curricula of Polish universities. Of more immediate consequence was the formation of two societies created to pursue further research in this area: the Institute for Polish-Jewish Studies in Oxford and its sister organization The American Association for Polish-Jewish Studies. Every year since 1987, these two associations have published a collection of scholarly essays, entitled *Polin: Studies in Polish Jewry*.

---

14 Jerzy Tomaszewski, email correspondence with the author.

Framed around one specific era or theme, each volume includes a plethora of thinkers and approaches.

The 1991 collapse of the Soviet Union permitted a deeper review of the Polish past. Archives previously closed off to foreign inquiry were declassified. Delving into the Soviet-era records, academics reinterpreted important historic events in Polish-Jewish relations. These academic writings have allowed me to reassess my own understanding of accounts of the past and the role that both Jews and Poles played over the centuries. Reading a range of works by well-respected American, British, Polish, Israeli, Christian, and Jewish thinkers in the field confirmed that American Jewry's twentieth-century education missed the mark on these topics. These works have supported not only my questioning of the beliefs mainstream American Ashkenazi Jewry has held sacrosanct, but also my new approach to the Polish people.

In the following pages, I present a different perspective on the relationship of Jews and Poles from the one I was taught. That I discuss a more nuanced approach to Polish-Jewish relations does not preclude me from recognizing antisemitism's role within the Polish collective as well as the downplaying of the Polish Jews' experience in order to elevate the Polish Christian experience. However, even at this present moment of memory confrontation and negation there remain Poles who devote their days to honoring the Jews' presence in Poland. As educator and activist Leora Tec often points out, "That's what happens when you grow up. You can hold two things at the same time that don't go together."[15] It is my hope that in presenting the nuances of the very long encounter between Christian and Jewish Poles, American Jewry will gain a better understanding, not only of the Polish and Jewish people who once lived in Poland, but also of those living there today.

This book reviews changing Polish-Jewish relations over a period of centuries, as generated by religious, economic, and political structures. Who were Poles and Jews before partition of the Polish-Lithuanian Commonwealth? Who did they become after its 1795 demise? Examining feudal Polish society and the middleman minority role Jews played in this culture helps to explain those early relationships, as do changing Polish and Jewish self-understandings after Poland was conquered, partitioned, and colonialized by the Russian, Prussian, and Austro-Hungarian empires. Additionally, late eighteenth-century ideals of liberty and equality as expressed in the French Revolution influenced Poles, Jews, and the Catholic Church in different ways. Threatened by this new worldview, Church leaders fought against their increasing loss of power by fomenting

---

15   Author's conversation with Leora Tec, January 13, 2022.

a backlash against the Jews who, as a people, had gained the most from modernity by breaching ghetto gates and leaping into secular society as leaders of the new capitalist economy. Jolted by the economics and social realities of capitalist industrialization, in the end Poles and Jews focused less on commonality than on their own particular group's perceived needs. The birth of antisemitism coupled with the continental-wide rise of nationalism met Polish feudalism's collapse and the Polish peasant's attempted elevation, all which wreaked havoc on Polish-Jewish relations.

Other oft neglected influences on Polish-Jewish relations in Poland and on American Jews' perception of those relations are rooted in early twentieth-century America. As we will see, the US government's approach to Poland and the Poles highly influenced American pop culture's presentation of the country and its people before, during, and after World War II and the Holocaust. These negative stereotypes still hold power, influencing contemporary American Jewry's attitude toward the Polish people.

A few words about both the literal and figurative territory covered here. In the section dealing with post-partition relations, I focus primarily on those Polish-Jewish relations within the Kingdom of Poland. However, given not only that the Kingdom of Poland was linked dynastically to the Russian Empire from 1815 to World War I, but also that Polish patriots saw their eastern neighbor as an enemy, I present a broader contextual understanding of Russian policies and personalities when needed. Grasping conflicts between the Romanovs and Polish insurgents enhances our view of both Jewish reactions in the Kingdom of Poland to Russian political supremacy and Poles' responses to it.

The impact of World War II and the Holocaust on Polish-Jewish relations is a topic in itself, and thus outside the purview of this book. However, in order to understand today's stereotypes and biases, I do raise specific issues stemming from the German and Soviet occupations of Poland, as well as from the Holocaust: I will explore genocide, the power of propaganda, the longevity of prewar antisemitism, the Jew-Bolshevik stereotype, Soviet deportations, the drive for survival, attempts at rescue, and blatant murder.

Furthermore, we will encounter Polish-Jewish relations in the immediate postwar period and during the Soviet colonialization of Polish land between 1947 and 1989. We will grapple with Polish pogroms, communist leaders of Jewish origin, internal political conflicts between two central Polish communist groups, and the March 1968 anti-*Zionist* purge.[16] We will also come to understand the

---

16   I follow Dariusz Stola's italicization of the term *Zionist* in this context. The government expelled thousands of people from the Polish People's Republic not because they affiliated

role played by the economy in fomenting Solidarity (the unusual cooperation among workers, the Church, and intellectuals) and the renewed interest in religious identity for Poles of Christian and Jewish origin.

My purpose in writing this book is to encourage North American Jews and Polish Christians to suspend judgment learned over the years from family, teachers, friends, books, movies, and the news media—and to welcome a reconstruction of the Polish-Jewish past. I am asking readers to examine the nuances of this long and complicated relationship in order to speak more reliably about present-day realities. I am suggesting that people step away from the clichés of the past and allow facts to inform them.

In learning and incorporating the complex details of past centuries, including those which have informed not only Jewish myths, but also Polish national myths, American Jews and Polish Christians have an opportunity to tackle the stereotypes each holds of the Other, of one's Self, and of one's homeland. I am not asking readers to accept violent behavior or antisemitism. I am asking that we take the time to unpack them and understand them. I hope the reader will find here a compelling argument for letting go of the hackneyed "good Jew, bad Pole" approach to Polish-Jewish relations that American Ashkenazi Jews tend to hold. For the Polish reader, I hope this more nuanced view of past Polish-Jewish relations will call into question the Jews-as-Poland's-enemy stereotype, while reasserting the importance of Polish Jews in the country's past. I ask you to dismiss the simple orderly image you have held of Poles and Jews. Indeed, the picture is quite messy. Let's jump into it!

Framework and Terminology

I present the relationship in Poland between Poles and Jews (in as much as these two groups are distinct) as well as that between Poles in Poland and American Jewry through the constructs of history, memory, and myth. One broad definition of *history* is that which occurred in the past. History includes *all* actors, contexts, and influences that shaped that past. Scholars insist on documentation and corroborating evidence to confirm the veracity of a historical event. People who chronicled events they experienced allow future generations to know about it. To *know* history, then, is to grapple with, grasp, and explain the documentation—the witnessing—of the intensely complex

---

as ardent supporters of and so-called spies for the State of Israel, but because they were of Jewish origin.

past. Seismic shocks and subtle details, new discoveries and revised perspectives shift understanding of that past, making history as a static noun elusive. What historians partake in is the active striving toward history. They uncover new information and look at the previously known through new lenses. Thus, history is an active process demanding constant reassessment and at times reconstruction.

Mistakenly, people apply the term *history* to everything they have learned and incorporated about the past. I, myself, tussled with misuse of the term at the start of my research. I questioned why my history was so different from Przemek's. What caused our conflict over the past was not history as a static noun, but rather our respective group's activation of memories of the past. *Memory* is that portion of the past that one recalls. Indeed, the relationship between history and memory is a difficult one as the latter does not necessarily correlate with the former. Renowned Jewish historian Yosef Haim Yerushalmi writes: "memory is always problematic, usually deceptive, sometimes treacherous." He adds that "what is remembered is not always recorded and, alas for the historian, ... much of what has been recorded is not necessarily remembered."[17] As such, the memory of a group's past is driven typically by what its leaders need to recover in order to deal with present-day problems. Thus, we find each community guards collective memories that have been handed down through the generations, memories which emphasize different stories as guides to the future.

The concept of *collective memory*—the experienced occurrences, images, and concepts of the past that bind a group in a meaningful way—is one that sociologists have studied since the early twentieth century. In the 1970s historian Pierre Nora popularized the idea.[18] However, four decades earlier French sociologist Maurice Halbwachs had already convincingly directed our understanding of memory away from a biological to a cultural framework.[19] Influenced by his teacher Emile Durkheim, Halbwachs further theorized the framework of collective memory to pertain to every group, including families, religious communities, social classes, political associations, and nations. These collectives form their respective identities based on having lived a shared experience.

---

17 Yosef Hayim Yerushalmi, *Zakhor: Jewish History and Jewish Memory* (Seattle: University of Washington Press, 1996), 5–6.
18 Nicolas Russell, "Collective Memory before and after Halbwachs," *French Review* 79, no. 4 (March 2006): 799.
19 Jan Assmann, "Collective Memory and Cultural Identity" (trans. John Czaplicka), *New German Critique*, no 65 (1995): 125–133.

If any one group's members are intent on group continuity beyond the first-generation iteration, it becomes essential to create a memory of that initial lived experience to pass onto successive generations.[20] Thought leaders have referred to these collective memory tools in various ways. I prefer Yerushalmi's expression "vehicles of memory." Whether experienced actively or more passively, within a group or by oneself, these vehicles transport a group member back to a foundational experience, helping to solidify one's connection with the collective. Jan Assmann explains that the group's collective memory is "concretized" through vehicles of memory, allowing the group "to reproduce its identity."[21] Thus, group representatives labor to write books, songs, liturgy, ceremonies, plays, films, and television shows; they create monuments, commemoration rituals, and museums. In essence these vehicles drive present-day individuals back into the past in order to transform them into future memory keepers.

Nicolas Russell argues that "when the nature of a group's collective memory changes, the group itself ceases to exist."[22] Thus, change represents group danger. Changing perceptions of the past raises an existential threat to any collective. The central challenge to every group is continuity. Therefore, group leadership must contend with how to present new historical discoveries and new cultural perspectives. Traditionalist authorities guard collective memory to maintain group cohesion. They will ignore or refute new discoveries and perspectives. They will fight to maintain unity of thought not only for the group's existence, but also for their own sense of Self—to maintain power, privilege, and purpose.

The rank and file also work to protect the group in order to defend the Self. People cleave to a group either because they are born into it or because they are drawn in by the collective memory that it forms or has solidified. The group brings meaning to individuals' lives. It anchors one in what otherwise could be experienced as a volatile, meaningless, and random existence. Thus, the group is intimately connected with the individual's own sense of meaning and purpose. To challenge the agreed upon memory is to challenge not only the unifying elements that bind individuals together in the group, but to challenge the meaning individuals have invested in their own lives.

A dialectical tension exists, then, between salvaging memories of a lived past and the drive to live in and respond to the present. How much room do we give the past in our present living and in our goals for the future? Halbwachs proposes that the present informs how we remember the past. When a collective's

---

20 Russell, "Collective Memory before and after Halbwachs": 796.
21 Assmann, "Collective Memory and Cultural Identity": 128.
22 Russell, "Collective Memory before and after Halbwachs": 797.

needs in the present change, it follows that a different memory from the group's past gets recovered. If the two memories are at odds with each other, one can expect trouble in the group, as members will not readily relinquish their long connection to a longer-held and better-known memory. It is the fight over conceding part of that salvaged past in exchange for another memory that drives this book. When and how do we allow change?

The American Jewish community has been wrestling against disintegrating group identification with the religious *myth* that had sustained the Jewish people for close to two millennium in the Jewish diaspora. Here, myth is that narrative that explains the group's understanding of itself, its origins, meaningful past and purpose vis-à-vis the chaotic world. A myth knits together the group's collective memories. Until the mid-nineteenth century, mainstream Jews accepted the concept of a God who operates in history; they understood the Jews' exile from Jerusalem in 70 CE as direct punishment for their unwillingness to follow God's commandments as set out in the Torah (Written Law) and Talmud (Oral Law); they believed that only if they were God-fearing, halakhic Jews (those who follow Jewish law) would God allow a return to the Land of Israel. In his seminal work *Zakhor*, Yerushalmi discusses the devastating break with this myth in parts of the Jewish community. This has led to a corresponding divorce from the central Jewish understanding of both group and the individual's role in it. Yerushalmi argues that nothing has replaced this myth for the Jewish people and thus Jews remain somewhat untethered.[23]

Those who have rejected the traditional Jewish religious myth might still participate in a modern Jewish denomination—Conservative, Reform, or Reconstructionist. But if the group's theology is not personally felt—and it takes tremendous individual work to understand and internalize it—the meaning of the denomination's myth might very well be lost to the individual. People who do not feel faith are often drawn to view with a zealot's certainty. Yerushalmi contends that "history becomes what it had never been before—the faith of fallen Jews."[24] Jews today, denominational and unaffiliated, rely on history, not faith, to find meaning in Jewish identity.

The Holocaust has become a centering stone for a great many Jews; they find meaning as a Jew in the fact of survival, in having repudiated Hitler's Final Solution by rebuilding Jewish life. Contemporary Jews continue to digest a large volume of Holocaust literature. I know friends and family members who focus on this literary niche. The struggle to survive speaks to readers' private struggles

---

23 Yerushalmi, *Zakhor*, 93–94.
24 Ibid., 86.

and gives them hope that they can survive the hell that life sends them. The problem, however, is that what we know about history changes with every generation's discoveries and evolving social perspectives.

The question remains: When will this obsessive connection with the Holocaust abate? How easily will Jews shift away from this negative framework for Jewish identity? While one may argue that the State of Israel offers a positive agenda for theologically bereft Jews, I see Israel as part of the Holocaust narrative: if Jews do not actively look out for themselves, then their very survival is at stake. I do not necessarily disagree with this perception. I am simply recognizing that this narrative acts as the centering device for many Jews' identities. It is an "us versus them" approach. And often, because it is a matter of physical survival, people find it difficult to allow for the gradations of gray within the curated stark black-and-white images of Jews and their enemies. I wonder when this particular sense of Jewish identity, which is rooted in the negative, will diminish. Unfortunately, the horrific October 7, 2023 Hamas attacks on Israelis, which left more than 1200 civilians murdered, numerous kibbutzim torched, over 253 hostages taken, and dislocated communities, has seared this perspective into the mainstream Jewish mindset.

A study on memory conducted in Israel by Barry Schwartz, Yael Zerubavel, and Bernice M. Barnett concludes that "when the future is uncertain, when the very survival of society is doubted or, at best, problematic" a past is appropriated, "one that matches and articulates the insecurity as well as the hopes of the present."[25] That past remains relevant while the present group members feel threatened. This notion is relevant not only to the Holocaust-Israel nexus, but also to a subtopic within it: American Jews' tight embrace of cliché relations between Poles and Jews in Poland. This process also plays out in today's Poland, where *Żydokomuna*—stereotypes of the Jew-Bolshevik enemy—still hold sway. When groups feel insecure, they gravitate to inspirational narratives and promote only positive images of their own group. It follows, when Poles and Jews feel the future is secure, leaders and group members will be more willing to take a deeper look at the enshrined black-and-white image of the collective past. Group security will enable deep self-reflection of historical nuances (often negative) that did not make it into the group's centering narratives, thus enabling better relations with groups previously conceived as threatening.

It is my contention that the challenge is to engage with these issues *before* a strong sense of security washes over the collective. For who knows how long that sense of security will remain? Indeed, I began this book at a time of liberalization

---

25 Barry Schwartz, Yael Zerubavel, and Bernice M. Barnett, "The Recovery of Masada: A Study in Collective Memory," *Sociological Quarterly* 27, no. 2 (1986): 161.

and freedom for Poles. I experienced their new assessment of the past after the Iron Curtain fell. But in just fifteen years that sense of tolerance and freedom has been overtaken once again by fear and insecurity. The challenge I present is no easy task.

Individuals participate in maintaining a group's collective memory by subconsciously filtering their own memories through this social sieve. The arduous task is for individuals to take agency and to permit deep reflection, recognizing the grays in what first appeared to be unambiguous snapshots of the past. The hope is that when individuals question, discover, and act they will move group leaders to do the same. This premise aligns with the principle of *distribution energy*, which Polish sociologist Sławomir Kapralski addresses in a 2017 article titled "The Holocaust: Commemorated but not remembered?" Distribution energy refers to individuals' capacity to fuel the building of collective memory by means of *social memory*, which includes those remembrances and recollections they have communicated and discussed amongst themselves. Kapralski recognizes the grass-roots dynamic of distribution energy and its ability to move what individuals discuss within social memory into collective memory.

Interestingly, and perhaps not surprisingly, the transport vehicles for that memory are quite similar to the vehicles of memory we noted earlier in this discussion. They include affectively charged events around a mobilizing narrative—"visual and verbal signs that serve as aids to memory; institutions of learning and the dissemination of mass media; sites and monuments that present palpable relics, commemoration rites that periodically reactivate the memory and enhance collective participation."[26] It is within social memory that space exists for the individual to raise perceptions and questions otherwise ignored by the previous or older caretakers of memory. The point is to do the work while understanding and respecting that all groups, not just your group, seek continuity.

This book focuses on Polish and Jewish groups' various ways of negotiating what each perceives as existential threats and their fears of collective repercussions. At the same time, it highlights individuals struggling against collective constraints. Fear of group disintegration pushes and pulls individuals to rally together to protect the group's identity and that of its members. All groups employ fear as a tactic. And, indeed, fear is very real at times. At the writing of this book, Vladimir Putin not only amassed thousands of troops along Russia's

---

26 Sławomir Kapralski, "The Holocaust: Commemorated but Not Remembered? Post-Colonial and Post-Traumatic Perspectives on the Reception of the Holocaust Memory Discourse in Poland," *Journal of Historical Sociology* 31, no. 1 (2018): 3, https://doi.org/10.1111/johs.12165.

border with Ukraine, but actually invaded the country, and he continues to wage a horrific military battle against the Ukrainian citizenry! Poles' fear has heightened, and they wonder if Putin will stop with its eastern neighbor.

American Jews are viewing the Poles anew, as a people that provides aid to fleeing refugees. They see a people that voted the illiberal Law and Justice party out of power. Perhaps this new image will encourage American Jews to discover "new" information concerning past relations and to discard tired categorizations of the Other. Perhaps this new image of Poles will influence American Jews to join in the important work groups of Poles and Jews in Poland have been advancing to reckon with difficult pasts and to drive toward a tolerant future.

Terms

Below I emphasize my understanding of a few essential terms and concepts employed throughout this book: *truth, myth, Pole, Jew,* and *Other*. *Truth* is that which a group deems to be true. Often biased, it is ever changing as new information, perspectives, and contexts emerge. I hope to take part in reconstructing truths held by Poles and American Jews as they relate to Poland, the Polish people, and Polish-Jewish relations.

Myth refers to a group's broad understanding of the past that brings meaning to that group and its individual members. I understand a myth's wholeness as having been stitched from the group's collective memories and made powerful by its members' identification with it. Neil Gilman (1933–2017), a rabbi and preeminent scholar in Jewish philosophy and theology, guided his students to locate their personal intersections of historical scholarship and faith. He encouraged them to create new meaningful myths that would carry them forward in their personal relationships with Judaism. Gilman's teaching has been a driving force for this book.

I recognize that *American* Jews are a diverse population, originating in a variety of lands. Most contemporary American Jews hail from Eastern Europe and are Ashkenazi. Those from the Iberian Peninsula (including Spain) are referred to as Sephardi Jews. While the majority of American Jewry has been accepted as white by American society, it has been argued that more than 20% is racially and ethnically diverse.[27]

---

27 Lewis Gordon, foreword to *In Every Tongue: The Racial & Ethnic Diversity of the Jewish People*, ed. Diane Kaufman Tobin, Gary A. Tobin, Scott Rubin (San Francisco: Institute for Jewish & Community Research, 2005), 21.

The term *Pole* is a complicated one. Living in the twenty-first century, most readers gravitate towards a civic classification, which accepts any person born in Poland as a Pole. But such a concept did not exist anywhere until the French Revolution unleashed it, permitting people of all races and religions to claim citizenship upon a declaration of loyalty to the nation. It took the populace decades to embrace this stated ideal. As such, until the mid-twentieth century, Christian and Jewish inhabitants of Poland consistently noted a difference between their two groups. Jews rarely called themselves Poles, and Polish Christians rarely accepted Jews as Poles. As such, in this book the word *Poles* does not include Jews. I recognize that such terminology passively promotes the very distinction in belonging against which some Jews argued, and which today's Polish Jews reject. Indeed, Stanisław Krajewski refers to those Jews living in twenty-first-century Poland as *Polish Polish Jews*, so important is their Polish identity.[28]

I refer to that group which stands outside the majority as the *Other*. Every society engages an Other. Sociologist Jan Assmann holds that when a group's identification is concretized its identity is determined in either a positive sense ("We are this") or in a negative sense ("That is our opposite"). The Other aids collective identity: by pointing to that which the group *is not*, one better understands what the group *is*. As such, a group's "cultural memory is characterized by sharp distinctions made between those who belong and those who do not, that is, between what appertains to oneself and what is foreign."[29] However, often people present the Other negatively to raise up the majority to which they belong. The Other refers to groups which hold different religious truths, economic roles, cultural norms, and political ideals from one's own group. For Jews, who lived amongst their own people in Polish villages, small towns, and urban neighborhoods from the Middle Ages to the interwar period (1919–1939), Christian Poles were an Other. For Poles who simultaneously inhabited the same land, the Other referred to all minority groups, including Jews. Because Jews heavily populated the entire Polish territory and were so visible in their distinctiveness from Christian Poles and other Christian minorities, Jews became the ultimate Other within the Polish nation.

---

28 Stanisław Krajewski, *Reflections of a Polish Polish Jew* (Kraków: Wydawnictwo Austeria, 2005).
29 Assmann, "Collective Memory and Cultural Identity": 130.

The ramifications of Otherness have waxed and waned throughout the near-millennium of Polish-Jewish relations. For the most part Otherness created separation between populations. Usually, people engaged peacefully with the Other at the marketplace and on the street. But during occasions which naturally stressed the Jews' differences, such as religious holidays and time of economic and political crisis, some Poles reacted aggressively to the Jews' Otherness.

Joanna Beata Michlic discusses the particular political embrace of the Jew as Poland's threatening Other. Beginning in the 1880s, the nationalist political party, Endecja, grounded its identity on proposing the Jew as the Poles' chief enemy.[30] Embracing antisemitism, Endecja's approach led to consequences that have lasted to this day.

I hold that Jews had multiple Otherness experiences throughout their long habitation on Polish land. Religious Otherness. Cultural Otherness. Educational Otherness. Linguistic Otherness. Social Otherness. Economic Otherness. But these Otherness experiences did not necessitate physical harm. As Kapralski notes, Poles and Jews "lived in the same physical space and historical time," but "did not share the same social space and time."[31] For more than eight hundred years Jews and Poles shared a separate coexistence. While relatively peaceful for the most part, during this long period there was an undercurrent of disrespect and resentment that at various times and in various locales erupted in violence.

***

I am from the United States, reared there and influenced by it. The American Ashkenazi Jewish (majority) community has shaped me, and in the following pages I respond to it. By raising issues and challenging perceptions I hope to introduce new ideas to American Jewry.

At the same time, I recognize that while I am drawn to Poland, and feel a sense of home when there, Poland is not my motherland. I do not have an instinctive understanding of the land, people, or culture. While I am an "outsider" in Poland, I have great respect for the people and their stories. It is my hope that individual Poles will read my work and reflect on it.

---

30 Joanna Beata Michlic, *Poland's Threatening Other: The Image of the Jew from 1880 to the Present* (Lincoln: University of Nebraska Press, 2006).
31 Kapralski, "The Holocaust: Commemorated but Not Remembered?": 8.

When one explores the past, one finds that what took place is not one thing or another, but rather a complex of events, deep and wrenching. In it one discovers humanity confronting its own limitations, failings, and desires. It is within this context that I offer my examination of the complex Polish-Jewish past.

There is an intrinsic danger in writing about a subject that has had such a polarizing effect on communities. I do not come here to take sides, but rather to show that no side is absolutely right. I am not writing with any political agenda. Because of that, people who are determined to read and "learn" only their group's perspective might well be angered by my work. This book throws the various rhetoric we have ingested over the decades into a pulsating blender. What I pour out is historiography's complexity and indeterminacy for you to examine and consider.

CHAPTER 1

Myth and Reconstruction

In 2005 I visited Auschwitz for the first time. I was shocked to learn that the Nazis initially built the camp not to enslave and murder Jews, but to enslave and murder Poles. In the museum I stood peering into the encased hoard of victims' eyeglasses, embarrassed by what I had not seen. I was the embodiment of the disconnect between Pole and Jew. Why as an American Jew had I not known of the Polish plight? And why has it been so difficult for many Poles to recognize Jewish suffering at the hands of their countrymen? The answers lie in both groups' unwillingness to acknowledge and study the Other's suffering, each fearing that to do so would erase their own identity. To recognize the painful past of the Other might jeopardize their own position in the world. Determined to untangle the twisted histories I had been taught regarding the Poles and their complex relationships with the Jews, I had to risk the security of *knowing* my place in this world. Here I explore this process by investigating not only American Jewish and Polish Christian myth making, but also the difficulty of challenging an accepted myth.

Each nation views history through its own distinct lens. Leaders and laypersons alike embrace perceptions of their country, culture, and its citizens that substantiate their own political and social tenets. We focus on what we wish to see clearly, while allowing other interpretations of the past to blur in our final assessment. Through this process collective memory takes shape, cropping out many historical facts.

For this reason, in place of the commonly used term *history*, I will often substitute the word *myth*. Here, myth signals a specific process of recording and integrating the past into the present. I ask the reader to suspend the usual understanding of myth as something deemed to be false. Instead, myth means a written or orally transmitted "structure through which a community organizes and makes sense of its experiences."[1] We have been trained to regard history

---

1 Neil Gilman, *Sacred Fragments: Recovering Theology for the Modern Jew* (Philadelphia: The Jewish Publication Society, 1990), 26.

as factual events which occurred in the past. The term *myth* allows for a more fluid approach, referring not only to the construction and deconstruction of our understanding of the past, but also to a nation's or group's relationship with it. Myth is a patchwork quilt of a group's collective memories.

Neil Gilman holds that "myths are the spectacles that enable us to see order, in what would otherwise be confusion."[2] This definition allows a fresh look at religious, cultural, and historical texts. It suggests we redefine truth as a belief rather than a fact. Releasing us from a literal reading of a text, it permits greater insight into the community's attitude toward Self and Other.

Each country and culture collects memories. Leaders stitch them into narratives of birth, survival, and growth in order to promote continued connection to the group and encourage future membership. The continuous reiteration of particular myths is vital for the group's continuity. It provides a "brand" with which members identify and leaders toil to ensure relevance for future generations.

Knowledge of, and respect for, another nation's myths are necessary for understanding its populace. To grasp the myth is to understand how a country or a people views itself. Accepting one's own myth as meaningful does not negate the ability, or the imperative, to recognize those of Others. To see one's own myth as a guiding force, but to know that it is not the *only truth*, is essential for living as an open participant in both dialogue and the reconstruction of positive working relationships.

Given that life is based on interactions between people, groups, cultures, and countries, it becomes critical to acknowledge that what one group chooses to salvage from an event is different from what another promotes. This is especially true when two nations are in conflict. Often their separate communal needs and understandings stand in opposition and are perceived as a threat to the other nation's well-being. Thus, politicians, historians, and educators offer only selective interpretations. Neither narrative may be totally false, nor will they be based on all the facts. All nations and groups are engaged in the same practice of preservationist mythmaking. American Jews and Polish Catholics are no exception.

---

2   Ibid.

Grains of Truth

It is true that people distort the past for their own needs. At the same time, there is often at least a grain of truth that props up a people's myth, including their stereotyping of the Others in their society. To understand why Poles latched onto their own simple views of Jews is not to condone that vision. It is to respect a group's historical context. This step may be difficult for some people to take, as to see and name the negative encased in one's own group requires courage. It involves uncovering and incorporating the messy and often ugly memories heretofore buried in collective denial. For example, Jews acted as moneylenders within Polish society. As such, they earned incomes by charging interest, something which Poles resented. More disheartening for Poles, when one could not pay back a loan, the Jewish moneylender took what little collateral the Pole possessed.

Countless Poles also characterized Jews as unpatriotic. The reality was that the majority of Jews rejected integration into Polish culture for a number of reasons. They refused full integration due to their religious practice, the perception that many Poles shunned such integration, and the rise of Jewish nationalism. Additionally, the Jewish communal policy of *dine demalkhuse dine*—the law of the land is the law—expressed Jews' loyalty to the ruling authority. For more than a century the Jews showed fealty to Prussians, Austrians, and Russians, but not to Poles. That Jews remained neutral during several border conflicts at the dawn of the Second Polish Republic provoked Poles' ire against the Jews as traitors to an independent Poland. Later, when Jews rose in the ranks of the Communist Party, Poles viewed the Jew as an internal enemy.

At the same time, American Jewry has painted Poland as an antisemitic nation. There is some truth to this stereotype. Anti-Jewish rhetoric had an extensive presence in the nineteenth- and twentieth-century Catholic Church, which greatly influenced the majority ethnic Polish population. Since the 1880s, antisemitism and consequent violence had erupted in historic Polish lands. This politicized Jew-hatred became fashionable in Poland before the Great War of 1914–1918, when Polish nationalists experienced the power that the Jewish minority voting bloc could exert. In response right-wing political players called for economic boycotts of Jewish businesses. The end of World War I did not bring relief. Pogroms besieged Jewish communities during the first years of the Second Republic, from 1918–1926. The years of World War II, 1939–1945, brought further bitterness and distrust between Jews and Poles. Despite the horrors Jews faced in the Nazi death camps of World War II, on July 4, 1946, a little more than a year after the war's end, Polish citizens massacred thirty-nine Polish

Jewish Holocaust survivors and wounded eighty others in and around the city of Kielce. Later in the 1960s, communist Poland carried out its so-called anti-*Zionist* purge of Jews. American Jewry extrapolated that all Poles held such hatred for Jews. Such categorizing is a natural self-defense reflex clung to by most groups, including both Jews and Poles.

Antipolonism in America

To begin myth reconstruction is to consciously recognize the possible existence of an alternative past reality to that generated by government, taught by teachers, or passed on by parents. It is to imagine Others as equal in worth to one's own group and to wonder how one's group affected the Other. Myth reconstruction demands that the Other's truth be expressed without typical unreflective opposition. It calls one to read the Other's telling of the past alongside one's own and to locate the inconsistencies between the two accounts. Myth reconstruction calls for scholars willing to dig into the Other's primary archives as well as their own in order to reconcile different interpretations. Ultimately, it also demands the public confront surprise, confusion, and conflict from a messy past.

In the mid-nineteenth century, Americans based their opinions of Poles on their experience with those Polish nobles who had emigrated to the United States after being defeated in the 1830–31 insurrection against Russian rule. Americans extrapolated from this limited demographic that all Poles were courageous, strong, and well educated. Nineteenth-century American playwright Oliver Cromwell presented Poles as "brave, patriotic, genteel, high-minded."[3] However, before the turn of the twentieth century, this generalized perspective shifted to view Poland and Poles with disdain. Between roughly 1880 and 1929 a new wave of migrants left Eastern and Southern Europe for American ports. Reaching well over two million people, the Polish immigrants—who included both Christians and Jews—were soon second to the Italians in population size.[4] Fleeing famine and extreme poverty, they arrived in the US in search of opportunity, only to be referred to derogatorily as "new immigrants." The more deeply rooted Americans viewed them as inferior and looked down on them.

---

3   Thomas S. Gladsky, *Princes, Peasants and Other Polish Selves: Ethnicity in American Literature* (Amherst: The University of Massachusetts Press, 1992), 12.
4   M. B. B. Biskupski, *Hollywood's War with Poland, 1939–1945* (Lexington: The University Press of Kentucky, 2010), 169.

People in power questioned the ethos and value of the Eastern European immigrant, and the Poles became the target of hostility due to their sheer numbers. In 1902, Woodrow Wilson (1856–1924) described Poles, along with Hungarians and Italians, as "men of the meaner sort" who possessed "neither skill nor energy nor any initiative of quick intelligence."[5] It did not help that the great majority of Polish Christian refugees came from rural areas with little formal education. Maintaining strong connections to both family and the Catholic Church, these immigrants planned to return to their motherland. As such, they resisted learning English and embracing American culture.

American social critics characterized this predominantly poor and unschooled population as representative of the Polish people as a whole.[6] Americans adopted the hateful and condescending Biegański stereotype in which "Poles are brutes. They possess qualities of animals. They are physically strong, stupid, violent, fecund, anarchic, dirty, and especially hateful in a way that more evolved human beings are not."[7] This stereotype also typified Poles politically as "thuggishly, primitively nationalistic. The special hatefulness of Biegański is epitomized in his Polish antisemitism."[8]

Americans misconstrued Poles' determination to retain their language and customs as signs of ignorance. Under pressure to assimilate, Poles living on American soil were called "simple" or "lazy," and this, as is the way with all stereotyping, was taken to include *all* Poles. Jokes about "Polaks" resounded.[9] That Protestantism dominated American Christendom only added to this damaging image of the Polish Catholic immigrant.

The new theory of scientific racism supported this derogatory perception of Polish immigrants. Madison Grant (1865–1937), the well-known figurehead of this movement, who professed that his racist beliefs derived from objective scientific studies, had the ear of two US presidents, Theodore Roosevelt

---

5   Ibid., 170.
6   Mieczysław B. Biskupski and Antony Polonsky, introduction to *Polish-Jewish Relations in North America*, ed. Mieczysław B. Biskupski and Antony Polonsky. Polin: Studies in Polish Jewry, vol. 19 (Oxford: The Littman Library of Jewish Civilization, 2007), 11.
7   Danusha Goska, *Bieganski: The Brute Polak Stereotype in Polish-Jewish Relations and American Popular Culture* (Boston: Academic Studies Press, 2010), 16.
8   Ibid.
9   Amazon still sells Polish joke books. What is shocking is that one was published as recently as 2011. Mark Geoffrey Young, *The Best Ever Book of Polish Jokes: Lots and Lots of Jokes Specially Repurposed for You-Know-Who* (N.p.: CreateSpace Independent Publishing Platform, 2011).

and Herbert Hoover. In his book *The Passing of the Great Race*, Grant argues that of the three European races he identified, the Nordic is superior to the Mediterranean, who in turn stands above the lowly Alpine. The latter includes Eastern Europeans. Grant argues that while members of a lower race could not elevate themselves, those within a higher race could be brought down through intermixing with those on lower rungs. He maintained that when two unlike races mix, the offspring is always a lower form.

Swayed by this theory, America's elites feared race suicide: that the "new immigrants" would captivate and corrupt the racial elite American, and through procreation would fill the land with racially inferior people. Diluted numerically, the master race would be weakened and robbed of its privileges. Among Grant's champions was Adolf Hitler, who found tremendous inspiration in this 1916 publication and lauded it as his "bible."[10]

So entrenched was this racial theory, that even some of those who dedicated their careers to countering it got sucked into it. The father of American Anthropology, Franz Boas (1858–1942), viewed all cultures as on the same plain. However, when it came to the 1880–1929 immigrants, this German-born Jew gave into racist stereotypes, portraying Christians and Jews from Poland as unintelligent with very little cultural worth.[11] However, unlike Grant, Boas argued that through assimilation immigrants could elevate themselves.[12]

This anti-Polish ideology did not exist only among elite academicians; it filtered down to the general populace through newspapers and films. The iconic American magazine *The Saturday Evening Post* was one of the most widely circulated and influential middle-class weeklies in the nineteenth and early twentieth centuries. The paper serialized novelist Kenneth Roberts's assessments of the "new immigrants" as highly problematic both culturally and politically. He characterized them as less than human in the November 6, 1920 edition where he stated resolutely, "They wear clothing that seems to have ripened on them for years, and they sleep in wretched hovels with sheep and cows and pigs and poultry scattered among them. They have been so for a great many centuries. It is almost impossible for them to slough the results of heredity and environment."[13]

---

10   Goska, *Bieganski*.
11   Ibid., 112–113.
12   Ibid., 117.
13   Ibid., 118.

Additionally, Roberts described Eastern Europeans as the source of "unrest, dissatisfaction, sedition, revolutionary and anarchist doctrines."[14] He characterized them as possessing a tragicomic mentality that created "a mess" of their countries. Not only did he view Poles as too stupid to open an umbrella when it rained, but he asserted that they were incapable of assimilation: "an ostrich could assimilate a cobble stone with about the same ease."[15] He admitted that "[p]ractically all of them, viewed individually, were hard-working, well-meaning, likeable persons,"[16] but he insisted—and convinced middle-class Americans—that when "[t]aken in the mass . . . , and viewed from an American standpoint, it is no more possible to make Americans out of a great many of them than it is possible to make a racehorse out of a pug dog."[17] Thus, the general American public learned to think of Poles as inferior.

Americans also came to judge Poles according to the jobs they held in the United States. Most Polish peasants entering the United States lacked formal schooling. In fact, given their former agricultural life, which included barter, they most probably had never even handled money prior to emigration. Despite their ability to turn dirt into food, and grain into clothing, urban America looked down on Polish immigrants and considered them unable to learn. They limited opportunities advanced to Poles. Labeled as most suited for heavy industry, Poles largely found jobs in factories where American industrialists needed bodies to fuel American progress. Indeed, the Polish immigrant soon embodied the prototypical American proletarian.

Poles labored under nightmarish conditions that killed and crippled many of their young.[18] When they organized strikes for higher wages and to improve conditions, they were met with middle-class fear. The popular acceptance of Eastern Europeans as less than, as Other, influenced the American populace's unsympathetic response to the Polish striker. During the early 1920s, civic and industrial authorities stopped strikes with the use of blunt force, beating men, women, and children indiscriminately and firing shots into unarmed crowds. The general American populace was antilabor and anti-immigrant.[19]

Confident of the Poles' inadequacies—intellectual, hygienic, and moral—and fearful of the dumbing down of America, politicians argued for restricting Polish

---

14   Ibid.
15   Ibid.
16   Ibid.
17   Ibid.
18   Ibid., 26–27.
19   Ibid., 31.

immigrants' entry to the country.[20] In 1907 the US Congress authorized the now famous Dillingham Commission, which determined in its 1911 report that Poles were intellectually and psychologically inferior to the American population. Believing Poles and others from Eastern Europe to be unassimilable, the report concluded their numbers should be restricted.[21]

It is important to note that because Poles and Jews migrated from the same territory, they have often been compared. While both experienced negative stereotyping in the United States during the "new immigration" and after, much has been done to counter the bigotry against Jews that academics, media, and government agencies promoted in the early twentieth century. Regrettably, "no such parallel effort has been made to renounce or deconstruct the devastating racist ideas about Poles and other Slavs (Bohunks)."[22]

Antipolonism among American Jews

American Jews growing up in the early twentieth century accepted these negative perceptions of Poles. In fact, this antipolonism corroborated the disdain of Poles that many early Jewish Americans, most of whom arrived from German lands, had carried with them from the Old World. The Jewish Prussians who reached America in the 1840s retained a cultural elitism, which castigated all inhabitants of Polish lands, Jews and Catholics alike.

Late nineteenth-century Jewish immigrants from partitioned Polish lands strengthened this belittling of Catholic Poles by transporting their own air of superiority over the Polish peasantry to American shores. Drawing on their past economic relationship—Jews as overseers and sellers of essential goods, Poles as laborers, farmers, and consumers—Jewish immigrants maintained condescending attitudes towards their Polish Christian compatriots. Reinforced by American antipolonism, most American Jews berated Poles who resettled in the US.[23] As we shall see, this negative relationship influenced American politics and culture.

It is vital to understand that the vast majority of Jewish immigrants from Poland did not regard themselves as Polish. They were Jews who happened to have lived

---

20 Ibid., 119.
21 Biskupski, *Hollywood's War with Poland, 1939–1945*, 170.
22 Ibid., 60.
23 Ewa Morawska, "Polish-Jewish Relations in American, 1880–1940: Old Elements, New Configurations," in Biskupski and Polonsky, *Polish-Jewish Relations in North America*, 77–79.

in the lands which made up the Polish-Lithuanian Commonwealth (today, not only Poland, but also Lithuania, Belarus, and Ukraine) and who left the area due to economic and political hardship. In America, as a whole, Polish Jews did not seek out broader Polish organizations to link them to the Old Country. Instead, they joined existing Jewish fraternities and societies, which helped them to Americanize. At the same time, however, Polish and Jewish immigrants settled in urban foreign enclaves, where they transferred their economic roles from Poland to the New World, with Jewish entrepreneurs providing the goods and services that the Polish peasants-turned-factory workers needed. As in the Old Country, these two communities retained a relationship of distant proximity.

Polish and Jewish Myths Diverge: The Holocaust, Hollywood, and "Polish Camps"

World War II and the Holocaust are perhaps the most important disputed issues within Jewish and Polish interpretations of the past. Despite the Nazis' responsibility for the Final Solution, the fact that they centralized this cataclysmic horror in Poland exacerbated American Jewry's contempt for the Poles. Human psyches operate through association. The inconceivable extent of torture and murder inflicted on millions of Jews on Polish soil created an image in the American Jewish mind of Poland as the heart of darkness. The Polish people were considered monsters who did not help their Jewish neighbors, allowing them to be slaughtered instead.

As we have seen, due to American scientific racism and xenophobia, the American public and, as a result, American Jews looked down on Poles and Poland. During the war years, Hollywood added to the accepted Biegański stereotype, feeding dangerous and calculated misperceptions of Poland and Poles to its American and foreign audiences. At a time when the studios released some five hundred films yearly and 74% of the US population went to the movies at least once a week, American cinema shaped the tastes and attitudes of its audience. For good or ill, Hollywood was "the foremost educational institute on earth."[24] In his book *Hollywood's War with Poland, 1939–1945*, historian Mieczysław Biskupski demonstrates that instead of portraying the heartbreaking heroics of the Polish resistance to the Nazis and Soviets, as well as Poles' horrific experiences under both occupying forces, studio heads chose to paint

---

24   Biskupski, *Hollywood's War with Poland, 1939–1945*, 1.

Poland as a weak nation that crumbled due to its own supposed appeasement tactics.

The American Communist Party members who founded and ran the Screen Writers' Guild, and US propaganda policies that presented its ally—the Soviet Union—in the best possible light, manipulated cinema audiences with this outrageous WWII fabrication. In addition, the various studio heads who were Jewish and already held some negative feelings toward Poland and the Poles played a role. Consequently, during the war, the Polish government-in-exile met an American ally teetering on this interplay of ideology, politics, and nationality.[25]

At the same time, Hollywood—pressured by US policy makers—directed Americans' perceptions by what it chose *not* to produce. The movie industry avoided making films about the Holocaust. Reasons for this omission included the Jewish studio heads' belief that Jewish-specific topics would highlight their own Jewish origins at a time of heightened American antisemitism. They were also following the Roosevelt administration's policy to steer clear of the subject as it might change public opinion, swelling demand to assist the Jews militarily—a position at odds with the US war plan.[26]

The American Jewish establishment believed that the Nazi authorities chose Poland as ground zero because Poles were supposedly "all-too-willing" to aid efforts to implement the Final Solution. Centuries of Catholic priests offering up theologically derived Jew-hatred, coupled with the more recent politicized antisemitism, made American Jewry certain that the Poles supported the Nazis. Due to the simplistic and misleading claim that Poles did nothing to stop the destruction of the six million, most American Jews felt justified in abhorring them. Additionally, given the coordination between the Roosevelt administration and Hollywood, it was relatively easy for American Jews to ignore the Poles' tremendous suffering during the war.

Although the Polish government had no part in planning or carrying out the Final Solution, American Jewry and Americans in general have come to refer to the Nazi camps on Polish territory as "Polish death camps." One must ask if a camp had been built in Hungary, would we call it a "Hungarian death camp?" Just as this description makes no sense, neither does the reference to "Polish death camps." It implies Polish involvement in Nazi Germany's scheme to murder the Jews and Poland's general national complicity in carrying it out. It reflects the American image of the brute Pole engendered by nationalism and realpolitik.

---

25 Ibid.
26 Ibid., 70.

American Jewry is not alone in making this serious mistake. Worldwide print media coverage of the sixtieth anniversary of the end of World War II made at least seventy such blunders.[27] While this might be due to numerous death camps built in Poland, the end result is that people have come to see the Poles as responsible in part for those killing centers. Seventy-five years since the end of the war, this gross error signifies a major gap between reality and perceptions of it. As we shall discuss in chapter 20, the Polish populist far-right Law and Justice Party (PiS) has exploited this accumulated misplaced guilt to create an enemy with which it must wage war.

American Jewry's Micro-Lens onto Poland

Until the wonderful Polish welcome of Ukrainian refugees in 2022, American Jews have tended to describe Poles as an immoral and savage people. They have focused on the tumultuous period of 1918–1968. Consequently, they have ignored more than eight hundred years of Polish-Jewish coexistence and its interethnic dynamics. They have pointed to the extreme antisemitism in Poland during the interwar period and ignored the freedom Polish Jewry had in the same period to develop Jewish nationalism and a Jewish print media. Concentrating on the Holocaust, American Jews referred incessantly to Poles who denounced Jews to the Nazis and disregarded the Poles who hid and saved Jewish lives. They remembered the Polish underground Home Army (Armia Krajowa, AK), which often treated the Jews in their ranks poorly and did not help the fighters in the Warsaw Ghetto enough during their dire time of need. At the same time, they do not remember the AK's own lack of weaponry and the Polish fighters' desperate circumstances under both the Nazi and Soviet occupations. While they knew about Poles taking over Jewish homes and then refusing to give them back to the few surviving owners at the end of the war, they discounted the original displacement of the general population and the systematic destruction they faced. American Jews fixated on Kielce while neglecting Soviet imperialism. All these events occurred. Yet how we understand these complex experiences is dependent on the collective memories and broader myths handed down by the respective culture in question. Human defense mechanisms lead us to see

---

27 Shana Penn, "American Press Coverage of Poland's Role in the Holocaust," in *Rethinking Poles and Jews: Troubled Past, Brighter Future*, ed. Robert Cherry and Annamaria Orla-Bukowska (Lanham: Rowman & Littlefield Publishers, Inc., 2007), 64.

only that which pertains to our own group. Such tactical instinct has negatively impacted Polish-Jewish relations.

This American Jewish conceptualization of Poland has been entrenched through generations of family lore, political debate, textbooks, the media, literature, and movies. We see it most clearly today in organized Holocaust tourism, which emphasizes Poland as a land of oppression, particularly for Jews. So passionate has American Jewry's disgust with the Poles been, it has often eclipsed its hatred of present-day Germans.[28] A despised people throughout history, Jews are not immune to hating Others.

I encountered this perception when speaking with a Jewish educator. A beloved teacher of Holocaust and Israel studies, she is someone I admire as a leader in Jewish education. However, her reaction in 2005 to my young children visiting Poland astounded me. She questioned our decision and saw no reason to step foot on *that land*. To her, it was a place filled only with death. Her walls were up and she had no desire to challenge their foundation. While frustrating, it is not surprising. She echoed the American Jewish establishment's myth. Polish Jewish leader Konstanty Gebert noted, in my November 2007 interview with him, that while academics may be breaking out from stereotypical thinking, most American Jews remain imprisoned by it.

In a survey regarding beliefs held about Polish-Jewish relations during the Holocaust, Robert Cherry demonstrates that Jewish teachers responded with the most negative judgments of any group. Cherry concludes that "Jewish non-historians have a substantially harsher assessment of the Polish people and the Catholic Church than Jewish historians and museum researchers have. . . . In particular this suggests that Jewish non-historians who teach Holocaust-related courses generally hold negative stereotypes that are inconsistent with the historical record."[29] My personal encounter with this Jewish educator gave me pause. Her anti-Polish bias revealed, she is one of many Jewish teachers consciously or subconsciously guiding our children and young adults to embrace a grim caricature of Poland and Polish people. She does not do so out of any ill intent. Rather, she is simply teaching what she learned without questioning those myths.

---

28 Most likely this sentiment is due to Germany's early ability to take responsibility for the Holocaust while Poles have been most reticent to accept the role their forbears played. Danusha V. Goska, "The Necesssity of 'Bieganski,'" in Biskupski and Polonsky, *Polish-Jewish Relations in North America*, 222–224.

29 Robert Cherry, "Measuring Anti-Polish Biases Among Holocaust Teachers," in Cherry and Orla-Bukowska, *Rethinking Poles and Jews*, 75.

Though historians might reassess historic events, in the end it is up to those who actually disseminate history to inform themselves more broadly and to bring a more nuanced view to the American Jewish community. It is up to rabbis, curriculum writers, teachers, authors, film producers, parents, and even friends. Yet Jewish leaders in the United States have found it difficult to move beyond the skewed view they themselves were taught.

Despite American Jews' experience of pronounced and prolonged antisemitism in the United States, and despite knowing that people of color have been physically, economically, educationally, and emotionally suppressed and exploited in this country, American Jews continue to see Poland just below Germany in terms of a nation's mistreatment of the Other. I hold that this stereotype resists decay because American Jews rarely have firsthand experience of any of the good that both existed in the past and that has emerged in contemporary Polish society. How will American Jews interpret the Poles' aid to Ukrainian refugees vis-a-vis the Polish-Jewish experience? We must wait to see if it redresses our attitudes or is construed to confirm them.

A Central Aspect of Jewish Myth: Victimization

A nation's myth reflects how its members understand themselves vis-a-vis Others and world events. It is undeniable that from ancient times, Jews have profoundly suffered as victims of oppression. The Israelites, the ancient Jews, were overrun, outmaneuvered, dispersed, and often murdered. During the Roman sacking of Jerusalem in 70 CE, thousands of Jews were slaughtered or sent into slavery. Those remaining were cut off from their religious center. Scattered to the winds, Jews regrouped, reviewed, and reworked their religious mode of expression. Although settlement outside of the Land of Israel proved to be an arena for collective creativity, Jews' rights and freedoms were always dependent on the host nation. The diaspora prospered when secular leaders embraced Jewish settlement for the economic welfare that Jews brought to society; danger dawned when those same services were no longer needed. When victimized in one place, the Jewish people moved to find more hospitable locales in which they would be welcomed for their economic contributions. And so, the cycle continued and with it the entrenched grounding Jewish myth of victimization.

As a people, Jews recall their oppression and resilience through holiday liturgy and ritual. Every year, Jews evoke their past to explain to Jewish youth their collective responsibility to group continuation. On the holiday of Purim, they recollect Haman's ancient scheme to rid Shushan of its Jews by reading the scroll of Esther. Around the Passover seder table, Jews remember Israel's enslavement and redemption from Egypt. The Chanukah celebration commemorates a Greek king's dominion over the Jews and their eventual revolution. In telling and retelling these stories, Jews emphasize their roles as underdog and ultimate victor. It is the knowledge that Jews have withstood and overcome oppression that bonds Jew to Jew.

This sense of responsibility to the past by securing the future is inherent in Jews' ritual practice. We learn that all generations of Jews should identify as slaves in Egypt because, had we been living then, we too would have been enslaved. Together all generations of Jews—past, present, and future—have stood at the base of Mount Sinai to receive the Torah. Accordingly, the Holocaust happened to *all Jews*. American Jews growing up from the 1950s onward learned to identify personally with the victims of Hitler's Holocaust. Dedication to the State of Israel is still couched in Holocaust references; practicing Judaism is considered a means of toppling Hitler. The message is that Jewish people will survive despite all efforts to obliterate us.

Explanations for Jewish victimization have changed over time. The biblical narrator blames the Israelites themselves for their victim status, linking it directly to the nation's disregard for God's commandments. The Book of Judges, the second section of the Hebrew Bible, clearly describes this relationship: when Israel follows God's ways, the nation prospers; when Israel sins against God, the nation suffers.

This justification of national trauma, however, does not resonate with most Jews today. A shift began with the eighteenth-century Enlightenment and German Jewry's particular expression of it in the Haskalah movement. As Jews emerged from the ghetto during the Enlightenment to encounter secularism, many of them shed their traditional outlook.[30] At the same time, socialism's growing popularity among a swath of mostly poor and young Eastern European Jews also influenced them to discard Old World interpretations of national trauma.

This deviation away from God's centrality and toward a modern secularized critical approach to the past took on seismic proportions during the post-Holocaust era. Did God really push millions of Jews into gas chambers and mass graves because they did not follow God's commandments? To understand the Jewish people's suffering, secular Jews narrowed their focus to the violent and overwhelming enemy. As such, most post-Holocaust Jewish writing denied

---

30 Yerushalmi, *Zakhor*, 82–85.

power to the so-called dangerous Jews within and targeted blame onto the Others who hated them, whether due to Jewish religious beliefs, cultural isolation, economic roles, or growing political leverage. The fault for Jewish oppression lies in the Others' inability to fully accept Jews, their differences, and their collective economic-political progress. Modern Jewry replaced one black-and-white belief system with another rigid conviction.

Jews protect our role as a fundamentally suffering people. When we argue against Others who apply the term *holocaust* to any experience outside of that faced by the Jews during World War II, Jews underscore their unique suffering. I do not suggest embracing a loose definition of *holocaust*. I am merely questioning what we fear will happen if other groups appropriate this terminology. Will a broader use of *holocaust* erase our specific communal past horrors, making them inconsequential? Are we afraid of becoming less significant if we are not defined by our suffering? Do we need antisemitism to preserve our Jewish identity? Victimhood has been essential to Jewish distinctiveness. Questioning its role challenges individuals, families, and communities to reflect on what it means to be Jewish. Subordinating our victimhood might very well help us to understand our relation to the Other more clearly.

Recognizing Poles as Victims

American Jews know little about the role that victimization plays in the Polish psyche. Oppression performs just as vital a part within the Polish national myth as it does within Jewish communal understanding. Indeed, the Poles' sense of persecution rivals that held by Jews, and at times it directly conflicts with the Jewish perception of the past.

The Polish people suffered through three partitions of the Polish-Lithuanian Commonwealth, in 1772, 1793, and 1795, losing control of their land until they regained sovereignty in 1918. Not only was their country torn into three segments, with the people divided by new foreign governing powers, but Polish culture and education also came under assault. Once the glory of Eastern Europe, the Poles were felled and emasculated. After losing two insurrections against Russian rule (in 1830–1831 and 1863–1864), the Polish people were punished by their Russian overlord who quashed their language rights, cultural freedoms, and employment possibilities. They were taxed heavily and disenfranchised. Although Poland briefly regained its independence in 1918, Polish freedom ended again with the Nazi-Soviet 1939 bifurcation of the country.

Unfortunately, most Jews forget, or never learned of, the horrors that the Poles endured under the Nazi and Soviet occupations. Germany brutally occupied Poland from 1939 to 1945. Hitler's henchmen slaughtered thousands of Polish intellectuals, religious leaders, and political activists. The Nazi oppressors built and managed concentration camps and death camps on Polish soil, killing millions of Jews, Poles, and other minorities, including the Romani. According to the Auschwitz Museum, roughly seventy-five thousand Gentile Poles perished in Auschwitz. During the same time, the Allies closed their eyes to Russian anti-Polish aggression, brutality, and murder. The 1945 Yalta agreement cemented this Entente offering of Poland as recompense for Soviet Russia's own grand military sacrifice.[31]

Postwar Poland met another phase of oppression. The Red Army occupied the country, giving the Polish people no choice but to accept their new conqueror; only the communist minority welcomed the situation. In the new Polish People's Republic, the Soviets controlled education and culture. Historians were free to promote only the party's perspective of the past.[32] Those who challenged the party could not publish their work. Concurrently, Cold War politics reverberated through all relations involving the East and West. Even dialogue among academicians soured, misunderstandings and rumors abounded, and negative perceptions of the Other deepened.

Few are aware that immediately following World War II, the All-Polish Anti-Racist League (Ogólnopolska Liga do Walki z Rasizmem) was founded in Poland. Its mission was to review Jewish-Polish relations prior to and during the war. However, it was soon shut down by the communist authorities. Its work conflicted with the government's desire to portray the Polish people as the most victimized group in Europe.[33]

Jakub Berman, a leading—and Jewish—member of Poland's 1946 communist regime, manipulated the numbers of Polish dead to establish an equivalence between Polish and Jewish wartime suffering. Thus, we have come to *know* that three million Polish Christians were killed during the war alongside three million Polish Jews. In his book *Bloodlands*, Timothy Snyder contends that by adjusting the then accepted figure of 4.8 million Polish citizens' deaths to six million,

---

31 Biskupski, *Hollywood's War with Poland*, 67–68.
32 Jerzy Tomaszewski, e-mail correspondence with author, July 8, 2012.
33 Ireneusz Krzeminski, "In Light of Later History," in *Why We Should Teach about the Holocaust*, ed. Jolanta Ambrosewicz-Jacobs and Leszek Hońdo, trans. Michael Jacobs (Cracow: The Jagiellonian University Institute of European Studies, 2005), 30.

Berman elevated Polish misery to that experienced by Jews.[34] Such statistics play a large role in the politics of memory. That its villages, towns, cities, and infrastructure were almost completely destroyed only increased Poland's status as Europe's most abject country.

Cold War geopolitics furthered this presentation of Poles as second only to the Jews in terms of misery. Denied access to any inflammatory documentation from the period, Polish historians only studied the "facts" to which the Polish communist government gave them access.[35] The Polish People's Republic presented its experience during World War II as that of total innocence versus pure Nazi evil. Very soon, memory of the Jews' particular experience was masked in all Soviet bloc countries including the Polish People's Republic. The history that young Poles learned in school was only that which the party approved.[36]

School textbooks stated that six million Poles died during the war. That three million of those murdered were Jews living in Poland no longer had relevance. Memorials set up by the communist government at death camps identified the victims simply as Poles, instead of as *Jewish* and *Christian* and *Romani* Poles,[37] even though it was the Jewish population in Poland which had teetered on the edge of annihilation. New generations of Poles did not learn to differentiate between the Nazi treatment of Jews and the Nazi treatment of Poles. All were Poles, and all Poles had been dealt with monstrously. Although most Poles who experienced the Nazi occupation directly had witnessed the Jews being singled out for ghettoization and mass murder, the fact that Poles suffered terribly and continued to suffer for decades under Soviet imperialism trained most Poles' attention on their own circumstances. They had little room for the Jews' suffering when they suffered themselves.

Only well after Stalin's death in 1953 were the Polish people permitted to examine national minorities within the Second Republic, the country's views

---

34　Timothy Snyder, *Bloodlands: Europe between Hitler and Stalin* (New York: Basic Books, 2012), 406.
35　Bozena Szaynok, "The Role of Antisemitism in Postwar Polish-Jewish Relations," in *Antisemitism and Its Opponents in Modern Poland*, ed. Robert Blobaum (Ithaca: Cornell University Press, 2005), 265, 279.
36　Zdzisław Mach, "The Memory of the Holocaust and Education for Europe," in Ambrosewicz-Jacobs and Hońdo, *Why We Should Teach about the Holocaust*, 22.
37　Due to current limited documentation and postwar Europe's ignoring the Roma genocide, historians estimate that Germans and their allies killed between 250,000 and 500,000 Roma during WWII. See United States Holocaust Memorial Museum, "Genocide of European Roma (Gypsies), 1939–1945," Holocaust Encyclopedia, accessed January 7, 2023, https://encyclopedia.ushmm.org/content/en/article/genocide-of-european-roma-(gypsies)-1939–1945.

of minorities, and the relationship Poles had with the Jews during World War II. And then only through the lens of Polish heroism. The first book on this subject came out in 1966. Written by Władysław Bartoszewski and Zofia Lewin, and constructed in part to dispel international slander against Polish society, *This is My Homeland: Poles Helping Jews 1939–1945* (*Ten jest z Ojczyzny mojej*) tells the story of Polish aid to the Jews while marginalizing Polish harm to Jews and their Polish rescuers.[38] Recognized by Yad Vashem, Israel's Holocaust museum, as Righteous Among the Nations, Władysław Bartoszewski was the deputy of the Jewish section of the Home Army and aided the establishment of Żegota (Council for Aid to Jews). Despite having experienced intense Polish opposition to his mission, he avoids highlighting its debilitating effect on Jews and their Polish rescuers. Instead, he and Lewin focus on the important work that Polish rescuers accomplished through an accepted Polish communist narrative.[39]

The degree to which the authorities censored manuscripts before permitting their publication depended on the leadership and public policy of the moment. Jerzy Tomaszewski and Henry Zieliński had great difficulty in the late 1970s and early 1980s printing and distributing their work on Poland's ethnic minorities. Zieliński's *Polish History 1914–1939* (*Historia Polski 1914–1939*) includes sections dealing with Polish violence against Jews in 1918 Lviv as well as several other passages regarding Jews in Poland. The censor refused to pass the book for publication. A dispute ensued. Zieliński was murdered in March 1981. It took his wife two more years of arguing with the censor before his manuscript could be published. For years, the censors had also denied Tomaszewski's first book on this topic, *Commonwealth of Nations* (*Rzeczpospolita wielu narodówa*), which was finally printed in 1985. His second title, *A Homeland Not Only for Poles* (*Ojczyna nie tylko Polaków*), was well received, but by the time the books were printed a political policy shift had occurred. Removed from bookstore shelves, all copies were sequestered in the publisher's cellar, not to be sold for years.[40] The Polish communist government's censorship of historiography greatly affected what Poles did and did not learn about Jewish life in their country, including the complexity of Polish-Jewish relations.

---

38 Tomasz Żukowski, ed. Mateusz Szepaniak, "'This Is My Homeland . . .' By Władysław Bartoszewski and Zofia Lewinówna (1966): A Critical Reading," Polin Museum of the History of Polish Jews, accessed January 7, 2023, https://sprawiedliwi.org.pl/en/o-sprawiedliwych/kim-sa-sprawiedliwi/ten-jest-z-ojczyzny-mojej-lektura-krytyczna.
39 Ibid., and Władysław Bartoszewski, introduction to *The Samaritans: Heroes of the Holocaust*, by Władysław Bartoszewski and Zofia Lewin (New York: Twayne Publishers, Inc., 1970), 20. First published as *Ten jest zojczyzny mojej* (Crakow: Znak, 1966).
40 Jerzy Tomaszewski, e-mail correspondence with author, July 8, 2012.

Due to such censorship, American Jewry refused the concept of the "righteous Pole," assessing it as an overall deception, a fiction.[41] In fact, rarely has the American Jewish establishment accepted that there were many Poles who, despite the threat to their own lives and those of family members, stood up against political and religious leaders to help Jews. When the 1969 British version of Władysław Bartoszewski's and Zofia Lewin's earlier work appeared, now titled *Righteous Among Nations: How Poles Helped the Jews*, American Jews received it with great skepticism. Although both authors had co-founded the underground organization ŻEGOTA, the Council for Aid to Jews, in 1942, and both had acted heroically to save Polish Jews during World War II, American Jewry was unwilling to accept their testimony. That the book reached publication just after an anti-*Zionist* campaign forced more than fifteen thousand Polish Jews to emigrate from the country likely played a role in its reception. To American Jews, such stories only underscored the belief that Poles were loath to recognize their own antisemitism. Just as Polish Americans may have gravitated to this positive presentation of Poles aiding Jews, American Jews were more likely to dismiss it as a ploy by Poles to manipulate American perceptions.

US Antisemitism Impacts American Jews' Call to Aid European Jewry

As for the American Jewish response to the Holocaust, many American Jews stated after the war that they did not know what was happening to the Jews until it was too late. It is true that the US State Department's policy suppressed news of the Holocaust and frustrated any possible American rescue attempts. Included in this agenda was Hollywood's agreement *not* to create films focused on the Jews' perilous situation. However, by November 1942 news of Hitler's Final Solution had become public knowledge. Yet, even before that time, news had been secretly couriered to American Jewish leaders. In January 1943, the same month the Nazis began the final liquidation of the Warsaw ghetto, the Jewish National Council in Poland addressed American Jewish organizations, such as the American World Congress of Jews and the American Joint Distribution Committee as follows: "Brothers! The remnants of the Jews in Poland live in the knowledge that in the darkest hour of our history you did

---

41 Jerzy Tomaszewski, e-mail correspondence with author, May 26, 2012, July 8, 2012, and July 10, 2012.

not help us. Say something. This is our *final* appeal to you" (emphasis mine).[42] Having requested weapons for self-defense, money for aid, and contacts in a neutral country, they received little acknowledgement. Though some Jewish leaders, such as Rabbi Stephen Wise, tried to convince President Roosevelt that more needed to be done to help European Jews, most did not get involved. There existed within the US government, and surprisingly amidst American Jewry itself, an ambivalence toward rescuing European Jews.

One profound government impediment to action on behalf of Jews remained the strict immigration policy in force since 1930.[43] Unwilling to fight the prewar isolationist and xenophobic sentiments in both Congress and the general population, President Roosevelt continued Hoover's restrictive policy into the war. After knowing about Nazi plans to exterminate all Jews in lands Germany controlled, Congress would not even allow a vote on bills sponsored by both Republicans and Democrats to permit temporary admission of all possible victims of German persecution.[44] While Roosevelt's War Refugee Board did manage to save some two hundred thousand European Jews, the fact that it was created only in January 1944 and was impeded by US bureaucracy points to lost opportunities and a US ambivalence regarding rescue.

Most Jewish leaders did not argue against this closed-door immigration strategy. Too many feared that an influx of unsponsored Jewish refugees from Eastern Europe would further promote the antisemitism which had increased dramatically in the US since the 1930s. During the war, American Catholics and Protestants filled their media, sermons, and textbooks with caustic antisemitism. Secular organizations debuted, such as We, the Mothers, and the Silver Shirts, which blamed the Jews for the war. Members of Congress expressed their hatred of Jews openly: Mississippi Senator Theodore Bilbo referred to a certain class of Jews in New York as "kikes" acting to "cram" the Fair Employment Practices Commission "down the throats of the American people."[45] Congressman Jacob Thorkelson of Montana propagated the conspiracy theory advanced popularly

---

42 Ryszard Zelichowski, "Pilate's Gesture," in *My Brother's Keeper: Recent Polish debates on the Holocaust*, ed. Antony Polonsky (Oxford: Routledge, 1990), 152.
43 Responding to the Great Depression and the following acute unemployment, President Herbert Hoover added restrictions to the already stringent 1924 nationality-based immigration regulations. Interpreting the 1917 ban on people "likely to become a public charge" within the context of the depression, Hoover even closed the door to professionals. See Leonard Dinnerstein, *Antisemitism in America* (Oxford: Oxford University Press, 1994), 131.
44 Ibid., 144.
45 Ibid., 131–137.

since the 1920s that international Jewish financiers were supporting communists' bid for world domination.[46]

A 1943 government report demonstrates that the middle class, especially those in Pennsylvania, Detroit, Cleveland, Minneapolis, and Los Angeles extolled vitriolic hatred against the Jews. Anonymous groups widely distributed antisemitic leaflets in factories and government buildings. The Massachusetts governor's investigation found the Boston police culpable of ignoring years of Irish and German Catholic gang violence against Jewish youths. Despite efforts made to raise tolerance, antisemitism also existed in the armed services. Even spokesmen and writers argued against the perceived overrepresentation of Jews in professions such as dentistry and psychology.[47] Before knowing the full extent of Nazi atrocities, the labor movement, which included many Jewish leaders, actively lobbied the government against issuing more visas to refugees so as to prevent competition. Initially, the government locked the gates.

Surrounded by a rampantly vocal antisemitic populace, too few people, even Jews, were willing to stand up and call for America to allow refugees entry. Jewish communal organizations could not agree on what approach to take. The fact remained that many Jews in America still busied themselves with assimilating into American culture. Too anxious about their own status, they could not see fit to make way for a large wave of Jewish immigrants. Those who did have the courage to speak against the system were often dismissed as radical elements within the community and fired from their leadership positions.[48]

Closer to the war's end, more American Jews felt guilty for their communal inaction on behalf of their besieged counterparts. After much infighting among leaders of America's Jewish organizations, the establishment united in 1944 to aid survivors in Europe. Much of this response translated into strong support for the creation of the State of Israel. Initially, after the war, American Jewish leaders continued to accept the closed-door immigration policy. Still insecure themselves as Jews in the US, and fearing job scarcity as soldiers returned to civilian life, they focused on the reconstruction of Jewish life on the European continent and settlement of survivors in British-controlled Palestine.

Only after President Truman himself not only grew incensed over Britain's own closed-door policy in Palestine, but also advised Congress to create provisions to permit some European refugees into the United States, did Jewish groups support a change in immigration laws. Beginning in November 1946,

---

46 Ibid., 134–136.
47 Ibid., 133 and 137.
48 Goska, "The Necesssity of 'Bieganski,'" 215–216.

the American Jewish Committee led a campaign to lobby Congress to adopt the Displaced Persons Act. Approved in 1948, this legislation permitted 205,000 refugees to enter the United States. By 1950, Congress passed new legislation that eliminated all antisemitic barriers to immigration, making it far easier for Jewish refugees to enter the country.[49]

Myth Reconstruction

How did American Jews' relative inaction on behalf of their fellow Jews in Europe play out in Polish-Jewish relations? Danusha Goska argues that postwar American Jews required a scapegoat, and they chose the Poles. She quotes Elie Wiesel's painful recognition that, due to their failure to act, American Jews held some culpability for the enormity of the Holocaust: "[I]f our brothers had shown more compassion, more initiative, more daring . . . if a million Jews had demonstrated in front of the White House . . . if Jewish notables had started a hunger strike . . . who knows, the enemy might have desisted."[50] Instead of accepting responsibility for their inaction, the American Jewish establishment directed its condemnation onto a viable "culprit"—the Pole. As we have seen, American pop culture had already condemned the Pole as a savage, uneducated brute prone to violence and dangerous nationalism.

Placing guilt on Poland made sense given emerging postwar geopolitics. To blame only Germany would conflict with America's new foreign policy, which assigned tremendous importance to supporting a reorganized West Germany. Instead, the Soviet Union and its satellites, including the Polish People's Republic, became the West's new enemy. The American initiative to promote

---

[49] This political move echoed the fervent social crusade against racism beginning in the US. Public disgust with both antisemitism and its spokesmen developed quickly in the postwar years. Beginning with soldiers who saw the camps, and extending to the general populace, antisemitism became socially unacceptable. Although it did not disappear fully, it was forced underground. Those places formerly closed to Jews, whether social clubs, elite higher education, or professional positions, began to welcome Jews. At the same time, the Americans were experiencing an economic boom and had little need to blame an Other for any lack of opportunity. Thus, from 1945 to 1965 there was a dramatic decrease in antisemitic incidents outside of the American South. This cultural transformation, together with the confidence Jews garnered by the 1948 declaration of the State of Israel's independence, made it easier for America's Jews to rally against religious bias. See Leonard Dinnerstein, *Antisemitism in America*, 161 and 150–165.

[50] Goska, "The Necessity of 'Bieganski,'" 215.

Europe's recovery, known as the Marshall Plan, echoed this new worldview. While the plan gathered and divided extensive resources to rebuild Western Europe, it provided no support for Soviet satellites. Eva Hoffman laments that

> instead of being modified by time and change, the bleak images of Poland were calcified by the Cold War. The Iron Curtain was a force of and for reductiveness. The countries behind that divide became relegated, even more strongly than before, to a category of Otherness, a realm of leaden, monolithic oppression.[51]

American Jewry followed this international political direction in its self-assessment of inaction on behalf of fellow Jews during the Holocaust. To escape blame and self-loathing, American Jewry denounced the Poles for what appeared to be their apathy toward Jewish victimization. By condemning the Poles, American Jews succeeded in ignoring their own unspoken shame and dishonor. Consciously or subconsciously, American Jews were desperate to place this shame anywhere but on themselves. That the Soviet system swallowed Poland created just the landing pad for it.[52]

As we have seen, like all religions, nations, and countries, both the Poles and the Jews have created narratives they teach to new generations in order to ensure group continuity. This mythmaking is a natural part of understanding communal identity and one's place in the world. Ironically, both Poles and Jews have withstood an inordinate amount of physical violence, political dismemberment, and social ostracism. To make sense of it all, each group has promoted their respective party lines.

Just as Poles continued to learn about only the positive behaviors of their fellow nationals towards Jews, American Jewry continued to view Poles only within their negative framework. Such defensive myths and stereotypes of the Other tend to have some kernel of truth, which allows for their inception and persistence. Stereotypes do not provide us with the full truth; instead, they bar us from it. Thus, the challenge in addressing the current cliche about Poles that so many American Jews hold is to distinguish between *all* Poles and *some* Poles, as well as to expose various contextual influences, both external and internal.

---

51 Eva Hoffman, *Shtetl: The Life and Death of a Small Town and the World of Polish Jews* (New York: Public Affairs, 2007), 4.

52 Raphael Scharf, "Janusz Korczak and His Time," in *Poland, What Have I to Do with Thee...: Essays without Prejudice* (London: Vallentine Mitchell, 1998); Elie Wiesel, "Eichmann's Victims and the Unheard Testimony," *Commentary* 32 (December 1961).

Here is my challenge: let us dig more deeply into what postcommunist historians, both Polish and American, both Christian and Jewish, have revealed about Polish-Jewish relations. Let us be bold and courageous, willing to read more carefully. It is through this more *intentional* work that we will reevaluate and reconstruct our internalized myths. To begin, it is imperative that we gain a broad contextual understanding of Poland's feudal past.

CHAPTER 2

Polish Feudalism and Its Middleman Minority

For centuries, the Polish Crown, landed nobility, and Catholic Church contended for control over land, levies, and laborers.[1] Extensive power and tremendous wealth awaited the victor after each bout. The sixteenth century marked the rise of the nobility (*szlachta*)—which included rich landowning magnates, as well as impoverished and landless gentry. At that point the szlachta accounted for 5–6% of the total population.[2]

Due to the elite szlachta's role in voting for a king, many royal suitors (typically foreigners) courted its ranks with promised privileges. Such bribes expanded the nobility's legal rights. By the end of the fifteenth century, the nobility directed the monarch to establish a central representative political body, the Sejm, with two legislative chambers. It filled the lower house with noble representation from provincial parliaments. Civil changes required full Sejm approval, while all royal appointments required Sejm ratification.[3] The szlachta had gained governmental control. In this chapter we will explore the feudal Polish-Lithuanian landscape and the Jewish middleman minority's role in it.

Poland's Feudal Estate Structure

Similar to other medieval European polities, Poland's agrarian feudal system supported a landscape divided into societal and economic strata, known as estates. Social status distinguished people, relegating ethnic origin to a relatively minor

---

1 Land and structures on it were denoted as royal, private, or Church owned.
2 Antony Polonsky, *The Jews in Poland and Russia*, vol. 1, 1350 to 1881 (Oxford: The Littman Library of Jewish Civilization, 2010), 166.
3 Ibid.

role. No matter whether one was Ruthenian, Belarussian, Lithuanian, or Polish, family lineage, landholdings, and assets determined noble status. Alongside the nobility, there were several other estates: the Christian clergy, the townspeople known as burghers, and the peasantry. In this caste-like system, one could rarely lift oneself into a higher social stratum.

With its increased political power, the nobility secured dominance over the peasantry and townspeople. It persuaded the king to strip the peasantry of its largely free status. Already in the early fifteenth century, it persuaded the Crown to impose a form of neo-serfdom on the peasantry. This shift restricted peasants' rights to leave their lord's estate without permission. In addition, it forced peasants not only to make payments to nobles in both money and kind, but also to provide increased *corvée*—the unpaid labor that peasants owed their respective lords—to at least three days per week.

Near the turn of the sixteenth century, Christian townspeople also came under szlachta assault. Known as burghers, these merchants and artisans tended to be non-Polish in ethnicity. Predominantly of German origin, Dutch and Italians also figured heavily in the burgher estate, with Armenians and Scots to a lesser degree.[4] They took up residence in Poland for the same economic opportunities as did the Jews. By barring burghers from purchasing land or holding either Church or state office, the szlachta prohibited their social and political advancement. The szlachta continued its self-serving approach to the law in 1539, when the Sejm gave all jurisdiction over those towns on noble estates to their owners, denying burgher residents a basic freedom—the protection of the royal courts.[5] Additionally, the nobility extorted monopolistic entitlements from the Crown, thus stealing manufacturing and processing rights from the burghers. Furthermore, the elite landholding nobility, known as magnates, shifted their own tax burden onto the burghers. In times of war, the nobility forced burghers to supply, without monetary compensation, housing for troops and military matériel.[6] By the mid-sixteenth century the szlachta was firmly in control—at the expense of the peasantry and burghers.

---

4 Ibid., 103.
5 Ibid., 167.
6 Ibid.

The Jewish Presence in Poland

An extremely modest Jewish presence in Poland began in the tenth century when Jewish merchants settled there due to the important trade routes traversing the land. While some early Jewish migrants came from the eastern land of Khazaria, a short-lived nomadic polity,[7] some Jewish traders also entered early on through Poland's western frontiers. Later, with rising persecution and expulsions of Jewish communities in Western Europe, large numbers of Jews migrated to find tolerance and refuge in Poland.[8]

By the mid-eleventh century Jews were sufficiently ensconced in the Polish state that they headed its coin manufacturing.[9] Duke Bolesław the Pious of Wielkopolska's 1264 Statute of Kalisz established the Jews' first legal foundation in Poland. In 1334, King Kazimierz the Great extended the statute throughout Poland and expanded Jewish privileges. With the reconfirmation of both rulings throughout the centuries, the Jews gained and maintained their legal position in Poland.

Within Poland's stratified milieu, the Jews were separated into their own distinct estate, with specific rights, obligations, and privileges. Unlike their situation in other parts of Europe at the time, Jews who settled in Poland's royal cities had the right to travel freely, as well as to engage in a variety of business ventures and artisan activities. Polish kings encouraged and enabled Jews not only to build synagogues and to hire Jewish clergy, but also to set up their own institutional leaderships—*kahals*. These Jewish councils dealt with internal Jewish communal affairs. Employing Jewish law (halakha), a kahal legislated over those cases involving only Jews.[10] Additionally, a kahal set limits on economic competition

---

7   For decades, Jewish historians have accepted the medieval legend that Khazaria's king converted both himself and the royal elite to Judaism to avoid political-religious conflicts between the Islamic Caliphate and Christian Byzantium. Recent scholars, however, dismiss this claim. See Yochanan Petrovsky-Shtern and Antony Polonsky, introduction to *Jews and Ukrainians*, ed. Yochanan Petrovsky-Shtern and Antony Polonsky. Polin: Studies in Polish Jewry, vol. 26 (Oxford: The Littman Library of Jewish Civilization, 2014), 3.

8   Janusz Tazbir, "Images of the Jew in the Polish Commonwealth," in *Poles and Jews: Perceptions and Misperceptions*, ed. Wladyslaw T. Bartoszewski. Polin: Studies in Polish Jewry, vol. 4 (Oxford: The Littman Library of Jewish Civilization, 1989), 21.

9   Currency dating to that era bears not only the Polish king's name in Hebrew letters, but also those of the Jewish minters. See Aleksander Gieysztor, "Beginnings of Jewish Settlement in Poland," in *The Jews in Poland*, ed. Chimen Abramsky, Maciej Jachimszyk, and Antony Polonsky (Oxford: Basil Blackwell, 1986), 16–19.

10 Jacob Goldberg, "The Privileges Granted to Jewish Communities of the Polish Commonwealth as a Stabilizing Factor in Jewish Support," in Abramsky, Jachimszyk, and Polonsky, *The Jews in Poland*, 31.

within the community, reviewed individual and communal relations with non-Jews, collected taxes, oversaw Jewish education, and provided for both the sick and the impoverished.[11] Indeed, the Jews' kahal system approximated the burghers' own communal autonomous structure, which included self-regulating tribunals.[12]

By the mid-sixteenth century, Jewish religious autonomy had reached its peak in the government-sanctioned Council of Four Lands (*Va'ad Arba Aratsot*). A Jewish institution unique to the Polish-Lithuanian Commonwealth, it acted on a semi-national level to promote Jewish communal autonomy. While European countries had long permitted Jewish communal autonomy through the singular kahal, the Polish-Lithuanian Commonwealth accepted a far more dynamic, extensive, and cooperative system. Each local kahal focused on its own administrative, judicial, legislative, and educational functions, whereas the *Va'ad Arba Aratsot* concentrated on relations with the government, tax collection from Jews, and adjudication of difficult matters among the commonwealth's Jews.[13] It acted more broadly and profoundly toward Jewish communal goals than any other individual kahal in Western Europe.[14] Indeed, while other countries, such as England, France, and the German principalities persecuted and expelled Jews, Poland welcomed them and established a legal format by which they could live full Jewish lives.

Although the Kingdom of Poland provided an array of communal freedoms to the Jewish people, it determinedly limited Jews' individual social and political advancement. The nobility designed a self-preserving social system by eliminating the threat of Others' encroachment. Just as the szlachta impeded those within the burgher estate from advancing into the nobility, it also erected similar barriers against Jewish infringement. For example, the szlachta blocked both Jews and burghers from jobs in the civil service. As owning land was a direct path into the nobility, the szlachta also denied land acquisition to burghers, Jews, and peasants. It is important to note that this was not a specific anti-Jewish policy. Rather it was a protective measure put in place by rulers to keep all

---

11   Gershon Hundert, *Jews in Poland-Lithuania in the Eighteenth Century: A Genealogy of Modernity* (Berkeley: University of California Press, 2004), 87.
12   Polonsky, *The Jews in Poland and Russia*, 1:17, 103–104.
13   M. J. Rosman, *The Lords' Jews: Magnate-Jewish Relations in the Polish-Lithuanian Commonwealth during the 18th Century* (Cambridge, MA: Harvard University Press, 1990), 37–38.
14   Chimen Abramsky, Maciej Jachimczyk, and Antony Polonsky, introduction to *The Jews in Poland*, 3. For a detailed description, see Gershon Hundert, *Jews in Poland-Lithuania* and Eva Hoffman, *Shtetl*, 54–62.

"foreigners" from challenging the elite's authority. However, by the early 1700s, this rule was challenged and often circumvented.[15]

From the thirteenth to the eighteenth centuries, Poland's leaders embraced the Jews for their economic connections. The country lacked financial relationships beyond its borders, and Jewish merchants ably created the links the country needed. Thus, when ousted by Western polities, Jews migrated to Polish territory. There they settled in Polish royal towns under the immediate jurisdiction of royal governors (*wojewoda*), connecting them directly to the king.[16] Until the mid-sixteenth century the king enjoyed tremendous authority over both the country, as well as the Jews. The Jews in turn contributed greatly to the ruling class's prosperity through trade, taxation, crafts, and moneylending.

Poland's Middleman Minority

Stemming from the Christian conviction that dealing in money and trade is a sin, ethnic Poles viewed commerce and moneylending as beneath them. Instead, owning and cultivating land was the pride of the ruling elite: kings, noblemen, and men of the Church. All relationships to the land commanded respect. Even peasants and serfs castigated those who did not till the soil.

While both Jews and Poles have viewed the economic role Jews played in Poland and their designated place in Polish society as distinct, it correlated to that void filled by outsider groups in various countries. According to Yuri Slezkine, "[t]here was nothing particularly unusual about the social and economic position of the Jews in medieval and early modern Europe. Many agrarian societies contained groups of permanent strangers who performed tasks that the natives were unable or unwilling to perform."[17] By migrating from their countries of origin to various European lands, and preserving a strict separation from their respective host societies, many outsider groups achieved positions of economic importance. They are referred to as middleman minorities. Some

---

15   In 1727, and again in 1760, Jews purchased a notable amount of land from Christian sellers. Additionally, in 1764 the Crown chose to ennoble hundreds of wealthy Jewish families who had converted to Christianity. See Rosman, *The Lords' Jews*, 47; Andrzej Ciechanowiecki, "A Footnote to the History of the Integration of Converts into the Ranks of the *Szlachta* in the Polish-Lithuanian Commonwealth," in Abramsky, Jachimczyk, and Polonsky, *The Jews in Poland*, 66.
16   Hundert, *Jews in Poland-Lithuania in the Eighteenth Century*, 3.
17   Yuri Slezkine, *The Jewish Century* (Princeton: Princeton University Press, Princeton and Oxford, 2004), 4.

examples include the Armenians, who collected taxes for the Ottomans and the Parsis of Mumbai and Gujarat, who filled artisan roles and moved into brokering, moneylending, shipbuilding, and international commerce.[18] By specializing in bringing goods and services to the surrounding agricultural or pastoral populations, they made a niche for themselves within their host societies.[19] Like the Jews, these groups took on the role of middleman minority.

Sociologist Edna Bonacich attributes the following traits to middleman minorities:

> a resistance to out-marriage, residential self-segregation, the establishment of language and cultural schools for their children, the maintenance of distinctive cultural traits (including, often, a distinctive religion), and a tendency to avoid involvement in local politics except in affairs that directly affect their group. They form highly organized communities which resist assimilation.[20]

If one accepts Bonacich's model, feudal Poland's Jewish population was the quintessence of the middleman minority.

Poland's need for the Jew to act as a middleman minority increased when sixteenth-century laws prohibited the nobility's participation in industry and commerce under penalty of losing legal rights and privileges.[21] Society had cast such activity well below the nobleman's status. Viewing agriculture as their only proper occupation, nobles and serfs alike shared the common belief that Jews' engagement in commerce was a necessary evil.[22] Likewise, they also criticized the burghers' commercial enterprises.

---

18   Ibid., 6.
19   Ibid., 7.
20   Edna Bonacich, "A Theory of Middleman Minorities," *American Sociological Review* 38, no. 5 (1973): 586.
21   Michlic, *Poland's Threatening Other*, 31.
22   Tazbir, "Images of the Jew in the Polish Commonwealth," 20; Michlic, *Poland's Threatening Other*, 45.

The Jewish Middleman Minority Threatens Burghers

From the outset, Jewish migration to Poland threatened burgher prosperity. Jews sought business opportunities in those fields they had experience, but which were already occupied by Poland's burghers. The early Jewish incursion into moneylending and trade, coupled with their later entry into craftwork, created great turmoil for the kingdom's burghers. As it did for all middleman minorities, communal solidarity, thrift, and low economic expectations allowed Jews to produce products at lower consumer costs than their burgher counterparts.[23] While the king and nobility appreciated the competitive pricing that the Jews brought, the burghers resented their shrinking profits. Not only did Jews compete with them, but they also eventually displaced a great many established burgher artisans and merchants.[24] According to Bonacich, this specific competition between Jew and burgher equates to a typical encounter between a middleman minority and those business groups which predated the middleman's immigration.[25]

Burghers attempted to salvage their economic monopolies against the Jews' incursion by requesting that the Crown set economic restrictions on Jewish competition.[26] However, despite legislation barring Jews from membership in the various artisan guilds, they succeeded in producing their cheaper wares while remaining a source of angst for the city burghers. At the height of the conflict, burghers in many royal cities lobbied the king to go one step further by expelling the Jews.[27]

The nobility's own demand for the Jews' business acumen only increased during the following centuries with Poland's eastern expansion. Some claim that so much did the nobleman believe he required the Jews' services that the szlachta safeguarded Jews to the detriment of the lower sectors of society.[28] Such

---

23   Family, regional, and ethnic ties lead to preferential economic treatment. In Poland, Jews either had family working long arduous hours for little to no pay or hired other Jews who accepted that middleman firms had to labor intensively while cutting labor costs to have any chance of success. Jewish non-family members willingly worked for less money than their Gentile counterparts, due to low economic expectations as well as a desire to connect culturally at work. See Bonacich, "A Theory of Middleman Minorities": 586.
24   Rosman, *The Lords' Jews*, 71.
25   Bonacich, "A Theory of Middleman Minorities": 590.
26   Bernard D. Weinryb, *The Jews of Poland: A Social and Economic History of the Jewish Community in Poland from 1100–1800* (Philadelphia: The Jewish Publication Society of America, 1972), 129.
27   Hundert, *Jews in Poland-Lithuania in the Eighteenth Century*, 46–47.
28   Tazbir, "Images of the Jew in the Polish Commonwealth," 22.

protection came not only in rights granted by the nobility to the Jews to compete with the burghers in trade and craft, but also in the nobility's condemnation of sporadic violence against Jews. While burghers argued for the Jews' expulsion, the szlachta rarely acted or spoke in such extreme terms against them.

The Kresy

In the late fourteenth century, Poland entered into a dynastic relationship with the Grand Duchy of Lithuania through the marriage of Grand Duke Jogaila and the young Jadwiga, Poland's only successor to its throne. Jogaila accepted Western Christianity and took the baptismal name of Władysław II Jagiełło. The Lithuanian court and nobility began a long process of Polonization by immediately accepting Roman Catholicism. This loose union provided both territories protective provisos in case enemies should invade either country. On July 1, 1569, leaders solidified this relationship between the two states through the Declaration of the Union of Lublin, thereby formally creating the Polish-Lithuanian Commonwealth, also known as the First Republic of Poland (1569–1795).[29]

The Polish-Lithuanian Commonwealth was the largest country in Europe at that time, with enormous power and natural resources. It consisted of 7.5 million people, with three million residing in Poland itself.[30] The szlachta referred to the great swath of land added to the core of Greater Poland (Wielkopolska) as the *kresy*. These borderlands included the Grand Duchy of Lithuania, as well as those lands it had previously conquered, which we know today as Ukraine and Belarus. The kresy played the important role as the physical buffer against neighboring aggression. Therefore, dominance over that territory was vital for maintaining the country's security.

By way of establishing Poland's control of the kresy, the king offered this vast eastern territory to the wealthiest of the noblemen, the magnates. As compensation for their military service defending the Crown,[31] this szlachta elite was

---

29 Although this commonwealth shared a monarch and a parliament, some division remained as each retained a separate government administration, treasury, army, and code of law. See Polonsky, *The Jews in Poland and Russia*, 1:167.
30 Ibid., 13.
31 Petrovsky-Shtern and Polonsky, introduction to Petrovsky-Shtern and Polonsky, *Jews and Ukrainians*, 5.

granted the right to organize and develop their huge expanses of land.[32] Known as a *latifundium*, each vast, though not necessarily contiguous territory, consisted of hundreds of villages and towns, with tens of thousands of inhabitants, representing hundreds of thousands of złoty in annual income and expenditures. Complexes dotted the territory. At the heart of each stood a manor, around which whirred several farming industries including cattle, poultry, fish, field crops, and timber. Most manors also had their own means to produce and sell liquor, grind grain, and mine salt.[33]

This sixteenth-century expansion into the kresy created a power shift. The magnate gained more land and thus more influence: on his property a magnate was sole lawmaker, lead manager, commander of his private army, and ultimate judge. Those few who achieved such status believed that they deserved to live like royalty. As such, each magnate family constructed multiple dwellings of massive proportions throughout their acquired lands. They furnished these extravagant residences at great expense, with exceptional art, lavish furniture, imported cloth, crystal tableware, and a full staff of butlers, maids, cooks, and soldiers.[34] Enjoying such excessive lifestyles, these aristocrat-magnates concerned themselves with accessing the cash flow needed to maintain it.

The new kresy territories were filled with limitless possibilities for generating the magnate's required funds. All house owners and renters on private lands belonging to a magnate had to pay the proprietor property taxes. Householders paid for the ability to fish in the owner's pond, as well as to graze their livestock in his meadows. Magnates also saved money by requiring those living on their property to supply a specified amount of free materials or labor (corvée). This system furnished magnates with free hay-cutting and baling and grain harvesting; proprietors also had to transport to market the owner's fish, honey, and grain.[35] Additionally, magnates derived income through legalized monopolies. Serfs and residents of private towns were obliged to purchase goods produced or sold by only the magnate who owned the town or from his lessees.[36] Holding villagers and townspeople responsible for acquiring their goods from magnate-owned industries, the owner received a steady income from his liquor and beer production, mills, and mines.

---

32 Rosman, *Lords' Jews*, 8n13 and n40.
33 Ibid., 11.
34 Ibid., 9.
35 Ibid., 53–54.
36 Ibid., 3.

Magnates employed managers and middlemen to oversee their huge territories, villages, towns, farms, and industries. Some magnates participated directly in their own business ventures, but more focused on the honorable duties of defense and politics. While landownership denoted honor, society viewed involvement with its management (revenue collection, property maintenance, and creating profit through agricultural industries) as less reputable. At the same time, the middle gentry—those from less affluent noble lineages—were skilled in agriculture and less trained as the Jews in commerce and industry. Thus, the magnate most often turned to the middleman minority, the Jews, to fill this important economic role.

Kresy Jews: The Epitome of the Middleman Minority

When they first migrated to Poland, Jews settled primarily in Polish royal cities, such as Kraków, Lublin, and Poznań. Due to intensifying burgher resentment of the Jews' economic competition, Jews readily answered the magnates' sixteenth-century call to pioneer the eastern kresy. The szlachta's appeal for Jews to create communities in the kresy was a remedy for both magnate and Jew, as the latter was known to have both business acumen and available cash to lease rights to real estate, agriculture, and industry.

So much did the magnates believe they needed Jewish assistance in creating their towns that many were willing to subsidize Jewish settlement.[37] They attracted Jews to kresy migration by less expensive costs of living, economic freedoms, special privileges, and broad communal rights. Jews were permitted to become lessees of towns, villages, and manors. Along with paying the magnate for the right to lease the land, the Jewish lessee also bought the right to collect and keep all taxes due from the residents on that land. Jews also leased the rights to various latifundium industries, such as liquor production, timber harvesting, and salt mining. This placed Jews in a very strong economic position within the eastern borderland.

Even Jews with little money enjoyed better economic opportunities in the kresy. Having obtained royal privileges to host annual fairs and market days, as well as to produce and sell liquor, every magnate needed people to develop his small private towns into market towns. The Polish elite required managers to run the markets and industries, as well as tradespeople and craftsmen to provide

---

37   Ibid., 40.

goods and services for the peasants. Thus, in exchange for the promise of legal residence, Jews moved far away from the royal cities, far from burgher resentment and influence, to pioneer the kresy. Jews were encouraged to take on trade and crafts, becoming apothecaries, bakers, blacksmiths, candlemakers, doctors, furriers, goldsmiths, haberdashers, launderers, moneylenders, musicians, parchment makers, shoemakers, soap-makers, storekeepers, tailors, and tar makers.[38] Although Jews had greater legal rights in royal cities due to the royal charters, their economic outlook was much better in the kresy.[39] The Jewish population in eastern Poland grew quite large as eastward movement coupled with prolific procreation. By the mid-seventeenth century, Jews numbered between 200,000 to 220,000.[40]

Traditionally, Jews refer to the private noble-owned town as a shtetl. Frenetic Jewish economic activity was central to defining a shtetl. A civilization specific unto itself, the shtetl was inhabited not only by Jews, but also Roman Catholics, Greek Catholics, Tatars, Armenians, Lutherans, and Eastern Orthodox. Here Christian townspeople typically engaged in economic relationships with Jewish townspeople. Contemporary historians underscore the unique quality of each shtetl. Population size did not define it. A shtetl could be large, with thousands of inhabitants, or quite small, with not even one hundred. Their commonality rested on having grown from Polish magnate privately owned towns, which fostered intense economic engagement between the Jewish and Christian populations.[41] A locale was considered a shtetl if the majority of its trading and urban estate was Jewish, if it was based on the Polish lease-holding economy, with an established trade, a marketplace, and a liquor trade all run predominantly by Jews, who themselves were organized into a traditional Jewish community.[42] Yohanan Petrovsky-Shtern suggests that "the shtetl for us is a place, but perhaps we need to re-conceptualize it also as an action, a whir of activity."[43]

The town was the epicenter of economic activity for the surrounding villages. There, Jews and burghers organized weekly markets and fairs in which peasants could sell their products and all parties could exchange goods. Merchants sold wares brought from outside the immediate area and artisans promoted their

---

38 Ibid., 50.
39 Hundert, *Jews in Poland-Lithuania in the Eighteenth Century*, 103.
40 Abramsky, Jachimszyk and Polonsky, introduction, 3.
41 Yohanan Petrovsky-Shtern, *The Golden Age Shtetl: A New History of Jewish Life in East Europe* (Princeton: Princeton University Press, 2014), 12.
42 Ibid., 26.
43 Ibid., 27.

trades. While the magnate did not get money directly from such town activities, he did receive it indirectly. When peasants or townsmen earned money, they used it to purchase items from the latifundium's industries. Although the magnate most likely leased out such business rights, in the future he would procure more rent for it if it was known as a successful industry.

Jews provided not only needed services for the kresy population, but also taxes for the town owner. Jews typically lived in the largest houses in the shtetls, which translated to high property taxes. By 1539, the Crown relinquished its jurisdiction over Jews in private towns, allowing the nobility not only to judge them in cases which involved non-Jews, but also to profit from them as well.[44] Thus, Jews' loyalty and tax revenue transferred to the noble landowner.[45]

Economic Crisis Effects Jews' Privileges

The economic privileges granted to Jews in the kresy came under assault in the mid-seventeenth century due to the acute poverty incurred by the nobility itself. Years of fierce Ukrainian uprisings had displaced many middle and petty gentry from landownership, causing extreme economic decline. Concurrently, the rich got richer as magnates took over land that the displaced could no longer afford. While about 90% of the commonwealth was owned by the nobility, only 25% of noblemen held land.[46] At the same time, there existed a sense of kinship within the nobility. Whether magnate or petty nobleman, the szlachta was one united estate. As such, magnates responded to those nobility suffering economically by reassessing land lease rights and allowing only those of noble lineage to lease land.

This enormous shift affected kresy Jews in that magnates now barred them from leasing real estate and agricultural land. However, they sustained the Jews' rights to participate in the *arenda* system, the leasing of latifundium industries. The magnates continued to sell Jews leases, usually from one to three years in duration, for the right to produce and sell liquor, flour, and salt, manage taverns, collect both property taxes and tolls, organize fairs, trade in grain, export wood, manage salt mines, operate tanning, fulling, grain, and timber mills, control

---

44 Goldberg, "The Privileges Granted to Jewish Communities of the Polish Commonwealth as a Stabilizing Factor in Jewish Support," 35; Hundert, *Jews in Poland-Lithuania in the Eighteenth Century*, 80.
45 Rosman, *The Lords' Jews*, 9.
46 Hundert, *Jews in Poland-Lithuania in the Eighteenth Century*, 40–41.

fishing ponds, store grain in warehouses, sell tobacco, produce and sell dairy products, and run very small stores.[47] Through legal contract, the noble landlord was assured an income, while Jews typically took the monetary risk and responsibility of securing the funds in the specific enterprises.[48] Arenda provided the magnate with the necessary cash flow to pay for his lavish lifestyle,[49] while supplying Jewish arendators with business opportunities.

The Jews in the Polish borderlands became so involved in this business system that the word *arendator* (*arendarz*) was often employed as a synonym for *Jew*.[50] As many as 15% of urban Jewish heads of households, and 80% of rural, were occupied in some aspect of arenda.[51] Usually, after an individual or group of Jews leased most of the industrial rights and monopolies in a given area, subarendators, often also Jews, would lease components of these rights from the general arendators.

This economic structure provided the nobleman with his much-needed funds. In return for the lessee's business, the nobleman protected his arendators when necessary. For if an arendator was unable to collect the revenues leased, the magnate would be incapable of securing a higher price for that lease in the next contract. In toll farming, for example, a lessee would hire his own large staff to collect tolls from those passing through noble property.[52] The staff had extensive legal autonomy and often charged excessive fees and used force to collect payment from those attempting to evade it.[53] In the end, the Jewish lessee usually profited and strove to continue this arrangement. As with all middleman minorities, the Jewish arendator subcontracted to family or community members, who in turn hired family or fellow Jews. Thus, Jews became the face of not only toll farming, but of all other such economic ventures which supported the Polish nobility.

---

47 Ibid., 115.
48 For a detailed description of *arenda*, see M. J. Rosman, *The Lords' Jews*, chapter five, as well as Bernard D. Weinryb, *The Jews of Poland*.
49 Arendators also acted as the magnates' checking accounts. When the owner needed to make a purchase, he would usually send a payment order to those whom he owed money. They in turn had to collect payment from an arendator, who would deduct that amount from the rent he owed the owner. At the end of the quarter, the arendator either paid the owner his remaining monetary obligation or he would show the magnate records indicating the owner already used his due rent money. See Rosman, *The Lords' Jews*, 128–9.
50 Ibid., 110.
51 Ibid., 107n2.
52 The king also leased out rights to both Jew and non-Jew to collect tolls on that property belonging to the Crown. See Weinryb, *The Jews of Poland*, 63.
53 Ibid.

Arenda was not unique to the Polish-Lithuanian Commonwealth. However, by the sixteenth century Poland was the only country in Europe which permitted Jews to participate in that system.⁵⁴ Given both the magnates' and general nobility's economic need for the Jews' services, the latter secured a confident position within Polish feudal kresy society. This economic relationship allowed Jews to flourish in sixteenth- and seventeenth-century Poland thereby casting the commonwealth of Poland-Lithuania was described as "heaven for the Jews, paradise for the nobles, [and] hell for the serfs."⁵⁵

Economic and Religious Conflicts in the Kresy: The Cossacks

Between the sixteenth and seventeenth centuries, agriculture flourished, and the Polish-Lithuanian Commonwealth became the breadbasket of Europe. To secure its harvest, magnates required people to work the land. Most Jews were involved in nonagricultural work. Though some Poles—peasant, burgher, and nobleman alike—moved eastward to benefit from this agricultural wealth, they remained a minority in the kresy. When the Polish magnates took over the land, native Ukrainian, Belarussian, and Lithuanian peasants were already tilling its soil. But they were relatively few in number. Realizing the drastic shortage of available labor to work the magnates' expansive land portions, the nobility steadily stripped the kresy peasantry of any personal freedoms to ensure the lords' access to them.⁵⁶ Simply put, Polish magnates reproduced Poland's feudal system in the kresy, subjugating peasants to the lord's rule. The szlachta not only decided on the type and number of levies to be imposed in the form of services, but also forced the peasants to purchase their alcohol and goods from the magnate's industries. Working the soil for almost no personal gain, the serfs resented not only the nobility's rule over them, but also the systemic use of violence to maintain their forced servitude.⁵⁷

---

54   Abramsky, Jachimszyk, and Polonsky, introduction, 4–5.
55   Ibid., 3.
56   Linda Gordon, *Cossack Rebellions: Social Turmoil in the Sixteenth-Century Ukraine* (Albany: State University of New York Press, 1983), 41.
57   John-Paul Himka, "Dimensions of a Triangle: Polish-Ukrainian-Jewish Relationship in Austrian Galicia," in *Focusing on Galicia: Jews, Poles, and Ukrainians, 1772–1918*, ed. Israel Bartal and Antony Polonsky. Polin: Studies in Polish Jewry, vol. 12 (Oxford: Littman Library of Jewish Civilization, 1999), 27.

While the commonwealth's nobility pressed the kresy's peasants into serfdom, the Polish Catholic clergy hindered them spiritually.[58] By the end of the seventeenth century, the Counter-Reformation had succeeded in this cause, bringing the majority of Poles, including the szlachta and burghers, into the service of the Church.[59] In turn, the Church's power increased. The numbers of Catholic clergy tripled, followed by a rise in church construction. A symbiosis developed between the Catholic Church and Polish culture. Mary, mother of Jesus, multitasked as Mary, queen of Poland. As the Church's authority increased, it—and, in effect, the commonwealth—perceived those who did not accept its religious truth as a possible threat.

Upon the establishment of the Polish-Lithuanian Commonwealth, Lithuania's predominantly Eastern Orthodox population (also referred to as Greek Orthodox) confronted the Catholic Church's demand for religious dominance. One significant difference between the Churches lies in religious authority. While the Eastern Orthodox look toward both Constantinople and Moscow, Catholics focus on Rome and the pope. In 1595–1596, the Catholic Church proposed what it viewed as a conciliatory agreement, the Union of Brest. The Eastern Orthodox community would surrender its allegiance to Constantinople, while maintaining its own separate liturgy. The many Orthodox who accepted this proposal became known derogatorily as Uniates.

Those skeptics who viewed this "compromise" as a masked attempt to co-opt the peasants' religious faith, referred to themselves as Disuniates. The Union of Brest created a deep fissure between the two. In the end, Catholics did not accept Uniates as equals, but rather treated them as second-class Catholics, whose own offspring rebelled by returning to Orthodoxy or by assimilating into mainstream Catholicism.

The Cossacks, a group of Eastern Orthodox Catholics, refused the Union of Brest. A corps of Eastern Slavs, the Cossacks dwelled in the sparsely populated and desolate area of southern Ukraine. Similar to North America's early western frontier, this territory was a choice destination for those evading the law's reach. Through banditry, the Cossacks earned both a living and a dynamic reputation. Not only did Poland's king and various magnates hire Cossacks as mercenaries to protect Polish interests, but neighboring enemies also purchased Cossack military service to wage war against the commonwealth. Cossacks attracted a variety of players into their ranks, such as the lesser gentry who had been squeezed off their lands by the magnate incursion, burghers living in Ukraine whose many

---

58   Ibid., 20.
59   Hundert, *Jews in Poland-Lithuania in the Eighteenth Century*, 57.

rights and privileges the magnates had erased in pursuit of their own economic desires, as well as Ukrainian peasants fleeing the magnates' imposition of serfdom.[60] Over time, the Cossacks attained popular support in the kresy given the Polish nobility's abuse of serf and burgher alike.

Cossacks pledged their allegiance to their own brotherhood. King Sigismund II Augustus (who ruled from 1548–1569) attempted to create among them a sense of devotion to the commonwealth by registering some Cossacks into the republic's army.[61] Receiving the rights of petty noblemen, units of registered Cossacks attained the status of free warriors. They crossed into the noble estate, a feat near impossible for most. Riding either to protect the Polish frontier or to serve as troops in Poland's numerous wars, registered Cossacks garnered economic and social privileges equal to those of the petty nobility.[62]

This hard-earned legal status, however, fell victim to the king's whims. He could take it away at any time by removing an individual Cossack from military service.[63] When dropped, in an instant that person reverted to his original lower social and legal ranking, with all previously gained freedoms forfeited.

Near the mid-1600s, the nobility recognized the Cossacks' growing strength and feared it. At the same time, Cossack leaders requested that *all* Cossacks attain societal and economic equality with the szlachta.[64] From the gentry's point of view, this scandalous idea threatened their fundamental standing. The government responded by sharply reducing the number of registered Cossacks. One estimate holds that whereas in 1621 forty thousand free Cossacks served Poland, by 1630 only some eight thousand remained.[65] This dramatic shift in prestige and privilege for tens of thousands caused intense discontent within the Cossack community.

Not only did this shift generate a conflict over ultimate societal rights and status, but it was also complicated by religious factors. Mostly Eastern Orthodox, the Cossacks refused to recognize the Union of Brest, which gave Poland's Roman Catholic Church authority over the Orthodox community. In 1596, the Cossacks launched the first of many rebellions against Catholic influence.[66]

---

60 Ibid., 73.
61 Ibid., 91.
62 Weinryb, *The Jews of Poland*, 181.
63 Ibid., 182.
64 Ibid.
65 Ibid., 181–182.
66 Nalewajko's Rebellion in 1596 was the first of many Cossack uprisings defending the Orthodox faith against Catholic influence. Less than twenty years later, such religious, social, and political grievances drove the Cossack leader to wage a violent struggle for secession from

The son of a petty nobleman, Boghdan Khmelnytsky entered the Cossack community in 1647. After Khmelnytsky ran into trouble with the law,[67] he fled and joined the Cossacks. Khmelnytsky encouraged the Cossacks to turn against the overbearing aristocratic Polish magnates. Due to their own economic and religious resentments, the Cossacks embraced his call for political independence and waged Khmelnytsky's violent 1648 "Deluge."

The first Cossack written chronicle of the Khmelnytsky uprising, known as the *Eyewitness Chronicle* (*Samovydets Chronicle*, which an unidentified author penned about twenty-five years after the events described), illustrates the Poles' degrading treatment of the Cossacks:

> The origin and cause of the Khmelnytsky War is solely the Polish persecution of the Orthodox and oppression of the Cossacks. Then the latter's freedoms were taken away and they were forced to do corvée labor, to which they were unaccustomed, and turned into household servants at the castles of the castle chiefs, who also used them to groom horses, stoke fires in the stove, groom dogs, sweep the yards, and perform other unbearable tasks.[68]

Reeling from their official return either to serfdom or the status of burgher with many obligations to the nobility, Cossacks rebelled against the commonwealth.

Myth Reconstruction

Jews mourn the Khmelnytsky massacre as a violent outburst specifically targeted against them, and as a forerunner of both late imperial Russian pogroms and the Holocaust.[69] My American Jewish educator, who vehemently disapproved of

---

the commonwealth, giving birth to a Ukrainian national ethos. See Norman Davies, *God's Playground: A History of Poland*, vol. 1, *The Origins to 1795*, rev. ed. (New York: Columbia University Press, 2005), 136; Weinryb, *The Jews of Poland*, 182.

67 With some of his property confiscated, Khmelnytsky was arrested, but released on bail. See *Encyclopedia Judaica*, 2nd ed. (2007), s.v. "*Chmielnicki, Bogdan.*"

68 *Eyewitness Chronicle*, cited in Zenon E. Kohut, "The Khmelnytsky Uprising, the Image of Jews, and the Shaping of Ukrainian Historical Memory," *Jewish History*, vol. 17, no. 2, Gezeirot Ta"h: Jews, Cossacks, Poles, and Peasants in 1648 Ukraine, 2003, 145, http://www.jstor.org/stable/20101495. Accessed 01/08/2012.

69 Kohut, "The Khmelnytsky Uprising, the Image of Jews, and the Shaping of Ukrainian Historical Memory," 141.

my family's trip to Poland, pointed directly to Boghdan Khmelnytsky's 1648–1654 massacres of thousands of Polish Jews as cause to detest Poland.[70] The confidence with which she held up Khmelnytsky as a prime example of Polish hatred for Jews challenged me. Did he prove this educator's point that Poland's history is embedded in such Jew-hatred that the Polish people cannot possibly free themselves from it?

Due to this educator's emphasis on the Khmelnytsky massacres as a major example of Jewish suffering in Poland, one would assume that Khmelnytsky, as a Pole, massacred the Jews and only the Jews in the name of Poland. Though Boghdan Khmelnytsky was raised within the petty Polish nobility, he fought for Ukraine's secession from Poland. His troops employed the terrifying Cossack methods of warfare, including rape, pillage, and murder. His rebellion targeted the Polish nobility, as well as Polish priests who not only led the gentry spiritually, but who at times also sought violent recriminations against Ukrainian Disuniates.[71] The fact is that Khmelnytsky rebelled against Polish rule, ordering his followers to slaughter a considerable number of Polish nobles, Catholic priests, and Uniates.[72]

Understanding the economic role Jews played as a middleman minority to the Polish establishment helps clarify the Cossacks' targeting of Jews. The economic reality demonstrates that Jews had been encouraged to pioneer the kresy. They achieved a higher standard of living and greater social status than the Ukrainian serfs in the Polish-Lithuanian Commonwealth. Even more damning was the fact that early Jewish lessees of towns and villages had not only access to free serf labor, but also control of the keys to open the churches.[73] Additionally, Jews acted as the nobility's tax collector. It was the Jew who

---

70 In 2003, Shaul Stampfer argued that of the forty thousand Jewish residents of Ukraine, some twenty to twenty-two thousand survived Khmelnytsky's forces either by fleeing, defending a locale with Poles, or by their towns not being invaded. Additionally, within that number some died at the hands of Tatars or due to disease. See Shaul Stampfer, "What Actually Happened to the Jews of Ukraine in 1648?" *Jewish History*, vol. 17, no. 2, Gezeirot Ta"h: Jews, Cossacks, Poles, and Peasants in 1648 Ukraine, 2003, 207–227, http://www.jstor.org/stable/20101498. Accessed 01/08/2012.

71 Weinryb, *The Jews of Poland*, 130.

72 Speaking about Volhynia, the author of the *Eyewitness Chronicle* states that Cossacks and their Tatar allies killed "not only Jews and nobles, but the common people of that land suffered the same fate." Kohut, "The Khmelnytsky Uprising, the Image of Jews, and the Shaping of Ukrainian Historical Memory," 146.

73 A 1710 circulated legend explaining the massacres stated that Jewish lessees had to approve the opening of the churches and often charged taxes for various Orthodox rituals to take place. See ibid., 147.

physically reached into Ukrainian serfs' pockets to take what little money they had. Though it was at the behest of the Polish magnate, it was the Jew who enforced the law and simultaneously benefited from it. In the kresy, the Jew was the face of the nobility's suppression of Orthodoxy, the burgher, and the peasant.

In unpacking these complex relationships and conflicts, it is worthwhile to note that kresy burghers fled to join the Cossack camp out of anger with the Polish magnates who had usurped freedoms granted earlier by the king, such as tax exemptions and trading rights. The magnates replaced the burghers' guilds and bypassed their institutions to deal directly with foreign merchants. The Jews facilitated this arrangement. Before peasants had accounted for the Cossack majority, the burghers had filled Cossack ranks. It is no wonder that the burghers turned against the szlachta, and against the Jews who helped the szlachta, to retain economic and thus political power. It was the Jew who had been a bone of contention for the burgher in the eastern borderland and against whom his fellow townsmen in Western Poland were still fighting.

However, according to Zenon E. Kohut, my American Jewish educator's presentation of Khmelnytsky falls completely within the Jewish historic myth:

> Jewish commentators . . . frequently have presented the massacres as a uniquely anti-Jewish phenomenon, paying little attention to the complex social, religious, and national context, and have mitigated or ignored the violence perpetrated against non-Jewish Poles and Ukrainian Uniates.[74]

Additionally, there has been a changing view among historians regarding the numbers of Jewish deaths caused by Khmelnytsky. Linda Gordon employs Israel Friedlander's 1915 scholarship to point to the hundreds of thousands of Jewish lives taken in the Deluge. Antony Polonsky accepts more recent research, which holds that roughly fourteen thousand Jews were murdered in the rebellion and that additional Jewish victims were killed during the subsequent Swedish and Muscovite wars. This does not change the grave effect Khmelnytsky had on the Jewish population in the eastern borderlands; indeed, Khmelnytsky's troops killed a much greater percentage of Poland's Jews than Polish Christians, given that the overall Jewish community was much smaller than its Polish Christian counterpart.

---

74 Ibid., 142.

When looking for a quick yet informed grasp of either a topic or a personage of Jewish interest, I often turn to the *Encyclopedia Judaica* for an overview. The problem is that this popular resource presents past events only through the lens of how events affected the Jews. Under the heading "Chmielnicki [Khmelnytsky], Bogdan," it states that the Cossacks massacred tens of thousands of Jews, but no mention is made of Polish or Uniate deaths. While it presents Jews as defenders of towns, it does not clarify that they worked together with armed Poles to secure those towns' safety.[75] In this scholarly resource, the Jews' collective memories are raised while the Poles' remain buried.

Indeed, collective memory gives rise to a loose and wobbly understanding of the past. In contrast to the *Encyclopedia Judaica*, the original Cossack chronicle of the war describes the rise of Ukraine, but rarely mentions the Jews. That the Cossack's own chronicler highlights the Polish problem as the cause of the uprising emphasizes the need for a broader, more nuanced image than that held by the Judeocentric perspective. Viewing the past through this wider lens points to Khmelnytsky's own desertion of Poland and to his urging people to rise against the commonwealth. It points to the role of the Polish nobility and clergy in subjugating the very people Khmelnytsky united. It shows the interconnectedness of Jews within this overarching system of economic use and abuse. The Khmelnytsky bloodbaths are not justified. However, a grasp of their context presents a better understanding of the past. In the end, it has been the simplistic Judeocentric understanding that American Jews teach, learn, remember, and pass down to future generations. The lack of a broader context is the difficulty.

During my early research in Poland, I interviewed Dr. Annamaria Orla-Bukowska, a professor at Jagiellonian University who researches genocide and its consequences, as well as majority-minority relations. Explaining the impetus behind my work, I raised my Jewish educator's challenge: that Khmelnytsky proves Poland as a land that disdained the Jews and did not welcome them. A perplexed look came over her face. Gently, and without condemnation, she led me through the documented historical past. I remember this as a salient moment. My face reddened with embarrassment, not only for not knowing this part of the story, but more importantly because I had not once thought to question either the context or the Polish perspective surrounding it. In this moment

---

75 When the author of the *Encyclopedia Judaica* article describes any sort of interaction between Poles and Jews during this period of carnage, he raises as the best example the town of Tulchin, in which "the Poles agreed to surrender the Jews to the rebels in exchange for their own lives." This illustrates the dominant Jewish narrative in which Jews are victims of the Poles' destructive forces.

I realized everything I knew regarding Polish-Jewish relations had to be reassessed. Thus, the need to view the Polish-Jewish past not only through a Jewish lens, but also a Polish one. In this chapter we have seen the important role the Jews played as a middleman minority for both the Crown in the West and the Polish magnates in the East. Especially in the kresy, Jews greatly benfitted economically, to the burghers' detriment.

To untangle oneself from an ingrained myth is quite challenging, for a group's definitional myth does not speak through one event. Rather, it pronounces itself time and again, and in every generation until it is reconstructed. Participating in myth reconstruction is especially difficult at the beginning of the process, when that myth resonates for the mainstream. To be resolute in understanding the past is thus to challenge the mainstream, not just once due to one misunderstood event, but manifold times to correct misconceptions of Self and Other.

CHAPTER 3

Tolerance and Resentment

Feudalism in Poland lasted until 1863, much longer than in Western Europe. Despite a shifting political structure, people remained separated into specific societal categories or estates. At first glance, clear and impenetrable boundaries seem to distinguish social status and economic opportunity, casting feudal relations as relatively simple. However, the mixture of nuanced associations, regional conflicts, and international sociopolitical trends challenged the stability of these alliances. This chapter explores the various and changing relationships the Jews experienced with several estates in the eighteenth and early nineteenth centuries when outside factors influenced internal dynamics.

Feudal Poland's Expansion

Since its inception, Poland's central position in Europe made it vulnerable to invaders. From the Middle Ages through the twentieth century, both Germany and Russia desired its territory. Landlocked and often enfeebled by weak leadership, the country frequently crumbled before invading armies that plundered its resources. While fear of the foreigner outside of its borders consumed Poland, fear of the foreigner living within did not appear until the eighteenth century. As the 1569 Declaration of the Union of Lublin suggests, to be "Polish" was to be part of the enormous Polish-Lithuanian Commonwealth.[1]

When Poland expanded eastward into the kresy, it gained not only an extensive and much-coveted buffer zone, but also the people who inhabited the land. Surprisingly, Polish leaders were not unnerved at the prospect of absorbing the kresy's varied population groups of Poles, Ukrainians, Belarussians, Germans, Italians, Armenians, Scots, Tatars, and Lithuanians with their multiplicity of different religious communities: Eastern Orthodox, Roman Catholics,

---

1   Norman Davies, *God's Playground*, 1:96.

Protestants in their various hues (including Calvinists and Lutherans), as well as Mennonites and Jews.[2] In fact, by the eighteenth century the kresy hosted the majority of Poland's Jews.[3]

Though comprised of a multiplicity of ethnicities, feudalism's socioeconomic landscape allowed for a type of mutual tolerance among its inhabitants. Until the dawn of nationalism in the late 1800s, the majority were peasants who had much less of a connection to their ethnicity than to their small villages.[4] Broader unity came from sharing allegiance to the same monarch. Minorities lived side by side, toiling to provide for both king and noble. Although tensions proliferated between religious groups due to entrenched superstitions regarding the Other, and conflict arose even amongst members of the same creed, outside of Cossack rebellions, internal violent outbreaks did not occur as often as they did in other lands. Indeed, for the most part, the commonwealth's kresy was an interethnic refuge where numerous cultures and religions lived and labored.

Tolerance was an unintentional consequence of feudalism. At the same time, a decentralization of political power left ecclesiastical courts unable to enforce the rare Church edicts calling for group expulsions.[5] Thus, in part, peaceful coexistence in the kresy was accidental.

Yet tolerance was also quite intentional. Those first leading the Polish-Lithuanian Commonwealth asserted the ideals of relative tolerance as a guiding principle. When the king died in 1573 without leaving behind an heir, the empowered nobility had to elect a new monarch. Protestant Sejm members worried that a foreign Catholic king would bring extreme anti-Protestantism to the commonwealth. Thus, they initiated the January 28, 1573 Confederation of Warsaw, which dramatically limited the king's powers and promised that "we who differ in matters of religion will keep the peace among ourselves, and neither shed blood on account of differences of Faith, or kinds of church, nor punish one another by confiscation of goods, deprivation of honour, imprisonment, or exile."[6] The Confederation of Warsaw also provided the ruling nobility with power over the king, since it could renounce allegiance to him if he disregarded these laws.

Though advanced by Protestant Sejm members for self-protection, the confederation's broad and inclusive legal language demonstrates the commonwealth's

---

2   Hundert, *Jews in Poland-Lithuania in the Eighteenth Century*, 21.
3   Michael Steinlauf, *Bondage to the Dead: Poland and the Memory of the Holocaust* (Syracuse: Syracuse University Press, 1997), 6; Weinryb, *The Jews of Poland*, 117.
4   Norman Davies, *God's Playground*, 1:44.
5   Ibid., 131–2; 155.
6   Ibid., 126.

desire for interethnic acceptance—something very different to the intolerance that characterized the rest of the continent. Although over time the country became less tolerant with foreign kings' ties to the Counter-Reformation and the Jesuit Order's proliferation in the country, this relative acceptance of minorities lasted for over two hundred years.[7] It was an essential factor in maintaining the comparative peace in what had become by the seventeenth century one of Europe's largest and most powerful countries.

Jews as Partners in Feudal Society

We have already seen that Jews occupied the important role of middleman minority within the Polish-Lithuanian economy. Like other middleman minorities, Jews filled a status gap in the kresy between the aristocracy and peasantry, often functioning as a shield for the nobility against the populace's animus.[8] It was much easier for the lowly peasants to direct their anger against the Jew who earned his living by collecting their taxes or by collecting their earnings at the local tavern than by addressing the source of the ruinous system—the nobility itself. As we saw with Boghdan Khmelnytsky's 1648 massacres, when leaders stirred the peasantry to rise against the system, they turned not only against the heads of it—the nobility—but also against those who supported and enabled it, that is, the Jewish middleman minority.

At the same time, the peasantry also needed the Jew to fulfill certain middleman minority roles. Occasionally, the Jew could intercede on its behalf, raising issues with the nobleman that affected the peasantry. The Jewish tavern keeper, who provided a social gathering place, read both newspaper articles and private letters to illiterate customers, and offered lay medical advice. Additionally, it was the Jewish trader, along with the burghers, who brought needed supplies to rural communities and created the weekly village market day at which peasants could sell their handicrafts. From the sixteenth through the eighteenth centuries, Jews played this important middleman minority role in the economic and social lives of the kresy population.

Given the lack of ethnic-national identification until the mid-nineteenth century, both nobleman and peasant typically ignored their own ambivalence toward the religiously foreign Jew out of their respective need for the Jew as

---

7 Polonsky, *The Jews in Poland and Russia*, 1:168.
8 José A. Cobas, "Six Problems in the Sociology of the Ethnic Economy," *Sociological Perspectives* 32. no. 2 (Summer, 1989): 210; Bonacich, 583.

middleman minority. Odd religious rituals, a separate language, and distinct clothing were all elements that Christians had learned to accept in relative terms. True, Judaism's theological rejection of Jesus as messiah did cause distrust of Jews within Christian society. Yet, both nobleman and peasant could usually be allayed of such discomfort given the benefits they derived from accepting this Jewish presence. Theological arguments were lodged against the age-old Israelites from church pulpits, while contemporaneous business transpired through arenda and market. Appreciation and disdain lived side by side.

The burgher estate, on the other hand, held no such appreciation for the Jew. Not even ambivalence. The burghers, who had been deleteriously affected by the Jews' migration, expressed only disdain. The former's economic well-being was scarred by the Jews' incursion into moneylending and trade. That the nobility chose to partner economically with the Jews from the sixteenth to the mid-nineteenth century presented enormous barriers to burgher prosperity. The nobleman trusted the Jew as leaseholder of his property much more than the Gentile, not only because he believed that the Jew acted with more industry in business, but also due to the entrenched myth of Jewish sobriety.[9] Jewish lessees often won the rights to lease a nobleman's distillery, tavern, cows, fishing ponds, and forests. The powerful nobility overlooked that its preference for Jewish arendators harmed the country's burghers. In the end, the szlachta perceived all other sections of society as existing purely to serve it.[10]

As a result, the burgher population nursed especial animosity toward the Jews. Burghers believed magnate development of private towns negatively impacted Crown cities and thus the state. Given that Jews as a middleman minority were central to this schematic, it followed for burghers to hold them responsible for it. Instead of accepting that Polish nobles acted voluntarily against state needs, burghers insisted that the Jews corrupted them.[11]

In pamphlets they penned and distributed, burghers fanned the memory of a century of terror against Poles into an active fear of the Other. Boghdan Khmelnytsky's bold and lethal assaults had overwhelmed the establishment. And they were not the last. Calls for Ukrainian national autonomy, continuous vicious Cossack attacks, coupled with burgher propaganda to convince the broader szlachta and burgher populations that the enemy included other ethnic minorities living within the commonwealth. For burghers, this enemy included the Jews.

---

9   Glenn Dynner, *Yankel's Tavern: Jews, Liquor, & Life in the Kingdom of Poland* (Oxford: Oxford University Press, 2014), 31–36.
10 Tazbir, "Images of the Jew in the Polish Commonwealth," 22.
11 Michlic, *Poland's Threatening Other*, 32.

Political Dysfunction and the Four-Year Sejm

Toward the late eighteenth century those in power took up the question of constituency in the commonwealth. The Enlightenment movement had stirred Western Europe, promising a measure of power to the disaffected. Anticlerical leaders united people who favored a separation of church and state. Enlightenment advocates battled the traditional authority of monarch and pope. The Enlightenment had led to the French and American revolutions. In France, these political shifts granted burghers access to citizenship rights and released ghettoized Jews to participate equally in society and economics. Polish conservatives feared a similar challenge.

Within the Polish-Lithuanian Commonwealth, most clergy and the conservative szlachta banded together against Enlightenment views. The government resisted true political reform by upholding the *liberum veto*, which established the legal right for any Sejm member, by a solitary vote, to defeat any prospective legislation. A single member's vote also had the power to dissolve the Sejm and to nullify all acts passed during that session. The commonwealth's foreign rulers bribed Sejm members to invoke it, dissolving Sejm sessions that threatened that respective ruler's interests.[12] The liberum veto hijacked governing.

Stuck in this political quagmire, the Polish-Lithuanian Commonwealth could not reach solutions to the conflicts dividing its two constituent parts, the Kingdom of Poland and the Grand Duchy of Lithuania. While observers marveled at its territory, which was larger than either Spain or France, and its tremendous population of eleven million, the commonwealth remained dysfunctional. The ruling nobility grew accustomed to selling the kingship to the highest foreign bidder. It did not have a central treasury, nor did it maintain an active army large enough to protect itself.[13] Having led the country to the brink of disaster, Sejm members could not protect the commonwealth and its population from political, cultural, and physical dismemberment.

In 1772, the Polish-Lithuanian Commonwealth lost complete control over part of its territory to a coordinated land seizure by the Russian Empire, the Kingdom of Prussia, and the Habsburg monarchy. Jolted out of complacency by this first partition, leaders struggled with how to fortify the commonwealth and prevent further political and territorial erosion.

---

12 Davies, *God's Playground*, 1:259.
13 Peter D. Stachura, *Poland, 1918–1945: An Interpretive and Documentary History of the Second Republic* (London: Routledge, 2004), 7.

By 1788, that segment of the nobility which embraced Enlightenment principles had gained control in the Sejm. This reform-oriented elite blamed ineffective, self-serving Sejm members for mismanaging the country's affairs. Emboldened by the rationalism and science intrinsic to the Enlightenment, they opposed religious influence in matters of state. Combatting the Church's role in government, they also opposed the Jews' designation as an independent estate. They sought a more integrated society, believing that all people should live under the same laws. Therefore, it followed for Polish Enlightenment leaders that the current separate Jewish estate, with its autonomous judicial system based on rabbinic law, was anathema to Poland's societal goals. Enlightenment ideologues held that religion, whether Christianity or Judaism, should play a smaller public role. Known as the Four-Year Sejm, this reform faction occupied political control from 1788 to 1792.

This coterie of Sejm reformers contained a variety of political ideologies that included extreme liberalism, centrism, and right-wing conservatism. What united them was the desire to embrace reform as a means toward regaining control of the commonwealth. By repealing the liberum veto, they successfully returned real legislative powers to the Sejm. Additionally, they increased the military five-fold while making sweeping reforms in taxation and administration. Their national reclamation process culminated in a new constitution adopted on May 3, 1791. But their success was short-lived.[14]

The Four-Year Sejm reformers sought a complete transformation of their state and society, which included economic and social reform. They believed peasant, burgher, and Jew alike needed to "improve" and change their ways in order to be part of the new society. They tackled difficult social issues that had been examined previously but left unresolved. Some argued for Jews' access to citizenship, aiming to transform them into "useful" participants in Polish society.[15] These reformers sought to shift the Jews' occupational structure away from moneylending and tavern keeping, which they viewed as base, to more so-called productive and positive work, such as tilling the earth. They believed that agricultural work would connect the Jews not only to the land itself, but also to the Polish state and culture.

---

14 Davies, *God's Playground*, 1:403.
15 Marcin Wodziński, "'Civil Christians': Debates on the Reform of the Jews in Poland, 1789–1830" (trans. Claire Rosenson), in *Culture Front: Representing Jews in Eastern Europe*, ed. Benjamin Nathans and Gabriella Safran. Jewish Culture and Contexts (Philadelphia: University of Pennsylvania Press, 2008), 54.

Given that Polish society deemed agriculture as the only useful and wholesome occupation, it follows that Polish society heretofore perceived the Jews as "not useful." According to Bonacich, host societies often charge middleman minorities with draining the host country of its resources, that is, "not engaging in productive industry."[16] For Poles, "productive industry" was agriculture. While this terminology conflicts with the fact that Jews fulfilled a vital economic function and furthered the country's development, the continued use of this degrading description of the Jewish middleman minority enabled Christians in the commonwealth, whether aligned with the royal, noble, Church, or peasant estate, to protect their own group's positive self-image.

Polish Enlightenment reformers also sought their ideal society by breaking down barriers that divided Jews and Poles. They admonished the Jews' separate Yiddish language and distinct attire, holding that each served to disconnect the two peoples. As such, reformers argued that the Jews needed to adopt Poland's language and dress. Additionally, reformers demanded that Jews stop adhering to their dietary law, known as kashrut, a custom that certainly divided the populations. Through language, dress, and food, reformers believed Jews should resemble the average Polish Christian. Only in private places, such as the home or synagogue, would Jews be expected to express their Jewish identity.

An attempt to regulate the position of the Jews within society occurred in 1790 when Sejm reformers established the Committee for the Amelioration of the Jews. Its members included ideologists along the political spectrum. Taduesz Czacki (1765–1813) argued that government must provide the Jews with full citizenship, guarantee them religious toleration, abolish special Jewish taxes, and annul the separate estate structure that supported their alienation from society.[17] Other reformers, such as Father Hugo Kołłątaj (1750–1812), held that the commonwealth would strengthen only through emancipating burgher and peasant, but maintaining the Jews' lower status.[18]

---

16 Bonacich, "A Theory of Middlema Minorities," 591.
17 Polonsky, *The Jews in Poland and Russia*, 1:210. Additional spokespeople with similar perspectives included Mateusz Butrymowicz and Walerian Łukasiński, according to Marcin Wodziński, *Hasidism and Politics: The Kingdom of Poland, 1815–1864* (Oxford: The Littman Library of Jewish Civilization, 2013), 15.
18 Richard Butterwick-Pawlikowski, "Jews in the Discourses of the Polish Enlightenment," in *Jews in the Kingdom of Poland, 1815–1918*, ed. Glenn Dynner, Antony Polonsky, and Marcin Wodziński. Polin: Studies in Polish Jewry, vol. 27 (Oxford: The Littman Library of Jewish Civilization, 2015), 52–53.

Burgher Influence on Sejm Reformers

Approaching social reform in 1790 from such varied positions, members on the committee debated the Jews' status particularly in royal towns. This dispute occurred within the context of Sejm debate over how to achieve economic restoration of both the royal towns and the burghers who inhabited them. The two had been in decline for a century. When Four-Year Sejm legislators permitted some Jews to settle in Warsaw, which until that time had maintained the status of *de non tolerandis Judaeis*, burghers in Warsaw raged against the Jews' incursion. Fearing increased economic competition, burghers authored pamphlets blaming the decline of Poland's towns on the Jews. The developing Jewish bourgeoisie retorted that the commonwealth's economic devastation had been due to wars and former kings' abuse of resources. Lobbying efforts by both sides followed suit. After three anti-Jewish riots during which burghers assaulted the szlachta for supporting Jews' evasion of settlement regulations, the committee capitulated.[19] The Sejm gave the burghers the rights of citizenship while stalling a vote on Jewish rights. Although liberal Sejm reformers raised additional bills that provided Jews with added rights, the marshal of the Sejm refused them a vote.[20]

While some of Poland's reformers aligned strictly with the burghers against Jewish rights, others argued for Jewish citizenship and opening more Crown cities to Jewish settlement. No doubt, the conservatives outflanked the liberals. But let us not forget that this opposition existed and took a stand. Too often, the opposition is forgotten.

---

19   Ibid., 215.
20   Ibid., 216. This type of power play often occurs in politics. One need only recall when the US Senate majority leader, Republican Mitch McConnell, maintained his public silence during the thirty-five-day-long US government shutdown. Instead of presenting the Senate with the House of Representative's bipartisan bills to re-open the government, he refused to bring them up for vote. Of course, this is the power of the Senate majority leader; the Democrats act in the same way when they have a majority. See Sheryl Gay Stolberg and Nicholas Fandos, "McConnell Faces Pressure from Republicans to Stop Avoiding Shutdown Fight," *New York Times*, January 3, 2019, https://www.nytimes.com/2019/01/03/us/politics/mcconnell-setate-republican-shutdown.html.

Taverns and the Jews Who Managed Them

For centuries, the tavern was a fixture of Polish villages, towns, and cities. Especially in rural areas, the tavern was not only a bar, but also a distillery, country store, hotel, stable, post office, and bank.[21] Usually, the only venue within miles in which musicians could perform, it also operated as the center for information and news due to the constant flow of travelers passing through it.[22] Many peasants preferred the tavern to church, immediately leaving the priest's congregation to rejoice in the tavernkeeper's assembly.[23] As part of their middleman minority role, Jews managed most taverns. In this role the tavernkeeper provided numerous social services to the peasantry, including giving medical and economic advice, lending money, reading newspaper articles and letters, and writing correspondence. Indeed, the tavern was the heart of a village.

The tavern also proved most detrimental to the village. Over time, peasant access to liquor grew and peasant drunkenness soon overwhelmed villages. Improvements in the distillation process elevated the potency of alcohol fourfold. At the same time, the increased cultivation of potatoes made production of vodka less expensive and drinking more affordable. Alcohol production became a boom industry, and the nobility doubled the number of distilleries in the kingdom between 1830 and 1840.[24] Additionally, the traditional respect for monopolies assured the magnate that his peasants would buy liquor only on his land. Some went so far as to require compulsory alcohol purchase, ensuring peasant impoverishment and noble wealth. Many landlords even paid peasants for extra work, not in cash, but rather in alcohol vouchers (*kwitki*) redeemable only in that lord's particular tavern(s).[25]

---

21 Ibid.
22 Dynner, *Yankel's Tavern*, 18.
23 Ibid., 22.
24 Ibid., 25–26.
25 Ibid., 72. The problem of noblemen paying the peasantry with drinking vouchers also plagued Austrian Galicia, where the Jewish tavernkeeper poured out the peasants' wages into their shot glasses. See Stauter-Halsted, *The Nation in the Village*. This same problem also existed in Russia proper. There they did not begin a crackdown on tavern laws until 1860. See R. E. F. Smith and David Christian, *Bread and Salt: A Social and Economic History of Food and Drink in Russia* (Cambridge: Cambridge University Press, 1984), 309–312. Paying with drink vouchers was a colonial practice. It occurred in late eighteenth to early nineteenth centuries in colonial Africa. European colonial companies owned the taverns and employed Africans (who had lost access to most of their land and were forced from subsistence agriculture to wage labor). Laborers received their paychecks in the taverns. But those paychecks would be delayed. Workers were permitted to drink the wages they were owed. In some cases, they

The tavern thus became a symbol for the social and economic decay of the Polish countryside. Peasant drunkenness not only shackled adults to idleness, illness, and poverty, but it also gravely affected their children:

> Children roamed around half-naked, their parents spending their days and nights in the tavern where "a great hubbub, screams, songs, or quarrels and brawls of the half-drunk and drunk resounded everywhere." Outside the tavern, draped across fences, lying in gutters or almost anywhere else, drunken peasants were as common as mushrooms and stones. The kingdom's villages had a plundered and abandoned look. One social critic witnessed tipsy mothers "soothing their crying children by pouring liquor into their mouths instead of food." Peasants were forgoing meat for vodka, as only the latter could be had on credit.[26]

While it was the Jew who sold the liquor to the peasants, it was the post-partition nobility who not only controlled alcohol production, but also benefitted most economically from the peasants' drowning in it. As discussed in chapter 2, just as the Jewish toll farmer gained the ire of the local populace when collecting monies owed to the nobleman, so too did the Jewish tavernkeeper attract public rebuke for a social ill controlled by the nobility.

In the early nineteenth century, Polish reformers attempted to rehabilitate society. As noblemen themselves, they avoided criticizing members of their own estate for this social ill by hoisting blame onto the Jewish tavernkeeper.[27] Stanisław Staszic, a reformer who promoted burgher and peasant rights, argued that "the Jews were the cause of the indolence, stupidity, drunkenness, and misery of the peasants."[28] Jews, on the other hand, attributed the reproachful condition of the tavern to its drunken Gentile clientele.[29] Although Christian and Jewish observers alike agreed to the physical and spiritual pollution of tavern life, most in each group refused responsibility for it.

---

were paid in scrip that could only be used at the taverns. See Timothy Burke, *Lifebuoy Men, Lux Women: Commodification, Consumption, & Cleanliness in Modern Zimbabwe* (Durham: Duke University Press, 1996).

26 Dynner, *Yankel's Tavern*, 72.
27 Ibid., 57.
28 Polonsky, *The Jews in Poland and Russia*, 1:202.
29 Dynner, *Yankel's Tavern*, 23.

Both liberal and conservative Polish reformers responded by eliminating Jews' access to tavern keeping.[30] However, this campaign against the Jewish tavernkeeper was more about economics than societal sobriety. By the decline of the Polish-Lithuanian Commonwealth, both Jews and Gentiles understood that taverns had developed into one of the most lucrative leases an arrendator could hold. Though it required hard work, if run diligently a tavern could provide enough earnings to feed and clothe a family. In territories plagued by poverty, it was an enviable business. The reformers' sought to remove the Jew from tavern keeping under the guise of establishing Jews in so-called acceptable work, such as farming. This strategy permitted Christian townspeople the rights to produce and sell liquor, thereby earning better livelihoods.

The representative noblemen concerned themselves with the burghers because they recognized that the nobility would need burgher support when it eventually rebelled against the partitioning powers. (They also required peasant sobriety to fuel this future rebellion.) To supplicate the burghers, reformers offered up the tavern. Sejm reformers, both liberal and conservative, sought to oust Jews from tavern keeping to grant burgher access to that lucrative field and, consequently, burgher political support for the full reform agenda.[31] Thus, they argued that fellow Christians would never allow their peasant Christian brothers to waste away drinking. Incentivized by political gain, reformers cloaked their collaboration in moral arguments.[32]

Enforcing this new policy proved quite difficult, though not for lack of Christians wishing to lease rights to tavern keeping. Rather, Jews retained their rights to lease taverns due to noble estate owners' refusal to change the economic relationship with them, which had long worked very well for both parties. Reformers believed that by following a similar protocol to Russia proper, which implemented excessive taxation of rural Jewish tavernkeepers, Poles would squeeze Jews out of this profitable business. However, the noble tavern

---

30 As with other leases, the nobility had reserved for Jews the right to run the nobles' taverns and inns because they believed Jews not only had a greater business acumen than non-Jews, but also because of the persistent myth of Jews' sobriety. Although Jews certainly did drink, and within many communities to excess—as Hassidic memoirs clearly note—they recognized the nobility's belief in their sobriety and thus kept their drinking to themselves for practical economic purposes. See Dynner, *Yankel's Tavern*, 31–38, 45.

31 Artur Eisenbach, *The Emancipation of the Jews in Poland, 1780–1870*, ed. Antony Polonsky, trans. Janina Dorosz (Oxford: Blackwell, 1991), 80.

32 This theory does not hold water given that throughout the innumerable Russian locales, Jews had either been successfully pushed out of tavern keeping or had never been involved in it. Yet Russian peasants remained inebriated.

owner, together with local Christians, aligned to secure the Jew's position. Local Christians entered economic relationships with Jewish lessees, posing as fronts to officials, and helped Jews to dodge debilitating state taxation.[33]

Despite laws prohibiting Jews from leasing roadside taverns, and later from even living in the countryside, the Jewish rural population remained steady. The conservative noble tavern owner, who believed the stereotype of Jewish sobriety, assisted Jews in retaining their hold on that industry. Economic desires created a pragmatic interethnic solidarity between the Jews and sections of the Polish nobility, the latter opposing the Polish reformers' anti-Jewish campaign and the post-partition absolutist Russian state.

Although Jewish tavernkeepers did not design this ghastly enterprise, it is imperative to recognize their complicity in actively maintaining it. As the industry's service sector, it was the Jewish tavernkeeper who handed more alcohol to an already inebriated peasantry. In it for business, just like the nobleman, the Jew wanted his customers to keep drinking. To do so, he created the concept of drinking on credit.[34] Despite funds running dry, drinks continued to pour, and the already drunk peasant did not have the wherewithal to stop. Polish peasants remained in a constant state of financial indebtedness to the Jewish tavernkeeper. Ignoring the nobility's role, Polish reformers transformed the Jewish tavernkeeper into the face of this epidemic.

Myth Reconstruction

Despite this interdependent economic relationship between Jew and noble, as well as Jew and peasant, the Jew as middleman minority remained separated from both sectors. Not only had feudalism demanded this social disconnect, but so too did the Jew. Rabbinic leaders erected barriers around their community to maintain Jewish cultural and religious integrity.

---

33 This arrangement was a natural extension of centuries-long Jewish-Christian cooperation in Poland to evade Jewish laws mandating the closure of Jewish businesses on the Jewish Sabbath. Christians would purchase the tavern lease from the Jewish lessee prior to the Sabbath and sell it back to him when it ended. While the rabbis often argued against such arrangements, this fiction filled a legal loophole, allowing both Jewish tavernkeeper and Christian clientele to meet their needs. The tavern stayed open, bringing in money for the Jew, while the Gentile sub-lessee earned his agreed upon amount. Thus, it was quite natural for both Jew and Pole to reach a similar solution when Polish reformers and the Russian government challenged traditional rural economics. See Dynner, *Yankel's Tavern*, 48–51.

34 Ibid., 65.

Jews distinguished themselves from Poles through language. Indeed, wherever they migrated, Jews either brought their own language or fashioned a unique Jewish version of the vernacular. One need only look at the rabbis' use of colloquial Aramaic in the Talmud, as well as Spanish Jewry's development of Ladino.[35] Their experience in Poland was no exception. Instead of Polish, the mainstream Jewish community spoke Yiddish, a hybrid language stemming from Hebrew, German, and Slavic roots. Totally illegible to most Gentiles, it utilized the Hebrew alphabet and was read from right to left.

Jews also separated themselves by following their own laws and rituals, such as wearing different clothing, observing the Sabbath on Saturday rather than Sunday, celebrating separate holidays from Christians, and maintaining complex dietary restrictions. By preserving specific dietary standards, Jews rarely broke bread with their Christian neighbors. Though children traversed boundaries relatively easily through play, adults typically did not share deep cross-cultural bonds of friendship. As Eva Hoffman writes, "separateness . . . precluded deeper familiarity between Jews and Poles and it is only superficial familiarity that breeds the superficial reaction of contempt."[36] To Poles, the Jews remained strangers: mysterious, magical, and therefore sometimes scary.[37]

It is important in this process of myth reconstruction that Poles also recognize truths that conflict with the history they have learned. Christians also set up and protected social boundaries to safeguard their own respective religion's truths. Although the clergy referenced the Israelites much more than the contemporary Jew, priests still taught the masses to hold the Jews in contempt. They preserved and disseminated inflammatory superstitions concerning the Jews: the belief that they desecrated the host, the supposition that they spread devastating diseases such as the bubonic plague, and the widespread conviction that Jews killed Christian children to use their blood in the baking of matzah (unleavened bread eaten during the Passover holiday).[38] Though permitted to cultivate economic livelihoods and autonomy through the Jewish communal kahal system, Jews were "a despised minority, tolerated in an inferior position to attest to truths of Christianity."[39]

American Jewry should note that just as the Poles did not want their Catholic children corrupted by the "dangerous, dirty, disease prone" Jew living down

---

35 Yuri Slezkine, *The Jewish Century* (Princeton: Princeton University Press, 2004), 18.
36 Hoffman, *Shtetl*, 62.
37 Jerzy Tomaszewski, e-mail correspondence with author, August 19, 2012.
38 Hoffman, *Shtetl*, 184.
39 Polonsky, *The Jews in Poland and Russia*, 1:184.

the road, the Jews did not want their children anywhere near the evil ways of the "wild, ignorant, boorish Pole."[40] Jewish religious leaders focused on group survival. While rabbis understood the importance of tavern keeping for Jewish economic endurance, they were also wary of its spiritual consequences. They feared that those Jews who earned their livelihoods by mingling daily with the peasantry would acculturate and disregard their faith and heritage.[41] Their worry was not without justification.[42]

Jewish religious leaders believed strongly that Judaism was *the only* way to connect with God. Indeed, Jews perceived themselves as the embodiment of religious truth: "The Jewish people were not simply the chosen, but were the only people of God: 'Israel and the Torah and the Holy one, blessed be He, are one' . . . Consequently, feelings of social involvement did not reach beyond their own people."[43] This Jewish sense of religious and cultural superiority predated its Christian counterpart. The need to guard the "one true path to God" from any possible destructive outside influence produced an insular community.

While village and town Jews knew their Polish neighbors and had cooperative business ties with Christians, religious leaders in each population were largely disconnected from one another. From the sixteenth to early nineteenth century, both Jew and Catholic Pole learned to distrust each other at a time of mutual economic dependency. Religious affiliation and belief in a *single* religious truth barred each group's acceptance of the Other. Thus, though relative economic tolerance existed from the sixteenth to early nineteenth century, the Poles' did not socially embrace the Jews.

Despite what many post-World War II American Jews assume, Poland was *not* always a terrible place for the Jews. Indeed, for centuries it was the one European country in which Jews could thrive economically, through trade, crafts, and arenda, while maintaining semi-self-rule through the Va'ad Arba Aratsot. The Polish-Lithuanian Commonwealth provided relative tolerance of the Jews' differences.

---

40 Hoffman, *Shtetl*, 62.
41 Dynner, *Yankel's Tavern*, 24.
42 As we have seen, Jewish tavernkeepers circumvented Jewish law requiring Sabbath rest by colluding with Christian peasants to keep the tavern open to customers. Additionally, rural Jewish tavernkeepers' children were on a particularly precarious trajectory: rural life was narrow in the choices it offered. Growing up with few options and within a small population, these Jewish children saw Catholic peasants in the tavern daily, learned their ways, at times married them, and many chose apostasy. See ibid., 69.
43 Rosa Lehmann, *Symbiosis and Ambivalence: Poles and Jews in a Small Galician Town* (New York: Berghan Books, 2001), 93.

But when challenged by political instability and economic distress, there arose an array of Polish voices that sought to change this situation themselves. True, Polish liberals existed; but most of these reformers believed that Jews were to blame for their negative treatment in Polish society. They argued that the only way for Jews to achieve relative civil equality with Poles was through assimilation and surrendering their rights to tavern keeping. Such reform proved difficult. The noble-Jew working dynamic and the latter's resistance to acculturation proved too strong. At the same time, the Church's demonization of the Jews precluded Catholic Poles from truly desiring to elevate Jews' status.

CHAPTER 4

Reform and Tradition

At the tail end of the eighteenth century the commonwealth faced political upheaval. Conflicts between reformers and traditionalists mushroomed in Polish politics and Jewish communal life. Both Poles and Jews in the commonwealth questioned to what extent people would fight to gain power, and how hard the threatened leadership would push back to retain it? This chapter explores the changing power dynamics within Polish politics, as well as in the broader Polish Jewish community in the late eighteenth and early nineteenth centuries.

Polish Conservatives Call In Russian Troops

Conservative Sejm members and the conservative nobility they represented had great difficulty reconciling themselves with Polish reformers' path to national recovery, which had included the Four-Year Sejm's 1791 liberal constitution. The aristocratic conservative elite feared the personal, social, economic, and political consequences of the new constitution. It posed an explosive financial threat to the szlachta by ending serfdom, and granting greater citizenship rights to burghers. Enraged, the powerful aristocratic elite went so far as to beseech Russia to intervene militarily, defeat the liberals, and restore the old order.[1] Russia complied, fearing its own impending loss of influence over the commonwealth if the liberals maintained political control. Indeed, the new Polish-Lithuanian constitution stripped foreign powers from direct governmental authority over Poland by calling for a hereditary monarchy. Thus, in 1793 Russia invaded and secured a second partition.

Polish reformers fought back against Russia through the armed support of Tadeusz Kościuszko, a Polish war hero who had trained in France and gained fame fighting for America's independence from the British. Kościuszko's 1794

---

1   Wanda Wyporska, "Poland, Partitions of," in Europe, 1450 to 1789: Encyclopedia of the Early Modern World, Oxford University Press 2004, accessed August 29, https://www.encyclopedia.com/history/modern-europe/polish-history/partitions-poland.

insurrection had brief success. Berek Joselewicz, a colonel in the Polish army, formed a Jewish military formation to fight alongside Kościuszko.[2] But eventually Russian prowess felled Kościuszko's troops in the Warsaw suburb of Praga, dismantling the new liberal Polish bureaucracy and its policies. Thus, Russia restored the conservative nobility to power, together with its old constitution and the liberum veto. With the 1795 third partition, Poland's deeply rooted elitist estate system was saved, at the expense of its sovereignty. The three partitions played an enormous role in generating Poles' sense of victimhood while provoking an intense fear of outsiders. Poland was not an independent state again until 1918.

By 1795, three carved out areas emerged from what had been the Polish-Lithuanian Commonwealth: Prussian Poland centered in Poznan; Austro-Hungarian Poland contained Galicia; and Russian Poland encapsulated the kresy, that immense territory the tsars would call the Jewish Pale of Settlement. It is important to note that there was not one Polish experience during partition. Rather, Polish reality differed depending on that region's ruler, as well as on the number of Poles in each locale. While Prussia enforced a program for Poles' assimilation into German culture, from the 1860s Austria provided a relatively high degree of freedom in which Polish nationalism could and did grow. Although Russia first permitted a measure of autonomy to that territory containing the majority of ethnic Poles, the Russian government later instituted harsh laws within Central Poland to combat Polish insurrections. The Jews in each territory were affected by the varied laws and attitudes of the respective regime.

The Duchy of Warsaw: Conditional Polish Citizenship

The year 1807 marked a political and cultural turning point for both Poles and Jews. Initially full of hope, both peoples were soon disappointed. The Poles had long been France's military allies. Having defeated Prussia with Polish military aid in the Franco-Prussian War, Emperor Napoleon reciprocated by restoring to the Poles the central Polish provinces that Prussia originally absorbed in the 1793 and 1795 partitions.[3] Napoleon offered the Poles a measure of pride. In establishing the Duchy of Warsaw, he carved out a fourth territorial component from the dismantled Commonwealth. Of the close to 3.3 million people living

---

2   Berek Joselewicz's 1794 Jewish military formation was one of the first ever created.
3   Piotr S. Wandycz, *The Lands of Partitioned Poland, 1795–1918*, ed. Peter F. Sugar and Donald W. Treadgold, A History of East Central Europe, vol. 7, rev. ed. (Seattle: University of Washington Press, 1984), 36–39, 43–45.

within the duchy's borders, 75% were Polish. The language of administration was Polish and only citizens of the new duchy could serve in public office.[4] Despite being ruled by a foreigner—Frederick August, the king of Saxony—the duchy operated as a Polish state.

The duchy's constitution emphasized the concept of citizenship, providing a platform not only for Polish political visionaries, but for Jewish dreamers as well. The promise in the constitution's article four that "all citizens are equal before the law" raised hope among the disenfranchised. However, after the conservative Polish political elite questioned the interpretation of "citizen," the right to vote and hold political office eluded both Jews and peasants in the duchy.[5] While French Enlightenment ideals inspired many reformers, they could not overcome majority szlachta self-interest. Was a citizen any male born on the land or did the term refer only to those who owned the land? How should a citizen demonstrate allegiance to the state? Just as there was not one clear-cut answer, so too were sides drawn over this issue well into the twentieth century.

By the time Napoleon had established the Duchy of Warsaw, so-called Polish liberal reformers had experienced the exponential political, geographic, and emotional consequences of the third partition. Partition negatively affected reformers' attitudes towards the Jews. Some, such as Stanisław Potocki (1755–1821), drew nearer to former conservative activists. He stressed growing Polish skepticism regarding possible Jewish fidelity to the Polish people. Despite Jews having fought alongside Kościuszko against partition, he believed that Jews' loyalty remained tied to the Jewish community: "The Jews form here a state within a state. They have their own courts, language, dress code, religion . . . their leadership mocks those governments which have sought for some time to civilize them."[6] As discussed earlier, most Jews embraced this separation, thereby proving the grain of truth in Potocki's words.

Marcin Wodziński argues that simple human habits also played a critical role in the reformers' approach to the Jews. While accepting the ideals of the Enlightenment, Wodziński holds that many could not put those ideals into practice: "I believe anti-Jewish attitudes in late eighteenth and early nineteenth-century Poland became a certain habitus. Those people did not believe it was

---

4   Glenn Dynner and Marcin Wodziński, "The Kingdom of Poland and Her Jews: An Introduction," in *Jews in the Kingdom of Poland, 1815–1918*, Glenn Dynner, Antony Polonsky, and Marcin Wodziński, Polin: Studies in Polish Jewry, vol. 27 (Oxford: The Littman Library of Jewish Civilization, 2015), 3.
5   Ibid.
6   Antony Polonsky, *The Jews in Poland and Russia*, 1:288.

right, but those people were not able to free themselves from certain reactions towards Jews."⁷ At the same time, Wodziński adds, there was a good deal of inconsistency in debate on the subject. Complete consistency in thought and action is, of course, unattainable. People are complex. They will not always do what they know to be best for themselves, let alone for society; and people often have weak and selfish tendencies.

We see this human nature at play when Napoleon promised the Poles a new constitution. The old guard, which retained the right to interpret and implement it, remained unwilling to give up its power and wealth despite the benefit such change would bring to a broader number of people. The Jews were not the conservative szlachta's only worry. Since article four of the duchy's new constitution abolished serfdom, the nobility also worked diligently to preserve the slave labor that secured its wealth. The szlachta contained the peasantry by imposing the feudal system of corvée labor.⁸ Peasants had to pay the lord for the right to reside on the land. As most did not have the funds for rent, they provided labor in its place.

It did not take long before reformers linked the question of citizenship for the Jews and the recently "freed" peasantry. Both groups wanted more rights. Though the peasantry had not yet organized, the rising Jewish bourgeoisie lobbied for privileges addressed in the constitution. But the ruling nobility held onto landownership as a prerequisite for accessing political power, and thereby barred both Jews and peasants from land rights, citizenship, and power. By the dawn of the Kingdom of Poland in 1815, all government positions had high property qualifications, a policy employed throughout the Russian Empire.⁹

Whether the duchy's Polish bureaucrats could not reconcile Jewish communal, legal, and cultural separatism with renewed hopes for Polish cultural and political revival, or whether they simply saw Jewish emancipation as a threat to the nobility's hold on power, the governing nobility brought the issue to the duchy's ruler, the king of Saxony. He himself believed the constitution granted Jews full equality.¹⁰ Polish conservatives, however, did not accept his response.

---

7   Similarly, it is near impossible for white people raised in a racist home and/or society to completely free themselves from racist inclinations. They may learn to disagree with them or bury them so others don't see them, but those initial internal reactions to race remain. Author's interview with Marcin Wodziński, Wrocław 2019.
8   For a thorough description of corvée, see Wandycz, *The Lands of Partitioned Poland, 1795–1918*, 46–47.
9   Ibid., 67 and 75–76.
10 Polonsky, *The Jews in Poland and Russia*, 1:284.

They sparred on this issue so intensely that the king eventually brought the question of duchy citizenship for Jews to Napoleon.

The emperor held Jews living in Poland to a similar criterion as he did French Jews: the Jews in the Duchy of Warsaw needed to submit proof of their loyalty to its government before gaining citizenship.[11] According to these French standards, by reforming their educational system and adopting Polish language and dress, Jews could prove themselves to be a part of society. Thus, in 1808 a royal decree suspended Jews' citizenship rights for ten years, demanding they take this time to demonstrate their full integration into Polish culture.[12] In the short term the conservative power-driven szlachta had won. They curtailed a potentially large citizenship expansion and its inevitable challenge to their political authority. When Napoleon proclaimed assimilation to be the only path which would lead Jews toward citizenship, he answered the debate over the "Jewish question" for the time being. A small Jewish acculturating community, known as Maskilim, accepted these preconditions for emancipation and lobbied their co-religionists to make religious, cultural, lingual, and educational reforms. However, while the Maskilim built a small following in Warsaw's growing urban center, the vast majority of Jews maintained their traditional and separate way of life.

To twenty-first-century Jews, the term *assimilation* has negative connotations. It smacks of the forced abandonment of one's Jewish heritage in order to meld into mainstream society. Nineteenth-century Jews, on the other hand, recognized assimilation as a pathway into living a modern *Jewish* life within Polish society. Some did discard their Jewish identity at the end of this process. Yet most did not pursue assimilation to the point of exiting the Jewish community. Integrationists (second-generation Maskilim in Poland) employed the term

---

11   Ibid., 283–287. Theodore Weeks points out that individual French Jews were able to obtain rights to citizenship once they accepted French language and culture. However, as a community, French Jews were barred from citizenship. Theodore Weeks email correspondence with author, October 30, 2011.

12   Wandycz, *The Lands of Partitioned Poland, 1795–1918*, 47. Although Jews did not gain citizenship, their rights in the duchy increased. Due to administrative and legal changes influenced by the constitution, the duchy's Jews, together with other inhabitants, experienced greater basic equality before the law. See Aleksandra Oniszczuk, "The Jews in the Duchy of Warsaw: The Question of Equal Rights," in Dynner, Polonsky, and Wodziński, *Jews in the Kingdom of Poland, 1815–1918*, 63–87.

assimilation with attached adjectives to underscore the type of assimilation being discussed: "linguistic assimilation" was good; "religious assimilation" was bad.[13]

In contrast, *acculturation* should be understood as the voluntary acquisition by Jews of some of the values and cultural traits of their host society. Most often in the Kingdom of Poland it included learning the Polish language and adopting contemporary clothing styles. However, acculturation did not necessarily lead to integration. Plenty of Hasidic Jews spoke Polish for business yet remained isolated from Polish society at large. Mainstream and Hasidic Jewry repudiated assimilation and those Poles and Jews who argued for it. Thus, when Napoleon gave Jews ten years to relinquish their traditional ways and take up not only the Polish language, but also Polish attire, food, and education, the vast majority had absolutely no desire to comply.

Jewish Enlightenment in Polish Lands

Like the Polish secular reformers, progressive Jews (Maskilim) followed Enlightenment ideals, albeit by way of the Jewish Enlightenment movement (Haskalah). The theories and goals of the French rationalists attracted Jewish intellectuals who yearned for civil rights. Relatively few in number, these mostly urban, well-educated, and wealthy Jews did not seek to divest from their religion.[14] Instead, they desired a fresh modern approach to it.

Maskilim shared Prussia's leading Maskil voice—Moses Mendelsohn (1729–1786)—with Jews in the Duchy of Warsaw. Mendelsohn advocated reducing Judaism's emphasis on ritual and tribalism. He theorized that host nations would welcome enlightened Jews as equals, and eventually give Jews equal civil rights.[15]

---

13   For a more thorough discussion on the term *assimilation*, and its application in the second half of the nineteenth-century Kingdom of Poland, please see Joseph Lichten, "Jewish Assimilation in Poland, 1863–1943," in Abramsky, Jachimczyk, and Polonsky, *The Jews in Poland*.

14   Marcin Wodziński, *Haskalah And Hasidism in The Kingdom Of Poland: A History of Conflict*, trans. Sarah Cozens (Oxford: The Littman Library of Jewish Civilization, 2005), 42–45. Early Maskilim in the commonwealth and in the later Duchy of Warsaw were either enlightened Jews who had immigrated to Warsaw from Prussia, where the Haskalah originated, or Polish Jews who had studied abroad in Prussia and brought their new progressive perspectives back to their Polish homes. See Alexander Gutterman, "The Origins of the Great Synagogue in Warsaw on Tłomackie Street," in *The Jews in Warsaw*, ed. Władysław T. Bartoszewski and Antony Polonsky (Oxford: Basil Blackwell in association with The Institute for Polish-Jewish Studies, 1991), 181–182.

15   Albert Lindemann, *Esau's Tears* (Cambridge: Cambridge University Press, 1997), 54.

Jewish reformers, who were literate and spoke in the language of their host country, presented a modern European aesthetic through their contemporary clothing, trimmed beards, or clean-shaven faces. Maskilim perceived Judaism as a living dynamic religion and culture that must respond to the times in order to proceed into the future. Polish Maskilim accepted the view that mainstream Polish Jews represented "a productive and basically honest people who, however, were oppressed by fanaticism and social backwardness."[16] They agreed with the Polish reformers, who argued that the Jewish population needed to reform its religious and social practices in order to enter modernity.[17] Maskilim longed for Jews to live fully in the secular world, while simultaneously maintaining a modernized and more private Jewish identity. (Note this goal's similarity to the early goal established by Polish reformers during the Four-Year-Sejm.)

By 1815, the Haskalah had amassed a moderately sized financially backed following in Poland, with its heartland in Warsaw.[18] Maskilim focused on language as the essential tool for Jews' entry into modernity. Like their Enlightenment counterparts in Western Europe, Maskilim regarded Yiddish as a garbled dialect that stunted its speakers' cultural progress: this "jargon" barred them from entering Polish secular society and culture. The rabbis viewed Yiddish as preventing Jews from crossing over into "dangerous" foreign cultural territory; from the Maskilim's perspective, Yiddish served only to cage the people. Maskilim insisted that Jews relinquish Yiddish. In its place, they proposed a linguistic dualism—firm knowledge of both the ruling government's language as well as Judaism's ancient Hebrew tongue.[19] However, while early proponents of Polish

---

16   As cited in Wodziński, *Haskalah and Hasidism*, 19. Salomon Maimon was born and raised in Poland-Lithuania. He moved to Berlin to take part in its intense Maskilic society.
17   Ibid., 23. Subscribing to *Hame'assef*, the first Hebrew journal of the German Haskalah, allowed Jews in the Kingdom of Poland to connect to these intellectual and spiritual changes. For a lengthier description of the development of the Haskalah movement in Russian Poland, see Israel Bartal, *The Jews of Eastern Europe, 1772–1881*, trans. Chaya Naor (Philadelphia: University of Pennsylvania Press, 2005), 90–101 and Wodziński, *Haskalah and Hasidism in the Kingdom of Poland*.
18   Ibid., 46. Other important towns with large Jewish populations, such as Zamość, Płock, and Kalisz, also developed sizeable Maskilic followings. However, Maskilim in these locales were often frustrated in their attempts to bring reform to their communities.
19   Haskalah took on particularized ideologies based on its thinkers' geographic and political situations. Marcin Wodziński points out "wherever a mono-ethnic national culture predominated, modernization processes in Jewish society led to linguistic assimilation with the native populations." Therefore, whereas Maskilim in the multiethnic Russian Empire coalesced around Hebrew, those in the Kingdom of Poland used a great deal of Polish in addition to Hebrew. See ibid., 65.

Haskalah read and spoke Polish, they favored German for intellectual discussion and writing—even in Warsaw's Reform synagogue, as German was their own language of secular intellectual initiation.[20]

The Kingdom of Poland: Reexamining the Jewish Question

The Duchy of Warsaw was short-lived. In 1812, Napoleon again militarily challenged Russia.[21] This time, however, he lost. The Russian Empire kept hold of the vast territory it had previously partitioned, and now it also acquired the defunct duchy through the 1815 Congress of Vienna peace negotiations. World leaders renamed it the Kingdom of Poland (also known as the Congress Kingdom and Central Poland) and cast it as a semiautonomous Polish state under Russian rule. While Austria and Prussia still retained portions of the former commonwealth, Russia's 1813 wartime victory gave it control over the largest swath of the partitioned land.

The Kingdom of Poland was the most ethnically and linguistically Polish region of the partitioned territories.[22] Polish served as the kingdom's official language and only citizens of the kingdom—the szlachta and burghers— could hold government posts. The kingdom acted as the center for all public debates regarding a reborn Polish state. One found there the Polish cause's most

---

20 Ibid., 158–159. The Reform synagogue on Daniłowiczowska Street was known derogatorily by mainstream Jewry as "di daytshe shul," the German synagogue, because from its 1802 inception well into the early 1860s, its rabbi, who came from Germany, delivered sermons in German rather than Yiddish. See Gutterman, "The Origins of the Great Synagogue in Warsaw on Tłomackie Street," 184. Not until 1852 did a Maskilic rabbi deliver a sermon in Polish—Rabbi Izaak Kramsztyk (1814–1899). By 1860, Rabbi Marcus Jastrow of the Daniłowiczowska synagogue had begun learning Polish in order, eventually, to speak to his congregation in Poland's vernacular. See Stefan Kieniewicz, "Jews, Polish Society and Partitioning Powers," in Bartoszewski and Polonsky, *The Jews in Warsaw*, 164.
21 Polish troops supporting Napoleon's war with Russia hoped French success would prompt him to grant Poles more of their land seized during partition. See Wandycz, *The Lands of Partitioned Poland, 1795–1918*, 57.
22 Dynner and Wodziński, "The Kingdom of Poland and her Jews: An Introduction," 5. An influential, anonymous 1785 pamphlet was followed by similar efforts by Mateusz Butrymowicz and Józef Pawlikowski in 1789, and later by Tadeusz Czacki. All believed that by breaking down social and economic fences, Jews would respond naturally by drawing closer to Polish society.

important political programs and cultural events.²³ Within this region the Jews accounted for a significant portion of the population, reaching 10%. By the late nineteenth century, one in four Jews living in the Russian Empire resided in Central Poland.²⁴ With its legal opposition and an independent judicial branch, the Kingdom of Poland resembled a sovereign Polish state. Having permitted the kingdom to retain its liberal political format generated by Napoleon, along with Polish culture, Russia's tsar hoped to win over Polish hearts and minds. It did not quite work out as he planned, however, when Poles realized how little power they actually held.

With the Kingdom of Poland tied dynastically to the Russian Empire, Alexander I also became known as the king of Poland. He appointed the administrative council and viceroy to govern the new acquisition, but Alexander I retained the right to rule over them. An inconsistent leader, concrete policy change did not follow from his political pledges. Although he promulgated the constitutional charter, he often ignored the Kingdom of Poland's constitution in order to achieve his ultimate goal—control.²⁵ Despite the Sejm's charge as a form of governmental oversight, it could not propose legislation.²⁶ As government censorship and ministerial disregard for Polish constitutional rights rose, Sejm members erupted in protest in 1820. Alexander reacted to the stormy Sejm session by granting permission to his ministers to abrogate the constitution in order to get the Polish house in order.²⁷ Polish enthusiasm for Tsar Alexander had abated.

In 1818, under the early promise of Alexander's reign, the First Sejm of the Kingdom of Poland took up the continuing question of the social and legal status of the Jewish population.²⁸ With what then looked like a seemingly autonomous state, Polish leaders believed they stood at a critical juncture, able to reevaluate and redefine the identity of their country and its inhabitants. In the newly developing Kingdom of Poland, much of the leadership remained the same from the days prior to the 1795 partition. Similar to the Four-Year Sejm, opinions differed regarding equal rights. As in the Polish-Lithuanian Commonwealth and the Duchy of Warsaw, the Kingdom of Poland retained the right of the landowning

---

23 Wandycz, *The Lands of Partitioned Poland, 1795–1918*, 65. Western Galicia did rival the Kingdom of Poland at the end of the nineteenth century for centrality in the Polish question. See Dynner and Wodziński, "The Kingdom of Poland and her Jews: An Introduction," 5.
24 Ibid., 3.
25 Nicholas V. Riasanovsky, *A History of Russia*, 5th ed. (New York: Oxford University Press, 1993), 318.
26 Dynner and Wodziński, "The Kingdom of Poland and Her Jews: An Introduction," 4.
27 Wandyz, *The Lands of Partitioned Poland, 1795–1918*, 83–84.
28 Wodziński, *Haskalah and Hasidism*, 144.

nobility to define who constituted a Pole. This self-appointed leadership consistently refused to let go of its powerful control over the Jews and peasants, who remained outside the concept of the "Polish people."[29] Reformers held several formal debates on the reform of Polish Jewry between 1815 and 1822.[30] However, given that they had been debating this issue for over thirty years with no progress, even those who had been more supportive of Jews' rights grew disenchanted with prospects for actual reform and moved further to the right.

Always a point of contention, Poles remained anxious about permitting Jews to own land.[31] Given the rise of a Jewish bourgeoisie, many noblemen feared that, if given the opportunity, Jews would buy up great swaths of territory and overtake the Polish population. Even some of the most liberal Polish reformers refused to give Jews the right to purchase land because landownership opened the door for Jews' citizenship and access to political power.

By maintaining that only Christians could purchase land, Poles contained Jews outside of the Polish sociopolitical power nexus.[32] Edna Bonacich contends that the Polish nobility responded to the Jews' desire for civil rights like other host societies in conflict with a middleman minority group. The Jewish arrendator and the Jewish sub-arrendators held relatively strong and entrenched economic positions, while a large segment of them maintained social and religious separation from Poles. "Such power appears devastating to host members, who believe their country is being 'taken over' by an alien group."[33] One could also argue that the Poles' recent political devastation underscored their need to prohibit another outside group from gaining power.

Other groups had already overtaken Poles through land seizures. They stole Poles' sovereignty. Prohibiting the Jews from buying land was a way to prevent another feared "attack" against Poles.

Concurrently, yet somewhat in contradistinction, reformers called on Jews to alter their occupational preferences and to engage in agriculture. However, prohibitions against Jewish (and peasant) landownership made it unattractive for Jews to pivot into farmning. Still, some Jews did answer the reformers' call to take up the plough, but they did so at a much slower pace and lower proportion

---

29 This relationship did not begin to change until the intelligentsia recognized it needed peasant support to carry out the 1863 Polish insurrection.
30 Dynner and Wodziński, "The Kingdom of Poland and Her Jews: An Introduction," 8.
31 Dynner, *Yankel's Tavern*, 159.
32 Theodore R. Weeks, *Nation and State in Late Imperial Russia: Nationalism and Russification on the Western Frontier, 1863–1914* (Dekalb: Northern Illinois University Press, 2008), 8.
33 Bonacich, "A Theory of Middleman Minorities": 592.

than Poles would have preferred. By 1859, there were fifty-six Jewish agricultural colonies established by noblemen and Jewish entrepreneurs, with a total of 4,405 members. Aside from this figure, an additional 25,600 Jews engaged in some form of farming.[34] Population numbers for the Jews in the Kingdom of Poland demonstrate that this was a very small percentage indeed. In 1820 Jews numbered roughly four hundred thousand. By 1880 that number jumped to 1.1 million.[35] Relative to their number in the Kingdom of Poland, Jews did not readily take up farming.

Polish responses to the "Jewish question"—how to transform the Jews into integrated members of society—changed over time. Partition's erasure of the commonwealth, coupled with Poles' later political insecurity as experienced in both the Kingdom of Poland and the duchy, greatly impacted the debate. After most Polish leaders accepted that restoring the Polish political state was not readily attainable, they began searching for new unifying forces. Moving away from the ideal of the political nation, they sought to promote an internal Polish cultural mindset, which could cross economic, social, and political borders.[36]

Polish reformers intensified their efforts to bring all of Poland's populace—Jews, peasants, burghers, and nobility—to a higher form of "civility and culture." For post-1815 reformers, this goal corresponded with the moral and cultural norms of secular Christian society. Opposed to the Church's power over the people, Polish secular reformers hoped to discard Church authority while maintaining secular Christian moral and cultural standards. They spoke about reform as creating "civil Christians." Viewing societies through a hierarchical model, they wished to elevate peasants, Jews, and burghers to their high Christian culture.[37] This morality-based language signified a shift in the reformers' outlook. Earlier, they had wanted outward signs of connection to Poland. Now they also angled for a deeper shared morality and way of life. Through language, education, and important cultural adjustments, they presented a new path toward Polish unity and continuity. For Jews, proving one's attachment to Poland became even more difficult.

---

34 Dynner, *Yankel's Tavern*, 158–160.
35 Polonsky, *The Jews in Poland and Russia*, 1:323.
36 For a discussion on the continuum between early debates on the Jews' reform and those occurring within the Kingdom of Poland, see Wodziński, "'Civil Christians': Debates on the Reform of the Jews in Poland, 1789–1830," 46–76.
37 Most reformers guarded against missionizing to Jews, as it deviated from the Enlightenment's concept of religious tolerance. See ibid., 55–57.

Language and Cultural Survival

Partition threatened Polish identity. Unless Polish leaders could create ties that were able to withstand physical, political, and economic divisions, the Polish people faced annihilation. Polish activists shifted their attention away from state political structures to the unifying forces of language and education.[38] The Polish intelligentsia created centers of learning in which Polish was the only language of instruction. In theory Tsar Alexander I supported cultural openness and the Poles' early attempt to save their native tongue. Thus, Polish reigned in several institutions, including the University of Vilna (within a region many Poles hoped to incorporate into the kingdom), the Royal University of Warsaw's law school and medical school, as well as three secondary schools.[39] By insisting on a common language, Polish people across political borders shared an immediate kinship, a common history, and hope for a collective future.

It is within this context that Polish reformers called on Jews to demonstrate fealty to the Polish people and Polish culture through language acquisition. The Jewish response varied. Mainstream Jews retained Yiddish as their lingua franca, while preserving Hebrew as a sacred language reserved only for prayer and study. Yiddish aided the Jews' own communal preservation. To replace Yiddish with Polish would serve no positive purpose in the eyes of traditional Jewish leaders. It would only bring their children (the future of Judaism), their women (the reproducers of Judaism), and their men (the stewards of Judaism) into greater direct daily contact with a form of life which threatened their own traditional convictions. Rabbis guarded loyalty and conformity to the Jewish faith by building a fence around the Jewish community. Maintaining Yiddish as their communal language, rabbinic leaders shut out secular enticements.

On the other hand, the fringe progressive Jewish community obliged Polish reformers. *Second*-generation Maskilim embraced Haskalah through the Polish

---

38 Inspired by the standardization of languages in other countries, the Polish intelligentsia founded the Society of Friends of Learning (Towarzystwo Przyjaciół Nauk), a grassroots academy of arts and sciences. In 1806, it sponsored the first monumental dictionary of the Polish language. Similar projects appeared contemporaneously—for example, Noah Webster's dictionary in the United States and the Grimm brothers' dictionary in Germany. The society counted among its members a wide range of intellectuals outside of the nobility, including the Jewish scientist Abraham Stern (1769–1842).

39 Wandyz, *The Lands of Partitioned Poland, 1795–1918*, 96.

language.[40] Born and secularly educated in the Kingdom of Poland, their language of intellectual initiation was Polish. They rejected their parents' old-school preference for German and Hebrew. To them, it made no sense. They lived their lives in the Kingdom of Poland; their affinity was to Polish culture, including its language. This intense and visceral connection with Poles separated them from their teachers. For them speaking Polish was part of their very essence. It symbolized their adoption of Polish culture and its people. Second-geeneration Polish Maskilim were known as *integrationists*.[41] Disconnecting from their parents' Maskilic ideological fidelity to the governing power (in this case, Russia), integrationists made Polish national interests their own. This generation's adaptation of Polish culture, coupled with the idealistic goal of bringing it to mainstream traditional Jews, would cement their positive relationships with Polish intellectuals in the 1850s and 1860s. Indeed, by the mid-nineteenth century, integrationists had been accepted as the de facto voice of Polish Haskalah.

Numerous integrationists focused their professional lives on attracting the broader Jewish population to Haskalah. Many accepted Polish reformers' offers to participate in joint ventures to transform backward religious followers into enlightened, civilized Jews. Establishing secular Jewish education was one such project. Working with Polish reform policy makers between 1818 and 1820, the integrationist leader Jakob Tugenhold (1794–1871) opened three secular elementary schools in Warsaw that accepted only Jewish children. By 1825, two additional schools opened, bringing the number of students to 432. Teachers taught all subjects in Polish. Other integrationists created the textbooks for these schools, which focused on ethics, Hebrew language skills, Jewish history, the Bible, Hebrew poetry, mathematics, astronomy, geography, history, as well as crafts and agriculture. While these schools had some success, when set up outside Warsaw they typically failed.[42] The issues of language and cultural

---

40 Throughout human history peoples have adopted the language of the powerful in order to rise economically and socially.
41 Wodziński, *Haskalah and Hasidism*, 155.
42 Compared to later Jewish participation in state schools in both Austrian Galicia, and the Russian Pale of Settlement, a smaller percentage of Jews in the Kingdom of Poland attended these modern schools. The density of the Jewish population—millions of Jews lived in this area and clung to their traditions—made educational reform challenging. With far fewer schools often provided to the general Jewish population in the Kingdom of Poland relative to other locales, a modern school did not exist where Jews lived, Additionally, a small number of Jewish children attended Polish state schools. Ibid., 48–51; Antony Polonsky, *The Jews in the Kingdom of Poland*, 255. Of note, in 1840s Galicia there were 355,071 Jews out of a population of 4,771,644. Fourteen towns had primary and secondary secular education.

survival remained central for nineteenth-century Poles and Jews (as it does for most migrating groups), begging the deeper question: Could Jews take part in the host culture and still retain a connection to their roots?

Jewish Traditionalists and Haskalah

As change assaulted the Jewish community in the Kingdom of Poland, fear of it readied traditionalists for war. Traditional rabbinic leaders created a full-blown campaign to block Haskalah and its new breed of Jewish thinker.[43] With the authority to judge Jewish community members through its separate rabbinic court, each kahal could fix penalties against modernization. To keep their flock in line, these guardians of halakha—Jewish law—fixed penalties against modernization, stoked societal pressure, and even employed physical force.[44] Their greatest weapon against radicalism, however, was the threat of excommunication.[45] The fact that the kahals required such an arsenal speaks to the likely presence of active opposition to rabbinic authority, which came not only from the Jewish populace, but also from Polish reformers.

Polish reformers believed that by limiting rabbinic authority, more Jews would assimilate. Thus, they denied rabbis the right of excommunication. By January 1820, reformers packed an even stronger punch when they dismantled the kingdom's entire kahal system. The state took on those municipal responsibilities the kahal had previously managed, leaving Jewish leaders with only religious matters to oversee. The additional 1822 state dissolution of all Jewish religious societies further degraded traditional Jewish leaders' sense of control.[46] Reformers replaced the old kahal structure, which had near unlimited power over the community, with a somewhat impotent Jewish community board system. Jewish traditionalists were under siege.

With approximately three thousand Jewish students in state schools, 0.0089 Jews attended state schools. In Russia's Pale of Jewish Settlement in 1844, there lived 1,041,000 Jews out of a population of 16,697,000. By 1855 there were seventy-one secular schools. With 3,700 Jews in state schools, 0.00356 Jews attended state schools. In 1825 in the Kingdom of Poland, there existed five state schools for 432 Jewish students at the height of attendance. At this time 0.00108 Jews participated in state lower education. Polonsky, *The Jews in the Kingdom of Poland*, 360, 370, and 273.

43   Author's interview with Marcin Wodziński, April 2019.
44   Wodziński, *Hasidism and Politics*, 242.
45   Polonsky, *The Jews in Poland and Russia*, 1:45, 62, and 254.
46   Wodziński, *Hasidism and Politics*, 241.

Maskilim and integrationists supported the government-driven changes. However, they were a minority. Despite the advances they had made in progressive religious communal organization, most Jews in the Kingdom of Poland neither followed the principles of the Jewish Enlightenment nor attended the new schools. The vast majority of Jews considered it heretical to espouse secular education as equal to long-established conventional Jewish learning. Additionally, mainstream Jewry objected to Haskalah's approach to the Hebrew Bible. In advancing textual criticism, a contemporary secular Christian methodology, Maskilim demoted the Bible from the traditional sacred word of God to a *human expression* of the divine. Contrary to mainstream Jews, Maskilim believed that humans helped to write and construct the Bible. Traditional Jews approached the Torah (also known as either the Five Books of Moses or Pentateuch), and the Talmud, which contains volumes of rabbinic discussion and law, as sacrosanct; they dedicated their energies to fleshing out the legal minutia within these texts. Rabbis garnered great respect for their intellectual prowess in textual study. Thus, it is not surprising that they responded to Haskalah as an attack against long-held rabbinic communal prestige and influence. Traditional Jews described Haskalah, its followers, and the later Warsaw Rabbinical School, as blasphemous.[47]

Jewish Traditionalists and Hasidism

While the Haskalah was establishing roots in the Kingdom of Poland, an additional yet distinct Jewish reforming element emerged. Born in the mid-1700s Podalia region of Ukraine, Hasidism spread slowly over decades throughout the eastern kresy. A form of Jewish mysticism, it created a spiritual and religious viewpoint removed from normative Judaism. Its central charismatic early figure was Israel ben Eliezer, better known as the Ba'al Shem Tov or by the acronym Besht (1698–1760).[48]

At its core, Hasidism held that ordinary Jews must be accepted, respected, and supported in their commune with God. This approach allowed the average Jew to feel appreciated and relevant. Hasidism focused on prayer as an experience. It endeavored to bring the petitioner closer to God by changing how one prayed.

---

47 Michael A. Meyer, *Response to Modernity: A History of the Reform Movement in Judaism* (Detroit: Wayne State University Press, 1988), 81.
48 For theories on the beginning of Hasidism, see Hundert, *The Jews in Poland-Lithuania*, 160–163.

To reach *devekut*, a cleaving to God, Hasidism not only added song and dance, but also alcohol consumption. Hasidism raised each individual Jew to partner with God: its concept of *tikkun olam* holds that every Jew must work with God to repair this world through individual good deeds.⁴⁹ Quite radical, Hasidism challenged the intellectually driven elitism of traditional rabbinic Judaism and replaced it with a populist, charismatic embrace of the Jew on the street.

By the early 1800s, traditional rabbis viewed Hasidism with great disgust. This response directly related to previous experiences with the quick rise and collapse of two other branches of Jewish mysticism, Shabbateanism and later Frankism. Both groups had rebuked the Talmud and encouraged behavior which violated traditional rabbinic morality. Their respective leaders (both self-proclaimed messiahs) eventually converted away from Judaism.⁵⁰ In 1750, two thousand Frankists also converted to Catholicism, dissolving into the Polish world. With only a generation dividing the rabbis from the Frankists' extreme denial of Judaism, one cannot overstate the panic many rabbinic leaders felt encountering yet another mystical outgrowth.⁵¹ For the rabbis, Hasidism posed a real danger to the community.

Because mainstream Jewry often responded against Hasidism aggressively, through verbal and physical assaults, Hasidim referred to them as Mitnaggedim, "opponents." However, not all traditional Jews aligned with the Mitnaggedim. Many remained ambivalent. A strong palpable opposition to Hasidism took form especially in the eastern kresy, where the Ba'al Shem Tov's followers proliferated.⁵² But Hasidism continued to attract not only the disaffected average poor Jew, but also young men from the learned elite.

Mitnaggedic testimonies abound through the mid-nineteenth century which attest to large numbers of young Jewish men leaving traditional Judaism for Hasidism. At a time when increased poverty prohibited more families from paying for elite Jewish education, the Jewish community continued to praise only those young men who had attained it. This disconnect between communal

---

49   Wodziński, *Hasidism and Politics*, 42.
50   Shabbatai Zevi converted to Islam. A significant portion of his followers went underground due to continued harassment from the rabbis. Jacob Frank claimed to be the reincarnation of Shabbatai Zevi. See Hundert, *Jews in Poland-Lithuania in the Eighteenth Century*, 121, 156.
51   Marcin Wodziński, *Haskalah and Hasidism in the Kingdom of Poland*, 11.
52   Immanuel Etkes, *Rabbi Israel Salanter and the Mussar Movement: Seeking the Torah of Truth*, trans. Jonathan Chipman (Philadelphia: The Jewish Publication Society, 1993), 4. As early as 1772 the phenomenon of Mitnaggedism arose at the behest of Rabbi Elijah, the Gaon of Vilna (1720–1797). Viewing Hasidism as a deviant sect, Mitnaggedim sought to publicly shame the group by exposing its heretical nature.

values and the economic means to fulfill them, created an intense social divide within the Jewish population. Hasidism (which opposed the type of rote study traditionalists valued) welcomed and accepted these young men snubbed by mainstream Jewish leaders. Hasidism gave them purpose and dignity.

Mitnaggedim assailed Hasidim not only for pilfering their young men, but also for their negative influence. Group pressure and physical force played a considerable role in Hasidic circles up through 1865.[53] However, both sides exhibited poor behavior, often allowing verbal confrontations to turn into physical altercations and even riots. Both groups dragged people away from the synagogue, broke windows, threw candles during services, and even bundled people into sacks and took them out of the city.[54]

Hasidim distinguished themselves from mainstream Jewry in their specific interpretations of Jewish law and by their zealous adherence to it. Prayer assembly and kosher slaughtering played a central role in separating Hasidim from ordinary Jews. Interestingly, the growing financial consequences of both most likely increased their importance to the two groups. Typically, when Hasidim took root in a community, they petitioned the government for the right to congregate in a private house (*shtibl*) to conduct separate prayer services.[55] In their petitions, Hasidim explained that they could not pray with the general community. Not only did they spend more hours in prayer than their opponents, but they also embraced the liturgical tradition prominent in the Land of Israel which differed from that traditionally used by Eastern European Jewry—Ashkenazim.

Requiring separate prayer houses had deleterious financial ramifications for the general Jewish population. The Jewish community generated tax income by selling synagogue seats and auctioning off the honor to read from the Torah.[56] When Hasidim prayed at a separate shtibl, they did not contribute to the community's tax burden. Thus, Mitnaggedim often sent requests to the government to shut down Hasidic prayer houses and to force the mystics to pay their share of taxes. They further argued that the Hasidim's example encouraged other Jews to congregate privately in prayer and thereby also escape their financial obligations to the community.[57] Local Polish officials in almost every province

---

53 Wodziński, *Hasidism and Politics*, 227.
54 Ibid., 248.
55 With growing unrest throughout Europe, coupled with anti-liberal repression, the government required all groups—whether Jewish or Christian—to petition for the right to gather. The government viewed all new assemblies with growing suspicion. Ibid., 117.
56 Ibid., 47.
57 Ibid., 236.

(voivoideship) raised the question of whether the Hasidim had the legal right to pray separately from the Jewish community. Officials advanced the question at least three different times at the state level.[58]

Jewish community leaders also lambasted the relationship between Hasidim and their spiritual leaders, known as tsadikim, or righteous ones. Often charismatic, a tsadik often had intensely loyal followers. There is evidence that by the 1820s five hundred to six hundred followers would make pilgrimages to the most famous tsadikim at their Hasidic centers on the High Holy Days.[59]

The traditional Jewish world lay in crisis. Both Hasidim and Maskilim rejected common Jewish means by which to reach God. Against both wings of the community stood a traditional rabbinic authority with diminishing power. The Mitnaggedim strove to remain at the helm of Jewish society at a time when challenges to its direction came not only from the Polish reformers outside, but also from within the Jewish world.

Myth Reconstruction

With the 1815 dawning of the Kingdom of Poland, political liberal elites believed they could eventually transform the semiautonomous region into an independent unified Polish state. However, Tsar Alexander I dashed those dreams. This failed attempt to regain sovereignty provides important context for grasping the Sejm reformers' negative response to the Jewish middleman minority group's continued pursuit for rights of residence and trade in royal towns, as well as citizenship. With the Enlightenment in decline by 1815, and hopes for a Polish nation state fading, the language of reform changed.

Prior to the partitions of the Polish-Lithuanian Commonwealth, most Sejm reformers were ambivalent about fully welcoming this large, separate, traditional Jewish mass of people as citizens. After another thirty-five years of territorial loss and lack of true power, the same reformers' ambivalence about the Jews had changed into fear of the Jews' consistently rising birth rates within the general population and impatience with their impertinence. Distressed by Russian disrespect and their own lack of authority in their country, Sejm reformers bristled at the Mitnaggedim's and Hasidim's rejection of Polish culture. By 1820, more statesmen blamed rabbinic Judaism for the Jews' "degeneration." Thus, many Polish reformers sought to curtail rabbinic influence over the Jewish population.

---

58   Ibid., 115.
59   Ibid., 44.

They no longer requested only outward signs of oneness with Polish culture. Now they set to change the very core of Judaism—rabbinic authority. Stanisław Staszic, the Catholic priest turned prominent Polish reformer, drew an extreme differentiation between biblical law and rabbinic law when he referred respectively to the two as "good Mosaism" and "bad Judaism."[60] Both liberal and conservative Polish reformers latched onto this ideal of the Jews' return to Mosaism. For Poles, Mosaism presented a far more comprehensible form of Judaism than rabbinic Judaism. At its heart, Mosaism valued only laws located in the Torah. It thereby discarded seventeen-hundred years of rabbinic law. By challenging the legitimacy of rabbinic Judaism, Sejm reformers reached a deeper level of contention with the Jewish population. While early political activists had not sought to change religion, only public ritual expressions of it, by 1815 Polish social crusaders were challenging both ritual and belief to realign Judaism with only the biblical period.[61]

In so doing, Polish reformers rejected the central position in which rabbinic Judaism placed the Talmud, a sixth-century codified multivolume legal text, written in Hebrew and Aramaic. Jewish traditional respect and authority stemmed from proficiency in this text. Reformers regarded the Talmud as the source for the Jews' supposed cultural and religious "primitivism." So fixated were Polish reformers on the Talmud that most misunderstand the traditional practices and core beliefs of traditional Jews.

Judaism is a religion concerned with behavior—following God's laws as revealed on Mount Sinai. The Jews believed God directly, and through inspiration, gave Moses not only the Torah (the Written Law), but also the Oral Law, which elucidated the Torah. Generations held that every syllable of the Torah could be understood through study of the Oral Law. The sages verbally handed down the Oral Law until the third century when they codified it into the Mishnah. Rabbis continued to ask questions of the Torah and provide responses. In the sixth century, they formed the Talmud by combining the Mishnah with centuries worth of rabbinic discussions and teachings pertaining to it. This codification of the Oral Law into the Talmud was the quintessential Jewish reaction to the destruction of the Second Temple in Jerusalem. Instead of imploding, the leadership reorganized. Instead of joining the burgeoning Christian community, Jews found their way to God through the interpretation of Jewish law. So

---

60 Wodziński, "Civil Christians," in *Culture Front*, 51.
61 Ibid., 51.

important was this rabbinic process that Jewish scholars recognize that for centuries the Talmud superseded the Hebrew Bible in importance for Jewish life.[62]

The rabbis' approach to living as Jews in this world placed the Talmud as a central pillar of Judaism. Studying it brought one closer to comprehending God's word, and each generation of rabbis took part in this sacred process of interpretation. The Talmud acted as their guide in resolving how best to follow God's Torah-based commandments within their "modern" context. In this pursuit, the rabbis acted as the descendants of Moses, receiving and deciphering God's word for the people.

Existing outside of the Jewish fold, Polish reformers grasped neither the significance of the Talmud nor the connection between it and Torah. Given that their own religion sprung from early Judaism, they accepted the sanctity of the Torah. However, for most Christians, rabbinic Judaism did not derive from God, but rather insulted God due to its rejection of Jesus as Christ. Polish reformers discarded the rabbis' "rules" on the grounds that the formulae had little in common with the Mosaic Bible. Stanisław Staszic argued for its elimination precisely because "Moses neither gave nor knew any Talmuds; he would not even have been able to understand them. For the whole of today's faith rests on the Talmud and that is its principal source of contamination."[63]

Polish secular Christian reformers focused their general disdain for rabbinic Judaism on the specifics of the Jewish dietary laws, kashrut. Over the centuries, the rabbis had elaborated a dense body of detailed law from several principles in the Torah covering dietary restrictions. The rabbis extrapolated from the biblical commandment "You shall not boil a young goat in its mother's milk" (Exodus 23:19) that one should not eat milk and meat together. With this conclusion came an array of legal fences to ensure Jews followed this law, including the prohibition against eating non-Jews' food. To grasp the Poles' intense response to kashrut, one must recognize that in Polish culture refusal to partake in a common Polish meal was a tremendous insult.[64] Although it was likely that a nobleman would not offer a seat at his table to a Jew (due to longstanding social barriers), the fact that a Jew would not accept a hypothetical invitation had great ramifications. Therefore, Poles necessarily viewed kashrut as an insult. For Jews, kashrut expressed their relationship to God and to the Jewish people. In this debate, two people's myths, which defined their respective places in the world, collided.

---

62 Adin Steinsaltz, *The Essential Talmud*, trans. Chaya Galai (New York: Basic Books, Inc., 1976, 3.
63 Wodziński, "Civil Christians."
64 Wodziński, *Hasidism and Politics*, 19n5

Polish reformers understood Jews' separateness as something to be changed rather than respected. The majority demanded Jews' acceptance of Polish cultural norms rather than Poles' acceptance of Jews' differences from Poles. They highlighted those excerpts from the Talmud that cast Christianity in a negative light as proof that the text was an enemy of Poland. They focused on the Talmud as the central basis for the Jews' marked departures from the host culture. In short, they tackled social reconstruction in a condescending manner. Did they want the general population to accept Jews by the latter drawing closer to Polish cultural norms, or did Polish reformers simply feel a need to assert authority?

Polish reformers derided a whole canon of literature and law without truly understanding its content. They homed in on pieces of text others had taken out of context and criticized. That they expected traditional Jews simply to follow their directives en masse was preposterous. Knowing their own conservative Polish peasants' reticence toward adopting more "civil" behavior, they could have predicted the Jews' ultimate rejection of change, especially that which was promoted by outsiders. That they expected mainstream traditional Jews to follow the Maskilim minority, which had made this return to Mosaism, was also naive. For observant Jews, Maskilim were the ultimate enemy within.

Traditionalists, whether Polish or Jewish, challenged Others and defended themselves through scheming, violence, and education. Both Poles and Jews wrestled with their respective communities, as well as with each other, to keep hold of some measure of control at a time when each felt its power diminished. While Polish reformers still debated Jewish citizenship, most had grown harsher in their demands. Bruised and bullied by partition and Russian authority, they set their sights on saving the Polish people.

CHAPTER 5

The 1830 Uprising and Its Consequences

In the Kingdom of Poland, Poles' hope for a Russian-approved path toward Polish sovereignty deteriorated. Despite Tsar Alexander I's initially liberal policy, the Russian ruler surrendered to his innate need for control. As Poles' own control decreased, they lost patience with mainstream Jewry's lack of social and political alignment with the general population. The change in Russian rule only further pushed younger Poles into rebellion. This chapter explores the 1830 Polish Uprising and the varied Polish and Jewish responses to it. It also attempts to understand the cultural punishments imposed by Tsar Nicholas I, as well as the Poles' assumptions about Jews that resulted.

Polish National Messianism

Poles were divided, often generationally, over how to respond to the kingdom's dynastic link to the Russian Romanov tsar. The older, conservative cohort accepted the tsar as king of Poland. While disapproving of the overreach of Russian ministers, they opposed any sort of Polish armed rebellion. The intellectual youth, on the other hand, sought a radical response to the tsar's harsh treatment of the kingdom.

Within the kingdom young intellectuals developed a particular brand of romanticism which focused on national messianism. They believed "the world was about to enter a new age in which injustice would be resolved, human consciousness would be elevated, and strife would come to an end."[1] Although they argued about the exact way this would occur, Polish romantics envisioned the

---

1 Brian Porter-Szűcs, *Faith and Fatherland: Catholicism, Modernity, and Poland* (Oxford: Oxford University Press, 2011), 84.

Kingdom of Poland as the essential force of change. They worked towards a free, reunified Poland, which would permit the cultural liberty of the individual.

Romantic writers, such as Adam Mickiewicz (1795–1855), generated immense patriotism among young Poles through ballads expressing a uniquely Polish love of fatherland, freedom, and the power of the people. As Brian Porter-Szűcs notes, Mickiewicz connected Polish patriotism to Church theology:

> Just as Christ was killed for his message, an evil trinity of monarchs destroyed Poland because they feared the freedom it embodied. But this apparent death was not the end, "for the Polish nation did not die. Its body lay in the grave and its soul had gone from the earth, that is, from public life, into purgatory, that is, into the domestic life of [those nations] suffering from slavery... And on the third day the soul will return to the body and the nation will rise again and free all the peoples of Europe from slavery."[2]

Though Mickiewicz invoked God in his presentation of the past, the Church banned his writing.[3] It could not accept linking Poland, or any other country, with the divine plan for salvation. According to its teachings, God had already provided salvation through Jesus Christ and the Catholic Church. The Kingdom of God existed already here on earth. The romantic belief in a future national rebirth as both a religious and political event, toward which people should strive, stood in absolute opposition to foundational Church doctrine. The conviction that God needed human help to move history forward departed radically from the long-standing Magisterial Catholic teaching: "all of us are free to choose the path of sin or salvation, but... we can no more transform the wider flow of history than we can alter the laws of nature."[4] For the Church, God was the soul actor in history: God determined political authority, raising kings and toppling them. It followed, therefore, that to act against Russia's political hold on the Kingdom of Poland was to act against God.

Young Polish intellectuals' discontent boiled over due to several impactful Russian polices. Russian authorities deported leaders, including Mickiewicz and other students, to the Russian interior. This punishment backfired, only intensifying young Poles' attraction to the ideals Mickiewicz described in his writings.[5] At

---

2   Cited in ibid., 87.
3   Ibid., 88.
4   Ibid.
5   Wandycz, *The Lands of Partitioned Poland, 1795–1918*, 84–86.

the same time, neither students nor cadets saw much future for themselves in the Kingdom of Poland due to the tsar's exclusion of Poles from higher education and military advancement. Fearing the influential student radicalism breaking out in Central Europe, the government had prohibited study abroad and cut funding for postsecondary studies for Poles.[6] Concurrently, Polish cadets' hopes for advancement were shattered, as the Polish army remained demobilized and humiliated under the command of the tsar's brother, Grand Duke Constantine. Though the army was the pride of the Polish people, Constantine's ineffectual use of it, constant inspections, and abuse of corporal punishment drove soldiers to despair.[7] The reactionary cycle continued when the tsar prohibited the right to gather in any political association, which spurred a surge of secret societies in the kingdom, including the popular Freemasons. Aware of this growing threat, by 1821 secret police and informants infiltrated these underground groups in an effort to quash expressions of Polish national sentiment.[8] The radicalized young nobility's yearnings for a strong Polish state only grew with such authoritarianism.

While this small fraction of the population concerned itself with policies and politics, most people living within the Kingdom of Poland could not occupy themselves with such frivolous matters. Theirs was a struggle for physical survival. Peasants focused on keeping starvation at bay. Though technically emancipated from serfdom under Napoleon's 1807 Constitution for the Duchy of Warsaw, and the Napoleonic Civil Code, their reality had hardly changed. With little to no land in their names, peasants remained subsistence farmers. They provided corvée, or free labor, to the landlord while struggling for their own survival.[9]

Rooted in Catholicism well before partition, the peasantry found even greater stability in the Church when their physical political reality offered little traction. The Church supported the weary peasant. Responding to the Poles' suffering, it recognized Poland as the "Christ of all nations," a country that died so that others could reach salvation. The Church supported the downtrodden peasant and in return the ethnic Polish population allowed Church influence to expand.[10] It follows that given the Church's staunch opposition to human interference in God's work directing the future, the peasantry had no imperative to act against the monarch.

---

6   R. F. Leslie, *Polish Politics and the Revolution of November 1830*, University of London Historical Studies, vol. 3 (Westport: Greenwood Press Publishers, 1969), 100.
7   Wandycz, *The Lands of Partitioned Poland, 1795–1918*, 78.
8   Dynner, *Yankel's Tavern*, 104–5.
9   Antony Polonsky, *The Jews in Poland and Russia*, 1:275.
10 Theodore R. Weeks, "Assimilationism, Nationalism, Modernization, Antisemitism: Notes on Polish-Jewish Relations, 1855–1905," in *Antisemitism and Its Opponents in Modern Poland*, ed. Robert Blobaum (Ithaca: Cornell University Press, 2005), 24.

The radical, more liberal szlachta, however, did have the ability and desire to act politically. Fantasies of an eventual reunification with other partitioned commonwealth territories filled their imaginations. Specifically, they dreamt of bringing the kresy back to Polish dominion. Erroneously, many had believed that the Kingdom of Poland's 1815 Constitution promised by Alexander I would further empower Poles to enact this political vision. However, while this interpretation might not have been far removed from Alexander's original statements at the Congress of Vienna, it was not even close to his 1820 agenda for the kingdom.[11] Although Alexander I's attraction to the Enlightenment disposed him toward creating reform policies, his fear of losing control over his varied and immense populations prevented him from making any real reforms. Thus, when autocracy infringed on constitutionality, and when dreams of reunification appeared frighteningly beyond reach, some Poles grew wary and impatient. It was during this time that radicalized Poles continued their underground activity, meeting and planning for the country's eventual freedom.

Tsar Nicholas I and Polish Rebellion

Much changed when Tsar Alexander I died unexpectedly in 1825. The ascension to the throne of his more autocratic brother, Nicholas I, promulgated further discontent among the kingdom's underground activists. Although he presented himself to the Poles as a ruler who would respect the constitution, Nicholas I worked deftly to defend autocracy.[12] Nineteen years younger than Alexander, Nicholas was influenced not by the Enlightenment's ideals of change, but rather by his coming of age during a time of warfare. Napoleon's earlier eastward march reminded him of the constant need for strong fortifications against political change.

Nicholas I's approach aligned with the growing European conservative reaction against Enlightenment ideals. To stave off change and societal discord, the new tsar created his doctrine of "Official Nationality," which emphasized religion, nationality, and autocracy. He supported the primacy of Russian Greek Orthodoxy (i.e., Eastern Orthodoxy) over other religions. In addition, he desired that all inhabitants embrace a love for Russia and articulate it through the Russian language. He guarded the Russian dynasty and the tsar's absolute sovereignty as necessary components for Russian statehood.[13] Having come to power in 1825 during the Decembrists' rebellion against Romanov rule, Nicholas worked

---

11 Wandycz, *The Lands of Partitioned Poland, 1795–1918*, 86.
12 Riasanovsky, *A History of Russia*, 324.
13 Ibid., 324.

feverishly to defend the existing order. Needless to say, Polish Catholics did not rank highly in his strategy.

Preoccupied with averting any rebellion by Polish youth, Nicholas enacted educational "reforms." By shutting down centers of higher education within the Kingdom of Poland, however, Nicholas I created a wider disconnect between Poles and their Russian overlord. Additionally, neither the growing discontent within the kingdom's army, nor the youth's rising national consciousness abated. With revolutionary fervor tearing apart Paris and Belgium, the Russian ruler could not prevent it reaching the Kingdom of Poland.[14]

Polish youth called for a revolution in the streets of Warsaw.[15] They wanted educational opportunities and cultural respect. A smaller, more radical element created the Patriotic Society, which demanded deeper social change: true emancipation for the peasants and the Jews.[16] On November 29, 1830, these calls for revolution bore fruit. Polish civilian conspirators attacked Grand Duke Constantine's residence at Belvedere Palace, while cadets marched toward Warsaw's old city.[17] Throngs of civilians as well as soldiers joined them. Due to a lack of skilled leadership, however, this mass effort soon broke down into mob violence, looting, and vandalism. During this upheaval, armed rioters killed those they suspected of Russian loyalties, including Polish military leaders and some Jews.[18]

The older, mostly wealthier szlachta attempted to quiet the uprising. As moderates, they did not want to break with Russia. They understood quite well that Poles could not sustain an armed resistance against Nicholas I and that a misguided rebellion would only result in physical devastation for Poles. Thus, leading members of the Polish nobility formed the National Guard, which sought not only to attain and then maintain public order, but also to prevent a political break from Russia.[19] The National Guard's goal was to secure the status quo, Russian rule. The middle-class householders and their sons who comprised the National Guard put on uniforms and grabbed weapons.[20]

---

14 Ibid., 331.
15 Shmuel Almog, *Nationalism & Antisemitism in Modern Europe 1815–1945* (Oxford: Pergamon Press, 1990), 17.
16 Norman Davies, *God's Playground: A History of Poland*, vol. 2, *1795 to the Present*, rev. ed. (New York: Columbia University Press, 2005), 237.
17 Wandycz, *The Lands of Partitioned Poland, 1795–1918*, 89 and 105.
18 Dynner, *Yankel's Tavern*, 105.
19 Polonsky, *The Jews in the Kingdom of Poland*, 1:198.
20 Ibid., 298.

Despite various secret attempts to obstruct the radical youth element, the conservative szlachta ultimately could not thwart the rebellion's momentum. Ironically, in its effort to organize reconciliation negotiations with the tsar, the aristocracy's leadership manipulated events to place itself at the helm of the very uprising it had failed to avert.[21] The tsar, however, did not believe that those now in control of the rebellion were moderates, who aimed only for harmony. Instead of reaching a nonviolent solution, Nicholas I sent an army of some 120,000 Russians against the Poles' roughly 60,000 fighters.[22] Soon, the radicals ousted their moderate leadership to take full charge of the uprising. After 325 days, Poland was defeated.

Brought on by romantic nationalism, the November Uprising collapsed due to a lack of clear leadership, direction, and support.[23] It polarized the population from the outset. Given the Church's view of Polish romanticism, it is not surprising that the peasants and clergy opposed the uprising; only a handful of priests supported it.[24] Moderates hoped to negotiate a de-escalation of force, while radicals pursued a military strategy. The failed uprising ended with thousands of Polish deaths, imprisonments, and refugees.

Jewish Participation in the Uprising

Like the aristocratic szlachta, most of Poland's Jews initially had no interest in rebellion.[25] The majority of Jews were loyal to the monarchy. At the same time, however, many members of Warsaw's Jewish bourgeoisie also felt a strong connection with Poland. They demonstrated this by supporting the conservative szlachta's attempt to maintain the kingdom's relationship with the Russian tsar. Believing it their civic duty to restore order to the city's streets, they joined the National Guard. The Jewish bourgeoisie aligned with the nobility: upholding Russian rule, it supported the Polish moderates' use of diplomatic channels to resolve the quagmire but ultimately helped object to Romanov autocracy.

As with any issue involving the Jews, disagreement existed among Polish leaders over how to respond to their support. The liberals General Józef

---

21 For a thorough discussion of attempts to limit the revolution to an insurrection, see Wandycz, *The Lands of Partitioned Poland, 1795–1918*, 105–117.
22 Davies, *God's Playground*, 2:234–245.
23 Wandycz, *The Lands of Partitioned Poland, 1795–1918*, 105–117.
24 Porter-Szűcs, *Faith and Fatherland*, 8.
25 Antony Polonsky, email correspondence with author, September 19, 2013.

Chłopicki (1771–1854), leader of the Polish army, and Governor Antoni Ostrowski (1782–1845), commander of the National Guard, took different positions toward Jewish participation in the armed forces.[26] Chłopicki was willing to accept only those Jews recognized as assimilated by their exemption from Warsaw's Jewish residential restrictions. A supporter of their quest for political emancipation and someone who categorically opposed anti-Jewish attitudes and behavior, Ostrowski took a more relaxed approach to Jews' military participation.[27] However, such forward thinking conflicted with mainstream Christian National Guardsmen, many of whom were in direct financial competition with Jews. For this element of the Christian populace, a Jew who served the fatherland militarily was at risk of becoming an even greater economic competitor.[28]

Ostrowski achieved a compromise with the guardsmen. Based on physical signs of acculturation, Polish leaders gave permission to those Jews who were willing to wear the National Guard uniform and shave off their beards. Just as the long sideburns of Austrian officials were considered proof of loyalty to the emperor in Vienna, so a clean-shaven face exhibited one's affiliation with Polish patriotism.

Historians clash over the number of Jewish men who took this extreme measure in order to join the approximately 5,700 Poles in the National Guard.[29] One volunteer, Joseph Berkowicz (son of the legendary Berek Joselewicz, who was the first Jewish colonel in the Napoleonic legions), formed a Jewish legion in the National Guard.[30] Stefan Kieniewicz argues that three to four hundred Jews joined Poles in this unit. Glenn Dynner portrays this number as erroneously inflated. He points to apologetics influencing Jewish historians to pronounce relatively large numbers of Jewish participants in Polish rebellions.[31]

For those Jewish men who could not bring themselves to shave their beards, another avenue opened to demonstrate allegiance to Poles. They established a

---

26   Polonsky, *The Jews in Poland and Russia*, 1:298.
27   Ostrowski published his thoughts on Jewish social reform in 1834. He believed that through access to secular education, military service, and agricultural colonization, the Jews could be readied for full emancipation into Polish society. See Dynner, *Yankel's Tavern*, 153.
28   Stefan Kieniewicz, "Assimilated Jews in Nineteenth-Century Warsaw," in Bartoszewski and Polonsky, *The Jews in Warsaw*, 161.
29   Ibid. In total, roughly six thousand men volunteered for the National Guard, of which Kieniewicz states three hundred to four hundred were Jews, with some reaching officer status. Glenn Dynner provides a smaller number of 137 Jews joining the National Guard. See Dynner, *Yankel's Tavern*, 105.
30   Ibid., 106.
31   Ibid., 105.

separate Jewish Civil Guard. Polish leaders spoke with respect of this organization, giving it full recognition. Historians agree that altogether some fourteen hundred Jews took part in the Jewish Civil Guard. This estimate includes traditional Jews, Mitnaggedim, and Hasidim. One memoirist, Pinhas Schweitzer, recalled a scene from his youth in which thirty Jewish traditionally dressed volunteers walked the streets of Bedzin, holding iron lances and wearing caps emblazoned with "Security Guard." "This was an unforgettable picture. Pious Jews in long *kapotes* abandoned their trade and their study houses and patrolled the town markets."[32]

Additionally, Hasidic tsadikim, such as Menahem Mendel of Kotzk (Kock) and Isaac Meir Alter of Ger (Góra Kalwaria), circulated decrees urging their followers to raise funds for the Polish National Guard. So well-known were they for their support of the uprising, that upon Russia's victory these Jewish leaders fled the Kingdom of Poland and changed their surnames.[33]

Although Mitnaggedim and Hasidim did not seek acculturation, many had formed an attachment to the Polish land and its people. They had lived for centuries in the same territory inhabited by Polish nobles and peasants. While many Jews aligned themselves with the governing authority, others felt inspired to support the Polish cause. Whether it was due to hatred for Russia and Nicholas I's decrees, hope for better conditions for Jews in a renewed Poland, fear of reprisals from Polish revolutionaries, or a genuine identification with the Polish cause, a number of traditional and unassimilated Jews either took up arms to defend the country or aided the uprising off the battlefield.[34]

Assessing Jewish Loyalty

Of those Polish elite insurrectionists whom the Russians did not kill, jail, or exile to Siberia, a significant number found refuge outside of the Kingdom of Poland. Some settled in Belgium, but most in Paris. Some seven to eight thousand activists took part in what became known as the Great Emigration.[35] They remained in exile for years, some for decades, assessing the revolt's failure and discussing

---

32 Gershon Bacon, "Messianists, Pragmatists, and Patriots: Orthodox Jews and the Modern Polish State (Some Preliminary Observations)," in *Netiot Ledavid: Jubiliee Volume for David Weiss Halivni*, ed. Yaakov Elman, Ephraim Bezalel Halivni, and Zvi Ari Steinfeld (Jerusalem: Orhot, 2004).
33 Dynner, *Yankel's Tavern*, 108–109.
34 Bacon, "Messianists, Pragmatists, and Patriots: Orthodox Jews and the Modern Polish State (Some Preliminary Observations)."
35 Polonsky, *The Jews in Poland and Russia*, 1:277.

Poland's future. Some liberal revolutionaries declared the leaders of the insurgence at fault for not encouraging the participation of both peasants and Jews, two groups that were politically disadvantaged by Russian rule. Liberal activists embraced those Jews who had acted on behalf of Poland's independence. In what Polish intellectuals had processed as a messianic battle of freedom against tyranny, Jews had served together with Christians, expressing their belief and trust in the spirit of Poland. Most of the uprising's romantic leadership found it meaningful that roughly two thousand Jewish men participated in the armed struggle for Poland's renewed independence.[36] In an 1837 declaration, Polish rebel leader Joachim Lelewel (1786–1861) promised Jews the right to citizenship if, in the future, they took up the sword for the nation's independence.[37] For these exiled patriots, to be Polish was to act for the country.

The more conservative activists in exile, however, did not give much weight to the Jewish demonstration of support for the Polish cause. Instead, they pointed to the Jewish monarchists, who benefitted from their economic ties to the Russian tsar. They focused on attempts by some Jewish communities to evade military service through bribery. During the rebellion Jews did use such tactics to escape conscription. Organizations such as the Warsaw Synagogue Council tried to offer double the recruitment tax in place of their Jewish members bearing arms.[38] However it is important to note the complicated history of Jews' participation in the Polish military. In both the Duchy of Warsaw and the Kingdom of Poland, despite the desire of assimilated Jews to be drafted, Poles instead requested an annual recruitment tax from the Jewish community in lieu of physical service. The seven hundred thousand florins paid annually by Jews living within Warsaw, coupled with the six hundred thousand florins provided by Jews outside the city, clothed the peasants who were drafted into service.[39]

Émigré conservatives, together with Polish conservative leaders who remained in Warsaw's underground movement, continued to demand acculturation as a prerequisite for societal acceptance. They maintained that the standard expectation for Jews' emancipation should be the Jews' transformation into "Poles of the Mosaic faith." Conservative Polish revolutionary leaders, and those who

---

36 For romantic Polish nationalists, Poles were not an ethnographic group, but rather people of different ethnic origins united not only by the ideal of Poland but also by actions taken to promote that ideal. See Brian Porter, *When Nationalism Began to Hate: Imagining Modern Politics in Nineteenth-Century Poland* (Oxford: Oxford University Press, 2000), 16.
37 Polonsky, *The Jews in Poland and Russia*, 1:300.
38 Dynner and Wodziński, "The Kingdom of Poland and Her Jews: An Introduction," 22.
39 Polonsky, *The Jews in Poland and Russia*, 1:287, 291, and 301.

succeeded them, advanced the belief that traditional Jewry, by definition, had detached from the Polish cause.

The Consequences of the Failed Uprising

Once he quashed the 1830 Uprising (also known as the November Uprising), Nicholas I targeted the Poles with punitive measures. He abolished the Sejm, which had dethroned him during the insurrection. He also installed a Russian viceroy, Ivan Paskevich, who died after twenty-five years at the helm.[40] Russia replaced the kingdom's 1815 Constitution with the 1832 Organic Statute, forcing Poland into "an indivisible part" of the Russian Empire. Additionally, St. Petersburg abrogated the 1822 commercial arrangement with the kingdom, which had given Poles preferential access to Russia's vast markets.[41] This policy shift negatively affected what little Polish industrial development had existed. While the Russian market had supported the unprecedented recent growth of Łodz's textile industry, this high tariff barrier stunted it temporarily.[42]

Nicholas also began emptying the government administration of Poles. At the same time, he rewarded several Jewish monarchists known to have helped the Russians during the insurrection by placing them in those freed positions. Propelled by a shortage of competent Russians to fill open offices, the government allowed not only Jewish monarchists, but also remorseful Jewish Polish nationalists to occupy low-level posts. Thus the promotion of Jakob Tugenhold (1794–1871), a committed Polish insurgent turned Russian loyalist.[43] By 1840, the highest civil government positions, which had once been reserved for Poles, were now filled by Russians.

Tsar Nicholas I fiercely attacked Polish culture through policies affecting language, religion, and education. Just as Polish intellectuals had understood the power of language, so too did the Russian tsar. (He did not completely abolish its usage from administrative offices and courts until 1867.) Tsar Nicholas I removed Catholic Church leaders from many of their posts and cracked down

---

40 On the Sejm's dethroning of Nicholas, see Wandycz, *The Lands of Partitioned Poland, 1795–1918*, 109; Riasanovsky, *A History of Russia*, 332.
41 R. F. Leslie, *Reform and Insurrection in Russian Poland 1856–1863*, University of London Historical Studies, vol. 7 (London: University of London and The Athlone Press, 1963). 264.
42 Polonsky, *The Jews in Poland and Russia*, 1:281.
43 Dynner, *Yankel's Tavern*, 110; YIVO Encyclopedia of Jews in Eastern Europe, s.v. "Tugenhold, Jakob," accessed February 15, 2019, https://yivoencyclopedia.org/article.aspx/Tugendhold_Jakob.

on the Uniate Church in order to encourage unification through Russia's preferred Eastern Orthodox.[44] In his assault on education, he left only thirty-some Polish schools with more than two grades. Because the level of instruction was quite poor, illiteracy reached mammoth proportions. Additionally, most of the school inspectors did not know Polish.[45] By the time of Nicholas's death in 1855, the Polish educational system was in ruins.[46]

It is significant that Nicholas did not treat all Poles equally. His approach to Poles inhabiting the kresy, Russia's western provinces, differed from that directed toward Poles in the Kingdom of Poland. While imperial Russia recognized the kingdom's unique political situation, it viewed the kresy as an historical part of Russia. The Russian state regarded Polish residents in the kresy—mostly noble landlords who lived dispersed among a majority of Belarussians and Ukrainians—as Russians. Nicholas I also reclassified thousands of poor Polish petty gentry as peasants or townspeople, hoping to engender identification with Russian culture inside the kresy.[47]

In order to assure steadfast Polish cooperation with the Russian authorities in the Kingdom of Poland, Nicholas I disbanded the sovereign Polish army. A strong proponent of using the military to fix the ills of society, Nicholas employed it to tighten his grip on the Polish male youth.[48] He incorporated many soldiers from the formerly independent Polish army into his own army, each for the Russian standard twenty-five year period of service.[49] Additionally, with the goal of staving off an independent Poland, the Russian tsar ordered nine- and ten-year-old sons of the Polish and Ukrainian nobility, who took part in the November Uprising, to serve in the old cantonist system until they reached

---

44 Wandycz, *The Lands of Partitioned Poland, 1795–1918*, 122–125.
45 Ibid., 156.
46 One popular theory regarding this targeted Russian devastation against the Polish people in the Kingdom of Poland holds that it was a "deliberate russification policy" aimed at defending the unity of the Russian Empire. Yet new research underscores that the Russian tsars did not deceive themselves in the early nineteenth century into believing that Poles in the Kingdom of Poland would ever discard their ethnic identity. By closing the University of Warsaw, cutting the number of high schools, and discriminating in admission policy against children of non-nobles, whom they viewed as potential revolutionaries, Nicholas I hoped to stop the growth of subversive elements. Here, the Romanov strategy was not Russification, but rather Polish neutralization. See Theodore Weeks, *Nation and State in Late Imperial Russia*, 14.
47 Riasanovsky, *A History of Russia*, 333.
48 Michael Stanislawski, *Tsar Nicholas I and the Jews: The Transformation of Jewish Society in Russia 1825–1855* (Philadelphia: The Jewish Publication Society of America, 1983), 14–15; Antony Polonsky, *The Jews In Poland and Russia*, 1:359.
49 Wandycz, *The Lands of Partitioned Poland, 1795–1918*, 122.

eighteen. At that age, they would feed into the military for another twenty-five-year term.⁵⁰ Through army discipline and years of programmed schooling, Nicholas I aspired to transform this group of Poland's youth from future rebels into Russian loyalists. Although Nicholas I had no intention of converting the army conscripts (but rather sought to neutralize their animus toward Russia), he did seek the conversion of the young boys in the cantonist system.⁵¹

More than his predecessors, Nicholas searched for solutions to societal ills through military structures, modifying their formats into tools for social change.⁵² As such, he envisioned the new cantonist system as a tool for social engineering.⁵³ Ideally, by growing up together, typically secluded from family and community, these boys would form a new sense of Self as useful subjects acting for the betterment of the Russian Empire. He also hoped to redirect the youth's religious affiliations. Though the Russian tsar guarded minority religious rights within the regular military ranks, he did not protect them in the cantonist organization. He sought to banish connections to *all* alien faiths within the

---

50 Stanislawski, *Tsar Nicholas I and the Jews*, 19; Weeks, *Nation and State in Late Imperial Russia*, 27.
51 Just as he had done with the Jews, Tsar Nicholas I targeted Catholics, Lutherans, Muslims, and pagans through the cantonist system with the intention to convert a diverse population to Eastern Orthodoxy. Though cantonist conscription alarmed Polish and Ukrainian families, contextually it was not a shocking stratagem because in the past it had provided some social benefits. It had served as early military training coupled with a separate schooling component for the children of Russian soldiers. Additionally, by opening the military to the children of criminals, vagabonds, and the homeless, his cantonist reconstitution also provided order for both orphans and the military's illegitimate children. Nicholas exploited the cantonist system to unify the empire's vast multiethnic population. The cantonist battalions also schooled those minors who were drafted in place of married adults with children, who needed to financially support their families and communities. These young draftees simply went into the cantonist system before their actual military service commenced. Indeed, Nicholas I embraced and exploited the military as the ultimate teaching tool. See Yohanan Petrovsky-Shtern, *Jews in the Russian Army, 1827–1917: Drafted into Modernity* (Cambridge: Cambridge University Press, 2009), 91.
52 Ibid. Nicholas also established a variegated draft for different sections of society. Jews within the Russian Empire were categorized similarly as guild merchants, and thus were able to pay a special tax in lieu of military service. Thus, the great majority of soldiers came from the peasantry, further demonstrating the economic division between Jews and peasants. However, the ability to avoid military service through taxation became more and more difficult. Later, Jews were forced either to serve directly or to pay for a Jewish substitute to serve in their places. See Polonsky, *The Jews in Poland and Russia*, 1:358–359. Survival by economic stratification within the Jewish community weakened Jewish communal unity. See Stanislawski, *Tsar Nicholas I and the Jews*, 28 and 32–33.
53 Petrovsky-Shtern, *Jews in the Russian Army*, 91.

cantonist battalions.[54] While he did not initiate the draft as a missionizing effort, by 1830 Nicholas I believed that making direct efforts to win the cantonist battalions to Russian Orthodoxy would only support efforts to construct his new, improved, homogenous population.[55]

The Conscription of Jews under Nicholas I

In 1827, Nicholas began drafting Jews (excluding those living in the Kingdom of Poland) into the Russian army. Together with other ethnic minorities, such as Poles, Estonians, Kazakhs, Tatars, and Uzbeks, Jews entered both the Russian military and the cantonist battalions.[56] Once a cantonist turned eighteen, he began his regular military service, which in the mid-1830s was reduced from a twenty-five-year term to a fifteen-year term.

Western Europeans recognized military conscription as a respectable path out of the Jewish ghetto and into the modern world. Many Jews in early nineteenth-century France and Germany employed it as a way to demonstrate allegiance to the state.[57] And while Nicholas attempted to expunge the youth's Jewish faith within the cantonist system, there is new research that suggests that close to two-thirds of those young Jewish recruits persevered to maintain their Jewish identity and ritual practice.[58]

To this day, American Jews learn that the cantonist battalions and the excruciatingly long regular military service term in mid-nineteenth-century Russia were created to break the will and survival of its Jews. American Jews have been reared on true horror stories about young Jewish men during the reign of Nicholas I who either maimed themselves or left their homes at incredibly young ages to escape conscription. However, Nicholas I's policies of conscription targeted many ethnic groups, not just Jews.[59] Each community was expected to provide a specified number of men for the military. It was left up to community leaders to decide who would fall into service.

---

54   Ibid.
55   Ibid., 92.
56   Ibid., 91.
57   Ibid., 9–17.
58   Ibid., 96–97.
59   After the 1830 insurrection, through special military ordinances, Nicholas I compelled several groups into military service which had been exempted previously, such as the Poles in the Kingdom of Poland, Ukrainian Cossacks, and the déclassé Polish gentry of the kresy. Stanislawski, *Tsar Nicholas I and the Jews*, 15 and 17.

According to Yochanan Petrovsky-Shtern, "neither Nicholas nor his military administration intended to flood the cantonist battalions with Jewish children. The number of teenagers selected by the Jewish communities and sent to the army—sometimes 50% of the levy—took the Russian military by surprise."[60] In order to secure Jewish heads of households' safety and continued financial support of their families and the community, Jewish authorities designated young male teens for the draft in their place.

As a rule, Tsar Nicholas I did not affront Jews in general with harsher military service than other groups. Just as he had treated Poles in western provinces separately from those residing in the kingdom, Nicholas dealt differently with Jews living within the Pale of Jewish Settlement from those living in the Kingdom of Poland. The Pale encapsulated most of the kresy, including the entire Grand Duchy of Lithuania and much of right-bank Ukraine. Starting in 1827, he subjected Jews in the Pale of Jewish Settlement—now regarded as part of Russia proper—to the cantonist battalions, while Jews in Congress Kingdom were not subjected to conscription into the Russian military and cantonist ranks until January 1, 1844.

While the tsar first drafted Jews and Poles in Russia proper in 1827, Nicholas dealt with these groups separately in the Kingdom of Poland. This decision bore consequences for Polish-Jewish relations. As a punitive measure, he conscripted Poles in the kingdom in 1832, more than a decade before the Jews in that same territory.[61] This highly unequal treatment fomented the belief among some Poles that the Jews worked as spies for the Russian enemy.[62] When the tsar finally drafted the kingdom's Jews in 1844, he did so to teach this group how to inhabit a more modern society. A tool for social engineering, military conscription was to bring ethnic populations into alignment with Russian social and cultural objectives. Tsar Nicholas I hoped that by moving closer to Russian societal norms Jews in the Kingdom of Poland would break their connections to Poles.

---

60   Petrovsky-Shtern, *Jews in the Russian Army*, 127.
61   Ibid., 18.
62   Dynner and Wodziński, "The Kingdom of Poland and Her Jews: An Introduction," 22.

Myth Reconstruction

Well into the twentieth century, Jews and Poles contributed to the mythology concerning the 1830–31 Polish Uprising. Jewish historians tended to highlight Jews who supported the uprising and Polish historians often denigrated Jews as spies who aided the Russians. Though Jews did support the Polish national enterprise, like the Poles themselves, they did not support it in droves. Most were ambivalent. They were pragmatic and did not want to get drawn into a battle that would prove disastrous for the Kingdom of Poland and for themselves.

The Polish myth indicting Jews as extortionists and spies cannot be discarded as merely propaganda. Numerous Jewish traders took financial advantage of the crisis by overcharging the insurgents for foodstuffs and textiles needed to carry out the rebellion. Additionally, many, like Abraham Kinderfraind, were willing to supply both sides, procuring materials for the Russian army as well as the Polish fighters.[63] At a time of political conflict, such behavior easily communicated enemy status.

There were also Jews, along with Poles, who acted as spies for the Russian military, providing information used later against Polish insurgents. Most commercial traders and spies, whether Jewish or Polish, were looking for personal economic gain. Assessing the situation, they placed their bets on the likely winner and hoped for a reward when political normality resumed. Several received compensation for helping Russia. After petitioning the Russian government, Jews who aided the Russians received monetary recognition, a low-level civil service appointment, or permission to manage a tavern at a time when the law prohibited rural Jews from tavern keeping.[64] Poles who observed Jews gaining such rights in the wake of the November Uprising, could not help but understand it as a sign that Jews favored Russia.

At this point, it is worthwhile looking back at Jakob Tugenhold's repositioning of himself. Prior to the insurrection, Tugenhold was a leading integrationist. He not only worked with Polish government officials as a liaison for Jewish affairs, but he also supported the insurrection. And yet, once the Russians crushed the uprising, Tugenhold changed sides. Having seen a highly regarded Jewish leader make this change, it is no surprise that some Poles felt slighted and began to generalize that Jews were either traitors to the cause or simply monarchists.

---

63   Dynner, *Yankel's Tavern*, 106
64   Ibid.

At the same time, it remains noteworthy that seventeen out of the 127 accused spies were Jewish. Although they accounted for only 13% of all spies on the list, Poles emphasized these Jews' treasonous acts. Highlighting Jewish espionage allowed Poles to mute the reality that 110 Polish Christians sold their nation and people to the Russians.[65]

The 1830–31 Polish Uprising was as a call to romantic nationalism that sputtered to its end, in part, due to the people's rejection of it. The majority of Poles repudiated this dangerous rebellion against Russian rule. The clergy and peasants ignored it. And those who did take part fled at its end, settling outside of the Kingdom of Poland to argue amongst themselves about the disappointing outcome. Polarized over questions of responsibility for losing the rebellion, conservative Polish émigré leaders focused on Jews betraying the cause, while liberal émigré leaders reflected more strongly on Jewish support for Polish sovereignty. Division spread wider in the kingdom when Russia appraised Poles and Jews differently for their respective participation in the revolt, creating suspicion among Poles that Jews were Russian agents.

It is true that the large majority of mainstream Jewry understood Russia as the rightful ruler. Following Haskalah values, most Maskilim continued to align themselves with the governing authority. Some integrationist leaders, who stood by the Poles during the rebellion and experienced the tremendous defeat, lost faith in a future Poland. They sidled up next to the Russian authorities to ensure their own personal and communal safety in the future. At the same time, however, many integrationists remained committed to the Polish cause as their own.

---

65 Ibid., 111.

CHAPTER 6

Fraternity and Skepticism

In 1855, Tsar Nicholas I died, opening up a more optimistic and promising period for Poles and Jews under Russian rule. His successor, Tsar Alexander II (who ruled from 1855–1881), initially attempted to demonstrate a new respect for his large Polish population. He expunged Nicholas I's harsh restrictions against Polish culture and personally visited Warsaw in 1856. However, while there he made it quite clear that his benevolent approach to the Kingdom of Poland had limits. Addressing his audience in French, rather than in Polish, he famously warned: "absolutely no daydreams."[1] Willing to permit a Polish cultural revival, he insisted that Polish autonomy, much less independence, remained out of the question. This chapter explores the changing economic, political, and interethnic dynamics within the Kingdom of Poland which led to Polish-Jewish cooperation in the 1863 Uprising. We will also examine the Russian repressive measures that divided Pole from Jew.

Marquis Aleksander Wielopolski

The Russian emperor sought advice on how to handle the Polish problem from a conservative Polish magnate, Marquis Aleksander Wielopolski (1803–1877). Although not pro-Russian—a pragmatist, rather—Wielopolski believed Poles' economic and cultural elevation would follow from cooperation with the Russians. In May 1862, Alexander II appointed Wielopolski head of Warsaw's civil government.[2]

Polish political activists perceived Wielopolski as an enemy who was willing to validate Poland's partition by actively maintaining it. Church leaders also recognized him as an adversary. Wielopolski was unimpressed and unmoved by his

---

1   Weeks, *Nation and State in Late Imperial Russia*, 95.
2   Ibid., 94–95.

countrymen's negative perceptions of him. He lambasted both the Polish gentry and the Catholic clergy for acting as a "government within a government."[3] At the same time, Wielopolski managed to convince Tsar Alexander II to make several important reforms for the Poles, including readmitting Poles to posts in the imperial administration, and re-establishing Polish institutions of higher education. He also supported the creation of the Agricultural Society, an elite body of landed Polish nobility which discussed various problems, such as agricultural backwardness and peasant dissatisfaction.[4]

These changes did not satiate the youth's thirst for some modicum of independence.[5] They launched diverse underground political organizations to gain greater Polish control over the kingdom, although their end goals differed in degree. The so-called "Reds" made a radical demand for complete independence from Russia. To achieve this objective, they were willing to stage an armed rebellion. The "Whites" offered a more moderate position, requesting cultural, economic, and religious reforms garnered only through legal channels.[6]

Alexander II soon took the view that any amount of freedom granted was too much freedom. "Give them your pinkie and they'll swallow the whole arm" is the Russian recollection of Polish gratitude for reforms.[7] For many Poles, limited liberty only underscored their lack of rights. By the late 1850s, Warsaw had become a hotbed of civil dissonance, and the tsar's aggressive reactions to it only deepened the Polish cause. Polish youth courageously demonstrated in the streets, singing hymns, and declaring their patriotic love of Poland. When a huge throng of people demonstrated in front of the viceroy's residence on April 8, 1861, and refused to disperse when ordered, Russian troops opened fire on them.[8]

---

3   Wandycz, *The Lands of Partitioned Poland, 1795–1918*, 165.
4   Andrzej Zamoyski, who disparaged Wielopolski's cooperation with Russia, headed the Agricultural Society. See Wandycz, *The Lands of Partitioned Poland, 1795–1918*, 162–163.
5   Ibid., 159.
6   Ibid., 160.
7   Theodore Weeks, comment on this manuscript, October 31, 2011.
8   Wandycz, *The Lands of Partitioned Poland, 1795–1918*, 164–165.

The Jews' Economic Rise in the Kingdom of Poland

The inter-insurrectionary period (1832–1862) witnessed impressive economic growth within the affluent Jewish bourgeoisie sector, which included both assimilating and traditional Jews. With some having gained their wealth by supplying armies with textiles and bankrolling national projects, they sought to attain those equal rights Jews had been awaiting since the Duchy of Warsaw days.[9] The Kronenberg family serves as one example. Associated with the progressive Daniłowiczowska Street Synagogue, this banking family headed by patriarch Samuel Kronenberg (1773–1826) established strong ties with Polish aristocrats and lived outside Warsaw's Jewish district. One son, Leopold (1812–1878), continued in banking and business, and, though converting to Calvinism, also remained tied to Jewish communal concerns.[10]

Despite the majority of Jews remaining impoverished, most Polish entrepreneurs could only see Jewish prosperity, and feared that its continued development would stymie ethnic Polish economic advancement.[11] We have seen this reaction in earlier chapters and understand it as a typical response from a host society to a middleman minority group when members of the former are in need of jobs. Additionally, the reconstructed and reiterated Jewish petition for equal rights gave Poles pause: What would happen if this wealthy Jewish population gained access to voting rights and government? Julian Ursyn Niemcewicz's publication *The Year 3333* (*Rok 3333*, also known as *The Incredible Dream*), written in 1820 but published in 1858, expressed Polish fears of a Jewish takeover of the Kingdom of Poland. For Niemcewicz, Jews' citizenship would lead to Poles' ruin:

---

9   Magdalena Opalski and Israel Bartal, *Poles and Jews: A Failed Brotherhood*, The Tauber Institute for the Study of European Jewry Series (Hanover: Brandeis University Press and University Press of New England, 1992), 15. In *Esau's Tears*, Albert S. Lindemann holds that it was this rise of the Jews throughout Europe which ignited modern antisemitism.

10 His extensive wealth allowed him the rare opportunity to purchase an aristocratic title, imbuing the family with the hereditary rights of Polish nobility. See Rafał Żebrowski, «Kronenberg Family,» YIVO Encyclopedia of Jews in Eastern Europe, accessed 29 August 2023, http://www.yivoencyclopedia.org/article.aspx/Kronenberg_Family; Jerzy Tomaszewski, email correspondence with author, October 12, 2012.

11 Opalski and Bartal, *Poles and Jews: A Failed Brotherhood*, 16.

[Jews] did not conquer the Poles with arms but with ruses, bribes and tricks ... once they received the right to hold public offices and to purchase landed estates, nothing could stop their tireless shrewdness and intrigues. As centuries passed, they crushed the Poles and other Christians and gained control of everything.[12]

Conservative Poles feared a Jewish economic, political, and social takeover. Polish ambivalence was clear: despite calling for Jews to assimilate into Polish society, Poles worried they would lose their limited control over Poland once Jews made inroads.

For a partitioned people still reeling from a failed rebellion, the fear of being conquered from within took on tremendous significance and intensity. *The Warsaw Gazette* (*Gazeta Warszawska*) went so far as to launch a press campaign against the Warsaw Jewish community in 1859 titled "The Jewish War."[13] Incensed by this smear campaign, that same year Leopold Kronenberg purchased the rival paper *Gazeta Codzienna*. He hired the popular novelist Józef Ignacy Kraszewski (1812–1887) as editor and tasked him with promoting understanding between Pole and Jew.[14]

Meanwhile, a significant number of Poles supported Jewish rights due to their own positive interactions with Jews, and because Jews took up the sword against Russia in 1830. They reveled in Adam Mickiewicz's iconic 1834 great epic poem *Pan Tadeusz* (Mr. Tadeusz), which contains a positive characterization of Yankiel, a Jewish tavernkeeper. A trusted, respected, traditional Jew who loves Poland, Jankiel is "a welcome guest in every quarter and a household counselor."[15] That Jankiel acts on behalf of the Polish nation in Mickiewicz's beloved poem makes him one with that nation. The tavernkeeper embodies the author's positive view of Jews as patriots. Mickiewicz portrays Poland as the new "chosen" nation, linked inherently to the ancient Israelites and thus to the Jews. For the poet, Poles needed to work together with their Jewish "older brother" to fulfill Poland's divine mission of freeing Europe from authoritarian rule.[16]

---

12 J. U. Niemcewicz, *Rok 333 czyli sen niesłychany, poprzedził wsstępem o sprawie żydowskiej w Polsce Nie Wiem Kto* (Warsaw: n.p., 1913), 8–9, as translated in Opalski and Bartal, *Poles and Jews: A Failed Brotherhood*, 30.
13 Ibid., 17.
14 Kieniewicz, "Assimilated Jews in Nineteenth-Century Warsaw," 165–166.
15 Adam Mickiewicz, *Pan Tadeusz*, trans. George Rapall Noyes (London: J. M. Dent & Sons, Ltd., 1917) , 98, https://www.gutenberg.org/files/28240/28240-pdf.pdf.
16 Opalski and Bartal, *Poles and Jews: A Failed Brotherhood*, 20.

His words were a beacon for Poles desperate for independence and encouraged Polish-Jewish collaboration.

Polish-Jewish Fraternity

Some Jews who self-identified as Poles felt it their duty to participate in Polish demonstrations against Russian rule in the 1860s. But most Jews involved in the fight for independence did so because they believed this path would secure those legal rights they desired. Liberal spokesmen for a renewed Polish state promised the Jews a more enlightened minorities' policy than had existed under Russia's dominance. Thus, thousands of Jews willingly stood up against Russia in anticipation of these rights.

Warsaw's Chief Rabbi, Dov Berush Meisels (1795–1870), fervently believed that a free Poland was the best proposition for the Jews. Orthodox in ritual, he had been politically engaged with the Poles since 1848. At that time, he had taken the Polish side in the Polish-German conflict. Simultaneously, he remained determined to secure equality for the Jews. Uniting with the Poles was his roadmap to achieving his loftier goal. Dr. Mordechai Jastrow, rabbi of the progressive Daniłowiczowska Street Synagogue, and Rabbi Izaak Kramsztyk of the "Polish synagogue" on Nalewki Street[17] were also active leaders within the Polish-Jewish alliance. Jastrow was known for his zealous Polish patriotism.[18] A pragmatist, he reasoned that if Jews rejected Polish attempts at brotherhood, Polish hostility towards the Jews would take its place.[19] He believed the Poles would interpret such dismissal as a sign the Jews had aligned with the Russian enemy. Rabbi Kramsztyk, on the other hand, was an ardent idealist who trusted completely in the promise of integration. Imbued with a love of both the Polish people and their culture, he preached cultural assimilation throughout his working life . . . and even preached it in Polish. He believed that assimilation, coupled with the reform of Jewish rituals, would offset the pressure of conversion felt by those Jews who longed for social acceptance.[20]

Meisels, Jastrow, and Kramsztyk often demonstrated publicly on the streets of Warsaw on behalf of Polish freedom. Their presence influenced large numbers of Jews to support the Poles' demand for greater freedom. All three rabbis joined in

---

17   Gutterman, "The Origins of the Great Synagogue," 193.
18   Wodziński, *Haskalah And Hasidism*, 163.
19   Gutterman, "The Origins of the Great Synagogue," 191.
20   Ibid., 193.

the funeral procession for five Polish activists who were killed on February 27, 1861, during a demonstration for land reform and autonomy.[21] The majority of Warsaw's middle class, of which Jews figured as a significant percentage, donned mourning clothes the day of the funeral to signify both support for Poles and hostility toward Russia.[22]

The decided change in Polish-Jewish relations, from perceived economic conflict to respect and appreciation, led to Jewish participation in Warsaw's 1861 political demonstrations. Poles were aware that Russian bullets felled Jewish activists during the April 8 demonstration. Conservative emigration leader Adam Czartoryski proclaimed:

> Today the Polish Jews, united with us by the enormous sufferings and tortures inflicted by the same hand, have ceased to be a nation within the nation and, having recognized as their mother this motherland, which has fed them for such a long time, have rendered it great services.[23]

Suddenly, it no longer mattered to Polish liberals what clothing the Jews wore and what food they ate. Of greater significance was Jewish action on behalf of Poland's freedom.[24] By 1861, that liberal voice seeking conciliation and cooperation with Jews gained strength. It led liberal Poles to accept Jews as compatriots without any presumption of cultural assimilation.[25] During this brief time, wide acceptance of cultural diversity reigned. Fighting for their mutual goal of greater civic and political rights, Jew and Pole accepted the Other's differences.

Joint demonstrations continued after April 1861, albeit within church sanctuaries for protection. On October 15, 1861, Russian troops surrounded and stormed two Warsaw Catholic churches in which a diverse gathering was singing hymns to Tadeusz Kościuszko, "the champion of liberty." Sixty years earlier, and with the combined efforts of Pole and Jew, he had attempted—yet failed—to thwart Poland's final partition.[26] According to Rabbi Marcus Jastrow's eyewitness testimony reported in *The Jewish Exponent*,

---

21 Antony Polonsky, *The Jews in Poland and Russia*, 1:309.
22 Marcus M. Jastrow, "Baer Meisel Chief Rabbi at Warsaw" (trans. Annie M. Jastrow), in *Jewish Exponent*, August 2, 1907, 9.
23 Porter, *When Nationalism Began to Hate*, 40.
24 Ibid.
25 Ibid.
26 Wandycz, *The Lands of Partitioned Poland, 1795–1918*, 10.

> at midnight the church doors were forced open, and amid cuffs and blows, all the male members of the assembly were escorted to the citadel, where, in the course of a few days, after careful scrutiny, the most intelligent of them, especially the students, were detained, to be afterwards sent to Siberia for compulsory military service.[27]

The Catholic clergy locked church doors and sent the keys to Rome in protest of this desecration of Catholic sacred space. Chief Rabbi Meisels and other Jewish leaders closed the main sanctuaries in synagogues to proclaim solidarity with their Polish brethren against the government.[28] According to Jastrow, this alliance between Jews and Poles, once inimical religious sects, created much anxiety for the Romanovs.[29]

In response, Tsar Alexander II threatened several Catholic leaders and silenced all three leading rabbis. The authorities arrested Rabbi Kramsztyk on November 9, 1861, and jailed him in the dungeons of Bobruisk. Released in 1862, he was later exiled to Saratov, where he remained until 1867.[30] They imprisoned Chief Rabbi Meisels for seventy-two days in the Warsaw Citadel and later deported him from the country.[31] In December 1862, they also deported Jastrow from Warsaw, having labeled him a firebrand who had agitated the Jews into joining the insurrectionary movement.[32]

The Polish leadership and laity noted the sacrifices made by Jews on behalf of Poland's freedom. They loved Chief Rabbi Meisels. After he emerged from Russian incarceration, Polish representatives bestowed on him a gift of twenty thousand rubles, which they had raised through sales of the rabbi's picture.[33] Polish writers celebrated Jewish action on behalf of Poland. Describing the Jews of Warsaw in a letter dated July 2, 1861, Władysław Mickiewicz, son of Adam Mickiewicz, wrote:

---

27 Jastrow, "Baer Meisel Chief Rabbi at Warsaw," 9.
28 Ibid.
29 Ibid.
30 Wodziński, *Haskalah And Hasidism*, 161.
31 Jastrow, "Baer Meisel Chief Rabbi at Warsaw," 9.
32 Gutterman, "The Origins of the Great Synagogue," 192; Wodziński, *Haskalah and Hasidism*, 164.
33 Opalski and Bartal, *Poles and Jews: A Failed Brotherhood*, 85–86.

The Jews here are the best in all of Poland. They sing national anthems in the synagogues. The sermons they give in the synagogues about love of the fatherland unite Poles and Jews in a single emotion, and the thought that a Poland will arise wakens hope in the Jews that their dispersal is coming to an end.[34]

In this feverish atmosphere of 1861–62, the story of Michał Landy crystallized the strength of Polish-Jewish fraternity. Tradition holds that during a demonstration against Romanov rule, Landy, a Jewish student, took the cross from the hands of a dying Catholic clergyman only moments before he himself was felled by a Russian bullet. Repeated throughout contemporary Polish literature, the Jew with the cross became a popular motif, paving the way for the Poles' collective elevation of the entire people of Israel.[35]

Russian Policy of Divide and Conquer

Aleksander Wielopolski had recognized people's increased frustration with Russian autocracy. The youth's rage grew over the lack of consequential cultural, educational, economic, and political reform under Alexander II. The people also demanded agricultural reform, which as a landowner Wielopolski resisted. Meanwhile, Polish-Jewish cooperation in the Polish patriotic movement had manifested Polish liberals' call for Jews' full equal rights. Wielopolski understood this alliance as detrimental to Russia. Fearful of growing Polish-Jewish fraternization, Alexander II followed Wielopolski's advice to divide and conquer.[36]

Soon enough, prominent Jews in Poland realized that the landed conservative Polish nobility intended to change very little regarding Jews' rights. In response, they turned to Wielopolski for support. They had some leverage given that both Poles and Russians needed Jewish assistance. On one hand, exiled Poles had broadcast the Jews' backing of Polish independence in order to entice European and American Jews to lobby their respective governments to assist the Polish cause.[37] On the other hand, Russian officials hoped that if Jews would quieten

---

34 Bartoszewski and Polonsky, *The Jews of Warsaw*, 17.
35 Opalski and Bartal, *Poles and Jews: A Failed Brotherhood*, 44–45.
36 Stanislaus Blejwas, "Polish Positivism and the Jews," *Jewish Social Studies* 46, no. 1 (Winter 1984): 24; Salo W. Baron, *The Russian Jew under Tsars and Soviets*, 2nd ed. (New York: Schocken Books, 1987), 41.
37 Eisenbach, *The Emancipation of the Jews in Poland, 1780–1870,* 462, 464, and 474.

their support for Polish sovereignty, Russia could silence the international pressure to pursue Polish independence.

Seeking to earn Jewish support for the monarchy, Wielopolski advised the tsar to broaden the Jews' civil rights in the kingdom. He believed that the Jews would play a foundational role as Poland's middle class and would improve the Polish economy.[38] On June 5, 1862, Russia's tsar promulgated legislation permitting Jews to purchase farmland and urban properties, be witnesses in Christian legal cases, hold some public offices, and take up trades from which they had previously been barred.[39] Understandably, many Jews celebrated Wielopolski and recognized Russian authority over Poland. And understandably, Poles interpreted this Jewish reaction as treachery.

Wielopolski's policy achievement did not please all Jews. The Jewish progressive periodical *Jutrzenka* sharply criticized it, portraying the legislation as weak, given that full equality was beyond Jewish reach.[40] Jewish leaders, together with Polish spokesmen, publicly questioned whether or not the tsar would actually implement this new law. Jewish émigré leader Ludwik Lubliner criticized the tsarist government for trying to dissolve the working relationship between Jew and Pole within the Polish national movement. Castigating the law as still limiting the rights of Jews, Lubliner underscored that only "[a]n independent, self-ruling Poland will declare that in the political field she knows neither Jews nor Christians, but only indigenous inhabitants, citizens who have equal civic rights and duties."[41]

Like many Jews who had earlier supported the Polish cause for their own personal and collective needs, not all Poles were moved by altruism to help the Other. Poles had made international inroads by demonstrating support for the Jews and presenting Poland as a land of equality.[42] While leaders existed on both sides who stood resolved to bring about both Polish independence and Jewish emancipation, there also existed plenty on each side who understood this situation more as an opportunity to make communal gains by diplomatic tactics.

---

38 Polonsky, *The Jews in Poland and Russia*, 1:310–311.
39 Blejwas, "Polish Positivism and the Jews," 24.
40 Eisenbach, *The Emancipation of the Jews in Poland, 1780–1870*, 470.
41 Ibid., 471.
42 Ibid., 475.

The 1863 Polish Rebellion and Jewish Support

Wielopolski knew that Polish activists, especially the Reds, held him in low esteem. Fearing the Poles' desire for revolution, Wielopolski attempted to prevent it. He introduced an army conscription which primarily targeted the thousands of urban Red affiliates.[43] In order to secure the Kingdom of Poland's fealty to Russia, he turned on those young Poles who stood directly in his way.

Although they argued for rebellion, the Reds had not fully prepared for it in January, when they heard about Wielopolski's planned conscription. Yet, despite the odds, in the winter of 1863 they called for a full-blown insurrection to derail Wielopolski's plans. Plagued by harsh weather, the uprising lacked both effective leadership and weaponry. Together with the moderate Whites, roughly two thousand Jewish Polish patriots also joined Polish battle units.[44]

Even before military clashes began, Jews aided the conspiratorial movement by delivering messages to leaders abroad. Their work as merchants involved much travel, which made them excellent facilitators of communication between émigré and domestic leaders. Some Jews purchased arms abroad and smuggled them into the kingdom.

Once the fighting started, many Jews supported the struggle for Polish independence off the battlefield by providing money, provisions, and leadership to the Polish troops. After the moderate Whites joined the rebellion, Leopold Kronenberg furnished the rebels with funds. Having played a very large role in forming the policy of the Whites, Kronenberg's ability to secure French credit for the rebellion enabled the revolutionary army to purchase much needed weaponry and food.[45] Other Jews also contributed their skills to enable the 1863 January Insurrection. Henryk Wohl (1842–1905) was the director of the revolutionary government's finance department.[46] Bernard Goldman (1842–1901), first the commissioner of Warsaw's underground police organization, later became an agent of the revolutionary body in Breslau.[47] Additionally, the

---

43 Wandycz, *The Lands of Partitioned Poland, 1795–1918*, 171.
44 Influenced by émigré Polish leaders, young Jewish activists travelled to Genoa to prepare themselves militarily to battle for the Polish motherland. Eisenbach, *The Emancipation of the Jews in Poland, 1780–1870*, 462; Israel Bartal, *The Jews of Eastern Europe, 1772–1881*, 87.
45 Wandycz, *The Lands of Partitioned Poland, 1795–1918*, 174; Jerzy Tomaszewski, email correspondence with author, October 14, 2012.
46 Polonsky, *The Jews in Poland and Russia*, 1:313.
47 Ibid., 313–314.

Hebrew book publisher, Isaac Goldman (1812–1888) printed the revolutionary leaflets which activists disseminated throughout the territory.

Other Jewish leaders voiced ambivalence about joining Polish forces against Russia. Though thankful for the relative peace Jews experienced in Poland, the Hasidic leader Abraham Isaac Kahana of Ciechanów worried about acting against the Russian rulers. In his letter of April 1861 to Rabbi Meisels, he explains that while he feels immense gratitude toward his local nobility who have lived harmoniously with the Jews, he feared Russia's warnings against supporting the insurgency. Based on his personal experience in the region, the szlachta's "generosity of heart awakens love among Jews . . . so that a people who a short time ago was scorned by every nation can now be counted on to gather together with them for the sake of the common good."[48] The nobility in his region had "miraculously" allowed Jews to join merchant guilds, own land, and engage in agriculture. Rabbi Kahana felt that most Jews "would like to fulfill the wishes of the nobility and not vex them" but were reluctant to oppose the will of the "actual regime."[49]

Other Jews did not care who ruled as long as they themselves profited. These individuals actively procured opportunities for economic gains. As was the case during the November Uprising, Jewish and Polish traders, who supplied needed materials to the Poles, also furnished the Russian military with provisions. Both Jews and Poles knew that Russia rewarded spies with free liquor permits, which they hoped to receive as a means to economic security. In his book *Yankel's Tavern*, Glenn Dynner supplies the names of Jews who sold Polish secrets to the Russian enemy in order to benefit financially. Leib Kroszyński, Abram Lubelski, Israel Ejzenberg, and Gershon Szyldyner all rendered services to the Russians, often causing the Poles direct harm.[50] Perhaps simply a crafty business play, it was also a betrayal of the Polish national movement.

Russian Repression

In the end, five hundred thousand Russian troops crushed the Polish rebellion. Russia retaliated by executing close to four hundred Polish revolutionaries and sending thousands of Poles into Siberian exile. Poland was placed under military occupation and martial law was imposed.[51] The Romanovs silenced

---

48 Dynner, *Yankel's Tavern*, 127.
49 Ibid., 123–124, 127. In retaliation against those tavernkeepers who aided the Poles, upon victory the Russians took away their liquor concessions.
50 Ibid., 123–124.
51 Porter, *When Nationalism Began to Hate*, 43.

Poles' diplomatic voice by abolishing the Polish secretary of state's post in St. Petersburg. All decisions regarding Poland were directed through Nicholas Miliutin (1818–1872) and his assistants, who steadily brought the kingdom's government administration into line with that of the Russian Empire. Only Russians could serve in higher administrative posts in Russian Poland, leaving Poles to subordinate positions.[52] In administrative offices and in all official documents, Tsar Alexander II made certain that the Kingdom of Poland was referred to as Vistula Land (Privislinskiy Krai), removing any official recognition of the area's particularly Polish heritage.[53]

Russian repression also extended into Polish culture.[54] Russia forbade speaking Polish in the courts and in government offices. Russian replaced Polish not only in all legal records and official correspondence, but also in the educational system.[55] Furthering the assault on education, tsarist officials ordered that teaching focus on Russian topics; Polish subjects and those who deigned to teach them were banned.[56] In 1869, Miliutin shut down the only Polish institution of higher education in the Russian Empire, Warsaw's Szkola Główna (Main School). He repurposed it as the Russifying University of Warsaw.[57] During the 1870s, the Russian administration converted the entire educational system in the Kingdom of Poland into an almost purely Russian enterprise, run by teachers imported from the interior of the Russian Empire. Because school attendance was not obligatory, two-thirds of the population of Vistula Land remained illiterate.[58] Those who did seek academic knowledge received a purely Russian interpretation of the past and present.

Alexander II also acted forcefully against the Catholic Church, closing those monasteries and houses of worship that Russia suspected of aiding the insurgents.[59] Perceived as pillars of Polish national resistance, Church leaders were prime targets of Russian harassment. Yet, examination reveals that only 10% of

---

52 Theodore R. Weeks, *From Assimilation to Antisemitism: The "Jewish Question" in Poland, 1850–1914* (DeKalb: Northern Illinois University Press, 2006), 53.
53 According to Theodore Weeks, even Russian officials continued to speak of Tsarstvo Pol'skoe well into the twentieth century, as noted on his review of this manuscript, October 31, 2011.
54 Andrzej Walicki, *Philosophy and Romantic Nationalism: The Case of Poland* (Oxford: Clarendon Press, 1982), 337.
55 Weeks, *Nation and State in Late Imperial Russia*, 99.
56 Leslie, *Reform and Insurrection in Russian Poland, 1856–1865*, 250–251.
57 Weeks, *From Assimilation to Antisemitism*, 52.
58 Weeks, *Nation and State in Late Imperial Russia*, 100–101.
59 Weeks, *From Assimilation to Antisemitism*, 52; Leslie, *Reform and Insurrection in Russian Poland*, 250–251.

the 3,200 Catholic clergy took the oath of loyalty requested by the so-called secreted national government.[60] In reality, having refused to aid the Polish insurgents, the vast majority of its leadership remained true to the Church's loyalist stance. The fact that Russian officialdom perceived the Church as an opponent, and punished all Polish Catholic clergy, eventually turned the Church into a true adversary of Russian rule.[61]

The tsar understood the importance of generating peasant loyalty to the empire. Therefore, Russia liberated the peasantry from their very real Polish oppression in both the kresy and the Kingdom of Poland.[62] Monarchist officials not only weakened the Polish nobility's influence, but at the same time strengthened Russian economic, cultural, and political power. Believing that the intelligentsia, szlachta, and the Catholic clergy sustained the "mutiny," and knowing that the latter two were big kresy landowners, Russian officials levied a special tariff on existing Polish landholdings. The enormous financial stress incurred by this tax burden forced many Polish gentry to sell their property at the extremely low prices offered by Russian purchasers.[63] The tsar also confiscated estates owned by insurrectionary activists, awarding them in turn to Russian officials who loyally served the empire.[64] Finally, to prevent any further Polish "corruption" of the provinces, on December 10, 1865 the Russian government prohibited persons of Polish descent from purchasing land in its western provinces.[65] Russia gained ownership of some eighteen hundred Polish estates in the borderlands. Within the Kingdom of Poland, about sixteen hundred Polish estates were also transferred to Russian ownership.[66]

In order to gain peasant allegiance, Alexander II's earlier March 1, 1861 Peasant Reform legislation not only entitled them to land confiscated from the nobility, but also obligated the lord to pay the peasants for their labor, finally making their emancipation economically meaningful. While the great magnates in the Kingdom of Poland and the kresy survived this economic warfare, due to their significant land and monetary holdings, the lesser gentry in both areas could not withstand it. Thus, this superficially benevolent policy toward the peasantry impoverished a large number of economically challenged landowning gentry,

---

60 Brian Porter-Szűcs, *Faith and Fatherland*, 165.
61 Ibid.
62 Jerzy Tomaszewski notes that Polish oppression of peasants was very real, being revealed often in many memoirs. See email correspondence with author, October 14, 2012.
63 Weeks, *Nation and State in Late Imperial Russia*, 99.
64 Ibid., 128.
65 Ibid., 99.
66 Wandycz, *The Lands of Partitioned Poland, 1795–1918*, 195.

driving them from their estates either due to higher taxes or peasant wages they could not pay.[67] While those with means increased their landholdings by purchasing the land peasants could not redeem, or for which they could not afford to pay taxes, most lesser nobility suffered from foreclosures, land confiscations, and the loss of peasant servitude. A great percentage of them had already been poor and now they were also landless.

Though the szlachta's education prepared them to take on government positions, Russian reaction to the uprising barred them from attaining political office. With few options, thousands felt forced to migrate to the cities. Job hungry, the déclassé nobility turned to commerce as a way to support itself. Once again, they ran into a wall. Jews, who had migrated earlier to the cities and at a faster pace than Poles, had those jobs that the new urban Polish population desperately wanted and needed.

And so, as economic opportunities shifted, significant numbers of nobles—which had once stood in a feudal partnership with the Jews—became fierce competitors with urban Jewry.[68] Polish resentment of the Jews' economic rise increased dramatically. At the same time that Russia unleashed these punishing economic and cultural policies against Poles, Russia did not target the Jews. Poles knew what they saw. While the Romanovs deprived Poles of their cultural, economic, and political rights, the tsar allowed the Jews to retain those civil rights granted to them in 1862. Thus, it appeared to many Poles that the Russians were treating the Jews better than the Poles, thereby stirring up Polish resentment of the Jews.[69] The very real economic and political frustrations experienced by the Polish intelligentsia and nobility created a ripe environment for anti-Jewish attitudes.

Myth Reconstruction

During the first decade after the 1863 Uprising, most Poles felt closer to Jews, not only for what they saw as Jewish support of Polish independence, but also because Polish writers continued to portray the Jews quite positively. Polish

---

67 Weeks, *From Assimilation to Antisemitism*, 51.
68 Ibid., 56–57.
69 What Poles tended not to notice was the actual Russifying efforts targeted towards the Jews. Wanting to break up the so-called Polish-Jewish fraternity, Russia sought to divide and conquer by prohibiting the use of Polish in the synagogues. Theodore Weeks, *From Assimilation to Antisemitism*, 53.

authors greatly influenced the literate segment of Polish society, creating examples of heroic Jews—insurgents and sympathizers—who stood in sharp contrast with the perceived egotistical and unpatriotic Polish gentry.[70] Often, the Jews who received the greatest accolades were spiritual leaders, such as Jastrow and Meisels, who fully embraced Poland. This liberal presentation of the Jews changed in the years after the rebellion when Polish writers reflected the separate realities Poles and Jews experienced following the uprising. Poles were devastated economically, while Jews seemed to profit financially from Russia's authoritarian success in Vistula Land.

Writers began expressing a shift in relations between Jews and patriotic Poles. Like so many other earlier advocates of Polish-Jewish brotherhood, Józef Kraszewski, the editor of *Gazeta*, reassessed his position after the failure of the 1863 Uprising.[71] In 1868, he wrote:

> The insurrection collapsed in a welter of blood and the Jews, making use of their thousand-year-old experience, raised themselves over our corpses. But when they sacrificed us and abandoned us in an evil hour, only to rescue themselves, they shook our faith in them and dampened our love. The fact is that in the [Congress] Kingdom none of those rescued offered their hands to help the drowning.[72]

The fact that the Jews created economic opportunities out of Polish despair proved to Kraszewski and his peers the Jews' disloyalty to the loftier cause of Polish freedom. He notes that in the end, the Jew is concerned about his own well-being and survival at the peril of Poland. He is concerned with himself, not with the Polish nation. Chastising the Jews for benefiting from the defeat of the uprising, several other Polish writers ceased praising Jewish involvement in it. Over time, the myth of Polish-Jewish fraternity lost its traction, again replaced by the caricature of the self-serving Jewish capitalist.[73]

During the same period, Jews developed their own negative images of Poles. Informed by Russian Maskilic writers, who lived in Russia but sold their stories to Warsaw publishers post-1864, Jews in the Kingdom of Poland became skeptical about the Polish-Jewish brotherhood. Though Russian Maskilim were not

---

70 Opalski and Bartal, *Poles and Jews: A Failed Brotherhood*, 58.
71 Ibid., 101.
72 As cited in Bartoszewski and Polonsky, *The Jews of Warsaw*, 21.
73 Opalski and Bartal, *Poles and Jews: A Failed Brotherhood*, 134.

from Congress Kingdom, they influenced a broad Yiddish, Hebrew, and Russian demographic in the Kingdom of Poland.[74] Additionally, Russian Jews, who accepted Russian culture and antagonistic Russian stereotypes of Poles, only further influenced these Russian Jewish writers and their Jewish audience in Poland to brand Poles negatively.[75] For Polish activists aware of this influence, it must have been quite frustrating. Depicting the Polish side as corrupt, unstable, vulnerable, and unreliable, these authors pointed to Polish nationalism as xenophobic, too Christian, and too demanding of Jews to assimilate.[76] Knowing the strong connection between the Catholic Church and Polish nationalism, they argued that Jews would never be accepted fully into Polish society.

For a short period, the robust and meaningful Jewish participation in the Poles' armed struggles against Russian rule steadily built a bridge of respect and brotherhood across a divide, which previous Sejm reformers had been unable to construct. That Jews demonstrated with Poles, suffered in prison with Poles, and died on the battlefield with Poles proved more meaningful than Jews' specific cultural adaptations. Jews demonstrated their love for Poland. But with military defeat came corrosive, and *intentionally unequal*, Russian reactive policies. Each group had to figure out how to respond. While Poles and Jews retreated to accept their overlord, Poles grew infuriated after seeing Jews benefit economically and politically from relations with Russia while Poles themselves suffered under Russian imposed cultural degradation.

---

74 Lev Levanda (1835–1888), Ayzik Meir Dik (also known as AMAD, 1807/14-1893) were Russian Maskilic writers who influenced Polish Jews. In their introduction to their book, Opalski and Bartal support their use of Jewish literature originating from outside of the Kingdom of Poland as representing and influencing a strong Maskilic voice within the kingdom. See Opalski and Bartal, *Poles and Jews: A Failed Brotherhood*, 10.
75 Weeks, *From Assimilation to Antisemitism*, 54.
76 Opalski and Bartal, *Poles and Jews: A Failed Brotherhood*, 96.

CHAPTER 7

Modernity and Fear

Modernity, that period initiated by the Enlightenment, released a wave of liberalization throughout Europe. Calls for greater minority rights and Jewish emancipation filled city streets and halls of government. In France, Prussia, Austria, and Italy, Jews breached ghetto walls. Assimilating relatively quickly into the host culture, Jews advanced socially, economically, and even politically. This progressive era experienced mass Jewish movement into European cities, where Jews provided inexpensive artisan and trade services. Already active in moneylending, Jews pioneered the banking system, which played part in funding railroad construction and wartime destruction. Jews steadily ascended into the middle class, with some even entering the ranks of the most wealthy and powerful. This chapter explores the post-1863 rise of the Jews in the Kingdom of Poland and the positivist circle that promoted them. It then shifts to the conservative backlash—due to international economic collapse coupled with the fears generated by modernity—that has ramifications to this day.

Modernity, progressive and liberal, pointed to traditional Jewish occupations as the new path of economic engagement for *all* peoples. The Jew—the standard-bearer of capitalism before the nobility and peasant were forced to enter it—exuded modernity in almost every sense. According to Yuri Slezkine,

> [t]here was a peculiar kinship between Jews and the Modern Age, that the Jews, in some very important sense, were the Modern Age. No matter what the standard—rationalism, nationalism, capitalism, professionalism, Faustian Prometheanism, literacy, democracy, hygiene, alienation, or the nuclear family—Jews seemed to have been there first, done it earlier, understood it best.[1]

---

1   Slezkine, *The Jewish Century*, 60.

Ironically, to become more like the Jew was to become more successful in the modern age.²

As typically occurs, liberal actions bred conservative reactions. Although the backlash mainly targeted Jews, this response was not about the Jews in and of themselves. Traditionalists agonized and raged against their lost power due to economic trends, secularism, and new migratory patterns—and the Jew became a symbol of everything they opposed.

Polish Positivism

A new generation of post-1863 Polish activists embraced this modern European view of Jews and capitalism. The youth waged an internal battle against not only the tsar's broadscale assault on Polish culture and political rights, but also the kingdom's traditional Polish leadership. The youth blamed the old guard for starry-eyed daydreaming and reckless actions that had led, by and large, to national disaster.³ Given that the romantic nationalists' methods had failed in two Polish rebellions, various thinkers developed new political outlooks for Poland's survival. One ideology, positivism, took hold and spread throughout the three partitions from the late 1860s to the mid-1880s.

Its boldest Polish advocates resided in the Kingdom of Poland.⁴ Their brand became known as Warsaw positivism, with its leadership emerging from students who attended the Warsaw Main School (Szkoła Główna Warszawska). The school itself represented all that was wrong with the Russian-censored educational system in the Kingdom of Poland. Though supposedly an institution of higher education, the Szkoła Główna was a pitiful excuse for a university: its faculty was incompetent and its library was sparse.⁵ A core intelligentsia emerged there that was dedicated to developing a new national vision based on cultural worth and economic strength. This group became known as the young press (*młoda prasa*).

Due to age, most of its young contributors had not participated in the 1863 January Uprising. They rejected Polish romanticism's myth of Poland as the chosen nation, as well as the belief that political independence remained of utmost necessity for survival. In its place, they presented the nation as a living organism

---

2   Ibid., 41.
3   Walicki, *Philosophy and Romantic Nationalism: The Case of Poland*, 337.
4   Ibid., 340.
5   Porter, *When Nationalism Began to Hate*, 45.

their positivism would strengthen, despite occupation by partitioning powers.[6] According to its acknowledged leader, the writer Aleksander Świętochowski (1849–1938), it was imperative to reconcile oneself as part of the Russian Empire. But Russian control could not prevent Poles from rebuilding their cultural and economic integrity. Poland would come back to life through the actual work being done within society.

Positivism did not dismiss change outright. It simply strove for achievable change. It was a delicate balance between progress and the status quo. Positivists believed that Poland would eventually gain independence, but that it would require great patience. The młoda prasa allowed the promise of a better future to ground them in the often tedious work of economic and social modernization. This was a rebellion from within. Positivism contended that work was necessary to create a "civilized" and "advanced" Polish nation which would reemerge not because of its military strength, but due to its intelligence.[7]

Positivism also sought to redesign the Polish soul. It aimed to replace traditionalism, religion, chauvinism, and superstition with rationalism, science, and capitalism. The młoda prasa knew that to achieve success it required the support of the multitudes, the very people they sought to transform. Their appeals contrasted the past marginalization of peasants, women, and Jews with a vision of future empowerment.[8] Their plans focused on industrial development, Jews' emancipation, women's rights, peasant modernization, and limited Church authority.

Distancing themselves from long-held feudal economic relationships, the młoda prasa looked to the West—England, France, and Germany—for economic growth strategies.[9] They focused on capitalism and industry to heal the kingdom's ailing economic system. Positivists celebrated those typically disparaged by the nobility, such as merchants and artisans. They regarded Jews and Polish burghers as shining examples of an essential middle class. And they expected the old szlachta to learn to do the same.

Positivists also derided the Church's grip on society.[10] In reimagining civil classifications, Świętochowski and fellow intellectuals such as Bolesław Prus (1847–1912) and Eliza Orzeszkowa (1841–1910) embraced a new view of

---

6   Wandycz, *The Lands of Partitioned Poland, 1795–1918*, 263.
7   Porter, *When Nationalism Began to Hate*, 70.
8   Ibid., 46, 65–69; Antony Polonsky, "The Dreyfus Affair and Polish-Jewish Interaction, 1890–1914," *Jewish History* 11, no. 2 (Fall 1997): 27.
9   Blejwas, "Polish Positivism and the Jews": 23.
10   Weeks, *From Assimilation to Antisemitism*, 57.

Jews.¹¹ No longer portraying them as those who denied Christ, positivists defined Jews in the kingdom as Poles with a religious foundation distinct from the Polish Christian majority. Having lived through the 1863 January Uprising, these three leaders believed in the brotherhood between Jew and Pole. Shared experiences of Jewish patriotism, coupled with a European shift toward tolerance of religious and ethnic minorities, supported their incorporation of the large Jewish population into their vision for national reconstruction.¹²

Positivists recognized that Jews living in partitioned Polish lands contributed greatly to Polish society as thinkers, entrepreneurs, and professionals. They also acknowledged the growing anti-Jewish sentiment expressed within those territories. Positivists agreed with contemporary European thinkers that the Jews' cultural isolation was the root cause of the problem.¹³ Świętochowski argued that Jew-hatred developed fundamentally from perception. Difference from the majority culture incited fear within mainstream society. He offered the European axiom that was taking hold as a solution: if the Jews would "reform," Jew-hatred would vanish.¹⁴ Other famous theorists, such as Prus and Orzeszkowa, understood the problem as a clash of cultures. They maintained that Poles would be more accepting of Jews if Jews were more accepting of Poland. In order to cross the extremely wide cultural divide separating the two peoples, positivists beseeched Jews to cast off their "backward" religious practices as well as their "jargon" (the Yiddish language). To relinquish their mother tongue and to replace it with Polish symbolized becoming one with the Polish nation.¹⁵ They also emphasized secular education to stimulate Jews' embrace of Polish culture. Polish positivists promised Jews all the rights, privileges, and responsibilities of Polish citizenship if they agreed to these suggestions.¹⁶

Positivists realized that the general Polish Christian population needed to play an active role in facilitating the Jews' transition into Polish society. In order for Jews to become one with the Polish people, the Poles themselves had to accept Jews as such. Świętochowski wrote in 1877: "We are convinced that the Jewish

---

11 While Orzeskowa did not define herself as a positivist, she held very similar views to them. Polonsky, *The Jews in Poland and Russia*, 1: 316.
12 Ibid., 62.
13 Shmuel Ettinger, foreword to Shmuel Almog, *Nationalism and Antisemitism from 1815–1945* (Oxford: Pergamon Press, 1990), xiv.
14 Lindemann, *Esau's Tears*, xviii.
15 Stephen D. Corrsin, "Aspects of Population Change and of Acculturation in Jewish Warsaw at the End of the Nineteenth Century: The Censuses of 1882 and 1897," in Bartoszewski and Polonsky, *The Jews in Warsaw*, 220.
16 Weeks, *From Assimilation to Antisemitism*, 58.

question does not exist. There exists only the urgent need for compulsory education for *Christians and Jews* to pull them out of isolation and furnish them with habits of thinking and everyday life common to the rest of humanity" (emphasis mine).[17] Pursuing a social engineering policy, they enlisted reason as their guide. According to Eliza Orzeszkowa, "all our social problems, including those with the Jews, will only be solved in a satisfactory manner when knowledge gives us the ability to think in a scientific, clear, and free way, and scientific, clear, and free thought teaches us to act energetically and intelligently."[18] They argued that to achieve national unity, people from all ethnic and economic backgrounds must dispense with antiquated views of the Other.

Integration: Challenges and Successes

The road to the Jews' integration into Polish society was strewn with blockades. Indeed, within its very ideology lay a barrier to success. In grounding its ideology in reason and scientific observation, positivism discarded the romantics' view that *action* proved one's belonging to the nation. As such, positivists reduced the nation to a noun. "'Poland' was now a community of Poles, not a transcendent 'national spirit' or 'essence' moving through and driving history."[19] Approaching the Polish nation as a social collective, the młoda prasa necessarily established ethnic boundaries and social discipline for belonging to it. Whereas the Polish romantic nationalists had finally come to understand anyone active on behalf of Polish patriotism, especially on the battlefield, as a participant in recreating the nation, the positivists limited their nation to those who belonged to it according to ethnographically demarcated rules. Once again, language, dress, and culture became a grave concern. Ironically, while positivism projected a liberal agenda, its founding, albeit ambivalent, rigidity would form the basis for radical conservatism's exclusionary principles in the future.[20]

Jewish integrationists accepted the positivists' ideas about how mainstream Jews could assimilate into Polish society. Working toward that end, both groups stumbled awkwardly due to their own misguided assumptions regarding their ability to transform traditional Jews. Encouraged by Haskalah's success in Germany, integrationists hoped to create similar results in the kingdom; but

---

17 Ibid., 62.
18 As cited in Antony Polonsky, *The Jews in Poland and Russia*, 1:316.
19 Porter, *When Nationalism Began to Hate*, 50.
20 Ibid., 56–57.

important distinctions between Germany and the Kingdom of Poland stood in the way. The German Jewish population constituted a very small percentage of that country's total inhabitants, rarely reaching more than 1% in any location.[21] Almost completely urban, and overwhelmingly made up of professionals, German Jews sought to mingle freely in secular culture. Raised on Haskalah ideals since the late eighteenth century, German Jews dreamed of complete, unfettered emancipation.[22] For decades, the German Jewish community had been providing their youth with secular educational opportunities.[23] These Jews had been primed and readied for a deeply filial relationship to Germany. The extremely large, mostly poor, secularly uneducated Jewish population in the Kingdom of Poland, which extended well beyond city limits, remained insufficiently prepared.

Of added significance stood the lack of interest in Haskalah, let alone in positivism, among Jews breaking into the Polish bourgeoisie. A diverse cultural profile defined the Jewish mercantile elite in Russian Poland. Most wished for acculturation only to the extent that it would enable them to secure those economic and residence rights beneficial to their immediate daily lives. Additionally, a large percentage of the kingdom's native Jewish bourgeoisie affiliated with Hasidism.[24] Thus, a limited integrationist mentality sustained their relative social and cultural isolation.

Problematic, neither integrationists nor positivists held the pulse of their target populations well enough to engage their new "enlightened" theories directly with them.[25] To connect, they would need understanding and respect. They had neither. Both groups fought against traditional beliefs by pushing the pen to rally others to join them. However, those they addressed did not read their journals and papers, if they read Polish at all. The intellectually charged positivists did not relate to the Polish rural, uneducated population; most integrationists discarded Jewish traditionalism and looked with disdain upon Jews wrapped so securely in it.

---

21 Miriam Rürup, "Demographics and Social Structure," IgDJ, September 22, 2016, https://jewish-history-online.net/topic/demographics-and-social-structure.
22 Emmanuel Etkes, "Haskalah" (trans. Jeffrey Green), accessed 29 August, 2023, www.yivoencyclopedia.org/article.aspx/Haskalah.
23 David Sorkin, "The Impact of Emancipation on German Jewry: A Reconsideration," in *Assimilation and Community: The Jews in Nineteenth-Century Europe*, ed. Joanthan Frankel and Steven J. Zipperstein (Cambridge: Cambridge University Press, 1992), 188.
24 Glenn Dynner, *Men of Silk: The Hasidic Conquest of Polish Jewish Society* (Oxford: Oxford University Press, 2006), 91.
25 Weeks, *From Assimilation to Antisemitism*, 65.

One could not even count on the newly emerging Jewish progressive spiritual leadership to extend itself to the broader Jewish public. Between 1826 and 1862, more than one thousand students graduated from the progressive Warsaw Rabbinic School.[26] These integrationist rabbis gravitated toward the assimilating Jewish community.[27] The slow growth of this Jewish sector prevented newly ordained rabbis from locating pulpits, forcing them into either education or commerce. Additionally, perhaps due to traditionalists' negative view of them, most Warsaw Rabbinic School graduates isolated themselves away from their "unenlightened co-religionists" instead of reaching out to them.

However, concurrently, a few integrationist leaders found new ways to connect with some Hasidic luminaries, tsadikim. Rabbi Marcus Jastrow and Daniel Neufeld (1814–1874, editor in chief of the short-lived periodical *Dawn* (*Jutzrenka*)[28] approached tsadikim anew—by patiently and respectfully communicating collective concern: if Jews refused modernization and integration, they would inevitably grow resentful of their leaders and discard Judaism.[29] They presented secular education as a panacea. The Gerer Rebbe (Isaac Meir Alter, 1789–1866), an intellectual giant within Hasidism, engaged in this discussion. Although known also for his polemics against integration, he called for teaching Polish in the *heder*, the traditional religious elementary school attended by most young Jewish boys.[30] Slow indeed, but progress, nonetheless. Whether or not positivists knew about it and understood its significance is another question. Concurrently, despite Daniel Neufeld's belief that many Hasidic leaders were on the cusp of permitting secular education, the actual number remained rather small at this point.[31]

Simultaneously, Hasidic leaders fought back against secularizing inroads the integrationists had achieved. Hasidism averted assimilation by making use of connections its members had with both the Jewish mercantile class and Polish government officials.[32] Ambivalence about the Jews' transformation plagued many Russian government officials, given that it originated in the Enlightenment, which opposed monarchy. Despite speaking highly of Maskilim's and integrationists' proposed reforms, both the ruling Romanov government and its

---

26 Katarzyna Person, *Assimilated Jews in the Warsaw Ghetto, 1940–1943*, ed. Henry Feingold (Syracuse: Syracuse University Press, 2014), 8.
27 Polonsky, *The Jews in Poland and Russia*, 1:305.
28 Russian officials shut down *Jutzrenka* after the January 1863 insurrection.
29 Wodziński, *Haskalah and Hasidism*, 185–198.
30 Ibid., 195–196.
31 Ibid., 186–187.
32 Dynner, *Men of Silk*, 90.

accommodationist Polish administrators feared reform. As such, the kingdom's tsadikim and their wealthy patrons from the mercantile class successfully lobbied and bribed officials to hinder those advances already made.[33] Thus, while progressive Jews worked in government offices creating programs to influence the Jews' assimilation, Hasidim secured government connections to minimize and even to negate such efforts. At the same time, larger issues plaguing the continent threatened the Jews' integration into Polish society.

Continental-Wide Growth of Antisemitism and Nationalism

In 1873, the stock market crash exploded free market economic theory and the mid-century European liberalism that championed it. The ensuing European-wide recession, known to contemporaries as the Great Depression, unleashed extreme economic adversity for close to two decades. Reactionaries, both Jews and non-Jews, lambasted liberalism for this disaster. They blamed shallow optimism—a belief in progress, science, and technology—and the often-corrupt practices of those in power for the economic devastation that enveloped European countries.[34] At the same time, some thinkers in Germany, France, and Austria linked the Jews' nineteenth-century ascendancy to the calamity.

In 1879, Germany's Wihelm Marr (1819–1904) called this new ideological assault on the Jews "antisemitism." Marr and his contemporaries directed political reactionaries away from Church anti-Jewish theology to focus instead on Jews' actions in the real world.[35] For modern antisemites, the Jews were a harmful race, capable of infecting supposedly superior races. "[S]ome had good reason to feel threatened, for Jews were in truth encroaching on arenas that had previously been exclusively Gentile, and Jews were helping to make life as those Gentiles had traditionally experienced it difficult or impossible."[36] Harnessing the impoverished masses' anger and angst, political antisemites argued against the modern, economically, socially, culturally, and politically influential Jew.

---

33 Ibid., 34.
34 Albert S. Lindemann, *The Jew Accused: Three Antisemitic Affairs Dreyfus, Beilis, Frank, 1894–1915* (Cambridge: Cambridge University Press, 1991), 29.
35 Ibid., 21.
36 Ibid., 12.

By the end of the nineteenth century, the "Jewish question" had turned into a consuming monomania for Europeans, be they French, German, Austrian, or Polish. The railroad and advances in the printing press enabled the quick dissemination of ideas between countries. Trains transformed not only travel, but also higher education, as students from one country could easily study in another state's universities. The printing revolution also greatly increased the interchange of ideas across physical borders. The steam-powered rotary press that replaced the hand-operated Gutenberg-style printing press facilitated printing on an industrial scale. It was now possible to reach hundreds of thousands. Higher literacy rates aided this movement of ideas. Thus, it should not come as a surprise that ideas germinated in Germany, Austria, or France impacted thinkers in Russian Poland.

Along with antisemitism's growth, nationalism came of age. Theorists throughout Europe arrived at the belief that only people of the same ethnic background or race should reside within the same territorial borders. There existed little space for diversity within a population. By emphasizing one nation's unique physical and cultural characteristics, nationalism ultimately drew attention to the Other's differences. Neighboring ethnic groups evolved into rival national movements.[37] Right-wing nationalism's approach to the Other gained even greater relevance when members of the alien group competed for individual economic survival and prosperity with native nationals.

In France, Maurice Barrès (1862–1923), a well-respected and influential thinker, turned to coupling antisemitism with nationalism.[38] Barrès grieved France's transformation from a traditional, rural, high quality handcrafted economy to one overrun by department stores, railroads, and factories. Blaming the Jews for creating and benefitting from these changes, Barrès cried: "France for the French!"[39] Similarly, French reactionary Édouard Drumont (1844–1917, of much lower intellect and societal respectability than Barrès), gained prestige when he incorporated antisemitic themes into his writing. Drumont challenged the French to regain control over its Jews, who had been at the center of several large debilitating economic scandals.[40] Looking into the civil service, the military, and the government, Drumont noted that there was an inordinate number

---

37 Almog, *Nationalism and Antisemitism in Modern Europe 1815–1945*, 10.
38 Those along the political spectrum, even Léon Blum, who would become France's first Jewish premier, considered this novelist and poet a leader of French literary culture. See Lindemann, *The Jew Accused*, 81.
39 Ibid., 83.
40 Ibid., 70 and 87.

of Jews in power relative to their 0.1 to 0.2% of the total population.[41] French Jewry's quick rise into the bourgeoisie through industry, banking, and politics also fed his anger. His linking of the French Jewish organization Alliance Israélite Universelle to a fantasy clandestine "Jewish Syndicate" that was working against French interests proved popular. His 1886 book *Jewish France* (*La France juive*), which included previously published antisemitic writings, became one of the best-selling books in the history of French publishing before World War I.[42] In time, these new theories crossed into the Kingdom of Poland.

The Growth of Antisemitism in the Kingdom of Poland

Concurrent to the positivists' and integrationists' call for reciprocal understanding, tolerance, and acceptance of one another, a growing antisemitic presence infiltrated Polish intellectual circles.[43] Nations throughout the continent made Barrès' exclusionary phrase their own. Thus, when right-wing Polish activists insisted "Poland for the Poles," they joined a movement already in progress. Bolesław Prus noted that "from France . . . there come to us not only fashions, but also opinions, not only women's hats, skirts and wine . . . but discoveries, slogans, even feelings. . . . Those social currents, which for decades had been developing in France appear today in our society, reproduced, although in a somewhat paler and less graceful form."[44] Polish-Jewish relations must therefore be seen within this broader context of European Christian-Jewish relations. Of course, this does not excuse violent antisemitic sentiment within Poland. It simply helps us to understand its eruption.

Antisemites resurrected and circulated old anti-Jewish tirades penned by long-dead priests and burghers. For young writers, the very longevity of these works proved their veracity. Contemporary authors borrowed similar language and arguments from them, painting the Jewish community as responsible for all that was wrong within Polish society.[45] This new generation of Polish writers also reiterated Stanisław Staszic's description of the Jews' "overpopulation"

---

41 The French Third Republic dismissed monarchists from their positions in various bureaucracies, replacing them with Léon Gambetta's Opportunists, who were often Jews. Ibid., 66.
42 While he did gain fame and wealth, Drumont failed at this time in turning antisemitism into a successful political ideology in France. Ibid., 83.
43 Weeks, *From Assimilation to Antisemitism*, 85.
44 As cited in Polonsky, "The Dreyfus Affair and Polish-Jewish Interaction, 1890–1914," 21.
45 Johanna Beata Michlic, *Poland's Threatening Other*, 39.

as the most permanent misfortune to affect Russian Poland.[46] He pitched his view as a battle over identity when he questioned whether "the Jews will end up becoming Poles, or the Poles become Jews."[47] Staszic's and his coterie's pamphlets targeted the intellectual elites. Thus, despite the constant presence of antisemitic thought in the Kingdom of Poland since its 1815 inception, the Polish masses remained ambivalent about the Jews until the last quarter of the nineteenth century.[48]

The slight movement that mainstream Jewry demonstrated toward integration, and the republication of old Polish priests' and burghers' anti-Jewish pamphlets, compounded European-wide antisemitic rhetoric. One of the first of the postinsurrectionary writers to fully anchor himself in antisemitism,[49] former positivist Jan Jeleński (1845–1909), launched a weekly titled *Rola* (Soil) in 1883. A conservative Catholic from a family of pauperized nobility, Jeleński portrayed the Jew as the reason behind all of Poland's problems: the Jew was Poland's enemy. Although this organ took years to capture the general Polish population's imagination, over its thirty-year circulation, he eventually succeeded in establishing the Jew as the ever-present Other within Polish society. Even more disturbing, Jeleński suggested that to protect itself Poland should isolate its Jews and compel them to emigrate from all Polish territory.[50]

Urban Migration and the Agrarian Crisis Spur Antisemitism

The general Polish populace grew more susceptible to such antisemitic and nationalist influences when their own personal economic relationships with Jews changed. In the past, peasants had compartmentalized societal and Church-based negative images of the Jews because the Jewish tavernkeeper, artisan, trader, and moneylender down the road helped them within feudal

---

46 Marcin Wodziński, "Reform and Exclusion: Conceptions of the Reform of the Jewish Community during the Declining Years of the Polish Enlightenment," in *Jews and Their Neighbours in Eastern Europe since 1750*, ed. Israel Bartal, Antony Polonsky, and Scott Ury Polin: Studies in Polish Jewry, vol. 24 (Oxford: The Littman Library of Jewish Civilization, 2012), 39.
47 Ibid., 40.
48 Ibid, 39–40.
49 Antony Polonsky, *The Jews in Poland and Russia, 1881–1914*, vol. 2 (Oxford: The Littman Library of Jewish Civilization, 2010), 97.
50 Michlic, *Poland's Threatening Other*, 55.

society. This dynamic shifted with the peasantry's economic transformation. As discussed earlier, the tsar had linked Aleksander Wielopolski's 1862 agrarian reform to an enormous tax burden, including imperial and Crown land levies. Due to the scant income they secured through their primitive farming techniques, the peasantry struggled in vain to meet their new financial obligations. Additionally, inheritance traditions mandated an equal division of land among all adult children, leaving most peasant farmers with an area of less than five acres to sow and harvest.[51]

The positivists theorized that urbanization and manufacturing would solve the Poles' economic woes. They had beseeched both peasant and Jew to urbanize, modernize, and secularize. By the late nineteenth century, the positivists' industrial vision materialized. Jewish and German manufacturers invested in the kingdom's modernizing capitalist boom, bringing factories, jobs, and workers to the cities. The Kingdom of Poland became the third leading industrial region in the Russian Empire, trailing only Moscow and Saint Petersburg. While only 7.3% of the empire's population inhabited Russian Poland, it produced a quarter of the empire's industrial output.[52]

The Russian tax retaliation for the 1863 insurrection had forced many Poles into the cities in search of income, where Jews held the majority of jobs. With many Jews having already transitioned out of lease-holding, Jews had found opportunity as urban artisans and petty traders. The agrarian crisis of the 1880s–1890s exponentially compounded the Poles' urban migration: steamships and railroads brought cheaper imports from America and Russia, challenging the kingdom's position as the breadbasket of Europe. Grain production in Russian Poland nearly halted, and the nobility sold most of its remaining land. By 1891, almost half a million landless agricultural laborers struggled in the cities.[53]

The dual impact of industrialization and serfdom's end created urban centers with hordes of landless peasants in search of economic opportunities. Warsaw's population alone expanded from 222,900 inhabitants in 1864 to 456,000 in 1890 and to more than 700,000 by the turn of the century.[54] With this urban

---

51 Stauter-Halsted, *The Nation in the Village*, 22–23.
52 Joshua D. Zimmermam, *Poles, Jews, and the Politics of Nationality: The Bund and the Polish Socialist Party in Late Tsarist Russia, 1892–1914* (Madison: The University of Wisconsin Press, 2004), 11.
53 Polonsky, *The Jews in Poland and Russia*, 2:90.
54 Porter, *When Nationalism Began to Hate*, 77.

population explosion there was an increase in crime, including armed robbery, theft, perjury, fraud, embezzlement, counterfeiting, and racketeering.

Both Jews and Christians were well represented in the kingdom's urban sex trade. The economic crisis and increasing poverty had sent countless young women to the cities looking for work, where a lack of jobs pushed many into prostitution. While the percentage of Jews in prostitution was high, reaching 35.7% of registered prostitutes in Łódz in 1902, their numbers were only slightly higher than their overall urban population percentage.[55] At the same time, a large portion of brothel keepers, pimps, and procurers were Jews.[56]

While *both* Jews and the German burghers built the cities, the Jews' dress, language, and sheer numbers made them the most visible. Thus, they symbolized not only urbanization, but also its problems. For traditionalists, Jews had debauched Polish culture. The Jews' activity on the criminal margins offered up new stereotypes for propagandists.[57]

Political antisemitism appealed to people who opposed modernity and secularism or who were simply unable to navigate the transformation of society.[58] Due to their agrarian roots, neither the nobility nor the peasantry had the skillset to adapt quickly to this new industrial age. For them, modernity was an impenetrable barrier to individual, familial, and national survival.

Rural Impoverishment and Antisemitism

The Jews also supplied an alibi for rural discontent. Those so-called emancipated peasants who chose to remain in the village despite their inability to afford their new tax burden often returned to the lord to work his land for payment. However, as already discussed, by compensating workers with drinking vouchers in lieu of money, some szlachta only worsened the peasants' dire situation.[59] The Jewish tavernkeeper who handed out the peasants' wages was most likely not colluding with the lord. However, peasants may have understood things

---

55 Robert Blobaum, "Criminalizing the 'Other': Crime, Ethnicity, and Antisemitism in Early Twentieth-Century Poland," in *Antisemitism and Its Opponents in Modern Poland*, ed. Robert Blobaum (Ithaca: Cornell University Press, 2005), 87.
56 Polonsky, *The Jews in Poland and Russia*, 2:92.
57 Blobaum, "Criminalizing the 'Other': Crime, Ethnicity, and Antisemitism in Early Twentieth-Century Poland," 81.
58 *The Jewish Century*, 63.
59 Nobles employed drinking vouchers (*kwitiki*) in the kingdom as early as the 1840s to pay peasants for additional labor. Dynner, *Yankel's Tavern*, 72.

otherwise.[60] Paying peasants for labor with drinking vouchers, coupled with the Jewish tavernkeeper's practice of permitting peasant drinking on credit, created and maintained a social disaster. The peasantry was caught in a cycle of poverty. Rural social activists portrayed the Jewish tavernkeeper as a metaphor for alcoholism, and therefore as the culprit for the peasantry's abjection.[61]

Social activists also harbored resentment towards Jews for their role as moneylender to the peasantry. In need of cash to pay their taxes, yet lacking formal credit facilities in the countryside, peasants frequently turned to Jewish moneylenders for help. In Galicia,[62] a southeastern region of Austrian-partitioned Poland, some Jewish lenders took extreme advantage of the combined lack of competition and exponential demand for credit, sending the interest rate on loans to the unfathomable amount of 250%, which was calculated weekly.[63] While lenders in the kingdom did not charge such excessive interest, the fact that many debtors reneged on their payments drove up rates.[64] Interest was commensurate with the risks involved in lending. While per lender the rate was reasonable, per borrower it was experienced as exorbitant.

The stereotype of the greedy Jewish moneylender, still persisting in the twenty-first century, has consistently failed to appreciate the high-risk nineteenth-century lenders took in extending credit. The value of money vacillated in the coin currency system, often falling in value between loan acceptance and repayment.[65] Commonly, crop failures or army conscription elevated the risk that peasants might fail to pay their debts. Additionally, once the peasantry began its mass migration to the United States in the 1880s, a loan's risk factor rose immeasurably.[66] At a time when the land spewed its poor onto distant shores, the Jewish moneylender faced undeniably greater danger that his debtor might flee. The difficulty for Jews to earn money by other means added to the high interest rates.[67]

---

60   Keely Stauter-Halsted, email correspondence with author, July 26, 2012.
61   Stefan Keiniewicz, "Polish Society and the Jewish Problem in the Nineteenth Century," in Abramsky, Jachimszyk, and Polonsky, *The Jews in Poland*, 72–73.
62   Jewish tavernkeepers and Jewish farmers often acted as moneylenders to the peasantry. While Galicia differed from the kingdom in its extensive grassroots activism, Poland's future was highly influenced by it. Several of the Second Polish Republic's (1918–1939) leaders emerged from Galicia.
63   Stauter-Halsted, *The Nation in the Village*, 50.
64   Glenn Dynner, email correspondence with author, September 8, 2013.
65   Weinryb, *The Jews of Poland*, 59.
66   Glenn Dynner, email correspondence with author, September 8, 2013.
67   Keely Stauter-Halsted, email correspondence with author, July 26, 2012.

Not surprisingly, peasants often could not pay back even small debts. Picture what happened when they could not pay back large debts. The only assets they could give to pay off a note were their animals, their homes, and their land. Steeped in poverty, when peasants borrowed they only became further entrenched in debt. Imagine the horror when their cherished land either became the outright property of a Jewish moneylender or he sold it to pocket the money. Indeed, the number of forced auctions of peasant farms increased dramatically in the late nineteenth century. Galicia was typical of this trend. While less than one hundred such liquidations occurred in 1868, by 1899 over three thousand farms were sold annually to meet debts.[68] That same year, 10% of agricultural land became owned by Jews.[69] Although this number correlates to population statistics, it was a vast change, and Jews crossed borders to take up landownership.

While the peasantry did not think much about the government, they did care about who owned village land. Both peasant and noble perceived Jewish "guests," who did not even recognize Jesus as Christ, as usurping the land of their hosts! This image of the Jew as a malicious, scheming, underhanded opponent lasted for quite some time. This narrow Polish perspective ignored the desperate poverty that was spread virally throughout Galician Jewry itself. As peasant and noble adjusted their economic relationship with Jews, they relinquished tolerance for the Jews' cultural separation, transforming the Jew into a target for Polish angst.

With the dramatic economic challenges facing Poles, new organizers arose to pull the Polish nation out of its misery. Some originated in Galicia, which had become a hotbed of radical Polish nationalism. These new Polish political voices not only became more appealing over the next several decades, but also maintained influence well into the twentieth century, with their ideas greatly affecting relations between Jews and Poles. When Galicia's Polish nobility recognized the need to tie their dreams of national resurrection to the masses, they rushed to promote a once unimaginable rapport with the peasantry.

As often happens when two historically opposed groups seek cooperation, they united over a shared hatred of another group.[70] Unfortunately for the Jews, countless embittered szlachta connected with the downtrodden peasant by propagandizing against the Jews. The two once antagonistic groups drew together over their shared inability to compete against the established middleman

---

68   Stauter-Halsted, *The Nation in the Village*, 50.
69   Ibid., 134.
70   Bonacich, "A Theory of Middleman Minorities": 589.

minority in business.[71] They painted the Jew as a greedy moneylender who exploited the peasantry, while also capitalizing on the peasantry's innate superstition about, and fear of, the foreign.[72] With all of their distinct physical, religious, and cultural differences from Poles, Jews became the ultimate Other. In sum, the szlachta sacrificed the Jew to gain Polish sovereignty.

The Catholic Church, Poland, and the Jews

As Europeans in general, and Poles in particular, turned to the new creeds of antisemitism and nationalism, the Catholic Church recast its own anti-Jewish doctrine. This trifecta of intolerance created a perfect storm for Poles' growing intolerance of Jews. Therefore, any serious discussion of Polish-Jewish relations must address the role of the Catholic Church and its influence within Polish society.

The Catholic Church secured the conversion of the szlachta and burghers during the Counter-Reformation in the seventeenth century. During the 1600s, Islamic, Greek Orthodox, and Protestant armies raced across borders to conquer Poland. Polish leaders tied Polish military victory to Catholicism. Believing that Catholicism, as the true path to God, had saved them, in 1717 Poles held a ceremonial coronation of the Virgin Mary at Częstochowa.[73] Having linked the Catholic Church with the political survival of the country, Polish nationalism thus became synonymous with the Catholic Church.

Church theology identifies Catholicism as an embattled hero, waging "eternal war with those implacable enemies: the world, the flesh, and the devil.'"[74] Depending on the historic period, priests either minimize or maximize military metaphors. Early nineteenth-century Catholic language focused on enemies such as alcohol, illicit sexual relations, or just laziness. But an enemy always existed.

For centuries the Catholic Church urged its flock to wage internals battle against worldly and bodily temptations. At the same time, sophisticated theological treatises and church sermons stressed the biblical injunction to "love one's neighbor." Catholic theologians worldwide emphasized that the word *neighbor* encompassed all of humanity. A neighbor should be loved whether Catholic,

---

71 Ibid., 590.
72 Stauter-Halsted, *The Nation in the Village*, 39
73 Norman Davies, *God's Playground*, 1:135.
74 Cited in Porter-Szűcs, *Faith and Fatherland*, 232.

Protestant, or Jew, Polish, Ukrainian, or Russian. This view allowed Catholics to hate the sin, but love the sinner; and this concept of "love thy neighbor" was the most popular theme in Polish homiletic, devotional, and catechetical texts in the nineteenth and twentieth centuries.[75]

Prior to the 1880s, then, the Polish Catholic Church did not single out the Jews as the national enemy. Until the very late nineteenth century every soul could be redeemed if pledged to Jesus as Christ. Despite taunting the Jews with its theology of supersessionism, the Church believed that even Jews could be saved.[76] However, conversion to Christianity remained a radical step for the kingdom's Jews.

Until the late nineteenth century, the Church remained firmly opposed to racial discrimination. This is not to say that priests did not communicate anti-Jewish sentiment in their sermons. They did. It was the *ancient* Israelites they derided, however—those who ignored Jesus during, and immediately after, his life in Palestine—rather than contemporary Jews living down the street. Any negativity about the Jews was theological, not racial.[77] Yet, when race-based fears filtered into the Church, theology necessarily transformed.

The Catholic Church Battles Modernity

The Enlightenment put traditionalists on the defensive, with its new liberal ideas about society, government, and religion. Nineteenth-century secularism forced the Church into a war for its very survival. The Freemasons[78] represented anti-clericalism in this battle. A society cloaked in secrecy, by the nineteenth-century Freemasonry required adherence to only very basic religious principles.[79]

---

75   Ibid., 235.
76   Pitting its theology against Judaism, supersessionism maintains that Christianity necessarily replaced Judaism as the true religion. A theological criticism of the Jews, supersessionism is not racially driven. Therefore, Jews would be accepted as individuals once they converted to Christianity. Ibid., 273.
77   Ibid., 275.
78   The masons originated in early eighteenth-century England and continued to proliferate throughout nineteenth-century Europe. Originally, the founders were concerned that Christians of different sects be given the opportunity to get along despite disparate theologies. See Ronad Modras, *The Catholic Church and Antisemitism: Poland, 1933–1939* (London: Routledge, 1994), 46.
79   In addition to the moral law, the Freemasons affirmed a belief in God, belief in the sacred law of the Bible, and belief in the immortality of the soul. Members were implored to keep any

Given that Masonic lodges regarded their members as equals, regardless of religion or social status, it should not be a surprise that the organization attracted assimilated Jews.

While not all lodges admitted them,[80] Masons in the Kingdom of Poland generally welcomed Jews.[81] Secular Poles recognized Freemasonry's radical stress on equality as a springboard not only to independence, but also to the alleviation of the miserable lot suffered by both peasants and Jews.[82] Although the Russian tsar outlawed Freemasonry in 1822, men continued to flock to its doors.[83]

Modernity's arrival, strength, and stamina stunned Church leaders. In this new age, which promoted science over theology, the Church continued to lose adherents and power. The pope's long-time control over the Papal States came under attack when the French helped to create the secular Kingdom of Italy. Pope Pius IX's sphere of influence was reduced to Rome and a small buffer surrounding it.[84] Concurrent demands for freedom of religion, the separation of Church and state, secular education, as well as calls for less ecclesiastical privilege, diminished the Church's power.[85] By September 20, 1870, as Rome fell to an Italian military siege, the Vatican had withdrawn behind its walls. Proclaiming himself a hostage of modernity, Pope Pius IX viewed the world through a conspiratorial lens. The beleaguered Church found itself in an existential fight. This situation shaped Catholic attitudes throughout the world, including those in Poland.[86]

Throughout this period of decline, the Church altered its definition of the enemy: it now opposed the perceived *sinner* rather than the *sin*. Priests denounced Freemasonry, anchoring their aggression in the pope's encyclical in which he proposed that the Freemasons were against God and were plotting the

---

other theological views to themselves in an effort to promote true acceptance and friendship. See ibid.

80 While England's lodges accepted Jews, German Freemasonry resisted their inclusion. See Jacob Katz, *Jews and Freemasons in Europe, 1723–1939* (Cambridge, MA: Harvard University Press, 1970), 1–2.
81 The Polish freemasons did not retain a disproportionate number of Jews relative to their percentage in Congress Kingdom's population. See Norman Cohn, *Warrant for Genocide: The Myth of the Jewish World Conspiracy and the Protocols of the Elders of Zion* (London: Serif, 2005), 35.
82 Wandyz, *The Lands of Partitioned Poland*, 85.
83 Ibid., 85.
84 David Kertzer, *The Popes against the Jews: The Vatican's Role in the Rise of Modern Antisemitism* (New York: Vintage Books, 2002), 125.
85 Modras, *The Catholic Church and Antisemitism: Poland, 1933–1939*, 49.
86 Kertzer, *The Popes against the Jews: The Vatican's Role in the Rise of Modern Antisemitism*, 126.

destruction of God's representative on earth.[87] In Polish lands, as elsewhere, this concern translated into a renewed interest in the ahistorical belief that the Masons were revolutionary conspirators.[88]

Church leaders needed to provide the people with a visual image of this modern foe. Yet the Freemasons remained incognito and therefore elusive. This lack of proof undermined the Church's anti-Masonic diatribes. To buttress its attacks, then, the Church advanced a Judeo-Masonic conspiracy theory. Catholic thinkers connected the evil of modernity to those who appeared to benefit the greatest from it: the Jews. Once separating them behind real or metaphorical ghetto walls, modernity had provided Jews with equal rights, job opportunities, and upward social mobility. The Jews were the definitive beneficiaries of modernity—that which threatened to ruin the Church. Thus, the Church labeled the Jews as the true force behind the Freemasons.[89]

The next pope, Leo XIII (who headed the Church from 1878–1903), repeated this conspiracy theory and succeeded in persuading more of the public to believe it.[90] Although Jewish participation in Freemasonry was more or less in proportion to the population, the public believed that Jews controlled the institution.[91]

---

87 Porter-Szűcs, *Faith and Fatherland*, 283. Late nineteenth-century Catholic leaders defended their seemingly radical departure from "love thy neighbor" as no real departure at all. It was merely a reevaluation of the concept. Under siege by modernity, the Church had to respond, putting "love" for the Church before that for Others. The definition of "neighbors" shifted to already ardent Catholics. In order to survive—in order to live out their God-determined role in bringing Christ to the people—Church representatives had to put love of God's mission before love of those perceived to be seeking the Church's destruction, and thereby God's destruction. We see this same spin in mid-1930s Poland when the paper *Mały Dziennik*, a Franciscan-run press based in Niepokalanów, defended Polish antisemitism as love for God and the Polish nation, in that they were saving both from the Jews' destructive forces. See Modras, *The Catholic Church and Antisemitism: Poland, 1933–1939*, 126.

88 Porter-Szucs, *Faith and Fatherland*, 283.

89 After denouncing Freemasons as leaders of modernity's battle against the Church, Pope Pius IX went so far as to add a postscript to his 1864 *Syllabus of Errors*, identifying the Jews as the hand that guides the masons: "It is from them that the synagogue of Satan, which gathers its troops against the Church of Christ, takes its strength." See Kertzer, *The Popes against the Jews: The Vatican's Role in the Rise of Modern Antisemitism*, 127. The Book of Revelation depicts the Jews' places of worship as "synagogues of Satan" (Revelation 2:9 and 3:9).

90 The pope's explicit depiction of personified evil within Freemasonry is an example of the radical departure the Church hierarchy was willing to take from its stance of hate the sin, not the sinner. Kertzer, *The Popes against the Jews: The Vatican's Role in the Rise of Modern Antisemitism*, 127.

91 Cohn, *Warrant for Genocide: The Myth of the Jewish World Conspiracy and the Protocols of the Elders of Zion*, 35.

Aided by popular and prolific traditionalist authors, the Church taught the public that the Jews had caused all harmful social and economic changes.[92] Writers insisted that countries reevaluate their relationships with the Jews: How could a government emancipate its Jews and give them free reign when those very Jews sought to take over the world?

An important question for this investigation into Polish-Jewish relations is whether or not the *Polish* Catholic Church supported this view. Following the Holy See's lead, mid-nineteenth-century Polish Catholic thinkers also argued that the Church's enemy was Freemasonry and, later, that the Jews plotted world domination.[93] The Vatican and Warsaw were united, and the Jews came to represent Freemasonry and its war against God's true Church. Thus, Catholicism effectively joined with the racially based antisemitism spreading rapidly throughout the secular world.[94]

The Catholic Church's Campaign against Modernity, That Is, the Jews

By the last decades of the nineteenth century, the Vatican employed the press as an important tool of persuasion. In so doing, it spread its opinions throughout the world and thereby restored some of its former strength. The pope trusted his communiqué to the Jesuit biweekly *Civiltà cattolica*. Known as the unofficial voice of the pope, *Civiltà*'s journalists believed it their task to defend the pope and to spread his message. Reaching a small, yet influential, eleven thousand subscribers worldwide, its impact proved titanic as Catholic papers throughout the world regularly quoted *Civiltà*'s articles in support of their own written "truth."[95] While popes and their secretaries of state publicly distanced themselves from antisemitic campaigns, *Civiltà cattolica* spread their views and accused the Jew of working toward the Church's destruction.[96]

In presenting the Jews as the cause of all of modernity's vices, *Civiltà cattolica* resurrected the blood libel. Society's fascination at the time with vampires,

---

92 Ibid., 37.
93 Porter-Szűcs, *Faith and Fatherland*, 284. Some Church leaders, including Bishop Leon Wałęga of Tarnów, vocally opposed targeting Freemasonry with hate. Though he recognized the Freemasons as enemies of the Church, he believed the individual needed to be more concerned with his own soul.
94 Ibid., 289.
95 Kertzer, *The Popes against the Jews: The Vatican's Role in the Rise of Modern Antisemitism*, 135.
96 Ibid., 213 and 135.

blood, and violence allowed the paper to revive the old falsehood that Judaism requires Christian blood in several of its ritual ceremonies and that, therefore, Jews capture, torture, and mutilate Christian children in order to drain their blood for ritual purposes.[97] Over time, communities accepted Passover as the dominant motivation, believing erroneously that Jews used Christian blood in the baking of matzah—the unleavened bread traditionally eaten during the holiday.[98] But often no motivation was tied to the blood libel trial, only the accepted "knowledge" that Jews murdered Christians, that Jews were dangerous. Over the centuries Jewish communities throughout Europe were falsely charged with murder when a Christian was found dead or a Christian child went missing.[99] First recorded in Norwich, England, 1144, this accusation followed the Jews as they migrated East from twelfth-century England and thirteenth-century German lands.[100]

The Vatican's interest in the blood libel has waxed and waned over the centuries. Several popes condemned it as an outrageous lie.[101] In 1759, Cardinal

---

97 Joshua Trachtenberg, *The Devil and the Jews: The Medieval Conception of the Jew and Its Relation to Modern Antisemitism* (Cleveland: Meridian Books and the Jewish Publication Society of America, 1961), 126. The earliest known charge of ritual murder against the Jews dates to the pre-Christian writer Democritus, who charged Jews with sacrificing a stranger every seven years in the Temple in Jerusalem and cutting the flesh into small pieces. Restructured over time, the legend resurfaced as a supposed reason Antiochus Epiphanes gave for pillaging the Temple. In the ancient world other peoples were also charged with ritual murder. In fact, Christians were vilified by pagans for sacrificing infants. The blood libel accusation reappeared in the Middle Ages and held Christianity's interest well into the twentieth century.
98 At the close of the nineteenth century, people also falsely believed that Jewish law demanded Christian blood as an ingredient in wine blessed to sanctify a wedding, and in a salve applied to heal circumcisions. In some centuries there even arose the notion that Jews ate the body parts of slain Christian children, including the heart, liver, lips, and ears. Tractenberg, *The Devil and the Jews: The Medieval Conception of the Jew and Its Relation to Modern Antisemitism*, 134; Charlotte Klein, "Damascus to Kiev: *Civiltà Cattolica* on Ritual Murder," in *The Blood Libel Legend: A Casebook in Antisemitic Folklore*, ed. Alan Dundes (Madison: The University of Wisconsin Press, 1991), 186–187.
99 Kertzer, *The Popes against the Jews: The Vatican's Role in the Rise of Modern Antisemitism*, 14. Human blood itself held significant meaning in both the ancient and medieval worlds as an important element for medicinal and magical purposes. While witches were believed to use blood to "write the compact with the devil," doctors used it, together with a long list of other body parts, to cure illnesses. See Tractenberg, *The Devil and the Jews: The Medieval Conception of the Jew and Its Relation to Modern Antisemitism*, 140–141.
100 Modras, *The Catholic Church and Antisemitism: Poland, 1933–1939*, 194,
101 Innocent IV (1247) issued the earliest pronouncement forbidding Church leaders from promoting this allegation, under punishment of suspension from office and excommunication. Gregory X (1272), Martin V (1422), and Nicholas V (1447), also refuted charges that Jews

Lorenzo Ganganelli, who would become Pope Clement VI in 1769, produced a key written refutation of the blood libel.[102] Later, however, some priests rebelled against such papal positions. Instead, they encouraged long-held fears of the Jewish people in sermons and writings. In 1881, the Greek Orthodox Church charged Jews with ritual murder in both Egypt and Crete.[103] In 1882, similar allegations against the Jews emerged from Tisza-Eszlar, Hungary.[104]

Within this larger context, Pope Leo XIII—head of the Church from 1878–1903—took advantage of growing antisemitism. Choosing not to refute the indictments against the Jews, he invented and advanced even more charges. He was fighting the battle of his life against secularism, against modernity, and against the Jews. In December 1881, *Civiltà* began a forty-month-long campaign against the Jews during which it published thirty highly inflammatory antisemitic articles. One "authority"[105] ordered his readers not to be misled by the foundational Christian tenet of "love thy neighbor." Christian love should not blind Church followers to the "sad fact of the evil the Jews do, nor prevent us from taking the actions needed to save the Church and Christian society from them."[106]

After "educating" its audience about the Jews' need for Christian blood, in May 1882 *Civiltà* repeated a forty-year-old story to support its theory that the Jew was the devil incarnate. In raising the 1840 Damascus blood libel accusation, the Catholic press deepened fear and hatred of the Jews; and worldwide

---

needed and used human body elements in their ritual practice. See Modras, *The Catholic Church and Antisemitism: Poland, 1933–1939*, 195; Tractenberg, *The Devil and the Jews: The Medieval Conception of the Jew and Its Relation to Modern Antisemitism*, 134.

102 Klein, "Damascus to Kiev: *Civiltà Cattolica* on Ritual Murder," 180.
103 Jacob M. Landau, "Ritual Murder Accusations in Nineteenth-Century Egypt," in Dundes, *The Blood Libel Legend: A Casebook in Antisemitic Folklore*, 199–202.
104 Lindemann, *The Jew Accused*, 42–43.
105 Father Giuseppe Oreglia di Santo Stefano, one of *Civiltà's* founders.
106 Kertzer, *The Popes against the Jews: The Vatican's Role in the Rise of Modern Antisemitism*, 138. In October, *Civiltà's* campaign shifted into demonstrating the Jewish ritual need for Christian blood. *Civiltà's* "proof" lay in the "fact" that neither Pope Innocent IV in 1247, nor Cardinal Ganganelli in 1759 were privy to important, supposedly damning, evidence against the Jews. These earlier pontiffs had claimed the Jews were innocent because there did not exist any support within Jewish law declaring the ritual need for Christian blood. However, according to *Civiltà cattolica*, the reason Catholic leaders could not locate the decree was because "the law was secret and had nothing to do with the original religion of Israel but was rooted in the Talmudic tradition." See Klein, "Damascus to Kiev: *Civiltà Cattolica* on Ritual Murder," 183–184.

Jewish protests simply proved the point that the accused were united in a conspiracy to control nations.[107]

In that 1840 case, eight Jews had been imprisoned in a Damascus jail on charges of ritual murder. After several of the prisoners died, there was widespread Jewish protest. Two renowned Jews, England's Sir Moses Montefiore and France's Isaac Adolphe Crémiux, had travelled to Cairo and to Damascus where together they successfully lobbied numerous consuls to pressure Mehemet Ali to release the remaining prisoners and exonerate them.[108] Though not the first blood libel charge of the nineteenth century, the Damascus affair gained the most notoriety as it demonstrated Jews' new position in society.[109] Not only had they attained economic and political power, they also "exploited" that power to benefit Jews worldwide.

Modernity had welcomed the Jew into its respective societies as faithful patriots. With the Damascus affair, the Church challenged this liberal position. French Jews' actions on behalf of Damascus Jews directly countered France's political interests in the region.[110] This reality proved to many that one's religious affiliation affected one's patriotism. The Damascus affair played Jew against state, with the host nation (this time France) losing to worldwide Jewish solidarity. It opened the door to recognizing the existence of world Jewry, which both French and English Jews cemented by forming organizations to continue fighting for Jewish honor and access to civil emancipation around the globe.

Civiltà refused to accept the Jewish leaders' procurement of innocence for the accused in Damascus. According to the publication, Jewish influence had shown its strength in 1840: "Montefiore had succeeded in bribing Mehemet Ali with Rothschild's gold, so that the truth of the affair should not become known."[111] In resurrecting the Damascus affair for the public in 1882, *Civiltà* reminded people that, by offering Jews equality, traditional state authority would continue to be overrun by Jewish interests. Antisemites recognized in Jewish solidarity a

---

107 In 1840, the authorities blamed the Jews of Damascus for murdering an Italian Capuchin friar, Father Tomaso, and his servant. Although the victims' bodies were never found, Syrian officials believed this to be a case of Jewish ritual murder. After exacting confessions through brutal torture or the fear of it, the authorities arrested a Jewish barber and seven leaders of the Jewish community. See ibid., 187.
108 Ibid., 187–188.
109 Lindemann, *The Jew Accused*, 35.
110 Ibid., 36.
111 Klein, "Damascus to Kiev: *Civiltà Cattolica* on Ritual Murder," 188.

growing enemy. Though the Jews denied such allegations, their actions in 1840 underscored Christians' fear of the social, economic, and political rise of the Other.

Myth Reconstruction

On Christmas day 1881, a pogrom erupted in Warsaw. By that December, Poles had succumbed to economic, social, and religious angst. The Great Depression (now known as the Long Depression), rural migration to the cities, and Catholicism under siege, generated poverty and fear. Polish traditionalists blamed the Jews—the representatives of modernity and builders of the city. On Christmas day of that year, Polish Catholics filled Holy Cross Church to capacity. Panic broke out to shouts of "Fire!" In the frenzy to escape, more than twenty people were trampled to death. Rumors quickly spread that Jewish pickpockets had planted a fake explosive in order to cause chaos and rob those fleeing the church. Poles expressed their fury by beating Jews and plundering their homes and shops.[112]

This pogrom horrified positivists and integrationists; they still clung to their dream of unity. They had believed their fellow Poles, especially in Warsaw, to be immune to such barbarity. Leading Polish intellectual Eliza Orzeszkowa wrote, "I feel unlimited shame . . . burning regret . . . that the efforts of enlightened minds . . . have fallen victim to the rekindled flames of hatred."[113] Speaking as the editor of *Izraelita*, the integrationist Samuel Peltyn implored Jews to persevere in their affection for Poland despite such difficult circumstances:

> Can we, veterans of adversity and most experienced masters of the art of perseverance, apply the principle: my country is only where we are happy? No! A thousand times no! Our country is the land where we were born and have grown up, our nation is the one in which we live, the one we wanted to become a part of in better times. And whatever happens, let it come, let volcanoes erupt here and there out of the womb of this earth, let the scum of this nation in moments of madness act with hostility

---

112 Michael Ochs, "Tsarist Officialdom and Anti-Jewish Pogroms in Poland," in *Pogroms: Anti-Jewish Violence in Modern Russian History*, ed. John D. Klier and Shlomo Lambroza (Cambridge: Cambridge University Press, 1992), 181.
113 Cited in Polonsky, *The Jews in Poland and Russia*, 2:88.

> against us—we have no right in such moments to be disloyal to this land, to this nation, and to ourselves. To renounce unity with this nation in order to look for a place that exists only in dreams would be a thoughtless act and it would bring not positive but only negative results.[114]

While pogromists caused considerable material damage, the moral damage completely overwhelmed both Poles and Jews.[115] For the former, it now appeared that they could no longer claim superiority to the Ukrainians who had carried out pogroms earlier that summer.

To save face, some Poles and Jews claimed that the Russian authorities had instigated the violence. They portrayed it as a continuation of Russia's policy of dividing the two groups, enforced since the 1863 Polish-Jewish Uprising against Russian rule. Others believed that Russia ordered it to redirect the world's attention away from Russia's own horrendous pogroms.[116] Poles readily adopted this position in order to assert their innocence.

Contemporary scholars challenge this myth, insisting on reconstructing it based on previously unpublished archival documents. They portray Poles themselves as the catalyst for the pogrom, suggesting that Tsar Alexander III (who reigned from 1881–1894) sought to prevent violence in both Russia and the Kingdom of Poland. The Russian authorities feared street violence—any popular mob violence—lest it morph into acts against the government itself. At a time when political terrorists were planting bombs in the streets, the tsar yearned for stability.[117] As such, the governor general of Warsaw inundated his governors with demands to hinder outbreaks of public disorder.[118] If a low-level Russian official encouraged anti-Jewish activity, they would suffer the consequences if discovered.[119]

---

114 Samuel Peltyn, *Izraelita*, no. 14 (April 2, 1882), cited in Polonsky, *The Jews in Poland and Russia*, 2:89.
115 Weeks, *From Assimilation to Antisemitism*, 80.
116 Ochs, "Tsarist Officialdom and Anti-Jewish Pogroms in Poland," 165 and 182.
117 I. Michael Aronson, "The Anti-Jewish pogroms in Russia in 1881," in Klier and Lambroza, *Pogroms: Anti-Jewish Violence in Modern Russian History*, 51.
118 Ochs, "Tsarist Officialdom and Anti-Jewish Pogroms in Poland," 167.
119 Ibid., 176 and 179.

The Polish people had grown weary of their economic and political impotence.[120] Three pogroms between 1881 and 1882 expressed their outrage.[121] The peasantry experienced little benefit from their emancipation. Forced to move to the city to find work, they could not create economically stable family lives; and the growing belief that Jews treated them unjustly added to the widespread simmering resentment. The pope's presentation through the Catholic press of the Jews as the Church's main enemy only encouraged this feeling. That those acting out against the urban Jewish community were very low wage earners, that pogroms took place usually during Christian rituals or festivals, and that such violence often occurred after some minor economic conflict between Jew and Christian points to the specific Polish economic and religious determinants of these atrocities.[122]

In May 1882, while *Civiltà* once again returned to the 1840 Damascus affair, the Catholic press not only accused the Jews of being evil, but also asked whether they could be Polish patriots at all. *Civiltà* had reminded its readers that French Jewry's support of Jews in nineteenth-century Damascus conflicted with French policies concerning the region. Poles naturally wondered if in an imagined future conflict, Polish Jews would side with their country or with world Jewry. Poles believed—and with reason—that the Jewish population was more concerned with its fellow Jews than with its Polish neighbors. Jews often acted as a group out of communal self-interest. Of course, many examples exist of Jews contributing to the welfare of the Polish people militarily, economically, and culturally. Indeed, less than three decades before, Poles and Jews had shared a mutual respect and brotherhood. But out of the hundreds of thousands of mainstream and Hasidic Jews living in the Kingdom of Poland, the great majority focused on the welfare of their families and the Jewish community.

We have seen that desperation often breeds irrationality. The Catholic Church and international political activists anchored themselves to antisemitic conspiracy theories to explain economic, political, social, and religious upheaval. Many Poles experiencing financial and social crises also succumbed to blaming Jewish success for their problems. By 1890, positivism was dying. The lack of

---

120 Artur Markowski, "Anti-Jewish Pogroms in the Kingdom of Poland" (manuscript version), 33.
121 Warsaw—1829; Kalisz—1878; Balwierzyszki—November 1881; Warsaw—December 1881; Iłowa—April 1882; Gąbin—April 1882; Podlasie—spring 1882; Preny—August 1882; and Częstochowa—autumn 1902. See ibid., 7–11.
122 Ibid., 16.

meaningful and measurable movement toward integration by mainstream Jewry convinced most positivists that their struggle to improve Polish-Jewish relations had been in vain. While an impressive number of Mitnaggedim and Hasidim had yearned to leave their traditionally restrictive Jewish lifestyles, they had dismissed the positivists' roadmap.

CHAPTER 8

Migration and Nationalism

By the 1880s, additional external political, economic, and social developments had compounded the positivists' evaporating hopes of the Jews' integration into Polish society. Already rising political antisemitism was given further impetus when Russian Jews (known as Litvaks) migrated to Congress Kingdom. A main consequence of this influx was the growing fear that Jews posed a serious threat to the kingdom's future. As we shall discover in this chapter, the Poles' antisemitism, and the Litvak's antipolonism left little room for improving Polish-Jewish relations.

Litvak Migration: Round One

Russian Jewish migration into the Kingdom of Poland began in 1868 after Russia permitted Jews not only freedom of movement between the Pale of Settlement and Congress Kingdom, but also the ability to reside in either locale.[1] This measure proved monumental. Until this point, the general population living in Russia had been prohibited from settling outside it. Russian Jews, specifically, had been restricted to the Pale of Jewish Settlement. By opening the border in 1868, the Russian tsar permitted Jews from the Pale to migrate to the Kingdom of Poland. Both Jews and Poles alike, residing in Congress Kingdom, reacted negatively to this development. They referred derogatorily to these Russian Jews as "Litvaks" because they came from the kresy, formerly part of the Grand Duchy of Lithuania, also known as Litva.[2] (Lithuanian Jews themselves adopted this terminology.)

Those first few Litvaks seeking residency in Poland in 1868 did so mainly for economic advancement. Primarily distributors of Polish industrial goods

---

1   Blejwas, "Polish Positivism and the Jews," 25–26.
2   Corrsin, "Aspects of Population Change and of Acculturation in Jewish Warsaw at the End of the Nineteenth Century: The Censuses of 1882 and 1897," 218.

eastward through the Russian Empire, they settled typically in either Warsaw or Łódź.³ The nascent Christian petite bourgeoisie, the displaced unemployed szlachta, and the urbanizing peasantry looked on these Jewish migrants with disdain. True, Litvak economic activity spurred industrial growth. Yet, at the same time, Russian Jewish migrants commonly received the higher paying jobs due to their Russian language skills, which enabled them to travel and sell goods throughout the empire. Banks and insurance companies also preferred to hire Litvaks due to their linguistic ability.⁴

At this time, only a small wave of Jews crossed borders. This lack of Jewish movement might be surprising given that the tsar emancipated Jews in the kingdom in 1862, while he retained restrictive laws against Jews in the Pale of Jewish Settlement. Classic migratory impediments held many in place: fear, family responsibilities, and religious commitment. Beyond these obstacles also lay the belief that life for Jews in the Pale had been improving since Alexander II's Great Reforms of 1855.⁵ The tsar's liberal policy, known as selective integration, looked very much like legal emancipation in all but name. A policy of gradual reform, the government acknowledged it could take generations. Russian Maskilim and the elite Russian Jewish mercantile class recognized that the government had already done the implausible by abolishing serfdom in 1861.⁶ They believed the Jews' emancipation would be next.⁷

By 1861, selective integration enticed Jews in the Pale to leave their traditional education behind, promising all Jewish university graduates the same privileges received by Christians. It underscored the right to unrestricted residence and the ability to choose any occupation.⁸ Jewish leaders, including clergy, pleaded with both the Jewish youth and their parents to grab hold of Russian secular schooling as their "salvation."⁹ The Jewish youth responded en masse, flocking to

---

3   Francois Guesnet, "Migration and Stereotype: The Case of Russian Jews in the Polish Kingdom at the End of the Nineteenth Century," *CAH. MONDE RUSSE* 41, no. 4 (October–December 2000): 509.
4   Ibid.: 510.
5   The tsar implemented this policy of gradual reform with the serf population as well, whose place in society the Romanovs sought to change, slowly. See Benjamin Nathans, *Beyond the Pale: The Jewish Encounter with Late Imperial Russia* (Berkeley: University of California Press, 2002), 48–49.
6   I prefer the term *secularizing* because this was a process for the Jews who took part in it.
7   Cited in Benjamin Nathans, *Beyond the Pale: The Jewish Encounter with Late Imperial Russia*, 52.
8   Ibid., 215.
9   Ibid., 216.

Russian education, which at this point did not exhibit the anti-Jewish prejudice that dominated Central European educational institutions.

Litvak Migration: Round Two

This trajectory for Russia's Jews changed markedly on March 13, 1881, when members of the terrorist group the People's Will (Narodnaya Volya) assassinated Tsar Alexander II.[10] Roughly six weeks later, on April 15, 1881, anti-Jewish mob violence erupted in Elisavetgrad, Kherson Province, spreading in fits and spasms over the following three years throughout the Pale's southwestern Jewish communities.[11]

The Russian government endorsed the popular charge that the pogroms expressed the people's anger against the Jews' economic exploitation of the peasantry. Liberals concerned with protecting the newly emancipated peasants rallied around this explanation.[12] Alexander III followed advice from his Judophobic new minister of the interior, Nikolay P. Ignatiev (1832–1908), to limit the Jews' economic power over the peasantry. In essence, the new governing authorities blamed the victims of violence for the violence. In 1882, he restricted Jewish-peasant interaction by introducing the so-called temporary

---

10 This date is based on the new calendar. The old Russian calendar date is March 1.
11 Historians have presented various theories regarding what prompted this pogrom surge. Generations of Jewish scholars have blamed Russian officialdom for sponsoring it—or at least for tolerating it as deflection from public anger and frustration with the Romanovs' slowing pace of reform. However, relatively new research contends that St. Petersburg did not seek to use the Jews as a scapegoat for societal problems. This new theory proposes that the pogroms actually erupted spontaneously, due to the centrifugal forces swirling within Russian society. The industrial depression burying Moscow and St. Petersburg prompted the new urban proletariat to head westward into the Pale in search of work. Unfortunately, they found little opportunity. Regional issues, such as crop failures and the ensuing near famine conditions, created pent-up popular frustration. That the Ukrainian peasantry resented the Jews' economic power over them added to the mix of despair, fear, and hunger. According to this theory, violence erupted not at the tsar's instigation, but despite his efforts to thwart it. Its vicious force often proved difficult to control, as the Russian police department had few men, and those that it did have were inadequately trained and lacking discipline. See John D. Klier, Shlomo Lambroza, "The Pogroms of 1881–1884," in Klier and Lambroza, *Pogroms: Anti-Jewish Violence in Modern Russian History*, 39–40; Aronson, "The Anti-Jewish Pogroms in Russia in 1881," 51–52; John D. Klier, "The Pogrom Paradigm in Russian History," in Klier and Lambroza, *Pogroms: Anti-Jewish Violence in Modern Russian History*, 20.
12 John D. Klier, "The Pogrom Paradigm in Russian History," 20.

May Laws.¹³ Further limiting Jewish settlement *to rural areas within the Pale*,¹⁴ the May Laws proved disastrous for Jewish economic life by limiting the workweek to five days.¹⁵ Thus, as the Jewish population increased over time, the territorial space available to it shrank. Overcrowding resulted in fierce competition for job opportunities between not only Jews, but also among Jews and Christian arrivals in the Pale searching for economic possibilities.

The May Laws coupled with the 1881–1883 pogrom wave heightened Jewish anxiety and forced young Russian Jews to reassess their status. Many progressive Jews who had previously believed they would be experiencing Russian Jewish emancipation in "this lifetime," radically shifted their views. Influenced in the universities by left-wing Russian student activists advancing cutting-edge political and economic theories, such as socialism, communism, and nationalism, they began to develop an array of new responses to the Jews' impoverishment and lack of civil rights.¹⁶ Zionism, the political ideology that Jews are a nation and should return to live in their biblical homeland of Zion, then called Palestine, gained an audience. Hebrew writer Moses Leib Lilienblum (1843–1910) pressed Russian Jews to change their direction:

> The pogroms taught me their lesson ... I became convinced that it was not lack of high culture that was the cause of our tragedy, but that we are aliens. We will still remain aliens when we are fully stuffed with education as a pomegranate is full of seeds.... We are aliens everywhere. We have to return home.¹⁷

Lilienblum spoke of returning to Zion.

Concurrently, however, wealthy Jewish merchants and bankers argued that poverty and population growth prevented most Jews from escaping the Pale. Although most Jews remained in Russia proper, hundreds of thousands searched for better living conditions in Hungary, Germany, Palestine, and North America. They also surged into the Kingdom of Poland, where the May Laws had not been enforced. This westward movement further provoked negative relations between Jews and Christians in the rest of Europe, in America, and in the Kingdom of Poland. Coinciding with the economic depression in Europe

---

13 John D. Klier and Shlomo Lambroza, "The Pogroms of 1881–1884," 40.
14 Nathans, *Beyond the Pale: The Jewish Encounter with Late Imperial Russia*, 323–324.
15 Weeks, *From Assimilation to Antisemitism*, 88.
16 Ibid., 244, and 252–253.
17 Cited in Polonsky, *The Jews in Poland and Russia*, 2:18.

and the United States, this 1880s population influx intensified Jewish-Gentile economic, social, cultural, and political tensions in the lands Jewish throngs entered.[18]

Reasons Poles and Jews Despised the Litvak Migration

Poles in the kingdom grew particularly wary of this second Litvak incursion. These foreigners insulted them by rarely trying to learn Polish. Due to the intensifying deployment of antisemitic tropes by both political actors and the Church in Rome, some Poles feared the Russian government had sent these Jews to destabilize the Kingdom of Poland.[19] Knowing that Jews (and Poles) had helped the Russians during both Polish insurrections, and that Polish Maskilim supported Russian rule, the idea that once again Jews were working for the Russian authority was incorrect... but not implausible.[20]

Russian Jews migrating to the kingdom in 1882–1889 formed a multidimensional group. Their numbers included intellectuals and laborers, secularists and traditionalists, the political and apolitical. They spoke Yiddish, Hebrew, or Russian, but rarely Polish.[21] Hebrew gave voice to integrationists, and Russian to secularists. Yiddish speakers made up a more complicated demographic. Poor religious Jews spoke Yiddish; Russian Jewish intellectuals and political activists advocated Yiddish as a tool to reach the general impoverished Jewish population.[22]

Litvaks created a completely separate community from native Jews, building their own synagogues, cultural organizations, and schools. Those Litvaks who had chased selective integration chose to employ Russian as the language for their schools' secular education.[23] They had spent years learning how to accommodate Russian culture into their lives. And although they moved into the Kingdom of Poland, where laws were less hostile to Jews, they retained their love and use of Russian. Litvaks looked down on Polish Jews. They challenged

---

18   Lindemann, *The Jew Accused*, 28–29.
19   Corrsin, "Aspects of Population Change and of Acculturation in Jewish Warsaw at the End of the Nineteenth Century," 223.
20   Blejwas, "Polish Positivism and the Jews," 26.
21   Corrsin, "Aspects of Population Change and of Acculturation in Jewish Warsaw at the End of the Nineteenth Century," 223.
22   Ibid., 222.
23   Piotr Wróbel, "Jewish Warsaw before the First World War," in Bartoszewski and Polonsky, *The Jews in Warsaw*, 253.

native Jews economically, politically, culturally, and religiously. According to the 1897 census, Russian Jews made up one sixth of the kingdom's Jewish population.[24] There is no doubt that by 1890 the kingdom's integrationists felt threatened by the steady growth of Litvak migration and its corresponding new Jewish politics.[25]

Contrasts between the lives of different cultural demographics drove the divide between Polish and Russian secular Jewish populations. Because there existed a very clear majority culture in Congress Kingdom, native Jews searching for a way out of Jewish traditional separatism naturally adopted it. They had little need to formulate experimental expressions for modern Jewish political life. Integration was their route into the new age.

Unlike the Kingdom of Poland, and despite its name, the Pale of Jewish Settlement did not host a culturally dominant group. Poles, Lithuanians, and Ukrainians living in the Pale developed their own respective national consciousnesses.[26] Instead of one dominant national voice, the Pale nurtured a collection of nation-specific groups. Without a clear path into modernity, but influenced by the politics of nationalism, kresy Jews yearning to escape traditionalism (and who had been discouraged by Russian policy and violence) constructed their own road. In person and in print, Russian Jewish thinkers who migrated to the Kingdom of Poland popularized the hot topics of Jewish nationalism, socialism, and various political combinations of the two.

The Dreyfus Affair and Antisemitism

Concurrent with the issues stemming from the Litvak migration, the Kingdom of Poland found itself once again debating "the rise of the Jews" due to the much publicized 1894 arrest of France's Captain Alfred Dreyfus. A Jew in the higher ranks of the French military, Dreyfus was charged with spying for Germany.[27]

---

24   Ibid., 513.
25   Guesnet, "Migration and Stereotype: The Case of Russian Jews in the Polish Kingdom at the End of the Nineteenth Century": 511.
26   Polonsky, *The Jews in Poland and Russia*, 2:22.
27   Throughout the proceedings Dreyfus adamantly denied working with the Germans against France. Despite the discovery of the actual traitor one year after Dreyfus had been court-martialed and sentenced to life (in isolation on Devil's Island), he remained a political prisoner off the coast of French Guiana for another four years. It took the French general staff a total of twelve years to exonerate Dreyfus. See Nicholas Halasz, introduction to Alfred Dreyfus, *Five Years of My Life: The Diary of Captain Alfred Dreyfus* (New York: Peebles Press, 1977).

French antisemitic writer Édouard Drumont recognized in Dreyfus a living proof of the secret "Jewish Syndicate" plot to take over France. In fact, it was Drumont's antisemitic newspaper *La Libre Parole* which first publicly declared Dreyfus a traitor to France. His accusation touched off an anti-Jewish frenzy in the press and country.[28]

Up until this juncture, France's populace seemed only moderately invested in promoting antisemitism, when compared with other countries, such as Germany and Russia. However, the trials and continuous press coverage attached to the Dreyfus affair provided antisemitic thinkers with increased notoriety. Monarchist traditionalists asserted that French republicanism had sacrificed the nation's security by allowing a Jew to reach such a position in the military. Throughout France, traditionalists rioted against liberalism by screaming, "Death to the Jews!" They desecrated synagogues, ransacked Jewish shops, and attacked Jews on the streets. They even launched anti-Jewish boycotts, hoping to squelch Jewish business competition.[29] At the same time, Dreyfusards—those rallying to defend the Jewish captain—were often non-Jews. Emille Zola, France's most famous contemporary writer, defended Dreyfus in his "J'Accuse!" There, he blamed ministers of war, prominent members of the general staff, and judges of having conspired to convict an innocent man through false evidence and an illegal trial.[30]

Newspapers worldwide reported on the Dreyfus affair. In the Kingdom of Poland, both left-wing integrationists and right-wing conservatives responded to France's scrimmage over Captain Dreyfus's contested guilt. The liberal Polish *Kurjer Warszawski*, with a daily run of twenty-five thousand by 1896, printed extensive reports from Paris about the trial, and sided with the Dreyfusards by presenting the captain as innocent. On the other hand, the Catholic National Democrats' antisemitic press, including papers like *Przegląd Katolicki*, *Rola*, and *Dziennik Dla Wszystkich*, whose circulations were much smaller than liberal publications, typically accepted anti-Dreyfusard arguments at face value.[31] While both socialism and antisemitism had gained only marginal acceptance before the Dreyfus affair, this international debate brought attention to nationalist papers, broadened their readership, and strengthened their positions.[32]

---

28   Ibid., 16.
29   Lindemann, *The Jew Accused*, 116.
30   Ibid., 114.
31   Antony Polonsky, "The Dreyfus Affair and Polish-Jewish Interaction, 1890–1914," in *Jewish History* 11, no. 2 (Fall 1997): 27.
32   Ibid.

Jewish Nationalism Gains Ground in the Kingdom of Poland

Within the kingdom's Jewish population significant conflicts erupted over how to interpret the ramifications from the Dreyfus affair with regard to Jewish-Christian relations. In the weekly *Izraelita*, Jewish integrationists defended not only Dreyfus, but also Jewish assimilation into the larger host society. They argued that through assimilation non-Jewish French Dreyfusards were ridding France of antisemitism.[33] The Yiddish press, which had far greater access to the masses than did *Izraelita*, countered that the affair demonstrated a need in Poland for Jews to take action against antisemitism. It would not be enough to have Others (as in France) fight these battles for Polish Jews. Jews would have to stand up and fight for themselves. Believing in Dreyfus' innocence, and angered by his long imprisonment, Yiddish authors moved ever further from accepting assimilation as a way into Polish society. Instead, they gravitated more dogmatically to themes of Jewish nationalism, be it through Zionism or socialism.[34]

There is no doubt that by the time of the Dreyfus trial, Litvak migration and its new Jewish politics hindered the kingdom's positivists and integrationists. Through grassroots activism, Jewish nationalism had gained ground in the Kingdom of Poland. Leon Pinsker's (1821–1891) 1892 pamphlet "Auto-Emancipation" had appealed to the kingdom's Jews with its modern *Zionist* ideal.[35] Just as it had helped to revolutionize Jews' thinking in the Pale of Settlement, so too did it spur Jews in the kingdom to reassess their approach to Jewish identity, national belonging, and antisemitism. A watershed moment, the Russian pogroms and the government's reactionism had galvanized Jewish secularists to turn inward for solutions to the Jewish problem. In "Auto-Emancipation," Pinsker urged Russian Jews to no longer accept the "degrading dependence of the ever alien Jew upon the non-Jew."[36] Pinsker called for Russian Jews to stop waiting for either an authority or the Messiah to emancipate them. He argued that Jews must emancipate themselves, not only by regenerating a national consciousness, but also by returning to independent territorialism. Soon thereafter,

---

33 Ibid.
34 Ibid.
35 Formerly committed to Alexander II's Great Reforms, Leon Pinsker shifted his thinking due to the pogrom waves following the tsar's assassination and "polite" society's blaming the Jews for the fire that consumed them.
36 Leon Pinsker, "Auto-Emancipation," Jewish Virtual Library, accessed July 15, 2021, https://www.jewishvirtuallibrary.org/quot-auto-emancipation-quot-leon-pinsker.

more than one hundred Jewish societies in the Pale joined Love of Zion (Ḥibat Tsiyon), an early *Zionist* organization, established by Perets Smolenskin, Eliezer Perlmann (later Ben-Yehudah) and Moses Leib Lilienblum.[37]

The second wave of Litvak migration had secured a following for Zionism by bringing Ḥibat Tsiyon to the kingdom's Jews. In Congress Kingdom, the *Zionist* message filtered through the joint leadership of Israel Jasinowski (1842–1917), a Litvak from the northwestern province of Grodno, and Yitzhak Grünbaum (1879–1970), a Warsaw journalist born in the Kingdom of Poland. The kingdom's Ḥibat Tsiyon iteration mirrored its parent organization by sending "preachers" out to synagogues in towns and villages. Speaking the people's language, Yiddish, these preachers linked nationalist messages to Torah. By strategically embracing the Yiddish language, Ḥibat Tsiyon "preachers" began the process of converting Jews in the Kingdom of Poland away from status quo traditionalism and toward a Jewish national consciousness.[38]

The *Zionist* movement also gained popularity in the kingdom with Theodore Herzl's 1897 First *Zionist* Congress, followed by the first, and clandestine, All-Russian *Zionist* Conference in Warsaw in August 1898. By 1899, the Warsaw and Łodz *Zionist* groups each boasted about fifty subordinate societies, with an organization-wide membership in the Kingdom of Poland totaling between four thousand and five thousand people. Though still small in number, compared with the Pale's close to seventy thousand membership,[39] *Zionists* in Congress Kingdom challenged the Jewish establishment by running for office on both communal boards and religious councils previously ruled by assimilationists.[40]

By 1900, Warsaw had become a center of *Zionist* activity due to the second wave of Litvak migration, which brought its political appetite and aptitude to the kingdom's Jews.[41] Litvak influence helped to cultivate Jewish national

---

37 Helena Stanislawki, "Ḥibat Tsiyon," Yivo Encyclopedia of Jews in Eastern Europe, accessed January 10, 2023, https://yivoencyclopedia.org/article.aspx/hibat_tsiyon.
38 In order to convert the masses of Jews away from their traditional acceptance of the Jewish lot, Ḥibat Tsiyon adapted the traveling traditional preacher to their own needs. While not as popular in the Kingdom of Poland as in Russia proper, due to the kingdom's large Hassidic population and relatively large number of Jewish integrationists, its proto-*Zionist* vision did take root in the Kingdom of Poland with the help of these preachers. Lecture and follow-up discussion with Joshua Karlip, "The Emergence of Modern Yiddish Culture," YIVO Summer Program, July, 2001.
39 Polonsky, *The Jews in Poland and Russia*, 2:27.
40 Ibid., 99.
41 Ezra Mendelsohn, *Zionism in Poland: The Formative Years, 1915–1926* (New Haven: Yale University Press, 1981), 34.

consciousness in the Kingdom of Poland through not only political pamphlets written in Yiddish, but also through the development of the Jewish nationalist press. This medium included the Yiddish weekly *The Jew* (*Der Yid* [Kraków/Warsaw, 1899–1903]) and the Yiddish daily *The Friend* (*Der Fraynd* [St. Petersburg/Warsaw, 1903–1913]).[42] In fact, until WWI "the most influential Yiddish cultural institution was the daily newspaper."[43] As such, journalists like the *Zionist* leader Yitzhak Grünbaum (in *Der Fraynd*) gained tremendous influence within Polish (and Russian) Jewry.

The Yiddish press gained greater influence following Russia's 1905 October Manifesto when the tsar eased censorship restrictions.[44] Five Yiddish newspapers were published in 1906 Warsaw. *Today* (*Haynt*—which was renamed in 1908 from *Jewish Daily* [*Yidishes tageblat*]) became the premier Yiddish paper. Its founder and publisher, Samuel Jacob Jackan (1874–1936), was a *Zionist*. Setting circulation records for a Yiddish daily at 150,000 in 1913, *Haynt* reflected and disseminated the *Zionist* views of its publisher.[45]

According to the Jewish historian Simon Dubnow (1860–1941), "the strength of the movement lay, not in the political aims of the organization which were mostly beyond reach but in the very fact that tens of thousands of Jews were organized with a national end in view."[46] Knowing it would take years to reach their goal of meaningful *aliyah*—immigration to Palestine—*Zionists* focused on educating their members in the history of anti-Jewish violence through a lens of Jewish powerlessness, reviving Hebrew as a modern language, and teaching farming methods.

The new mass politics attracted young Jews who renounced integrationist ideology, but who also desired separation from the stifling traditional Jewish lifestyle. Prior to the second Litvak wave, Jews in the kingdom escaping traditionalism had basically one path: integration into Polish society. Both positivists and integrationists grew alarmed with this new alternative. If Jews perceived themselves as their own nation, why would they want to merge with the Polish nation? And why would Poles want them? Jewish nationalism threw integrationists and positivists under the bus.

---

42 David E. Fishman, *The Rise of Modern Yiddish Culture* (Pittsburgh: University of Pittsburgh Press, 2005),12.
43 Ibid., 13.
44 Polonsky, *The Jews in Poland and Russia*, 2:103–104.
45 Ibid., 2:104–105.
46 Simon Dubnow, *History of the Jews in Russia and Poland*, vol. 3, trans. Friedlaender (Philadelphia: The Jewish Publication Society of America, 1920), 46.

Zionists believed that they were acting assertively, taking the people's future into their own hands. From a Polish perspective, however, Zionism only further encouraged alienation. Until Zionism's development, political antisemitism in the kingdom had remained on the fringe. With Zionism's spread in the Polish kingdom, however, Poles grew ever more anxious of Jews, allowing antisemitism into the mainstream.[47]

National Socialism: Jews and Poles

In the last quarter of the nineteenth century, Russian and Polish youth became viscerally aware of the travails of the working class. Jewish secularizing youth joined efforts to combat economic and social disparities. Poverty linked Jew to non-Jew, and many young Jews led the fight for the proletariat.

In 1890, secularized Russian-educated Jews organized themselves in the kresy's urban center of Vilna. The Jewish Social Democratic Group in Russia—also known as the Vilna Group—originally sought to implement an internationalist socialist agenda.[48] They sought to efface any particular Jewish consciousness from the Jewish worker in order to draw him closer into the Russian revolutionary movement. Yet after several years, Vilna Group Jewish-born ideologues, including John Mill (b. Yoysef Shloyme Mill, 1870–1952), Tsemakh Kopelzon (1869–1933), and Shmuel Gozhanski (1867–1943), recognized that despite sharing similar concerns with the general proletariat, Jewish laborers experienced particular difficulties due to their Jewish identity. The Jews' actual "factory" experience differed completely from that of Christians. While Christians labored in large production factories, most Jews worked in quite small cottage industries. Not only did the two groups not labor together, but they also had to deal with different work-related problems. Vilna Group leaders acknowledged in 1894 that "the Jewish worker suffers in Russia not merely as a worker but as a Jew [...] that, together with the general political and economic struggle, the struggle for civil equality must be one of our immediate tasks."[49] The May Laws and the Sunday Rest Law, together with antisemitic violence, further inspired Vilna Group leaders to relinquish internationalism.

The Vilna Group preached its own form of autonomism through Jewish nationalism in order to solve Jewish workers' concerns. Although in theory the

---

47   Polonsky, *The Jews in Poland and Russia*, 2:111.
48   Zimmerman, *Poles, Jews, and the Politics of Nationality*, 39.
49   Cited in ibid., 52.

group's long-term goal remained a merger with the worldwide proletariat, it acknowledged that it must first ensure that socialist leaders would both accept the Jewish worker as an equal to the general proletariat and demonstrate this respect through appropriate laws and protocols. Jewish socialist leaders realized that their followers could not rely on the Russian or Polish workers' movements to care enough about Jews' specific problems to ensure their fair treatment. Shmuel Gozhanski—a former extreme anti-Yiddishist—argued that Jews "must develop a consciousness among the Jewish proletariat strong enough so that it will be prepared to attain its rights and defend them once they have won."[50] Jews had to depend on themselves. In its transition to a frontline Judeo-centric socialist ideology (with a shift in linguistic tactics), the Vilna Group proclaimed itself the chief representative of the Jewish proletariat throughout the entire Russian Empire. This included not only the kresy, but also the Kingdom of Poland.

At the same time, in 1892, the Polish Socialist Party (Polska Partia Socjalistyczna, PPS) was formed, a consolidation of the kingdom's three active and decidedly Polish socialist organizations. Led into this union by the wealthy Polonized Jew Stanisław Mendelson (1858–1913), a cadre of Warsaw secular Poles and assimilated Jews organized with the primary objective of breaking free from foreign reign. Polish and assimilated Jewish socialist leaders had been raised on heroic tales retold from the 1863 Polish Uprising against Russian rule. And they felt broken by the outcome. PPS leader Józef Piłsudski (1867–1935)[51] wrote of growing up with a bitterness that "ate away at my father's soul, drew tears from my mother's eyes and deeply impressed a child's mind. That was the memory of the national defeat of 1863."[52] The Russian educators sent by the Russian government to quash Polish pride greatly impacted Piłsudski's youth:

> The atmosphere of the gymnasium crushed me, the injustice and the politics of the schoolmaster enraged me. . . . [I]n these circumstances my hatred for the Tsarist administration and Muscovite oppression grew with every year. My cheeks burned, that I must suffer in silence while my pride was trampled upon, listening to lies and scornful words about Poland, Poles and their history. . . . The feeling of oppression weighted on my heart like a millstone.[53]

---

50 Cited in ibid., 50.
51 Piłsudski became a PPS leader upon his 1897 return from five years of Russian imprisonment.
52 Cited in ibid., 26.
53 Cited in ibid.

PPS leaders, both Jews and Poles, embarked on a two-part struggle for Polish sovereignty and proletarian rights, while also emphasizing Jews' civil rights.

PPS activists believed that only by reuniting the partitioned territories of the former Polish-Lithuanian Commonwealth would the people of Poland specifically, and the West in general, outmaneuver Russian despotism.[54] A united proletarian struggle—built by all workers throughout the partitioned commonwealth lands, despite different national and religious affiliations—would arise to quash Russian bourgeois tyranny. The PPS's 1895 May Day leaflet called on Jews to recognize their commonality with Christian Poles: "Brothers! Comrades! The same yoke oppresses both the Christian and the Jewish worker. Our interests are one in the same! ... We must boldly demand our rights together!"[55] In establishing a politically independent Polish state, the PPS would seek to create a society based not only on socialism's economic principles, but also on equality among the citizenry regardless of sex, race, nationality, and religion. However, the fact that the PPS envisioned complete equality for the nationalities, did not negate the fact that the party's leaders described the new republic as a Polish state.

The PPS viewed Poland's national sovereignty as a sacred ideological talisman. Creating an independent democratic Polish republic (which would respect the rights of the many nationalities and religious groups inhabiting its lands) distinguished the PPS from other socialist organizations. Indeed, the party insisted on securing Polish independence before fighting for the general socialist revolution. Some Polish socialists, including Rosa Luxemburg (1871–1919), argued that Poland must be a part of, not separate from, the Russian Socialist Federation.[56]

The Vilna Group, on the other hand, did not oppose Poland's drive for political independence. It did dispute, however, the planned timing of the country's rebirth. John Mill, who led the Vilna Group's 1894–1895 advance into Warsaw, asserted Poland's right and need for political renewal, while demanding that it conduct that battle only after the successful Russian Revolution.[57] When this conflict erupted between the PPS and other socialist parties the Vilna Group took a neutral position. The PPS's directors interpreted the Jewish group's neutrality as opposition to the party's goals. In the March 4, 1893, edition of the journal *Przedświt*, Piłsudski wrote, "no socialist for whom any manifestation of

---

54   Ibid., 4.
55   Cited in ibid., 77.
56   Rosa Luxemburg split from the PPS due to this very issue and formed Social Democracy of the Kingdom of Poland (Socjaldemokracja Królestwa Polskiego, SDKP).
57   Ibid., 55.

oppression is loathsome . . . has the right to hold a neutral position on this question, not to any extent."[58]

The PPS and the Vilna Group: Division

The PPS and the Vilna Group shared similar societal concerns, such as attaining workers' rights and closing the economic chasm between the proletariat and bourgeoisie. Yet, each held core values which diametrically opposed the other's, especially surrounding "nationhood." Infused by the century-long yearning for territorial reunification, the PPS's leaders—both assimilated Jews and secular Poles—argued for the traditional connection between land possession and nation status. Therefore, for the PPS, it simply followed that the Jews' lack of land barred them from nation status.

Litvak activists directing the Vilna Group ultimately rejected the traditional land-based definition of "nation." Arkadi Kremer (1865–1935) and his colleagues embraced radical continental ideas, including extra-territorialism—the understanding that a nation did not require land. This broadening definition of nation allowed Jews to view themselves as more than a religious group. Accordingly, Jews were elevated to a nation and considered themselves entitled to the same rights as other nations. Thus, the conflict revolved not only around the timing of Poland's fight for independence, but also around whether the Jews were a nation. The Litvak socialists demanded it; the Polish socialists refused it. In 1897, the Vilna Group agitated to recognize Jews as separate from the general population among which they lived; the PPS proposed that Jews integrate into their "host" nation.

The PPS believed Jews would and should eventually assimilate into their host nation's culture, as they had done in the United States. Jewish PPS leaders, such as the staunch assimilationist Maksymilian Heilpern (1858–1924), held that they must embrace the Polish language to move out of isolation and into Polish society. To become conscious socialists, working with their Polish brethren, Jewish laborers had to learn the language.

For the PPS, Jewish workers shared basic aims with the Christian Polish proletariat: labor rights and territorial independence. Jews living on Polish land belonged to both the Jewish religion and to the Polish nation. Thus, the party held that all Jewish laborers inhabiting previously Polish ruled territory should

---

58   Cited in ibid., 28.

align with Poland's independence campaign. Jewish PPS leaders, such as Felix Perl (1871–1927), argued that only by creating this breakaway democratic Polish republic would the Jews gain economic and civil rights.

PPS theorists believed Jews would eventually integrate politically and culturally with the Polish people. Indeed, that many Polish Jewish workers and *polu-intelligenty* (worker-intellectuals) fervently supported the PPS program, remaining bitter opponents of a separate Jewish workers' movement, demonstrates that the integrationist ideology of the Polish Jewish intelligentsia had trickled down to a section of the Jewish working class.[59] By the early 1900s, the general Jewish worker in the Kingdom of Poland was learning the Polish language. In fact, as the General *Zionist* party leader in Congress Kingdom, Yitzhak Grünbaum claimed in 1919 that while Jews argued among themselves about which language to use as the Jewish national language—Yiddish or Hebrew—the real problem remained Yiddish versus Polish. The Polish language and Polish culture had been making deep inroads into Jewish life.[60] Other *Zionist* leaders concurred. Yitzhak Nissenbaum's 1917 *Ha-tsfirah* article proclaimed that "Polish assimilation . . . destroyed all national Jewish sentiments not only within its own ranks but among all Jews who come into contact with it."[61]

The PPS and the Vilna Group: Competition

Aiming for the unification of all Jewish workers throughout the empire into a single all-Russian organization, the Vilna Group began a process of colonization by which they created centers of agitation in the industrial cities of both the Pale of Jewish Settlement and Russian Poland. By 1894, the group had advanced into Warsaw.[62] This move alarmed and infuriated PPS activists.

Warsaw became an ideological battleground. From the perspective of Jews in the PPS, John Mill's Vilna Group was

---

59 Ibid., 82.
60 Mendelsohn, *Zionism in Poland: The Formative Years, 1915–1926*, 65 and 186.
61 *Ha-tsfira*, 8 November 1917, 10, cited in Mendelsohn, *Zionism In Poland: The Formative Years, 1915–1926*, 43.
62 Having immigrated to Congress Poland from Vilna during the last wave of Litvak migration (between 1890–1891), Lithuanian Jewish students aided Tsivia Hurvitsch in organizing a small group of Jewish workers. See Zimmerman, *Poles, Jews, and the Politics of Nationality*, 73.

heaping slander at us Jews and at the whole PPS. What's more they have a tendency to falsify the whole PPS program, persuading Jews that the PPS does nothing for them . . . that the behavior of the PPS demonstrates total indifference to Jewish workers and that only their party is concerned with Jewish issues.[63]

This twisted perspective soon took hold. It even took root across the Atlantic.

If American Jews remember anything about the PPS, it most likely involves the Jewish historiographic consensus, wrong though it was, that the PPS had no interest in the Jewish worker. In actuality, Józef Piłsudski placed great emphasis on winning over the Russified Jewish intelligentsia and Jewish workers.[64] He viewed the Jewish population as exceptionally important to the Polish cause, given the millions of Jewish workers living on previous Polish land. The PPS itself later advanced into Vilna, deepening the intense competition between both socialist entities. Concentrating on reuniting pre-partition Polish territory into one breakaway federal republic, PPS leaders committed themselves to gaining influence over—and therefore manpower from—millions of Jews (and Lithuanians) living in the kresy. So important to Piłsudski was Jewish cooperation with the PPS that not only did he express great concern for the Jewish worker, but he was also the first to reach out to Jews in their own language—Yiddish.

While Polonized Jews in the PPS derided Yiddish, and early Vilna Group Jews ran from it as essentially isolationist and separatist, Piłsudski alone recognized and respected it as, paradoxically, the only pathway to integrating the Jewish worker with the general Polish-Lithuanian proletariat. He understood that before one could assimilate the Jews, one had to meet them where they lived, and in their own language. Thus, the PPS illegally trafficked 955 Yiddish socialist brochures into Vilna, between 1893–1894, along with fifty copies of the Galician-produced Yiddish socialist organ *The Worker* (*Der arbeyter*). Piłsudski also had a mimeograph machine with Yiddish typeface smuggled into Russian Poland so that socialist Jews there could create their own Yiddish propaganda.[65] Such PPS efforts influenced the Vilna Group to change its own course—to demote Russian and accept Yiddish as its primary language.

However, problems plagued Piłsudski's mission. While he appreciated the immense value of incorporating Yiddish into PPS propaganda efforts, émigré

---

63 Cited in ibid., 78n37.
64 Ibid., 82.
65 Ibid., 31.

leaders who controlled the PPS's purse strings did not. Additionally, the party lacked the ability to generate its own Yiddish material for distribution: its Jewish leaders had grown up in assimilated homes, knew little about Jewish life, and could rarely speak Yiddish. As such, most could not produce their own Yiddish literature.[66] The non-Jewish PPS leader Leon Wasilewski (1870–1936), a descendent of the Polish szlachta, went so far as to learn Yiddish himself in order to continue producing the PPS's *Der Arbeyter* after its Jewish editor Maks Horowitz (1877–1937) was imprisoned in 1899.[67] Leadership priority conflicts and a dearth of Yiddish-speaking Jewish leaders challenged the PPS's goal of bringing more Jewish workers into the organization.

For the PPS, the Vilna Group's expansion into Congress Kingdom was a provocation, and they saw these Litvak socialists, who had been schooled to love Russian culture and disdain Poles, as Russifying agents.[68] Although Piłsudski eventually attempted to persuade Vilna Group leaders to join Polish and Lithuanian workers in their struggle for independence, the two parties could not move past the seemingly insurmountable obstacles of nation status and the timetable for establishing Poland's political sovereignty. In 1897, the Vilna Group changed its name to the General Jewish Workers' Bund in Russia and Poland. That it demanded autonomy from the PPS (and all other socialist parties), and refused to fight alongside Poles for Poland's independence, proved to Piłsudski that it was the enemy.

PPS propaganda coached its audience to perceive these Litvaks as working for the tsar. Though nothing could be further from the truth, several conflicts pointed to the Bund's possible treachery: the Vilna Group frustrated PPS approaches to the Jewish proletariat; it did not teach that the Russians oppressed Poles and Lithuanians linguistically and culturally; and it supported a united Russia (including the Kingdom of Poland) because it would retain the Jews' unity and therefore secure their political strength through numbers.[69] Educated in the Russian school system, which was fundamentally dismissive of Poles, most Litvaks were not interested in the Polish question. The PPS position against the Russian Jewish socialists was ideological, not antisemitic.

Despite conflict between Piłsudski and the émigré leadership about funding for Yiddish material, and the PPS's inability to persuade the Vilna Group to work

---

66 For years PPS Jewish members requested that more effort be placed on procuring Yiddish socialist propaganda from the United States and Galicia.
67 Ibid., 132 and 137.
68 Zimmerman, *Poles, Jews, and the Politics of Nationality*, 86.
69 Ibid., 28, 182, and 187.

symbiotically with it, the party developed a large Jewish following.[70] In 1902, the PPS sanctioned the creation of a Jewish Committee (Komitet Żydowski, KŻ), through which its Jewish leaders could focus on specifically Jewish work, such as producing and disseminating party literature and speeches in Yiddish. The PPS also voted to give the committee representation in the PPS's central committee.

To counter the Vilna Group's incursion into the kingdom, the PPS relocated Jewish Committee leader Feliks Sachs (1869–1935) to Vilna. Though he arrived with theoretical arguments to draw Litvaks away from an anti-Polish stance, his actual encounter with Jews in the Pale led to a clearer understanding of their attitude. Meeting Litvaks in their own environment, Sachs better understood Lithuanian Jews' attraction to Russian culture and their alienation from Poland. Instead of condemning Litvaks as Russifying agents, he suggested regarding them in terms of Lithuanian nationalism. Rather than insisting that Lithuania become part of Poland, Sachs suggested that Poland respect an independent Lithuania. "'We will have to unambiguously stress [that we view] Lithuania as a sister, *not* a daughter, of Poland.'"[71] In 1900, Piłsudski reformed his position on the Jews as a nationality, and he came to embrace Lithuania's desire for independence.

Piłsudski never shifted his thinking about Russia, however. He remained adamant about maintaining independence from the tsar, and in 1905 a schism occurred. A PPS Left emerged (Young Faction) which cooperated with striking workers in Russia.[72] The PPS Left agreed to an autonomous Polish state attached to an emancipated socialist-governed Russia. This transformation, which now aligned with the General Jewish Workers' Bund's consistent all-Russian orientation, allowed the Young Faction to cooperate with the Bund in strikes in Russian Poland.

Polish Integral Nationalism

Nationalism took on a variety of forms. Particular to the Jews was the General Jewish Workers' Bund's socialist agenda, and the *Zionists*' multiplicity of ideological factions. Poles expressed their nationalism not only through the PPS socialist program but also via the extreme ideology presented by Roman Dmowski (1864–1939), the chief theoretician of Endecja. Opposing Piłsudski, he argued

---

70 Ibid., 79.
71 Cited in ibid., 173.
72 Ibid., 198.

that Germany posed the greatest threat to the Polish people. And though he desired independence from Russia, he did not wish to launch a military campaign against the behemoth. Dmowski embraced the relatively new political concept of integral nationalism, in which the citizen is expected to place the needs of the country above everything else. He reiterated the French antisemitic trope that the Jews' supposed attempt to rule the world made them an internal enemy. Influenced also by social Darwinism, he held that "if Poland was to survive as a nation it would have to abandon the naive belief in international brotherhood."[73] Dmowski concluded that Poland must be selfish, placing its own needs ahead of others in order to move forward and to endure as a political, national, and cultural entity. Accordingly, he proposed that Poles "pursue a policy of ruthless 'national egotism' and create an organic national movement which would defend their interests."[74]

Although not a socialist, by 1905 Dmowski recognized the importance of gaining favor with the laboring Polish masses. In response to the tsar's disproportionate abuse of workers as frontline fodder in the 1904–1905 Russo-Japanese War, as well as the concurrent factory firings and wage cuts,[75] more than one hundred thousand Polish workers (from the General Jewish Workers' Bund and the PPS Left) joined Russian socialist strikes.[76] During these industrial strikes the National Workers' Union (Narodowy Związek Robotniczy, NZR) took shape. Essentially Endecja's labor division, the NZR presented workers with arguments against following a socialist agenda. Its leaders knew that laborers feared poverty when participating in strikes. Many workers believed the tsar had already responded to the people's grievances with his October Manifesto, so right-wing nationalists plied them with promises to end their "outrageous socialist" strikes.[77]

Against both class struggle and internationalism, the NZR promoted Polish national solidarity. Waging an anti-strike and anti-socialist crusade, it blamed Jewish factory owners for the deplorable job losses and wage cuts. NZR activists did not dig deeper into the root cause of the economic downturn, the Russo-Japanese War. Thus, when Endecja transformed the socialist message from one of "proletariat versus bourgeoisie" to the nationalist "Pole versus Jew," many workers bought into it. Although socialists viewed antisemitism as a

---

73 Antony Polonsky, *The Jews in Poland and Russia*, 2:96.
74 Ibid., 96.
75 Zimmerman, *Poles, Jews, and the Politics of Nationality*, 196.
76 Ibid.
77 Ibid., 202.

middle-class phenomenon, and believed that it would not appeal to the worker, in the end they were wrong.[78] Workers had already been fed antisemitic rhetoric that connected Jews to the ills of the city. The growth of Jewish nationalism only further corroborated Endecja's argument that the Jews did not care about Polish collective needs.

The Church also factored into the workers' eventual embrace of Dmowski's integral nationalism. A large percentage of Poles viewed their priests not only as religious guides, but also as key interpreters of political and social events. Village priests caught in the Church's fight against modernity, and thus against the Jew, steered their congregants toward Dmowski's radical Polish nationalism. The growing number of conservative activists publishing antisemitic pamphlets and weekly papers also aided this effort. For example, for thirty years Jan Jeleński's paper *Rola* had poured antisemitic thought into the minds of conservative Roman Catholic Poles.[79] Thus, Polish nationalist extremists made inroads into labor, splitting Polish workers' support for the now fractured Polish Socialist Party.

Nationalisms Collide in Russian Duma Elections

Following the 1905 Russian Revolution, Tsar Nicholas II attempted to subdue the revolutionaries with his placatory October Manifesto. This momentary liberalization granted universal male suffrage to all citizens throughout the empire. Despite the many limits to Russia's new constitutional monarchy, the fact remains that both Jews and Poles gained the vote.[80] However, the Election Law of the same year favored the gentry and middle class, providing workers with a very small percentage of the actual vote: one landowner received the same voting rights as forty-five workers combined.[81]

Protesting this inequality, socialists in the Kingdom of Poland decided to boycott the 1906 Duma elections. Running against Endecja stood an alliance between the liberal Progressive Democratic Union (Związek Postępowo-Demokratyczny), a very small yet highly influential group of which one-third of its members were Jewish. It included noteworthy positivists such as Aleksander Świętochowski and the Jewish Electoral Committee formed by the League

---

78 Ibid., 130.
79 Michlic, *Poland's Threatening Other*, 54.
80 Wandyz, *The Lands of Partitioned Poland, 1795–1918*, 316.
81 Zimmerman, *Poles, Jews, and the Politics of Nationality*, 215.

for the Attainment of Full Rights for the Jewish People of Russia.[82] Dmowski responded with a bitter campaign focusing on the Jewish representation in both groups. His National Democrats denounced the Progressive Democrats as "Judaized." The Endecja party press warned against the so-called Jewish danger lurking over Warsaw. A leaflet declared, "We must show that we are the rulers of this country—that our vote predominates here."[83]

Preventing mass consumption of antisemitic rhetoric proved quite difficult. The Jewish Section of the PPS requested more literature condemning antisemitism. However, émigré leaders refused to fund it. They believed that workers were immune to such propaganda.[84] Only after Dmowski targeted the socialists as a Jewish conspiracy to control the kingdom did the PPS condemn Endecja for inciting Poles to hate Jews.

Dmowski was victorious in this contest to represent Warsaw's Poles in the first Russian State Duma. With the PPS having boycotted the election, 54% of the sixty-seven thousand votes favored Endecja, while the Progressive-Democratic-Jewish Electoral Committee alliance took 40%.[85] Surely this does not speak of a purely antisemitic population, especially given the vacuum caused by the socialist boycott. It does, however, point to the birth of political antisemitism in Polish party politics. Employing antisemitism again in the 1907 elections, the right-wing nationalist bloc, consisting of Endecja and the National Concentration, took 53% of the vote, while 45% went to the Progressive Alliance Jewish Electoral Committee. Those three Duma seats reserved for worker representation went to the bloc of the General Jewish Workers' Bund-SDKPiL (Social Democrats of the Kingdom of Poland and Lithuania, PPS Left).[86]

Competing in 1912 for a seat to represent Warsaw in the fourth Russian State Duma, Dmowski's extremism grew even more intense. While sparring with the moderately conservative National Concentration, he was pressed on his conciliatory tone towards the Russian authorities, which made him look rather weak in the public eye. He retorted by underscoring that Jan Kucharzewski, the Concentration candidate, had been unwilling to be vocally antisemitic, thereby "proving" that he bowed to the Jews. Believing that his loud antisemitic rhetoric

---

82   Ibid., 216.
83   Cited in ibid., 217.
84   Cited in ibid., 219.
85   Ibid., 217.
86   Ibid., 218.

demonstrated his own strength, Dmowski focused the National Democrats' campaign on Poland's struggle with the Jews.[87]

After Kucharzewski's ambivalent attitudes toward the Jews in general and Jewish rights specifically emerged, Jewish voters had but two options: they could either abstain from voting in the election, allowing the Poles alone to choose a representative, or they could cast their 40% of the electoral votes for an altogether different candidate.[88] Despite some Jews' pressuring electors to abstain from the vote, the Warsaw Jewish electoral body acted to block both Dmowski's and Kucharzewski's election, raising a relatively obscure Polish socialist, Eugeniusz Jagiełło, to the seat in their stead.[89]

In defeating Dmowski, Warsaw's Jewish population showed itself for the first time to be an actual political rival to the right-wing Polish nationalists. The Jews' ability to act in concert toward achieving their own particular desires incensed Dmowski. While they did not put a Jew in his seat, for Endecja the Jews' candidate was the next worse possibility: a socialist.

The Jews' political move also infuriated National Concentration's backers, who had championed the Jewish position on several matters, including the Dreyfus affair. A November 8 article in *Kurjer Warszawski*—the main liberal paper which supported National Concentration—expressed dismay over the Jewish vote:

> Today's election by the Jews is the most flagrant demonstration imaginable.... In voting for Mr. Jagiełło, the Jews have attempted to show that our national will means nothing here, that they can impose their will on us, that they will seize the first opportunity to give the Polish nation a challenge to battle....
>
> ... We have lost our seat despite the fact that we made the greatest efforts to save it for the national cause. In exchange, we have gained a clear understanding of an important aspect of internal affairs, the knowledge of a danger which stands before us; we have recognized the features of the internal enemy.[90]

For right-wing and moderate conservative parties, that the Jews could and did block Polish national interests proved them to be the Poles' enemy within.

---

87 Antony Polonsky, *The Jews in Poland and Russia*, 2:108.
88 Ibid., 109.
89 Michlic, *Poland's Threatening Other*, 64.
90 Excerpt from Kurjer Waszawski, Nov. 8, cited in Polonsky, *The Jews in Poland and Russia*, 2:109.

Dmowski Retaliates with an Economic Boycott of the Jews

Dmowski responded to the Jews demonstrated political strength with a powerful gesture. Calling on Poles to take Poland back from the Jews, he insisted that Poles engage in an economic boycott of Jews.[91] Not only had Jews in 1912 barred his political agenda, but according to the Endek perspective, for centuries Jews had been preventing the full development of the Polish people. Beyond the immense size of the Jewish population, its visibility, and perceived immunity to assimilation, Endecja focused on the Jews as an impediment against Polish economic growth. According to Dmowski, Jews harmed Poles by their role as the central middleman minority in the commonwealth and kingdom, and by controlling the middle class, the social strata which Dmowski believed was vital for a modern society to thrive.

Dmowski argued that Jews performed those jobs Poles would have naturally taken had the Others not been present and willing to fill such positions. He specified the Jewish arrendator who helped manage the Polish nobleman's estate. Had Jews not been present, Dmowski argued,

> the Polish people would have organized itself to perform the social functions which they [the Jews] fulfilled and would have emerged as a rival force to the nobility as a third estate which has played such an important role in the development of European societies and has become the principal force in modern social life.[92]

But the Jew had been present ... in both rural and urban Poland.

Indeed, per the positivists' requests, Jews had built and filled the city centers. According to Dmowski's reasoning, had Jews not turned to the city for their own economic welfare, plenty of room would have existed there for the peasantry to find a new source of income after the agrarian crisis. However, as it stood, once the peasantry finally migrated from its rural comfort zone (due to agricultural reform's failure), it found the cities full of Jews who had already established dominion over urban commerce. By 1921 Jews in Poland constituted 14.25 per cent of the population. With industrialization, Jews had found new working

---

91 Wandyz, *The Lands of Partitioned Poland, 1795–1918*, 326.
92 Dmowski, *Myśli nowoczesnego Polaka*, 40, cited in Polonsky, *The Jews in Poland and Russia*, 2:97.

opportunities as artisans, constituting 39.7 per cent of that field. 34.6 per cent of all economically active Jews still worked in trade and insurance; 88.9 per cent of them were employed in the retail goods trade. Dmowski's economic boycott was especially difficult for this group.[93]

Sociologist Edna Bonacich sympathizes with nations which attempt to take control of their economies after periods of colonialization, in which typically a middleman minority served the colonizer. Regarding Poland, one may point to two stages of colonization: 1) the nobility's takeover of the kresy and 2) the later commonwealth partitions. During both periods, the Jewish middleman minority played key roles in aiding the colonial power. The Jewish arrendator and moneylender maintained the nobility's command over the kresy; the Litvak entrepreneur opened Poland's markets to Russia. When positivists embraced modernity and capitalism, the Jews not only remained entrenched as merchants and artisans, but they proved formative in building the kingdom's economic centers. Bonacich writes that the "efficient organization of the middleman economy makes it virtually impossible for the native population to compete in the open market."[94] It makes sense that as part of a host nation Poles would clash with the Jewish middleman minority once Russia loosened its colonial reigns and Poles attempted to regain economic control. However, recognizing the real conflict at hand does not equate to embracing the extreme measures Dmowski pushed to dislodge the Jewish middleman minority from its economic position.

Dmowski demanded that Jews give their middle-class status to the Poles by the latter taking the formers' jobs. The Jews did not budge. Thus, Polish right-wing politicians looked to wrest economic and professional power from the Jews through an economic boycott. Dmowski praised those who participated in the boycott as loyalists to the Polish cause, while he denounced those Poles who refused to take part in it as national traitors.[95]

Myth Reconstruction

Today, one can hardly speak candidly about Polish-Jewish relations without raising the topic of Polish antisemitism. Both Polish Christians and American Jews draw on myths to support their narrow view of the general past and of this topic in particular.

---

93 Polonsky, *The Jews in Poland and Russia*, 3: 61–62.
94 Bonacich, "A Theory of Middleman Minorities": 590.
95 Michlic, *Poland's Threatening Other*, 64.

Part of the standard American Jewish myth includes the belief that all Polish political groups embraced antisemitism. However, once one explores the contextual nuances of Polish politics in the early twentieth century, the myth falls apart. Just as the Vilna Group reconstructed its original internationalist socialist agenda into the General Jewish Workers' Bund's empire-wide Jewish nationalist program, so too did the PPS transition from denying Jews nation status to recognizing it. This reality negates the consensus in mainstream Jewish historiography that *all* Polish political parties up until WWI, including the socialists, acted against granting Jews national rights.

In fact, the PPS was the first European Socialist Party to officially recognize the principle of extraterritorial autonomy for Jews, including the freedom to develop their own culture by speaking their native language in schools, administration, and courts of law.[96] For Piłsudski, this transition occurred in 1900 after his personal interaction with the General Jewish Workers' Bund leader Arkadi Kremer in London. By 1902, Piłsudski recognized the old PPS program, which demanded Jewish assimilation, as bankrupt. He agreed with other PPS leaders that if the Jews identified as a nation, Poland could not expect full assimilation. At the sixth party congress, Piłsudski proposed adding to the party manifesto the promise that Jews would have both nation status and that Poland would defend their rights as a nationality.[97] In return for accepting Jewish nationality, the PPS demanded that Jews demonstrate their loyalty to the general interests of the country. Jews must, then, put the needs of the state before those of the Jewish nation.

It is true that Piłsudski yearned for the General Jewish Workers' Bund's support in prioritizing Polish independence. He hoped that his nation status concession would bring Jewish socialists to his cause. At the same time, this ideological change grounded Piłsudski's politics well after he abandoned socialism. So much did he embrace this new understanding that he changed his vision of a renewed Polish state: having wished for a multicultural country, based on the American model, he now sought a federation of nationalities. This transition from national assimilation (*asymilacja narodowa*) to state assimilation (*asymilacja pánstwowa*) marked Piłsudski's attitude towards national minorities in interwar Poland.[98]

While the PPS did not base its political decision-making on antisemitic ideology, Endecja did. Dmowski's following accepted political antisemitism, casting Poland's large Jewish population as the reason for the Polish people's economic

---

96   Zimmerman, *Poles, Jews, and the Politics of Nationality*, 191.
97   Ibid., 168.
98   Ibid., 166.

and political troubles. Urban demographics only underscored Dmowski's argument. The rooted urban Jewish population that migrating peasants and unemployed szlachta met at the end of the nineteenth century caused tremendous concern. In 1897, Jews made up 33.7% of Warsaw's population. By 1910–1914, official estimates put the Jewish population at 36–39%. It was growing faster than the Catholic population, which roughly retained its 1897 share of between 54–57%.[99] Supplying a good deal of the city's mercantile, trade, and artisan needs, the Jews left little room for the Poles.

But one must ask whether the Jews created this problem. The Endek argument posits that if the Jews had not been present, there would have been more opportunity for the urbanizing peasants. But reason proposes that once those limited jobs had been taken, the tens of thousands of other peasants streaming into the cities would have found few opportunities. Even the positivists' factory-filled cities could not sustain the enormous wave of unemployed people, whether or not Jews had settled in the cities prior to the peasant and gentry migration.

Part of the standard Polish myth concerning troubled Polish-Jewish relations during the early twentieth century purports that the animus Poles exhibited toward Jews remained fundamentally a question of economics. Indeed, I recall my friend Przemek explaining that Polish antisemitism is a made-up construct. It never existed. He and his generation had learned that the conflict between Pole and Jew lay rooted in economic competition, not nation status and not religion. The problem with this argument is that while economics certainly played a role in the spiraling relationship, it ignores other contextual truths that we have explored in this chapter, including the nobility's embrace of the Jewish arrendator, partitions of the commonwealth by foreign powers, and the landless szlachta's decline toward peasant status. The economy-focused position also overlooks two failed rebellions and Russia's uneven retaliatory measures against Poles and Jews in the Kingdom of Poland. The argument further ignores traditionalists' fear of modernity. Liberalism, technological advances, and urbanization offered hope, but also caused economic and social disaster. The dominant economic theory also ignores the Catholic Church's influential campaign against the Jew as the primary enemy in the Church's fight to survive modernity. By the time Roman Dmowski called for the Jews' economic removal due to pauperization of the peasantry and landless gentry, all these factors had already formed his point of view.

---

99   Corrsin, "Aspects of Population Change and of Acculturation in Jewish Warsaw at the End of the Nineteenth Century: The Censuses of 1882 and 1897," 214.

This economy-centric argument also ignores mainstream Jewry's refusal to integrate into Polish society. A people which had already been conquered, the Poles desired some sense of control over their land and future. They yearned for support in their political and cultural battles with Russia. Once the migrating Litvaks reached the kingdom, any hope of gaining broad Jewish support for a specific Polish agenda dissipated. The Litvaks brought with them the radical idea that the Jews were themselves a nation and deserved the same cultural, communal, linguistic, and educational autonomy that Poles sought. In the name of Jewish autonomy, they discouraged assimilation into the Polish society. The Litvaks instead called for Jews to take ownership of their lives through politics, and rallied their brethren in the Kingdom of Poland to prioritize Jewish needs above the Poles' goals and desires.

Progressive Poles blamed the influx of Litvaks into Warsaw and Łódz for the sharp turn from talk of assimilation to that of antisemitism. While the antisemitism engendered by the Dreyfus affair in France made its way onto Polish streets, positivism's final shift away from assimilation came in reaction to both Jewish nationalism and the general Jewish population's continued resistance to integration.[100] Whether scorned or simply frustrated, positivists quieted their calls for brotherhood, thereby allowing antisemitic rhetoric to spread and take root. With little to show for their decades defending tolerance, by 1905 the great majority of positivists adopted a more cynical view of the Jews' relationship to Poland.

Jewish integrationists also accused the Litvak migration of upsetting Polish-Jewish coexistence in the Kingdom of Poland by bringing Zionism and Jewish socialism across its border. In 1910, the integrationist newspaper *Israelita* announced gravely, "the influx of the Litvaks and the 'Judaisation' of the kingdom had brought about the death of assimilation."[101] Is it any wonder, then, that contemporary Jews and Poles in the kingdom spoke of the "Litvak invasion?" At roughly 250,000, the number of Litvaks could not exactly overwhelm a population of millions. However, the force with which Litvaks asserted their separateness from Poles, while compelling native Jews in the kingdom to establish new ideologies vis-à-vis the compatriots, created this perception. And perception is reality.

This period's complexity spreads wide and deep. Following Enlightenment principles, positivists and integrationists cooperated in their attempt to secure the Jews' civil rights and cultural assimilation. Though they made strides, their efforts were stymied when political issues in other countries crossed borders

---

100 Polonsky, "The Dreyfus Affair and Polish-Jewish Interaction, 1890–1914," 32.
101 Wróbel, "Jewish Warsaw before the First World War," 252.

and affected the Kingdom of Poland. France's Dreyfus affair and the Church's battle with modernity presented the Jew as a dangerous foreigner intent on taking over the world. During the same period, Russian pogroms pushed hundreds of thousands of Litvaks into the kingdom. Their Jewish nationalism changed the political situation for their counterparts in the Kingdom of Poland, as the Litvak Vilna Group not only insisted that Jews have nation status, but also put Jewish collective needs in the empire ahead of the PPS's drive for Polish autonomy. Despite Piłsudski's enormous efforts and the inroads he made by employing Yiddish and transitioning to accept the Jews' nation status, in the end the PPS lost some power to Jewish socialism. At the same time, the *Zionist* Ḥibat Tsiyon gained a foothold in the kingdom and attracted Jews away from the concept of integrationism. By the beginning of the twentieth century, Jewish integrationists recognized their dream had died.

CHAPTER 9

Destruction and Rebirth

For decades, Polish and Jewish activists created new political identities and generated competing forces. As one century transitioned to the next, the rift between mainstream Poles and Jews widened. By 1917, as WWI ground towards its conclusion, right-wing conspiracy theories that projected Jews as the main threat to the world order had grown exponentially. When the Russian Revolution morphed into the Russian Civil War between the tsarist Whites and the Bolshevik Reds, the Jew-enemy stereotype became even more powerful, and not only in Russia. In this chapter, we will explore how these developments impacted the contest between Roman Dmowski and Józef Piłsudski to determine the nascent independent Poland's direction.

The Great War

By late 1915, Russia responded to its military defeats with a scorched earth policy in Congress Poland: if Russia could not have the land, Germany would gain only devastated, unusable, terrain. Thus, those regions inhabited by most of the Polish population were destroyed wholesale at the behest of the Russian authorities. Poles endured massive dislocation and suffering, as soldiers carried out orders to burn villages, slaughter livestock, and wreck food supplies.[1]

Germany's march into the kingdom brought further disaster. Requisitioning all materials for the war effort, the victorious army stripped industrial cities and farms of everything of any possible use.[2] The German's had a particular need for leather. They seized the thick leather transmission belts that factories could not function without, and turned them into soles for their soldiers' boots. The army

---

1   M. B. B. Biskupski, *The History of Poland* (Westport: Greenwood Press, 2000), 42.
2   Davies, *God's Playground*, 2:130.

also sent machine parts back to the fatherland. The result was the shuttering of factories and the unemployment and immiseration of thousands upon thousands of Poles.

In his book *The Brothers Ashkenazi*, contemporary Polish Jewish writer I. J. Singer describes the German destruction of rural Poland:

> Every stalk of wheat, every potato in the cellar, every new-born chick, calf and piglet had to be reported. The fruit was plucked from orchards, the grass from pastures, the fleece from sheep. Hunters were stripped of guns, and fishermen of nets, so that all the game and catch were left for the victors. Even stray dogs and cats were rounded up and rendered for their fat. Their flesh would feed the animals in German zoos.[3]

Poverty and malnourishment ensued.

Although the Germans provided ration cards to Poles so they could get bread, it was an ersatz bread

> that wasn't made of flour but from an abomination of chestnuts and potato peelings. It stuck to the gums and ruined the digestion. The rich bought food from the army of smugglers that had proliferated since the occupation, but the poor dropped like flies from malnutrition and disease.[4]

The now jobless workers starved. Unable to fend off disease, they and their offspring died one after the other as epidemics ravaged the populace.

The "war to end all wars" took a colossal toll on the Kingdom of Poland. Reeling from more than 1.5 million military casualties and an untold number of civilian deaths, the traumatized survivors were expected to create a new Polish society.

---

3   I. J. Singer, *The Brothers Ashkenazi*, trans. Joseph Singer, with a foreword by Rebecca Newberger Goldstein and an introduction by Irving Howe (New York: Other Press, 2010), 324.
4   Ibid., 324.

The *Protocols of the Elders of Zion*, Russian Pogroms, and *Żydokomuna*

As the conflict wore on, the *Protocols of The Elders of Zion* gained immense popularity among conservative Christian monarchists. It tells of a fanciful, invented, centuries' long sinister plot by Jews for world domination. Its ever-widening audience processed their wartime experiences through this contrived story. Readers concluded that the Russian Revolution and WWI had been instigated and manipulated by the Jews to achieve their supposed goal of world domination.

This conspiracy theory was not new. Its origins, though, had remained obscure given the text was published anonymously as stolen notes from a secret midnight meeting of Jewish elders. For quite some time scholars had named Pyotr Rachkovsky, the Paris-based head of the Russian secret police (Okhrana), as fabricator of the *Protocols*.[5] However, new research, elucidated by Steven Zipperstein in his book *Pogrom: Kishinev and the Tilt of History*, points to Russian nationalist writer, publisher, and well-known antisemite Pavel Krushevan as the *Protocols*' author, or at least co-author.[6] In 1903 Krushevan serialized a shorter version of this text in his then newly acquired antisemitic daily *Znamia* (The Banner). That first printing remains the least known of the *Protocols*' Russian-language iterations.[7]

Near the time of its printing, some contemporaries called out the document as a forgery. Indeed, large chunks of it had been lifted directly from fantasies penned in the 1860s: the French political satirist Maurice Joly's 1864 *Dialogue in Hell between Machiavelli and Montesquieu* and Hermann Goedsche's 1868 novel *Biarritz*.[8] A 1921 three-part series in the London *Times* went so far as to feature side-by-side passages from the *Protocols* and Joly's book, demonstrating that 70% of the *Protocols*' words came directly from the novel.[9] As is often the case, especially during times of crisis, people discarded complicated truths and favored lies that offered an easier grasp of convoluted circumstances.

---

5   Ibid., xi.
6   Steven J. Zipperstein, *Pogrom: Kishinev and the Tilt of History* (New York: Liveright Publishing Corporation, 2018), 168–172.
7   Ibid., 170.
8   "Protocols of the Elders of Zion," United States Holocaust Memorial Museum, accessed January 23, 2023, https://encyclopedia.ushmm.org/content/en/article/protocols-of-the-elders-of-zion.
9   Zipperstein, *Pogrom: Kishinev and the Tilt of History*, 168.

The perception of the Jews as a dangerous "enemy within" had already gained credence in Russian government circles with the 1881 assassination of Tsar Alexander II. Most ministers saw the Jews as an alien people, which due to dogged isolation and particularism posed a threat to Russia's national essence. Millions of Jews also proved dangerous due to their very poverty. Believing that Judaism was a breeding ground of subversion, Russian officials translated the masses of impoverished Jews into likely future political radicals.[10] By the early twentieth century, the Russian military trained its soldiers to recognize the Jew as an alien hostile to Russian culture.[11] Russian political institutions still clung onto a culture of eighteenth-century absolutism; as a consequence, the country was "on a collision course with modernity."[12] For many conservatives, the Jew symbolized modernity.

Pavel Krushevan transmitted these concepts through his 1896–97 novel *Chto takoe Rossiia?* (What Is Russia?). A member of the Right, he pinpoints Jews as Russia's primary enemy. He argues that the Jews' insistence on cultural and religious separation from the Russian Christian world threatened Russia's survival. He suggests that the Jews cause the pogroms themselves through their resistance to assimilation and their focus on commerce. He insists their growing political radicalness and dismissiveness of the Christian world will bring their downfall.[13]

Krushevan also spread his antisemitic exhortations in the pages of the daily Kishinev newspaper *Bessarabets*, for which he acted as writer and editor. In spring 1903, *Bessarabets* published weeks of threatening attacks on the Jews. Though Krushevan had recently sold the paper, he maintained editorial control of it.[14] Articles with accusations of ritual murder implored Christians to take revenge on the Jews. Krushevan's colleagues, who believed the Jews were plotting against the Gentiles, augmented his messaging by distributing leaflets that urged anti-Jewish violence.[15]

---

10 Hans Rogger, *Jewish Policies and Right-Wing Politics in Imperial Russia* (Oxford: Macmillan in association with St. Antony's College, 1986), 64. While most Russian ministers regarded the Jews as a dangerous problem, they differed on how best to reduce the threat to the country. Some sought harsher restrictions while others wanted to dissolve the Pale of Settlement and do away with other if not all the May Laws. See ibid., 56–111.
11 Oleg Budnitskii, *Russian Jews Between the Reds and the Whites, 1917–1920*, trans. Timothy, J. Portice (Philadelphia: University of Pennsylvania Press, 2012), 228.
12 Shlomo Lambroza, "The Pogroms of 1903–1906," in Klier and Lambroza, *Pogroms: Anti-Jewish Violence in Modern Russian History*, 195.
13 Zipperstein, *Pogrom: Kishinev and the Tilt of History*, 161–164.
14 Ibid., 97–98.
15 Ibid., 97.

On Easter Sunday, April 6, 1903, a bestial pogrom erupted in Kishinev (now Chișinău, Moldova). Neighbors, seminary students, and villagers from the city outskirts coalesced into a seemingly organized operation. Having begun with rock throwing and extensive looting, it soon devolved into property destruction, physical assaults, and the ferocious rape of women and girls. The second day's terror escalated with continued gang rapes and heinous murder. In the end, pogromists butchered forty-nine Jews, raped close to forty women and girls, injured some five hundred Jews, looted roughly six hundred Jewish businesses, and destroyed nearly seven hundred Jewish homes.[16]

News of the pogrom spread quickly, thanks to mid-level Jewish community activist Jacob Bernstein-Kogan. On the second night after the streets grew quiet, he went door-to-door to collect funds from Kishinev's remaining Jewish residents. He used a large portion to telegram news outlets, organizations, and influential figures throughout Europe and the US about the massacre. Journalist Michael Davitt arrived in Kishinev soon thereafter because of one of the telegrams.[17] His meticulous reporting for the *New York American* prompted immediate global horror about the atrocities. Photographs of Kishinev's butchered Jews filled newspapers. The London *Times* published the so-called Plehve letter—a forgery, attributed to Minister of the Interior Vyacheslav Konstantinovich Plehve. Reprinted widely, this shocking document requested local authorities not to respond too harshly to the pogromists, who were frustrated by the Jews' exploitation of them. Jews (and non-Jews) worldwide accepted this fanciful proof of Russian government complicity in the Kishinev pogrom.[18] Globally, people reacted in shock to Kishinev and contributed mightily to relief efforts.

---

16 "From Haven to Home: The Kishinev Massacre," Jewish Virtual Library, accessed January 31, 2023 https://www.jewishvirtuallibrary.org/from-haven-to-home-judaic-treasures.
17 Zipperstein, *Pogrom: Kishinev and the Tilt of History*, 179–181.
18 The Plehve letter became fixed in the Jewish mind, as did Russian official blame for the pogrom. However, despite so many officials' disdain for the Jews, they were terribly afraid of mob violence. Hans Rogger writes, "It was, moreover, almost certain that pogroms were not manufactured, inspired or tolerated as deliberate policy at the highest level of the central government. The available evidence suggests rather that an important and continuous aim of policy was not to indulge but to control mob violence and to that end the law of 1891 was adopted establishing criminal liability 'for open attacks of one part of the population upon another.'" See Rogger, *Jewish Policies and Right-Wing Politics in Imperial Russia*, 109. For a discussion of the Plehve letter's forgery and the Jews' misinterpretation of Plehve as the ultimate Russian bogeyman who studded his career with antisemitic actions, see Zipperstein, *Pogrom: Kishinev and the Tilt of History*, 92–96.

The Jewish community soon likened the Kishinev pogrom to the worst of Jewish history's catastrophes, including the destruction of the temples in Jerusalem.[19]

Jews recognized the pogrom as a catastrophe, for which in part they blamed the victims. In his now infamous poem "In the City of Killing," Jewish writer Hayim Nahman Bialik built a *Zionist* anthem around the monstrousness of Gentiles and the passivity of Jews. Although examples of Jewish male martyrdom existed in Kishinev, he canonized the image of Jewish male cowardice, of men escaping or hiding while pogromists took turns raping their women.[20]

> This terrain of violation is
> Spied by brother, husband, father, son.
> From behind the cellar casks & boxes, his
> Gaze is fastened to the Christ-emboldened, clammy ton
> Of defilement that wincing maidens gasp
> Underneath . . .[21]

Bialik argues that had the "heirs of Maccabees" defended themselves with greater force, the pogromists would have backed down from the slaughter.

At the same time, and somewhat ironically, the pogromists blamed Jewish aggression for the escalated violence. Courtroom defendants argued that Jewish men fighting back at the onset of the pogrom and Jewish bar keepers' unwillingness to give pogromists free liquor were the reasons for the explosion. Krushevan and his Black Hundreds pro-monarchist cohort twisted the pogrom into proof of Jewish power. In court proceedings, defendant Georgi Pronin, one of Krushevan's close associates, insisted that his instigation of the pogrom was necessary to prevent the Jews' supposed plotting against the Gentiles.[22] Such beliefs had percolated for decades in Russian officialdom.[23]

Krushevan responded quickly to the April Kishinev pogrom by printing in late August and early September of that year "proof" that Jews had been plotting world domination. Through his St. Petersburg newspaper he published nine

---

19   Ibid,, 103.
20   Ibid., 137.
21   Chaim Nachman Bialik, *In the City of Slaughter*, trans. Jeffrey Burghauser (Orlando: Argus Huber, 2021), 13.
22   Zipperstein, *Pogrom: Kishinev and the Tilt of History*, 97.
23   Even the relatively moderate Nikolai Bunge, the tsar's minister of finance in 1881, believed the Jews' stubborn isolation created for them a state within a state through which they could manipulate international finances to rule the world. See Rogger, *Jewish Policies and Right-Wing Politics in Imperial Russia*, 71.

consecutive pieces attributed to the "World Union of Freemasons and Sages of Zion." His headline read: "The Program of World Conquest by Jews."[24] When slightly altered and transformed by others into the *Protocols of the Elders of Zion*, and published in several book editions in 1905–1906, this conspiracy theory gained a wider following. The *Protocols* offered monarchists straining against the workers' stubborn rise a clear enemy to blame.

When millions of workers and peasants demonstrated in 1905 for new political and economic rights, Tsar Nicholas II and many of his ministers believed that half the revolutionaries were Jews and condemned them for spreading unrest. It did not matter that no more than 2.5% of Russia's four million Jews were in revolutionary organizations.[25] As we have seen already, it is often perception, not reality, that directs people's actions. After Nicholas II signed the October Manifesto, propagandists on the developing Russian Right blamed the Jews for the changes befalling their country. When they accused the Jews of being enemies of Christianity who endeavored to dominate the world, they portrayed Bolshevism as a Jewish movement.[26] Known as Żydokomuna, this conspiracy theory saw Bolshevism as the path by which international Jewry planned to take over the world. The Jews, then, were quickly transformed into the ultimate enemy.

Żydokomuna rapidly spread and intensified when various pro-monarchist reactionary groups, known collectively as the Black Hundreds, organized against the tsar's 1905 October Manifesto.[27] Groups mushroomed in Russian provincial towns with the assistance of clerics, police, and army officers (and the rank and file), as well as some governors. Following the continental trend, the Black Hundreds blamed Jews—who they labeled as liberals, cosmopolitans, and revolutionaries—for modernity and the demise of conservative political ideals. These

---

24 Zipperstein, *Pogrom: Kishinev and the Tilt of History*, 146.
25 Lambroza, "The Pogroms of 1903–1906," 221. Right-wing vigilante groups even blamed Jews for the devastation wrought on the Russian Empire due to the earlier Russo-Japanese War. At a time when thousands of Russian troops were dying in Manchuria, right-wing printed pamphlets and leaflets blamed the Jew for Russia's ruination, as both the financial backers for Japan's war effort and traitors to Russia at the front. It is true that Jewish financier Jacob Schiff did back the Japanese war effort with monetary loans. He hoped a Russian loss would force the government to make necessary social reforms, especially regarding Jewish life in the empire. At the same time, however, the Jewish banking house of Rothschild funded Russia's own war effort. See ibid., 214–215.
26 Rogger, *Jewish Policies and Right-Wing Politics in Imperial Russia*, 193.
27 The term *Black Hundreds* later applied to the larger and more permanent extreme right wing groups, such as the Union of Russian People. See ibid., 198.

paramilitary groups fought back with pogroms against Jews, liberals, socialists, and students. However, heads of the central government, who feared mob violence and unequivocally denounced pogroms, opposed the Black Hundreds and the extreme right wing they represented.[28] Not only did the Black Hundreds seek specifically to forestall the promised constitutional monarchy, but they also fought to block the general liberalization of the Russian Empire. They stopped at nothing to achieve a sharp political readjustment.[29]

The Black Hundreds adopted the pogrom as its preferred form of protesting the Jew-Bolshevik enemy and launched into a violent, insane assault on Russia's Jewish communities. Publishing pamphlets which coupled theological anti-Judaism with political antisemitism, the group called for physical revenge on the Jews:

> Do you know brethren, workmen and peasants, who is the chief author of all of our misfortunes? Do you know that the Jews of the whole world . . . have entered into an alliance and decided to completely ruin Russia? Whenever those betrayers of Christ come near you, tear them to pieces, kill them.[30]

Pogrom instigators also distributed inflammatory leaflets to officials in the army and police, and to local and provincial government authorities.[31] Between 1903 and 1906, more than 650 pogroms pummeled Russian Jewish communities, killing more than five thousand Jews, injuring thousands more, leaving families impoverished, children orphaned, women raped, and property obliterated.[32] By World War I, Russian military policy had adopted the

---

28 Ibid., 109, 198–199.
29 Peter Kenez, "Pogroms and White Ideology in the Russian Civil War," in Klier and Lambroza, *Pogroms: Anti-Jewish Violence in Modern Russian History*, 304.
30 Lambroza, "The Pogroms of 1903–1906," 235.
31 Though relatively new research has debunked the myth linking Nicholas II to such instigations of social upheaval and pandemonium, some high-ranking government officials and military leaders are known directors and accomplices. Those advising Tsar Nicholas II were of two minds: on the one side was Count Witte, who authored the October Manifesto, allowing for reform and the demise of autocracy; on the far other side sat General D. F. Trepov, who supported right-wing reactionism, and knew about these antisemitic printing presses, at times even reviewing their contents before people distributed them. See ibid., 235–236.
32 Polonsky, *The Jews in Poland and Russia*, 2:48–63; Lambroza, "The Pogroms of 1903–1906," 227–229.

pogrom as policy along the Western front to rout out the Jew-Bolshevik enemy.[33]

Almost a decade later, when the Great War and Russian Revolution unfurled fear and destruction, the *Protocols of the Elders of Zion* provided supposed proof that the Jews should be blamed for it all.[34] Russia's monarchist White Volunteer Army printed hundreds of thousands of copies of the *Protocols* for distribution, placing the fault for World War I, the revolution, and the consequent Russian agonies, squarely on international Jewry. At this time, Zionism gained political momentum, with Great Britain's 1917 Balfour Declaration and promises of Jews ruling over Jerusalem's Christian holy sites. Christian conservatives pointed to this decision as part of the Jews' so-called masterplan. The creation of other Jewish-centric political movements throughout the latent Polish territories provided fodder for antisemites.[35]

By 1920, the *Protocols* had been translated into German, French, Polish, and English. It did not take long before this claim of Jewish world economic and political ambition gained worldwide attention.[36] Already anxious about a Judeo-Masonic conspiracy, the Catholic Church embraced the ideas contained in the *Protocols* in the immediate post-WWI years and used them to explain the tremendous chaos exploding and ripping through the European continent.[37] Communism—the political anti-Christ—was the enemy and, according to Żydokomuna, the Jews controlled it.

---

33 Alexander Victor Prusin, *Nationalizing a Borderland: War, Ethnicity, and Anti-Jewish Violence in East Galicia, 1914–1920* (Birmingham: University of Alabama Press, 2006), 26.
34 Segel, *A Lie and a Libel: The History of the Protocols of the Elders of Zion*, 16.
35 Paul R. Mendes-Flohr and Jehuda Reinharz, eds. *The Jew in the Modern World: A Documentary History* (Oxford: Oxford University Press, 1980), 299. According to historians Paul Mendes-Flohr and Yehuda Reinharz, "the term *elders of Zion* is apparently an allusion to the First *Zionist* Congress, which was held at the time the Protocols were written. It's very name points to the new Jewish nationalists in their *Zionist* garb as the enemy with which the world will have to contend.
36 Today, one may still purchase this flagrantly antisemitic work on such notable and trusted sites as Amazon. The company adds a disclaimer under the book's description, as well as a statement from the Anti-Defamation League. The question is whether or not it should be for sale.
37 Segel, *A Lie and a Libel: The History of the Protocols of the Elders of Zion*, 5.

Jews and Bolshevism

Jews did support the early twentieth-century revolutions in Russia, but not to the degree that the Russian monarchists claimed. That numerous revolutionary political parties also actively opposed antisemitism, made them attractive to Jews. After the 1903 Russian Social Democratic Workers' Party schism, a higher percentage of Jews preferred Martov's heterogenous Mensheviks to Lenin's then homogenous Bolsheviks.[38] Jewish membership in both parties rose when it was believed—erroneously—that the Black Hundreds' pogroms were government-sponsored.[39]

Yiddish writers, such as I. J. Singer, Chaim Grade, and Sholem Asch, filled their pages with young Jews' wish for change and equality:

> there would no longer be the oppressors and the oppressed, distinct classes or nations, hatred and envy. All men would be free. All worldly goods would be equally apportioned. And the happiness would be universal since all of man's troubles, all worldly evil derived from unjust economic conditions.[40]

Revolutionary socialist activity did indeed attract people of Jewish origin.

In fact, many Jews reached the upper echelons of the Bolshevik Party. Yakov Sverdlov (1885–1919), Grigori Zinoviev (1883–1936), and Lev Kamenev (1883–1936), among others, were in leadership positions, further fueling the distorted conspiracy theory of Bolshevism as a Jewish phenomenon. However, it is vital to make distinctions. Most revolutionaries of Jewish origin did not belong to the Bolshevik Party before 1917. A Bolshevik Party census reveals that merely 958 Jewish members joined prior to 1917—roughly 4% of its membership on the eve of the Romanov's fall. Some 1,175 Jews joined the Bolsheviks in 1917.[41] Although Jews held some high-ranking leadership roles, the Bolsheviks were not a Jewish party. The majority of its members identified as Russians of Christian origin. That opponents of Bolshevism claimed *all* Jews were

---

38   Jacob Miller, "Soviet Theory on the Jews," in *The Jews In Soviet Russia since 1917*, ed. Lionel Kochan, with an introduction by Leonard Schapiro, 3rd ed. (Oxford: Oxford University Press, 1978), 47n1.
39   Budnitskii, *Russian Jews Between the Reds and the Whites, 1917–1920*, 39.
40   I. J. Singer, *The Brothers Ashkenazi*, 237.
41   Antony Polonsky, *The Jews in Poland and Russia*, vol. 3, *1914–Present* (Cambridge: Littman Library of Jewish Civilization in association with Liverpool University Press, 2012), 9.

communists is a terrible distortion. But it worked to ferment peoples' fear and encourage them to fight the Jew enemy. Again, perception is everything.

After the Bolshevik's shocking overthrow of the Russian Provisional Government and deadly usurpation of the Constitutional Assembly, most revolutionaries (including Jews) affiliated with the party. They understood that to survive in this new political climate one had to participate in the power structure.[42] Jewish attachment to the Bolsheviks also expanded precipitously due to the White Army's antisemitic violence during the Russian Civil War.

Initially, thousands of Jews had joined the tsarist White Army. But several generals permitted its recruits, fresh from the front lines of World War I, to release their anger on the so-called Jew-Bolshevik enemy. Having witnessed extreme antisemitism in the White Army, many Jews defected to the Bolsheviks. The Bolshevik Red Army pursued the ideal of unity through tolerating different ethnic and religious origins. By 1918, then, Jewish membership of the Bolshevik Party had risen swiftly to 16% and approximately 30% of its central committee members were Jews.[43]

Young Poland and the Jew-Bolshevik

When Poles declared their independence near the end of World War I, many understood two things: the Bolsheviks were young Poland's enemy and communism's Jewish leaders were Poland's nemesis. Indeed, Lenin's right-hand man, Leon Trotsky (born Lev Davidovich Bronshtein, 1897–1940), bore responsibility for the Bolsheviks' intensifying military strength.[44] Many Poles interpreted their own social and political problems through the situation in Russia. Holding that *their* Jews would never assimilate into Polish culture—especially given Jewish nationalism's emergence—and aware that many Jews in Russia fought alongside the Reds, Poles perceived their own Jews as willing recruits for the Bolshevik enemy.[45] As it stood, the vast majority of Polish Jews did not side with Lenin and Trotsky. Yet quite a number did.

---

42 Leonard Schapiro, introduction to Kochan, *The Jews in Soviet Russia Since 1917*, 5; David G. Roskies, introduction to S. Ansky, *The Dybbuk and Other Writings*, ed. David G. Roskies and trans. Golda Werman (New Haven: Yale University Press, 2002), xxi.
43 Polonsky, *The Jews in Poland and Russia*, 3:9
44 Ibid.
45 World leaders and their advisors also made assumptions about the Jews' ties to the Bolsheviks, not only because of the preponderance of Jews within the Party, but also due to Russian monarchist propaganda. Many in Britain's foreign office believed that the Jews were behind the

The youth were particularly drawn to the Bolsheviks. In his memoir *My Mother's Sabbath Days* Chaim Grade makes an accounting of the many Jewish youth who subscribed to Soviet propaganda pumped into Poland through radio waves. In the Second Polish Republic, jobs were scarce, higher education elusive, and material comforts few. The Soviets, however, promised the youth employment and homes. Young Poles and Jews—susceptible to propaganda portraying their idyllic dreams as attainable—believed "[i]n the Soviet Union, everyone can realize his ambitions. If you want to become an engineer, you become an engineer; if you want to be a doctor, you become a doctor."[46] In Grade's memoir, his girlfriend, Baylka, is a broken, poorly paid seamstress who latches onto the hope offered by the Bolsheviks. Baylka represents the many Jewish and Christian Polish youth who not only sought party membership, but who also often stole across borders into their promised land.

Looking eastward in 1918, Polish nationalists interpreted the build-up of Bolshevik forces as a sign of imminent invasion. Given that the Catholic Church had already inundated Poles with Judeophobia through an antisemitic press campaign, and Roman Dmowski's Endecja proclaimed Jews the economic enemy of Poles, the Polish people were more than ready to view Jews as their political adversary. Pamphlets promoting Żydokomuna, combined with an increasing awareness of the *Protocols of the Elders of Zion*, convinced many Poles that the Jew-Bolshevik would soon invade Poland.

Poland: One Country, Two Voices

Despite the collapse of those powers which had previously carved up the Polish-Lithuanian Commonwealth and divided it amongst themselves, the Polish state's rebirth was not a fait accompli towards the close of World War I.

Russian Revolution and the ensuing struggles with the Russian Provisional Government. In the summer of 1919, an American Jewish captain, Jacob Harzfeld, brought proof against two British colonels showing they were disseminating antisemitic propaganda among Russians. In an effort to influence the war, the British ostensibly distributed pamphlets calling on "the Red Guards to throw off the Jewish yoke and unite with the Whites." Indeed Britain's General Knox stood by the belief that Britain was in a "full-scale crusade against 'the blood-stained Jew-led Bolsheviks.'" See Mark Levene, *War, Jews, and the New Europe: The Diplomacy of Lucien Wolf 1914–1919* (Liverpool: The Littman Library of Jewish Civilization in association with Liverpool University Press, 2009), 132–135 and 243–244.

46 Chaim Grade, *My Mother's Sabbath Days: A Memoir*, trans. Channa Kleinerman Goldstein and Inna Hecker Grade (Lanham: Rowman & Littlefield Publishers, Inc., 2004), 56.

The future republic would require both international support and internal cooperation. And though those in the kingdom had lived through partition's political and cultural consequences, at the dawn of a renewed Polish state Poles did not agree on what form that body politic should take. The very definition of Poland was up for discussion, as ideologues argued over who constituted a Pole. Despite numerous political parties and their respective factions, by 1918 two main camps dominated the debate: the National Democrats (Endecja) led by Roman Dmowski, and the Polish Socialist Party led by Józef Piłsudski.

Dmowski's training in the biological sciences, and consequent belief in Darwinism, provided him with a black-and-white worldview. This foundation led him to apply Darwin's theories of biological evolution to the theory of social evolution. Dmowski believed that some nations—the Poles among them—were better suited for survival than others. Dmowski's Poland would close its borders to any nations deemed either weak or a danger to the country's economic well-being. A Russophile, the Endek leader categorized Jews as one of the forces that would undermine the new nation's Polish ethnic core.

Dmowski welcomed the Ukrainians and Belarussians, believing they would eventually assimilate into this new Poland. Additionally, because these minorities lived primarily in the East[47] Dmowski asserted that the Poles could handle them. However, nearly a millennium of Jewish life in Poland proved that the Jews were steadfast loyalists to their own cultural, religious, and linguistic traditions. Dmowski's Poles rejected the Jews. That the Jews were so large in number, and held desirable jobs, allowed him to portray them as an internal enemy which, if not stopped, would rule over a renewed Poland. Thus, for Dmowski, "the Jews, the most alien of minority peoples, infidels in a land of Christians, merchants in a land of farmers, should be apprised instantly and decisively of their second-class status in a newly independent Poland."[48] His presentation of the Jew as Poland's ultimate enemy resonated with his traditionalist audience, which had been schooled by the Church, the *Protocols of the Elders of Zion*, and the spread of Żydokomuna.

Józef Piłsudski presented Poles with an alternative vision for a renewed Poland. Though he too got caught up in the nationalist surge sweeping Europe,

---

47 Despite the fact that the territory Dmowski pursued would retain a minority population of roughly 40%, Dmowski believed that the Poles could assimilate most of them, aside from the Germans, reasonably quickly. See Biskupski, *The History of Poland*, 58; Stachura, *Poland 1918–1945*, 12.

48 Howard M. Sachar, *Dreamland: Europeans and Jews in the Aftermath of the Great War* (New York: Vintage Books, A Division of Random House, 2002), 24.

his thinking had been informed by his time in the Polish Socialist Party (PPS). Many of his PPS cohorts had been Jewish, so he saw Jews as a welcome minority in an ethnically diverse Polish state. Despite having abandoned his socialist roots, Piłsudski maintained an abhorrence of integral nationalism, ethnic chauvinism, and right-wing clericalism.[49]

While Piłsudski's Poland would provide freedom of religious affiliation and expression, Dmowski's Poland would be defined by Catholicism. Thus, while Piłsudski acknowledged the rights of ethnic minorities, Dmowski's Endecja provided little room for them: "The Polish nation, it was felt, had not shed its blood and sacrificed its sons in order to establish a state in which vast territories and important financial resources would be controlled by non-Poles."[50] While Piłsudski extended himself to the Other, Dmowski believed that Poland should be reserved only for ethnic Poles, and those minorities willing to assimilate into his homogenous ideal.[51] Unlike Dmowski with his impoverished urban origins, Piłsudski was rooted in the landed Lithuanian gentry. He looked to the Polish nobility's military insurrections of 1794, 1831–32, and 1863–64 with pride. It was Piłsudski who, during the 1905–6 general strike against Russian rule, created a fighting organization for the PPS (Organizacja Bojowa), which took armed action against tsarist officials and government offices.[52]

Piłsudski yearned to re-establish the Polish-Lithuanian Commonwealth's grandeur. Dissimilar to Dmowski and his Endecja, which argued for Western expansion into German land, Piłsudski's territorial vision focused on the eastern borderland—the kresy.[53] While Dmowski sought to limit the role of minorities in a reborn Poland, whether by border placement or by excessive assimilation, Piłsudski welcomed minorities. He recognized the role interethnic toleration had played in maintaining Poland as a European power. He believed,

---

49 Sarunas Liekis, *A State within a State?: Jewish Autonomy in Lithuania 1918–1925*, ed. Edvardas Tuskenis (Vilnius: Versus Aureus Publishers, 2003), 45; Joseph Rothschild, *East Central Europe between the Two World Wars*, ed. Peter F. Sugar and Donald W. Treadgold, *A History of East Central Europe*, vol. 9 (Seattle: University of Washington Press, 1992), 33.
50 Mendelsohn, *Zionism in Poland*, 37.
51 Rothschild, *East Central Europe between the Two World Wars*, 34.
52 Wandyz, *The Lands of Partitioned Poland, 1795–1918*, 320.
53 Dmowski called for a renewed Poland to extend westward into German held territory. His initial border desires did not include the eastern kresy, given not only its preponderance of minorities, and Jews, but also the conflicts with Russia over the land. By swapping land for peace with Russia, he hoped to be able to stand solidly against Germany, the country which he considered the true, historical, enemy of Poland. See Dmowski, "Memorandum on the Territory of the Polish State," March 26, 1917, as cited in Stachura, *Poland 1918–1945*, 23; Biskupski, *The History of Poland*, 57.

writes Biskupski, that "the minorities were . . . the source of Polish greatness."[54] Given that Poland's enlarged borders would encroach on other peoples, who also desired political and cultural sovereignty, such as the Lithuanians and Ukrainians, Piłsudski sought coexistence within a loose confederation of states. Yet, Poland would have ultimate control.[55]

Piłsudski was not a diplomat, however. Shaped by a lifetime battling against Russia's absolute power over the Poles, Piłsudski was not concerned about being liked. A leader with a strong will, he "inspired either adoration or hate, but fondness never."[56] In contrast, during World War I Dmowski had established himself internationally as the representative voice of the Polish people. Yet, by aligning himself with the Polish National Committee—a 1917 coalition of right-wing émigrés and political parties—Dmowski actually spoke only on behalf of the most reactionary elements in Polish life. Despite this lack of true representation, Allied leaders turned to him as the recognized mouthpiece for the entire Polish population! When Dmowski visited the Allies and promised them Poland's future loyalty and support, he cemented their perception of him as the Poles' unequivocal spokesperson.[57] As such, it was also Dmowski to whom Jewish American leaders turned in order to understand the fundamental Polish view of Jews in a restored Polish state.[58] Unfortunately, Jews in the US came to equate Dmowski's outspoken antisemitic views with *all* of the Poles he purportedly represented.[59]

During this same period, a coalition of Polish Jews—Bundists (the General Jewish Workers' Alliance), General *Zionists*, territorialists, socialists, and Jewish national autonomists alike—galvanized support for Jews' legal recognition as

---

54 Biskupski, *The History of Poland*, 59. Ibid., 59.
55 Rothschild, *East Central Europe between the Two World Wars*, 40.
56 Davies, *White Eagle, Red Star: The Polish-Soviet War 1919–1920 and 'the Miracle on the Vistula'* (London: Pimlico, 2003), 64. The Allies did not trust the marshal due to his pragmatic collusion with the Central Powers. When Piłsudski recognized that Germany's promise of Polish independence was a smoke screen, he refused further cooperation and was imprisoned by the Germans in July 1917.
57 Levene, *War, Jews, and the New Europe*, 190.
58 George J. Lerski, "Dmowski, Paderewski and American Jews (A Documentary Compilation)," in *Jews and the Emerging Polish State*, ed. Antony Polonsky, Polin: Studies in Polish Jewry, vol. 2 (Oxford: The Littman Library of Jewish Civilization in association with Liverpool University Press, 2008), 95–116.
59 Other liberal Polish voices tried to gain access to the Allied powers, such as August Zaleski and Stanisław Patek who led the Polish Progressive Party, but given that their positions were similar to Piłsudski's, the British government eschewed them and the liberal Polish voice. See Levene, *War, Jews, and the New Europe*, 188–189.

a nation while still living in the Jewish diaspora. They argued that the Polish government should distinguish Jews as a landless nation. As such, they hoped to gain the same rights other national minorities sought, such as public funding for their (minority) schools and the right to speak their own language in both said schools and in public places. Ironically, these requests paralleled those Dmowski had made in 1907 on behalf of the Poles living in Russian Poland.[60]

Just prior to the Paris Peace Conference (January 18, 1919–June 28, 1919), at which world leaders convened to create treaties to end World War I, Dmowski campaigned for international support for a renewed Polish state. Unwilling to recognize the new political theory of landless nationhood, he argued for the traditional definition of a nation—that is, territory. As the Jews had no territorial claims to Polish land, Dmowski could deny them nation status and all its privileges. For him, the Jews remained the ultimate minority.

Independence and Border Expansion

The Great War's termination ended the reign of empires and granted power to nation states. Despite the cessation of hostilities in Western Europe, however, separate conflicts raged throughout the borderlands. The Bolshevik Revolution of November 1917 had extended its insidious hand of destruction into corners and crevices, terrorizing land and populations.[61] Now, emerging succession states unwilling to wait for the Allies' border determinations, bloodied the field. Ukraine, Latvia, Belarussia, Lithuania, and Poland, each sought to construct their own nation's political and cultural destiny by fighting one another as well as the Red and White Russian forces.[62]

On November 10, 1918, Piłsudski returned to Warsaw from German imprisonment in Magdeburg Castle. Recognized as commander in chief of the Polish armed forces and provisional head of state on November 11, 1918—before the world was ready—he declared independence on behalf of the Polish people.[63] Although disliked by diplomats worldwide for his disrespect for international

---

60 Wandyz, *The Lands of Partitioned Poland, 1795–1918*, 319.
61 Bolsheviks were considered Reds. Initially the Russian counterrevolutionary legions grew from an amalgamation of army officers, Cossacks, the bourgeoisie, students, intellectuals, and political groups, such as socialist revolutionaries. See Riasanovsky, *A History of Russia*, 480.
62 Almog, *Nationalism and Antisemitism in Modern Europe 1815–1945*, 144.
63 Stachura, *Poland 1918–1945*, 28.

authorities, he was highly favored by the Poles themselves. They cherished him as the hero who had led the Polish Legions during WWI, and they propelled him into the undisputed role of military and political leader of the resurrected Polish state.[64] As Piłsudski took command, two daunting issues challenged Poland's future: one, the actual determination of its borders, and two, the insistence of the Allies on safeguarding minority rights.

When the Allies first began stitching together nations torn apart by gluttonous power and catastrophic warfare, they envisioned a limited territory for Poland. This plan would make the Second Polish Republic the smallest Polish state since the Piast rule in the fourteenth century.[65] Angst-ridden Polish leaders did not know how such a small landmass could survive past infancy, flanked as it was on either side by historically aggressive countries. Believing Germany would seek retribution for Poland's westward expansion at the former's expense, and knowing that Soviet Russia needed to conquer Poland to extend its workers' revolution into Central and Western Europe, Piłsudski fell upon a military solution.

Aside from craving kresy land for strategic advantage, the Poles felt emotionally tied to the eastern borderlands. Even the average person who supported Dmowski still had a difficult time letting go of the kresy. Though it held far more ethnic minorities than it did ethnic Poles, Polish leaders spoke of it as being innately Polish.[66] Poles had a longstanding love affair with the kresy, as it symbolized the breadth and romance of the beloved Polish-Lithuanian Commonwealth. Thus, when the Germans evacuated the eastern borderlands near the close of WWI, creating a power vacuum, Poles sparred with many groups to establish governance over it.[67]

Piłsudski's call to battle for the kresy resulted in the formation of the Second Polish Republic's defense forces. A broad assortment of leftover units that had survived the Great War, their one commonality was an allegiance to Piłsudski as commander in chief.[68] Polish units arrived from abroad, but combining these disparate entities and leaders into a single force was difficult and slow. Generals and soldiers alike had to adapt to a new order.

---

64 Davies, *White Eagle, Red Star*, 63; Rothschild, *East Central Europe between the Two World Wars*, 33; Levene, *War, Jews, and the New Europe*, 190–192.
65 Biskupski, *The History of Poland*, 56.
66 Antony Polonsky, introduction to *Focusing on Jews in the Polish Borderlands*, ed. Antony Polonsky, Polin: Studies in Polish Jewry, vol. 14 (Liverpool: The Littman Library of Jewish Civilization in association with Liverpool University Press, 2001), 4.
67 Davies, *White Eagle, Red Star*, 24–25.
68 Ibid., 41.

Equipment—including uniforms, boots, and blankets—was extremely limited,[69] causing much physical suffering due to the harsh conditions confronting borderland battalions. Bootless soldiers scrimmaging for land faced minus forty degree winters. It only took one night's brutal frost to rob unblanketed men of their fingers and toes. Nor did such elemental struggles end with the change of seasons, as summer brought a sweltering, scorching heat.

The former Entente powers watched in disbelief and alarm as Piłsudski brazenly directed his troops to regain hold of the kresy. Opposing Dmowski's position, he aimed to take cities in East Galicia inhabited by relatively large populations of Poles. Disparate Russian units, as well as the Ukrainians and Lithuanians, met the Poles' attempt to expand their eastern borders.

War's Toll

Most of those soldiers straining to gain hold of kresy land had already seen the horror of war in 1914–18. Yiddish novelists addressed the human toll of war and the inability for soldiers to maintain a moral compass. In Sholem Asch's novel *Three Cities*, his main Jewish character Zachary Mirkin acknowledges, "'I've seen war with my own eyes—I know what war is: it turns men into beasts. Even the most righteous war turns men into beasts.'"[70] In his 1924 book *The Street*, Israel Rabon gives voice to the emotional catastrophe people experienced in both World War I and the ensuing Polish-Soviet War. Having spent four years serving in the Polish army, Rabon's Jewish narrator recalls a harrowing experience during the Polish-Bolshevik hostilities. After a steely winter night's carnage, the lone, desperate Polish battalion survivor drags himself over a steppe of frozen corpses in search of warmth. When he trips on a dying Belgian draft horse, he loses his mind:

> I thought I would die of the cold. Suddenly I had a wild thought that made me shudder. [...] In the space of a single breath I had my carbine knife out and *whack*! Gritting my teeth, I plunged the knife into the horse's belly with all my strength [...]
>
> A spurt of thick warm blood gushed over me. A caressing warmth, soft and heavy, flowed over my fists—which still

---

69 For a detailed listing of various military equipment, see ibid, 45–46.
70 Sholem Asch, *Three Cities: A Trilogy*, trans. Willa and Edwin Muir (New York: G. P. Putnam's Sons, 1943), 833.

grasped the carbine knife. [...] [W]ith my whole body I tore at the horse's belly till I had ripped its entrails out.

[...] Finally, the body was empty. I jumped for joy; then, squeezing myself together on the ground beside the horse, I crawled into its belly.

I was warm.[71]

But the next morning,

[t]he horse's blood shrieked accusations at my body. It tortured me. It choked me. It sucked my breath. [...]

[...] I wept. I yelled. I tore the hair, the bloody hair from my head.[72]

Rabon's Jewish soldier presents the extreme darkness of war, when survival overrides social values. Rabon's Jewish soldier had been felled by war's horrors.

Lieutenant Colonel Dave Grossman, former US Army Ranger and paratrooper, and a psychologist at West Point, confirms what World War I soldiers describe. Focusing his research on the individual and collective toll of war, Grossman's *On Killing* has become the standard text in the field.[73] He underscores that the drive to kill another person is not innate to human nature. We fight against it. In fact, throughout history a very large percentage of soldiers have refused to fire their weapons.[74] Grossman writes of soldiers' terror about the responsibility of protecting their fellow soldiers by killing the enemy. A study of soldiers who spent more than sixty days in sustained combat shows that 98% of survivors experience mental trauma.[75] Awash in fear that they will let their units down, soldiers face physical and emotional conditions civilians rarely know: pure exhaustion, raging inculcated hate for the enemy, and horror at the sounds, smells, and site of killing. "[T]he irreconcilable task of balancing these with the need to kill, eventually drives the soldier so deeply into a mire of guilt and horror that he tips over the brink into that region we call insanity."[76] The probability of a soldier

---

71 Israel Rabon, *The Street* (New York: Four Walls Eight Windows, 1990), 70–72.
72 Ibid., 73.
73 Lt. Col. Dave Grossman, *On Killing: The Psychological Cost of Learning to Kill in War and Society*, rev. ed. (New York: Back Bay Books/Little Brown and Company, 2009), xv.
74 Ibid., 23.
75 This data comes from Swank and Marchand's much-cited World War II study. See ibid., 43–44.
76 Ibid., 53.

becoming a psychiatric casualty of war was greater in World War I than that of his being killed by the enemy.[77]

Numerous writers understood that those lucky enough to survive war's brutality were hard-pressed to escape its influence. Rabon insists that his readers understand that a generation was ruined:

> Young people. Children, still at their mother's breast—eighteen-year-olds rounded up and thrown into battle—there they learn to kill people, to shoot, to slaughter each other. And they come back and God is gone from their hearts; they are wild, undisciplined, ruined—wandering about in the streets like birds of prey, ready to twist someone's head off or to cut their throats for a thousand marks. [...] A pity. A pity. They're such children.[78]

In the iconic rendering of World War I— *All Quiet on the Western Front*—Erich Maria Remarque also concludes that the youth who fought in the war were forever destroyed. Hospitalized, his German protagonist Paul Bäumer reviews what he has learned from war:

> I am young, I am twenty years old; yet I know nothing of life but despair, death, fear, and fatuous superficiality cast over an abyss of sorrow. [...] What do they expect of us if a time ever comes when the war is over? Through the years our business has been killing; it was our first calling in life. Our knowledge of life is limited to death. What will happen afterwards? And what shall come out of us?[79]

For Poles, the end of the Great War did not end the fighting. Polish soldiers fresh from the battlefields marched eastward to contend for Poland's expansion into the kresy.

---

77 Ibid., 54.
78 Rabon, *The Street*, 24.
79 Erich Maria Remarque, *All Quiet on the Western Front*, trans. A. W. Wheen (New York: Random House Trade Paperbacks, 2013), 194.

Kresy Pogroms

Although killing another human being is not innate to people, "with the proper conditioning and the proper circumstances, it appears that almost anyone can and will kill."[80] One important factor is the ability to maintain distance from the enemy, whether it be physical, emotional, cultural, or moral.[81] One is able to kill by separating oneself from the victim. Thus, to kill and survive, one must assert the enemy's inferiority and inhumanity. In the previous chapter, we discussed the Catholic Church's branding of Jews as the essential moral enemy. Roman Dmowski marked them as the central economic and political enemy. The spread of Żydokomuna and the impact of war on the national psyche made Jews the perfect target for violent responses to trying circumstances.

Towards the end of WWI, Poles in Galicia unleashed attacks on Jewish communities. Pushed by fuel shortages, hunger (which "compels the most law-abiding man to use force"),[82] and political anxiety, as well as inculcated antisemitism, many Polish civilians—especially right-wing youth—joined in looting Jewish-owned stores.[83] Poles portrayed Jews as traitors and enemies to a renewed Polish state, especially in Endek-filled towns. When Poles learned that Chełm and other kresy land they desired would go to the nascent Ukrainian state, numerous "Chełm protests" broke out. But in February 1918, rioters in Milówka launched a pogrom instead. Poles also blamed Jewish merchants for setting outrageous food prices. On April 16, 1918, Poles stormed into Kraków's Jewish Kazimierz district. Over six days, Jewish stores were sacked and Jews assaulted. The police were mostly passive.[84] During border expansion battles over the next few years Polish anti-Jewish violence surged and intensified. Such behavior is clearly upsetting and unacceptable. What I want to do here, however, is draw out nuance and provide context.

By 1918, all parties struggling for control over kresy territory took their grievances out on the Jewish communities in their midst.[85] The Ukrainian People's

---

80 Grossman, *On Killing*, 4.
81 Ibid., 158–162.
82 From the diary of Anna Kahan, cited in William W. Hagen, *Anti-Jewish Violence in Poland, 1914–1920* (Cambridge: Cambridge University Press, 2018), 3.
83 Ibid., 95.
84 Ibid., 97–99.
85 Prusin, *Nationalizing a Borderland: War, Ethnicity, and Anti-Jewish Violence in East Galicia, 1914–1920*, 19, 22, 26–27. For an extremely detailed explanation as to why these fighting armies targeted the Jews also see Polonsky, *The Jews in Poland and Russia*, 3:32–43.

Army was the worst.[86] Ill-disciplined and forced to plunder for provisions, the Ukrainian forces were responsible for some 439 pogroms.[87] While they were the most brutal, the 213 pogroms brought to bear on the Jewish population by the White Russian troops elicited the most casualties.[88] Even the Bolshevik Red Army, which stood ideologically opposed to antisemitic violence, could not always control its soldiers' behavior. Troops often switched sides, making it difficult to impose a single ideology on them. Those who left the White Army (led by Lieutenant General Anton Denikin [1872–1947]) or who abandoned the Ukrainian army to join the Soviets, often took their anti-Jewish agenda with them.

The most reliable estimates of the Jewish death toll throughout not only the Russian Civil War but also the Russian-Ukrainian conflict and the Soviet-Polish conflagration are that fifty to sixty thousand Jews were killed, with hundreds of thousands wounded, orphaned, and/or suffering psychologically.[89] Pogromists devastated Jewish communities economically through plunder and structural destruction. And while ruin, rape, and murder were not new to pogrom victims,

---

86 Sachar, *Dreamland*, 23; Polonsky, *The Jews in Poland and Russia*, 3:36–40. Jewish representatives in the Ukrainian Central Rada and Mala Rada were willing to promote an autonomous Ukraine within a federal Russia, organized under Russia's Provisional Government. The Bolshevik putsch of 1917, however, completely changed the Ukrainians' willingness to maintain any ties to Russia. The Ukrainians responded with their Fourth Universal, a declaration of independence from the Russian Bolshevik government. At this point, the Jews' own political loyalism could not let them align with the Ukrainians against Russia. Jewish political representatives did not support the Ukrainian's Fourth Universal. "Their opposition was received with particular bitterness, since the Rada had just passed the historic Law of National-Personal Autonomy: '. . . the Ukrainians were convinced that by this act they had won at least the moral right to a solemn and unanimous vote for the Universal of the Central Rada, including all its members, Ukrainians and non-Ukrainians.'" Henry Abramson, *A Prayer for the Government: Ukrainians and Jews in Revolutionary Times, 1917–1920* (Boston: Ukrainian Research Institute of Harvard University, 1999), 66. This lack of Jewish assistance, coupled with a growing Jewish national political mobilization, enraged supporters of an independent Ukraine; they later took vengeance on the Jewish communities through large-scale looting and killing. The Ukrainian peasantry went along with the violence as they viewed Jews as exploiters, who had brought about their economic woes. The peasants also associated Jews with not only the dreaded city and modernity, but with the whole Soviet regime itself. Clearly, for so many peasants, the Jew was the enemy. See Abramson, *A Prayer for the Government*, 53, 59–66.
87 Polonsky, *The Jews in Poland and Russia*, 49. For his numbers, Polonsky relies on records maintained of pogroms by Nakhum Gergel, who was a former deputy minister of Jewish affairs in the Ukrainian government.
88 Ibid., 53.
89 Ibid., 40.

by 1919 their intensity had reached fever pitch, mirroring the violence meted out in both the Russian Civil War and the numerous national battles.[90] Describing the Gorodishche pogrom of May 1919, Rogovoj, the inspector of EKOPO [the Jewish Committee for the Aid of War Victims], wrote that

> the *shtetl* is drowning in the down from beddings and mattresses, the local hospitals are full of women, many of whom are dying, on the streets there are piles of the young women (presumably dead) with their bellies swollen from being raped and cases of people losing their sanity.[91]

The death toll of the pogrom was anywhere from 350–500.[92]

That same month, in the large central Ukrainian town of Cherkasy, the worst of several pogroms in that vicinity occurred. In a little-known yet extraordinarily important archive compiled by historian Elias Cherikover, one finds a report by the Red Cross inspector Tsifranovich in which he describes the atrocities committed by Petlyura's Ukrainian People's Army "Cossacks."[93] "[T]he male Jewish population aged from sixteen and over was killed almost completely, bodies were mutilated so horribly that it was almost impossible to recognize them, with their arms and legs cut off."[94] The report goes on: "The rapes were of a horrible character. The victim was tortured by 8–10 people consecutively, and they gathered the Jews to make them watch the barbaric atrocity."[95] It is with this context that we explore Polish pogroms in the kresy at the close of World War I.

---

90 Irina Astashkevich, "Gendered Violence: Jewish Women in the Pogroms of 1917 to 1921" (PhD diss., Brandeis University, 2013), 206.
91 Ibid.
92 Ibid.
93 Here, *Cossacks* does not refer to the isolated, self-governing, military communities of the Don and Kuban Cossacks which provided excellent military service to the Russian tsars and who demonstrated loyalty to them by putting down uprisings and revolutions. The new Ukrainian People's Army lifted the term *Cossacks* in an effort to create an identity around which all disparate fighters could coalesce. The Cossacks evoked pride for Ukrainians given their freedom and military capabilities. While the 1917 people's militia referred to itself as "Free Cossacks," later the Ukrainian People's Army troops called themselves, simply, "Cossacks." See ibid., 185–186.
94 Ibid., 267.
95 Ibid.

Lviv, November 1918

Poles, Jews, and Ukrainians inhabited the Galician capital Lviv, (also known as Lwów and Lemberg). During November 22–23, 1918, Polish soldiers and civilians advanced against Lviv's Jews. Poles murdered at least seventy-two Jews and left more than three hundred wounded. The monetary damage is estimated at 110 million crowns (equivalent to more than twenty million contemporary US dollars), with Jewish shops, homes, apartment buildings, and synagogues plundered and then set ablaze.[96] Jews worldwide were aghast. Despite ninety anti-Jewish attacks having already been committed since the spring of 1918 by not only Galician Poles, but also Polish soldiers deserting the Austrian military, and Polish prisoners of war returning from Russia, Lviv shocked people in its enormity and breadth.[97] November 22–23 marked the beginning of large-scale Polish military pogroms that added to the Russian terror Jews had been facing in the eastern countryside. In reaction, American Jewry flung accusations far and wide about the new Polish nation that was celebrating its rebirth by robbing Jews of their existence.[98] "Lviv, 1918" is not just an individual event, then: it is a metaphor for both the violence which followed it and the unraveling of Polish-Jewish relations.

As we have seen time and again, context helps us understand conflict. When Austrian troops withdrew from eastern Galicia, Poland launched its first military campaign on its own behalf. Between November 1–22, 1918, Poles challenged the Ukrainian nationalist claim to Lviv as the capital of the new West Ukrainian Republic.[99] In their desperation to expand Poland's borders, the Polish army set itself up against the Ukrainians' own hunger for political national autonomy.

Lviv's Jewish population, which neared 82,000 out of 219,000, or roughly 37% of the city populace, chose to remain militarily and politically neutral during the 1918 fight for the city.[100] They did the only thing they could think of which would have the least negative consequences: nothing. They were not all

---

96 Polonsky, *The Jews in Poland and Russia*, 25; Hagen, "The Moral Economy of Popular Violence: The Pogrom in Lwów November 1918," 138, 142–143.
97 Polonsky, *The Jews of Poland and Russia*, 3:25.
98 Andrzej Kapiszewski, *Conflicts across the Atlantic: Essays on Polish-Jewish Relations in the United States during World War I and the Interwar Years* (Kraków: Księgarnia Akademicka, 2004), 58.
99 Mendelsohn, *Zionism in Poland*, 40; Davies, *God's Playground*, 2:287–288.
100 Hagen, "The Moral Economy of Popular Violence: The Pogrom in Lwów, November 1918," 126. While the Poles reached a slight 51% majority, the Ukrainian population rested at close to 12%.

necessarily against Polish political and territorial gains. But neither were they willing to take a stand against the Ukrainians' hold of the city. A minority surrounded by two powerful forces, Lviv's Jews helped neither the Poles nor the Ukrainians.

The Poles took Lviv, and many other cities, without the aid of the local Jewish communities. However, deeply concerned with world opinion, the Poles craved international support for expanding their borders. Polish diplomats believed that to have Lviv's Jews—one-third of the population—stand behind their demand for the city's inclusion within a renewed Polish state would greatly aid their cause in the international arena. Thus, despite many Poles accepting Żydokomuna's pretext of the Jews' enemy status, Poles still craved the Jews' support. If Allied leaders (from Britain, France, Russia, Italy, Japan, and the US) perceived the city's Jews to be taking a stand against Polish control of Lviv, world opinion could easily be swayed to support Ukrainian sovereignty over the city.[101] For the Poles, the Jews' attempted neutrality equated to acting on behalf of the Ukrainians. It equated to treason.[102]

Poles living in Lviv entered the conflict already predisposed to believing that the Jews opposed Polish national interests. Despite enjoying better relations decades earlier, when the Jews and other minorities received the right to vote, tensions emerged. The spread of Zionism in the Jewish population, with its call for neutrality, exacerbated these tensions.[103] Jews established a separate national identity at the same time that Poles had reasserted their own national cause. The surge in Endek antisemitic rhetoric and the spread of the Jew-Bolshevik conspiracy theory had primed Poles to view the Jews—with their neutrality and their Zionism—as enemy combatants.[104]

The fact that the city's Jews created an armed militia added to the Poles' disgust with the community's self-proclaimed neutrality. Polish soldiers believed

---

101 David Engel, "Lwów, 1918: The Transmutation of a Symbol and Its Legacy in the Holocaust," in *Contested Memories: Poles and Jews During the Holocaust and Its Aftermath*, ed. Joshua Zimmerman (New Brunswick, N.J.: Rutgers University Press, 2003), 40.

102 Hagen, "The Moral Economy of Popular Violence: The Pogrom in Lwów, November 1918," 144; Kapiszewski, *Conflicts across the Atlantic: Essays on Polish-Jewish Relations in the United States During World War I and the Interwar Years*, 57.

103 John-Paul Himka, "The Polish-Ukrainian-Jewish Relationship," in Bartal and Polonsky, *Focusing on Galicia: Jews, Poles, and Ukrainians 1772–1918*, 24, 36–37; Hagen, "The Moral Economy of Popular Violence: The Pogrom in Lwów, November 1918," 127, 136.

104 Though most Jews remained neutral in the Polish-Ukrainian battle, there were some pro-Ukrainian Jewish militia fighters. See Engel, "Lwów, 1918: The Transmutation of a Symbol and Its Legacy in the Holocaust," 35.

the stories Polish inhabitants of Lviv told them of Jews firing at and pouring boiling water from apartment building windows onto Polish soldiers.[105] Convinced that Jews had physically turned against the Poles, a large number of Lviv's Poles accepted the soldiers' celebration of their victory with anti-Jewish violence.

What Polish citizens and soldiers did not know, or chose to ignore, was that Jews had formed this militia in response to Jewish shops being vandalized and robbed from the outset of the Polish-Ukrainian battle for Lviv. On November 9–10, both Polish and Ukrainian military and civilian leaders sanctioned a Jewish armed militia of two hundred men to patrol against the looting of essential goods and foodstuffs.[106] For if the looting continued, populations would suffer. The authorities had set municipally fixed prices for such goods to insure public access. The Polish Foreign Ministry's initial investigation into the riot (prepared December 17, 1918, yet unpublished for years)[107] concurred that the militia formed due to police unresponsiveness to the attacks on Jewish shops. Having obtained two hundred rifles, Jews "captured Ukrainian and Polish bandits almost daily."[108] Most were former criminals just released from prison into the conflict's mayhem, who the Polish army readily outfitted to serve as manpower for the cause.[109] These were the Polish soldiers who Polish civilians saw Jews shoot. However, the Polish agents who authorized the Jewish militia did not explain to Lviv's Poles that military and civilian leaders had approved the Jewish militia. This lapse alone suggests, at least, an ambivalence over Poles fanning falsehoods and igniting their vengeance on the Jews.

That the Polish leadership had no idea how to respond to the violence against the Jewish population intensified the impact of this one pogrom. Until this time, Polish representatives had asserted Poland's exceptional moral merit in their international campaign for sovereignty.[110] The Lviv pogrom challenged this myth of a heroic victimized people. It also raised worldwide speculation over how

---

105 Hagen, "The Moral Economy of Popular Violence: The Pogrom in Lwów, November 1918," 127.
106 Ibid.
107 Poles began their investigation into the pogrom with a predisposed belief that the honorable Polish soldier and citizen would never take on such malicious, carnal behavior. They believed they would find evidence to support the Poles. In the end, they did not. As such, they felt compelled to silence the report in fear of international repercussions. This report was followed by others which tried to shed a brighter light on the aspiring Polish nation. See Engel, "Lwów, 1918: The Transmutation of a Symbol and Its Legacy in the Holocaust", 34.
108 Ibid., 35
109 Ibid., 36.
110 Ibid., 40.

Poles would deal with other ethnic minorities. As a direct consequence of this pogrom, the Allies severed 70% of Upper Silesia and its ethnic German majority from the emerging Polish state. The Polish nation came to understand "Lviv, 1918" as a tragic turning point in its dreams of national renewal. International opinion had turned against Poland: once the victimized underdog, the country now looked to the world like a chauvinistic victimizer. Yet according to Poland's national myth, the Jews' neutrality had caused this disaster.

Myth Reconstruction

American Jewish perception holds that Polish military policy institutionalized antisemitism and pogroms. However, a close look at the history of the region demonstrates that this view is a misperception. Unlike the Russian White Army, Polish military policy condoned neither antisemitism nor pogroms. However, the fact that pogroms occurred demonstrates an acceptance of them on some level. If a general held antisemitic views, there was a good chance that he would permit his troops to rob, harm, and even kill Jews. His soldiers had permission to direct their angst and frustrations at those they could overpower. Unable to control so little in this war, they violently devoured often unarmed or at best poorly armed communities to assert power.

Three generals in the new Polish army, well known for permitting pogroms, had been seasoned in the tsar's army. Not only did they wage battle for Mother Russia during World War I, but they also took part in the Volunteer White Army's struggles against the Bolshevik enemy. General Józef Dowbór-Muśnicki, leader of the anti-Bolshevik cause in Belarus, and General Lucjan Żeligowski, who campaigned with the Russian Whites in Odessa, southern Ukraine, permitted and encouraged Polish pogroms in Pinsk, on April 5, 1919, and in Vilnius (also known as Wilno and Vilna) in 1920.[111] Former Russian officers and soldiers who joined the Polish army brought with them a profound fear and activated hatred of Jews.

General Józef Haller, commander of the White Army, was notorious for his antisemitism, which he inflicted on Jewish volunteers who served in his ranks.[112] General Haller recruited about fifty thousand Polish soldiers from France and the United States during a time of strained Polish-Jewish relations in North

---

111 Davies, *White Eagle, Red Star*, 41–43.
112 Polonsky, *The Jews in Poland and Russia*, 53.

America.[113] Additionally, Haller's soldiers from France were known to entertain themselves in the spring and summer of 1919 by cutting off the beards of traditionally dressed Jewish men.[114] Indeed, these antisemitic sensibilities led Haller's "Blue Army" to double the number of casualties already inflicted by Poles on Jews during the first one and a half years of border conflicts.[115] Fending off Russian troops which had reached the gates of Warsaw, Haller's Blue Army took its desperation out on the supposed Jew-Bolshevik enemy in their midst. Officers encouraged their soldiers to view Jews not as people, but as invaders; the suffering they received was not cruel and unjust, but deserved and necessary for the defense of Poland. The army's leaders, in short, fanned their men's fears and frustrations into evil actions.

At the same time, it is important to recognize that, despite the intense buildup of antisemitic rhetoric throughout the region, Polish military atrocities did not increase exponentially, as they did with the Ukrainian and Russian forces. One significant preventative influence was Józef Piłsudski's commitment to a Poland in which national minorities would be treated with respect. After hearing of the atrocities that the Ninth Division inflicted on the Jews in Pińsk (April 5, 1919) under General Antoni Listowski, who had previously served in the tsar's army, Piłsudski ordered a change of command.[116] With careful consideration, he appointed as the new commander of the Polesie Division on the Lithuanian-Belarussian front the more refined General Władysław Sikorski (1881–1943), "a cultured man, free of the barrack-room psychology which prevailed to a greater or lesser degree in an army which had been through five years of war."[117] Although Sikorski had very little actual battle experience, Piłsudski knew that his soldiers needed a leader who would model behavior suited to an open, minority-friendly Poland.

---

113 According to the Polish perspective, Jews had turned on the Polish people during World War I, when the latter needed public international support for a renewed Polish state. Instead of providing political and monetary assistance, most Jewish representatives only defamed Poles globally by blaming them for economic boycotts and antisemitic agendas. (That such things took place was not the issue for the Poles. They did not want to be called out for them on the international stage.) Kapiszewski, *Conflicts across the Atlantic*, 33–53.
114 Jerzy Tomaszewski, "Pinsk, 5 April 1919," *Poles and Jews: Renewing the Dialogue*, ed. Antony Polonsky, Polin: Studies in Polish Jewish Studies, vol. 1 (Oxford: The Littman Library of Jewish Civilization, 2004), 234.
115 Sachar, *Dreamland*, 25.
116 Józef Lewandowski, "History and Myth: Pińsk, April 1919," in Polonsky *Jews and the Emerging Polish State*, 51.
117 Ibid., 50 and 52.

Of course, in order for the head of government to learn about alleged pogroms someone needed to step forward to tell him. Those who held to the so-called "Belvedere camp" took a public stand against the military's right-wing excesses. In his diary, Wiktor Tomir Drymmer, then a young second lieutenant and information officer at the Ninth Division's headquarters, explained how a group of "like-minded people" strongly objected to the character of the division. Not only did it violate their vision for a renewed Poland, but it dramatically reduced any pro-Polish sympathies in the area. They did not stand by idly, but acted, despite possible personal consequences. The group sent a grim account of the Pińsk atrocities through secret channels to both Sejm deputies and the press.[118] When these allegations reached the Sejm, thirty deputies signed the motion to set up a special parliamentary commission to investigate the execution of thirty-three Jews in that city.[119]

The left did not remain silent. It employed both the media and parliamentary procedures to change the leadership of the Polish army and of Poland. Turning in thirty-six officers to the courts, Sikorski recognized that "[i]n Gen. Listowski's time the most despicable scum in our resurgent army ran wild."[120] Although Piłsudski did not respond quickly enough to prevent all pogroms, his actions and those of his base prevented them from becoming much more commonplace. The American Jewish media could not see this fact. Blinded by heightened emotion, a lack of information, and confusion, it chose to portray Poland as a one-dimensional antisemitic monster.

In moral support for their fellows in Central-Eastern Europe, American Jewry portrayed Poles as wholly antisemitic thus, worsening relationship between Poles and Jews in the Second Republic.

---

118 Ibid., 57–58.
119 Ibid., 56.
120 Ibid., 60.

CHAPTER 10

Offense and Defense

Prior to Piłsudski's preemptive declaration of Polish independence and his pursuit of the kresy, the Poles had been seen as the darling of the Allies. As the Great War neared its final months, an internationally renewed independent Polish state was all but certain.[1] Along with his cohort, US President Woodrow Wilson saw hope for a new Europe in the Poles. Flanked on either side by Germany and the Soviet Union, a renewed Poland would help to stabilize Europe, acting as a buffer against past aggressors.[2] Indeed, the Entente took seriously Soviet Russia's own description of its worldwide socialist agenda: "Over the dead body of White Poland shines the road to worldwide conflagration. On our bayonets we shall bring happiness and peace to toiling humanity. To the west! March!"[3] Resurrecting Poland, a country torn apart by 146 years of Russian, Prussian, and Austrian partition thus became one of President Wilson's top priorities.[4] In fact, a year prior to the Paris Peace Conference, Wilson drew up his Fourteen Points as principles for peace, declaring in point thirteen a renewed Polish state.[5] This chapter explores the Paris peace talks, where Roman Dmowski's antisemitism intersected with the American Jewish misrepresentation of kresy pogroms as Polish.

---

1   Sachar, *Dreamland*, 25.
2   Kapiszewski, *Conflicts across the Atlantic*, 56.
3   M. Tukhachevsky, commander in chief of the Red Army on the Western Front in his Order of the Day, 2 July 1920. Cited in Stachura, *Poland 1918–1945*, 39.
4   Davies, *God's Playground*, 2:286.
5   Stachura, *Poland 1918–1945*, 25.

Dmowski Asks American Jews for Aid

By mid-1917 representatives of the emerging Polish state had formed the Polish National Committee. Endecja leader Roman Dmowski and world-renowned pianist Ignacy Paderewski (1860–1941) traveled throughout the United States to lobby on behalf of the committee for the realization of Poland's renewed sovereignty.[6] They hoped to gain Congress's support for Polish independence while securing financial and political backing from various influential groups.

Paderewski reached out to the leadership of the American Jewish Committee (AJC), which had been a vocal political advocate for Central Eastern European Jewry. A Jewish philanthropic organization, the AJC's leadership sprang from Jewish German immigrant families who had made a financial and social mark in their new country. Louis Marshall (1856–1929), a brilliant appellate lawyer who had argued more cases before the Supreme Court than any other lawyer of his time, presided as AJC president. Paderewski understood the importance of establishing strong ties with him.[7] As such, Paderewski met with Marshall in September 1918 and organized a meeting between Marshall and Dmowski for the following month.

The initial October audience in Dmowski's New York Plaza Hotel suite took an immediate turn for the worse after Marshall raised the recent pogrom activity and demanded that Dmowski end the Polish economic boycott that had devastated Jewish livelihoods since 1912.[8] Dmowski let it be known that such an end could be accomplished if Jews in the United States and other Western countries would "furnish capital with which to develop commerce and industry in Poland."[9] Angered, Marshall noted Dmowski's veiled effort at extortion. In turn, he made his own arrogant demand. He did not stop at insisting that Jews have greater legal rights in a renewed Poland. He presented Dmowski with an already drawn up bill of rights and insisted that it be incorporated into the Polish Constitution. The Polish contingent was aghast at the gall of the American Jew to press himself so forthrightly into Polish legal institutions.

The two men met again, but to no avail. Each side remained unmoved. While Dmowski asserted the Polish National Committee's commitment to a democratic constitution under which all Polish citizens would be treated equally

---

6 Polonsky, *The Jews in Poland and Russia*, 27.
7 Sachar, *Dreamland*, 30.
8 Ibid.
9 Ibid., 30–31.

before the law, the AJC representatives denounced it as too vague. They wanted specific guarantees—a bill of rights—for the Jews in a renewed Poland.[10]

So intent was Marshall on protecting Jewish rights in Poland, that he sent a copy of the bill of rights to not only Senator Henry Cabot Lodge of the Foreign Relations Committee, but also to President Wilson. In requesting that the US delegation impart to the Poles the absolute necessity of curtailing antisemitism, Marshall argued that such a bill of rights ought to be the basis for international acceptance of Poland as a new nation.[11] In the end, it would be this very concept, this dependency on accepting legislation guarding its minorities, that would drive much of the diplomatic endeavors surrounding the new Polish state.

American Jews and *Polish* Pogroms

Louis Marshall's argument for an international mandate protecting Poland's Jews grew stronger as one year transitioned to the next. Just prior to the start of the initial Paris Peace Conference, news broke of the Lviv pogrom. Hearing about pogroms was not a new phenomenon in the American Jewish experience. As a collective, American Jews had responded to the 1903–1906 wave of Russian pogroms. However, learning of Poles joining in this monstrous activity was new. Although the Polish right had been engaged in an economic boycott against the Jews since 1912, Poles were not known for extreme anti-Jewish violence. American Jews responded through the press and political channels.

Polish representatives resisted referring to anti-Jewish "excesses" as pogroms. They feared that for Westerners such a term would link Poland to Russian pogroms. Instead, Polish diplomats explained the assaults as acts of war, claiming that Jews killed by Poles were Bolsheviks, whose own goal was to take control of Poland. Polish spokespeople enlisted Żydokomuna as a defense strategy to shut down the disparaging talk of *Polish* pogroms, which threatened international validation of Poland's professed borders.[12]

The American Jewish press refused this explanation of events. In December 12, 1918, *The Jewish Advocate* remarked on Lviv with the headline: "Jews the Only Victims of Polish Pogroms."[13] The article included accounts of the Polish

---

10   Naomi W. Cohen, *Not Free to Desist: The American Jewish Committee 1906–1966* (Philadelphia: The Jewish Publication Society of America, 1972), 111.
11   Ibid., 112; Polonsky, *The Jews in Poland and Russia*, 27–28.
12   Biskupski, *The History of Poland*, 72.
13   "Jews the Only Victims of Polish Pogroms," *Jewish Advocate*, December 12, 1918.

Municipal Council's debate over the nature of the violence, during which two Jewish council members asked: "How does the chief of the Citizens' Militia, who claims that the pogroms were not anti-Jewish in character account for the singular fact that the only victims were Jews?"[14] The American Jewish press too would not be duped by Polish diplomatic word choice.

At the same time, the American Jewish press often conflated the complicated situations on the ground in the eastern borderlands, eventually charging the Poles with most of the atrocities carried out against Jewish communities. Whilst Poles, Lithuanians, Latvians, and Ukrainians struggled to consolidate their political independence, the Bolsheviks were embroiled in a civil war with Russia's White Army. Between 1918 and 1920, each nascent state encountered multiple conflicts while fighting for political survival. Poland challenged the Soviets, Ukrainians, and Lithuanians in various land grabs, thus engaging in six concurrent wars for control of the kresy.

With multiple shifting war fronts fought by fluctuating combatant army combinations, confusion and misrepresentation erupted. Thus, while the Poles targeted force against Jews, the press and the American Jewish public also held Poles responsible for devastating anti-Jewish brutality which Poles did *not* commit. Instead of deciphering the specifics of many conflicts, reporters and editors led people to cast the post-WWI pogrom crisis as Polish-led. Consequentially, American Jews developed a particularly virile antipolonism, which exists to this day.

The American Jewish press changed from recognizing pogroms as "the worst horrors of Czarist Russia"[15] to naming the Poles as most responsible for the continued violence:

> It used to be one of the boasts of the Poles that their country was unstained by pogroms and the boast was more or less warranted until Mr. Dmowski—the gentleman whom the Foreign Office accepted as the representative of Poland—and his friends took to specializing in antisemitism as a political doctrine. Once the Poles started to learn the lesson from the Russians they rapidly improved upon their teachers, and they are taking over the practice of pogroms when the Russians are abandoning it.[16]

---

14 Ibid.
15 "The Polish Pogroms," *American Israelite*, January 9, 1919.
16 Ibid.

Citing the secular *Manchester Guardian*, the *American Israelite* promoted the position that Poland, independent for less than three months, had become the hotbed of antisemitic violence surpassing even that of Russia.

Breditschew

For the American Jewish press, Poland morphed into a metaphor for pogroms and antisemitism. We can see this clearly in a quick analysis of two articles grounded in the same initial reporting. The *Cornell Daily Sun* reported on January 15, 1919: "Several Hundred Jews Killed at Breditschew." Basing its story on a January 13, 1919 report by the Associated Press in Warsaw, the paper presents the massacre having "occurred as a result of an attempt by *peasants* to disarm the militia which the Jews were organizing for their protection in all centers, which they anticipated would be necessary when the Moscow government breaks up" (emphasis mine).[17] Here, "peasants" erupt into antisemitic brutality. But which peasants? Russian, Ukrainian, or Polish?

After indicating that several hundred Jews had been killed, the correspondent provides some insight into the criminals' nationality: "It is considered here that the control of Petlyura, the Ukrainian leader, has weakened, as otherwise he would not have permitted the massacre, his policy previously having been to protect the Jews when possible."[18] Symon Petlyura's permission would be relevant for people who followed him, or whom he controlled militarily—Ukrainian peasants. Other nationals, vying for their own freedom, did not need this Ukrainian leader's permission to act. It follows that those who committed the atrocities against the Breditschew Jewish community were Ukrainian peasants, not Polish peasants.

Yet, on January 16, 1919, the Cincinnati based *American Israelite* presented the exact same article provided by the Associated Press under this tell-all caption: "Polish Pogroms Multiply." By simply changing the headline, the *American Israelite* portrayed the Breditschew massacre as a Polish-led atrocity. Despite the last few sentences that assess Petlyura's shrinking power base, the average reader could easily put the paper down without connecting the dots, or without reading to the end. What stands out is that "Polish Pogroms Multiply." Headlines are powerful. Quick. To the point. Readers scan headlines to garner some general

---

17 "Several Hundred Jews Killed at Breditschew," *Cornell Daily Sun*, January 15, 1919, http://cdsun.library.cornell.edu/cgi-bin/cornell.
18 Ibid.

sense of world events. Unfortunately, headlines don't tell the story.[19] The problem here is apparent: a voice in the American Jewish press blames Poles for outrages that they did not commit. And because people were so enraged by what Poles actually did do in Lviv from November 22 to 24, 1918, it did not become clear to the Jewish community, or perhaps even matter to many, that in this case, as in others, the American Jewish media had pointed a finger at the wrong party.

What American Jewry has retained erroneously from this irresponsible journalism, is that Poland played an enormous role in kresy pogroms and that thousands of Jews died due to Polish antisemitism. The fact that Poland's lead international diplomat, Roman Dmowski, had long voiced hatred for the Jewish middle class and instituted the 1912 Jewish economic boycott only further encouraged American Jews' willingness to misread the kresy situation. Although Piłsudski held a completely different political, economic, and social orientation from Dmowski regarding the Jews, American Jews ignored the marshal. Mirroring the US government, American Jewry permitted Dmowski—whom Paderewski had referenced as "Poland's ablest and strongest statesman"—to represent *all* Poles in attitudes toward Jews.[20] American Jews had reduced Poles to a single one-dimensional image against which they protested.

New York Demonstration Against *Polish* Pogroms

On May 21, 1919, after the April 5 Pińsk pogrom, American Jews, Christians, World War I veterans, and public officials gathered in New York City to demonstrate against *Polish* pogroms. According to a *New York Times* article detailing the public protest, hundreds of thousands of people, wearing black armbands as

---

19 In an article written by Julius H. Greenstone, the author discusses the Vilna pogrom and the Polish accusation that the Jews had turned against the Polish forces, accepting Bolshevism. Greenstone also notes other pogroms, which took place in Galicia. The last paragraph mentions a pogrom in Zhytomyr, in which two thousand Jews were murdered. The average American Jew did not know where Zhytomyr was located. The article also fails to attribute the pogrom to a particular group. I would argue that many readers would have connected Poles to the Zhytomyr pogrom, despite it having been carried out by Ukrainians, given that they had just read in the same article that Poles led the Vilna pogrom. See "House of Israel: More Pogroms Reported in Poland and Galicia," *Jewish Exponent*, May 30, 1919, 7.

20 "The Representative of the Polish National Committee (Paderewski) to President Wilson," Office of the Historian, accessed June 6, 2021, https://history.state.gov/historicaldocuments/frus1917Supp02v01/d701.

"a way of mourning their fellows murdered in Poland,"²¹ converged in parades throughout New York City. Despite reporting on crowds that decried the "massacres of Jews in Poland, Galicia, and Romania," the article proceeded for two pages to blame only Poland for the spate of pogroms. Only Poland was named after the introduction. Not Russia. Not Ukraine. And yet, this city-wide demonstration took place during the worst year of pogrom violence, when other nations played an incredibly large role in it. Readers understood that American Jews, and those government representatives speaking at the event, blamed Poland—specifically—not only for the most recent Pińsk pogrom, but also for the other atrocities.

When the marchers gathered at Madison Square Garden that evening, former New York Governor and Supreme Court Justice Charles Evan Hughes welcomed them. He proclaimed that "these outrages are a betrayal of the cause for which we fought; they are a betrayal of the victory that has been won."²² Jacob Schiff, a prominent Jewish banker, businessman, and philanthropist pointed to all of the Jewish servicemen in the audience, who had risked their lives fighting for newly emerging nations to attain justice. And yet, justice seemed in short supply. The Poles, now free, were wreaking havoc on Jews. The philanthropist Nathan Strauss, owner of two major New York department stores, called on the Polish government to "realize the dreadful consequences of inaction in not preventing massacres of innocent people. They can do it if they want to and we won't take any excuse. It has got to stop."²³

Former Governor Hughes added,

> The question is, whether the peoples, with this new vision and this new opportunity [for political freedom] will be able to save themselves by their own self-restraint . . . whether these people can safeguard this opportunity and make democracy real. . . .
>
> The whole test comes when any one is singled out and discriminated against by reason of creed or of race . . . [Our men went to war] not to fight for something vague and unascertainable, but for very definite principles of American liberty. . . .

---

21 "Call On Nations to Protect Jews," *New York Times*, May 22, 1919, 1.
22 Ibid.
23 Ibid.

> I stand here against all violence, all manifestations of a desire to gain by force at the expense of justice . . . ; against all that the Hun represented; against all that is represented in these terrible persecutions in *Poland*.[24] (emphasis mine)

Governor Hughes' audience could not miss the jarring correlation between the "Huns" and the Poles. At a time when the Entente powers were gathering in Paris to discuss new nation states' borders, Jews and US leaders reflected the belief that Poles, more than any other party, bore responsibility for the bestial violence unleashed against kresy Jews.

Polish Leaders Respond to Accusations of Polish Pogroms

Polish leaders found the international press coverage of Polish pogroms insulting and demoralizing. Poles had long believed that the honorable Polish soldier and citizen would never exhibit such malicious, carnal behavior.[25] The Poles needed global support at this delicate political juncture. Although having already declared independence, Polish nation status and acceptance of its expanded borders, with access to the sea, felt very much tied to the Entente's meeting at Versailles.[26]

Prior to any pogroms, world opinion had cast the Poles as the much-respected underdog. People respected the Poles' internal struggle to maintain their national identity. By 1914, the Polish leadership had demonstrated a steadfast dedication to preserve the integrity of the Polish people and to reunify its land. The Poles' struggle and determination impressed the Allies. But this perception changed with the press coverage of Polish pogroms. Allied leaders grew concerned that in asserting their own rights, Poles (and other new nation states) would end up disregarding national minorities' rights in their regions.

---

24 Ibid. Governor Hughes also spoke out vociferously against Jim Crow. As the keynote speaker at the opening session of the first National Conference on Lynching, May 5, 1919, Hughes underscored that the Allied victory in WWI would not be complete until the US rid its own land of hatred. He stated, "We have not destroyed the menace of force because we have licked the Kaiser; the menace of force resides in every community." See Maury Thompson, "Charles Evans Hughes Was a Consistent Voice against Racial Inequality," *Post Star*, July 11, 2020, https://poststar.com/charles-evans-hughes-was-a-consistent-voice-against-racial-inequality-copy/article_59b63fad-c1da-5fcf-b1b2-7192f7cf42b7.html.
25 Engel, "Lwów, 1918: The Transmutation of a Symbol and Its Legacy in the Holocaust," 34.
26 "The Representative of the Polish National Committee (Paderewski) to President Wilson."

Dmowski denied that the violence committed by Poles was specifically targeted against Jews. He chose to see the conflict within the context of rivals at war, defining those Jews killed as the Bolshevik enemy. That some Polish left-wing leaders also denied such charges is more surprising: caught in the throes of literally fighting for the fulfillment of their people's dream of independence, they did not accept that their heroic soldiers could act so immorally.[27]

In a June 1919 interview with the *New York Times*, Polish Premiere Ignacy Paderewski explained that the world misunderstood Poland because it knew little of Eastern Europe. He outright denied Polish violence against Jews, holding that only two pogroms had taken place that were led by Poles, and that those had occurred before he took office. He asserted, "I can unhesitatingly state that the events as represented in the New York meeting have not occurred."[28] Declaring that the bloody scene in Pińsk did not constitute a pogrom, Paderewski explained that the country had been battling the Bolsheviks in the city, where Jews led the revolutionary movement. Poland responded to the Reds' killing of sixty Polish soldiers by killing Bolsheviks.

Prince Lubomirski, then Polish minister to the United States, formally addressed *Polish* pogroms in an interview with the *New York Times* on July 27, 1920.[29] With the goal of demonstrating that the Ukrainians bore responsibility for much of the anti-Jewish violence misattributed to Poles, Lubomirski singled out one particular pogrom:

> Rumors of pogroms in Poland have of late again become frequent in the American press. At the end of May came the first news of a Jewish pogrom by Polish soldiers in Balta; ... A glance at the map would, however, have sufficed to show that Balta was inside the Bolshevist lines and that the Polish Army never occupied that town, so that if there really was a pogrom it was perpetrated by the Bolsheviki.[30]

A city in Odessa district, Ukraine, Balta repeatedly changed hands between the Bolsheviks and Petlyura's forces.[31] Over a two-month period, three pogroms

---

27 Polonsky, *The Jews in Poland and Russia*, 49.
28 "Lemberg Pogroms Were Not by Poles," *New York Times*, June 2, 1919.
29 The *New York Times* article was reprinted in the *Jewish Exponent*, July 30, 1920.
30 "Jewish Ill Treatment Denied by Lubomirski," *Jewish Exponent*, July 30, 1920.
31 Jewish Virtual Library, s.v. "Balta, Ukraine," accessed August 29, 2003, http://www.jewish-virtuallibrary.org/jsource/judaica/ejud_0002_0003_0_01949.html.

took place. Pogromists killed some hundred Jews, raped at least 120 women, and bombed thirty-five houses.[32] With violence ravaging the city, Jews fled to Odessa. Jews ran not from Polish aggression, but from that inflicted by Ukrainians, Russian Bolsheviks, or both.[33] Unfortunately, due to months of reading not only about *Polish* pogroms but also articles in which Premiere Paderewski had denied responsibility for all pogroms but two, Jews responded to Minister Lubomirski's argument with derision.[34]

American Jewish Influence at the Paris Peace Conference

Recalling his failed meeting with AJC president Louis Marshall, Roman Dmowski wrote, "When my sojourn in the United States came to an end, I knew... that during the Peace Conference we would have in the Jews the most vehement enemies of our cause."[35] As continued media coverage of *Polish* pogroms ignited the press, Dmowski and Paderewski landed in Paris to lobby on behalf of a renewed Poland. They believed that the Jews who journeyed from the United States, Western Europe, and Eastern Europe to advocate for the besieged Jewish communities would attempt to lay out conditions, that is, roadblocks to the Poles' national liberation process. They could not have foreseen just how impactful the multiple Jewish groups would be in birthing the European successor states.

However, the various Jewish representatives differed in their agendas. Specifically, they disagreed on the actual definition of the Jewish people: Were the Jews a religious group or a nationality? Should lobbyists expect Jews to assimilate fully into the host country's culture or work doggedly to retain all aspects of their separate identity, such as language, dress, and education? The French and British Jewish community representatives held staunch antinationalist proclivities. They feared Jewish nation status would foster the age-old stereotype that Jews living in any country posed a threat as "a state within a state."[36]

---

32 Elias Heifetz, *The Slaughter of the Jews in the Ukraine in 1919* (New York: Thomas Seltzer, Inc., 1921), 402–403.
33 Ibid.
34 "Give Data on Polish Pogroms," *Jewish Exponent*, June 6, 1919, 6.
35 Sachar, *Dreamland*, 31.
36 Oscar I. Janowsky, *The Jews and Minority Rights: 1898–1919* (New York: Columbia University Press, 1933), 17–22.

Several representatives from the nine-man American Jewish delegation also aligned privately as anti-nationalists. However, they traveled to Paris as emissaries of the new American Jewish Congress, which had voted in 1917 to define Jews as a nation in need of communal and cultural autonomy.[37] Led by Marshall as vice president and Julian Mack (1866–1943) as president,[38] the American Jewish Congress delegation advocated for the Jews to have international protections through minority rights legislation.[39] In Paris, the American Jewish Congress group consolidated its lobbying efforts with the Central East European Jewish delegates, who categorized themselves as Jewish nationalists or *Zionists*.[40] They created the Committee of Jewish Delegations at the Paris Peace Conference. This committee often clashed with British and French Jewish representatives over Yiddish and the autonomy of Jewish schools.[41]

Acknowledging both the prestige of the United States and the fact that its lead representatives had already established contacts with President Wilson, the Committee of Jewish Delegations named Marshall chairman of its crucial human rights subcommittee.[42] Through backdoor diplomacy, Marshall and Mack made the ingenious suggestion of including safeguards for all minorities, not just Jews, in both successor states and defeated states.[43] Their contact carried this idea through the chain of command vetting process.[44] That large-scale pogroms devastated Jewish communities in the kresy during this same period (e.g., Pińsk, April 5, 1919) only increased the Jewish delegation's need to secure rights for the Jews and all minorities in those regions.

---

37 The American Jewish Congress formed as a result of surging conflict between the "establishment" American Jewish Committee, defined by its German Jewish leadership, and the new political *Zionist* voice demanded by East and Central European Jewish immigrants. See Sachar, *Dreamland*, 33.
38 Julian Mack was also a German Jewish Harvard educated federal judge.
39 The American Jewish Congress, in its pro-*Zionist* stance, advocated also for a renewed State of Israel in Palestine. See Sachar, *Dreamland*, 33; Cohen, *Not Free to Desist*, 112.
40 The vast majority of Jews inhabiting Central and Eastern Europe still identified themselves within a religious orientation, not a Jewish national one. See Levene, *War, Jews, and the New Europe*, 21.
41 Swiss political leaders also argued for linguistic rights for national minorities. See Janowsky, *The Jews and Minority Rights*, 259.
42 Sachar, *Dreamland*, 35.
43 Polonsky, *The Jews in Poland and Russia*, 29.
44 Marshall and Mack's contact was David Hunter Miller, a friend and legal adviser to the American Peace Commission.

President Wilson sanctioned the Jewish Delegations' plan in April 1919, creating the Committee on New States and for the Protection of Minorities.[45] This committee would be charged with drafting the bill of rights—those clauses to be incorporated into binding treaties with each successor state—guaranteeing, at least on paper, the civil rights of minorities, while providing them with some form of communal autonomy.[46] In essence, Marshall succeeded in bringing to Versailles that which Dmowski refused in New York.[47]

While drafting the minority bill of rights legislation,[48] a main point of contention between Jewish and Polish leaders lay in providing Jews full national autonomy, which included linguistic autonomy—the full use of Yiddish in civil institutions and some schools. Those Jews sitting at the table insisted Yiddish was a central component of the Jews' national identity and, therefore, a right necessitating protection. They insisted on maintaining Yiddish as it was

> the vernacular of six million Jews, the growth of 700 years of separate Jewish history, the medium of a considerable and highly respectable Jewish literature, the spontaneous dialect of the Polish Jew in his home and in the market place and an indispensable element in the intricate social and economic relations of the Jewish community which lives in great masses and which would be completely disorganized without it.[49]

Without the right to Yiddish in all activity, Jewish representatives argued that Jews would suffer culturally and economically: "Without it there . . . [can] be no liberty of meetings or school education, no political life, no justice or legal protection."[50] Polish leaders contended that affording Jews linguistic rights

---

45 Sachar, *Dreamland*, 36.
46 Polonsky, *The Jews in Poland and Russia*, 29.
47 Marshall and Mack met with President Wilson at the White House on March 2, 1919, one week prior to Marshall's trip to Paris. While in that discussion they presented a "Jewish Bill of Rights," by the time the concept reached the president again, they had decided to include all minorities. See Sachar, *Dreamland*, 34–35.
48 Miller and his associate Manley O. Hudson worked closely with the American Jewish lobbyists before presenting their final draft to the Allied peacemakers. Together with head British Jewish delegate Lucien Wolf (1857–1930), who began to understand the necessity for at least limited national linguistic and educational autonomy for the Jews of Central and Eastern Europe, they formed the basic provisions of Poland's Minorities Treaty. See Cohen, *Not Free to Desist*, 116–117; Polonsky, *The Jews in Poland and Russia*, 30–31.
49 Levene, *War, Jews, and the New Europe*, 203.
50 Ibid., 189.

would not only encourage further separation, by nullifying any true need to learn Polish, but also spur persistent cultural divisions, thereby promoting continued distrust and animosity between Poles and Jews.[51] At the same time, they understood the importance of maintaining one's group language. In Russian and Prussian partitioned Poland Poles had been denied linguistic rights in public spaces including schools and courts.[52] Dmowski himself had lobbied the 1907 Russian Duma to allow Poles this basic right. His efforts were unsuccessful.

With the help of Ignacy Paderewski, who respected the Yiddish language's relevance to the Jews,[53] Lucien Wolf ably navigated the solution. He respected that Poles felt threatened by complete Jewish national autonomy. Including such extensive linguistic freedoms for the Jews and other minorities challenged the Poles' sense of control over the internal civil direction of their reborn state. Wolf presented linguistic duality as the solution. Jews would use Yiddish in their schools only up until the sixth grade, while teaching Polish throughout the Jewish educational system. Subject to state supervision, Jewish school curriculums would be assimilated to the statewide curriculum.[54] In the end, this bill of rights did not differ much from the one that Louis Marshall had first presented to Dmowski in New York City. The main difference was in Wolf's compromise, that is, refrain from conceding maximalist national rights to the Jews.[55]

Poland's Minorities Treaty

In providing full civil, religious, and political rights to all citizens of the new Poland, article two of Poland's National Minorities Treaty required that naturalization be extended to all persons either born or habitually residing in the state.[56] Article seven recognized the importance of language, protecting the free use of

---

51 A similar debate has gained prominence among Americans in the twenty-first century, who question the place Spanish has gained in US culture. As nationalist currents increase in the US, so too have calls to curb Spanish use. Although the Jews' situation in Poland differed greatly from that of Spanish-speaking US immigrants in that Polish Jews had lived in that land for centuries, both groups chose to retain their respective separate identity through language, alienating and infuriating many in the "host" society.
52 Email correspondence between the author and Jerzy Tomaszewski, December 23, 2013.
53 Jerzy Tomaszewski explained this situation concerning Yiddish. Wolf, and Paderewski to the author in an email dated December 23, 2013.
54 Levene, *War, Jews, and the New Europe*, 219–220.
55 Polonsky, *The Jews in Poland and Russia*, 30–31.
56 Levene, *War, Jews, and the New Europe*, 312.

"any language in private intercourse, in commerce, in religion, ... in publications of any kind."[57] Additionally, "adequate facilities" (interpreter services) were to be provided minority members who testified in their own language before courts of law. Article eight also supported privately funded primary schools in which ethnically non-Polish children would be instructed "through the medium of their own language."[58] Articles nine and ten detailed the creation and autonomous management of public funding for public primary schools within a community in which a "considerable proportion of Polish nationals of other than Polish speech are residents" in order that they may receive instruction in their own language.[59] On paper, it appeared that Poland (and other successor states) would support the Jews' and other minority populations' self-preservation.

Only two articles of Poland's Minorities Treaty single out the Jews from other minorities. Article ten states that elected Jewish Educational Committees are responsible for the distribution of state funds for Jewish public primary schools discussed in article 9. Article eleven protects Jewish religious practice. It exempts Jews from "performing any act which constitutes a violation of their Sabbath," which begins Friday evening at sunset and lasts through Saturday at dusk, when three stars are visible.[60] The state is also prohibited from holding national elections on the Jewish Sabbath.

Clearly, the American-led Committee of Jewish Delegations and Britain's Jewish leader Lucien Wolf had great sway at the Paris Peace Conference due to networking and back room diplomacy. While Polish Jews themselves could not get any concessions from their meeting in Poland with Dmowski held prior to the peace conference, international Jewish leaders forced his acquiescence.[61]

Dmowski's Response to the Jews' Power at Versailles

On June 24, 1919, after German and Allied representatives signed the Treaty of Versailles, relinquishing former German-held Polish territories, Roman Dmowski and Ignacy Paderewski sat in stony silence in the Hall of Mirrors and

---

57   Ibid., 313.
58   Ibid., 314.
59   Ibid.
60   Ibid.
61   Ezra Mendelsohn, *The Jews of East Central Europe between the World Wars* (Bloomington: Indiana University Press, 1987), 35; Michlic, *Poland's Threatening Other*, 72–73.

signed the National Minorities Treaty.⁶² Poland's internationally recognized status as a nation became tied to her acceptance of the National Minorities Treaty and the Jews' protections within its articles.

An enormous number of Poles seethed with anger that a minority would hold so much power over their hard-won independence—a minority that had not demonstrated, from the Poles' perspective, the support Poland required during its border expansion conflicts. In the end, that Jews enlisted a political figure to whom most people did not have access—the president of the United States. The fact that political figures from all corners of the globe converged at an international peace conference only strengthened Poles' conviction that Jews had global power.

From Dmowski's perspective, this international Jewish lobbying effort to achieve both minority and Jewish rights represented the first calculated step in creating Judeo-Polonia—a Polish Jewish state in Poland.⁶³ As one who had already fought against Jewish economic predominance, this apparent Jewish political triumph solidified Dmowski's belief that the Jews' represented not only Poland's definitive internal enemy, but its external enemy as well.⁶⁴ Certainly, if one was persuaded by the increasingly popular conspiracy theory presented in the *Protocols of the Elders of Zion*, then the supposed Jewish enemy had moved at least three steps closer to world domination.

Of course, international Jewish leaders' descent on Versailles did not signify a Jewish conspiracy to take over the world. Rather it illustrated a concerted effort to bring aid to fellow Jews who had been targeted violently in pogroms led by multiple nationalist military campaigns associated with Central Eastern European succession states. This Jewish-led effort to secure civil rights and physical protection for Jews and other minorities equated to a human rights campaign. Yet many Poles could not see this. Their suffering physically and culturally under partition had clouded their vision. They knew that for the most part, when the Poles were in difficult situations, other nations did not come to their defense; and now, at the moment their country was finally becoming the darling of nations, with the world poised to help it, the Jews had turned the world against it. The peacemakers forced Poles to treat the Jews better than Poles themselves had been treated. Of course, this was the very point of the Paris Peace Conference: to stop the cycle of internal conflict and oppression within and between nations. However, to be on the receiving end of such directives

---

62 Sachar, *Dreamland*, 40; Polonsky, *The Jews in Poland and Russia*, 31.
63 Michlic, *Poland's Threatening Other*, 73.
64 Mendelsohn, *The Jews of East Central Europe between the World Wars*, 35.

elicited negative reactions from not only Poland but from the other successor states as well.

Poles Claim Hypocrisy: US Race Relations

Just prior to signing the Minorities Treaty, Poland organized a rebellion with the other emerging new states, each of which would also be required to sign a version of this accord before it could join the international community of nations. They argued that while the treaty infringed on each new state's sovereignty, world leaders did not hold other larger countries to the same standards, including Germany, the war's initiator.[65] They decried the Allies' disregard for their own minorities, which conflicted with the rights granted in the Minorities Treaty. For example, American Jews living in heavily Jewish populated centers did not speak Yiddish in public schools. And succession state leaders believed the US government would never accede to such a request if made.

Indeed, it can be argued that President Wilson rejected the American Jews' request that succession state minorities have the right to bring complaints of infractions of the Minorities Treaty directly to an international body in fear that American minorities would be granted similar rights and would assert that privilege.[66] Wilson was well aware that US government policy had not treated its minority populations, especially Indigenous peoples[67] and Asian immigrants,[68]

---

65 Janowsky, *The Jews and Minority Rights, 1898–1919*, 353.
66 Ibid., 29.
67 In one late nineteenth century example, the US government forced tens of thousands of young Native Americans to leave their families and homes and attend "assimilation" boarding schools. In these 150-plus boarding schools, established expressly to "kill the Indian in him and save the man," children were not permitted to use their given names, speak their native language, or practice their religion and culture. Through this inhumane policy the US government tried to force Native American assimilation into the white man's culture. See Becky Little, "How Boarding Schools Tried to 'Kill the Indian' through Assimilation," History, July 11, 2023, https://www.history.com/news/how-boarding-schools-tried-to-kill-the-indian-through-assimilation.
68 American hatred and abuse of the Chinese in the late nineteenth century brought carnage to this immigrant population. Massacre upon massacre erupted in the American West with nodded approval from government authorities and politicians. This anti-Asian stance grew and solidified itself further in aggressive anti-Japanese legislation. The Gentlemen's Agreement of 1907 slowed Japanese immigration to the US. But not enough. By 1910, the census showed a tripling of the Japanese population, from 1900, to roughly seventy-two thousand. See Gary Dean Best, *To Free a People: American Jewish Leaders and the Jewish Problem in Eastern Europe, 1890–1914* (Westport: Greenwood Press, 1982), 3. Horrified,

with the same cultural, political, and economic respect it demanded from the emerging states. Despite well-known US maltreatment of these groups, Wilson's administration made no apology for or sought to rectify such malfeasance.

The most glaring American hypocrisy at the time lay in Wilson's acceptance of the segregated Jim Crow South. A shorthand for the violently enforced codes of the Southern caste system, the Jim Crow regime reigned from the 1880s to the 1960s.[69] True, the US could insist that it had fought and won a war against slavery. It could assert that Reconstruction had afforded freed slaves rights previously denied them, such as the right to vote, marry, attend school, open a business, and run for political office. Yet the US government could not demonstrate that it actually protected this minority population as it expected the newly emerging Central Eastern European states to do with their minorities. Once Northern troops left the South after a mere decade, Southern leaders dismantled the flimsy dais of Reconstruction on which Black Americans stood and sent them toppling back onto the parched dusty ground from which they had risen.

In her acclaimed work *The Warmth of Other Suns*, Isabelle Wilkerson proposes that post-Reconstruction Southern white society simply reestablished the socioeconomic structure originally imposed by slavery. This reclaimed "caste system [was] based not on pedigree and title, as in Europe, but solely on race, and which, by law, disallowed any movement of the lowest caste into the mainstream."[70] Many Southern whites perceived Black Americans' freedom as an assault on true Southern culture, economic well-being, and political power. Jim Crow and its white supremacy rhetoric became embedded at all levels of government. Approving the "equal but separate" policy, even the Supreme Court bowed to its influence. Its 1894 Plessy v. Fergusson ruling permitted the definition of Black Americans as less than human. Jim Crow's separation of Black Americans and white Americans reached into all aspects of life, including education, work, housing, transport, prayer, medicine, recreation, and even sanitation.

---

anti-Japanese groups influenced the passage of the 1913 California Alien Land Law, which barred Japanese migrants from purchasing land. It also prohibited Japanese from becoming naturalized citizens, no matter how long they lived in the United States. See Heart Mountain: WWII Japanese American Confinement Site, accessed August 29, 2023, https://www.heart-mountain.org; du.com, accessed June 19, 2019, https://www.du.edu/behindbarbedwire/history.html.

69 Isabelle Wilkerson, *The Warmth of Other Suns: The Epic Story of America's Great Migration* (New York: Vintage Books, 2011), 10.
70 Ibid., 38.

Along with establishing that Black Americans were less than, reactionary traditionalists also portrayed them as the dangerous Other. By characterizing Black men as violent animalistic threats to white civilized society, the 1905 novel *The Clansman* and its nationally acclaimed 1915 film version *Birth of a Nation* fed white society's panic over the Black minority's economic, social, and political freedom. The first major motion picture of its kind, *Birth of a Nation* was seen by millions of people within the US. Lauded by President Wilson, members of the US Supreme Court, and Congressmen, the film engaged its audience with the frightening image of Black equality as an unleashing of the Black Beast.[71] Both explicitly and implicitly, it argued that Black men did not have the mental fortitude to hold political office. And due to its supposed raging sexuality, the Black Beast would prove a constant danger to the vulnerable white woman and thus to white society.[72]

Armed with these two alarming and widely accepted allegations—that the inferior Black Beast was dangerous to both society and white women—Southern local law enforcement found every reason to arrest and imprison Black Americans, especially Black men. Sheriffs ignored the 1868 Fourteenth Amendment to the US Constitution, which grants the right to due process and equal protection to anyone born in the United States.

With the 1915 release of *Birth of a Nation*, the Ku Klux Klan's (KKK) membership skyrocketed.[73] The KKK surged into mainstream white culture as a grassroots security force for the preservation of white womanhood, the white man's political birthright, and white masculinity.[74] The need for such so-called protection against the Black threat permeated American white society, especially in the Jim Crow South. While the North had won the civil war, the South had won the culture war.

By the time President Wilson led the Entente at Versailles, minority relations at home had reached appalling levels. Clearly the new European states were being held to standards that did not apply to the Allies. While Jewish lobbyists, who did not understand the multilayered nuances of Polish-Jewish relations,

---

71 Travis D. Boyce and Winsome M. Chunnu, "Toward a Post-Racial Society, or a "Rebirth" of a Nation? White Anxiety and Fear of Black Equality in the United States," in *Historicizing Fear: Ignorance, Vilification, and Othering*, ed. Travis D. Boyce and Winsome M. Chunnu (Colorado: University Press of Colorado), 125.
72 Ibid., 125–126.
73 Ibid., 122.
74 Wilkerson, *The Warmth of Other Suns*, 40.

had moved the Allied leaders at Versailles to involve themselves in other countries' internal policies, the Entente would never tolerate such a breach of their own members' sovereignty.[75]

The Morgenthau Report

On June 2, 1919, the *New York Times* ran an interview with Poland's premier, Ignacy Paderewski. After roughly seven months of negative press covering *Polish* pogroms, the New York City demonstration, and the tumultuous minority rights negotiations, Padereski called for an American commission to visit Poland and to assess the Jews' situation. Stating that "I and my colleagues in the Polish Government have nothing to conceal,"[76] Paderewski endeavored either to reset the conversation, or to get ahead of the latest news and control the story. Weeks earlier, on May 16, 1919, Louis Marshall and Julian Mack had visited President Wilson's Paris apartment and pressed for an inquiry into widespread *Polish* pogroms. Wilson acquiesced, thus creating an investigative committee to review matters on the ground.[77] He later charged this mission to Henry Morgenthau Sr. (1856–1946), the former US ambassador to the Ottoman Empire during World War I.

An American Jewish lawyer born in Germany, Morgenthau spent two months in Poland (July 13, 1919–September 13, 1919) investigating what American Jews claimed was rampant *Polish* pogrom activity.[78] Influenced by his personal belief that Jewish communities should integrate fully into their respective host nations' cultures, Morgenthau did not agree that the Jews should be given such broad linguistic and educational rights as the Minorities Treaty granted. Meticulously and vigorously fulfilling his duties, Morgenthau traveled to Jewish communities throughout the country where pogromists had destroyed

---

75 Although the Allies worked deftly to underscore Poland's sovereignty by avoiding the designation of the Jews as a national minority, they obfuscated this fact by providing the Jews and other minorities with such broad communal and cultural autonomy.
76 "Paderewski Asks American Inquiry," *New York Times*, June 2, 1919.
77 Sachar, *Dreamland*, 36.
78 Henry Morgenthau was also present in Paris during the peace conference as part of President Wilson's entourage. As ambassador to the Ottoman Empire, Morgenthau was one of few American officials who wrote about the Armenian genocide. Ibid., 28, 35.

property and people, and he interviewed both Jews and Poles.⁷⁹ In the end, his report, which focused on the eight most recent large pogroms, placed no blame on Polish government policy, thereby dismissing the American Jewish media's claims. Instead, it pointed to a confluence of conditions, including the undisciplined and ill-equipped Polish recruits, the long-held view of Jews as cultural aliens, and Roman Dmowski's Endecja's intensifying antisemitic press with its increasing number of proponents.⁸⁰

In a rather stark tone, Morgenthau determined that "[t]hese excesses were apparently not premeditated, for if they had been part of a preconceived plan, the number of killed would have run into the thousands instead of amounting to about 280."⁸¹

Furthermore, he stressed that "It is believed that these excesses were the result of a widespread antisemitic prejudice aggravated by the belief that the Jewish inhabitants were politically hostile to the Polish state."⁸² He begged restraint from stereotyping the Polish criminals as *all Poles*.

Morgenthau argued that "just as the Jews would resent being condemned as a race for the action of a few of their undesirable coreligionists, so it would be correspondingly unfair to condemn the Polish nation as a whole for the violence committed by uncontrolled troops or local mobs."⁸³ In the end, he noted that the Polish government should devise a "plan for Jews to secure the same economic and social opportunities as are enjoyed by their coreligionists in other free countries."⁸⁴ He added, "[t]he fact that it may take one, or two generations to reach the goal must not be discouraging."⁸⁵

The Poles Claim Morgenthau Report Hypocritical

The Poles did not respond well to the October 1919 Morgenthau Report. Though based on good intentions, and well researched, it reflected the patronizing hypocrisy that Poles believed cradled the Minorities Treaty. Morgenthau closed his report with:

---

79   Ibid., 28.
80   "Fixes Blame for Polish Pogroms," *New York Times*, January 19, 1920.
81   Ibid.
82   Ibid.
83   Ibid.
84   Ibid.
85   Ibid.

> All citizens of Poland should realize that they must live together. They cannot be divorced from each other by force or by any court of law.... The Polish nation must see that its worst enemies are those who encourage this internal strife. A house divided against itself cannot stand. There must be one class of citizens in Poland, all members of which enjoy equal rights and render equal duties.[86]

US race relations directly contradicted the advice Morgenthau presented to the Poles. The Jim Crow laws enforced in the South made the US's suitability to dictate other country's civil standards questionable to say the least.

Poles knew that Black populations in the US suffered from the unjust socioeconomic and political inequality imposed by the US government. Poles also knew that intolerance of the Other often turned to violence. The Ku Klux Klan set enormous crosses ablaze on Black people's property. Terror lynchings persisted as a preferred local means of punishment for perceived transgressions by Black people against the white supremacist social code.[87] Across the South an Black American was hanged or burned alive every four days from 1889–1929.[88] Suspended from a tree branch by a noose, often set ablaze or riddled with bullets, Black men, women, and children swayed to their deaths before cheering crowds of white men, women, and children. Largely tolerated by state and federal officials,[89] between 1877 and 1950 white people conducted 4084 lynchings.[90] Lynch mobs symbolized white solidarity, strength, and superiority. They battled what they perceived as an immense socioeconomic and political threat.[91] Contemporaneous to pogrom terrorism in the borderlands, terrorism by lynching permeated the American South.

---

86 Ibid.
87 Philip Dray, *At the Hands of Persons Unknown: The Lynching of Black America* (New York: The Modern Library, 2003), iii-iv.
88 Arthur F. Raper, *The Tragedy of Lynching* (New York: Dover Publications, 1933); Wilkerson, *The Warmth of Other Suns*, 39.
89 Brian Stevenson and the Equal Justice Initiative, *Lynching In America: Confronting the Legacy of Racial Terror* (Montgomery: Equal Justice Initiative, 2017), 3.
90 Ibid., 4. Recent research has found eight hundred more lynchings than had previously recorded in collections, as well as three hundred lynchings that took place in eight states outside of the Deep South.
91 James H. Madison, *A Lynching in the Heartland: Race and Memory in America* (New York: Random House, 2001),14.

The *Chicago Defender* described an October 12, 1917 lynching in Houston Texas:

> Eight hundred oil-field workers ... employed at Goose Creek, a suburb of this city, seized Bert Smith, a member of the Race, and brutally hung him to a tree and riddled his body with bullets and horribly mutilated it with sledge-hammers and butcher knives after cutting it down.
>
> ... a number of oil drillers ... placed a rope around his neck, hammered his mouth in with a sledge and pierced his body with sharp instruments, and then forced a 10-year-old white lad who carried water around the camp to take a large butcher knife and unsex him. Smith, who was still alive, begged that all his feelings be taken from him. He was dragged down the main thoroughfare near the camp houses and viewed by citizens including women.[92]

Lynching continued in the United States because the very idea that Black men could rise in social stature and respect elicited unpunished outrage in the South. Black leaders who challenged white social norms were lynched simply because they brought a sense of self-worth to those in their communities. Instead of hanging Black community leader Eli Cooper from a tree, the mob released white anxiety by shooting him to death in an Ocmulgee, Georgia church. The white mob burned down the church and other vital Black communal property after accepting the rumor that Blacks were planning to exterminate white residents.[93] This conspiracy theory paralleled that launched against the Jews in the *Protocols of the Elders of Zion*. Both groups, American white nationalists and the Russian Right, feared annihilation—economic, cultural, and physical.

Racially motivated mobs also razed *whole* Black communities. While pogromists raged against Jews in the eastern borderlands of Poland, white mobs descended on Black communities throughout the United States. In 1917, at least forty Black people were killed during a race riot in East St. Louis, Illinois sparked by white anger at the increase in the Black population. In 1919, a slew of race riots terrorized numerous Black communities, including Charleston, SC., Chicago, IL., Knoxville, TN., Omaha, NE., and Washington, DC. According to government documentation, eight whites were injured and eighteen white

---

92 "Boy Unsexes Negro before Mob Lynches Him," *Chicago Defender*, October 13, 1917; reprinted in Ralph Ginzburg, *100 Years of Lynchings* (Baltimore: Black Classic Press, 1988), 113–114.
93 "Lynch Negro, Burn Church," *New York Sun*, August 29, 1919, reprinted in Ginzburg, *100 Years of Lynchings*, 123.

people were killed. That same documentation shows that a total of 769 Black Americans were injured and at least ninety-four were killed.[94] Estimates of fatalities provided by the Black community are much higher than those offered by government agencies.[95]

The racially triggered violence continued in June 1921 when a group of white residents in Tulsa, Oklahoma attacked Black-owned homes and destroyed Black businesses in the city's Greenwood District. There, white mobs destroyed thirty-five blocks in what was known as Black Wall Street, killing at least three hundred Black residents and injuring another eight hundred. The 1923 Rosewood massacre claimed a minimum of six Black lives, with the probability that closer to 150 Black people were murdered.[96] From 1917 to 1923, which included what is known as the Red Summer of 1919, race riots raged in more than thirty cities, terrorizing Black citizens in the United States.

While the horrors of World War I certainly influenced events, it should be noted that little was done on a local level to protect the victims or to punish the perpetrators. Neither did a governmental review or accounting take place.[97] Indeed, although asked to launch an investigation into the 1917 East St. Louis riots, President Wilson refused. It took an act of Congress to forge an investigative committee.[98]

It is imperative to acknowledge US racist legislation, terror lynchings, and race riots in order to understand the Poles' response to both the Minorities Treaty and the Jewish influence on its creation. During that time in which Poland's borders were being redrawn on the world map, and numerous media outlets were misattributing most pogroms to the Poles, structural racism permeated the United States (not just the South). Yet, in Versailles, those world leaders trying to stitch nations back together focused only on *Polish* pogroms, successfully compartmentalizing their countrymen's own uncivil behavior back home.

---

94 Keisha L. Bentley-Edwards et al., "How Does It Feel to Be a Problem? The Missing Kerner Commission Report," *RSF: The Russell Sage Foundation Journal of the Social Sciences* 4, no. 6 (September 2018): 24, https://www.jstor.org/stable/10.7758/rsf.2018.4.6.02.

95 Nan Elizabeth Woodruff argues that in the Elaine, Arkansas 1919 massacre, soldiers, police officers, and white mobs killed hundreds of people in an attempt to halt union organizing. "Homes were burned with Black families inside, and the victims included men, women and children." See Mike Ives, "Beyond Tulsa, Overlooked Race Massacres Draw New Focus," *New York Times*, June 29, 2021, https://www.nytimes.com/2021/06/29/us/elaine-massacre-history-lessons.html.

96 Bentley-Edwards et al., "How Does It Feel to Be a Problem? The Missing Kerner Commission Report": 20–40.

97 Ibid.

98 Ibid.: 29n8.

Myth Reconstruction

Americans, both Jews and non-Jews, identified Poland as the heart of the evil enacted against Jewish communities in the immediate postwar scramble for border expansion, when in fact Poland bore responsibility for a mere fraction of it. American Jews and non-Jews looked down on the country, castigating its violent behavior despite knowing that America had its own evil social norms. They painted a one-dimensional portrait of the emerging Polish state. With an unwillingness to provide economic, political, social, and religious context, American Jews saw in Poland only Roman Dmowski's popular Endecja.

I admire American Jews' endeavors to call Poland to account for its actions against the Jews. But knowing of America's own contemporaneous racial intolerance and consequential violence against Black people, I do query American Jewry's lack of curiosity and unwillingness to discover other dimensions within Polish society. Certainly, American Jews knew that not *all* white people (which included the majority American Jewish population) behaved barbarically against African Americans. They knew that some white people even rose up and protested this horrific abuse, at times putting their own lives in jeopardy to protect minorities.[99] Despite the racism present in the country's majority white population, American Jews knew that not *all* white people (including white Jews) hated Black Americans. Given the ability to distinguish among varying approaches to minorities in the United States, one would expect those same US Jews to recognize that not *all* Poles viewed Polish Jews as the enemy of Poland and that they would not take part in pogroms.

But in this time of rage, stereotyping prevailed. Perhaps because mainstream American Jews defined themselves within the white American collective, and white Jews living in the United States inherently recognized their own multi-dimensionality, it followed that white American Jews could extrapolate that the white American population itself remained multi-dimensional. Americans included both racists and anti-racists. Some Jews were racist, and some were anti-racist. But, since most American Jews did not identify closely with Poland's majority population, they did not feel compelled to dig beyond the surface to locate the Poles' own complexity.

It is important to underscore that the number of Jews killed specifically by Polish soldiers and Polish armed civilians in pogroms rests between 350 and

---

99 "Sheriff Nearly Lynched," *Providence Bulletin*, August 31, 1916; reprinted in Ginzburg, *100 Years of Lynchings*, 107.

500. Poles struck out against Jews, leaving numerous communities traumatized and devastated—physically, economically, and psychologically. This sad truth is not in question. Yet Polish-inflicted terror against Jews did not reach anywhere near that attained by either the Ukrainian or Russian forces. Importantly, the very discussion of real numbers makes it clear that the Polish government did not authorize the devastation of Jewish civilian life and property. Soldiers on all fronts could be manipulated to act against the Jews. What separated the Polish troops from others was their leadership: not only had many Polish officers been trained in the Austro-Hungarian military where pogroms were not sanctioned, but Piłsudski himself stood against pogroms and acted relatively early to limit them. A central problem, however, lay in the fact that within the newly formed Polish military, which looked to various countries for officers and soldiers, the line of command from military chief to soldier could be obfuscated. Generals who had authorized pogrom violence in past conflagrations allowed their men to abuse Jewish communities despite Piłsudski's antipathy.

However, the Polish leadership's lack of transparency regarding Polish brutality against Jewish communities made Polish crimes even more alarming. This lack of ownership of Polish pogroms not only set Poles and Jews up for difficult future dynamics, but also made accepting the truth that much harder once Poles revealed it decades later.

Given that the *Protocols of The Elders of Zion* had soared in popularity, and that the Roman Catholic Church depicted Jews as the main enemy facing both Church and God, it should not be surprising that people accepted the dangerous myth of Żydokomuna, the Jew-Bolshevik who clamored for world domination. In her 1920 memoir, Maria Kamińska describes the power of Polish right-wing propaganda posters plastering the city during the Polish-Soviet borderland battles:

> On the wall enormous posters appeared: skulls, skulls, and more skulls all piled up, and on them an enormous wild cutthroat was sitting with a knife between his bared teeth. He had a Red Army cap on his unkempt head. The face of a degenerate—hideous and vicious. One is struck by the fact he is an exclusively Semitic figure. People stop, terrified. "A Jew, a Bolshevik," you can hear them saying. One or two whisper astutely: "Trotsky."[100]

---

100 Szyja Bronsztejn, "Polish-Jewish Relations in Memoirs," in Anthony Polonsky, Ezra Mendelsohn, and Jerzy Tomaszewski, eds., *Jews in Independent Poland, 1918–1939*, Polin: Studies in Polish Jewry, vol. 8 (Oxford: The Littman Library of Jewish Civilization, 2004), 81.

It took very little to jump from recognizing Jewish leaders in the Bolshevik Party to believing that the Soviet drive westward signaled the realization of decades, even centuries, of scheming by the purported Elders of Zion.

We have seen that when people believe dangerous tales spun about whole groups of people, violence often ensues. We pinpoint this trajectory from stereotype to violence not only in the actual Polish pogroms, but also in the lynch mobs white Americans formed in the Deep South. While both majority cultures had layered attitudes concerning minorities, American Jews did not look for Poles' multi-dimensionality. Lacking curiosity and in need of a villain, most American Jews labeled *all* Poles antisemitic. Although Polish society held two main distinct attitudes toward the Jews, American Jewry identified Roman Dmowski's antisemitic rhetoric and economic boycott as representative. This misreading gave rise to the American Jews' own arrogance in dealing with Dmowski. This false perception coupled with the American media's conflation of most pogroms into *Polish* pogroms has ramifications to this day: American Jews' continue to stereotype Poles. At the same time, the Jews' influential role at the Paris Peace Conference only helped many Poles to solidify stereotypes of Jews as striving for international power.

Poland's leaders were horrified not only by the American (as well as British and French) Jews' influence on the Minorities Treaty, but also by the later hypocritical Morgenthau Report. Indeed, while Poles did commit some horrific outrages against Jews in the kresy, the United States' treatment of its minorities was abysmal. Poles knew that Jim Crow legislation, lynch mobs, and widespread terrorism plagued African Americans in the United States. Poles were chastised and punished for their terrible behavior, but the Entente members continued without consequence to abuse their own minority populations. Right-wing and traditionalist Poles would not soon forget the role played by the Jews at this unjust and humiliating moment.

CHAPTER 11

Instability and Identity

In those heady days immediately following their declaration of independence, Poles moved about in a state of euphoria. Reality, however, cast a heavy shadow: rural overpopulation, minimal industry, and excessive unemployment. Formerly divided among three powers, the country and its backward infrastructure required legal and economic consolidation. Yet its leaders had hardly been schooled to run an actual state. Although skilled in military maneuvers as well as uniting people against a common enemy, they knew close to nothing about connecting three disparate lands into one economically sound and cohesive body politic. In this chapter we will explore the overwhelming economic, social, and political challenges facing the Second Polish Republic and how they impacted Polish-Jewish relations.

Economic Instability

Following Poland's resurrection the existence of one central currency eluded the state. Rather, one could make purchases with the German mark, Polish mark, Gdańsk mark, Russian ruble, Ostruble, and Polish zloty.[1] Indeed, the endurance of six different currencies only heightened the general anxiety. People on the street never knew if that money in their pockets actually would be accepted by a merchant. Given its relative worth, one might demand payment in only German marks or Russian rubles. In addition, hyperinflation racked the nation. The Polish government could not collect enough taxes for the extremely high

---

1 Andrzej Zawistowski, "The Mark, the Lech and the Zloty, or How Poland's Currency Was Born: When the Bank of Poland Began Issuing the Zloty," Polishhistory, accessed February 14, 2023, https://polishhistory.pl/the-mark-the-lech-and-the-zloty-or-how-polands-currency-was-born/.

cost of running the country. In reaction, leaders chose to overprint note currency.[2] According to J. Słomka, in his *Memoirs of a Polish Village Mayor, 1842–1927*,

> paper marks were issued without restraint, and their worth degenerated. If anyone sold something and did not at once buy something else with the money, he would lose heavily.
> ... There were endless heaps of money, one had to carry it in briefcases or baskets. Purses and the like were useless. For things for the house one paid in thousands, then millions, and finally in billions.[3]

Maintaining a connection to the German mark only intensified the problem. In 1923 when the mark plunged due to the Franco-Belgian occupation of the Ruhr, the Polish notes also plummeted.[4] It was only in 1924, after the introduction of the zloty and its tie to gold, that Poland's currency attained some stability.

The Second Polish Republic also faced immense social problems, including access to basic healthcare and a staggering 23.1% illiteracy rate.[5] The rural population was hit hardest, with one third of all rural women unable to read or to write. Indeed, 45.5% of rural inhabitants in the eastern provinces were illiterate according to the 1931 census.[6] While these troubles would be addressed with improved health and education systems, the most overwhelming challenge— overpopulation—proved more onerous to solve. Between 1921 and 1937 Poland's population experienced an increase of seven million people: a 26% increase in new jobs would be needed to support this growth.[7]

A dearth of economic opportunity wracked this country in which the majority eked out a living through small farm agriculture. At a time when the republic contained thirty-two million people, 52% of them (16.2 million) endured as peasants. Close to 90% of these peasants subsisted on between 2.5 and 24.7

---

2 Stachura, *Poland, 1918–1945*, 49.
3 J. Słomka, *From Serfdom to Self-Government. Memoirs of a Polish Village Mayor, 1842–1927* (London: Minerva, 1941), 262, as reprinted in Stachura, *Poland, 1918–1945*, 55.
4 Polonsky, *The Jews in Poland and Russia*, 69.
5 Edward D. Wynot Jr., *Polish Politics in Transition: The Camp of National Unity and the Struggle for Power 1935–1939* (Athens: University of Georgia Press, 1974), 19.
6 Brian Porter-Szücs, *Poland in the Modern World: Beyond Martyrdom* (Malden: Wiley Blackwell, 2014), 112.
7 Wynot, *Polish Politics in Transition: The Camp of National Unity and the Struggle for Power 1935–1939*, 11.

acres of land.[8] While the few wealthy landholders prospered, the peasantry sank deeper into poverty as each family followed tradition and divided amongst the adult children the little land it owned. Yet while peasant land holdings dwindled in size, the peasant population soared, throwing the peasantry into severe poverty and angst.

One response to population growth is a buildup of industry to promote concurrent job growth. The Second Polish Republic, however, proved unable to raise the requisite capital to pull the country out of its post-World War I industrial slump.[9] While industrialization intensified in other east European states, Poland's lack of capital stifled such economic development.[10] Although both France and the US made limited investments, both were far more consumed by their own internal problems to do much more for Poland.[11] In addition, the textile industry, for which Russian Poland had been known prior to World War I, had lost its complete market share due to the territorial shake-up.[12] With its dried-up markets, what little industry Poland retained fell into disrepair. Jobs that once existed, disappeared.

The prevalent negative cultural stance toward industry and urban growth compounded this problem. Traditionalists pointed to modernity and its many foibles as the bane of Polish society. The link the Catholic Church asserted between industry, the city, and the evils of modernity sanctioned a simpler, traditional way of life.[13] Additionally, the majority of Poles, who lived in the provinces, attributed so much importance to working the land that the idea of leaving it seemed almost sacrilegious. And so, most citizens retained their rural addresses and remained mired in poverty rather than look for a better livelihood.

In the past, Poles had been able to escape economic hardship through emigration. For example, from the 1870s to the 1920s some two million sailed toward American refuge.[14] But the Great Depression sealed off that escape route. When

---

8   Ibid., 5.
9   Norman Davies, *God's Playground*, 2:130.
10 Wynot, *Polish Politics in Transition: The Camp of National Unity and the Struggle for Power 1935–1939*, iiiix.
11 Stachura, *Poland, 1918–1945*, 47.
12 While the Polish-Soviet peace treaty signed in Riga brought a formal end to the exhausting war for border expansion, it conversely created an economic cold war. Having once been the Russian Empire's top textile producer, Polish factories were cut off from their former lucrative client. See ibid.
13 Modras, *The Catholic Church and Antisemitism: Poland, 1933–1939*, 132.
14 John J. Bukowczyk, *A History of the Polish Americans* (New Brunswick: Transaction Publishers, 2009), 15.

their own nationals suffered tremendous high unemployment, countries which had previously welcomed Poles to their shores now locked their gates.[15] With both industry and emigration closed off to them, the Polish peasantry fell into an economic abyss.

The Depression also assailed the peasantry's earning capacity, stripping them of any chance to make enough money through work. While peasants' earnings through agricultural products dropped 51% during this crisis, the cost of industrial goods decreased by only 36%. The discrepancy drove many agricultural workers into wretched poverty.[16]

Poland's stewards lacked both the necessary imagination to find solutions and the courage to implement them. While Poland's leaders called for land reform, what they managed to produce resembled the status quo. Already in 1920, legislation had passed demanding the state's right to expropriate land from large estates and parcel it out to small land holders.[17] The actual enforcement of this law, however, was much more difficult than its creation. The landed gentry and the Church, which itself retained significant landholdings, fought against it. Additionally, the almost constant change in governments during those first years provided a veil for inept leadership. Indeed, even after Poland reached political stability with Marshal Józef Piłsudski's 1926 military coup, land reform did not adequately reach the people. Instead, Piłsudski's deal making with the conservative block of Church and szlachta stymied it. In return for the latter's support for the coup, Piłsudski would not divvy up their land for those working it.[18] Although Piłsudski cared deeply about the people, his chief aim was to maintain Poland's independence.

Political Instability

During its first fitful years, the Polish government sputtered through multiple iterations, affecting its ability not only to govern in general, but also to address its relationship with Jews living in Poland. Poles engaged one another in a perpetual struggle for control over their country's future. Sejms rose and Sejms fell.

---

15 Wynot, *Polish Politics in Transition: The Camp of National Unity and the Struggle for Power 1935–1939*, 11–12.
16 Ibid., 6.
17 Stachura, *Poland, 1918–1945*, 48.
18 Wynot, *Polish Politics in Transition: The Camp of National Unity and the Struggle for Power 1935–1939*, 38.

Indeed, in less than eight years the Polish Republic went through 118 changes in government, including fourteen different cabinets.[19]

Political dysfunction drew attention to the electoral system, which the republic based on proportional representation rather than on the winning party's automatic majority control of the legislature.[20] No fewer than ninety-two political parties existed by 1925, with a third of them gaining seats in parliament.[21] Therefore, governing necessitated the formation of coalitions comprised of politicians with markedly different ideologies. Government officials needed to find compromise for the greater good of the country. A challenge for even well-versed politicians, it proved near impossible for those with little to no experience.[22] What resulted were groups of politicians working against one another, rather than a governmental body working toward the common goal of nation building. Piłsudski and Dmowski, however, remained at the epicenter of this Polish political landscape.

Piłsudski's followers included Poland's growing number of liberals and Freemasons. Polish Freemasons, typically bourgeois intellectuals, opposed the Endecja agenda. The Freemasons advocated for an enhanced republican form of government, separation of Church and state, state control of the youth's secular education, and rights for national minorities.[23] Fiercely secular, Piłsudski's inner circle was perfectly in step with the Freemasons.[24]

The Church hierarchy and parish priests, on the other hand, galvanized around Roman Dmowski, the founder of Polish integral nationalism. Like the Russian Right, Dmowski linked his political ideology to his portrayal of the Jew as the threatening Other. In his 1902 popular book *Thoughts of a Modern Pole* (*Myśli nowoczesnego Polaka*), Dmowski presents Jews as the cause of all past and present problems facing Poles as a nation. In it, he insists that the Jews had taken over the middle class and locked Poles out. In addition to understanding Jews as an economic threat, he also portrays Jews as a cultural and racial danger to Polish identity. Charging that the Polish "national organism should absorb only

---

19   Sachar, *Dreamland*, 56.
20   Ibid., 44.
21   Ibid., 63.
22   In 1919, Dmowski's Endeks held 30% of the Sejm's seats. While not a majority, this right-wing position could not be ignored. Despite the Left having claimed a solid 20%, it needed to secure compromise with the Centre's 40% in order to hold back Dmowski's plan for a closed, narrowly envisioned Poland. See Biskupski, *The History of Poland*, 76.
23   Modras, *The Catholic Church and Antisemitism: Poland, 1933–1939*, 58.
24   Neal Pease, *Rome's Most Faithful Daughter: The Catholic Church and Independent Poland, 1914–1939* (Athens: Ohio University Press, 2009), 14.

those [foreign elements] that are capable of assimilating," he argues that Jews do not fall into this category. He continues, positing that "it is the Jews who are in a better position to assimilate our majority into their culture and even to assimilate part of us in a physical sense."[25] Dmowski contends that the Jews "have far too many characteristics that are alien to our moral code and that would play a destructive role in our lives."[26] For Dmowski, the Jew posed a danger to the Polish individual's national identity. Thus, he concluded that "[m]ingling with the majority of them would lead to our destruction."[27] Dmowski's ideal solution to these social and economic dilemmas would be the Jews' emigration.

Like Piłsudski, Dmowski opposed Church power in government, and he denied its supernatural essence. Still, Dmowski embraced the Church as a pragmatic political ally.[28] The Church appreciated Dmowski's rancor against liberalism, Freemasonry, and the Jews. Bishop Sapieha of Kraków steered his flock toward Endecja while labeling Piłsudski a bandit who wished to construct a "socialist and Jewish Poland."[29] Parish priests gravitated towards Endecja's provocations of the threatening Other and sense of Polish victimhood. They transported Endek themes to the provinces, where Dmowski's nationalist anti-Jewish message took hold.[30]

Piłsudski chose not to run for president in the first election (November 1922) due to Endek manipulation of the constitution to limit the executive's power.[31] However, Piłsudski and his loyalists still labored against Endecja. Despite forming the strongest electoral bloc, the Endeks lost their bid for the presidency. Cooperation among the Left, Piłsudski, some Centrist groups, and the Bloc of National Minorities (headed by Jewish leader Yitzhak Grünbaum) secured the presidency for Gabriel Narutowicz, a moderate leftist.[32] Surprised by the machinations underlying the democratic process and horrified that this coalition stole Dmowski's "rightful" position, the Right unleashed a smear campaign branding the new president a pawn of minorities, especially the Jews. In response, right-wing mobs attacked deputies outside parliament. One fanatic pushed the Polish

---

25 Roman Dmowski, *Myśli nowoczesnego Polaka* [Thoughts of a Modern Pole], 214–215; quoted in Michlic, *Poland's Threatening Other*, 66.
26 Ibid.
27 Ibid.
28 Pease, *Rome's Most Faithful Daughter: The Catholic Church and Independent Poland, 1914–1939*, 10.
29 Ibid., 14–15.
30 Ibid., 23–24.
31 Polonsky, *The Jews in Poland and Russia*, 67.
32 Biskupski, *The History of Poland*, 77.

political world to the brink of civil war when he assassinated Narutowicz on December 16, 1922.[33]

Jewish Demographics

Due to Piłsudski's military charge eastward, a move which Dmowski viewed as reckless folly, Poland had incorporated a territory which, while part of the former Polish-Lithuanian Commonwealth, contained relatively few ethnic Poles.[34] Saturated with minorities, the kresy brought a much larger Jewish population to Poland than Dmowski and his right wing had ever envisioned. For the Right, incorporating such a massive Jewish population into the Second Republic seemed absurd.

Reviewing Jewish population numbers relative to other countries reveals why people, who already viewed Jews through the lens of militant conspiracy theories, were outraged by the numbers of Jews incorporated into the new Polish state. By 1931, Jews in the United States numbered four million, comprising 3% of the general population.[35] At the same time, in the relatively miniscule Polish territory, the Jewish population had reached three million. With a general population of approximately thirty million, Poland's Jewish population constituted 10% of the country's interwar inhabitants and the second largest ethnic group.[36]

That most European countries' Jewish populations rarely surpassed one hundred thousand only highlighted the pronounced and unmistakable Jewish presence in Poland. Indeed, more Jews resided in one city, Warsaw, than in all of France.[37] After more than a century of partition, Poles had finally arrived at their chance to govern themselves. But for right-wing nationalists, who were appalled

---

33 Polonsky, *The Jews in Poland and Russia*, 69–70.
34 Ibid., 67.
35 Robert Cherry and Annamaria Orla-Bukowska, eds., *Rethinking Poles and Jews: Troubled Past, Brighter Future* (Lanham: Rowman & Littlefield Publishers, Inc., 2007), xiv.
36 Wynot, *Polish Politics in Transition: The Camp of National Unity and the Struggle for Power 1935–1939*, 15.
37 Exceptions were Germany and France, where the Jewish populations were 240,000 and 320,000, respectively. See Tomasz Gąsowski, "The Second Republic and Its Jewish Citizens," in *The Jews in Poland*, vol. 2, ed. Sławomir Kapralski (Cracow: Jagiellonian University Printing House, 1999), 126.

by the number of villages, towns, and regions in which Catholic Poles were a minority, reality did not match their dreams.[38]

Traditionalists' desire to forge the Second Polish Republic's future were further thwarted by its 1921 constitution, which embodied a liberal democratic vision, based on pluralism, capitalism, and the fair treatment of minorities. A radical departure from prevailing European norms, this political vision proved difficult to realize due to a traditional population and constant national crises.[39] At the very time that the new Polish state battled the Soviets to expand and maintain its freedom, it was embroiled in internal political crusades to determine how to express that freedom. Faced with a long list of deep-rooted social challenges including rural overpopulation and a call for land reform, Jewish representatives in the Sejm took up the struggle for equal rights for Jews.

Poles' Ambivalence over the Minorities Treaty and the Jews

Dmowski and Paderewski had signed the Minorities Treaty in Versailles June 28, 1919. The Jews expected its implementation in Warsaw. Conservative Poles were not in a rush. Jews openly requested that Poland ratify and apply the Minorities Treaty. Emasculated by international Jewry's role in designing the Minorities Treaty, and demanding that Poland sign it, Poles delayed ratifying it for eighteen months, allowing ethno-nationalism to fester.[40]

Dmowski's followers couched their anger in growing Europe-wide doubts about the Jews' allegiance to the state. Since the days of the French Revolution, traditionalists fighting against modernity had battled the Jew as its symbol. They

---

38 Norman Davies, "Ethnic Diversity in Twentieth Century Poland," in Bartoszewski, *Poles and Jews: Perceptions and Misperceptions*, 145.
39 When the PPS's leading activist, Stanisław Wojciechowicz joined the new Polish government as minister of the interior he knew that numerous Poles chafed against its concept of equality for Jews and all other minorities. He also understood that his government's liberal vision was beholden to subordinate administrative functionaries to implement it. On February 1, 1919, he wrote:

> I feel compelled to remind you that the Jewish population enjoys the Polish civil rights just as the aboriginal Polish population does and must not be subjected to violence or abuse of law. In independent Poland the citizens are not divided into categories.

Quoted in Jerzy Tomaszewski, "The Civil Rights of Jews 1918–1939," in Polonsky, Mendelsohn, and Tomaszewski, *Jews in Independent Poland, 1918–1939*, 115.
40 Polonsky, *The Jews in Poland and Russia*, 60.

contended that the Jews formed a state within a state, remaining loyal to their Jewish community rather than to the country. Endeks argued that many newly incorporated Jewish communities had not rallied to the Poles' aid during recent borderland battles. The Jews' choice of neutrality in the struggle between Poles and Ukrainians over East Galicia exemplifies this tension. In the fight for Vilnius, at times Jews even supported the Lithuanians over the Poles. Thus, Endeks asked rhetorically: Could Poles trust the Jews to truly view Poland as their homeland, to act on its behalf, and to prioritize Poland above Jewish identity?[41]

Most likely, these same Polish leaders also extrapolated conclusions about the Jewish minority from their experiences of German and Ukrainian active opposition to Polish rule. Germans in the western borderland, who published anti-Polish propaganda, hoped to be reunited with their fatherland. The Endecja hoped either to "de-Germanize" the lot or to eject them completely from the land.[42]

The large Ukrainian population in the east had waged a violent struggle against the Poles in their 1918 clash over Lviv, and in their fight to control East Galicia. Numbering 4.5 million in 1931, Ukrainians worked primarily as small farmers and agricultural laborers concentrated along the Polish eastern frontier. Ukrainian resentment of Polish landowners and Polish rule fueled not only a continual political push for Ukrainian independence, but also a powerful underground terrorist organization, which pursued Polish targets.[43] Those who did not bother to consider the subtle differences which separated the Jews from these two ethnic minorities inferred from German antipolonism and Ukrainian radicalized nationalism that the Jews held a similar propensity to act against the Polish state. Indeed, for those who accepted the rampant conspiracy theory of Żydokomuna—that Jews, dressed in Soviet garb, battled Poles as part of their

---

41 One could see this conflict of national interest also within the socialist camp. Just prior to 1918, the Bund (the General Jewish Workers' Alliance) which was the largest Jewish organization in Russian Poland, rejected Polish independence in its entirety. In declaring its fealty to Russia, its members pressed for an autonomous Congress Kingdom within the Russian Empire. At that juncture, Bund members had placed Poland's national aspirations second to creating safety for international Jewish workers. See Zimmerman, *Poles, Jews, and the Politics of Nationality*, 109

42 Germans controlled a large percentage of remaining Polish industry. Even though Germans (and Jews) had helped to build this infrastructure, Poles resented their holdings. Stachura, *Poland, 1918–1939*, 80–81.

43 Wynot, *Polish Politics in Transition: The Camp of National Unity and the Struggle for Power 1935–1939*, 13–14.

effort to rule the world—the image of the treacherous and dangerous Jew made sense.⁴⁴

The Sejm finally ratified the Minorities Treaty in December 1920; right-wing legislators continued their battle against it through interpretation. The Minorities Treaty established that non-Poles who had been "habitually resident" in those territories now forming the Second Polish Republic were entitled to Polish citizenship, with the right to vote and run for political office. Politicians argued over the definition of "habitually resident." Signing the Polish-Soviet treaty over the eastern borderland elevated the problems with requiring proof of habitual residence. Extensive property damage during the Russian Civil War and battles for expansion left personal documents lost or destroyed and administrative records in shreds.

Additionally, the sharp distinction between national leadership and local administration paralyzed policy implementation. Although consecutive ministers of the interior created avenues for en masse citizenship for minority populations, including the Jews, right-wing local administrators impeded the process by demanding additional unnecessary documentation. Though by 1928 most cases had been settled, more than thirty thousand Litvaks residing in the eastern territories remained stateless.⁴⁵ Polish ethno-nationalists painted these Litvaks as radicalizing Jewish nationalists or Bolshevik implants. They argued that granting these "revolutionaries" the right to vote and run for office would be national suicide.

The government's ambivalence toward accepting the Jewish minority as equal to Poles also bore out in the debate over leftover discriminatory legislation produced by the three partitioning powers. Each had subjected the Jews to different prejudicial regulations. Jewish legal rights had been most impaired in the kresy, where the May Laws and specifically the Sunday Rest Law impacted the Jews economically. While the former Kingdom of Poland had prohibited Jews from

---

44 In an effort to address the Poles' mistrust of the Jews, Jewish Sejm deputies drafted legislation in 1925 stating that while the Jews "promised to act to preserve the state's borders, and internal cohesion," giving their full support to the Polish nation, the state would in turn provide for their rights. Although an agreement to this effect was reached, government leaders mishandled it not only by insisting that it remain secret, but also by refusing to sign it formally. While this type of backdoor diplomacy might have been effective in the long run, it undermined Jewish faith in the republic's intentions and further derailed trust in the process. Clearly, ambivalence regarding the overwhelming Jewish presence in Poland prevailed. Szymon Rudnicki, "The Jews' Battle in the Sejm for Equal Rights", in Kapralski, *The Jews In Poland*, 156.

45 Tomaszewski, "The Civil Rights of Jews 1918–1939," 116–119.

owning agricultural land and holding high office in small towns, Austrian-ruled Galicia permitted its resident Jews to own land. Although close to 10% of Jews there became landholders, Jews still experienced discrimination with the prohibition of speaking Yiddish or Hebrew in public.[46]

The Polish courts addressed this confounding legislation through a variety of interpretations of the constitution's provision of equal rights for the Jews. In 1924, the General Meeting of the Supreme Court held that the constitution's language already gave equal rights to Jews and thereby effectively removed all preexisting partition-era discriminatory laws. However, that same year the Supreme Court of Administrative Law ruled that while the constitution called for equal rights, until a formal document abolishing each prejudicial regulation was written and passed, tsarist and Habsburg anti-Jewish laws had to be enforced.[47] While the 1926 Grabski-led government did away with some anti-Jewish legislation, it was unable to nullify most of it.[48] Thus, partition-era discriminatory legislation continued to affect the Jewish community until 1931 when, after a number of crises, including the depression linked to the German mark, Piłsudski's government could focus on the topic and pass necessary legislation through its autocratic barring of right-wing opposition.[49]

---

46 Ibid., 121–123.
47 Ibid.; Rudnicki, "The Jews' Battle in the Sejm for Equal Rights," 157.
48 Polonsky, *The Jews in Poland and Russia*, 71, 75.
49 The power of the courts is tremendous. In the US, the Left and Right continue the long battle over voting rights. Though provided to the emancipated Black population during Reconstruction (1865–1877), right-wing conservatives fought this legislation, first by ignoring it and later by challenging it in the courts. In almost every era, Americans do this dance with voting rights: the Left pushes forward and the Right reflexively pulls backward. One would imagine that a country such as the United States, which symbolizes the potential of democracy for those ruled by autocrats and oligarchs, would have solved such problems as inequality long ago. Joe Biden won the 2020 election against Donald Trump with an outpouring of voter participation by communities of color. One might view such high voter turnout from marginalized communities as a sign of democracy at work. But the Right has responded with court cases and legislation, inundating the courts with challenges to the validity of this election and calls of voter fraud. Failing to win the argument, not only have republican leaders continued to brand the 2020 election "rigged," but republican lawmakers throughout the United States have brought forth legislation that curtails the strides the Left has made in securing voting rights, especially for people of color. Democrats are responding in the courts. See Ronald Brownstein, "The Democrats' New Voting Rights Obstacle," *Atlantic*, July 8, 2021; Pete Williams and Nicole Via y Rada, "Trump's Election Fight Includes over 50 Lawsuits. It's Not Going Well," nbcnews.com, November 23, 2020.

The Polish Catholic Church

As previously detailed, the Catholic Church's centuries-old condemnation of the Jews was the basis for many Poles' receptiveness to political antisemitism. In 1913, Poles had watched in real time the medieval Church's blood libel charge against Menachem Mendel Beilis (1874–1934). Though the Russian court acquitted him of ritual murder, it did not rule out ritual murder itself. The international attention given to the Beilis trial (in Russia, Europe, the United States, and Poland itself) resulted in fresh, and damaging, interest in the blood libel itself.

Continuing the Church's battle against secularization that had begun in the eighteenth century, Polish Catholic leaders professed the foundational myth that Poland was a fundamentally Catholic country.[50] The Minorities Treaty, with its promise of equal rights to all people, regardless of religion, threatened their definition of the nation—for it gave the Jews—branded by the Church as an enemy—the right to vote, and thus the right to undermine Poland.[51] As such, many Catholic leaders found in Roman Dmowski's extreme ethno-nationalism an echo of and justification for their own anger and fear.

Through the pope, pulpit, and press, the Church played a large role in spreading the Jew-communist stereotype in Poland. In a 1927 sermon, Father Feliks Bodzianowski stoked fear of and revulsion towards the Jews when he connected them with Satan, Freemasonry, communism, and a hatred of Poland. Bodzianowski presented the Church in a fight against the Jews for the country's soul. He contended that not only had Jews killed Jesus in antiquity, but that twentieth century Jews continued that same battle against Christ by destroying Poland, the country known as "the Christ of Nations:"

> When, nineteen centuries ago, the sons of Israel proclaimed in one voice "crucify Him, crucify Him," willingly bringing the blood of Christ onto them and all their descendants until the end of the world, the Jews sold themselves to Satan. From then on their relentless hatred for Christ, for those who represent

---

50 Modras, *The Catholic Church and Antisemitism: Poland, 1933–1939*, 59.
51 The idea that Poland's identity as a Catholic country was threatened by incorporating a large Jewish population with voting rights into its territory provides some added perspective to the current debate over Palestinians' right to return to the State of Israel as full citizens. While the two sociopolitical situations are not the same, they each offer an opportunity for sensitivity and nuance to Jews engaging these topics.

Him on earth and who lead us to Him, has persisted.... So we understand why, in relations with Poland, the Jews of the entire world and the Masons hiding behind them burn with particular hatred. For was Poland not always the bastion of Christianity, did it not defeat the victorious march of the sons of the "Star of Zion" during those memorable August days of 1920, does it not separate the openly Bolshevik-Jewish Moscow from the half-open Masonic Germany?[52]

Bodzianowski blamed the Jews for communism's intense present threat against the Polish state's territory and the Catholic Church's truth, framing the Jew-communist as Poland's penultimate threat.

The Church waged war against not only Jews but also a plethora of secularist organizations run by self-described liberal Catholics. They included the Women's Civil Service Union (Związek Pracy Obywatelskiej Kobiet), through which medical doctors and a large number of women gained influence. The Youth Legion (Legion Młodych) disseminated secularist ideas among the younger generation.[53] Additionally, periodicals such as the *Freethinker* (*Wolnomyśliciel*), the *Morning Courier* (*Kurier Poranny*), and the *Literary New* (*Wiadomości Literackie*) spread ideas of tolerance, civil rights, and other anti-Church ideas including birth control.[54] Indeed, Dr. E. Muszyński stated, "[t]here is no lack of progressive Catholics today."[55]

---

52 Feliks Bodzianowski, "Fałszywi prorocy shwili obecnej," *Nowa Biblioteka Kaznodziejska*, 33, nos. 14–15 (July-Aug. 1927), 38–40; quoted in Brian Porter-Szucs, *Faith and Fatherland: Catholicism, Modernity, and Poland* (Oxford: Oxford University Press, 2011), 300–301.

53 Other liberal Catholic organizations included, the Polish Free Thought Union (Polski Związek Wolnej Myśli) headquartered in Warsaw, with branches in several cities. Separate reformists spearheaded the Society for the Defense of Freedom and Conscience in Poland (Stowarzyszenie Obrony Wolności i Sumienia w Polsce), the League for the Defense of Human and Civil Rights (Liga Obrony Praw Człowieka i Obywatela), and the Polish Ethical Society (Polskie Stowarzyszenie Etyczne). See Modras, *The Catholic Church and Antisemitism: Poland, 1933–1939*, 67.

54 Ibid., 61. A possible solution, in part, to Poland's economic woes, birth control ignited tensions between secularists and Church adherents. Liberalizing Poles formed the Society for the Promotion of Birth Control (Towarzystwo Krzewlenia Świadomego Macierzyńsłwa), for which Jewish Polish writer Tadeusz Boy-Żeliński was a spokesperson, given his professional training as a gynecologist and pediatrician.

55 Quoted in ibid., 59; *Wiara i Życie*, December 1932, 173–178. Collaborating in the Union of Village Youth (Związek Młodzieży Wiejskiej), and its periodical *Wici* were numerous liberal authors, all critical of the Church. They included Wojciech Szuza, Stanisław Młodożeniec,

Against them all the Church wielded its Jewish-Masonic conspiracy theory. It believed that fear of Jewish world domination would save Catholics from secularism. Polish bishops supported Polish authors, such as Dr. Kazimierz M. Morawski, who joined their battle against the dangers of Masonry. Morawski gave a paper at the Warsaw June 11–12, 1938 anti-Masonic convention. In it he linked Masonry to Judaism, claimed that it served the interests of international Jewry, and that Polish Freemasons work to unite Polish Jews.[56] *Mały Dziennik*, the largest daily Polish periodical, which consistently voiced this clerical-nationalist argument, reported the convention's declaration of "readiness for war on behalf of Poland's cultural and political-economic independence against masonry and the Jews behind it."[57]

To the Church's age-old fear of the secularist Jew, it also attached the idea of the Jew-communist. The contemporary threat of communism consumed Pope Pius XI,[58] who further cultivated the notion of the Masonic-Jewish-Bolshevik enemy. This message resonated in Poland. Through sermons and media, the Polish Catholic Church clamored against this dangerous trifecta, which it claimed would stop at nothing until it had destroyed the Catholic Church, Christian values, and the Polish nation.[59] With varying degrees of urgency, the clergy spread this anxiety about the supposed unholy alliance of Freemasonry, communism, and the Jews.[60]

In 1921, a large number of Jews from eastern regions once held by Russia proper returned to Poland.[61] According to the Polish-Soviet peace treaty signed in Riga, these Jews could repatriate to Poland and become Polish citizens. That they chose to live in Poland, but were proficient in both the Russian language and its culture, prompted Poles to see them as Soviet implants, that is,

---

Leon Lutyk, Tadeusz Rek, Stanisław Kot, Tomasz Nocznicki, Stanisław Thugutt, and Ignacy Solarz. See ibid., 61.
56 Ibid., 70–71.
57 Quoted in ibid., 71; *Mały Dziennik*, June 14, 1938.
58 Pease, *Rome's Most Faithful Daughter: The Catholic Church and Independent Poland, 1914–1939*, 114–115.
59 Modras, *The Catholic Church and Antisemitism: Poland, 1933–1939*, 70.
60 Pease, *Rome's Most Faithful Daughter: The Catholic Church and Independent Poland, 1914–1939*, 29.
61 In the past, people assessed the number of incoming Litvaks to be about six hundred thousand. Today, historians estimate them at thirty-three thousand. The main point in our discussion remains that it was a large group of incoming Jews from the enemy's land, speaking the enemy's language. There was a vast difference between Polish Jews and Lithuanian Jews, not only in Yiddish dialect, but in terms of culture, politics, and religion as well. Polish Jews also saw them as a foreign element. See Rudnicki, "The Jews' Battle in the Sejm for Equal Rights," 158.

the enemy within. Poles derogatorily referred to these Jews as Litvaks, a term which the latter embraced for themselves. Litvaks had migrated to Poland in the late nineteenth century, bringing Jewish nationalist ideology, and creating what appeared to be immovable barriers to Jews' integration into Polish society. Poles feared that this 1921 Litvak migration would infect the Polish nation by further destroying its cultural and political distinctiveness.[62]

In his memoir *Memories* (*Wspomnienia*), Ludwik Krzywicki blamed Litvak retention of Russian culture and language for rising antisemitism in Poland's eastern city of Vilnius: "Even after independence had been long established, the Vilna Jews were more persistent in their use of Russian than native Russians. This has not been forgotten in Vilna to this very day and had a great influence on the widespread antisemitism there."[63] Researcher Szyja Bronsztejn, who has studied 150 memoirs dealing with interwar Poland, concludes that "the numerical preponderance of the so-called "Litvaks" among Jews in the central and eastern areas of Poland undoubtedly had a negative influence on Polish-Jewish relations."[64]

The majority of Catholic periodicals fomented an aggressive presentation of the "Jewish question" in Poland.[65] Accounting for 27% of press publications in Poland, the Catholic press had a significant sway over Poles.[66] Of those targeting a non-clerical audience, two journals focused extensively on the "Jewish question," while most others touched on it in each issue.[67] Convinced that the Jews threatened Catholicism and its adherents, the Church colored the Jew as a looming threatening Other, waiting to terrorize the Christian world. To keep Catholics safe, the Church called for isolation from all minorities. To stoke fear of the Jew-enemy, the Catholic press accused them of crucifying Christ, persecuting Christians, spreading atheism, and sometimes killing Christian children to bake matzah. They filled columns with allegations of Żydokomuna and quotes from the *Protocols of the Elders of Zion*. The Jew-Mason-Bolshevik-*Zionist* nexus sprang to life in the pages of numerous Catholic publications; and though

---

62 Polonsky, *The Jews in Poland and Russia*, 61.
63 Quoted in Bronsztejn, "Polish-Jewish Relations in Memoirs," 70.
64 Seventy-five of the memoirs were composed by non-Jews. See ibid.
65 Alina Cała, *Jew. The Eternal Enemy?: The History of Antisemitism in Poland*, trans. Jan Burzynski and ed. Mikołaj Gołubiewski, Polish Studies Transdisciplinary Perspectives, vol. 22 (Berlin: Peter Lang, 2018), 216.
66 Anna Landau-Czajka, "The Image of the Jew in the Catholic Press during the Second Republic," in Polonsky, Mendelsohn, and Tomaszewski, *Jews in Independent Poland, 1918–1939*, 146.
67 Ibid., 147.

some periodicals remained tolerant of the Jews, such as *Rycerz Niepokalanej*, those attracting the average person on the street, including the Congregation of Marian Fathers' *Pro Christo* and the Franciscans' *Mały Dziennik*, instigated aggressive antisemitism.[68]

Monsignor Stanisław Trzeciak, a prolific contributor to *Mały Dziennik*, insisted on the *Protocols*' truth, having attended at least one European conference on it. No Polish cleric wrote more about the *Protocols* than Trzeciak. While many clerics did not believe the *Protocols*, they still quoted Trzeciak often, allowing his ideas further access into the mainstream.[69]

The conservative Polish Catholic press demanded the eradication of the Jewish danger. Otherwise, Poland would lose its Catholic influence. Father Hetnal in *Przewodnik katolicki* urged his readers to realize that "native Poles who have inhabited these lands for centuries . . . are sinking in increasing numbers to the level of servants and slaves of the Jews."[70] According to him, the Jews had invaded Poland, created discriminatory laws in favor of themselves, and were now establishing their own "Judeopolska." Another periodical underscored this threat: "A terrible danger hangs over Poland. Day by day, hour by hour, we are gradually ceasing to be masters of our own land! Poland is becoming a Judeopolska!"[71] With an obsessive and aggressive depiction of the Jew-enemy, *Pro-Christo* urged university students to act more assertively against those who did not desire "ritual slaughter but the slaughter of the Polish people."[72]

Piłsudski's Coup D'état

Józef Piłsudski left the political helm in 1923 after being denied the ability to form his federalist vision. However, after realizing that internal political chaos would continue to weaken Poland within its borders and internationally, he wrested control of the new state in a 1926 coup d'état. Despite his overwhelming popularity, such a move almost launched Poland into civil war.[73] His seizure of the reins of power, with the active support of at least half of the army, at the

---

68 Ibid., 149; Modras, *The Catholic Church and Antisemitism: Poland, 1933–1939*, 91–92.
69 The Church appreciated his armor and weaponry and promoted him to lead one of Warsaw's largest churches. See ibid., 95.
70 Quoted in Landau-Czajka, "The Image of the Jew in the Catholic Press during the Second Republic," 173.
71 Quoted in ibid., 173–174.
72 Cała, *Jew. The Eternal Enemy?*, 222–223.
73 Biskupski, *The History of Poland*, 77–78.

expense of the country's constitution, inflamed those who stood up to him and who he had defeated. Establishing a military dictatorship, he led a "centralized authoritarian oligarchy," avoiding the emerging European pull toward fascism.[74] While he permitted Poland's established constitutional, parliamentary, and political institutions to survive, his incessant interference with them threatened to eviscerate the country's structural foundation.[75] When the opposition rose again, he jailed its leaders.[76] Splintered parties, a submissive legislature, and an obedient president supported his rule.[77]

Piłsudski cemented his reign by establishing the Sanacja, a combination of various political players who blindly followed the marshal's strong and charismatic leadership. He set them up as his eyes and ears in second rank, yet crucial, government posts.[78] They did not admire his political ideology, for in effect he had no real doctrine: Piłsudski's modus operandi was simply to retain Polish independence. As war minister and inspector general of the armed forces, he amassed support from the military and conservative landowners, while further distancing himself from his former PPS comrades.[79]

The populace accepted him as the right man for the task. He garnered mass support based on his past military heroism and on his strength of character.[80] Raising himself above party politics, Piłsudski often espoused contradictory views to secure the people's following. He also found popular support when, in 1926, the depression embroiling Poland ended.[81] While his rule was harsh, a sense of economic, political, and social stability developed.

Despite his autocratic reign, Piłsudski permitted a breadth of freedoms. At first, even parliamentary elections afforded the political opposition a seat at the table. However, this did not last long. When the opposition proved itself still surprisingly vital, the marshal pushed through various constitutional amendments to strengthen the executive at the expense of the Sejm. In 1930, he imprisoned many Center and Left opposition leaders; in 1933, he banned

---

74 MacMillan, *Paris 1919, Six Months That Changed the World*, 22.
75 Rothschild, *East Central Europe between the Two World Wars*, 56.
76 Polonsky, *Jews in Poland and Russia*, 76.
77 Rothschild, *East Central Europe between the Two World Wars*, 56.
78 Ibid., 58.
79 Stachura, *Poland, 1918–1939*, 66.
80 Ibid., 63–64.
81 A British coal miners' strike had lifted Poland out of its malaise by engaging Poland's own coal mines in greater international trade. That these years of recovery and growth occurred on the tails of Piłsudski's coup solidified for many Poles his right to rule the nation. Rothschild, *East Central Europe between the Two World Wars*, 66.

Dmowski's Endecja (then called the Camp of Great Poland); and in 1934 the regime interned dissident activists.[82] These actions culminated in 1935 when he replaced the constitution with one far more autocratic.

Piłsudski and the Jews

Most Poles expected the Piłsudskiites, with their renowned pro-federation past, to inaugurate a new stage in nationalities policy.[83] Polish Jewry was no exception. But while Piłsudski acted on behalf of the Jews, he too showed some ambivalence to their cause. The "Jewish question" was but one of many issues he faced; and his ultimate objective remained the security of Poland, not the happiness of one group.

Although the marshal did not support the minorities to the extent they desired, the Jews clearly preferred him over his political opponents. He did not antagonize them by blaming all of Poland's problems on their large numbers, unlike the Endeks. Rather, he accepted their right to equality under the law. While previous government coalitions faltered in enforcing the Minorities Treaty, the marshal tried to provide the Jews and other minorities with the many rights due to them. His minister of the interior, Kazimierz Młodzianowski, presented the government's liberal agenda when he argued before the cabinet on August 18, 1926 that "the goal of national assimilation should be renounced; instead, conditions should be created for assimilation to the state structure as citizens."[84]

Regarding the Jews specifically, Piłsudski set out to create state primary Yiddish-language schools and to provide government aid to Jewish private schools. His government legally instated the Jews' right to speak Yiddish at public meetings, which many Jews themselves opposed. In addition, he issued a decree to extend and restructure Jewish communal organizations through elections, stimulating Jewish political life.[85]

Under the marshal, the thirty-three thousand Litvaks from Russian Poland had finally been granted rights of Polish citizenship.[86] Prior to the coup,

---

82 Stachura, *Poland, 1918–1939*, 66–67.
83 Andrzej Chojnowski, "The Jewish Question in the Work of the *Instytut Badań Spraw Narodowościowych* in Warsaw," in Bartoszewski, *Poles and Jews: Perceptions and Misperceptions*, 159.
84 Polonsky, *Jews in Poland and Russia*, 73–74.
85 Chojnowski, "The Jewish Question in the Work of the *Instytut Badań Spraw Narodowościowych* in Warsaw," 161.
86 Rudnicki, "The Jews' Battle in the Sejm for Equal Rights," 158.

various ministers of the interior had attempted to streamline the citizenship process, but the right-wing administrative bureaucracies in towns and villages barred it.[87] Despite the failure of previous efforts, Jews' civil rights improved significantly only after Piłsudski focused on enacting legislation to abrogate the remaining partition-era anti-Jewish prohibitions.[88] It is no wonder, then, that the right-wing opposition vehemently described him as bending to the Jews' demands.

Piłsudski's government also prevented the National Democrats' proposal to legalize a *numerus clausus* in the university system, which would limit the number of Jews permitted access to higher education. In March 1932, a majority of the Sejm Education Committee condemned this right-wing tactic.[89] However, in practical day-to-day terms, Piłsudski did little to affect the unofficial *numerus clausus* which some universities employed. Additionally, although his representatives spoke out against economic antisemitism, the Right continued using it as a rallying cry to their followers.

The Piłsudski government stringently opposed antisemitic violence, seeking to protect its Jewish citizens from radicalized reactionaries. In August 1929, the National Democrats attempted to initiate a violent anti-Jewish campaign in Lviv with allegations that Jews there profaned a Corpus Christi procession. The minister of the interior, then Felicjan Sławoj-Składkowski, derailed this agitation immediately.[90] Jews responded by placing both their hopes and trust in Piłsudski.

A sign of the new regime's openness toward ethnic minorities was also signaled by the reemergence of the Warsaw Instytut Badań Spraw Narodowościowych, an independent institution for research into nationality matters. This group of Polish politicians, journalists, and scholars with democratic and socialist convictions included several Jewish figures. The institute addressed questions facing the Poles' relationship with various ethnic minority groups, including how to effectively assimilate them into Polish culture.

A Jewish commission within the institute focused on Jewish communal concerns. It struggled with ways to negotiate such issues as the Sunday Rest Law, kahal elections, Jewish schools, and reasons behind Jewish poverty, while

---

87 Tomaszewski, "The Civil Rights of Jews 1918–1939," 119.
88 Although Jewish representatives in the Sejm, with the support of left-wing groups, had been trying to tackle this very issue for years, it did not get rectified until Piłsudski focused on it and fought for it. See ibid., 125.
89 Polonsky, *Jews in Poland and Russia*, 78.
90 Ibid., 75.

concomitantly awakening within the Jewish community a firm connection to Poland and its security.[91] A think tank of sorts, the institute submitted reports to the Presidium of the Council of Ministers, while also receiving government financial support.[92]

The 1929 worldwide Depression greatly impacted the marshal's rule. National morale dropped precipitously and social tensions sharpened. Inordinately severe in Poland, the Depression led to a 25% decline in national income between 1929 and 1933.[93] As lower wages and joblessness assaulted Poles, Piłsudski's ability and willingness to deal specifically with problems plaguing minorities waned.[94]

He focused his efforts on fighting the growing opposition. Piłsudski's hostile manner deepened into an anti-parliamentary "command" style of rule.[95] At this point, he gave his World War I military cronies, known as "the colonels," more powerful ministerial offices. Their sole job amounted to following the marshal's instructions.

Six left and center opposition parties created a bloc by which they hoped to force Piłsudski's resignation. Jewish political parties refused to participate because three noted antisemitic parties were involved in it: the Christian Democrats, the National Workers' Party, and the Piast Polish Peasant Party.[96] Additionally, they feared that any change in government would negatively affect their own legal standing within the state. As such, the Jews, along with other minority groups, chose to remain neutral. As in both the 1912 Duma elections and the 1922 Polish general elections, when Jewish compacts dashed Roman Dmowski's political ascent, Jews also played a critical role in the 1930 election. The opposition's political coalition failed to evict Piłsudski from power: the Jews clung to neutrality and Piłsudski clung to control. Right-wing resentment of the Jews only grew.

---

91 Chojnowski, "The Jewish Question in the Work of the *Instytut Badań Spraw Narodowościowych* in Warsaw," 167.
92 Ibid., 160.
93 Polonsky, *The Jews in Poland and Russia*, 76.
94 Chojnowski, "The Jewish Question in the Work of the *Instytut Badań Spraw Narodowościowych* in Warsaw," 163.
95 Rothschild, *East Central Europe between the Two World Wars*, 57.
96 Polonsky, *The Jews in Poland and Russia*, 76.

Jewish Nationalism and Language

During the two decades which spanned the Second Polish Republic, the Jewish community experienced not only a hostile right-wing political campaign, but also the freedom to respond to it. As Polish right-wing nationalism spread, Jews answered it in kind. Nationalism begot nationalism.[97] Jewish nationalist political ideologies developed and expanded exponentially. Zionism, diaspora nationalism and Jewish socialism had made inroads well before World War I through Ḥibat Tsiyon, Simon Dubnow's Folkspartei, and the General Jewish Workers' Alliance (known as the Bund). Additionally, continuous splintering and new approaches to orthodoxy begot the modern orthodoxy of Agudat Yisrael, the religious *Zionists* in Mizrachi, as well as both the left and right wings of the *Zionist* Workers Party (Po'alei Zion). These and other groups vied for representation in Jewish autonomous communal elections. Throughout Poland, roughly six hundred Jewish community boards (replacements for the dismantled kahal system) held elections.[98] Jewish political parties campaigned to gain representation on them and thus power in the Jewish community.

Polish Jewry continued to develop its various identities through language. Jews collaborated through and collided over Yiddish, Hebrew, and Polish. Because the Polish language was a mandatory subject in Jewish private schools and given that most Jewish students now attended free state schools, young Jews attained an almost universal proficiency in Polish.[99] At the same time, however, most Jews did not assimilate into Polish culture. First, most Jews remained traditional. Second, interwar Poland included what had recently been Russia's Pale of Jewish Settlement (the kresy). Jewish secularists there had already experienced not only the post 1905 counterrevolutionary pogroms, but also the disappointing Russian reaction to them. In response, Jewish secularists veered off their path, embraced Jewish nationalism, and urged other Jews to "return to the kehillah."[100]

When Russian Jewish secularists embraced their Jewish roots and developed a stronger sense of Jewish peoplehood they did so through Yiddish. Influenced by past stateless nations, including Poles and Ukrainians, Jewish nationalists

---

97 I. L. Peretz moved toward Jewish nationalism only after experiencing Roman Dmowski's Polish nationalist Endeks. Joshua Karlip, "The Emergence of Modern Yiddish Culture," lecture at Yivo Summer Program, July 20, 2021.
98 Andrzej Paczkowski, "The Jewish Press in the Political Life of the Second Republic," in Polonsky, Mendelsohn, and Tomaszewski, *Jews in Independent Poland, 1918–1939*, 181.
99 Ibid., 178.
100 Fishman, *The Rise of Modern Yiddish Culture*, 34.

understood language as *the* essential element for curating and securing a peoplehood. It provided a concrete, daily expression of the Jews' unique culture.[101] Though secular Jewish nationalism would have many political iterations, one common thread running through each was the right of Jews to their mother tongue, Yiddish.

Not only did Yiddish provide political organizations access to the Jewish masses, it also symbolized the active taking back of what the Russian tsar had stolen: the Jews' right to express their specific culture in their specific language.[102] Actively engaging the Yiddish language symbolized the building of a national consciousness and the Jews' struggle for their national rights. In this vein, "Yiddishists demanded recognition of Yiddish by the state, within the framework of its granting Jews national autonomy. They also pressed for Yiddish, rather than Polish (or Russian), to be the language of instruction in modern Jewish schools and of public discourse in communal bodies and organizations."[103] As David Fishman argues in his book *The Rise of Modern Yiddish Culture*, the politics of Yiddish reinvigorated a new generation's relationship to the Jewish people.

Already in 1908, leaders of the Czernovitz Yiddish Conference had made it clear that the Jewish secularist intelligentsia had transformed its attitude toward the jargon, that is, the Yiddish their predecessors had taught them to berate.[104] We see such a conversion with I. L. Peretz, who in his first published story apologized for writing in Yiddish, a lesser language. Peretz would later be revered as Yiddishism's prophetic voice.[105] The key resolution at the Czernovitz conference stated, "The first conference for the Yiddish language recognizes Yiddish as a national language of the Jewish people, and demands for it political, social, and cultural equal rights."[106]

---

101 Cecile Esther Kuznitz, *YIVO and the Making of Modern Jewish Culture: Scholarship for the Yiddish Nation* (Cambridge: Cambridge University Press, 2014), 4.
102 Russia had banned Yiddish in both the press and theatre out of the tsar's fear that otherwise these cultural mediums would act as conduits for political nationalism.
103 Fishman, *The Rise of Modern Yiddish Culture*, 15.
104 Nathan Birnbaum, Chaim Zhitlovsky, and Isaac Leib Peretz led the 1908 Czernovitz Yiddish conference. See ibid., 15.
105 Karlip, "The Emergence of Modern Yiddish Culture." Karlip notes that Jewish intellectuals had gleaned from the multiple stateless nations in pre-WWI Eastern Europe the imperative of retaining one's culture until the state politic could be reestablished. They all viewed language as the device to secure culture.
106 Fishman, *The Rise of Modern Yiddish Culture*, 32. Yiddishists did not make up a cohesive cohort. Specific tensions emerged and remained concerning the importance of and respect for the old Jewish religious culture. This conflict could be traced back to the leaders of the

For Jews, one's language symbolized to some degree one's approach to the range of issues facing Polish Jewry. The Hebraist movement, as famously represented by Ahad Ha'am (1856–1927), contended that whether or not Jews established a Jewish national homeland in Palestine, Jewish life in the diaspora must be Hebraized in order to retain its national authenticity and unity.[107] Hebraists argued that Hebrew should be the dominant language of Jewish education, culture, and communal life given its role as the original written and ritual language of the Jewish people and its having secured intellectual standing among the secularized Jewish intelligentsia since the Haskalah.

A significant number of secular Jews—who had been raised in the Russian Pale of Jewish Settlement to embrace one of the various forms of Jewish nationalism, whether it be subsumed under Zionism or diaspora nationalism—now resided within Polish borders. These Jews would be hard pressed to accept the Polish language and culture as their own. Acculturation into Polish society would also be hampered by the explosion of Yiddish cultural mediums that energized the secular Jewish population in interwar Poland.[108]

Interwar Jewish Culture: Yiddish Press and Yiddish Theatre

As opposed to Jews in the Soviet Union, during the interwar period Jews in Poland had the freedom to explore their linguistic national identity through a range of mediums, including the press and theater. Soviet policy banned Hebrew due to its religious and political centrality. At the same time, the Soviets coopted the Yiddish press, theater, and schools in a successful bid to hasten the Jews' linguistic and cultural Russification. The Second Polish Republic, on the other hand, provided favorable conditions for the continuation of a free Yiddish

---

1908 Czernovitz conference, who held opposing positions. For Dr. Chaim Zhitlovsky's radical cultural Yiddishism, the language was the sole requirement for maintaining the Jewish people in the diaspora. He argued that as long as one's daily language was Yiddish the content of that language was insignificant. However, for I. L. Peretz's national romantic Yiddishism, the cultural content of the language was of tremendous import. He strove to nurture a modern Yiddish culture that would perpetuate the spirit found within the traditional Jewish continuum from the Bible through Hassidic thought. See ibid., 101–102.

107 Ibid., 99.

108 David Fishman argues that had the tsar not outlawed both the Yiddish press in the 1870s and 1890s and the Yiddish theater from 1883 to 1905, these cultural outlets would have had wide audiences prior to 1905, when the explosion of Yiddish culture actually took place. Ibid., 21.

culture which could raise Jewish national self-consciousness. Thus, Jews in interwar Poland acculturated much more slowly than did Jews in the Soviet Union.[109]

As Jewish literacy and the Jewish reading public grew in the interwar period, the demand for new material increased. Medium and small towns saw the greatest literacy development.[110] The variegated Polish Jewish community required an array of reading material, mostly in Yiddish. The general populace consumed the daily press, which included afternoon sensationalist tabloid papers. Jewish newspapers shared the goings on in Jewish towns, Poland, and the world. The daily Jewish press also provided room for budding and popular Yiddish writers to print their stories. By the 1930s, in Warsaw alone there were nine major Jewish dailies: five Yiddish morning papers, two Polish-Jewish papers, and two afternoon Yiddish papers. The Yiddish papers averaged a daily circulation of 161,450, with the Zionist leaning *Today* (*Haynt*, 1908–1939) and *The Moment* (*Der Moment*, 1910–1939) in the lead.[111] Even Orthodox Jewry now embraced this modern medium, reading Yiddish dailies, weeklies, and magazines.[112] And though *Zionists* argued for the primary status of Hebrew over Yiddish, they published their papers in Yiddish in order to meet the populace where it stood.

Our Review (*Nasz Przegląd*, 1923–1939) stood out as the top Jewish paper in the Polish language which also supported a Jewish national political outlook. Far from the previous Polish Jewish weekly *Izraelita* (1866–1913), which encouraged the Jews' assimilation into "Poles of the Mosaic faith," *Nasz Przegląd* presented a general *Zionist* message and warned against the dangers of complete assimilation.[113] Calling for Jewish civil and national rights in Poland, it also consistently translated literary works in both Yiddish and Hebrew for its audience.

Yiddish writers flourished in interwar Poland. Nobel Prize winner Isaac Bashevis Singer launched his literary career in 1933 with his prized novel *Satan in Goray*. Numerous Yiddish modernist and avant-garde poets and writers found a home in interwar Poland, including Avrom Sutzkever (1913–2010), Kadya Molodovsky (1894–1975), I. J. Singer (1893–1944), and Chaim Grade

---

109 Ibid., 84–86.
110 Paczkowski, "The Jewish Press in the Political Life of the Second Republic," 187. The percentage held by the Jewish press among the minorities fluctuated. While in 1922 it stood at 69.6% in 1931 it fell to 38.2% and by 1937 it stood at 29.7%.
111 Steinlauf, *Bondag to the Dead: Poland and the Memory of the Holocaust*, 225.
112 Fishman, *The Rise of Modern Yiddish Culture*, 85–86.
113 The Polish-Jewish papers accounted for 20.6% of the Warsaw Jewish dailies. Two sister papers to *Nasz Przegląd* were Kraków's *Nowy Dziennik* [New Daily, 1918–1939) and Lviv's *Chwila* (Moment, 1919–1939). Steinlauf, *Bondage to the Dead: Poland and the Memory of the Holocaust*, 219, 220, 225, 227.

(1910–1982). A number of Yiddish publishing houses emerged. Kultur-Lige provided the intelligentsia with the Yiddish literary weekly magazine *Literary Pages* (*Literarishe Bleter*, 1924–1939); the printing house Vilner Farlag fun Boris Kletskin issued the first European editions of the collected works of Sholem Aleichem in twenty-eight volumes and I. L. Peretz in eighteen volumes. Libraries and reading rooms abounded, filling the needs of the expanding Yiddish readership. Indeed, the Yiddish literary culture in Poland augured such acclaim that, for the first time, PEN International, the poets', essayists', and novelists' organization, "recognized a literature without a state, rather than the literature of a country" when it formed a Yiddish division in Poland.[114]

Alongside the Yiddish press and serious Yiddish writers, the Yiddish theater in interwar Poland also thrived. Warsaw was the heart of the Jewish stage, where several Yiddish theaters were active, including the Kamińska Theatre, the Vilner Trupe, the Tsentral Teater, and the Warsaw Jewish Art Theater (Varshaver Yidisher Kunst Teater, VIKT).[115] Theatre troupes also toured throughout the region.

While rabbis and Hasidic rebes—tsadikim—viewed the Jewish theatre as a frivolity and opposed the mingling of men and women, the art form was tremendously popular. Enormous audiences made up of both Jews and non-Jews paid to see Yiddish-speaking actors perform. On the Jewish stage, one could see Yiddish classics, such as those by Avrom Goldfaden (1840–1908), "the father of Yiddish theatre"; one could watch Ester Rachel Kamińska, known as "the mother of Yiddish theatre," perform the lead role of Jacob Gordin's Yiddish drama *Mirele Efros* at the Jewish-owned Kamińska Theatre. On the same stage, one encountered works by a new generation of Yiddish writers—Sholem Aleichem, S. Y. Ansky, Sholem Asch, and Isaac Leib Peretz, for example. Translated plays by non-Jewish playwriters allowed Yiddish-speaking audiences to enjoy Shakespeare, Victor Hugo, and Eugene O'Neill.[116] Ida Kamińska's company produced a range of plays in Yiddish, from Sholem Aleichem to the Russian and French classics, including adaptations of Dostoevsky's *The Brothers Karamazov* and Molière's *The Miser*.

In this public space, one saw Jews dressed in traditional garb, with caftans flowing, and Jews dressed in Western fashion. As Alyssa Quint notes in her book *The Rise of the Modern Yiddish Theater*, Jews experienced the Yiddish theatre as a

---

114 Fishman, *The Rise of Modern Yiddish Culture*, 88–89.
115 Laura Quercioli Mincer, "Ida Kamińska," Jewish Women's Archive, December 31, 1999, https://www.jwa.org.
116 Polonsky, *The Jews in Poland and Russia*, 138–139.

"shock of the familiar," which produced among Jewish attendees a greater sense of collective cultural identity and pride.[117] By the interwar period, audiences in Poland expected Yiddish theatre companies to "achieve the artistic level of Polish theatre and reflect the social experience of Jews in Poland."[118]

Interwar Jewish Education

Several Jewish educational options arose in Poland. In 1918, the government had set up universal primary education and created schools specifically for Jewish students which would be closed on Saturdays and opened on Sundays. Most Jewish students received their education in these tuition-free state schools.[119] As such, most young Jews attained fluency in Polish, and reached for Polish reading material as much as or even more than they did for Yiddish literature. With the Polish-language Jewish press gaining in readership and prestige, Yiddishists worried that Polish would soon outpace Yiddish among Poland's Jews.[120] Thus, while Jews were slower to acculturate in Poland than in the Soviet Union, the process had been set in motion.

Various political groups also developed private educational alternatives, though most Jews did not have access to them due to location and lack of tuition funds. Bund supporters founded the TSYSHO [Di Tsentrale Yidishe Shul-Organizatsye, the Central Yiddish School Organization] school network in 1921 in Warsaw. Its mission provided for a Jewish national, diaspora-focused, secular education for Jewish primary and secondary students. The language of instruction was Yiddish. Self-identifying as proletarian, the TSYSHO schools had a strong socialist orientation. As a rule, its teachers ignored religious subjects and Hebrew. The schools introduced progressive educational ideas and practices, including but not limited to coeducation, physical education, and "non-frontal" learning through creative activity. They were most popular among private school attendees in Vilna where they tempered their political orientation.[121] While the schools reached some twenty-four thousand pupils in 1929, largely in the kresy, enrollment declined in the following decade,

---

117 Alyssa Quint, *The Rise of the Modern Yiddish Theater* (Bloomington: Indiana University Press, 2019), 2.
118 Mincer, "Ida Kamińska."
119 Mendelsohn, *The Jews of East Central Europe Between the World Wars*, 64.
120 Fishman, *The Rise of Modern Yiddish Culture*, 86.
121 Ibid., 91.

as parents wondered about the practicality of learning Yiddish culture to this depth.[122]

Concurrently, General *Zionists* along with moderate left-wing *Zionist* parties created the Hebrew language Tarbut system, which served 46,839 students in the 1936–1937 academic year.[123] Highly successful in the kresy, it promoted a less politically radical agenda than the TSYSHO schools.

The most impressive numbers for Jewish private education, however, belonged to the then newly formed modern Orthodox Agudat Yisrael network of Beys Yankev schools for girls, and Horev schools for boys. Sara Schenirer established the first Beys Yankev school in 1917 as an attempt to stem secularization's appeal to Orthodox women who had been attending the free Polish state schools.[124] For the first time, traditional Jewish girls would be afforded formal Jewish education. In 1936–37, Agudat Yisrael's schools served 84,209 students.[125] Smaller Yiddish educational endeavors also existed, such as technical schools, Yiddish-language crafts schools, agricultural schools, a nursing school, a conservatory, a theater school, and the Yiddish teachers' seminary.[126]

In 1925, Yiddishists finally addressed the lack of scholarly Yiddish literature when they created the Yiddish Scientific Institute (Yidisher Visnshaftlekhe Institut), known as YIVO. Though it struggled to maintain an a-political orientation, there is no doubt that its founders embraced a form of diaspora nationalism. Influenced by the preeminent Jewish historian and father of diaspora nationalism, Simon Dubnow (1860–1941), they underscored the ongoing vitality of the

---

122 Mendelsohn, *The Jews of East Central Europe between the World Wars*, 65.
123 Polonsky, *The Jews in Poland and Russia*, 132–133. The Tarbut school system was grounded in the Russian *Zionists heder metukan* (reformed heder), which they created in the 1890s through a Russian legal loophole. Traditional religious heders were not regulated by the Russian government. Thus, *Zionists* created a new type of heder, which would teach Hebrew language and literature, Jewish history, and the Bible, all in Hebrew. See Fishman, *The Rise of Modern Yiddish Culture*, 31.
124 Asaf Kaniel, "Beys Yankev" (trans. Carrie Friedman-Cohen), The Yivo Encyclopedia of Jews in Eastern Europe, accessed December 27, 2021, https://yivoencyclopedia.org/article.aspx/Beys_Yankev.
125 Polonsky, *The Jews in Poland and Russia*, 132–133; Mendelsohn, *The Jews of East Central Europe between the World Wars*, 66. Other schools served the Jewish community: the Religious *Zionist* party Mizrachi ran Yavne; bilingual schools included Braude high schools which taught in Hebrew and Polish, and the Shul-Kult schools, which promoted Yiddish and Hebrew.
126 Fishman, *The Rise of Modern Yiddish Culture*, 93.

Jewish people, stressing ordinary Jews' agency as the central figures in Jewish history.[127]

Its founders, scholars, and supporters understood YIVO's work as the culmination of having transformed Yiddish "from a lowly 'jargon' to a modern language, the equal of any European tongue and a fitting vehicle for a sophisticated high culture."[128] Located in Vilnius, YIVO's research included philology, history, economics, statistics, psychology, and pedagogy. Its research focus on the past blended with YIVO's painstaking study of contemporary Eastern European Jewish society. "By taking as their subject the collective actions of large numbers of ordinary people, YIVO's scholarship implicitly asserted the importance and agency of the Jewish masses. At the same time YIVO 'served the folk' by disseminating its research findings to a wide audience."[129]

An enormous amount of YIVO's energy concentrated on developing its library and archives. With the help of volunteer collectors known as *zamlers* (often poor and uneducated individuals dedicated to preserving folk songs, terminology, and historic documents),[130] YIVO's library swelled to forty thousand books and some ten thousand volumes of Jewish periodicals; the archive accumulated 175,000 catalogued files. In 1936, YIVO introduced a graduate training program in which fifty-three students participated during the next three years.[131]

For the Jews, interwar Poland provided a cornucopia of paths into Jewish identity and expression. Responding to Polish society, antisemitism, and one another, Poland's very large Jewish community created an unprecedented autonomous Jewish cultural center in the diaspora.

Myth Reconstruction

Despite the relatively recent dramatic shift in Jewish historiography toward understanding a spectrum of Polish perspectives on Polish-Jewish relations, most American Jews who are in their forties and beyond, fixate on Poland's interwar period as one that epitomizes extreme antisemitism. They have retained what they learned in the 1970s, 1980s, and 1990s from Jewish historians. Among this cohort are numerous Israeli academicians who bring with them

---

127 Kuznitz, *YIVO and the Making of Modern Jewish Culture: Scholarship for the Yiddish Nation*, 8.
128 Ibid., 5.
129 Ibid., 6.
130 Ibid., 7.
131 Fishman, *The Rise of Modern Yiddish Culture*, 96.

personal experiences of having been born and raised in Poland, where many joined *Zionist* youth organizations. They lived in Poland during the height of the struggle in which both Jews and non-Jews tried to solve the "Jewish question": How should Jews and non-Jews best respond to post World War I Europe and the antisemitism engendered therein? Could they stay and make a meaningful existence for their communities, as the secularists, diaspora nationalists, and Bund held, or should they leave to establish their own homeland? According to noted historian Ezra Mendelsohn, these Israeli academicians' research supports their specific worldview that the State of Israel is necessary for the Jewish people's continuation.

These earlier Jewish historians did not view the interwar period in its own right, but rather, saw it colored by Polish Jewry's destruction in the Holocaust.[132] For them, so Mendelsohn's argument goes, interwar Poland was one period of intense antisemitism, which attacked its Jewish population and pushed it to its demise. Lucy Dawidowicz's masterpiece *The War against the Jews* elucidates this point. The book, a text which college students find on most syllabi for introductory level classes on the Holocaust, focuses on the Nazis' relationship with the Jews.

In a very short afterward, however, Dawidowicz presents the Second Polish Republic as a "torrent of antisemitic legislation, brutal pogroms and an official government policy of 'evacuating' the Jews from Poland."[133] Her quick phraseology leads her reader, often vulnerable due to lack of knowledge, to believe that interwar Poland passed one anti-Jewish law after another. But the truth is otherwise. Whereas there was often discussion in the various Sejms concerning possible anti-Jewish legislation, only one specific law passed, which after opposition and modification restricted kosher slaughtering to Jews, Muslims, and Karaites living in various regions.[134] While this restriction was targeted against the Jewish population and had negative impacts on the community, it was not a "torrent of legislation." The many anti-Jewish laws Dawidowicz likely refers to were the debilitating partition-era anti-Jewish laws that remained intact for a decade, despite Polish liberals' attempts to excise them.

Furthermore, Dawidowicz's statement that the Poles had an official emigration policy to deal with its so-called Jewish problem also leads one erroneously to assume that the government was actively evacuating Jews from the country.

---

132 Ezra Mendelsohn, "Jewish Historiography on Polish Jewry," in Polonsky, Mendelsohn, and Tomaszewski, *Jews in Independent Poland*, 4.
133 Lucy Dawidowicz, *The War against the Jews* (London: Weidenfeld and Nicolson, 1975), 472.
134 Tomaszewski, "The Civil Rights of Jews 1918–1939," 125.

In fact, while emigration was a tactic seriously researched and accepted by the right-wing ethno-nationalist government in the late 1930s, it was never implemented. Dawidowicz presents a true statement regarding interwar Poland. Yet by choosing to describe it broadly, and with very little explanation, the average reader is left with a false understanding of the country's policies regarding the Jews.

Dawidowicz's work was published in 1975. Years later, despite a growing desire by some academics to review anew relations between Jews and Poles, many historians chose to remain loyal to their teachers' viewpoints. In his 1990 *Nationalism and Antisemitism in Modern Europe, 1815–1945*, Shmuel Almog informs us that

> Polish antisemitism . . . became part of the national ethos and acquired a semi-official status following independence. . . . Antisemitism in Poland, then, tended to be nearly total, and it intensified with the deterioration of the political and economic situation in the inter-war period.[135]

While antisemitism did garner a position within the post-1936 governing body, it did not become "part of the national ethos" and acquire "semi-official status following independence." Yes, Poles launched violent pogroms against Jewish communities during the battles for expansion. Once politicians agreed to delineated borders, this intense antisemitic violence abated. And while the Church and Endecja rhetoric against the Jews continued and even ratcheted up at the end of the interwar period, one need recall the numerous government and liberal organizational efforts made on Jews' behalf during that same time. Almog acknowledges quietly that his understanding of Poland is that state existing after Marshal Piłsudski's death in 1935. That Poland which he presents to readers is based on a very short four-year period, 1935–1939, in which antisemitism and its violence increased dramatically.

It is no wonder that so many American Jews have learned to view Polish-Jewish interwar relations outside of its own contemporary context, given the vacuum in which teachers have presented it. Early Jewish historians tended to present a one-sided image of Polish-Jewish relations. They offered little understanding of Poland's struggles with its different minorities and were unwilling to view the large Jewish population as a *real* challenge for a burgeoning Polish nation still in

---

135 Almog, *Nationalism and Antisemitism in Modern Europe, 1815–1945*, 107.

search of its identity. Indeed, they did not present much of the Polish perspective on this relationship at all.[136] As such, many histories written through 1990 on Polish-Jewish relations have most often portrayed interwar Poland as "an extremely, perhaps even uniquely, antisemitic country."[137]

The American sociologist Celia Heller, who was born in Poland and emigrated in 1938, goes so far as to present Poland's antisemitism as an innate precursor to the "final disaster."[138] This noted sociologist published her bestseller *On the Edge of Destruction* in the 1970s, when Jewish antipolonism had already been well established. She published her work after communist Poland's 1968 expulsion of close to twenty thousand Jews had further scarred Polish-Jewish relations and thereby underscored her claim. Like others in her generation, it is not what Heller stated that is problematic. What is troubling is how Heller states it and what she chooses to leave out of the discussion. By not describing events in full, and their impact on both Jews and Poles, she leads one to a misunderstanding of history and relations between the two peoples.

One example is Heller's discussion of the Polish resentment of the Minorities Treaty. While she spends several pages on Polish abuses of Jews, which led the Allies to create the Minorities Treaty, and on the great impact this had on the Poles' historic sense of honor, only three sentences explain that Poles targeted their resentment of the Minorities Treaty against Jews due to international Jewish influence over the legislation.[139] While she admits to Jewish faults in this situation, Heller glosses over the details so quickly that she leaves the reader with a profound sense of Polish wrongdoing.

This one-sided version of many events would not be so troubling if today's Jewish leadership were keenly aware of it and searched out new sources. However, not only was Heller's work something Jews grabbed onto then, it is also the foundation of modern leaders' understanding of current Polish-Jewish relations. While discussing these relations with a friend who is a congregational rabbi, he proudly took down a copy of *On the Edge of Destruction* from a shelf in his book-lined study. He seemed pleased to have produced a work on the topic of our conversation. The problem is that this book, written in 1977, is his only text on this very specific topic. While he and his colleagues have learned about relations between Poles and Jews, for the majority it has been through a very

---

136 Mendelsohn, "Jewish Historiography on Polish Jewry," 13.
137 Ibid., 4–5.
138 Celia S. Heller, *On the Edge of Destruction: Jews of Poland between the Two World Wars* (Detroit: Wayne State University Press, 1977, 1994), 10.
139 Ibid., 54–57.

narrow lens. Due to the nature of their work congregational rabbis are, admittedly, generalists. Although they must have intellectual access to a plethora of topics, they are not able to go study most of them in depth—and this includes the subject of Polish-Jewish relations. Unfortunately, until rabbis, teachers, and community leaders take the time to learn more about the complex relationships between Poles and Jews in interwar Poland, American Jewry's communal understanding of Poland will be unjustly skewed.

As we have seen, Polish political leaders on the Left and Right wrestled to secure their respective vision of Polish identity. Would Poland welcome all minorities as promised in the Minorities Treaty or would it take on a nationalist character? The Church brought its own angst about secularism's advancing influence to this struggle. For both right-wing politicians and most Church leaders, the enormous Jewish population symbolized the threat they felt Catholic Poland faced. Many Poles followed their lead and expressed contempt for the "Jew-Bolshevik" enemy.

At the same time, to the Church's ire, liberal and secularizing Poles created sociopolitical organizations to shape Poland's future. There were consecutive contests in the political arena about this matter, which displayed at times the Left's coordinated strength and a desire to enforce the Minorities Treaty. Right-wing nationalists countered these efforts and drove Jews into a civil rights struggle. Yet despite these clashes, interwar Poland's Jewish population attained the extraordinary freedom to affirm its nationhood through the explosive expansion of Yiddish secularist culture and Jewish political nationalism. The relative stability that Marshall Józef Piłsudski secured for the country during his tenure remains one reason Jews were able to thrive culturally. However, the country and its Jewish population would soon discover the horrible implications of Piłsudski's former colleagues' political impotence.

CHAPTER 12

Instability and Violence

Marshal Józef Piłsudki's unexpected death on May 12, 1935 created an immeasurable leadership vacuum within his ruling authoritarian party, known as the Sanacja. Sanacja members' only ideological connection was their reverence for Piłsudski. With its charismatic leader buried, the party struggled to fill the political void. The post-Piłsudski Sanacja required both a face and a message to maintain legitimacy. Government jobs, power, and influence were at stake. In this chapter we will explore the Sanacja's transformation into a right-wing nationalist party, which turned a blind eye to antisemitic violence.

Three factions within the party vied for control. Though two leaned left, they failed to unite and gain power. As president of the republic, the moderate leftist Ignacy Móscicki had some factional support within the Sanacja; but the political, economic, and social realities challenged his rise.[1] Neither did Colonel Walery Sławek's campaign end well. Piłsudski's right-hand man, Sławek believed that the Sanacja should reestablish long broken ties with the Polish Socialist Party.[2] The Sanacja disagreed.

General Edward Rydz-Śmigły, one of the marshal's most trusted generals, emerged as the dominant leader. For those who desired continuity and stability, this high-ranking military leader could not be more suitable.[3] Unlike Piłsudski, however, Rydz-Śmigły was not charismatic; besides, to maintain power the party would need more than personality. It required an arresting political ideology. Lacking these necessary ingredients, and with little imagination, the Sanacja resorted to mirroring the popular opposition: the party attained a renewed grip on power by coupling a call for rapid industrialization with an ultra-nationalist definition of country and Self.

---

1 Wynot, *Polish Politics in Transition: The Camp of National Unity and the Struggle for Power 1935–1939*, 35.
2 Joseph Rothschild, *East Central Europe between the Two World Wars*, 71.
3 Wynot, *Polish Politics in Transition: The Camp of National Unity and the Struggle for Power 1935–1939*, 36.

The Depression-era economic crises had broadened the opposition.[4] Yet, despite resisting the Sanacja, the opposition remained disjointed. Numerous parties with internal factions weakened the opposition's left and right camps. The Polish Socialist Party (PPS) and the Peasant Party (SL), the centrist Labor Party (SP), the Christian Democrats, the National Workers' Party, Dmowski's National Democrats (known as Endecja), and the more extreme National Radical Camp (ONR) all vied for political and social control. Politicized peasants and workers conducted food strikes against the cities. Political activists held mass rallies, made agitation speeches, and launched armed attacks. The government countered with violence.[5] Although the strikes and violence rocked the country, the opposition was not united enough to take down the Sanacja government.

While the Left had portrayed class struggle as Poland's core socioeconomic problem, the extreme Right continued to focus the country's fury on the "Jewish enemy." As the country's various crises unfolded, blaming Poland's problems on the growing Jewish population appealed to larger numbers of Poles. People sought simple answers to complicated problems, with more individuals blaming the supposed Jew-Bolshevik enemy within for the disasters they faced.[6]

The younger generation, which had been raised on promises of a glorious future, had grown disillusioned by Poland's continuous economic pitfalls. Highlighting the dearth of jobs and sense of cultural insecurity, extreme ethnonationalist pundits prompted younger people to vent their frustrations on Poland's Jewish minority.[7] Focusing their political protests not only at the university but also in the town market, the outraged and resentful Christian youth attacked the Jews' dominance of higher education and trade.

Embittered by their plight and fearful of Poles' wholesale economic and cultural displacement by Jews, the Polish youth based its arguments not in fantasy but in statistics. In 1921, Jews accounted for 7.8% of Poland's population.[8] And yet there was a preponderance of Jewish students in higher education. For the 1923–24 academic year, as per Vice Minister of Education Miklaszewski: Jews made up 25.04% of the students at Kraków University; 33.78% at Lwów

---

4   Rothschild, *East Central Europe between the Two World Wars*, 68.
5   Wynot, *Polish Politics in Transition: The Camp of National Unity and the Struggle for Power 1935–1939*, 156.
6   Anne Applebaum, *Twilight of Democracy: The Seductive Lure of Authoritarianism* (New York: Doubleday, 2020), 12. Applebaum notes that people—one by one—are drawn to authoritarianism "like a flock of moths to an inescapable flame."
7   Gąsowski, "The Second Republic and Its Jewish Citizens," 132.
8   Stachura, *Poland, 1918–1945*, 52. According to the 1921 census, Poland had 27,177,000 inhabitants.

University; 32.91% at Warsaw University; 19.57% at Wilno University; and 62.88% in the Dental Institute.[9] In the halls of higher education, Jews accounted for far more than their general population numbers would predict.

University Anti-Jewish Violence

Beginning in the 1930 fall term and again a year later, right-wing Polish university students protested the Sanacja's continued hold on power. Piłsudski had won the 1930 election due to the Jews' neutrality and his imprisonment of opposition leaders.[10] Because most Jews were delighted with Piłsudski's hold on government, students grew convinced that his anti-democratic rule was connected to the Jews: They believed the Jews controlled Piłsudski.

For extremist ethno-nationalist student organizations, such as All-Polish Youth (Młodzież Wszechpolska, MWP), which had been formed and buttressed by the National Democrats, the call for violence against Jewish students appeared quite justified.[11] Indeed, by the late fall of 1931 Endecja resolved that

> [t]he number of Jews in this country and their strong position in its economic life, which has only strengthened under the present government, are threatening our economic future. Their destructive influence on the population's morals and on national spiritual life, and their hostile attitude toward the Polish raison d'être, prove that the rightful aim of Polish national politics has to be opposition to the Jewish Threat.[12]

---

9   Szymon Rudnicki, "Anti-Jewish Legislation in Interwar Poland," in *Antisemitism and Its Opponents in Modern Poland*, ed. Robert Blobaum (Ithaca: Cornell University Press, 2005), 156n32.

10 Outraged by the marshal's original seizure of power and later by his autocratic style, university professors proved the most vocal and best-organized Polish critics of opposition leaders' arrests. In 1930 over 320 professors (60%) signed resolutions condemning this internment of political prisoners. In retaliation, the government liquidated fifty-three professorial positions. Clearly animosity stoked this relationship between higher education and the Sanacja government. See John Connelly, *Captive University: The Sovietization of East German, Czech, and Polish Higher Education 1945–1956* (Chapel Hill: The University of North Carolina Press, 2000), 81.

11 Michlic, *Poland's Threatening Other*, 112.

12 Quoted in ibid., 121.

The National Democrats lauded the student protesters, who violently assailed Jews and thereby "protected" Poland's economic self-interests and Catholic identity.

Between 1935 and 1937, a large segment of Polish students sustained a second, more intense wave of anti-Jewish violence at the universities. Hitler's 1933 rise to power, his Brown Shirts' assaults against Jews, and the Nuremberg Laws, coupled with Piłsudki's death, gave extreme Polish ethno-nationalists permission to intensify their violence and demand anti-Jewish policies.[13] They created "spontaneous manifestations of antisemitism ... as proof that the Jewish issue is a pressing one, that it requires immediate and radical solutions."[14] Their solutions included the establishment of "ghetto benches," segregated seating for Jewish students meant to humiliate them until a *numerus nullus*—the de-Judaization of Poland's higher education system—could be achieved.

Maria Dąbrowska (1889–1965), a novelist, journalist, playwright, and moral authority in Polish intellectual circles, spoke against the particular and commonplace assault on Jews at universities.[15] Her November 24, 1936 article entitled "Annual Shame," which was published in the leftist *Dziennik Popularny*, criticized those Polish students "who today make clubs, knives, brass knuckles, and iron crowbars hidden in a schoolbag into symbols of the Polish student."[16] For Dąbrowska, they wanted "to blame Jews for all the bad things taking place in Poland."[17]

According to Dąbrowska, by 1936 "the student pogrom epidemic has spilled out from universities into the streets. Students are smashing windows, breaking into shops, and using metal weapons to hit people who are calmly going about their business."[18] In 1934, students at the University of Warsaw attacked the historian Marceli Handelsman from behind and hit him on the head with brass

---

13 Szymon Rudnicki, "From 'Numerus Clausus' To 'Numerus Nullus,'" in Polonsky, *Jews and the Emerging Polish State*, 259.
14 Maria Dąbrowska, "Annual Shame," in *Against Antisemitism: An Anthology of Twentieth-Century Polish Writings*, ed. Adam Michnik and Agnieszka Marczyk (New York: Oxford University Press, 2018), 47.
15 In 1965, forty years after her death, Maria Dąbrowska's private journals were made public. Based on numerous entries, critics have come to question the commitment and reasoning behind her writings which oppose antisemitism. Some suggest that her concern for Poland's international reputation influenced her, rather than her desire to end discrimination of Jews for its own sake. See Laura Darling, "Maria Dąbrowska," Making Queer History, March 17, 2020, https://www.makingqueerhistory.com/articles/2020/3/17/maria-dbrowska.
16 Dąbrowska, "Annual Shame," 47.
17 Ibid.
18 Ibid., 48.

knuckles, "with obviously murderous intension."[19] In 1936, they threw eggs at the world-renowned physicist Mieczysław Wolfke during a lecture. Dąbrowska implored her readers to realize that "great thuggery is coming to Poland not from below but from above; and if it encounters no resistance, it will soon turn against all that is lawful, enlightened, noble, and judicious."[20]

Alone, or supported by organizations, many Polish students stood by their fellow Jewish students during this harrowing time. Some joined their Jewish peers, who stood during lectures, rather than participate in legitimizing the shameful ghetto bench. A collection of diverse student groups protested the violence and opposed anti-Jewish sanctions in the university: Communist Life (Życie), the Union of Independent Socialist Youth (Związek Niezależnej Młodzieży Socjalistycznej), the Youth Legion—Faction (Legion Młodych-Fracja), the Union of Young Polish Democrats (Związek Polskiej Młodzieży Demokratycznej), and Wici, the academic youth movement of the Peasant Party. Several of these groups cooperated to form the Committee for the Defense of Students' Honor (Komitet Obrony Honoru Akademika).[21] Students affirmed that another Poland existed: the country of Tadeusz Kotarbiński, who as an esteemed philosophy professor had influenced a group of academics to stand while giving lectures to demonstrate solidarity with students protesting unjust treatment of Jews.[22]

Other academics rose up to condemn the antisemitic violence. For example, Professor Stanisław Kulczyński (1895–1975), rector of the Jan Kazimierz University in Lviv chose to resign from office rather than to acquiesce to violent pressure to install ghetto benches. In an open letter he characterized "ghetto benches" as defiling the sound reputation of the university: "Learning cannot develop under conditions of compulsion . . . because learning is free thought."[23] Although his replacement, Rector Longchamps, ordered the imposition of segregated seating, in a letter of protest the prorector, Professor Ganszyniec, refused to follow through with such "absurd demands."[24]

Nearly one hundred academics, one-sixth of the total number at Polish universities, signed protest letters to their institutions.[25] At Lviv's polytechnic,

---

19 Ibid.
20 Ibid.
21 Rudnicki, "From 'Numerus Clausus' To 'Numerus Nullus,'" 258.
22 Connelly, *Captive University: The Sovietization of East German, Czech, and Polish Higher Education 1945–1956*, 82.
23 Stanisław Kulczyński, as quoted in Peter D. Stachura, *Poland, 1918–1945*, 110.
24 Szymon Rudnicki, "From 'Numerus Clausus' To 'Numerus Nullus,'" 263.
25 Polonsky, *The Jews in Poland and Russia*, 406.

Kazimierz Bartel (who had served earlier as Poland's prime minister under Piłsudski) led a demonstration with twenty-six professors against any form of segregation. In December 1937, fifty-eight esteemed professors from various backgrounds and political viewpoints publicly opposed university restrictions based on religion, nationality, or race. A number expressed solidarity with Jewish students also by lecturing while standing.[26]

However, it cannot be missed that five-sixths of professors remained silent, with some actually approving the outcome. According to historian John Connelly, "[h]ere the professoriate failed to take a courageous stance. In some cases, this was due to sympathy for the student radicals, especially in strong National Democratic *środowiska*, like Lwów [Lviv] or certain faculties in Warsaw."[27] Some academics remained quiet to avoid the fray. They hoped that giving into the bullies' demands would bring peace back to the campuses. Furthermore, they saw that colleagues who expressed concern for Jewish students risked right-wing retribution. Polonist Konrad Górski of Vilnius, who had publicly supported Jewish students, survived an assassination attempt.[28]

A variety of intellectuals publicly railed against this travesty to Polish enlightenment.[29] Writers, artists, political activists, and public figures condemned the hate-filled attitude toward Jewish students and the violence inflicted upon them. Antoni Sobański's scathing article "In Reply to Mr. Dembiński" appeared in the conservative periodical *Czas*. It was one of the most critical pieces of the student-led violent campaign against the Jews.[30] Despite intimidating violence aimed at them, such as explosive charges laid at apartment entries, rotten eggs pelted at them, and smoke canisters thrown into lectures, many intellectuals defended Poland's liberal and democratic views.[31]

In the end, however, universities bent to the will of extreme ethno-nationalists. Despite Minister of Education Wojciech Świętostowski's January 1937 statement that the establishment of ghetto benches was "impossible," nine months later the segregation of Jewish students in Polish universities and polytechnics became common practice. Świętostowski changed his mind due to the number

---

26 Rudnicki, "From 'Numerus Clausus' To 'Numerus Nullus,'" 263.
27 Connelly, *Captive University: The Sovietization of East German, Czech, and Polish Higher Education 1945–1956*, 82.
28 Ibid.
29 Władysaw Bartoszewski, "Some Thoughts on Polish-Jewish Relations," in Polonsky, *Poles and Jews: Renewing the Dialogue*, 281.
30 A. Sobański's article, "W odpowiedzi panu Dembińskiemu" was published in *Czas*, November 8, 1936. Rudnicki, "From 'Numerus Clausus' To 'Numerus Nullus,'" 258–259.
31 Ibid., 261.

of requests from university rectors who feared further violence.[32] In an effort to stem the violence, the Sanacja allowed universities to regulate seating and separate Polish and Jewish students. But violence continued when Jews refused to take up their assigned seats on the bench.[33]

In her article titled "Annual Shame," Dąbrowska casts a finger not only at students for their horrid violence, but also at priests who "have never used their authority to condemn the brawls and violence perpetrated in the name of Catholicism and the cross."[34] She blames those who belonged to the education system, the press, as well as family members and professors for not speaking out against the violence. She concludes: "But we—old sinners, corruptors, and passive enablers—we should know that we are responsible for others' mortal sins, sins that bring nothing but harm, ill repute, and shame to Poland."[35]

Professional organizations also succumbed to the menacing antisemitic drumbeat. Physicians at the May 1937 conference of the Association of Doctors voted and narrowly passed a motion on *"numerus nullus* for Jews at all medical departments, and *numerus nullus* for Jewish professors and doctoral candidates at all medical departments and hospital wards."[36] This group of educated elites viewed "the present status as an insult to the dignity of the Polish nation."[37] Other medical, dental, and architectural societies followed suit, ousting Jewish members.[38] In March 1937, the Warsaw section of the Confederation of Polish Electrical Engineers voted 107 to twenty-three to admit only "Aryans" to its membership. Two months later, the League of Polish Lawyers voted to prohibit Jews from entering the profession.[39]

---

32 Polonsky, *The Jews in Poland and Russia*, 87.
33 Michlic, *Poland's Threatening Other*, 113.
34 Dąbrowska, "Annual Shame," 49–50.
35 Ibid., 49–50.
36 As cited in Henryk Grynberg, *Drohobycz, Drohobycz and Other Stories: True Tales from the Holocaust and Life After*, trans., Alicia Nitecki and ed. Theodosia Robertson (New York: Penguin Books, 2002), 12. Also see Polonsky, *The Jews in Poland and Russia*, 87.
37 As cited in Grynberg, *Drohobycz, Drohobycz and Other Stories*, 12. Also see Polonsky, *The Jews in Poland and Russia*, 87.
38 Grynberg, *Drohobycz, Drohobycz and Other Stories*, 14–17.
39 Polonsky, *The Jews in Poland and Russia*, 87–88.

Market Stall Anti-Jewish Violence

Since his early writings, Dmowski had argued that "[t]he Jewish population is an undeniable parasite on the body of the society in the country where it lives."[40] Through exploitation, the so-called Jewish parasite feasted on the host population for sustenance, growth, and power. As we have already learned, Dmowski urged the elimination of the Jewish middleman, who he portrayed as stealing the Pole's economic prosperity. Though most Jewish traders were poor, the fact remains that Jews, who had reached 10% of the general population in the mid-1930s, had been overly represented in trade: Jews accounted for 62% of individuals earning a living in trade and insurance. Of that number, 88.9% was employed in the retail goods trade.[41]

By mid-1935, Dmowski had called for a national boycott of Jewish stores, including market stands. To force Jews out of this occupation, Dmowski instructed National Democracy squads to plunder Jewish market stalls and beat up the Jewish owners. His eventual goal remained the Jews' emigration. For Dmowski, that Polish society permitted Jews citizenship equated to weakness, backwardness. To secure Poland's health, Poles needed to reclaim the nation from the Jews.

Franciszek Ksawery Pruszyński (1907–1950), a conservative journalist, writer, and diplomat, who opposed right-wing ethno-nationalism, emphasizes in a July 12, 1936, article that "[t]he fight for the market stand does not break out because market stands could provide jobs for all the unemployed in the countryside. The fight breaks out because there is nowhere else to go."[42] Poland's rural youth found itself at a dangerous socioeconomic inflection point: the nation had "no equal in Europe when it comes to the size of its agrarian population and the scale of its rural destitution."[43] Thus, when prompted, people were ready to take what they could grab: "the market stand is close at hand. It is what's most easily available, most immediately profitable."[44]

---

40 Grzegorz Krzywiec, *Chauvinism, Polish Style: The Case of Roman Dmowski (Beginnings: 1886–1905)*, trans. Jarosław Garliński (Frankfurt am Main: Peter Lang, 2016), 269.
41 Polonsky, *The Jews in Poland and Russia*, 62.
42 Franciszek Ksawery Pruszyński, "The Przytyk Market Stands," in Michnik and Marczyk, *Against Antisemitism*, 41.
43 Ibid.
44 Ibid.

One may argue, however, that it did not make sense to go after Jewish market stands, given that most of their owners were poor. Yet peasant perception overrode reality:

> [T]oday's countryside views the merchant as a rich man—he is the owner of a treasure trove with sugar, petroleum, matches, and iron. Only if we look on from above do we see that this petty Jewish merchant is actually a pauper. For the peasant . . . [t]he man in a yarmulke eats herring and potatoes, while the peasant in the sheepskin coat eats only potatoes. Simply put, a group whose standard of living is even lower than that of the Jewish Ghetto is now challenging this Ghetto.[45]

As we have seen previously, too often it is perception that matters.

Boycotts against Jewish shops peaked in 1936. The Church and the Sanacja government declared their support for the boycotts as long as they did not include violence, sabotage, or physical force. However, much violence did occur. And when Jewish youth met Polish ethnic nationalist violence with guns and *Zionist* militancy, the fighting only intensified. One instance took place in the small town of Przytyk, south of Warsaw, near Radom. Responding to continued material destruction and violence, Przytyk's Jewish youth formed a self-defense group.[46] On March 9, 1936, these Jews retaliated against Jewish property destruction. After close to an hour of brawling, a Jewish fighter, Szolem Leska, shot and killed a Polish assailant, Stanisław Wieśniak. Poles answered by escalating the violence: crowds of ethnic Poles spilled out into the Jewish neighborhoods of Podgajek and Zachęta, destroying Jewish property, working over Jewish individuals and crushing the Jews' confidence in their Polish citizenship. Polish rage sacked the Minkowski home and pummeled the children and parents. An ethnic Polish neighbor saved the children, but both parents died.[47] The Przytyk market stand boycott had morphed into the Przytyk pogrom.

Moses Schorr, an independent senator in the Sejm, condemned the massacre on March 12. Soon thereafter the Bund and the Polish Socialist Party called for a one-day nationwide general strike. During the trial, guilty sentences were reached for eleven of the fourteen Jewish defendants and twenty-two of the

---

45 Ibid.
46 Adam Michnik and Agnieszka Marczyk, introduction to "The Przytyk Market Stands," in Michnik and Marczyk, *Against Antisemitism*, 34.
47 Michlic, *Poland's Threatening Other*, 129.

forty-three Polish defendants. Important is the fact that Jews received much longer prison terms than did the Poles; and while the Jewish murderer, Leska, was sentenced to eight years in prison, the four Poles accused of murdering the Minkowskis were acquitted on "insufficient evidence."[48] Several judges empathized not only with the Poles' economic resentment, but also "the movement of the Polish people towards economic independence."[49] The Polish historian Jolanta Żyndul suggests that the courts' apparent minimization of punishment for the Poles who had instigated interethnic violence made such aggression more acceptable.[50]

Comparable devastation also occurred in Myślenice, south of Kraków. On June 22–23, 1936, the Endecja member Adam Doboszyński (1904–1949) led close to 150 people in acts of terror against the local Jewish community, destroying its material goods.[51] Endecja portrayed Doboszyński as a national hero. In response to the Myślenice pogrom, Prime Minister Felicjan Sławoj Składkowski told the Sejm, "My government considers that nobody in Poland should be injured. An honest host does not allow anybody to be harmed in his house. But an economic struggle? That's different."[52] This construct—that the Jews, as guests, do not belong to the collective Polish nation—was at the very heart of the problem.

Though the Church did not support violence, it clearly agreed with a social and economic separation of Poles from Jews. In February 1936, in the midst of violence at both university and market stall, the Polish primate August Hlond (1881–1948) issued a lengthy pastoral letter entitled "On Catholic Moral Principles." He lamented the brutality sweeping Poland. By blaming it on the so-called process of Bolshevization, he blamed it on the Jews, who he portrayed as essential to the Bolshevik cause. He did not mention the non-Jews who remained essential to the Bolshevik cause nor the Polish non-Jews, specifically, who aided the growth of communism in Poland. Focusing on the Jewish enemy, the Church deflected attention away from the Polish Catholic enemy, thus denying its danger.

Hlond went on to argue that the "Jewish problem exists and will exist as long as Jews will be Jews."[53] Jews remained problematic for Catholic Poland:

---

48   Adam Michnik and Agnieszka Marczyk, introduction to "The Przytyk Market Stands," 34.
49   Polonsky, *The Jews in Poland and Russia*, 86.
50   Michlic, *Poland's Threatening Other*, 122.
51   Ibid., 121.
52   Quoted in Polonsky, *The Jews in Poland and Russia*, 86.
53   Quoted in ibid., 84.

> It is a fact that the Jews are fighting with the Catholic Church, that they are embedded in freethinking, that they constitute the avant-garde of godlessness, the Bolshevik movement, and revolutionary activities. It is a fact that Jewish influence on morality is pernicious, and that their publishing houses spread pornography. It is true that the Jews permit fraud and usury, and that they carry out trade in live merchandise [a euphemism for prostitution—JS-B]. It is true that in the schools the influence of the Jewish youth on the Catholic [youth] is, in general, negative from the religious and ethical point of view.[54]

But though he recognized that "[n]ot all Jews are like that," he made it clear that "[o]ne must close oneself off to the harmful moral influences of Jewry, separate from its anti-Christian culture."[55] Although in this 1936 letter he spoke against inflicting violence on Jews, he and the Church had finally accepted violence as a necessary evil to save the Self—that is, Catholic Poland.

Anti-Jewish violence erupted in centers of learning and trade. It spread throughout the former kingdom, including the provinces of Kielce, Warsaw, Białystok, and Łodz. It engulfed some 150 small towns (shtetls) where local sections of National Democracy confronted the Peasant Party in heated political debate.[56] The National Democrats turned up their antisemitic rhetoric to whip up fear and poverty into political support. The historian Jolanta Żyndul estimates that beatings of villagers and townspeople, students at universities, and commuters on trains led to fourteen people killed and close to two thousand injured.[57] This four-year period between 1935 and 1939, in which antisemitic attitudes and violence assailed Jewish university students, Jewish professors, and Jewish market stall owners, often defines interwar Poland in American Jewish minds.

Sanacja, Antisemitism, and Anti-Jewish Violence

Dmowski was not alone in promoting anti-Jewish violence. To maintain its own power, sections within the post-Piłsudki party focused on cultivating the disgruntled youth. Adopting a more nationalistic approach by deploying

---

54 Quoted in ibid.
55 Michlic, *Poland's Threatening Other*, 114.
56 Ibid.
57 Polonsky, *The Jews in Poland and Russia*, 86.

antisemitic tropes, Sanacja hoped to attract the National Democrat's youth to its own voting bloc. In 1937, Sanacja's new Camp of National Unity, or OZN (Obóz Zjednoczenia Narodowego), took up the bullhorn for this co-opted brazen nationalism. By 1938, Sanacja was warning that Poles would become "a nation of a very strange construction . . . a nation of Polish workers and peasants, directed by an intelligentsia of a different national origin."[58] The party presented "national security"— be it political, economic, or social—as the answer to Poland's problems.[59] In the name of Poland's political survival, the OZN attempted to unite two hitherto opposing messages—Piłsudski's authoritarianism and Dmowski's Polish exclusivism.

While the OZN jumped on the "Jew-enemy" bandwagon, commandeering nationalist rhetoric and policy to gain political support, opponents to this message stepped forward. The Polish Socialist Party (PPS) was the strongest opposition entity, as it had the largest following.[60] Together with its central committee comprised of trade union leaders, the PPS decried the use of antisemitism as a political tool.[61] Tellingly, the PPS showed incredible success in local elections held during the winter of 1938 and the spring of 1939. In fact, the Polish Socialist Party fared better than the OZN, controlling six cities on its own and nine more in alliance with various Jewish parties. Additionally, the PPS won more seats than either the OZN or the Endeks, claiming over 25% of the total vote of the 160 locales where the socialists ran.[62] Its significant gains in the major urban areas demonstrates that even during a challenging and unstable time, many Poles were willing to view the Jews as relatively equal with themselves.[63]

Despite a substantial percent of Poles desiring a tolerant Polish society, life for Poland's Jewish community worsened during the last four years of the Second Polish Republic. People's fears of de-Polonization fueled a violent unease. Hitler's growing military aggression only strengthened it. And though a deep-rooted opposition to antisemitism emerged, by mid-1939 this segment of the population prioritized Poland's defense against German aggression and renounced opposition to Sanacja.[64]

---

58   Wynot, *Polish Politics in Transition: The Camp of National Unity and the Struggle for Power 1935–1939*, 110.
59   Ibid., 53.
60   Ibid., 32.
61   Ibid., 148.
62   Ibid., 234–235.
63   Ibid., 33.
64   Ibid., 243.

Prior to 1984, Polish historians played down the charge of interwar antisemitism by casting it as the result of "objective social and economic conditions."[65] They legitimized antisemitism as necessary for Poland's national self-defense. Jews were guests. They did not belong in the country. Today, many Polish historians have come to recognize the problem with this viewpoint. However, I would argue that, like American Jews, a great many Poles who were taught this older perspective still hold onto it either because of a lack of continuing education on the subject or because of renewed need to attain a type of nationalist confidence. In short, they find it necessary to ignore or erase past Polish brutality.

Myth Reconstruction

It is my contention that American Jews have bought into the idea of Poland as a terrible place not only because antisemitism flourished in interwar Poland, and Jewish historiography stressed it, but also because an antisemitic Poland allowed American Jews to avoid confronting their own decision to live in an American society rife with antisemitism and racism. According to the *New York Times* editor Jonathan Weisman, "the 1920s and 1930s was perhaps the darkest age for American Jewry, a period of fear and menace."[66] Henry Ford's newspaper the *Dearborn Independent* blamed so-called international Jewry for the horrors of World War I. His mouthpiece argued that Jews had orchestrated the global conflagration in order to kill off the Christian population and thereby gain even greater worldwide influence. For eighteen months, Ford's paper rebuked Jews by serializing the *Protocols of the Elders of Zion*. Later, he widely disseminated the *Protocols* in his book entitled *The International Jew*.[67] Ford influenced the spread of American antisemitism, which impacted Jews in real ways.

American nativism and immigration restrictionism blossomed. US immigration expert Peter Schrag writes in *Not Fit for Our Society* that the post-World War I era was just one of many times since the country's founding when xenophobia, racism, and restrictionism gained power over the more accepted and well-maintained image of America as a beacon of hope for the imperiled immigrant. Numerous influential, white Christians, be they in academia or politics,

---

65 Quoted in Michlic, *Poland's Threatening Other*, 110–111.
66 Jonathan Weisman *((Semitism))): Being Jewish in America in the Age of Trump* (New York: St. Martin's Press, 2018), 53.
67 Sheldon Marcus, *Father Coughlin: The Tumultuous Life of the Priest of the Little Flower* (Boston: Little, Brown and Company, 1973), 149.

had learned American exceptionalism from its English origin story (similar to Poles viewing Polish Catholics as the epitome of Polishness). Benjamin Franklin warned in 1751 that Pennsylvania was becoming "a Colony of Aliens, who will shortly be so numerous as to Germanize us instead of our Anglifying them and will never adopt our Language or Customs."[68] In the 1850s, Know-Nothingism flourished as a secret society that disparaged Irish Catholic immigrants. Shop signs said, "No Irish Need Apply." In later decades, American cartoonists branded Jewish, Italian and Polish immigrants on ships as pirates, naming their vessels "socialism," "disease," and "Mafia."[69]

Entering the twentieth century, nativist and immigration restrictionists took up the new purported scientific theory of eugenics to "prove" that America's *original* settlers from England and their offspring bore superior intellectual, physical, and moral traits compared with other racial and religious groups. Henry Ford's racism and antisemitism fell in line with such thinkers as Henry H. Goddard, a prominent American psychologist and pioneer of intelligence testing, who claimed that 60% of Jews who immigrated through Ellis Island prior to World War I could be classified as "morons."[70]

Eugenics "experts," including Harry Laughlin who promoted eugenic sterilization, advised Representative Albert Johnson's House Committee on Immigration and Naturalization. Its recommendations led to race-based national origins immigration laws in both 1921 and 1924, which targeted East European nations with large Jewish populations; the 1924 Johnson-Reed Act slowed Jewish immigration to a trickle.[71] This "scientific" acceptance of Jews as inferior also set up numerous roadblocks against social and educational advancement for Jews who had already immigrated. Country clubs barred Jews. In 1922, Harvard University set a de facto quota on Jewish admissions. Colleges and universities across the country followed suit.

Representative (later Senator) Henry Cabot Lodge of Massachusetts described Jews as "birds of passage." Taking advantage of the United States at the expense of honest American workers, they had no intention of embracing American language and culture, let alone remaining in the country. In response to such prejudicial statements, Jews taught future generations the imperative to

---

68 Quoted in Peter Schrag, *Not Fit for Our Society: Immigration and Nativism in America* (Berkeley: University of California Press, 2010), 3.
69 Ibid., 3.
70 Ibid., 8.
71 Ibid., 8–9.

assimilate.⁷² Those Jews who had taken the risk of leaving their homeland, their families, their friends, their jobs, and their culture, constituted a self-selected Jewish population willing to move away from tradition. These Jews sought to show that they belonged by giving up Yiddish and their Old World Jewish culture. When American Jewish papers featured articles on the eruption of antisemitism in the Polish borderlands during the 1918–1922 wars of expansion, Jews in America could assuage their own fears about America.

The United States did not lack in populist leaders who employed antisemitic rhetoric to secure a base. A charismatic and highly influential Irish Catholic priest, Father Charles E. Coughlin, spewed antisemitism during his 1930s radio broadcasts.[73] Each week, up to thirty million listeners heard his Sunday afternoon sermons and commentary. One of the most influential figures in American culture, Father Coughlin's oratory grew ever more extremist in 1938. He depicted international (read: Jewish) bankers as the enemy who had brought the Great Depression to the American populace. Like Roman Dmowski, he furthered the Żydokomuna conspiracy theory that portrayed the Bolshevik enemy as inherently Jewish.[74] His weekly magazine *Social Justice* reprinted the fraudulent *Protocols of the Elders of Zion* and viewed Hitler as a solution to the international Jew. He called for the creation of the Christian Front to defend the nation from threats posed by Roosevelt, Jews, and communists. Many Christian Fronters espoused Nazi ideals. They organized "buy Christian only" movements and between 1938 and 1940 they made many cities' streets, subways, and movie theaters unsafe for Jews. The police in New York City often ignored the Christian Front's physical assaults on Jewish women, children, and elderly people.[75]

Contemporary Jewry felt the rage of not only Father Coughlin and the Christian Front, but also the myriad of right-wing extremist organizations and leaders who championed white Anglo-Saxon Protestant America. As in Poland, their influence gained ground after Hitler rose to chancellor of Germany. Several

---

72 Ibid., 14.
73 Sheldon Marcus opens his book on Father Coughlin:

> It was a sad, low period in history. All over the world it appeared that democracy was buckling under its problems and challenges. In Europe many people, embittered either by the frustrations of World War I or by the conditions wrought by depression, looked to dictatorship to alleviate their discontent.

> How incredibly similar our own time is. See Sheldon Marcus, *Father Coughlin: The Tumultuous Life of the Priest of the Little Flower*,

74 Ibid., 4, 7.
75 Ibid., 154–156.

Americans retained connections with high-ranking Nazi officials, including Julius Streicher, the editor of the vicious antisemitic *Der Stürmer* newspaper and one of twelve major German war criminals condemned to death at Nuremberg. Some even met with Hitler himself. Each right-wing leader reached hundreds of thousands of followers through printed media that accused the Jews of organizing an international communist conspiracy to overtake the United States. Some even charged that to destroy American values the Jew paid Black men to rape white Christian women.[76]

By 1939, a Roper poll published in *Fortune* magazine uncovered that 53% of American respondents believed that "Jews are different and should be restricted."[77] In a speech at the September 11, 1941 pro-Nazi America First Committee rally, American hero Charles Lindbergh proclaimed that three forces were driving the nation into another world war: the Jews, Roosevelt, and Churchill. Lindbergh insisted that the Jews' influence had to be limited.[78] American Jews often responded by keeping their heads down, trying not to instigate anti-Jewish responses. They also reminded themselves that Jews remaining in Poland had it much worse.

---

[76] Ibid., 146–154. Marcus points out William Dudley Pelley, who founded the Silver Shirts the day of Hitler's coronation. He patterned it after the Nazi SS. With his own publishing company, he distributed Hitler's *Mein Kampf* throughout the United States along with a mass of other antisemitic literature. Marcus also points out Fritz Kuhn, who was influenced by Henry Ford's paper, met with Hitler, and created the German-American Bund which packed Madison Square Garden on February 20, 1939 with nineteen thousand members, swastika flags unfurled, officials dressed like Hitler's Storm Troopers, banners reading "Smash Jewish Communism" and "Stop Jewish Domination of Christian America."

[77] Quoted in Weisman *(((Semitism))): Being Jewish in America in the Age of Trump*, 54.

[78] Ibid., 55–56.

CHAPTER 13

Genocide and the Poles

On August 23, 1939, Soviet Foreign Minister Vyacheslav Molotov met in Moscow with his German counterpart, Joachim von Ribbentrop, to sign a non-aggression accord between the two countries. The Nazi-Soviet Pact partitioned Poland between the two signatories. Immediately thereafter, on September 1, 1939, Germany thundered eastward into Poland.[1] As Poland had only recently achieved independence, its newly formed military lacked modern weaponry. Poorly deployed, the Polish army could not hold back the sixty-five German formations numbering 1,850,000 men equipped with some ten thousand guns and mortars, 2,800 tanks, and more than two thousand airplanes.[2] On September 28, 1939, Warsaw fell. The Nazi war machine had begun its colonial task of securing lebensraum—living space, growing space—for the German people.

On September 17, 1939, just sixteen days after the Nazi invasion, Soviet troops marched westward through Poland up to the Curzon Line.[3] On October 5, 1939, the Red Army took Vilnius. The following day, the last operational Polish unit surrendered. The Soviets occupied Poland's eastern provinces until the summer of 1941 when Germany turned against the USSR and invaded that very

---

1   Upon the German invasion, both Poles and Jews recognized quickly the implicit need to move beyond antisemitism and to unite against their common enemy. One hundred twenty thousand Jews joined fellow Poles to defend their country. People equated this cooperation between Pole and Jew in defense of Poland as reminiscent of the 1861–63 Polish-Jewish brotherhood. See Wladyslaw Bartoszewski and Zofia Lewin, *The Samaritans: Heroes of the Holocaust*, 2.
2   Richard C. Lukas, *Forgotten Holocaust: The Poles under German Occupation 1939–1944*, rev. ed. (New York: Hippocrene Books, 2005), 2.
3   The Curzon Line is the border proposed by the Allies in Versailles to demarcate the separation between Poland and the Soviet Union, but which Polish troops ignored in the border expansion wars. See Norman Davies, *God's Playground: A History of Poland*, 2:294.

region to further extend its empire. In this chapter, we will explore World War II's impact on the Poles. We will dig into German and Soviet crimes against Poles, recognize how each occupier set Jews and Poles against one another, and discuss Polish anti-Jewish wartime violence within this context.

German Colonialism

Hitler justified his eastward European expansion with the claim that he was merely taking back formerly German land from the "savage" Poles and Ukrainians who had "mismanaged" it. With this argument, he employed the same rhetoric imperialists had used for centuries.[4] In the genocide scholar Jürgen Zimmerer's words, "the German war against Poland and the USSR was without doubt the largest colonial war of conquest in history."[5]

Hitler's imperial fantasy mirrored America's beliefs about its own nineteenth-century westward expansion: for the Führer, the East would replenish the German spirit and people. From the newly won territories the Germans would create a racial paradise, a "Garden of Eden." Upon Poland's surrender, Germany implemented the General East Plan (*Generalplan Ost*), the blueprint for that "Garden."[6] Having annexed western Poland and parts of southern and central Poland, Germany recast the territories into two new administrative regions—Reichsgau Danzig-Westpreussen and Wartheland. To administrate German-occupied Poland, which included Warsaw, Kraków, and Lublin, Hitler formed the General Government. The German Hans Frank (1900–1946), headed its government and placed Germans in every post. Like all imperialists, Hitler not only controlled the land and its resources, but also mercilessly forced the native people into submission. European powers had long believed in the moral legitimacy of colonial conquest. Hitler turned it against them as he began his own conquest of the East.

---

4   David Furber and Wendy Lower, "Colonialism and Genocide in Nazi-Occupied Poland and Ukraine," in *Empire, Colony, Genocide: Conquest, Occupation, and Subaltern Resistance in World History*, ed. A. Dirk Moses (New York: Berghahn Books, 2008), 373.
5   Ibid., 374.
6   Ibid.

Genocide

It is within this framework of colonialism that recent scholarship understands genocide in general and the Holocaust in particular. People often conflate genocide with the Holocaust, the Jewish genocide implemented during World War II.[7] But the Holocaust was a specific and isolated campaign against the Jews which took place during World War II. In fact, throughout human history genocide has repeated itself again and again, with variation.[8] Indeed, since the Roman destruction of Carthage in 146 BCE to the twenty-first-century, political leaders have launched genocides against populations in efforts to expand power. A form of foreign conquest and occupation, genocide is "necessarily imperial and colonial in nature."[9] Left unnamed for centuries, people began investigating it only in the early twentieth century.

In the early 1920s, Raphael Lemkin (1900–1959), a Polish Jewish linguist and soon-to-be law scholar, recognized common threads among minorities' collective experience of violence. Reviewing these traumas together with the 1915 Turkish assault on the Armenian people,[10] Lemkin created a new term: *genocide*.[11]

---

7   Samantha Power affirms that "the link between Hitler's Final Solution and Lemkin's hybrid term would cause endless confusion for policymakers and ordinary people who assumed that genocide occurred only where the perpetrator of atrocity could be shown, like Hitler, to possess an intent to exterminate every last member of an ethnic, national, or religious group." See Samantha Power, *"A Problem from Hell": America and the Age of Genocide* (New York: Harper Collins, 2007), 43.
8   John Cox, *To Kill a People: Genocide in the Twentieth Century* (Oxford: Oxford University Press, 2017), 12–25.
9   A. Dirk Moses, "Empire, Colony, Genocide: Keywords and the Philosophy of History," in *Empire, Colony, Genocide: Conquest, Occupation, and Subaltern Resistance in World History*, ed. A. Dirk Moses (New York: Berghahn Books, 2008), 10.
10 Power, *"A Problem from Hell": America and the Age of Genocide*, 1. Here Power provides two chapters on the Armenian genocide, the man who presided over the implementation of genocide (Mehmet Talaat), and reactions to it. The genocide killed nearly one million Armenians in Turkey.
11 Adam Jones, *Genocide: A Comprehensive Introduction*, 3rd ed. (London: Routledge, 2017), 14–15. Lemkin focused more on non-Jewish minorities. His understanding was presented at a 1933 European legal scholars' conference in Madrid (though not by the author because Poland had denied him a travel visa). Countries did not accept it given they did not see reason to challenge states' sovereignty on this matter. Lemkin continued after the war to advocate for an international acceptance of the definition of genocide, which he achieved in 1948. However, the United States did not officially recognize it.

He fused the Greek *genos*, meaning race or tribe, with the Latin *cide*, for killing, to name the "coordinated plan of different actions aiming at the destruction of essential foundations of the life of national groups, with the aim of annihilating the groups themselves."[12] Lemkin elaborated:

> By "genocide" we mean the destruction of a nation or an ethnic group.... Generally speaking, genocide does not necessarily mean the immediate destruction of a nation, except when accomplished by mass killings of all members of a nation.... The objectives of such a plan would be disintegration of the political and social institutions of culture, language, national feelings, religion, and the economic existence of national groups, and the destruction of the personal security, liberty, health, dignity, and even the lives of the individuals belonging to such groups. Genocide is directed against the national group as an entity, and the actions involved are directed against individuals, not in their individual capacity, but as members of the national group.[13]

Not until World War II's end and fifteen years of Lemkin's stalwart, obsessive, and exhaustive lobbying, did government representatives accept such a notion.[14] While scholars continue to argue over the definition, Lemkin's remains the UN standard in addressing the "calculated destruction of a group's ability to maintain its identity and its collective existence."[15] According to article 2 of the General Assembly's Convention on the Prevention and Punishment of the Crime of Genocide,

---

12 Raphael Lemkin, *Axis Rule in Occupied Europe: Laws of Occupation, Analysis of Government, Proposals for Redress*, 2nd ed., Foundations of the Laws of War (Clark: The Lawbook Exchange, Ltd., 2008), 79.
13 Lemkin notes: "Genocide has two phases: one, destruction of the national pattern of the oppressed group: the other the imposition of the national pattern of the oppressor. This imposition, in turn, may be made upon the oppressed population, which is allowed to remain, or upon the territory alone, after removal of the population and the colonization of the area by the oppressor's own nationals." See ibid.
14 Power, *"A Problem from Hell": America and the Age of Genocide*, 17–85. Power provides a detailed dissection of Lemkin's lobbying to bring about an international law against genocide.
15 Cox, *To Kill a People: Genocide in the Twentieth Century*, 4.

> [g]enocide means any of the following acts committed with intent to destroy, in *whole or in part*, a national, ethnical, racial or religious group, such as
>
> (a) Killing members of the group;
> (b) Causing serious bodily or mental harm to members of the group;
> (c) Deliberately inflicting on the group conditions of life calculated to bring about its physical destruction in whole or in part;
> (d) Imposing measures intended to prevent births within the group;
> (e) Forcibly transferring children of the group to another group.[16] (emphasis mine)

Unfortunately, the term *genocide* is often employed carelessly to define any mass slaughter. As the above definition indicates, the term refers to a specific set of actions. There exists a notable difference between acts of war and acts of genocide. While the mission of warfare is to cripple an opponent's forces into ceasing aggression or surrendering territory, genocide seeks to eradicate the people who inhabit an occupied land—not only as individuals, but as an ethnic group or culture. Indeed, for Lemkin the relevance of cultural destruction to the genocidal process proved key. Without its cultural institutions and leaders, a nation disintegrates. However, the UN refused Lemkin's insistence on the cultural aspect of genocide.

In his book *Axis Rule in Occupied Europe*, Lemkin generated a list of eight genocidal techniques the Nazis imposed on their victim groups. It is worth our time to list them here, with commentary by the genocide scholar A. Dirk Moses, to provide a fuller understanding of the genocide process, thus enabling us to name it when it exists. Lemkin's words are in quotes.

> *Political* techniques refer to the cessation of self-government and local rule, and their replacement by that of the occupier. "Every reminder of former national character was obliterated."

---

16 Quoted in Jones, *Genocide: A Comprehensive Introduction*, 18.

Social techniques entail attacking the intelligentsia, "because this group largely provides the national leadership and organizes resistance against Nazification."

Cultural techniques ban the use of native language in education and inculcate youth with propaganda.

Economic techniques shift economic resources from the occupied to the occupier.

Biological techniques decrease the birthrate of the occupied. "Thus, in incorporated Poland marriages between Poles are forbidden without special permission of the Governor (Reichsstatthalter) of the district; the latter, as a matter of principle, does not permit marriages between Poles."

Physical techniques mean the rationing of food, endangering of health and mass killing in order to accomplish the "physical debilitation and even annihilation of national groups in occupied countries."

Religious techniques try to disrupt the national and religious influences of the occupied people. In Poland, the Germans conducted "the systematic pillage and destruction of church property and persecution of the clergy," in order to "destroy the religious leadership of the Polish nation."

Moral techniques are policies "to weaken the spiritual resistance of the national group." This technique encourages moral debasement, elevating "cheap individual pleasure" above the desire for collective ideals.[17]

Though rarely recognized by American Jewish leaders, and perhaps Americans in general, the Nazis committed genocide against the whole Polish and Ukrainian nations. (Here I focus only on the Polish case of genocide.) The Nazi machinery did not seek merely to gain control over Polish territory. The Germans also intended to manage the population in that land by destroying its capability and resolve to act as a collective force. They did not want to rule over the Polish people. They desired the demise of the Polish people as a nation, which had been held together through a shared language, culture, history, and idea of the future. In short, the Nazis sought to eradicate the Poles' language, culture, and history.

---

17   Lemkin, *Axis Rule in Occupied Europe: Laws of Occupation, Analysis of Government, Proposals for Redress*, 82–90; Moses, "Empire, Colony, Genocide: Keywords and the Philosophy of History," 14.

Since the late 1800s, "scientific-based" racism had justified imperial conquests and concurrent genocides. By the early twentieth century, racism had become an obsession within European societies as well as in the United States.[18] Within this context Nazi race ideology presented Poles as inferior to Germans. The Nazis placed Poles only slightly higher than Jews on the racial superiority ladder, referring to both peoples as *untermenschen*, subhumans.[19]

Hitler drew an important distinction between peoples considered related by blood to the Germans (such as those from the Netherlands, Norway, and Luxemburg, as well as the Flemings) and peoples not related by blood (such as the Poles, Slovenes, and Serbs). In *Mein Kampf*, Hitler wrote that only the first group was worthy of Germanization.[20] "With respect to the Poles in particular, Hitler expressed the view that it is their soil alone which *can and should be profitably Germanized.*"[21] He did not desire the Germanization of the Poles because he believed the Poles would never assimilate.

To acquire their coveted lebensraum, the Nazis stormed across borders to decimate the Poles (and all Slavs) as a collective and take over Polish land. Various documents demonstrate the Germans' intention to eliminate the Poles as a nation.[22] Ultimately, Hitler plotted to destroy the Polish nation by annihilating their elite and reducing the remainder to slaves.[23] The Germans targeted the Poles through political, social, cultural, economic, biological, and physical means in an effort to crush any ability to preserve their national character. While in the end, the Germans attacked the Jews most viciously, it remains that from

---

18   Cox, *To Kill A People: Genocide in the Twentieth Century*, 17.
19   Polonsky, *The Jews in Poland and Russia*, 3:365.
20   Lemkin, *Axis Rule in Occupied Europe: Laws of Occupation, Analysis of Government, Proposals for Redress*, 81–82; Adolf Hitler, *Mein Kampf* (New York: Reynal & Hitchcock, 1939), 590.
21   Ibid.
22   Robert Rozett, "Distorting the Holocaust and Whitewashing History: Toward a Typology," *Israel Journal of Foreign Affairs* 13 (2019): 4.
23   In Hitler's statement to Hermann Rauschning he writes: "The French complained after the war that there were twenty million Germans too many. We accept the criticism. We favor the planned control of population movements. But our friends will have to excuse us if we subtract the twenty million elsewhere. After all these centuries of whining about the protection of the poor and lowly, it is about time we decided to protect the strong against the inferior. It will be one of the chief tasks of German statesmanship for all time to prevent by every means in our power, the further increase of the Slav races. Natural instincts bid all living beings not merely conquer their enemies, but also destroy them. In former days, it was the victor's prerogative to destroy entire tribes, entire peoples. By doing this gradually and without bloodshed, we demonstrate our humanity." Quoted in Lemkin, *Axis Rule in Occupied Europe: Laws of Occupation, Analysis of Government, Proposals for Redress*, 81n7.

September 1939 to March 1941 the Nazis implemented their plan to destroy the Polish nation through racially discriminatory German legislation, expulsion, hard labor, cultural dismemberment, economic devastation, starvation, and murder.[24] This complex of atrocities falls under the definition of genocide. That the war ended before they advanced their efforts into progressive phases saved the Poles. However, that Hitler did not decimate the Poles to the degree that he destroyed the Jews does not take away from the pain and suffering inflicted on the former group and the fact that the cultural and physically destructive mechanisms were already in motion.

In his 1994 study, Israel Charney names various types of genocide. He recognizes the existence of "multiple intentional genocide," where one perpetrator commits genocide against more than one victim group at the same time or in closely related or contiguous actions.[25] Such parallel persecutions took place during World War II. The Holocaust was a Jewish genocide. Bearing down simultaneously, on the same soil, yet at a different speed and intensity, was a Polish genocide.

Polish Genocide

Surviving notes from an August 22, 1939 meeting with Hitler's high command make it clear that the campaign against Poland would be genocidal. "The Polish nation was to be destroyed, its 'living forces' (*lebendige Kräfte*) eliminated":

> It is not a question of reaching a specific line or a new frontier, but rather the annihilation of the enemy, which must be pursued in ever new ways. . . . Execution: Harsh and remorseless. We must steal ourselves against humanitarian thinking![26]

On Himmler's orders, Reinhard Heydrich formulated Operation Tannenberg, which organized five Einsatzgruppen—mobile killing squads—to murder Poland's national, political, cultural, and religious leaders in Poland's western

---

24 Ibid., 79–90, 221–231.
25 Tatiana E. Sainati, "Toward a Comparative Approach to the Crime of Genocide," *Duke Law Journal* 62, no. 1 (October 2012).
26 Phillip T. Rutherford, *Prelude to the Final Solution: The Nazi Program for Deporting Ethnic Poles, 1939–1941* (Lawrence: University Press of Kansas, 2007), 41–42.

region.[27] By September 8, 1939, the Einsatzgruppen were executing two hundred Poles daily. With alarming speed, they decimated the ranks of Poland's leadership.[28]

Following their September 1939 campaign, the Germans launched a broader effort to kill off the Polish elite in annexed western Poland and parts of southern and central Poland, known as Reichsgau Danzig-Westpreussen and Wartheland. Based on claims of anti-German activity, the Nazi SS-Einsatzgruppen[29] executed nearly forty-two thousand Polish citizens, including many from the intelligentsia and nobility, and roughly seven thousand Polish Jews, over a two-month period.[30]

The situation for Poles in the General Government was similarly fraught. Hans Frank, its head, understood his primary responsibility as establishing an exploitive colonial system that would take resources found and grown within his domain and funnel them into the German war effort. Through requisitions, the General Government provided food for Germany's soldiers and administrators at the expense of the native population. Lack of nutrition gave way to disease, especially rickets and tuberculosis in children.[31] Germans kicked Poles and Jews from their homes and confiscated their businesses, warehouses, and shops. People were robbed of their earning capacity. By imposing higher taxes and devaluing the złoty, the Nazis financially wrecked both Poles and Jews.[32]

To subdue resistance and extract all resources, Frank strove to ensure that "the backbone of the Poles is broken for all time."[33] He implemented policies similar to those employed in the annexed western regions. To prevent public education and cultural preservation he took aim at the broad intelligentsia, including political, cultural, educational, and religious leaders. In just one example, the Nazis arrested 183 Kraków scholars on November 6, 1939 and sent them to the Sachsenhausen concentration camp.[34] They never returned. Frank's "Polish

---

27 Ibid.
28 Ibid., 43.
29 The SS-Einsatzgruppen were Operational Groups, which later executed more than a million Jews in the kresy in the June 1941 Operation Barbarossa.
30 Rutherford claims the number of Poles murdered was closer to fifty thousand. See Polonsky, *Jews in Poland and Russia*, 3:365; Phillip T. Rutherford, *Prelude to the Final Solution: The Nazi Program for Deporting Ethnic Poles, 1939–1941*, 9.
31 Lukasz, *Forgotten Holocaust: The Poles under German Occupation 1939–1944*, 30.
32 David Engel, *In the Shadow of Auschwitz: The Polish Government-in-Exile and the Jews, 1939–1942* (Chapel Hill: The University of North Carolina Press, 1987), 157–158.
33 Quoted in Polonsky, *The Jews in Poland and Russia*, 3:367.
34 Bartoszewski and Lewin, *The Samaritans: Heroes of the Holocaust*, 3.

intelligentsia" included prosperous merchants, large landowners, doctors, dentists, veterinarians, officers, teachers, writers, journalists, nuns, and anyone who had attended high school.[35]

On March 15, 1940, during a meeting of the commandants of Nazi camps in Poland, Himmler stated: "All Polish specialists will be exploited in our military-industrial complex. Later, all Poles will disappear from this world. It is imperative that the great German nation considers the elimination of all Polish people as its chief task."[36] In spring 1940, the Nazis murdered more than six thousand Polish politicians and members of the intelligentsia in a far-reaching program to pacify, according to SS Brigadeführer Bruno Szreckenbach, "the spiritual and political leaders of the Polish resistance movement."[37] Known as the A-B Plan (*Ausserordentliche Befriedungsaktion*),[38] it ensured that in June 1940 thousands of Polish men were sent to Auschwitz, a death camp built explicitly to crush Polish resistance.[39] The first non-German prisoners of the camp, Poles constituted the largest group of inmates until 1942 when Jews surpassed them in numbers. Three hundred Poles and seven hundred Soviets were the first prisoners gassed at Auschwitz.[40]

As part of their war against Polish culture, the Germans denied Polish youth access to formal education past primary school. Prohibiting teachers from passing on Polish history, Germany sought to eradicate Polish identity. To achieve this aim, they also confiscated history books, removed public statues of Polish heroes, and closed all scientific, artistic, and literary institutions.[41] As is part of cultural genocide, the Germans also burned Polish library collections, forbade the playing of Polish composers' music, and ravaged most of the country's archives.[42] The goal was to destroy Polish national memory. The Germans even

---

35 Polonsky, *The Jews in Poland and Russia*, 3:367.
36 Tadeusz Piotrowski, *Poland's Holocaust: Ethnic Strife, Collaboration with Occupying Forces and Genocide in the Second Republic, 1918–1947* (Jefferson: McFarland & Company, Inc., Publishers, 1998), 23.
37 Władysław Bartoszewski, "Polish-Jewish Relations in Occupied Poland, 1939–1945," in *The Jews in Poland*, ed. Chimen Abramsky, Maciej Jachimczyk, and Antony Polonsky (Oxford: Basil Blackwell, 1986), 150.
38 Bartoszewski and Lewin, *The Samaritans: Heroes of the Holocaust*, 5.
39 Bartoszewski, "Polish-Jewish Relations in Occupied Poland, 1939–1945," 149–150; Polonsky, *The Jews in Poland and Russia*, 3:368.
40 Lucasz, *Forgotten Holocaust: The Poles under German Occupation 1939–1944*, 38.
41 Ibid., 12.
42 Piotrowski, *Poland's Holocaust: Ethnic Strife, Collaboration with Occupying Forces and Genocide in the Second Republic, 1918–1947*, 21.

restricted Poles from speaking Polish.[43] The Nazis published the only Polish-language newspapers.

To ensure Poles' obedience, the German administration not only organized mass arrests and secret executions, but also collective punishments. In retaliation for two known Poles' killing of two German noncommissioned officers, the Nazis executed 108 men near Warsaw on December 27, 1939.[44] In December 1941, a German special criminal code for Poles and Jews demonstrated the lowly status of the occupied by decreeing, in both the Gestapo and criminal courts, the death penalty for most violations. The Nazis executed people who hid fire hoses, damaged agricultural machinery, or illegally slaughtered animals.[45]

At the same time, Germany divided Polish families who lived in the General Government by sending hundreds of thousands of Poles to the Third Reich or to annexed Western territory to do agricultural and industrial jobs left vacant due to German enlistment. In January 1941, the Nazis forced 798,000 Poles into such slave labor. By August 1943, that number had reached 1.6 million Poles.[46] German policy required these Poles to wear an identifying violet letter "P" on their clothing, banned them from fraternizing publicly and privately with Germans, and housed them in poor conditions with minimal food.

As part of its plan to reduce the Polish population, Germany abducted roughly two hundred thousand Polish children and sent them to the Reich for Germanization. Demanding they join Nazi youth groups and prohibiting them from speaking Polish, the Nazi leadership hoped to break the children's Polish familial and cultural ties. In changing their names and making false birth certificates, the Germans robbed them of their Polish identities.[47]

These policies did not appear all at once, nor did the Nazis implement them to the same degree in all German-occupied Poland. At the start of the war, they focused more feverishly on the annexed territories. Given that the roughly six hundred thousand ethnic Germans inhabiting that land were far outnumbered by the 8.9 million Poles and 603,000 Jews, Hitler endeavored to expel those deemed nationally, politically, and racially "dangerous"—all Poles and Jews—to the territory administered by the General Government.[48] To create a cultural

---

43 Polonsky, *The Jews in Poland and Russia*, 3:66.
44 Bartoszewski and Lewin, *The Samaritans: Heroes of the Holocaust*, 5.
45 Polonsky, *The Jews in Poland and Russia*, 3:66.
46 Lukasz, *Forgotten Holocaust: The Poles under German Occupation 1939–1944*, 33.
47 Ibid., 25–27.
48 Rutherford, *Prelude to the Final Solution: The Nazi Program for Deporting Ethnic Poles, 1939–1941*, 203.

and economic German ideal in previously Polish land, from September 1939 to March 1941, Nazi policy focused on removing Polish and Jewish inhabitants and replacing them with migrating Germans and Volksdeutsche.[49] To aid Germanization, the Nazis seized exiled Poles' and Jews' money, property, and businesses, and transferred it all to the incoming ethnic Germans. This policy swiftly pauperized hundreds of thousands of Poles and Jews.[50] For one and a half years this Germanization settlement policy remained a Nazi priority.

By the end of 1944, the Nazi regime murdered 330,000 Poles in the annexed territory and expelled roughly 860,000 additional Poles either to forced labor in Germany or to the Nazi administered General Government in central Poland.[51] By 1940, they had also expelled some two hundred thousand Jews to the General Government's territory.[52] Deporting Poles into homelessness, poverty, and hunger, as well as subjecting them to slave labor amounted to eradication policy, as disease and death often followed.

As David Furber and Wendy Lower argue, in the spring of 1941 the two contending Nazi imperialist agendas came into conflict. Hans Frank's exploitive colonialist agenda could not withstand the pressure from the SS settlement-oriented program.[53] One plan had to give. In this instance, it was the resettlement campaign. In June 1941, despite the Nazi branding of Poles as an inferior, intolerable enemy requiring expulsion, Germany needed them.[54] The Germans knew they would soon abrogate the Molotov-Ribbentrop Pact (the Nazi-Soviet Pact). Invading the Soviet Union by first capturing the kresy necessitated increased production of munitions and food for the military. Therefore, German policy shifted to keep Poles in the annexed territories where they manned the armament factories and ploughed the fields. Most deportation efforts halted.[55]

---

49 Ukrainians also lived in that land, were forced to resettle, and were devastated by the war. However, given the limited space, I keep my discussion to the implications for Poles and Jews. See ibid., 6–8.
50 Ibid, 8.
51 Polonsky, *The Jews in Poland and Russia*, 3:65.
52 Ibid.
53 Furber and Lower, "Colonialism and Genocide in Nazi-Occupied Poland and Ukraine," 376–7.
54 Rutherford, *Prelude to the Final Solution: The Nazi Program for Deporting Ethnic Poles, 1939–1941*, 203–207.
55 Ibid., 6–7.

The Nazis suspended their anti-Polish policy to the extent that they even registered (sometimes forcibly) hundreds of thousands of Poles as Germans.[56] However, historian Phillip T. Rutherford suggests that

> the relaxation of the anti-Polish resettlement policy was only temporary and that if the German army had emerged victorious on the eastern front, destructive anti-Polish action, be it in the form of deportation or physical liquidation or both, would have resumed and radicalized with a vengeance.[57]

The Soviet defeat of Germany at Stalingrad saved the Poles (and other Slavs) from Germany's destructive wrath.

As Nazi Polish policy shifted, so too did its Jewish strategy. Hitler had always viewed the Jews as Germany's primary enemy, as "the anti-race." The Nazis instituted ghettos (most between 1940–1942) to separate Poles and Jews. In Warsaw, the Germans removed 113,000 Poles from the ghetto's circumscribed area and forced 138,000 Jews into it.[58] By dividing the people, the Germans intentionally created a situation in which each experienced their tragedy in isolation. For Poles, prewar antisemitism combined with German propaganda and segregation to poison the context in which they understood the Jews.[59]

Once the Nazis sealed the ghettos, completely cutting off legal contact between the populations, the campaign against the Jews intensified. Food distribution told the story: in Warsaw 1941, Germans received 2,613 calories every day, Poles 760, while Jews were allotted only 213 calories daily.[60] Starvation soon gripped the ghetto population. Poles learned of the dire situation through the black-market smuggling labyrinth jointly run by Poles and Jews. Like most groups who witness an Other's tragedy while also suffering themselves, the Poles responded in various ways. Some tried to help the Jews. Some harassed them for profit. But most Poles ignored the Jews: they too were "totally absorbed in the day-to-day battle for the most basic means of survival."[61]

---

56 Ibid., 210–211.
57 Ibid., 216–218.
58 *"Żegota": The Council for Aid to Jews 1942–1945*, ed. Andrzej Krzysztof Kunert (Warsaw: Rada Ochrony Pamięci Walk I Męczeństwa, 2002), 12; Bartoszewski, "Polish-Jewish Relations in Occupied Poland, 1939–1945," 154.
59 Yisrael Gutman and Shmuel Krakowski, *Unequal Victims: Poles and Jews during World War II*, trans. Ted Gorelick and Witold Jedlic (New York: Holocaust Library, 1986), 44–45.
60 Ibid., 45.
61 Bartoszewski, "Polish-Jewish Relations in Occupied Poland, 1939–1945," 153.

Soviet Invasion and Jewish Welcome

While people suffered under Nazi control in western and central Poland, the kresy endured Soviet occupation. Yet perceptions of the Soviets differed between Jews and Poles. Kresy Jews knew that Nazi propaganda had labeled them the ultimate enemy. Nazi ideologues had leaned on the well-known Jew-Bolshevik conspiracy theory to cast Jews as not only the fundamental global danger, but also Germany's specific enemy. They perceived Jews as having already dispossessed Germans of their power and prestige during and following World War I.[62] The 1935 Nuremberg Laws, made race-based Nazism official.[63]

The Soviets accepted Jews. True, Jews of means would have to give up their land and businesses to the communist authorities. But so too would all peoples. Although the Soviets swiftly dismantled organized religious and communal Jewish life and restructured Jewish cultural and educational institutions to fall in line with communist ideology, kresy Jews recognized that Soviet ideology did not single them out for mistreatment.[64] The Soviets provided Jews safety from antisemitism by outlawing it; the Germans wrote it into law.[65]

Whereas kresy Poles did not know the extent of Nazi aggression waged against their fellow compatriots in the annexed western territories, kresy Jews had already heard about it from Jews who had survived anti-Jewish Nazi brutality in nearby towns. They learned that in early September the Nazis forced six hundred Jews in Przemyśl to dig a mass grave and then massacred them.[66] Jewish fears of Nazi terror intensified as thousands of Jewish refugees fled eastward to escape Nazi barbarity.[67] According to one Jewish inhabitant of Slonim, "Who cared about communism? Who paid any attention to theoretical problems of national economy, when one faced an immediate danger to life? The question of

---

62　Furber and Lower, "Colonialism and Genocide in Nazi-Occupied Poland and Ukraine," 375–377.
63　For a review of the Nuremberg Laws see, Polonsky, *The Jews in Poland and Russia*, 3:72.
64　Engel, *In the Shadow of Auschwitz: The Polish Government-in-Exile and the Jews, 1939–1942*, 61.
65　Andrzej Zbikowski, "Polish Jews under Soviet Occupation," in *Contested Memories: Poles and Jews during the Holocaust and Its Aftermath*, ed. Joshua D. Zimmerman (New Brunswick: Rutgers University Press, 2003), 56.
66　Polonsky, *The Jews in Poland and Russia*, 3:386.
67　Engel, *In the Shadow of Auschwitz: The Polish Government-in-Exile and the Jews, 1939–1942*, 61. Partly as a result of the refugee incursion, and concern over an impending Soviet-German war, Soviet paranoia about enemy infiltrators grew and corresponding policy radicalized. The Soviets enforced four waves of deportation from the kresy into the Soviet interior beginning in June 1940.

whether the regime was good or bad was irrelevant."⁶⁸ While kresy Poles considered the Soviets worse than the Nazis—evidenced when hordes of kresy Poles fled westward into Nazi-occupied Poland following the Soviet invasion—kresy Jews perceived Nazi rule as far worse than the Soviets' reign.⁶⁹

Importantly, kresy Jews also experienced the Soviets as rescuers from ethnic violence. During those two chaotic weeks between the Soviet invasion and occupation, Ukrainian peasant mobs looted both Polish and Jewish property. Some soon-to-be-disbanded Polish soldiers, who harbored anti-Jewish and anti-Ukrainian sentiments, threatened violence. Rumors spread about impending pogroms. Jews organized self-defense units. Still, the earlier than expected arrival of Soviet troops brought a burst of joy and relief for shtetl Jews. Despite many Jews' apprehensions about communist rule, "at the moment of first encounter, the dominant sentiment in 'the Jewish street' was that they were rescued."⁷⁰

This Jewish response differentiated between the Red Army and former tsarist battalions. Since 1881, the tsar's army had served as an arm of Russian antisemitism; the new Soviet soldier appeared polite and respectful. The tsar's forces carried out pogroms; the new Soviet man passed out cigarettes. The tsar's warriors looted Jewish stores; the Soviet officer paid for goods with cash. According to one Jew in Lipniszki, this transformation made an even stronger impression on Jews when, for the first time, "we saw officers speaking Yiddish. We could not believe our eyes . . . We had bright hopes for a great future.'"⁷¹ Seeing a reflection of themselves in power, some Yiddish-speaking Jews saw hope in the Soviet occupation.

Some Jews also welcomed Soviet troops because they had embraced communism as a response to social and economic injustices. While most Jewish traditionalists still viewed communism as an abomination, many young Jews embraced it. Throughout the interwar period, secularism had challenged Jewish tradition, even in the shtetl—that place usually regarded as the bastion of Jewish

---

68 Quoted in Polonsky, *The Jews in Poland and Russia*, 3:387; Kalman Lichtnestein, ed., *The History of Slonim* (Heb.), 2 vols. (Tel Aviv, 1961–1979), xii, 18.
69 Shmuel Krakowski, "The Polish Underground and the Extermination of the Jews," in *Jews, Poles, Socialists: The Failure of an Ideal*, ed. Antony Polonsky, Israel Bartal, Gershon Hundert, Magdalena Opalski, and Jerzy Tomaszewski, Polin: Studies in Polish Jewry, vol. 9 (Oxford: The Littman Library of Jewish Civilization, 1996), 139.
70 Ben-Cion Pinchuk, *Shtetl Jews under Soviet Rule: Eastern Poland on the Eve of the Holocaust* (Oxford: Basil Blackwell, 1990), 21.
71 Ibid., 24.

tradition.⁷² Not only did secularism push many young people to move to the city or migrate across the Atlantic, but many young Jews remaining in the shtetl were also secular. Distanced from Jewish tradition, they could not help but delight in radio broadcasts that promised the educational and employment opportunities that Jews in the Soviet Union had enjoyed since 1921.

To serve its own needs of modernization and industrialization, the Soviet regime dissolved restrictions against Jewish higher education. By 1939, 26.5% of all Jews in the Pale of Settlement had a high school education (as compared to 7.8% of the USSR's general population). In 1939, Jews constituted 15.5% of all Soviet citizens with higher education, and one-third of all Soviet Jews of college age (nineteen to twenty-four years old) attended universities, as compared to 4 to 5% of the general Soviet population.⁷³ Such recent educational opportunities opened new employment options for Soviet Jews. In 1939, 40% of Jewish earners held state administrative posts, while 364,000 identified as members of the intelligentsia. Jews were highly represented within the ranks of managers, accountants, technicians, teachers, doctors, cultural workers, academicians, agronomists, engineers, and architects.⁷⁴

Such educational and economic promise, coupled with Stalin's 1926–1932 campaign against antisemitism, as well as the government creation of an albeit chimerical secular Soviet Yiddish nation in the 1920s, offered broad possibilities for Jews under Soviet occupation.⁷⁵ "No wonder that in the God-forsaken shtetlach of eastern Poland, without electricity, running water or decent roads, the impact of the [broadcast] Soviet promises on the young was tremendous."⁷⁶ An unnamed young *Zionist* from Lutsk reported in 1942 to the Warsaw Ghetto underground Oyneg Shabbos⁷⁷ group that in his town "[t]he majority of the youth expressed great enthusiasm. They kissed the soldiers, climbed the tanks,

---

72 Ibid., 14–15.
73 Antony Polonsky, "Jews and Communism in the Soviet Union and Poland," in *Jews and Leftist Politics: Judaism, Israel, Antisemitism, and Gender*, ed. Jack Jacobs (Cambridge: Cambridge University Press, 2017), 151.
74 Ibid.
75 Ibid., 158.
76 Pinchuk, *Shtetl Jews under Soviet Rule: Eastern Poland on the Eve of the Holocaust*, 25.
77 The Jewish Historical Institute (Żydowski Instytut Historyczny or ŻIH—founded in 1947 in Warsaw) houses the Warsaw Ghetto Archive, known also as the Ringelblum Archive, which was created by the clandestine Warsaw Ghetto group Oyneg Shabbos. ŻIH also archives countless other testimonies from Holocaust victims.

they gave an ovation."[78] Not all Jews expressed such outward joy at the Soviet incursion, but many did: young Jews, secular Jews, rural shtetl Jews, and poor Jews were more likely to embrace the new Soviet order than older Jews, traditional Jews, wealthy Jews, urban Jews, and Jewish nationalists and *Zionists*.

Poles took great offense when watching Jews welcome the Red Army. The image quickly came to represent the wartime Polish experience of the Jew-Bolshevik enemy. Jan Karski, a Polish underground courier and spy, reported that "it is generally believed that the Jews betrayed Poland and the Poles, that they are basically communists, that they crossed over to the Bolsheviks with flags unfurled."[79]

Soviet Occupation and Jewish Collaboration

Based on both Jewish and Polish testimony, Polish-Jewish relations soured dramatically during the Soviet occupation, due in large part to Jewish behavior.[80] Not only did many Jews welcome the Eastern invaders, but during the first several weeks prior to the Red Army's arrival and those next months before Soviet administrators' appearance, communists of Jewish origin inserted themselves into the power vacuum left by besieged Polish functionaries. Jews played a prominent role in voluntarily establishing and running local temporary executive committees which would govern the towns until the Soviets arrived. They also supported the committees' efforts through local self-defense organizations armed with weaponry taken from retreating Polish soldiers. Often, these Jewish-led executive committees initiated "socialist" reforms, which included taking property from wealthy Jews and Poles and redistributing it to the poor. At other times, Jewish communists felt empowered to settle scores with Polish policemen and Polish administrators.[81]

---

78 Quoted in Andrzej Zbikowski, "Jewish Reaction to the Soviet Arrival in the Kresy in September 1939: Why did Jews Welcome the Soviet Armies?," in *Focusing on the Holocaust and Its Aftermath*, ed. Antony Polonsky, Polin: Studies in Polish Jewry, vol. 13 (London: The Littman Library of Jewish Civilization, 2000), 67.

79 Quoted in David Engel, "An Early Account of Polish Jewry under Nazi and Soviet Occupation Presented to the Polish Government-in-Exile, February 1940," *Jewish Social Studies* 45, no. 1 (1983): 10. Interestingly, Karski notes on the same page that for the "Jewish proletariat, small merchants, artisans, and all those whose position has at present been improved *structurally* and who had formerly been exposed primarily to oppression, indignities, excesses, etc., from the Polish element—all of these responded positively, if not enthusiastically, to the new regime. Their attitude seems to me quite understandable."

80 Zbikowski, "Polish Jews under Soviet Occupation," 58.

81 Pinchuk, *Shtetl Jews under Soviet Rule: Eastern Poland on the Eve of the Holocaust*, 25–26.

One Jewish kresy fugitive, who had fled to Warsaw, contextualized his report with the fact that the three different kresy nationalities held a mutual disdain for one another. He recalled that after the Soviets entered his town "the Jews, they took revenge on Poles sometimes in a very nasty way; the expression 'Your time is over' was not only much used, but, by and large, overused."[82] Another Jewish witness affirmed that,

> the Jews themselves stirred up this hatred [. . .]. The coming of the Bolsheviks was greeted by Jews with great joy. Now they felt proud and secure, they almost considered themselves in charge of the situation; towards the Poles they were condescending and arrogant, and they often let them feel their powerlessness and scorned them because of it.[83]

Jewish words gave rise to Polish invective.

Jan Karski notes many cases in which Jews actively took revenge on Poles:

> they [the Jews] denounce the Poles [. . .] when they direct the work of the Bolshevik police force from behind their desks or are members of the police force [. . .]. Unfortunately, it is necessary to state that such incidents are quite common, more common than incidents which reveal loyalty toward Poles or sentiment toward Poland.[84]

Later, Poles pointed to the Jewish embrace of the Soviets as the central factor which exponentially worsened Polish-Jewish relations, and which some Poles argue negatively affected many Poles' willingness to provide aid to Jews during the war.[85] The Jewish testimonies presented here thus support Jan Karski's 1940 evaluation that Polish-Jewish relations in the kresy deteriorated exponentially

---

82 Quoted in Zbikowski, "Jewish Reaction to the Soviet Arrival in the Kresy in September 1939: Why did Jews Welcome the Soviet Armies?," 68.
83 Ibid.
84 Quoted in Engel, "An Early Account of Polish Jewry under Nazi and Soviet Occupation Presented to the Polish Government-in-Exile, February 1940": 10. Karski notes on the same page that the intelligentsia and the wealthiest Jews long for Poland and would welcome a return to Polish independence.
85 Quoted in Zbikowski, "Jewish Reaction to the Soviet Arrival in the Kresy in September 1939: Why did Jews Welcome the Soviet Armies?," 68.

not only due to Soviet policy, but also because "the Jews created the situation in which the Poles regard them as devoted to the Bolsheviks."[86]

Polish animosity against the Jews also piqued due to the Soviet preference for Jews over Poles within the Soviet occupation administration. True, Poles did not necessarily wish to work for the Soviets for fear of being branded traitors to Poland. At the same time, however, they were barred from the new administrations due to Soviet mistrust of Poles. One Jewish observer confirmed that in his village,

> [w]hen the Bolsheviks entered Polish territory, they were very mistrustful of the Polish population, and they fully trusted the Jews. They deported to Russia the more influential Poles and those who before the war held important jobs, and all offices were given mostly to Jews, who everywhere were trusted with positions of power. For these reasons, the Polish population at once assumed a very hostile general attitude. Hatred became even stronger than before the war. The Poles, however, could not vent it in any way, and therefore nourished and cherished it.[87]

In the early transition to Soviet rule, Polish functionaries had been replaced by Jews, who in turn often mistreated the Polish population. This aspect of the Soviet occupation deepened Polish resentment of the Jews in general.

According to a separate Jewish testimony, Jews experienced the Soviet occupation very differently from Poles: "The changes which began to occur in the village after the Russians' arrival were a total surprise ... To the Jews, they could only consider it a dream, as if the messiah had come."[88] Due to Soviet mistrust of Poles and even of Polish communists, Jews rose to occupy a disproportionate number of mid-level Soviet administrative positions in the first few months of Bolshevik occupation.

However, most Jews did not hold administrative posts. Yet because Poles had not seen many Jews in positions of authority, they experienced this new Jewish rise as

---

86 Quoted in Zbikowski, "Polish Jews under Soviet Occupation," 59. Karski adds to his 1940 report that "one can safely say [the Poles] wait for the moment when they will be able simply to take revenge upon the Jews. Virtually all Poles are bitter and disappointed in relation to the Jews; the overwhelming majority [first among them of course the youth] literally look forward to an opportunity for 'repayment in blood.'" See Engel, "An Early Account of Polish Jewry under Nazi and Soviet Occupation Presented to the Polish Government-in-Exile, February 1940": 11.
87 Quoted in Zbikowski, "Polish Jews under Soviet Occupation," 57.
88 Quoted in Polonsky, *The Jews in Poland and Russia*, 3:87.

massive. Indeed, the Soviet governing system comprised mainly Ukrainians and Belarussians in an effort to placate local nationalist groups. Yet, due to their lack of formal education, neither Ukrainians nor Belarussians could handle much of the new ruler's administrative needs. As a result, the Soviets gave the Ukrainians and Belarussians the titles but allowed communists of Jewish origin who had secular education to do the work.[89] This disproportionate number of Jews in mid-level positions of authority began to shift in the middle of 1940 when the Soviets replaced locally recruited officials with so-called *Vostochniki*—people brought in from the Soviet interior referred to as Easterners.[90]

That many Jews welcomed the Red Army is clear. That many Jews accessed authority over Poles during Soviet occupation is also clear. And yet the Jews' stance toward the Soviets is not black and white. Jews also suffered alongside Poles under Bolshevik rule. When the Soviets shattered the Polish economy in the east, both Poles and Jews suffered.[91] The Soviets imposed exorbitant taxes on everyone, as well as mandated corvée, unpaid work service. (Here it included cutting wood and building roads.)

The Soviets also deported Poles and Jews to the northern and central regions of the USSR, where many died. During four stages of deportations from February 1940 to June 1941, the Soviets displaced at least eight hundred thousand people. The Polish government-in-exile estimated the population breakdown: 52% Poles, 30% Jews, and 18% Belarussians and Ukrainians.[92] They journeyed eastward in cattle cars:

> They froze in unheated cattle cars in February and suffocated in the June heat four months later. They were locked in for weeks with only meager rations of food and water, with a hole in the car's floor for all facilities. . . . [M]any died, and the corpses traveled with the living before being discarded at some railway stop.[93]

---

89 Pinchuk, *Shtetl Jews under Soviet Rule: Eastern Poland on the Eve of the Holocaust*, 7.
90 Ibid., 8; author's correspondence with Antony Polonsky, September 21, 2019.
91 The Soviets confiscated all Polish private and state property, reducing factories to pieces and shipping the parts out of the regions. They redistributed landed property to peasants, and plundered durable goods, such as food commodities, cattle, and oil. See Piotrowski, *Poland's Holocaust: Ethnic Strife, Collaboration with Occupying Forces and Genocide in the Second Republic, 1918–1947*, 11.
92 Pinchuk, *Shtetl Jews under Soviet Rule: Eastern Poland on the Eve of the Holocaust*, 10.
93 Grudzińska-Gross and Jan Tomasz Gross, ed. *War Through Children's Eyes: The Soviet Occupation of Poland and the Deportation*, trans. Ronald Strom and Dan Rivers (Redwood City: Hoover Institution Press Stanford University, 1985), xxii–xxiii.

For Poles, Jews came to symbolize these destructive Soviet anti-Polish policies despite Jews amounting to a significant proportion of those deported into the Soviet interior. It is one reason why Poles ignored Jews' pleas for help during the Nazi anti-Jewish brutality.

Rural Polish Violence against Jews: Jedwabne and Other Pogroms

Just as Jews must wrestle with the facts regarding Polish victimization, historical context, and Jewish behavior, so too must Poles wrestle with truths that contradict their own national myth. The standard depiction of the Polish past is filled with Polish battalions rushing into battle to save the state from the enemy. Military uprisings in 1794, 1830–31, 1848, and 1863–64 attest to the myth of Polish heroism in the face of grave oppression. These same memories often reflect Polish self-perceptions of the Polish responses to the Nazi and Soviet occupations. It is true that Poles bravely battled the enemy and thousands risked their lives to save Jews hiding from the Nazis. But it is also true that while Poles were victimized, and some Poles were heroes, some Poles were also victimizers.

In 2000, the Polish-born Jewish historian Jan Gross unleashed a devastating moral tsunami with his publication of *Neighbors: The Destruction of the Jewish Community in Jedwabne, Poland*. According to the Warsaw daily *Rzeczpospolita*, Gross's work

> generated a shock as no other book had done in the preceding half century. Why? Because Professor Gross showed, on the basis of documents, that the crime against the Jews was not performed by Germans with the participation of the Poles, but on the contrary, by the Poles with the participation—likely slender—of the Germans [. . .]. [T]he crime was not committed behind barbed wires in an extermination camp or in some prison, but in a small, ordinary, poor township, where everyone knew each other, met daily and lived together for centuries. Jedwabne is the new kind of Holocaust: the murder of neighbors by neighbors.[94]

---

94 Jan T. Gross, *Neighbors: The Destruction of the Jewish Community in Jedwabne, Poland*, 2nd ed. (New York: Penguin Books, 2002).

Neighbors forced Polish society to face heinous truths buried for close to sixty years. Gross also introduced more general "provocative claims regarding Polish antisemitism and collaboration with the Nazis in the extermination of the Jews."[95] A passionate national debate ensued.

The book divided families and friends. Some viewed the Jedwabne pogrom as pure fabrication created to sully Poland's good name; others—often from the intelligentsia—accepted it in full, rejecting all critiques.[96] Many within the Polish intelligentsia have since reviewed their uncompromising stance and recognized some of the book's methodological problems.[97] At the same time, as Bogdan Musiał asserts, "[n]evertheless, no serious Polish historian has ever expressed any doubts about the Polish participation in this crime."[98] Gross's problems do not deflect from the fact that a group of more than one hundred persons, made up of local Poles and peasants from nearby villages, unleashed their hostility on the Jews of Jedwabne in a monstrous fashion. Rounding them up and first murdering those who appeared strong and able to resist, they forcefully marched the roughly seven hundred remaining Jews into Bolesław Śleszyński's barn and then set it on fire with the Jews inside.[99]

The Polish Institute of National Remembrance, IPN (Instytut Pamięci Narodowej), conducted its own research into the June 1941 massacre. According to Joanna B. Michlic and Antony Polonsky, the IPN corroborated Gross's findings, with relatively minor differences.[100] To its credit, the Polish study also

---

95 Jeffrey S. Kopstein and Jason Wittenberg, *Intimate Violence: Anti-Jewish Pogroms on the Eve of the Holocaust* (Ithaca: Cornell University Press, 2018), 18.
96 Piotr Wróbel, "Polish-Jewish Relations and *Neighbors* by Jan T. Gross: Politics, Public Opinion, and Historical Methodology," in *Lessons and Legacies VII: The Holocaust in International Perspective*, ed. Dagmar Herzog (Evanston: Northwestern University Press, 2006), 387.
97 In a 2006 essay, the historian Piotr Wróbel explains that "numbed and outraged" by Poles' vicious behavior, he had once stood among those who had voiced only the strengths of Gross's argument. Though Wróbel remains convinced that the basic ideas of the work have not been disproved—"I still consider *Neighbors* an outstanding and important book"—he stresses that it is not a sacred text. See ibid., 388.
98 Bogdan Musiał, "The Pogrom in Jedwabne: Critical Remarks about Jan T. Gross's Neighbors," in *The Neighbors Respond: The Controversy over the Jedwabne Massacre in Poland*, ed. Antony Polonsky and Joanna B. Michlic (Princeton and Oxford: Princeton University Press, 2004), 304.
99 Wróbel, "Polish-Jewish Relations and *Neighbors* by Jan T. Gross: Politics, Public Opinion, and Historical Methodology," 393.
100 The number of victims that Gross cited was 1600 based on a memorial stone. The IPN assessed that roughly one thousand Jews died in the blaze and several dozen others were killed in other ways. Historian Dariusz Stola in "A Monument of Words," *Yad Vashem Studies*

shows that during that same summer of 1941, in the kresy region of Suwałki, in sixty-six towns and villages, other Poles massacred their Jewish neighbors. In Radziłow and Wiżna towns, Poles murdered hundreds of Jews.[101] In a 2002 article written in the Catholic weekly magazine *Tygodnik Powszechny*, the co-editor of the IPN report, Krzysztof Persak, provided the Polish public with a forthright review: "[t]he intensity of these events attests that they had not been isolated incidents, but rather fragments of a more common phenomenon."[102]

Like in Jedwabne, the IPN found that in the sixty-six pogroms it examined most of the atrocities committed by Poles against their Jewish neighbors were incited and supervised by German Einsatzgruppen units, which had been tasked with emboldening "self-cleansing actions" by the local population.[103] At the same time, it is imperative to note that "although the 'resolution, decision, signal, recommendation or order to kill was issued by Germans,' the Poles were not coerced into taking part."[104]

In that time of raging chaos, during the Soviet retreat from and German advance into the kresy, Poles organized temporary Polish authorities and sometimes armed so-called Citizens' Guards in many towns and villages.[105] Many Poles felt entitled to seek retribution against the Jews for what they perceived as Jewish crimes. From the perspective of Poles who witnessed Jews rise in status at the Poles' expense, the Jews' collaboration with the Soviets caused Poles excruciating physical, emotional, economic, and cultural suffering. According to the IPN researchers, "members of the [Polish] Citizens' Guards often initiated or performed the anti-Jewish pogroms."[106] Additionally, many of the perpetrators were local Polish and Ukrainian peasants who had recently been released

---

30 (2003), https://store.yadvashem.org/en/a-monument-of-words-8, numbers the victims at closer to six hundred with scores killed elsewhere. Joanna B. Michlic and Antony Polonsky, letter to the editor, *History* 93, no. 1 (January 2008): 155–156, https://www.jstor.org/stable/24428687.

101 Ibid.: 155.

102 Krzysztof Persak, *Not Only Jedwabne*, trans. David M. Dastych, *Tygodnik Powsechny*, 10 November 2002; "IPN (Institute of National Remembrance) Presents the Results of the Inquiry into the Crimes in Bialystok Region," Canadian Foundation of Polish-Jewish Heritage, Montreal Chapter, accessed 7/30/2007, http://www.polish-jewish-heritage.org/eng/grudzien_not_only_jedwabne.htm.

103 Based on Edmund Dmitrow's essay found in the IPN study, *Around Jedwabne*, vol. 1 (Warsaw: IPN, 2002), 273–352. Quoted in Michlic and Polonsky, letter to the editor: 155.

104 Quoted in ibid.

105 Persak, *Not Only Jedwabne*, 3.

106 Ibid.

from Soviet prisons and sought revenge on both the real and presumed Soviet collaborator.

The IPN's Krzysztof Persak states that "[t]he truth about the participation of Poles in the anti-Jewish actions in the Łomza District and in the Białystok Region had been for a long time forgotten." He recognizes that "only the recent discussion about 'the case of Jedwabne' brought it back to the Polish national conscience, in a very painful way. But nobody can run away from the truth."[107] When the IPN report *Not Only Jedwabne* reached publication, many Polish leaders and the general populace found it difficult to process such information. Immediately following the 2001 revelations in *Neighbors*, one seventy-year-old Pole expressed general Polish sentiments: "We were taught as children ... that we Poles never harmed anyone. A partial abandonment of this morally comfortable position is very, very difficult for me."[108]

1941 Pogroms: Increasing or Rare?

The political scientists Jeffrey Kopstein and Jason Wittenberg investigated this pogrom wave in their 2018 book *Intimate Violence*. Broadening the geographic lens to include five kresy provinces, all of which experienced Soviet withdrawal and subsequent German invasion, they found that pogroms were "relatively rare events."[109] Out of the more than 2,400 localities studied in which Jews and non-Jews dwelled together, 9%—219 localities—erupted in pogroms.[110] Kopstein and Wittenberg found that in the 219 pogroms they examined, Germans were not always present.[111]

Kopstein and Wittenberg sought to discover what tipped some localities into a pogrom frenzy while others stayed peaceful. They concluded that the prior interwar political rivalry among nationalisms remained the central predictive element of summer 1941 pogrom violence. Polish nationalists and Ukrainian nationalists could not tolerate Jewish nationalists, as they clashed over future agendas. Linking their research to power threat theory, first introduced to

---

107 Ibid., 5.
108 Cited in Michlic and Polonsky, *The Neighbors Respond: The Controversy over the Jedwabne Massacre in Poland*, 1.
109 Kopstein and Wittenberg, *Intimate Violence: Anti-Jewish Pogroms on the Eve of the Holocaust*, 2.
110 Ibid.
111 Ibid.

understand race relations in the US South, they hold that "pogroms were most likely to break out where non-Jews perceived a Jewish threat to their political dominance."[112]

Kopstein and Wittenberg's findings do not diminish the horrors of those hundreds of pogroms. They face the fact that in these "rare events" Poles (and Ukrainians) savagely attacked Jews, who suffered devastating brutality. As suggested in chapter nine, anti-Jewish violence grew ever more gruesome as wartime atrocities infected already existing interethnic tensions. Indeed, these pogroms often included not only the burning of large groups of people, but also beheadings, dismemberment, and ripping fetuses out from wombs.[113]

What Kopstein and Wittenberg offer here is a nuanced perspective on the explosive immorality unleashed in those summer 1941 pogroms. Viewing them as relatively "rare events" that erupted in response to a perceived political threat, they move the conversation from one of general Polish responsibility to one of localized Polish guilt. This theory refines the core issues twenty-first-century Poles have been struggling to understand and articulate. The 2001 debate between Adam Michnik, the editor of *Gazeta Wyborcza*, and Leon Wieseltier, the editor of the *New Republic*, demonstrates the difficulty of addressing the guilt. To whom does it belong? Michnik scoffs at the general concept of collective guilt or collective responsibility. However, he asserts that Jedwabne "must weigh on the collective consciousness of the Poles."[114] In response, Wieseltier, admonishes Michnik's rejection of Polish collective guilt. He argues that

> individuals belong to groups, and it is a cost or benefit of their belonging that they are morally implicated by their groups, which are moral agents, too. One can oppose the misdeeds of one's group, but one cannot secede from it, I mean not neatly after the fact [...]. Indeed, I could not permit myself to feel pride about the accomplishments of my people and my country if I did

---

112 Ibid., 14; For a review of power threat theory in its original context of US race relations in the South, see, Stewart E. Tolnay, E. M. Beck, and James L. Massey, "Black Lynchings: The Power Threat Hypothesis Revisited," *Social Forces* 67, no. 3 (March 1989): 605–623.
113 Kopstein and Wittenberg, *Intimate Violence: Anti-Jewish Pogroms on the Eve of the Holocaust*, 2.
114 Adam Michnik, "Poles and the Jews: How Deep the Guilt?" *New York Times*, 17 March 2001, in Michlic and Polonsky, *The Neighbors Respond: The Controversy over the Jedwabne Massacre in Poland*, 437.

not require myself to feel shame about the perfidies of my people and my country.¹¹⁵

The various potholes each fall into along the way jolt both writer and reader into acknowledging the difficult nature of Polish-Jewish dialogue across the Atlantic.¹¹⁶

Here I will further my correlation between America's historic racism and past Polish antisemitism. Though America's harshest expressions of racism were localized, factors existed throughout American society which could tip into physical violence and racist legislation. This fact has necessitated changes in the United States including controversial legislative, educational, and economic responses, as well as a deep, broad, and ongoing national discussion. Similarly, while the localized reality of pogroms places responsibility for these terrible crimes on those specific local populations, that such pogroms could erupt in 1941 requires not only an ongoing difficult national conversation, but also education to tackle the very real layers of anti-Jewish and antisemitic bias that exist to various degrees throughout Polish society. As we shall see later, both non-Jews and Jews in today's Poland have been working intensely towards these aims.

The Home Army's and Polish Partisans' Crimes against Jews

Polish ethnographer and cultural anthropologist Johanna Tokarska-Bakir's examination of archives uncovers that assaults on Jews by segments of the Home Army (AK) and various partisan units, even leftist, prevented many Jews' survival.¹¹⁷ Poles revere the AK as a symbol of their national struggle against

---

115 Leon Wieseltier, "Washington Diarist: Righteous," *New Republic*, 9 April 2001, in Michlic and Polonsky, *The Neighbors Respond: The Controversy over the Jedwabne Massacre in Poland*, 441–442.

116 In his 17 April 2001 reply to Leon Wieseltier, Adam Michnik explains what he meant when he "wrote that there is no Polish family that was not wounded by the war. You call it 'the usual Polish apologetics.' But the truth is, Leon, that is a simple Polish fact. And although such facts should not be used to relativize the crime in Jedwabne, to know them is a prerequisite to understanding Polish-Jewish relations." Adam Michnik, "Reply of Adam Michnik," *New Republic*, 17 April 2001, in Michlic and Polonsky, *The Neighbors Respond: The Controversy over the Jedwabne Massacre in Poland*, 443.

117 Johanna Tokarska-Bakir, *Pogrom Cries: Essays on Polish-Jewish History, 1939–1946* (Frankfurt am Main: Peter Lang, 2017),

Hitler. The truth that untamed segments contributed to Hitler's Jewish genocide by killing Jewish refugees has been buried for so long that, like other ugly truths, many Poles resist it. One Polish historian recalled his father, a former AK member, telling him about "a specific order (it is not really clear by whom) and killing, in the spring of 1944, of certain Jews who had been hiding for almost 4 years."[118] However, because the "AK currently constitutes a kind of a myth or symbol,"[119] he worried that bringing this chapter to the broad Polish society would "raise strong emotions."[120] Fearing some people would misunderstand it as a prevailing phenomenon, and create a "distorted picture,"[121] he preferred to remain silent. Tokarska-Bakir understands this particular situation as influenced by the AK's spring 1944 incorporation of members from the radical National Armed Forces (Narodowe Siły Zbrojne, NSZ)—a far-right underground organization, which held intense animus for Jews.[122]

Tokarska-Bakir also demonstrates that Polish partisan units proved extremely dangerous to both Jews and the Poles hiding them. In one testimony given by Urełe (Aron) Sztarkman, we learn about Pawel, an impoverished farmer who provided him and another Jew with shelter: "Our host tries to provide us with news every day: that the partisans are searching for Jews in order to eliminate them. The partisans announce in the village that anyone found keeping Jews will be punished by death."[123] Well known in the vicinity for his dire poverty, Pawel caused a stir when he could afford to marry and provide his wife with fashionable church clothes. Several times the partisans appeared at his tiny house to interrogate him. Sztarkman testified that "Our host is quite scared . . . The partisans believe what he says. On their way out, they tell him that this is the last time they are sparing his life. If they have to come again, he will be shot dead and his house burnt down."[124]

Even Polish communist partisans murdered Jews. Research into the Świt combat unit that supported the Polish communist military force, Armia Ludowa (AL), reveals that many members had antisemitic attitudes.[125] In her review of archived interrogations of former "Świt" members, Tokarska-Bakir shows that on various occasions, Poles with top authority within the unit—Władysław

---

118 Quoted in ibid., 365.
119 Quoted in ibid.
120 Quoted in ibid.
121 Quoted in ibid.
122 Ibid., 49.
123 Quoted in ibid., 40.
124 Quoted in ibid., 41.
125 Ibid., 86.

Sobczyński and Eugeniusz Wiślicz—ordered the elimination of groups of Jews seeking to join the communist AL partisan movement. Commander Tadeusz Maj carried out, in part, one such order, when he shot two Jews asking to join the unit. He told the other eight Jews to run. Świt partisans who later found those Jews, shot them dead.[126]

During his interrogation, Maj explained that prewar antisemitism had influenced his wartime attitude towards the Jews:

> I was still in the grip of prewar prejudice toward the Jews as speculators and exploiters, which was caused by the Sanation [Sanacja] regime propaganda. Accordingly, my attitude toward Jews was disdainful, and I believed that there was no place for the likes of them in the new Poland. [...] Murdering these Jews by carrying out Sobczyński's orders [sic] without any resistance was a kind of offshoot of the antisemitic influences and nationalist upbringing and social environment in which I found myself during the war.[127]

As we have seen in Poland's battles for expansion in chapter 12, urgent war needs can supersede ideology. Immediately following WWI, Poland's tremendous need for soldiers and generals allowed military chiefs to ignore recruits' past anti-Jewish violence in the tsar's White Army. Such generals permitted pogroms until the top leadership reigned them in. It should not be surprising that during World War II, numerous Polish fighters who had been schooled in the intense prewar Endecja and post-1935 Sanacja Jew hatred released that same violent contempt onto Jews fleeing Hitler.

Theories on Rural Polish Complicity in the Jewish Genocide: Barbara Engelking

Recent research into atrocities against Jews by Poles during World War II has shocked Poles, who often prefer a prettier picture of the past. Documentation, however, has refuted this simple image. Additional research by the Polish historians Barbara Engelking, Jan Grabowski, and Tomasz Frydel has further challenged the nation's sense of Self. Plunging into what she terms a "nocturnal

---

126 Ibid., 91.
127 Quoted in ibid., 107–108.

history, dark and difficult," Engelking's moving 2016 book *Such A Beautiful Sunny Day*[128] explores the Jews' "sense of self-worth and belonging to the human world that were put into question by the Germans."[129] In doing so, Engelking reminds us that Poles had very little influence over the fate of Jews who had been separated into ghettos and deported to slave labor and concentration camps. Some Poles supplied food. Some even offered hideouts to Jews. But the reality is that relatively few Jews fled the ghettos prior to July 1942, when many finally linked mass deportations with mass murder. Until that fateful summer, most Jews had stayed in the ghettos, fearful of the very real Nazi threat to shoot any Jewish escapee. When more Jews eventually considered escape, the Germans had already conditioned Poles to be too afraid to help.

Such was the experience of Rózia Reiner, who detailed in a diary her wandering with her infant son:

> I spent the first night in the quarry, and other nights in the field, on the ground, cradling the freezing child. I was not breastfeeding anymore, and for the past two weeks, I could not feed him anything warm. Some people saw me the next day, took pity on me and brought some milk and bread. [...] People were afraid. Someone would throw a piece of bread without breaking stride. Just on one single occasion did some woman bring me two hard-boiled eggs. I went into the forest with the child and together we cried helplessly. [...] Sometimes, in the evenings I would sneak into houses I knew to wash the diapers. [...] Finally I reached the village of Dale (Racławice Commune, Miechów County), where I started living in some old woman's house; she was afraid to be alone and accepted me. However, I had nothing to live on, so I made the rounds of manors, where I got food and even clothing for the child, and returned to this woman for the night.[130]

---

128 Engelking bases her findings on three hundred records of postwar Polish court cases which tried Polish citizens for cooperating with the Germans, as well as five hundred Jewish diaries written in hiding and postwar testimonies of survivors. Her work focuses on rural areas, which bely not only a specific peasant mentality of "consciousness isolation" and a history of overpopulation, but also tremendous unemployment, and exacerbating hunger.

129 Barbara Engelking, *Such a Beautiful Sunny Day... Jews Seeking Refuge in the Polish Countryside, 1942–1945* (Jerusalem: Yad Vashem Publications, 2016), 31.

130 Quoted in ibid., 64–65.

While many Poles helped Różia, they did so with small bits of isolated aid. Even the lonely old woman could no longer shelter her, most likely due to fear of reprisal. This withdrawal of aid forced Różia and her child to "wander for weeks on end, without being able to settle down anywhere."[131] Engelking points to this period—after a ghetto liquidation—when Poles had greater influence over Jews' lives as more Jews escaped and trudged through the countryside looking for refuge.

Theories on Rural Polish Complicity in the Jewish Genocide: Jan Grabowski

In his book *Hunt for the Jews*, Jan Grabowski details the attempt by Jews who escaped ghetto liquidations to find safety and shelter among rural Poles in Dąbrowa Tarnowska, a southeastern farming region. He explains why Poles not only feared providing Jews with aid, but also hunted them down. This region lay outside of territory occupied by the Soviets from September 1939 to June 1941; thus, Grabowski asserts, in this specific region revenge against Soviet collaborators did not push Poles to seek retribution against the Jews.[132] (Though it did remain a factor in other regions.) In fact, prior to spring 1942, the countryside in "Lesser Poland" (Małopolska) had been a comparably good place for Jews to find refuge, with numerous Polish peasants assisting Jews with food and shelter.[133]

A noted change occurred after the ghetto liquidations. When Nazi authorities discovered a discrepancy existed between the Jewish ghetto registration lists and those ghetto Jews inventoried for "resettlement," they realized Jews were hiding and with probable Polish help. Grabowski estimates that roughly 250,000 Jews—about 10% of the Jews still alive in the summer of 1942—escaped. Less than fifty thousand survived.[134] This sizeable numerical disparity between

---

131 Quoted in ibid., 65.
132 Jan Grabowski, *Hunt for the Jews: Betrayal and Murder in German-Occupied Poland* (Bloomington: Indiana University Press, 2013), 10.
133 Given that this region had been part of Galicia prior to 1918, Jews in that area had been permitted to buy and sell land (whereas Jews in Russian Poland were prohibited from owning land). As such, a much larger percentage of Jews were farmers in Dąbrowa Tarnowska than were in what had been Russian Poland. However, although Jews had closer ties with Poles in this rural area known as "Lesser Poland" due to a shared vocation, relations began to erode in the 1930s as nationalists, aided by the Catholic anti-Jewish press campaign, gained ground in the area. See ibid., 17–19.
134 Ibid., 172–173.

escapees and survivors requires our attention, as it raises questions about Poles' influence on this limited opportunity for Jewish survival.

Jewish fugitives from the surrounding rural area often sought aid from Polish peasants they knew. Those from outside the region typically hid in the forest. To locate and kill these Jews, the Germans invoked the *Judenjagd*, the Jew hunt. Although such a hunt already existed for the purpose of turning over any fugitives to the Nazis, be they Soviet POWs, Roma, "bandits" (partisans), or Jews, after ghetto liquidations the hunt for the Jews became more focused and determined.

A Judenjagd had two stages. The first occurred immediately following the liquidation of a ghetto and involved various sectors of Polish society. The Nazis insured that the Polish Blue Police, Polish youth from the Baudienst (forced labor construction service), and the Jewish Police,[135] as well as local helpers and volunteers, aided in hunting down Jews who had escaped deportation. Those Jews who remained in the ghetto hid in underground bunkers and concealed spaces. Responsible for locating such hideouts, often the Polish Blue Police organized Jew hunts. Indeed, in their 1953 trial, the station commandants from Wiązowna (Otwock County), Władysław Kądziolka, Bolesław Wiesztort, and Marian Chodnicki, admitted to participating in manhunts. Leon Posesorski, a carpenter from Wiązowna, testified that "[t]he entire crew from the police station often staged manhunts against Polish citizens of Jewish nationality who were still alive."[136]

During this first phase of the Judenjagd, the German authorities also involved the local peasantry with promises of rewards. In Dąbrowa Tarnowska, the chief of the local German administration offered two kilograms of sugar for each denounced Jew. In Mielec County, the authorities offered up to five hundred zlotys for each surrendered Jew.[137] Some Poles also craved the clothing and shoes off the Jews' bodies.

In this early stage, Jew hunters either killed Jews on the spot, took them to the local execution site and murdered them, or put them on a train bound for a concentration camp.[138] During this phase of the Judenjagd, the number of captures

---

135 Tomasz Frydel, "*Judenjagd*: Reassessing the Role of Ordinary Poles as Perpetrators in the Holocaust," in *Perpetrators and Perpetration of Mass Violence: Action, Motivations and Dynamics*, ed. Timothy Williams and Susanne Buckley-Zistel (London: Routledge, 2018), 193–194.
136 Quoted in Engelking, *Such a Beautiful Sunny Day . . . Jews Seeking Refuge in the Polish Countryside, 1942–1945*, 172–173.
137 Grabowski, *Hunt for the Jews: Betrayal and Murder in German-Occupied Poland*, 57.
138 Ibid., 52.

and Jewish deaths peaked. The stage ended when the hunters had located and killed all Jews hiding in the ghetto. The second phase centered on the villages and surrounding forests. For this, the Nazis required additional eyes and ears throughout the region.

Theories on Rural Polish Complicity in the Jewish Genocide: Joanna Tokarska-Bakir

Joanna Tokarska-Bakir provides numerous archival testimonies which document the greed that directed many Poles living in Lesser Poland's south-central provinces of Kielce and Kraków to find and kill Jews for the Nazis. Szymon Sztrumpf's testimony reveals that his brother and family were murdered by "the Siudak brothers, [who] belonged to a band of robbers that hunted Jews."[139] With the approval of the village mayor, five local men allegedly murdered Szymon Sztrumpf's mother, Cylka, and her eight-year-old granddaughter Słupska. Tokarska-Bakir notes that after they murdered the mother, "they removed her boots, extracted her gold teeth and tore out the earrings."[140] For their effort, this group appropriated the following goods: "a down pillow, 12 meters of silk cloth for shirts and a scarf."[141]

According to this testimony and others, there is evidence that in several villages, including Zapusty, "a fairly large group of people enhanced their livelihoods by capturing and robbing Jews."[142] Given the long-accepted myth that all Jews were wealthy and hid their gold, these Poles participated in the Judenjagd likely with hopes of discovering such loot.[143] A rural teacher and prewar Polish Socialist Party member from Łuków, Stanisław Żemiński, wrote about one Jew hunt in his diary:

> On November 5 [1942] I drive through the village of Siedliska. I enter the local community store. The peasants are buying scythes. The sales lady tells us "the scythes will come handy for today's hunt." "What hunt?" I ask. "The Jew hunt," they tell me. "And how much do they pay you for each captured

---

139 Quoted in Tokarska-Bakir, *Pogrom Cries—Essays on Polish-Jewish History, 1939–1946*, 25–26.
140 Ibid., 26.
141 Quoted in ibid.
142 Ibid., 27.
143 Grabowski, *Hunt for the Jews: Betrayal and Murder in German-Occupied Poland*, 102, 109.

Jew?" Embarrassed silence is the answer. The hunters followed the fugitives into the forests, hoping for prizes offered by the Germans: vodka, sugar, potatoes, oil, but also personal items taken off the victims.[144]

To entice the general local population into joining this second stage of the Jew hunt, by March 1943 German authoritied codified that in addition to alcohol and food, "[p]ersons who have helped to apprehend the Jews can receive up to 1/3 of the seized property."[145] In a hunger-ridden and depraved climate, in which many peasants had accepted political and Church antisemitism, such promises could move some people to act like beasts.

One person's envy birthed another's fear. If Poles aiding Jews showed signs of having more money than usual—a new dress or new shoes—neighbors grew jealous and some dangerously hostile. They assumed the "wealthier" neighbor was being paid. Peasants already knew that some Poles' envy and greed for the "Jewish gold" led them to kill both the Jews and the Poles helping them. Tokarska-Bakir argues that this knowledge convinced peasants who might have been inclined to help Jews to ignore them instead or even denounce them. For Poles had learned to fear their neighbors more than they feared the Germans.[146]

Theories on Rural Polish Complicity in the Jewish Genocide: Tomasz Frydel

The historian Tomasz Frydel, who carried out research in Lesser Poland's historic Western Galicia, focuses on fear as the central factor in everyday Poles' willingness to murder Jews. Were Polish peasants overwhelmed by fear of their fellow Poles due to the latter's greed? Frydel suggests otherwise. To enlist needed peasant support for the Jew hunts, and thereby "co-opt segments of Polish society into active complicity in genocide," the German occupation authorities leaned on the local dynamics of communal fear for survival that was instituted when

---

144 Quoted in ibid., 52–53, 256n12. Stanisław Żemiński's diary was found in a garbage heap in the Majdanek concentration camp, where he most likely died.
145 Quoted in ibid., 57.
146 Ibid., 53.

they invaded Soviet territory in June 1941.[147] For Frydel, "this is not to suggest that antisemitism, like greed, did not coexist with this system or to say that Gentiles were otherwise waiting to jump forward to save the Jews."[148] But since Lesser Poland had earlier been a territory of relative refuge for Jews, we cannot claim it a hotbed of antisemitism. Behavior changed there because survival was at stake. Through strategic manipulation, the Nazis transformed ordinary Poles into perpetrators of genocide.

To meet their own extraction quotas of both food to feed the German army and people to fill slave labor demands in the Third Reich, the Germans reconfigured locally run village administrations.[149] They made the elected village head (*sołtys*) responsible for meeting these quotas and enforcing all Nazi orders. Knowing that Germans viewed job resignation as sabotage and that they were replaceable, most village heads tried to retain their jobs by satisfying German demands. For cooperating, the village head received tremendous authority: the Germans introduced the death penalty for insulting Polish village heads.[150] This policy further separated the village heads from the people, causing communal conflict public.[151] Similar to the Judenrat (Council of Jewish Elders) system established in the ghettos (which will be covered in the following chapter), the Nazis set up a divisive power dynamic in the rural regions, which pitted Pole against Pole.

This occupation strategy also included a second-tier power base of village guards (Ortschutzwache), whose members often drew from the local fire brigades. A type of local militia, it included night watches, couriers, and deputy elders. Responsible for aiding the sołtys in fulfilling Nazi quotas of food and people, and thereby for hunting down those peasants who refused to comply, it also served as another set of watchful eyes. Night watch section leaders received modest compensation from the Germans with the expectation they would inform on village events and the village head.[152] Knowing he was under surveillance, the sołtys himself was more likely to comply with Nazi orders. Additionally, both the village head and the militia were also responsible for

---

147 Frydel, "*Judenjagd*: Reassessing the Role of Ordinary Poles as Perpetrators in the Holocaust," 188.
148 Ibid., 200.
149 Ibid., 190.
150 Grabowski, *Hunt for the Jews: Betrayal and Murder in German-Occupied Poland*, 64.
151 Ibid., 64–65
152 Ibid., 65.

reporting and delivering fugitives—that is, Soviet POWs, Roma, partisans, and Jews—to the nearest gendarmerie or Polish police station.[153]

Frydel holds that during the second stage of the Judenjagd, when the Nazis believed peasants knew about and aided Jews who had escaped ghetto liquidations, the village elder remained responsible for finding them. The night watch had to assist in the Jew hunt.[154] Even official couriers and cart drivers faced punitive grain quotas, arrest, or even death if they refused to aid the process of searching for and delivering Jews in hiding.[155]

To ensure success, Nazi officials ordered each village head to designate "hostages": appointed for limited periods of time, hostages were held personally responsible by the Germans for any threatening anti-German behavior, including hiding Jews. Thus, these hostages also watched villagers carefully. If they refused to denounce villagers' illegal activity to the Polish Blue Police, they risked deportation to a labor camp.[156]

In this second stage, the Nazis also intensified their fear campaign. They plastered propaganda sheets on walls to stoke fear that Jews carried typhus: hiding a Jew could mean putting one's whole family at risk of contagion and death.[157] Furthermore, after the Nazis pivoted to locating Jews in hiding, they revised the punishment for aiding and abetting Jews. While Hans Frank's October 15, 1941 third regulation called for capital punishment, it was typically enforced only against Jews. More commonly, those Poles discovered to have been helping Jews were imprisoned or sent to concentration camps. Now "death" meant death. A person who housed a Jew or provided food to a Jew would be killed. Indeed, even a Pole who hid knowledge from the authorities of another peasant aiding a Jew, even that Pole would be killed in retaliation.[158] One physical example of Nazi follow-through generated toxic fear throughout a village.

Franciszek Kotula recorded such examples in his wartime chronicle of the "voice of the street" in Rzeszów. He described the stark consequences Poles faced if they provided Jews with any aid: "In the region of Hyżne, twenty Jews were killed and 10 Poles, who had given them food and shelter. Three sons of the forester in Hadle Szklarskie were killed for sheltering Jews and five peasants

---

153 Frydel, "*Judenjagd*: Reassessing the Role of Ordinary Poles as Perpetrators in the Holocaust," 190.
154 Grabowski, *Hunt for the Jews: Betrayal and Murder in German-Occupied Poland*, 71–73.
155 Ibid., 69.
156 Ibid., 66.
157 Ibid., 55–57.
158 Frydel, "*Judenjagd*: Reassessing the Role of Ordinary Poles as Perpetrators in the Holocaust," 190.

in Grzegorzówka."¹⁵⁹ It became much more difficult for Jews to find help in this atmosphere of surveillance and physical intimidation.

The Nazis introduced communal retribution into their fear campaign. One Pole giving refuge to a Jew could result in retaliation against all Poles in the same village, even those not involved. In effect, this device created a village of "hostages." Nazi disciplinary efforts included burning down not only homesteads, but also whole villages. In their own struggles for individual and familial survival, then, Pole set upon Pole. In June 1943, the German mayor of Jasło called a meeting of surrounding village elders. Andrzej Wojtowicz, sołtys of the village of Markuszowa, heard him berate the Poles present because Jews had been hiding successfully. The mayor threatened them with collective reprisals for hiding Jews, including killing five peasants per village.¹⁶⁰

In the besieged provinces, Poles grew ever more obedient to Nazi sanctions. They knew that informers working for the German police lurked everywhere.¹⁶¹ It is no wonder that when Polish peasants sheltering Jews feared they would be discovered, they often wanted the Jews to leave. But by 1943, when the consequence for aiding Jews was death, Poles recoiled from casting them out lest, when most likely captured and tortured, the Jews might betray them.¹⁶² Often they killed the Jews themselves.¹⁶³

By coupling the fears of contagion, resident surveillance, and collective responsibility, with the desire for food, alcohol, and any looted property, the Germans secured a steady stream of aid from Poles, even the Jews' murder. Family survival trumped prewar relationships and moral standards. The reality of imposed fear and the urge to survive made many Polish peasants complicit in the Nazi's plan to kill all Eastern European Jews.

Certainly, it is impossible to know what any of us would do in the same situation. Would any of us even have the initial desire to aid a hunted person? In the film *Hiding and Seeking*, Menachem Daum asks his grandfather, who had been saved by a rural Polish family, if he himself would have reciprocated that righteous act. He answers, "I think I wouldn't."¹⁶⁴ He of all people understands the daily risk taken and terror encountered by Poles aiding Jews. What would

---

159 Quoted in ibid., 196.
160 Grabowski, *Hunt for the Jews: Betrayal and Murder in German-Occupied Poland*, 77.
161 Frydel, "*Judenjagd*: Reassessing the Role of Ordinary Poles as Perpetrators in the Holocaust," 192.
162 Quoted in ibid., 196.
163 Ibid., 198.
164 *Hiding and Seeking*, dir. Menachem Daum and Oren Rudavsky (First Run Features, 2004).

we do if our cardinal value of helping humanity directly conflicted with that of protecting our families?

Myth Reconstruction

Numerous American Jewish historians who study either Polish-Jewish relations or the Holocaust pay respect to the agonies the Polish people suffered under German occupation.[165] Yet, I have not encountered one who calls it what it is: genocide. Why has it been so difficult for Jewish scholars, rabbis, and teachers to attribute this one word to the Poles' experience under the Nazis? Poles suffered neither "brutal repression" nor "genocidal tactics" (a term which suggests genocide-like behavior that is not equal to genocide), but rather the implementation of genocide against the Polish nation. While these two genocides—the Jewish genocide referred to as the Holocaust or Shoah (Hebrew for "catastrophe") and the Polish genocide—shared features, they did not look the same.

As we noted earlier, Nazi ideology met Germany's annexation of western Poland and initial successful military drive eastward with a push to cleanse the Reich of both Jews and Poles.[166] In that early period, the Nazis eliminated large numbers of Poles. But by 1941, Hitler was reacting to the war's development. No longer did a quick euphoric Nazi victory appear likely. Extended battles were dwindling Germany's military supplies. The Nazis needed manpower to aid the war effort. At this point, Nazi ideology precluded employing Jews, as the German authorities had labeled them its primary adversary, and, as such, the Jews had been condemned to complete eradication. But Poles were another story. Nazi ideology understood most Poles as subhuman—stupid, lazy, dirty, ill-clothed—but still worthy of life if that life benefited the German nation. Thus, while the Nazis' Jewish genocide took on greater momentum in 1941, their Polish genocide took a more gradual approach.

The historian David Engel writes that "[t]he persecution of the Poles was ruthless. During the war 3 million of them were murdered by starvation, forced

---

165 Antony Polonsky and David Engel are two Jewish historians who provide detailed portrayals of this Polish genocide in all but name. They go to great lengths to describe the targeted economic, cultural, and religious actions the Nazis employed against Polish individuals and institutions to defeat the Poles as a nation. See Polonsky, *The Jews in Poland and Russia*, 3:364–369; Engel, *In the Shadow of Auschwitz: The Polish Government-in-Exile and the Jews, 1939–1942*, 157–158.
166 Polonsky, *The Jews in Poland and Russia*, 3:67.

labor, or execution."[167] Although he argues that the Nazis created from the Polish people a "reservoir of slave labor for the German Reich,"[168] he is unwilling to state unequivocally that the Nazis intended to inflict genocide on the Poles. This decision requires reflection, given that according to the 1948 United Nations Convention on the Prevention and Punishment of Genocide the Nazis' actions against the Poles did amount to genocide. As a necessary reminder, the following is the accepted definition of genocide:

> By "genocide" we mean the destruction of a nation or an ethnic group.... Generally speaking, genocide does not necessarily mean the immediate destruction of a nation, except when accomplished by mass killings of all members of a nation.... The objectives of such a plan would be disintegration of the political and social institutions of culture, language, national feelings, religion, and the economic existence of national groups, and the destruction of the personal security, liberty, health, dignity, and even the lives of the individuals belonging to such groups. Genocide is directed against the national group as an entity, and the actions involved are directed against individuals, not in their individual capacity, but as members of the national group.[169]

---

167 Since the 1987 publication of David Engel's book *In the Shadow of Auschwitz*, detailed scholarship has further developed, establishing the number of Poles and Jews who died at the hands of the Nazis. Polish studies have found that a maximum of 1.5–2 million Polish Christians were killed by the Germans during the war. These studies, carried out by Professor Krystyna Kersten and others, have corroborated the figure of roughly three million Polish Jews killed. Their findings were published in 1994 in the Warsaw journal *Dzieje Najnowsze* 26, no. 2. Other scholars suggest lower figures: Timothy Snyder, in his *Bloodlands: Europe between Hitler and Stalin*, numbers the Polish Christian civilian deaths at around one million; Czesław Łuczak in his study "Szanse I trudności bilansu demograficzego Polski w latach 1939–1945," *Dzieje Najnowsze* 21 (1994) estimates the number of ethnic Polish civilians who died under Hitler at 1.5 million. Wojciech Materski and Tomasz Szarota's 2009 work *Polska 1939–1945. Straty osobowe I ofiary represji pod dwiema okupacjami* proposes that some 2,270,000 ethnic Polish Christians died under Nazi occupation.

168 Engel, *In the Shadow of Auschwitz: The Polish government-in-Exile and the Jews, 1939–1942,* 158.

169 Lemkin, *Axis Rule in Occupied Europe: Laws of Occupation, Analysis of Government, Proposals for Redress*, 79: "Genocide has two phases: one, destruction of the national pattern of the oppressed group: the other the imposition of the national pattern of the oppressor. This imposition, in turn, may be made upon the oppressed population which is allowed to remain, or upon the territory alone, after removal of the population and the colonization of the area by the oppressor's own nationals."

Based on this definition, genocide rarely reaches the complete extermination of a people, or the unthinkable numbers of Jews the Nazis murdered. The UN definition holds that "genocide itself may be partial. Indeed, it usually falls far short of the total extinction of a group."[170]

Engel hints at why he (and others) do not call the Poles' experience "genocide": "Indeed, of all the peoples of occupied Europe, their [the Poles'] suffering was the greatest—except for the Jews. For though they were destined for extinction as a nation, most of them still had a definite if ignominious function to perform as individuals in the Nazi 'new order.'"[171] Here, Engel affirms his conviction that the Germans sought to destroy the Poles as a nation—the core of genocide. And yet he refuses to name it as such—I hold—to stress the Jews' role as Hitler's primary target. The Jews certainly had it worse than the Poles. At least for the moment. If the Nazis had achieved victory in World War II, and accomplished their plans to completely decimate the Jews, some studies indicate that they would have turned next to the Poles to feed the furnaces at Auschwitz, while perhaps saving some Poles for a slower demise through slave labor.[172]

This unwillingness by Holocaust historians (and the Jewish public) to call the atrocities inflicted against the Poles a "Polish genocide" results from several issues. First, the Holocaust looms so large as an example of genocide that other genocides tend to appear "minor" in comparison. The genocide scholar Martin Shaw contends that there is a problem with "the erection of 'the Holocaust' as a maximal standard that other episodes must reach if they are to be recognized: not surprisingly they mostly fail."[173]

Second, the two genocides occurred during the same war, by the same actor, on the same soil. As a result, people either conflate the two into one, as the Poles did for decades under the communist Polish People's Republic, or they negate one, as the Jews have done regarding the Polish genocide. In communist Poland, Poles grew up learning that the Nazis murdered six million Poles. They did not focus separately on the Nazi goal to annihilate the Jews. Unwilling to recognize the Holocaust's special status lest their own national myth of victimization

---

170 Ben Kiernan, *Blood and Soil: A World History of Genocide and Extermination from Sparta to Darfur* (New Haven: Yale University Press, 2007), 15.
171 Engel, *In the Shadow of Auschwitz: The Polish government-in-Exile and the Jews, 1939–1942*, 158.
172 Ibid., 284n2.
173 Martin Shaw, *What Is Genocide?*, 2nd ed. (Cambridge: Polity Press, 2015), 53.

appear diminished by comparison, the Polish communist authorities ignored the Jewish genocide. The Poles remained the central victims in their narrative.

Conversely, by cultivating a hatred for Poles since the end of World War I, due to American Jews' misperception of widespread *Polish* pogroms, and the rise of interwar Polish antisemitism, American Jews labeled Poles in general as supporting Hitler's destruction of Polish Jewry.[174] American Jews have feared that to give full credence to the Poles' pain, to the Poles' national destruction, would detract from the Jews' own victimization, which at times Poles themselves caused. Would recognizing Poles' pain disrespect those Jews murdered in the Holocaust or trivialize the catastrophe itself?

Third, scholars in the field of Holocaust studies have been slow to publicly name the Polish genocide as such due to anxiety of losing ground in the absurd and continuing victimhood rivalry between Poles and Jews. By withholding the term from Poles (and other groups including the Romani, homosexuals, and the disabled), Jews retain the position of "most victimized." In resisting the characterization of the Poles' WWII experience as a Polish genocide, Holocaust scholars assert the uniqueness of the Holocaust, a topic widely discussed in academic circles and dear to the American Jewish community.[175]

The uniqueness argument emerged in the 1970s and 1980s as a way to express the unfathomable devastation wrought by the Holocaust. The historian Tom Lawson writes:

> First and foremost it was an articulation of despair, an attempt to draw attention to the scale of the challenge that the murder of Europe's Jews posed. It also gave vent to anguish at the lack of attention that the Holocaust apparently received both in the historical profession and in Western culture more generally. Uniqueness also articulated a fear of the potential consequences

---

174 Some Poles did desire Jews' mass emigration from Poland prior to the war. During the war, the Polish government-in-exile considered plans with Jabotinsky's Revisionist *Zionists* to conduct voluntary large-scale Jewish emigration to Palestine after the war. They believed this aligned with the Jewish nationalists' agenda and would be seen positively by international Jewry. See Engel, *In the Shadow of Auschwitz: The Polish government-in-Exile and the Jews, 1939–1942*, 95.

175 For a discussion of the uniqueness of the Holocaust, see Martin Shaw, *What Is Genocide?*, 53–65; Tom Lawson, *Debates on the Holocaust* (Manchester: Manchester University Press, 2010).

of antisemitism in a world where threats to the state of Israel were growing.[176]

That people claimed uniqueness to the Jewish disaster is understandable in human terms. Yet such claims disregard, and consequently deny other genocides, Others' pain.

Thus, I have to ask the discomforting question: Can one people be both victim and victimizer? Those who desire a simple tale of the past would say "No!" But reality is complex. It is messy. Within any one group, there are both good and bad people. Indeed, within one person there are both good and bad inclinations. Moreover, because genocide is an act of collective aggression, and under the direction of a leadership that relies upon fear, misinformation, and enticements to persuade one group of its superiority over another group's threatening presence, anyone can—under the right circumstances—become vulnerable to the social pressures and manipulations that persuade one not only to fear the Other but also to take action to destroy it.

It is crucial for people to acknowledge and accept that within their national group there are both oppressed and oppressor. In fact, one individual can inhabit this seeming contradiction. There is nothing inherent in human beings that prevents the victim from becoming a victimizer. Both Nazi and Soviet policy subjugated the Polish peasantry through deportations, forced labor, slave labor, and levies, as well as by murdering individuals and families, destroying thousands of farmsteads, and confiscating resources. Between 1939 and 1945, some 675,000 peasant farmsteads were completely or partially destroyed, the land and the people were thoroughly exploited.[177]

It has been estimated that roughly 10% of Polish Jewry's three million tried to escape Nazi annihilation.[178] Given that the number of Jews living under the General Government and in the Białystok district prior to Operation Reinhardt was 1.6 million, it follows that the number of escapees would number close to 160,000.[179] However, only thirty to forty thousand Jews survived in occupied Poland. This means that, at the least, some 120,000 Jews lost their lives during this final stage of the Nazi destruction of Polish Jewry. It must be recognized that

---

176 Lawson, *Debates on the Holocaust*, 6.
177 Engelking, *Such a Beautiful Sunny Day . . . Jews Seeking Refuge in the Polish Countryside, 1942–1945*, 12.
178 Ibid., 165n1.
179 Engelking notes the calculation by Krzysztof Persak, the co-editor of the IPN's report *Not Only Jedwabne*. See ibid.

Poles massacred Jews out of revenge for a partial Jewish alliance with the Soviet occupation, and took part in Jew hunts, due to prewar transmitted antisemitism, greed, or fear. The victimized can be the victimizer.

At the same time, it is also imperative to understand that the victimizer can be a savior. Within the Polish population, thousands of people risked their lives and those of their families to aid Jews in hiding. An untold number helped Jews who were later betrayed and killed. The Institute of National Remembrance identifies 704 cases of Poles who were executed for helping Jews in hiding.[180] Of the 337 Jews in hiding studied by Jan Grabowski, fifty-one Jews survived. Of that number, twenty-seven owed their lives to the selfless help offered by their Polish hosts.

If Jews are honest, we need to concede that during the war communists of Jewish origin oppressed Poles. Does this mean that all Jews were communists or that all Jews harmed Poles, or that there was some Jewish policy to target Poles? Absolutely not. We have seen that Poles formed generalizations about *all* Jews based on those Jews who welcomed the Soviets with flowers, as well as those who worked within the tyrannical Soviet apparatus. Those Poles claimed that such behavior proved the decades-old Żydokomuna conspiracy theory and therefore, Jews—all Jews—were traitors to Poland. In so doing, they also sidestepped the fact that many of their countrymen supported communism in the interwar era and during the war. American Jews know that to extrapolate a segment of society's actions onto the whole society is irrational and wrong. We reject it when groups do it to us ... whether in the US or in Poland. So why do we do it to Others ... to Poles? Why do we judge *all* Poles for only *some* Pole' actions? This basic mistake plagues us to this day.

WWII and the Holocaust evoke painful emotions for both Poles and Jews. We have seen that several Polish academics have confronted national memory with historical documentation. Since Poland brought down the Iron Curtain, diverse scholars have engaged in a reevaluation of the country's central myth concerning Poles, Jews, and the Holocaust. Jedwabne, the Judenjagd, and AK Jew hunts are as much part of Poland's past as is victimization, martyrdom, and bravery. The historians' research not only contradicts the comforting Polish myth of *all* Poles' benevolence toward Jews during the Holocaust, but has also forced the population into dialogue over it.

As a collective, American Jews have rarely grappled with our own construction of an identity through the myth of the Holocaust's uniqueness. Is there room in

---

180 Grabowski, *Hunt for the Jews: Betrayal and Murder in German-Occupied Poland*, 56.

our identity to recognize other contemporaneous genocides? What do we fear will happen by teaching about the Poles' pain and categorizing it as genocide? Will Jews' pain shrink in the eyes of the international community? I argue that to move forward in forging a meaningful relationship between contemporary Poles and Jews we must be able and willing to name each group's tragedies, and acknowledge both victims and victimizers within each population.

As I demonstrate in the following chapter, when evaluating this tragic history buried by communist Poland, it is vital to view it as part of broader Nazi policy. Like village heads and the Polish Blue Police, among others, Jews too were Nazi pawns: Jew was set against Jew. Like Poles, they were victim and victimizer.

CHAPTER 14

Genocide and the Jews

According to Emmanuel Ringelblum[1] (1900–1944), lead chronicler of the Warsaw Ghetto, the Polish-Jewish joint military response to the September 1939 Nazi invasion of Poland reawakened a strong sense of solidarity between Jews and Poles. Paralleling the 1860s Polish-Jewish brotherhood, Ringelblum notes that in 1939 "the feeling of harmony and cooperation in defense of the country spread throughout all classes and strata of the country."[2] Unified action against a common enemy tore down divides antisemitic groups and antisemitic policy had built up, especially since Piłsudski's 1935 death. Barbara Engelking-Boni writes that "Citizens of Warsaw—Poles and Jews—jointly dug trenches, jointly put out fires, and jointly defended the city."[3]

However, when occupation realities overwhelmed Poles and power dynamics split the populations, this Polish-Jewish rapprochement could not withstand

---

1   Born in 1900, Emmanuel Ringelblum received a PhD in 1927. For ten years he taught Jewish history in Polish language secondary schools for Jewish girls. He also worked at the mutual Aid Funds Center which provided no-interest loans within the Jewish community. In the Warsaw Ghetto Ringelblum organized several secret Jewish social aid campaigns. He is best known for establishing a group of dedicated writers, researchers, teachers, underground members, and ordinary Jews to contribute to the clandestine chronicling of facts about and perspectives on life in the ghetto. It should be noted that longtime involvement with the Jewish leftist political party Po'alei Zion tinted the lens through which Ringelblum and many of his chief collaborators viewed ghetto life. Leaders buried the Ghetto Archives, known as Oyneg Shabbos, in three containers. Due to the complete destruction of the Warsaw Ghetto two containers were never found. Ringelblum's manuscript on Polish-Jewish relations survived. See Samuel D. Kassow, *Who Will Write Our History?: Rediscovering A Hidden Archive from the Warsaw Ghetto* (New York: Vintage Books, 2007), 1–16.
2   Emmanuel Ringelblum, *Polish-Jewish Relations during the Second World War*, ed. Joseph Kermish and Shmuel Krakowski, trans. Dafna Allon, Danuta Dabrowska, and Dana Keren (Evanston: Northwestern University Press, 1992), 25.
3   Barbara Engelking-Boni, "Psychological Distance between Poles and Jews in Nazi-Occupied Warsaw," in *Contested Memories: Poles and Jews During the Holocaust and Its Aftermath*, ed. Joshua D. Zimmerman (New Brunswick: Rutgers University Press, 2003), 47.

the inclination to revert to old habits. Catholic Church anti-Jewish diatribes and prewar political antisemitism had been instilled in society, and had rapidly escalated since spring 1935. Hunger and fear lowered resistance to what contemporary observer, Alexander Donat saw as "[p]oisonous Nazi propaganda [that] soon reawakened native antisemitism."[4] For most Poles—who were focused first on fighting and then resisting the German enemy—the problems facing the Jews were of less importance. This view intensified, given that Nazi treatment of the two populations was similar in various locations at the early stage of the war and Poles in the west were treated even more severely.[5] This chapter further explores Germany's antisemitic policies and the discord that followed within both the Polish and Jewish populations, including American Jewry. While some Poles participated in anti-Jewish terror, some fought against it. Among Polish and American Jews, we find complicity, resistance, and exhaustion.

German Occupation and Polish Collaboration

By saturating the Polish citizenry in the General Government with antisemitic propaganda, Germany extended to the Poles what Jan Karski described as a "narrow bridge upon which the Germans and a large portion of Polish society are finding agreement."[6] Karski emphasized that the Nazis transmitted the message that "the Germans, and the Germans alone, will help the Poles to settle accounts with the Jews."[7] Prewar Poland's growing antisemitism prepped a portion of the population to grasp firmly onto German messaging. The Germans engineered this bridge with radio and loudspeaker systems in public spaces. They also tasked a German-operated Polish-language press with disseminating antisemitism through its newspaper, brochures, leaflets, and posters.

---

4   Quoted in Engelking-Boni, "Psychological Distance between Poles and Jews in Nazi-Occupied Warsaw," 48.
5   Ibid.
6   Quoted in David Engel, "An Early Account of Polish Jewry under Nazi and Soviet Occupation Presented to the Polish Government-in-Exile, February 1940": 12. Karski differentiates between the Polish masses, who were vulnerable to Nazi antisemitic propaganda, and those who he believed could resist it: "The Germans are attempting at all costs to win over the Polish masses—not the intelligentsia, not the upper classes, not the wealthy and enlightened landholders or townspeople, but the masses—the peasants, the workers, the artisans, etc." See ibid., 11.
7   Quoted in ibid., 12.

According to Czesław Miłosz (1911–2004), who lived under the General Government, the Nazis' antisemitic propaganda appealed to those Poles who already perceived Jews as an economic enemy due to Jewish overrepresentation not only in the population, but also in the universities, white-collar professions, and trade.[8] Hans Frank's administration physically, and ultimately emotionally, separated these two victimized groups by emphasizing their differences and thereby sowing greater disharmony. Once the occupation had stretched into 1941, those Poles with entrenched antisemitic views were able to compartmentalize the Nazis' actions against Jews from those against Poles.[9]

Poles heard stories about Jews abusing their Christian fellows in the Soviet-occupied kresy. By late 1941, when thousands of Polish soldiers returned to the General Government from eastern territories (first taken by the Soviet Union and later captured by Germany), they brought back tales of terrible treatment by the Red Army—that is, it was suggested, *the Jews*. Since World War I, global antisemitic propaganda had been linking the Jews to the Soviets through the Żydokomuna conspiracy theory. Roman Dmowski's interwar Endecja promulgated this lie. Now Poles blamed the Jews for the Soviet abuse of Polish soldiers. When Poles grieved for the fifteen thousand Polish officers murdered in the Katyń forest (which, in fact, included seven to eight hundred Jewish officers), many people who blamed the Soviets connected Jews to this outrage.[10]

Given this multi-layered context—which included anti-Polish Nazi repression—most Poles did not engage with the Jews in a positive manner. Some harassed them for monetary profit. Known as *szmalcowniks*, these young ruffians gathered mostly from the fringe ONR (Obóz Narodowo-Radykalny—the National Radical Camp) and other interwar peripheral extreme right-wing antisemitic political groups. Having struggled with high unemployment, these Poles had already accepted Jews as Poland's economic enemy. They moved from antisemitic violence at universities to collaboration with the Gestapo. Szmalcowniks ran in gangs that terrorized Jews seeking aid from "Aryans." They pointed out Jews to the Nazis unless the Jews could bribe their way to safety.

---

8   Polonsky, *The Jews in Poland and Russia*, 3:403.
9   Engelking-Boni, "Psychological Distance between Poles and Jews in Nazi-Occupied Warsaw," 52.
10 Ringelblum, *Polish-Jewish Relations during the Second World War*, 39. The thousands of Polish officers murdered included seven hundred to eight hundred Jewish officers. The Polish mass graves were found in the Katyń forest. The Soviets refuted any involvement in the Katyń massacre until April 1990 when President Gorbachev finally apologized to the Polish people for this Soviet crime. Until then, Soviet authorities blamed Germany for Katyń.

These blackmailers also included the Polish police, Polish agents of the Gestapo, smugglers, speculators, and members of the criminal underworld.[11]

Ita Diamant, a nurse in the Warsaw Ghetto, testified to the szmalcowniks' power:

> When we made the first three steps on the other side of the ghetto, we were assaulted by a swarm of boys, blackmailers [...]. They started chasing us and [...] shouting that we should give them money. Of course we were not wearing the armbands. [...] But they were like a swarm. [...] We could not beat it. [...] To put it briefly: when we [got on the train]—we had no money, no rings, no watches or shoes left. We had nothing.[12]

Polish szmalcowniks kept up this debilitating aggression throughout the war.

An October 1943 report by Żegota (the Polish Council for Aid to Jews) underscored the szmalcownik problem to the delegate of the government-in-exile:

> The great plague that can be called a social curse, is the pandemic growth of extortion, whose victims have been and continue to be large numbers of Jews residing within the Aryan areas. These victims are brutally robbed of their life's possessions, of money, valuables, clothing, linens and other valuable items. In result, the victims of blackmail lose their apartments and become a burden to their relatives, friends.[13]

Żegota appealed for official countermeasures including sentencing blackmailers and their helpers to death. Despite the council's own distribution of twenty-five thousand flyers condemning blackmailers and beseeching the Polish population to aid Jews, blackmailers plagued Jews and the Polish Christians who helped them.[14]

---

11 Ibid., 42.
12 Quoted in Engelking-Boni, "Psychological Distance between Poles and Jews in Nazi-Occupied Warsaw," 50–51.
13 23 October 1943, Warsaw. Report on the Activity of the Council for Aid to Jews "Żegota" (Rada Pomocy Żydom "Żegota") at the office of the Minister Plenipotentiary/Delegate of the Government of the Republic of Poland to the Homeland (Pełnomocnik/Delegat Rządu RP na Kraj) for the period: December 1942-October 1943. Located in Kunert, "Żegota": The Council for Aid To Jews 1942–1945, Selected Documents, 94.
14 Ibid.

Polish Aid to Jews

Truth has many facets. The truth is that individual Poles collaborated in the Nazi annihilation of Polish Jewry. Thousands of Poles inflicted tremendous harm on Jews who tried to escape ghettos and Nazi "resettlement" Aktions. Szmalcowniks' persistence chased Jews back into the ghettos, sealing their fate. At the same time, it is also true that despite the enormous personal risk, many Poles helped Jews. Aware of this, the German authorities legislated against it.

On November 10, 1941, the Nazis posted public notices, making it clear that Jews leaving ghettos illegally would be killed. They also warned Poles that assisting Jews would result in execution.[15] One poster in the Radom district read:

> The experience of the last few weeks shows that the Jews, in order to evade evacuation, tend to run away from the smaller Jewish residential districts.
>
> Those Jews must have been taken in by Poles. I am requesting all mayors and village heads to advise the population that every Pole who takes in a Jew is guilty of crime. Those Poles who feed the runaway Jews or sell them foodstuffs are to be regarded as accomplices, even if they do not offer shelter. In either case, such Poles are subject to the death penalty.[16]

Nightly executions of Poles who had provided help to Jews rattled the Polish citizenry.[17] In mid-1942, German propaganda again stressed that Poles who assisted Jews would be subject to the death penalty. A list circulated the names of 270 people murdered for helping Jews.[18]

As in villages, the Nazis also announced collective responsibility and applied collective punishments in towns and cities. Polish fear intensified. If one Pole hid a Jew in his apartment, the entire building or even block could be condemned to death. The chief of the SS and police in the Government General expanded the definition of "aid" to include anyone "who knew about Jews being hidden but failed to report those Jews and Poles hiding them."[19] As well as death, Poles

---

15 Ringelblum, *Polish-Jewish Relations during the Second World War*, 83.
16 Bartoszewski and Lewin, *The Samaritans: Heroes of the Holocaust*, 12.
17 Ringelblum, *Polish-Jewish Relations during the Second World War*, 154.
18 Ibid., 152n1 and n2.
19 Bartoszewski and Lewin, *The Samaritans: Heroes of the Holocaust*, 13.

risked internment in a concentration camp. Indeed, as Ringelblum noted, a "Jew living in the flat of an intellectual or a worker or in the hut of a peasant is dynamite liable to explode at any moment and blow the whole place up."[20] This threat to their survival transformed Polish neighbors into spies.

A Pole hiding a Jew in his apartment worried about any noise that might draw a neighbor's attention and therefore elicit questions. How would one explain extra food brought home? Should one disconnect from family and friends to avoid detection? Would the creation of such distance draw even more questions? Ringelblum does not disparage those Poles who took money from Jews to hide them. Instead, he asks whether there was "enough money in the world to make up for the constant fear of exposure, fear of neighbors, the porter and the manager of the block of flats, etc."[21] Poles, who hid and helped Jews, were themselves in danger every minute of every day.

To repeat, Poles both harassed and helped Jews. Some scholars connect the decisions Poles made with regional prewar levels of antisemitism. As described earlier, Poles in the region referred to as Lesser Poland had relatively good prewar relations with the Jews. In 1940 and 1941, Poles in Lesser Poland treated the Jews well, in both large provincial towns (e.g., Lviv, Kraków, Grodno, and others) and in rural areas. Some Polish peasants guided Jews to the forests. Some fed Jews imprisoned in nearby camps and provided food to those hiding in forests. Some peasants sheltered Jews. However, this benevolence declined after the Nazis retaliated by enforcing the death penalty and collective punishments. From this point, most peasants in Lesser Poland chose their own survival over their Christian values.[22]

Polish aid to Jews came from all segments of society. Some of the Polish railwaymen who discovered that "resettlement" from a ghetto really meant murder in Treblinka informed the Polish underground, which in turn warned Jewish communities and, indeed, the world; a few railway men even gave Jews tools to

---

20 Ringelblum, *Polish-Jewish Relations during the Second World War*, 226.
21 Ibid.
22 Ibid. In *When Light Pierced the Darkness: Christian Rescue of Jews in Nazi-Occupied Poland*, Nechama Tec concludes with a list of characteristics shared among rescuers. One is the recognition in that chaotic and dangerous environment rescuers tuned out the ramifications of being caught aiding Jews, lest they be paralyzed by them. Tec also discusses Christian Polish rescuers' grounding in independent thought, freedom, and a longstanding tradition of helping the downtrodden. See Nechama Tec, *When Light Pierced the Darkness: Christian Rescue Of Jews In Nazi-Occupied Poland* (New York: Oxford University Press, 1986), 190.

open transport wagons and helped Jews who leaped from them.[23] Polish clergy, scientists, peasants, doctors, and maidservants put their lives on the line to support Jews. Some Polish sewer workers helped Jews find their way out of the ghetto through the labyrinth of underground tunnels. Polish smugglers, despite the penalty of death, cooperated with Jews in the Warsaw Ghetto to create an economy by smuggling material into the ghetto and Jewish-manufactured goods out of it: according to Ringelblum, "many Polish common people displayed human magnanimity with regard to smuggling and were ready to make sacrifices for the sake of the Jews."[24]

In assessing Polish aid to the Jews, Władysław Bartoszewski (1922–2015),[25] wartime Polish journalist and Żegota member, reminds one that during this time Poland was under siege. The Nazis decapitated Poland and devoured its resources. Until the ghettos were sealed neither Poles nor Jews believed Jews would be treated much worse than Poles.[26] Before any world leader knew of Hitler's Final Solution, before Hitler had laid out his plan in Wannsee in January 1942, neither the Poles nor the Jews foresaw the Germans' plan to exterminate the Jews. Implementation of the Final Solution began in the spring of 1942. Until the railwaymen returned with news about Treblinka, from a Polish perspective the Nazis were destroying an entire country, including the Jews living within it.

However, some Poles realized that the Germans were starving Jews to death in ghettos and working them to death in labor camps. A few had also attempted to draw Poles' attention to the specific German focus on the Jews. Aleksander Kamiński (1903–1978), the editor of the Home Army's secret paper *Biuletyn Informacyn*,[27] reported in the January 9, 1941 edition:

---

23 Ringelblum, *Polish-Jewish Relations during the Second World War*, 200–203.
24 Ibid., 80.
25 Born in 1922 to a Roman Catholic family, Władysław Bartoszewski grew up in a Jewish Warsaw neighborhood. In 1939 he fought with his countrymen against the Nazi invasion and later joined the Polish Red Cross. Rounded up with several thousand other Polish men after the 1939 surrender, he was an early inmate at Auschwitz, bearing the number 4427. After the Red Cross obtained his release, he joined the Polish underground as a writer in the Home Army's Information and Propaganda Bureau. He is best known for his involvement in the clandestine Council for Aid to Jews, known by its codename Żegota. See Rick Lyman, "Wladyslaw Bartoszewski, 93, Polish Activist Who Battled Both Nazis and Communists," *New York Times*, April 28, 2015 A 25.
26 Bartoszewski, "Polish-Jewish Relations in Occupied Poland, 1939–1945," 149–150.
27 Aleksander Kamiński also served as chief of the Bureau of Information in the Warsaw district of the Home Army. See Andrzej Paczkowski, *The Spring Will Be Ours: Poland and the Poles from Occupation to Freedom*, trans. Jane Cave (University Park: The Pennsylvania State University Press, 2003), 101.

> The Jewish labor camps hardly differ from Auschwitz.[28] People who are completely unfit to work in the fields, poorly dressed for the winter weather, terribly undernourished, are driven from farms and villages where they are quartered in unheated barns and sheds, to work on fortifications. The guards treat them in a sadistic manner. There is a very high death rate.[29]

Kamiński sought to expose the Jews' situation. Having close ties with Warsaw Jews before the war, he printed information passed secretly to him by friends in the ghetto.[30] The underground press also informed Poles that acquiescing to a voluntary request to help the Germans guard the Jews' barracks would be considered treason against Poland.[31]

Today, we know all too well the form and scope of Hitler's terror against the Jewish people. But initially, when Jews heard from both Jewish witnesses and the Polish underground that "resettlement" Aktion was code for mass murder, they dismissed it as inconceivable; and by staggering their ghetto liquidations, the Nazis helped solidify Jewish denial. In spring 1942, Hans Frank began liquidating Lublin's ghetto. From July to September 1942, the Warsaw Ghetto "resettlement" Aktion ensued. In that short time span, the Nazis deported roughly three hundred thousand Jews to their deaths.[32] When the remaining sixty thousand ghetto Jews were informed that resettlement meant mass murder, most refused to believe it.[33] Of those who heard and believed, many thought it an anomaly. It would not happen *here*, in *this* ghetto. Only a few succeeded in hearing the news, internalizing it, and responding to it through armed resistance.

Zofia Kossak-Szczucka (1889–1968), a well-known Catholic writer and prewar antisemitic thinker, drew a moral distinction between murdering Jews and desiring a Poland free from economic, religious, and political problems,

---

28 At this time, Auschwitz was still designated for Polish prisoners.
29 Bartoszewski and Lewin, *The Samaritans: The Heroes of the Holocaust*, 4–5.
30 Ibid., 17.
31 Ibid., 7.
32 Yisrael Gutman and Shmuel Krakowski, *Unequal Victims: Poles and Jews During World War II*, trans. Ted Gorelick and Witold Jedlicki (New York: Holocaust Library, 1986), 157.
33 From a Warsaw March 1944 report by Yitzhak Cukierman which the Polish underground sent to London on May 24, 1944. Yad Vashem Archives, 0-25/96. See *Documents on the Holocaust: Selected Sources on the Destruction of the Jews of Germany and Austria, Poland, and the Soviet Union*, ed. Yitzhak Arad, Yisrael Gutman, and Abraham Margaliot (Jerusalem: Yad Vashem, in cooperation with the Anti-Defamation League and Ktav Publishing House, 1981), 277–278.

which she blamed on the excessively large Jewish population. Kossak-Szczucka founded a Catholic anti-fascist organization called the Front for the Rebirth of Poland (Front Odrodzenia Polski—FOP). The FOP focused on ethics, working toward "the moral rebirth of the nation." It also provided aid to the most needy, especially among the Jewish population.[34] Confronting the Warsaw Ghetto summer deportations, the FOP recognized death as the Jews' eventual fate. The FOP appealed to the collective conscience, calling the whole of society's attention to the ongoing atrocities against the Jews.

In the first days of August 1942, with Warsaw Ghetto deportations at their height, the FOP illegally printed and distributed through the Polish underground five thousand copies of a leaflet titled *PROTEST!* It reads in part:

> In the Warsaw Ghetto, behind walls that separate it from the outside world, several hundred thousand condemned await death. There is no hope of rescue, no help is coming from anywhere. The executioners race through the streets shooting at anyone who dares to leave their home. They shoot similarly to anyone who stands in a window. The unburied dead lie in heaps in the roadways.
>
> The daily list of requisitioned victims totals from 8–10 thousand. The Jewish Police are required to deliver them to the hands of the German executioners. If they do not fulfill this tally, they will be killed themselves. . . .
>
> . . . Wagons wait at the loading ramps. The deathsmen cram the condemned into them, up to 150 into a car. A thick layer of quicklime and chlorine dampened with water lies on the floor. [. . .] those dying slowly from the fumes of lime and chlorine [are] denied air, or a drop of water, or food—no one will survive. . . .
>
> . . . What is occurring in the Warsaw Ghetto has been occurring for the past half year in various smaller and larger cities of Poland. The total number of Jews killed already exceeds a million and the number enlarges with each passing day. Everyone dies. . . .

---

34 Maciej Kozłowski, *The Emissary: The Story of Jan Karski*, trans. Joanna Maria Kwiatowska (Warsaw: The Ministry of Foreign Affairs, 2007), 21.

> ... The world looks at this atrocity, more horrible than anything ever seen in the annals—and stays silent. The slaughter of millions of unarmed individuals is committed in the midst of a widespread, ominous silence.[35]

It is important to note that Kossak-Szczucka expressed her own antisemitic views in the leaflet: "Our feelings towards Jews have not changed. We have not stopped considering them the political, economic and conceptual enemies of Poland."[36] She viewed the rise of Jewish national politics a threat to her beloved Polish Catholic society; she regarded the overwhelming numbers of Jewish tradesmen, shopkeepers, and artisans as directly preventing the formation of a healthy and necessary Polish middle class. However, during the German occupation, she had the courage to prioritize this moral crisis over ideology. Speaking to the world watching in silence, she argued, "This silence cannot be tolerated any longer. [. . .] Who remains silent in the face of slaughter—becomes an enabler of the murderer. Who does not condemn—then consents."[37] Speaking as a Catholic Pole, Kossak-Szczucka warned that if Poland betrayed its ethical foundation it would be lost.

Kossak-Szczucka did not wait for someone else to save Poland's moral essence. In the same summer that *PROTEST!* was distributed, together with PPS activist Wanda Krahelska-Filipowicz (1886–1968) she formed a special agency under the leadership of the delegate of the government-in-exile to help Jews in occupied Poland. It evolved into the Council for Aid to Jews—its cryptonym Żegota. The council assisted Jews in hiding by locating apartments, providing money and clothing, and by making forged documents, such as identity cards, work cards, birth certificates, employment certificates, passes, and marriage certificates, all at no cost to the Jews.[38] It opened branches outside Warsaw, helping Jews in more rural areas. It set up a children's section, headed by the underground activist Irena Sendlerowa, which rescued some 2,500 Jewish children. It also operated a medical section to help Jews in hiding.[39] Though the government-in-exile funded

---

35 Zofia Kossak, "Protest!," in Kunert,*"Zegota": The Council for Aid to Jews 1942–1945 Selected Documents*, 77–79.
36 Ibid.
37 Ibid.
38 23 October 1943, Warsaw. Report on the Activity of the Council for Aid to Jews "Żegota" (Rada Pomocy Żydom "Żegota") at the office of the Minister Plenipotentiary/Delegate of the Government of the Republic of Poland to the Homeland (Pełnomocnik/Delegat Rządu RP na Kraj) for the period: December 1942-October 1943. 92.
39 Bartoszewski and Lewin, *The Samaritans: Heroes of the Holocaust*, 24.

Żegota, most of the required money was first raised from Jews living outside Eastern Europe and funneled by Polish underground couriers into the region of the General Government. While in January 1943 the government-in-exile provided the council with only 150,000 złoty, by August 1944 it offered two million, and in December 1944 it handed over six million.[40] In both populations—Polish and Jewish—there arose heroes and villains. One need only compare members of Żegota with the szmalcowniks to see that good and bad lived within each population at the same time.

We began this book by noting that whereas the righteous gentile Raoul Wallenberg was recognized early on for his activity, Irena Sendlerowa's efforts took much longer to receive the attention they deserve. Thanks to Kansas high school students and their teacher, the world has come to celebrate Sendlerowa. At the same time, Henryk Sławik (1894–1944), who has been dubbed the "Polish Wallenberg," is hardly known outside of Poland. A journalist and prewar member of the Polish Socialist Party, Sławik escaped occupied Poland. He crossed over into Hungary (with roughly 120,000 Polish refugees) where, as a representative of the Polish government-in-exile, he ran the Citizens' Committee for the Care of Polish Refugees in Hungary. Together with Hungarian Commissioner for Refugees József Antall, Sr. (1896–1974), he took care of some thirty thousand Polish refugees. In an orphanage created in Vac, he sheltered roughly one hundred Jewish orphans, claiming they were Polish officers' children. He rescued about five thousand Jewish refugees when he secured their escape from transportation to Nazi death camps. Denounced in 1944, Henryk Sławik was arrested, sent to Mauthausen-Gusen concentration camp, and murdered there. He never gave up the names of those who worked with him in these rescue efforts.[41]

Historiography and Polish Aid: The Underground and Government-in-Exile

Historiography is a tricky beast. Secret archives are opened and "new" documents are discovered. Historians ask some questions, but fail to ask others. Despite a desire for objectivity, subjectivity often insists on playing a role.

---

40   Ibid. 26–27.
41   Łukasz Kobiela, "Poles Rescuing Jews under German Occupation—Henryk Sławik," accessed August 31, 2023, https://ipn.gov.pl/en/news/7913,POLES-RESCUING-JEWS-UNDER-GERMAN-OCCUPATION-HENRYK-SLAWIK.html?search=515396.

Historians themselves are aware of these problems: they know that current understandings of the past could be upended by future revelations. It is the public that remains less aware of this never-ending process of writing history. Thus, the public holds as sacrosanct the "truths" presented in their own time, and cling to them despite new research. At the same time, when a specific point of a historian's theory is proven problematic, it is important not to reject their entire work.[42] This dynamic has appeared in discussions concerning Polish-Jewish relations during World War II. Just as Poles continue to wrestle with new information regarding Polish pogroms in the summer of 1941 and Polish participation in the Judenjagd, Jews too must grapple with recent insights which subvert the standard Jewish view of official Polish aid to the Jews during the Holocaust.

In his 1987 book *In the Shadow of Auschwitz: The Polish Government in Exile and the Jews, 1939–1942*, David Engel reacts to what at first appears as Polish reticence to share intelligence with the West concerning the Jews. Already in June 1942, the Polish government in London had details of the German plan to destroy Polish Jewry. Engel posits that the Poles chose not to share that intelligence with the British until December 1942 for several reasons. He theorizes that because a significant portion of the Polish electorate held antisemitic positions,[43] the government-in-exile could not be seen as putting Jewish needs before those of ethnic Poles who themselves were suffering under the Nazis.[44] Engel also proposes that Poles' feared that elevating the Jews' victimhood could override current world sympathy for the Poles; Polish officials had grown incensed and impatient with Jewish leaders publicizing complaints internationally about antisemitism in Poland, especially within the Polish army. The Jews' portrayal of a hostile Poland sullied its international reputation at a time when

---

42 David Engel has greatly improved our understanding of the dynamic between the Polish government-in-exile and the Western Jewish establishment, both sides' expectations and disappointments, as well as the role self-interest played for each party.

43 Jan Karski delivered a report in February 1940 to the government-in-exile then located in Angers, France. Karski, who had stolen into Soviet-held Poland, spoke with Polish underground sources regarding Polish-Jewish relations. They shared their perceptions of the positive reception "the Jews" gave the Red Army and "the Jews'" subsequent negative treatment of Catholic Poles. Though Karski states that one should not generalize about all Jews, he presents relations between the two groups in the Soviet-held eastern borderland as rather polarized. See David Engel, *In the Shadow of Auschwitz: The Polish Government-in-Exile and the Jews, 1939–1942* (Chapel Hill, The University of North Carolina Press, 1987), 60.

44 When Jan Karski suggested the need to create common cause with the Jews against the Nazi assault and division of the populace, he recognized that the government would be reticent to act jointly with Jewish leaders because it was fearful of losing the support of that part of the Polish constituency that was overtly antisemitic. See ibid., 63.

the nation needed global support to secure its future.[45] Hence, numerous reasons existed for the Poles' apparent decision to withhold critical information regarding the Jews.

Engel argues that the Poles changed their position only out of self-interest. (Importantly, he writes that the Jews too based their actions vis-à-vis the Poles' desperation out of Jewish self-interest.) While at first Polish leaders did not believe they needed Western Jewry as an ally, they shifted their position by the end of 1940. Engel contends that as they feared losing Poland's prewar eastern border to the Soviets, and believed international Jewish opinion could influence postwar political decisions,[46] the Poles attempted to win the sympathy of *Western* Jewry by demonstrating solidarity with and action on behalf of *Polish* Jewry.[47]

This negative perception of the government-in-exile has long been the accepted narrative among both Holocaust scholars and Jewish leaders. The historian Michael Fleming flips this narrative on its head when he examines Poland's entire intelligence transfer system, including the danger inherent in sending radio transmissions and working in Poland's courier system. To evade German capture, Poles severely limited the length of radio transmissions. For expansive reports, they enlisted couriers who crossed Europe by foot, rail, and plane to reach London. Fleming points out that between April 1, 1940, and April 1, 1943, just over 50% of official Polish reports sent to London were received. This number rose the following year to roughly 61%.[48] Of the total number of 114 reports sent to London throughout the war, seventy arrived. This data demonstrates the fragility of the intelligence relay system. It also provides perspective on the efforts made by the delegate to inform the West about the Jews' destruction: the Polish information that reached London between November 1942 and June 1944 included news of Germany's murder of the Jews at an average rate of two reports a month, which the Polish London government routinely passed to the Allies.[49]

---

45 Ibid., 102.
46 Ibid., 84, 93.
47 Engel holds that despite Western Jewish pressure, the Poles resisted releasing a statement affirming equal rights for Jews in postwar Poland. Per Engel they eventually acquiesced to a statement, known as the "Stańczyk declaration" (given it was written by Labor Minister Jan Stańczyk), because they realized that world leaders cared about how Poles treated the Jews. See ibid., 79–80.
48 Michael Fleming, *Auschwitz, Censorship and the Allies* (Cambridge: Cambridge University Press, 2014), 24.
49 Ibid., 27.

In his seminal work, Adam Puławski provides detailed documentary evidence of "the systematic, organized and structural nature of the Polish underground's effort to inform London of the ongoing Holocaust."[50] In fact, he demonstrates that alerting the Polish government-in-exile to the specific assault on Poland's Jews became a regular Polish Underground State activity. (However, he acknowledges that the central issue for the underground state and the government-in-exile remained the safety of Poland's ethnic Polish population.) Numerous unknown individuals made the dangerous trek across Europe to bring intelligence on the Jews' destruction to the West.[51] For an especially important report, the delegate would enlist multiple couriers, each secreting a copy along a different route at a different time to ensure that at least one copy arrived in London. By November 1942, multiple couriers, including Jan Karski, had transported the Bund's *Report on the Situation of the Jews in Poland*.[52] The document alerted Western leaders to Nazi massacres of Jews, new killing techniques employed at the Chełmno death camp, as well as Bund leaders' pleas for action.[53] The government-in-exile received at least one copy in July. Karski arrived November 15 with his eyewitness account of the Warsaw Ghetto.[54]

The question at hand is what did the Polish government-in-exile do with this intelligence?[55] Engel is right that the Polish government-in-exile was the principal vehicle through which news of Polish Jewry's situation under the Nazi regime could be relayed from the underground state. However, Fleming elaborates on the next step in disseminating such intelligence overlooked by Engel: the role

---

50 Michael Fleming, review of *Wobec "niespotykanego w dziejach mordu": Rząd RP na uchodźstwie, Delegatura Rządu RP na Kraj, AK a eksterminacja ludności żydowskiej od "wielkiej acji" do powstania w getcie warszawskim*, by Adam Puławski, American Association for Polish-Jewish Studies, accessed March 3, 2022, http://www.aapjstudies.org/index.php?id=262.
51 Ibid., 2–3.
52 The underground State's Bureau of Information and Propaganda had prepared a microfilm version of the Bund report for their curriers.
53 Ibid., 30.
54 David Engel, *Facing a Holocaust: The Polish Government-in-Exile and the Jews, 1943–1945* (Chapel Hill: The University of North Carolina Press, 1993), 16, fn9.
55 Fleming points out that many Holocaust scholars have blindly followed the relatively early analysis by Martin Gilbert (*Auschwitz and the Allies*, 1981) and Walter Laqueur (*The Terrible Secret: Suppression of the Truth about Hitler's "Final Solution,"* 1980) about when the West knew of and internalized the decimation of the Jews in Auschwitz. Gilbert stresses that the June 1944 Verba/Wetzler report, written by two Jewish escapees from Auschwitz—Rudolf Verba and Alfred Wetzler—gave the West its first full view picture of the Nazi death machine. Fleming upends this theory, and in so doing upends the assault on the Polish government-in-exile, by claiming that British (and American) censorship and antisemitism delayed public knowledge of Auschwitz and the Holocaust. See Fleming, *Auschwitz, Censorship and the Allies*, 2.

of British wartime censorship and how British antisemitism and antipolonism influenced it.⁵⁶ On July 25, 1941, Britain's Ministry of Information delineated what to publicize:

> It should not be too extreme. Sheer "horror" stuff such as the concentration camp torture stories [...] repel the normal mind. [...] A certain amount of horror is needed, but it must be used very sparingly and must deal always with treatment of indisputably innocent people. Not with violent political opponents. And not with Jews.⁵⁷

Indeed, the BBC followed this policy, and British officials often blocked information concerning Jews. For example, "the Polish representative, Count Baliński, repeatedly complained through 1942 and 1943 that information supplied by the Polish Government in Exile was not being broadcast and that texts were being cut."⁵⁸

The Polish government-in-exile responded to the reports on the deportation and mass killing of Jews. The Jewish representatives on the Polish National Council in London, the *Zionist* Ignacy Schwarzbart (1881–1961) and the Bundist Szmul Szygielbojm (1895–1943), forwarded information and wrestled with how to generate British press interest.⁵⁹ In early July 1942, the BBC related the Jews' situation, but failed to mention important details—including the fact that seven hundred thousand Jews had already been murdered. For Fleming, this "error" indicates British censorship. A week later, on July 9, 1942, the Polish government in London held a press conference to present all the facts relayed by the Bund regarding the dire situation facing the Jews in Europe, including the estimated number killed.⁶⁰ However, British censors determined what was reported. The government-in-exile also published that same month a pamphlet entitled *Stop them now. German mass-murders of Jews in Poland*.⁶¹ Additionally, on December 1, 1942, it released a four-page press bulletin on that summer's

---

56   Ibid., 35, 38.
57   Ibid., 58–59.
58   Ibid., 57.
59   Ibid., 177. That the Jewish community had representation on the council was quite remarkable given prewar antisemitism and the lack of much Jewish representation in other countries, including the US.
60   David S. Wyman, *The Abandonment of the Jews: America and the Holocaust 1941–1945*, (New York: Pantheon Books, 1984), 21.
61   Bartoszewski and Lewin, *The Samaritans: Heroes of the Holocaust*, 21.

deportations from the Warsaw Ghetto entitled *"Extermination of the Polish Jewry: What Happened in the Warsaw Ghetto."*[62]

The Polish National Council appealed to the Allies for joint efforts to end the extermination of the Jews. Minister Edward Raczyński (1891–1993) took the radical measure of sending a seven-page document to the Allied governments, dated December 10, 1942, about the "horrifying picture of the position to which the Jews in Poland have been reduced."[63]

> The new methods of mass slaughter applied during the last few months confirm the fact that the German authorities aim with systematic deliberation at the total extermination of the Jewish population of Poland and of the many thousands of Jews whom the German authorities have deported to Poland from Western and Central European countries and from the German Reich itself.[64]

He closed by stating his "confident belief" that the governments of the League of Nations would find "means offering the hope that Germany might be effectively restrained from continuing to apply her methods of mass extermination."[65] Four days later, he addressed the occupied Polish population via radio regarding the plight of the Jews.

The Polish politicians in London knew that it was in no military position to stop the Nazi death machinery; but it could bear witness to it and inform the world. It walked a tightrope, aware that the British Foreign Office typically buried news of German atrocities against Jews. As Poland needed UK support, the government-in-exile typically aligned with British Foreign Office policy. Thus, Poles had to determine whether the information it obtained concerning the Jews was momentous enough, and trustworthy enough, to challenge British policy.[66]

Raczyński's diplomatic note of December 10, 1942 proved of great significance. It formally brought the knowledge of the systematic attempt to annihilate Polish Jewry to the "civilized countries." David Engel contends that by confronting the

---

62   Kunert, *"Żegota": The Council for Aid to Jews 1942–1945 Selected Documents*, 72–76.
63   Republic of Poland, Ministry of Foreign Affairs, "The Mass Extermination of Jews in German Occupied Poland. Note addressed to the Governments of the United Nations on December 10th, 1942, and other documents, in Kunert, *"Żegota": The Council for Aid to Jews 1942–1945*, 101–108.
64   Ibid.
65   Ibid.
66   Fleming, *Auschwitz, Censorship and the Allies*, 53.

"special peril greater even than that faced by the Poles" the Polish government-in-exile "gave the issue of assistance to Jews a far greater urgency than it had ever possessed."[67] The Allies responded with a twelve-nation joint statement condemning the Nazi brutality. Beyond words, however, the Allies did not take further steps. The Polish government in London did its job. The Allies did not.[68]

Western Jewry's Support and the Changing War

Though Jews in Britain and the United States attempted to help their endangered brethren in the ghettos and camps, their efforts bore little fruit. During Jan Karski's December 1943 mission to the United States, he met not only with US government officials, including President Roosevelt, but also with America's Jewish leadership. Karski's meetings with Jewish heads yielded several national initiatives but minimal wartime results. The Reform Rabbi Stephen Wise brought a unified Jewish voice to this crisis by creating the Joint Emergency Committee on European Jewish Affairs (JEC), which represented seven American Jewish organizations. The JEC held forty rallies in twenty states to inform people of the Holocaust. It succeeded in creating a day of mourning that people observed throughout the country, and it achieved the promise of a postwar war crimes trial.[69] Additionally, the American Jewish Congress's March 1, 1943 demonstration in Madison Square Garden informed more than twenty thousand people about the plight of Jews under Hitler, while the rogue Committee for a Jewish Army's "We Will Never Die" pageant took its message to more than one hundred

---

67 Engel, *In the Shadow of Auschwitz: The Polish Government-in-Exile and the Jews, 1939–1942*, 10.
68 The Polish government in London continued to put pressure on the Allies to take action to save the remaining Jews in Europe. In April 1943 Karski wrote another pamphlet with world-renowned authors Aleksey Tolstoy and Thomas Mann, entitled *Terror in Europe: The Fate of the Jews*. They printed and distributed several thousand copies. Still the Allies did not act. Karski made another trip in the summer of 1943, this time to the United States. However, his meeting with President Roosevelt bore little fruit. See Kozłowski, *The Emissary: Story of Jan Karski*, 50.
69 The various Jewish organizations that constituted the JEC included the American Jewish Committee, the American Jewish Congress, B'nai B'rith, the Jewish Labor Committee, the Synagogue Council of America, Agudat Yisrael of America, the Union of Orthodox Rabbis, and the American Emergency Committee for *Zionist* Affairs. See Wyman, *The Abandonment of the Jews: America and the Holocaust 1941–1945*, 93.

thousand people.[70] However, American Jewish leaders were rather ineffectual at persuading the United States government to help European Jewry.

Indeed, despite the positive optics of a British-American refugee conference in Bermuda, very little came of it. The organizers did not invite Jewish representatives, nor did they consider the eleven-point rescue plan the JEC drew up. With only five press agents permitted, and the conference's conclusions kept secret, both countries intentionally thwarted a feared influx of Jewish refugees. Rabbi Israel Goldstein of the Synagogue Council of America charged that the "victims are not being rescued because the democracies do not want them."[71]

Poles have long believed that Western Jewry did little to help Polish Jews and that this lack of action was due to mistrusting the Polish messenger who brought news of the Holocaust. They understood American Jews as viewing Karski's efforts—and by extension the Polish government-in-exile's efforts—as propaganda to manipulate both American Jews and the US government into supporting the Polish State and its postwar agenda. However, while American Jewry, as a whole, did not trust the Polish government-in-exile, the lack of a US response to the situation did not result from Jewish Americans' inaction, but rather from their ineptitude. Their inability to persuade the US and Britain to rescue the remaining Jews in Europe drove many community leaders into despondency. Politically impotent, they quieted their requests lest they be viewed as anti-American.[72]

During the war's first year, American Jews supported Poland. They genuinely empathized with Polish suffering, seeing it as basically identical with their own, and recognized Poland as an important ally in the fight against Hitler. At this stage, Western Jews clamored for a Polish statement regarding postwar Jewish civil rights in a reconstituted state. However, the Polish government-in-exile was silent on the subject and put off any declaration in fear of alienating voters. Polish government officials were leery of making a statement in support of the Jews when they and their constituency had heard stories about Jews joining Soviets against the Poles in the kresy. Poland's position changed only after it concluded that Western Jews did in fact have international political influence.

---

70 Ibid., 90–91.
71 Ibid., 110–122.
72 Bartoszewski and Lewin, *The Samaritans: Heroes of the Holocaust*, 21; Wyman, *The Abandonment of the Jews: America and the Holocaust 1941–1945*, 122–123.

Thus, only on November 3, 1940 did Labor Minister Jan Stańczyk make a public statement in support of postwar Jewish civil rights.[73]

For American Jewry, this announcement was too little, too late. By April 1941, US Jews viewed the November statement as "nothing more than a paper promise."[74] Jewish leaders chose not to understand the substantial political risk that the government-in-exile had taken by publicly supporting Jewish interests at a time when stories from the East seemed to confirm Żydokomuna—that Jews were the backbone of the Soviet enemy. America's Jewish leadership missed the opportunity to demonstrate respect for this weighty internal Polish decision.

At the same time, Polish leaders did not grasp the Jews' intense need for a signal that the November announcement was meaningful.[75] Western Jewish leaders, and those Polish Jewish leaders who had fled Europe and made it to the United States, pressed the government-in-exile to eradicate antisemitism in the Polish army that had recently been formed from returning deportees to Russia. Although high-ranking officials had taken measures against antisemitism, lower ranked officers still permitted it. Learning of continued hatred of the Jews in the Polish armed forces, Western Jewish leaders believed the government-in-exile was not acting in good faith.[76] In the end, neither party got what it desired. Each expected too much from the other and was resentful.

Western Jewry completely changed its approach to Poland with the German invasion of the Soviet Union on June 22, 1941. Allied Jews shifted to align with the Soviets after the USSR joined the fight against Hitler because they perceived Stalin's large army as much more likely than the Poles to stop Hitler. They also believed that the Soviets would assume an influential role in both international and regional postwar politics, especially those affecting Jews.[77] Thus, the Jews remained quiet concerning Poland's desired postwar eastern border.

---

73 In stating that the present Polish government stood opposed to all antidemocratic political ideas, Stańczyk's remarks included a vision of postwar Poland's Jewish community: "The Jews, as Polish citizens, shall in liberated Poland be equal with the Polish community, in duties and in rights. They will be able to develop their culture, religion, and folkways without hindrance. Not only the laws of the state, but even more the common sacrifices on the way toward Poland's liberation and the common sufferings in this most tragic time of affliction will serve to guarantee this [pledge]." See Engel, *In the Shadow of Auschwitz: The Polish Government-in-Exile and the Jews, 1939–1942*, 80.
74 Ibid., 57–94.
75 Ibid., 93–94.
76 Ibid., 96, 100–102.
77 Ibid., 122.

With this shift, Western Jewish leaders fell into the Soviet trap of deflection regarding who should control the kresy after the war. In 1941, the Soviet-Polish Pact allowed Polish citizens who had been deported to the Soviet interior in 1939 to return to Poland. Yet few Polish citizens had returned. The Soviets explained: Jews wished to stay within Soviet borders and retain Soviet citizenship because Polish policy discriminated against them. (We have already seen that while the USSR had created a welcoming secular Yiddish culture, the authorities manipulated it as propaganda to Sovietize Jews.) In reality, the USSR had made it more difficult for Jewish Polish citizens than ethnic Poles to return to Poland.[78] Why would the Soviets work so hard during the war to keep Jews in Soviet-controlled territory? The Soviets used the Jews to claim that since "Soviet citizens" lived in the disputed borderlands that territory should be given to the Soviets at the end of hostilities.[79]

Just as the Poles had been reticent—out of self-interest—to embrace a partnership with the West's Jewish leadership, so too, out of self-interest, did Western Jewry's support for the Poles fluctuate. At various junctures during the war both Jews and Poles realized that they needed to ally with the Other; but neither fully understood the Other's complex position. This lack of understanding in turn led to a deepened mistrust of the Other. Furthermore, at different points during WWII both sides were so drunk with posturing about the postwar world that, though they met, they could not really see one another.

Jewish Councils

As we have seen, within one population there are heroes and villains, everyday people who respond to the same dire situation in grossly different ways. Within the wartime Jewish population, courageous people took part in a variety of resistance endeavors. These people included smugglers, clandestine chroniclers and gatherers of testimony, teachers in secrete schools and universities, underground writers and printers, escapees in hiding, as well as organizers of, and participants

---

78 When the Soviets invaded in 1939, they insisted that all people take Soviet citizenship. However, as opposed to ethnic Poles who could regain their Polish citizenship in 1941, kresy Jews were forced to retain Soviet citizenship.
79 Engel, *In the Shadow of Auschwitz: The Polish Government-in-Exile and the Jews, 1939–1942*, 130.

in, uprisings in ghettos and death camps.[80] Currently, it is toward this half-truth about Jewish heroics that American Jews gravitate. We are pulled much more readily to learning about Jewish resistance than toward considering questionable Jewish behavior within ghetto power structures.[81]

The collective American Jewish message has become one of pride in Jewish resistance. It is certainly a more appealing topic than the darker aspects of ghetto life. Students attending Jewish day school or afternoon Hebrew school learn about small and large acts of resistance within the ghettos—theater, libraries, underground newspapers, secret worship, welfare systems, medical facilities, and orphanages, as well as revenge schemes and armed opposition. In fact, when I interviewed American Jews who lived during the Holocaust, they themselves had forgotten long-ago Jewish communal debates over the major role Jewish ghetto leaders played in enforcing Nazi policies.[82] I had to give them evidence of the Jews' active part in the Nazis' twisted design, which they then recalled. Such people are not unique. Although I learned in college classes about this critical, if discomforting, aspect of our past, I had let the memory fade. I too had focused on Jewish resistance. Research for this book has reminded me that it is by embracing this complex past, which includes many Jews' moral failings, that history becomes more fully human.

On September 21, 1939, Reinhard Heydrich[83] issued a *schnelbrief* ordering the establishment of a Council of Jewish Elders (Judenrat; plural, Judenräte) in every Jewish community numbering ten thousand or more souls.[84]

---

80 A broad literature reviews forms of Jewish resistance to the Nazis. Nechama Tec has written extensively on the subject. Her book *Defiance* brought the three Bielski brothers and their forest refuge to print and screen. In his book *Jewish Resistance against the Nazis*, Patrick Henry looks at Jewish resistance throughout Europe and the Yishuv (Palestinian and Jewish community pre-Israel statehood).

81 In the 1960s, Raul Hilberg presented and Hannah Arendt popularized a hard line against the negative behavior of ghetto Jews with power. They argued that the Judenräte (plural of the word *Judenrat*) facilitated the Nazi repression and destruction of the Jewish people. Stunningly, the public embraced this position. In 1972, Isaiah Trunk offered a new, more nuanced, point of view. Instead of labeling ghetto chiefs as complicit in the murder of millions of Jews, Trunk strove to understand the unfathomable situation they were in, uncovering veiled attempts at resistance. On his telling, most of the Jewish ghetto leaders cooperated with Nazi mandates in order to save the remaining Jews in the ghetto. But most were not to the Nazis collaborators. American Jews have been fascinated with Jewish resistance ever since.

82 Author's interview with Sandra Katz (née Stark) and Arthur Stark, June 2019.

83 In 1934, Reinhard Heydrich was appointed head of the SD (Sicherheitsdienst), the Intelligence branch of the SS.

84 Arad, Gutman, and Margaliot, *Documents on the Holocaust: Selected Sources on the Destruction of the Jews of Germany and Austria, Poland, and the Soviet Union*, 173–178; emphasis Heydrich's.

Each Judenrat consisted of either twelve or twenty-four councilmen, depending on the size of the community. The Germans ordered prewar Jewish communal leaders to fill these positions. The interwar Jewish community boards—which had replaced the former kehillah structure—were filled primarily with assimilated Jews who had risen to community prominence due to wealth and access to Polish society: industrialists, doctors, and lawyers, by and large.

Connections to authority, rather than merit, qualified one for a job within the growing council bureaucracy. Thus, members of the Polish intelligentsia of Jewish descent who had been moved into the ghetto, sat with assimilated Jewish professionals behind Jewish council desks, pushed paper, and signed orders.[85] In ghetto life the assimilated reigned over the traditional. Given that those with power had access to much higher living standards, community tensions and further fragmentation followed. Certainly, some council members maintained strong connections to the people they served. However, most ghetto inhabitants felt abandoned by those at the top.[86]

One could argue that the Judenräte had a dual—contradictory—mission: to serve the Jews and to fulfill Nazi orders. Each council was "made *fully responsible*, in the literal sense of the word, for the exact and prompt implementation of directives already issued or to be issued in the future."[87] In his September 21, 1939 directive to all Einsatzgruppen of the Security Police, Heydrich demanded that the Jews, themselves take a census of their population, breaking it down according to age, gender, and occupation. In this same order, Heydrich directed the Council of Jewish Elders to be financially responsible for both the evacuation of the Jews from the annexed territories and resettlement in the various cities administrated by the General Government. It should not be surprising then that ghetto populations perceived Judenräte officials as the face of Nazi policy.[88]

Jewish community leaders were conflicted about whether to oppose the order to organize an administration that answered to the Germans. Of those prewar Jewish leaders who did not escape Poland and who the Nazis first charged with directing the Jewish councils, some refused participation in the Nazi government structure. They suffered serious consequences. The Germans shot many

---

85 Katarzyna Person, *Assimilated Jews in the Warsaw Ghetto, 1940–1943* (Syracuse: Syracuse University Press, 2014), 58.
86 Ibid., 40.
87 This same document ordered the expulsion of Jews from the Reich's newly annexed Polish territories. See Arad, Gutman, and Margaliot, *Documents on the Holocaust: Selected Sources on the Destruction of the Jews of Germany and Austria, Poland, and the Soviet Union*, 173.
88 Polonsky, *The Jews in Poland and Russia*, 3:477.

on the spot, arrested others, and deported some with their families.[89] In the end, the Germans filled the councils with much less honorable representatives. However, numerous prewar Jewish community leaders, including Adam Czerniaków (1880–1942), acquiesced to Nazi demands, believing it their duty to help their people through the crisis.

Jewish Council Collaboration with the Nazi Authorities

Per Heydrich's plan, since the majority of the ghetto population experienced the Judenrat as the effective legitimate government, they often blamed it—not the Germans—for the oppression they experienced.[90] Heinz Auerswald's November 24, 1941 letter to Berlin spoke of the success of the Nazi strategy: "When conflicts occur in the Ghetto, the Jewish population directs their discontentment primarily against the Jewish administration, not the German authorities."[91] Each Judenrat had been charged with providing all infrastructure needs, including housing, sanitation, water, gas, and electricity to the ever-expanding and impoverished ghetto population. It also distributed the meager food supplies permitted by the Germans. Thus, ghetto inmates saw Judenrat functionaries as responsible for the constant lack of necessities, such as coal and food. The Judenräte were Nazi tools of deflection and division.

Judenräte officials were at an extreme disadvantage. While Nazi policy expected Jewish leaders to extract payment for all maintenance from the Jews it also stipulated the banning of most Jews from work and the confiscation of their businesses and money.[92] Through taxes, Jewish councils were responsible for feeding, clothing, and housing not only their immediate communities but also the overwhelming influx of impoverished refugees. Each Judenrat would pay with commandeered valuables Jews still possessed and permitted bank withdrawals. The people blamed council members for the unending and unjust taxation—payroll taxes, head taxes, taxes on rationed bread, payments for exemption from forced labor, rental taxes, cemetery taxes, postal surcharges,

---

89 Isaiah Trunk, *Judenrat: The Jewish Councils in Eastern Europe under Nazi Occupation* (New York: Macmillan, 1972), 20–21.
90 Ibid., 528.
91 Letter of 24 November 1941 from Heinz Auerswald to Juliusz von Medeazza, Hans Frank plenipotentiary in Berlin. Cited in Katarzyna Person, *Policemen: An Image of the Jewish Order Service in the Warsaw Ghetto*, chapter 6, fn18 (forthcoming).
92 Trunk, *Judenrat: The Jewish Councils in Eastern Europe under Nazi Occupation*, 61–72.

and fees for drugs and registration.[93] For the people, the Judenräte represented everything vile in the ghettos.

One particular ghetto hardship terrorized Jews—forced labor. On October 26, 1939, the Nazi authorities commanded the Judenräte to impose forced labor on all Jewish men fourteen to sixty years of age.[94] In almost every ghetto, there quickly arose a "voluntary" tax for exemption from this slavery. These funds paid for forced labor substitutions. Although the ransom provided those too poor to escape forced labor with their only source of income,[95] they often died due to harsh conditions. Ghetto inmates quickly came to resent not only the Jewish council's roundups of forced laborers, but also the fact that the poor paid the highest tax of all by having to serve in these brigades:[96] "[O]nly poor Jews are doing compulsory labor; the rich twist out of it."[97]

Prewar Jewish national political activists (often Yiddish secularists) also drew a stark divide between themselves as Jewish leaders and those sitting on the councils. In the Warsaw Ghetto, Jewish nationalists (as discussed earlier, Bundists and members of varying *Zionist* groups, who advocated speaking Yiddish and Hebrew respectively) often fought the council, which was filled with Polish speakers. Attempting to establish their own control, Jewish nationalists organized grass-roots efforts. Of most interest is Self-Help, popularly known by its Yiddish name Aleynhilf. It provided soup kitchens and medical aid, nurtured Jewish identity,[98] and supported Emmanuel Ringelblum's Oyneg Shabbos Archive, which documented Jewish life in the Warsaw Ghetto.[99] However, Aleynhilf fell short because it lacked the power to tax those Jews who still possessed resources to pay for expanding aid to the poor.[100]

---

93 Raul Hilberg and Stanislaw Staron, introduction to Adam Czerniaków, *The Warsaw Diary of Adam Czeriaków: Prelude to Doom*, ed. Raul Hilberg, Stanislaw Staron, and Josef Kermisz, trans. Stanslaw Staron and the Staff of Yad Vashem (Chicago: Elephant Paperback in association with the United States Holocaust Memorial Museum, 1999), 92.
94 Trunk, *Judenrat: The Jewish Councils in Eastern Europe under Nazi Occupation*, 242.
95 Ibid.
96 Ibid., 534.
97 Emmanuel Ringelblum, *Notes from the Warsaw Ghetto: The Journal of Emmanuel Ringelblum*, ed. and trans. Jacob Sloan (New York: Schocken Books, 1984), 37.
98 Given that many assimilationist council leaders had ignored their Jewish religious, cultural, and political identity, Aleynhilf nurtured it within the ghetto as a form of opposition to the Jewish councils.
99 Katarzyna Person, *Assimilated Jews in the Warsaw Ghetto, 1940–1943* (Syracuse: Syracuse University Press, 2014), 86–87.
100 Ibid., 92.

Perception obscures reality. Necessarily biased, it usually ignores relevant information either by choice or mistake. When exploring Jewish council members' responses to circumstances confronting and confounding them, it is essential that one recall the unprecedented situation the Judenräte faced. Given their role in serving the Nazi overlords, they could hardly fulfill the ghetto inhabitants' needs.

The Jewish Councils' Agendas Shift

One study by Abraham Weiss attempts an objective review of Judenräte behavior vis-à-vis the Jewish community they ostensibly served. Weiss finds that until that time when it was clear that Jews would be deported to their deaths, Judenräte officials tried to aid the Jews in their charge more often than not.[101] Weiss notes four patterns of possible behavior: complete noncooperation with the Nazis; cooperation regarding property, but noncooperation in delivering people for deportation; sacrificing the lives of some people in the hope of saving others; and full cooperation with the Nazis in the hope of saving their own lives. The study concludes that during the first stage of ghetto existence, 68.7% of Jewish council leaders behaved "positively." At this point, the majority cooperated with the Nazi authorities when they believed Jews could be saved, either through intercessions and bribery or making Jews useful to the German war economy. Weiss's work shows that 21% acted "negatively" and 17.1% in an "intermediate" way.[102] In this vein, many council chiefs who struggled with Nazi-imposed famines—designed to murder ghetto Jews slowly through starvation and related diseases—collaborated with Nazi officials to create ghetto industries that would support the German war effort. To feed the people and save Jewish lives, they put Jews to work for their oppressors.

In the Warsaw Ghetto, roughly sixty-one thousand Jews out of nearly half a million worked for German and Jewish manufacturers producing leather products, adding machines, clothing, mattresses, shoes, furs, furniture, uniforms, toys, and cosmetics, as well as electrical, mechanical, and photographic products.[103] Judenräte officials, also including those in Łodz and Kovno, reasoned

---

101 Polonsky, *The Jews in Poland and Russia*, 3:479. For his study, Abraham Weiss analyzed 146 council leaders during the first period of the war, and one hundred in the second period.
102 Ibid.
103 Hilberg and Staron, introduction to *The Warsaw Diary of Adam Czerniaków: Prelude to Doom*, 51–53.

that if the Nazis needed the Jews, the Nazis would feed those workers, thus sustaining them physically until the Allied victory. (The unemployed majority, however, remained highly vulnerable.) Given that assimilated Jews filled most Judenräte seats, the assimilated intelligentsia received these supposed life-saving work assignments, not traditional Jews.

This same study points to a marked reversal of Judenräte behavior in the second stage of ghetto existence—when council elders knew the deportation trains led to death camps. In this stage, 60.4% of Jewish leaders chose to respond negatively towards their charges: they filled the trains with Jews bound for death in order to save their own lives. Meanwhile, 29.6% of the leadership continued to make positive decisions and 10% acted between the two extremes. This changed approach by council heads was also due to the Nazis already having replaced many of the first-tier leaders.

The Nazi's killed numerous Judenräte leaders—due to either their unwillingness or physical inability to comply with orders. The Nazis arrested Ignatz Buchner, the first chairman of the Judenrat in Zawiercie (eastern Upper Silesia), and sent him and his family to Auschwitz in the summer of 1942. He had opposed cooperating with the Germans and protested against crimes committed by other functionaries, such as wanton bribery.[104] The Nazis murdered Lviv's first council chairman, Dr. Joseph Parnas, for refusing to deliver several thousand Jews ostensibly required for forced labor.[105] The Nazis deported the lawyer Adolf Weinberg, chairman of the Dąbrowa council (eastern Upper Silesia), with his family, after he refused to provide a list of "resettlement" candidates and to tell the authorities where some people were hiding.[106] Often less honorable characters filled emptied positions.

Some of those first drafted into Judenräte service, but who resisted extreme collaboration, took their own lives. The assimilated Jewish engineer Adam Czerniaków, head of the Warsaw Ghetto Judenrat, realized that he had underestimated the degree of Nazi barbarism. Despite his collaboration by procuring Jewish workers for ghetto industries that served the German war effort, the Nazis continued to request thousands of Jews for deportations. Czerniaków chose suicide in an act of defiance. It has been reported that before swallowing potassium cyanide, he wrote two letters. In his last message to his wife, he expressed his anguish about giving in to SS pressure; he believed that he had, in

---

104 Trunk, *Judenrat: The Jewish Councils in Eastern Europe under Nazi Occupation*, 439.
105 Ibid., 437.
106 Ibid., 441.

effect, killed Warsaw's Jewish children with his own hands.[107] To the council, he wrote: "I am powerless, my heart trembles in sorrow and compassion. I can no longer bear all this. My act will show everyone the right thing to do."[108] What exactly Adam Czerniaków hoped to accomplish through his suicide we do not know for certain. But his words indicate a desire for defiant action.

The Łodz Ghetto chief Chaim Rumkowski[109] (1877–1944) took an even more radical approach to the same situation. For Rumkowski, extreme collaboration paved a way to community preservation. In his address to the Jewish public on September 4, 1942, he pleaded,

> [i]n my old age I am forced to stretch out my hands and to beg: "Brothers and sisters, giver them to me!—Fathers and mothers, give me your children..." (Bitter weeping shakes the assembled public.) ... Yesterday in the course of the day, I was given the order to send away more than 20,000 Jews from the ghetto, and if I did not—"we will do it ourselves." The question arose: "Should we have accepted this and carried it out ourselves, or left it to others?" But as we were guided not by the thought: "how many will be lost?" but "how many can be saved?" we arrived at the conclusion—those closest to me at work, that is, and myself—that however difficult it was going to be, we must take upon ourselves the carrying out of this decree. I must carry out this difficult and bloody operation, I must cut off limbs in order to

---

107 Hilberg and Staron, introduction to *The Warsaw Diary of Adam Czerniaków: Prelude to Doom*, 70.
108 Quoted in Hilberg and Staron, introduction to *The Warsaw Diary of Adam Czerniaków: Prelude to Doom*, 23.
109 In book one of the trilogy *The Tree of Life*, mid-twentieth century Yiddish writer Chava Rosenfarb depicts Chaim Rumkowski as a broken man prior to the war. A childless widower who heads an orphanage, in the book Rumkowski makes abhorrent secreted sexual advances on girls under his care. Impatient with everyone, he is an impulsive and jealous man whose temper flares easily and without concern for the pain he causes. He is a powerless man outside of his orphanage, always asking the wealthy Jewish men of Łodz to donate to maintain it. Most Jewish communal leaders do not like him and avoid him. In this text, he is elevated to lead the Judenrat because of his thirst for power, which the Nazi authorities believe can be manipulated. See Chava Rosenfarb, *The Tree of Life: A Trilogy of Life in the Łodz Ghetto*, book 1, *On the Brink of the Precipice, 1939*, trans. Chava Rosenfarb and Goldie Morgentaler (Madison: The University of Wisconsin Press, Terrace Books, 1985), 85–102, 245–253.

save the body! I must take away children, and if I do not, others too will be taken, God forbid ... (terrible wailing).[110]

Although he convinced himself that sending off the children would save those who had a better chance of surviving the war, in the end the remaining ghetto inhabitants met their death at Chełmno—Rumkowski among them.[111]

Systemic Ghetto Corruption and Demoralization

While some who accepted leadership roles within the Jewish councils did so out of moral obligation to the Jewish community, many who ascended to power did so for self-advancement. There exist numerous examples of Jews working within the vast Judenräte bureaucracies who ignored the duality of their mission. They manipulated misfortune not only to preserve themselves and their families, but also to achieve social and economic status.[112] They received broad protections, including better housing, larger food rations, and immunity for themselves and their families from both forced labor and random home searches[113] As the Nazis eliminated the top-tier leadership, however, more room emerged for immoral practices. In some cases, even first-choice leaders welcomed the new value system.

Another testimony[114] charges that Dr. F. S., a physician and member of the Baranowicze Judenrat and chief of its sanitation department, "together with two other members, A. and B., informed, collaborated, and entertained lavishly at

---

110 Chaim Rumkowski, "Rumkowski's Address at the Time of the Deportation of the Children from the Łodz Ghetto, September 4, 1942," in Arad, Gutman, and Margaliot, *Documents on the Holocaust: Selected Sources on the Destruction of the Jews of Germany and Austria, Poland, and the Soviet Union*, 283.
111 Some believe Rumkowski's strategy would have prevailed had the war ended earlier; unfortunately, it did not. Polonsky, *The Jews in Poland and Russia*, 3:490.
112 Trunk, *Judenrat: The Jewish Councils in Eastern Europe under Nazi Occupation*, 360.
113 Polonsky, *The Jews in Poland and Russia*, 3:477.
114 In another example of corruption, this time in the Siedlce Judenrat, an eyewitness testified regarding the vice chairman, C.: "As soon as the Council was established, he instantly upgraded his standard of living. [...] The fact that all of a sudden large amounts of money came into his hands, and that other opportunities also came his way, simply turned his head. He believed that he had limitless powers and took advantage of his position, profiting by the general misery. He took a lion's share of the large sums of money and jewelry which were entrusted to him for safekeeping against a time of emergency when it would be necessary to pay off the Germans." It has been questioned whether the Jewish council vice chairman in

the expense of the starving community."[115] It further states that "[i]n company with policemen, Dr. F. S. searched out and beat-up Jews who had hidden themselves with the intention of joining the partisans."[116]

Numerous councils enlarged their networks to meet the needs of a continued influx of refugees, as well as to provide some sort of protection for the new hires. The Jewish community bureaucratic system in Warsaw swelled from 532 prewar functionaries to 1,741 by July 1940. Prior to the July 1942 deportation, it surged to over six thousand staff. By early August 1942, it peaked at the unwieldy number of 9,030 employees.[117] With such an expanded operation, the ghetto leadership could not quash the sweeping corruption, especially since the most grievous corruption existed at the top. Numerous councilmen held silent partnerships in the myriad nightclubs, cafes, and brothels run by the Jewish underworld (which itself had ties to the Gestapo).[118] Bribery, patronage, and nepotism were rife not only in the Warsaw Ghetto, but also in most ghettos.[119] Money and connections to powerful people were invaluable, keeping suffering at bay. Many leaders got caught in the Nazi power web, harming other Jews to increase their own power and chance of survival.

The most common form of corruption was bribery. The Warsaw Ghetto archivist and political leftist Emmanuel Ringleblum raged: "You have to bribe the mailman for your mail. Janitor service costs three hundred zlotys; mail, five hundred zlotys. Every service has a charge... A gang of operators and swindlers, and there's no control over them."[120] The disparity between rich and poor expanded exponentially, as almost every physical need was met through taxes and bribery. The wealthy could buy their lives; the poor were doomed.

---

this case was Hersh Eisenberg. Trunk, *Judenrat: The Jewish Councils in Eastern Europe under Nazi Occupation*, 448–449, 637, fn194.
115 Ibid., 447.
116 Ibid.
117 Hilberg and Staron, introduction to *The Warsaw Diary of Adam Czerniaków: Prelude to Doom*, 43.
118 Person, *Assimilated Jews in the Warsaw Ghetto, 1940–1943*, 64.
119 Trunk, *Judenrat: The Jewish Councils in Eastern Europe under Nazi Occupation*, 354.
120 Ringelblum, *Notes from the Warsaw Ghetto: The Journal of Emmanuel Ringelblum*, 107.

Ghetto Poverty and Disease

Without funds, the majority of ghetto inhabitants lived in overcrowded and squalid conditions with little heat in the winters. They battled vermin—bed bugs, cockroaches, lice. Despite scorching them with boiling water, ammonia, and hot irons, people's clothes and hair teamed with lice. Bogdan Wojdowski, who spent two years as a child in the Warsaw Ghetto, recounts:

> [T]he lice keep on multiplying. They gather on the wall in a prominent place, fall onto the bed on their backs and clumsily paw at the air with their little feet until they turn over onto their bellies, and then, indefatigably, they come closer seeking warmth, shelter on human skin, and blood.[121]

Ghetto housing contracted as the Nazis flooded it with refugees. Such crammed confines provided the ideal breeding grounds for lice-born typhus. On July 1, 1941, Czerniaków noted that "[w]ith a corpse in the entrance of an apartment house, the lice spread through the entire building."[122]

Starvation also concerned ghetto inmates daily. In his remarkable portrayal of the Warsaw Ghetto, Wojdowski describes the pervasive, constant, and crippling hunger: "The darkness that enveloped his mind, the cold that made his body stiff, the gnawing in his stomach merged into a single entity: hunger. First comes fear of expending any energy, then nervous rage, and finally apathy, quiet, blissful indifference, and the first signs of starvation."[123] Starvation descended first on those refugees from the eastern regions, who had neither shelter nor work, and who were forced into begging: "The naked skeletons shook their begging tins, cried out, and stuck their legs out in front of passersby. They were rotting in the sunshine, and blue flies kept landing on their sticky wounds. Here, people became carrion while they were still alive."[124] Despite efforts to combat it, the ghetto could not conquer starvation.

In the Warsaw Ghetto, Adam Czerniaków faced these crushing forces. He placed a copy of a July 22, 1941 inspection report in his journal:

---

121 Bogdan Wojdowski, *Bread for the Departed*, trans. Madeline G. Levine and Henryk Grynberg (Evanston: Northwestern University Press, 1997), 198.
122 Hilberg and Staron, introduction to *The Warsaw Diary of Adam Czerniaków*, 54.
123 Bogdan Wojdowski, *Bread for the Departed*, 208.
124 Ibid., 96.

> In front of 16 Krochmalna Street I was stopped by a commander of a military sanitary column and shown the corpse of a child in an advanced stage of decay.... [I]t was established that the body was left behind by its own mother, Chudesa Borensztajn, residing at 14 Krochmalna Street apartment 67, and that the child's name was Moszek, age 6. In the same apartment there was the body of Malka Ruda, age 43.... [T]he child's mother Chudesa Borensztajn testified in the presence of the commander of the sanitary column that she had abandoned the corpse because the Community Authority refuses to bury anyone without payment, and that the child had died and she will soon die precisely because she had no money. It was ascertained that the child had indeed died of hunger and the mother's extremities are swollen from starvation.[125]

A cyclical deluge tormented the bulging and impoverished ghetto population. Hunger and lice infestations led to starvation and typhus, which led to death, which led to decaying bodies (due to lack of burial funds), which led to more disease and more death. The ghetto population was besieged from all sides.

Some Jews committed suicide.[126] Others chose to adapt to the outrageous "new normal" by burying their prewar moral compasses. Some sunk so low as to blackmail fellow Jews and become informants for the Gestapo. A number helped the Nazi authorities locate Jewish shops and Jews in hiding.[127] On May 11, 1941, Ringelblum admitted that Jews were afraid of one another: "The demoralization of the Jews of Warsaw is frightful. It has reached the point where, when two Jews meet, one says to the other; 'One of us must be serving the Gestapo!'"[128] Abraham Gancwajch (1902–1943) was one such collaborator in the Warsaw Ghetto.

Gancwajch co-headed a force of some five hundred Jewish men known as the "Thirteen" due to its address at 13 Lezno Street. With the official title, Control Office for Combatting the Black Market and Profiteering in the Jewish District,

---

125 Adam Czerniaków, *The Warsaw Diary of Adam Czerniaków: Prelude to Doom*, ed. Raul Hilberg, Stanislaw Staron, and Josef Kermisz, trans. Stanislaw Staron and the Staff of Yad Vashem (Chicago: Elephant Paperback in association with the United States Holocaust Memorial Museum, 1999), 261–262.
126 Ibid., 205.
127 Ringelblum, *Polish-Jewish Relations during the Second World War*, 41.
128 Ringelblum, *Notes from the Warsaw Ghetto: The Journal of Emmanuel Ringelblum*, 175.

its informants and agents provided information to the Nazis.[129] Set up in the autumn of 1940, the "Thirteen" extorted ghetto businesses and controlled smuggling operations. It remained the only institution in the Warsaw Ghetto not subordinate to the Judenrat.[130] Instead, it answered to the Germans. While corruption flowered under Czerniaków's watch, he himself was known as a decent man who did not take particular advantage of his role. Gancwajch, on the other hand, often requisitioned items from Jews for his own benefit, made numerous threats, and threw parties, which Germans attended along with powerful Jews.[131] Gancwajch reportedly made several attempts to take over the Judenrat, and at some point the council considered him for vice president. Having written in his diary about Gancwajch at least thirty times between April 1941 and August of that same year, it is clear that the threat Gancwajch posed consumed Czerniaków as much as the danger of hunger, disease, and deportation.

The Jewish Order Service: Corruption

Prior to resettling Jews into a ghetto, the Nazis ordered the formation of not only a Judenrat but also a Jewish Order Service—Jüdisher Ordnungsdient. Also known as the Jewish Ghetto Police, it fell under Jewish council control. Its mission was to maintain order within the Jewish population as the Germans imposed vast transformations. At first, ghetto inhabitants welcomed the service, seeing in its unarmed force a more palatable presence than the Polish Blue Police or Gestapo. However, they soon came to resent this new Jewish authority.[132]

The traditionalist majority in each ghetto viewed the Jewish Order Service as a foreign element, given that most of its members were either assimilated or former Jews who had been baptized. In the Warsaw Ghetto, for example, the first superintendent of the Jewish Ghetto Police, Colonel Józef Szeryński, was baptized and in the prewar Polish police. Szeryński surrounded himself with other Christian converts, establishing baptized Jews as the elite of the ghetto police. Most others who entered the force did so through connections and bribery. Thus, in contradistinction to the general populace, the Warsaw Ghetto Jewish Order Service was filled with converts, assimilationists, and people who entered

---

129 Hilberg and Staron, introduction to *The Warsaw Diary of Adam Czerniaków*, 44.
130 Person, *Assimilated Jews in the Warsaw Ghetto, 1940–1943*, 68.
131 Czerniaków, *The Warsaw Diary of Adam Czerniaków*, 234.
132 Person, *Assimilated Jews in the Warsaw Ghetto, 1940–1943*, 75.

the ghetto with wealth. It demonstrated the fundamental "us" versus "them" ghetto dynamic.

The populace reviled the service, especially for its enforcement of Nazi policy. The Jewish ghetto policemen ensured that people paid their endless stream of taxes, that housing blocks followed the disastrous protocol for typhus disinfection, and individuals produced property for confiscation.[133] Jews' bitterness grew when they saw their own with legal power, able to use physical force against other Jews.[134] The historian Katarzyna Person dissects the nuanced relationship between the Jewish police and ghetto Jews in her masterful book *Policemen: An Image of the Jewish Order Service in the Warsaw Ghetto*. She cites an anonymous police officer who stated, "[People] could not believe [. . .] that some distant friend of theirs, their relative, a son or a son-in-law of their neighbor, was allowed to give them commands, mistreat them, push them around."[135] Reflective of the populace's grievances with this new Jewish power structure were the numerous hateful rumors spread about its members.

Unlike earlier historians who accepted survivors' testimonies about the Jewish Ghetto Police as the whole truth, Person has a more complex understanding of it. She describes the great discrepancy between high-ranking officers and the common service members. Jewish men joined the Jewish Order Service to secure a job at a time when Jews had been robbed of most earning opportunities. To their dismay, however, the rank-and-file went without pay for long periods, leaving their families hungry and vulnerable. Person gives Tadeusz Witelson as an example: "For a year and a half or longer I have been working [for free], our children are starving and freezing, we are formally dying from exhaustion, lack of vitamins and food, while our managers and commanders get salaries for themselves, and they tell us to survive on . . . air!"[136] Person also points out that while high-level police were in a good position to receive bribes to ignore smuggling operations "over the wall" and "protect" small businesses, the rank-and-file saw little of these earnings.[137]

Over time, however, lower ranked police gained access to bribery rights. Officers conceded this reward and created a culture of plenty and envy, luring others in the service to participate. Such permission, coupled with an internal moral shift, enabled the police to rationalize their actions. They justified their

---

133 Ibid., 60–62.
134 Person, *Policemen: An Image of the Jewish Order Service in the Warsaw Ghetto*, chapter 6, p. 1.
135 Ibid., 2.
136 Ibid., 3.
137 Person, *Assimilated Jews in the Warsaw Ghetto, 1940–1943*, 77.

immorality: not only did they risk their lives by working in such proximity to the German military police—who harassed them—they also worked harder than officers, who got paid much more than they did.[138] Separated from the main populace due to their work, Jewish Order Service members relied on one another for validation of their individual behavior.

It is noteworthy that a legal office functioned within the Jewish Order Service to assess its members' actions. Though in theory the Order and Disciplinary Section (Referat Porządkowo Dyscyplinarny) introduced some transparency into the Jewish police force, its legal functionaries covered up the abuse at the top. Testimonies berate the section, particularly its leaders who reviewed all Judenrat misconduct, for focusing on minor offenses committed by the rank-and-file while ignoring the excessive fraud perpetrated by police elite.[139] All of the attempts to introduce order were "dramatically inadequate when compared to the scale of the fraud committed by the Order Service."[140] Additionally, not only did the service widen the Nazi-imposed divide between "us" and "them," its failed attempts at justice also expanded the internal divide within the Jewish Order Service itself.

At the same time, Jewish men applied to work for the Jewish Ghetto Police for both its perks and relative power. They accessed better living conditions and more food than regular ghetto inmates. Policemen were exempt from curfew, forced labor, paying imposed communal contributions, and from deportations to labor camps.[141] Though still hungry, underpaid, and for long periods unpaid, they were important to maintaining the ghetto power structure.

The Jewish Order Service: Forced Labor and Deportation Quotas

Prior to the Germans' initiation of ghetto deportations, the most terrifying order enforced by the Jewish Order Service entailed filling forced labor quotas. Although some probably found this task terribly problematic, soon the Jewish Ghetto Police concluded that "it is better to catch than be caught."[142]

---

138 Person, *Policemen: An Image of the Jewish Order Service in the Warsaw Ghetto*, chapter 6, pp. 5–7.
139 Ibid., chapter 7, p. 4.
140 Ibid. 5.
141 Trunk, *Judenrat: The Jewish Councils in Eastern Europe under Nazi Occupation*, 488; Polonsky, *The Jews in Poland and Russia*, 3:477.
142 Person, *Policemen: An Image of the Jewish Order Service in the Warsaw Ghetto*, chapter 6, p. 8.

Person writes that during the roundups in spring 1941 and spring 1942, the Warsaw Jewish Order Service acted severely against fellow Jews on labor lists. They caught men on the streets, surrounded apartment blocks, and dragged people out of their homes in the middle of the night. Witnesses, such as pianist Władysław Szpilman, recall service members imitating the Germans' loud and brutal shouting and beating Jews with rubber truncheons.[143]

In the Warsaw Ghetto, the first stage of forced labor roundups sent Jews daily out of the ghetto and into local areas from whence they returned in the evening. Yet, beginning in August 1940 Jews were transferred further away to labor camps. Most of these employed torture. A letter from prisoners of the Tyszowice labor camp to the Warsaw Jewish Council expressed their harrowing situation:

> We are beaten and maltreated and, added to this, we are in mourning for three of our colleagues who died a tragic death—executed by shooting... Here the freezing temperature falls as low as minus 10–12 degrees, and we stand waist-high in water. We have been eaten alive by lice and an epidemic is unavoidable. We are half dead with hunger. It is high time to end this torture. We now face a winter camp, which we are not likely to survive. It is you who will bear responsibility for this.[144]

"[T]he never-ending crying of mothers of the workers in the camps begging for help"[145] haunted the Warsaw Jewish Council elder Adam Czerniaków. And though those enslaved blamed Judenrat officials for not doing enough on their behalf, they also reviled the Jewish Order Service for enforcing this harshest of policies.

By the time the Nazis commenced ghetto Aktions, the service had widened the chasm between "us" and "them" through bribery and violence. Policemen closed ranks, seeking acceptance and validation for their behavior from within their group. This is especially true during deportations: the Jewish Order Service employed violence not only to pacify the crowds of agitated and scared Jews, but also to draw an impregnable boundary between the captives and themselves. In part, violence defined their belonging to the service.

---

143 Person, *Assimilated Jews in the Warsaw Ghetto, 1940–1943*, 76.
144 Ibid., 60.
145 Czerniaków, *The Warsaw Diary of Adam Czerniaków*, 212.

According to the noted historian Isaiah Trunk, the Jewish Ghetto Police everywhere, to a larger or lesser degree, physically enforced the Nazi "resettlement" Aktions and the terrifyingly brutal measures that accompanied them.[146] Trunk describes the ruthlessness of most as a combination of environmental influences and individual tendencies. Person acknowledges the negative impact "the poisoned ghetto environment ... [and] constant struggle for bare physical survival"[147] had on the Jewish Ghetto Police. However, unlike Trunk, Person holds that given such an environment most individuals would have eventually fallen into disgrace. By their very belonging to the Jewish Order Service or the Judenräte, members "cut themselves off from the people, becoming instruments of the Nazis."[148]

Calek Perechodnik[149] (1916–1944), an Otwock Ghetto Jewish policeman, confronted this moral decay as it related to participating in an Aktion:

> The Jewish police receive the order to provide the people for the square. The police, numbering two thousand, go about their task vigorously. Each one congratulates himself that he had the good sense to sign himself up for the police, secure in himself and his family. Everyone is certain that at such a time the "wardrobe will

---

146 Trunk, *Judenrat: The Jewish Councils in Eastern Europe under Nazi Occupation*, 508.
147 Ibid., 556.
148 Ringelblum, *Polish-Jewish Relations during the Second World War*, 62–63.
149 The Polish translation of Calek Perechodnik's journal has come under scrutiny by David Engel, who compared the original handwritten Polish account located in Yad Vashem, with not only two postwar typed copies of the journal, but also the 1993 published account, which was edited by Paweł Szapiro. Engel finds that Szapiro cut passages that he thought might have jarred mainstream Polish sensibilities regarding their views on Polish-Jewish relations during World War II. For Engel, "Perechodnik can no longer add to the ongoing discussion of Polish-Jewish relations during the Second World War. But precisely because he cannot respond to those who find fault with his portrayal today, he is entitled to have his one and only entry in the discussion heard in its entirety, exactly as he wrote it, without even the most minor alterations, let alone the highly obtrusive ones forced on his journal in the published Polish editions. This must be so even if in the end it can be shown beyond the slightest doubt that his portrait was overdrawn, unfair, or even downright malicious. To do otherwise—to concoct the bowdlerized version that the published Polish editions put forth—is to perpetrate a travesty upon memory and to vitiate whatever value the testimony of Holocaust diarists and memoirists may have for understanding this most painful, soul-wrenching, and divisive period of the recent past." See David Engel, "On the Bowdlerization of a Holocaust Testimony: The Wartime Journal of Calek Perechodnik," in *Focusing on Galacia: Jews, Poles and Ukrainians, 1772–1918*, ed. Israel Bartal and Antony Polonsky, *Polin: Studies in Polish Jewry*, vol. 12 (London: The Littman Library of Jewish Civilization, 1999), 327–328.

play for him," and sets about his task.¹⁵⁰ And before anything else, they break open shops with food provisions, rob the goods so that they themselves don't go hungry... If someone has pangs of conscience, he will deaden it with vodka.¹⁵¹

On that day, "Otwock police became famous among Jewish police in other ghettos because they made a pile of money after the Aktion," robbing deported Jews' homes.¹⁵² Perechodnik acknowledged that on the day of the Aktion "reason did not guide us but blind instinct that revealed to us the real human face, the nobility of some, the vileness of others."¹⁵³ American Jews respond with alarm to learning that Poles robbed deported Jews' houses. What do we say about Jews who robbed other Jews' homes?

Jewish Ghetto Police in all ghettos believed what Nazi commanders told them: Ghetto policemen's wives and children would be safe from deportation, as long as the Jewish policemen directed ghetto inhabitants to the deportation gathering site and maintained order. Indeed, to save their individual family units,

> [t]he policemen lead their own fathers and mothers to the cattle cars; themselves close the door with a bolt—just as if they were nailing the coffins with their own hands. [...] [T]here is an unbearable pain in the heart and a single thought that we will soon take our wives and children away and run from this accursed place.¹⁵⁴

The promise of safety for their families overtook them.

In Warsaw, the Germans ordered every Jewish policeman to supply five "heads" daily to the *Umschlagplatz*—the central gathering site for deportations. They did so having been threatened by the commandant of the Warsaw Ghetto Polizei that if they did not comply then their wives and children would be deported.

---

150 A "playing wardrobe" is a term for a prominent bribe taker. The Jewish police hoped to profit during the Aktion. See Calel Perechodnik, *Am I a Murderer? Testament of a Jewish Ghetto Policeman*, ed. and trans. Frank Fox (Boulder: WestviewPress, 1996), 17.
151 Ibid.
152 Ibid., 111–112.
153 Ibid., 44.
154 Ibid., 45.

He assured them "today is the last day for deportation." Yet every day for three months he gave the same speech. [...] Their hearts turned to stone [...]. They grabbed people, they carried in their arms infants from the apartments, they robbed if there was an opportunity.[155]

Corrupt, they ransomed lives for valuable commodities; they enforced deportation through unremitting brutality.[156] The Jewish Order Service even joined the Judenjagd, and hunted down Jews who remained hiding in the ghetto after an Aktion.[157] In dividing the Jewish community, the Germans set Jew on Jew, brother on brother. This is a typical genocidal strategy imposed on a targeted population.

Myth Reconstruction

Does the collective American Jewish community accept this nuanced reality? Jews too acted for their own survival. Moral decay set in among an enormous swath of Jews the longer they fought for their survival. Just as war hardens those who fight it, so too does genocide transform those who experience it. Situations which once would have caused great emotional angst, faded into the landscape: "There is a marked, remarkable indifference to death, which no longer impresses. One walks past corpses with indifference."[158] Ringleblum chronicles the desperate, starving, orphaned children as a sign of the ghetto's fall into disgrace: "There is an evident and terrible slackening of the sentiment of compassion. Walking through the streets, one passes children as emaciated as skeletons, barefoot and naked, who put out frozen-blue hands for alms—in vain. People have grown as hard and unfeeling as stones."[159] Seeing dead, frozen children became an ordinary sight.

By October 1941, the ghetto populace expected misery. And what one expects no longer surprises. What one expects, one can ignore . . . to survive. Marek Edelman, a Warsaw Ghetto resistance fighter and survivor, wrote of Warsaw

---

155 Ibid., 104.
156 Trunk, *Judenrat: The Jewish Councils in Eastern Europe under Nazi Occupation*, 512.
157 Ibid., 513.
158 Ringelblum, *Notes from the Warsaw Ghetto: The Journal of Emmanuel Ringelblum*, 194.
159 Ibid., 225.

Ghetto Jews that "[t]he instinct of self-preservation slowly changed people's psychology in the direction of saving themselves even at the expense of others."[160]

Just as the Nazis created a socially divisive ghetto administrative structure, which facilitated the perversion of ghetto society, turning Jew against Jew, so too did the Germans implement such a governing tool among the Poles. In the previous chapter, we learned that village elders, along with locals working in various capacities, aided the Nazis in order to save their villages and themselves. Poles turned in other Poles who were helping the so-called Jew-communist enemy. Poles participated in Jew hunts, because either they desired loot or feared their absence might target them for village reprisals.

Today, neither Poles nor Jews seek out bad actors in their respective groups. Each attempts to ignore its role as victimizer, while nursing its victimization. Jews avoid focusing on those who participated to some degree in the Nazi's murderous scheme: Judenräte bureaucrats, Jewish Order Service members, Jewish scoundrels, and Jewish thieves. Jews also belittle the role Jews played in demeaning, destabilizing, and deporting Poles during the Soviet occupation. Equally, Poles often deny levels of Polish complicity and collaboration with the Nazis against the Jews.

At the war's end, both populations attempted to reestablish social mores. Just as the Poles conducted postwar trials against alleged Polish traitors for their role in killing Jews or sabotaging Jews' hiding efforts, Jewish courts endeavored to confront the bad actors in their own community. Established in the Jewish displaced persons' camps in Germany and Italy between 1945–1948, Jews judged members of the Jundenräte and Jewish Order Service.[161] Interestingly, just as most trials in Poland were inconclusive or handed down inconsequential sentences to perpetrators, the Courts of Honor convicted few Jewish Ghetto Police and Jundenräte officials. They recognized the horrific and oppressive fear the Nazis inspired in the defendants. On the rare occasions when they passed a guilty verdict, the sentence was lenient.[162] In only thirteen of the forty-two cases did the courts declare defendants as traitors to the Jewish people, forbid them from holding any Jewish public positions, or entirely excommunicate

---

160 Bartoszewski and Lewin, *The Samaritans: Heroes of the Holocaust*, 10.
161 See Grabowski and Engelking, who base much of their research on the court documents from these Polish trials. Grabowski, *Hunt for the Jews: Betrayal and Murder in German-Occupied Poland*, 11–13; Engelking, *Such a Beautiful Sunny Day . . . Jews Seeking Refuge in the Polish Countryside, 1942–1945*. The Jewish trials also tried Jewish kapos who inflicted great pain on their fellow Jewish inmates.
162 Piotr Wróbel, "The 'Judenrate' Controversy: Some Polish Aspects," *Polish Review* 42, no. 2, 228.

them from the community. They denied rehabilitation to some without punishment. In nine cases, they permitted rehabilitation. Fifteen cases did not result in any sentences.[163] Between 1950 and 1964, the Israeli courts tried a number of former Jewish policemen and Jewish kapos (prisoners in the Nazi camps who held authority over other prisoners), but no Jewish Council of Elders members. Again, the results were lenient due to the fact that the refusal to carry out German orders placed a person's life in danger.[164] Given such outcomes, if Jews condemn Poles' laxity in confronting Polish perpetrators in the courts, we must also revisit Jewish courts which did not confront Jewish collaboration in a long-lasting meaningful way.

This comparison necessitates reflection on the victimization and agency of each group and upon the legacies of genocide borne by subsequent generations. I do not equate the two groups' situations during the Second World War, nor their responses to it. But I do acknowledge their similarity and the corresponding and persisting consequences shared by Jews and Poles. In so doing, I must stress that, within each group, many succumbed to the terrifying occupier's repression; and that in each group some soared above it.

I propose that each party dive deep into its own well of treacherous waters, again and again, to truly understand itself and the Other. This task is scary, as it threatens the narrative each side has cultivated for decades. It risks a loss of identity. But a sharper understanding of both Self and Other will result.

We have seen that for several decades Polish researchers have engaged the nation in new perspectives on the past, challenging Poland's identity myth that the great majority of Polish Christians helped Jews during the Holocaust. Though a backlash has ensued, the process still continues. American Jewry, on the other hand, has given little time to understanding the nuances that challenge our own stalwart anti-Polish outlook. It is time for American Jewry not only to acknowledge and respect the hard work some Poles have taken on, but also to engage in it ourselves.

To be aware of the complexity of the past elevates our ability to find compassion for those who experienced it. It elevates our own humanity. Discovery and acceptance of the Polish genocide heightens our respect for the Polish people's experience as a whole and for that segment that risked their lives and those of their loved ones to bring aid to Jews. Uncovering the ugly relationships among

---

163 Ibid.
164 Ibid.

Jews in the ghettos enables us to relate to the Poles who also chose to demote Jewish life. Too often, members of a ghetto's Judenrat or Jewish Order Service put their own needs above those of their fellow suffering Jews. If we so choose, such knowledge can lead to meaningful dialogue concerning Polish-Jewish relations and the impact war, power dynamics, and divisive propaganda have on the individual and the collective.

CHAPTER 15

Communism and the Jews

World War II decimated Poland, its land, infrastructure, and population. By September 1945, the war had destroyed most farms and livestock, smashed cities and towns and shattered bodies and psyches. Prior to September 1939, some thirty-five million people had inhabited Poland. By the war's end, German and Soviet policies of starvation, deportation, forced labor, and execution had killed close to three million ethnic Poles.[1] Most fatalities were civilians.

Millions of people also underwent forced migration both during and after the war. The "Big Three"—the United States, Great Britain, and Soviet Russia—mapped out the future of the East, including, of course, Poland. The new Polish eastern border was drawn as an approximation of the Curzon line, running southward into Galicia and its western border along the Oder-Neisse river line. Poland lost cities in the east and gained them in the west. The Allies believed that forced migration would solve the ethnic strife in East Central Europe and thereby created a homogenous Polish state where a multinational one had once existed. By 1949, millions of Poles had been forced to leave their homes, communities, and a way of life in the east, only to find themselves lost and untethered in new western Polish territories.[2] In this chapter, we will see that Polish postwar pogroms erupted at the intersection of postwar trauma, lost national sovereignty, and conspiracy theories.

---

1 Engel, *In the Shadow of Auschwitz: The Polish Government-in-Exile and the Jews, 1939–1942*, 158.
2 Michlic, *Poland's Threatening Other: The Image of the Jews from 1880 to the Present*, 196–197. For details on the various population movements including ethnic Poles, Jews, Germans, Ukrainians, and Lemkos, see ibid., 208–209.

Soviet Encroachment

As the war reached its end, Poles looked to rebuild their society—its political structure, however, was a point of heated debate. The government-in-exile planned for a parliamentary system. Stalin, though, had jockeyed for control over Poland's (prewar) territory by exploiting the Soviet Union's high military standing among the Allies. Long before the war concluded, the Soviets positioned themselves to envelop Poland. At the December 1943 Tehran Conference, Roosevelt and Churchill secretly acquiesced to Stalin's wish for an Eastern sphere of influence, thus changing prewar frontiers and abrogating the August 1941 Atlantic Charter.[3] Without the Polish leaders' consent, Roosevelt and Churchill gave Stalin Poland's eastern borderland.[4] Roosevelt and Churchill kept this under wraps, hoping to steer the Poles, themselves, into making the offer of land for peace.[5]

Excessively manipulative, Stalin achieved his endgame of Westward expansion.[6] On New Year's Eve 1943–1944, communist activists established the foundations of a postwar Polish government—the National Council of the Homeland (Krajowa Rada Narodowa, or KRN). The KRN declared itself the only legal and authentic representative of the Polish people.[7] Of course, this could not have been further from the truth, as it ignored the Polish underground and government-in-exile. But Stalin believed Goebbels's observation that if one told the same lie often enough people would eventually believe it. In the spring of 1944,

---

3   Polonsky, *The Jews of Poland and Russia*, 3:594; Paczkowski, *The Spring Will Be Ours: Poland and the Poles from Occupation to Freedom*, 117. The Soviets insisted on establishing Poland's eastern border along the Curzon Line, thus depleting Poland of territory in the east while expanding its Western borders to the Oder River at Germany's expense.
4   The USSR had stolen the kresy in the 1939 Molotov-Ribbentrop dissection of Poland but were forced to return it when the Soviets were in dire need of Allied aid.
5   For a contemporary discussion of this secret land for peace deal, see Arthur Bliss Lane, *I Saw Poland Betrayed: An American Ambassador Reports to the American People* (Indianapolis: The Bobb-Merrill company, 1948), 42–88.
6   Already in January 1943 Stalin had made the startling declaration that all people—including Poles—who resided in the eastern territories were considered Soviet citizens. This stance intended to defeat the Polish position that the borderlands were to revert to Poland, given they were part of the pre-1939 independent Polish state. To further combat Polish claims to the territory, in May 1943 Stalin ordered the formation of the Tadeusz Kościuszko Infantry Division, a Russian-led amalgam of Poles who had been released from their gulag internments. This force looked the part of the Poles supporting Stalin's policies. Paczkowski, *The Spring Will Be Ours: Poland and the Poles from Occupation to Freedom*, 97, 110, 112.
7   Ibid., 97.

the Soviets parachuted more and more communist partisans into German-occupied Poland, intensifying communist activity among Poles. Stalin's July 22, 1944 creation of the Polish Committee of National Liberation (Polski Komitet Wyzwolenia Narodowego—PKWN)—set up in the city of Lublin—was a government structure run by Polish communists who took their orders from Moscow. The Lublin PKWN then formed and grew the Polish Workers' Party, along with its corresponding military wing.

The Soviet dictator deflected any onlooker's gaze by engaging Polish political leaders in dialogue. Against the other political parties' position, anticommunist Peasant Party activist Stanisław Mikołajczyk met with Stalin, hoping to assert influence. Mikołajczyk had replaced Sikorski as prime minister after the latter's death in a spring 1943 plane crash.[8] In his Moscow meeting with Stalin, Mikołajczyk attempted to negotiate with the Soviet leader. However, his effort fell flat due to Stalin's unwillingness to concede anything to the Poles.[9] At the same time, Mikołajczyk's willingness to negotiate frontiers with Stalin created a debilitating and irreparable fracture in the Polish government-in-exile.

Circumstances changed on December 31, 1944, when by Stalin's orders the PKWN—the Lublin government—transformed itself into the Provisional Government of National Unity (Tymczasowy Rząd Jedności Narodowej, TRJN). When Stalin recognized it officially on January 5, 1945, he made it clear that he no longer needed or wanted Mikołajczyk or any other political dissenters in *his* government.[10]

The Final Military and Political Fall of Poland

At the same time that Stalin had been working to acquire Poland, the AK—Poland's Home Army—planned a large-scale unified uprising against the Germans: Operation Tempest. The AK finally found its opportunity for Operation Tempest in August 1944, when its leadership chose to piggyback on

---

8   Like Sikorski before him, Mikołajczyk held the very unpopular view that large Polish concessions to Stalin would be necessary for the Poles to regain sovereignty. This included the possibility of land concessions. However, Mikołajczyk believed it was Poland's right to make that decision, not the Western Allies (who had secretly already done so at the 1943 Tehran Conference). See ibid., 128.
9   Ibid., 115, 129.
10 Ibid., 129; Krystyna Kersten, *The Establishment of Communist Rule in Poland, 1943–1948*, trans. John Micgiel and Michael H. Bernhard (Berkeley: University of California Press, 1991), 79.

the successful Soviet offensive that pushed the Wehrmacht westward through Poland. According to Arthur Bliss Lane, the US ambassador to Poland (1944–1947), it seemed that Moscow had given the AK the go-ahead for its plan. Although Moscow had not responded to Polish radio messages, the Poles received an encouraging Polish-language broadcast from Moscow on July 29 at 8:15 pm: "Poles the time of liberation is at hand! Poles to arms!"[11] The Polish government-in-exile received a similar broadcast the following day urging them to aid the Soviet crossing of the Vistula; Stalin had welcomed the government-in-exile's prime minister, Stanisław Mikołajczyk (1901–1966), to Moscow for talks; the Red Army was actually nearing the Vistula—all of these events led AK General Bór-Komorowski to believe that the Soviets would support a Polish uprising against the Germans.[12] Bór-Komorowski had been played.

The Warsaw Uprising stalled and failed in a most terrible way. Soviet troops halted their advance along the bank of the Vistula River. In addition, they denied the Allies use of Soviet airfields to transport food supplies and needed artillery to the Poles.[13] Although the Polish Home Army captured two-thirds of Warsaw in the first few days,[14] bitter disappointment soon took hold. Kazimierz Pużak wrote to fellow PPS leaders in London: "I am convinced of the complete isolation of our uprising . . . I state for the record that the last minutes are passing."[15] For sixty-three days the Soviets waited, watching as a reorganized and resurgent Nazi force killed some 180,000 Poles and nearly levelled Warsaw.[16] By the time the Soviets crossed the Vistula into the destroyed city, the Polish Home Army was no more.

The Polish government-in-exile lost its political relevance, having drawn its power from the AK's allegiance. In October 1944, the head of the Polish Home Army disbanded his units, acknowledging their total defeat by the Germans and later to the Soviets. A power vacuum emerged for which Stalin had long been preparing.

Stalin had rejected the Poles' many pleas for help, calling the uprising a "reckless adventure." Through his official mouthpiece *Tass*, he asserted that "the

---

11 Poles believe that this incitement to arms, issued by the Union of Polish Patriots, of whom many were members of Moscow's Lublin government, was authorized by Moscow. The Soviets did not take responsibility for the broadcasts. See Lane, *I Saw Poland Betrayed: An American Ambassador Reports to the American People*, 43, 51.
12 Ibid., 43–44.
13 Ibid., 49–51.
14 Ibid., 45.
15 Quoted in Kersten, *The Establishment of Communist Rule in Poland, 1943–1948*, 73.
16 Polonsky, *The Jews in Poland and Russia*, 3:595.

only people responsible for the results of the events in Warsaw are the Polish émigré circles in London."[17] He argued that it was only due to the Red Army that Warsaw was liberated on January 17, 1945. Furthermore, he contended that since the communist-run Provisional Government was already functioning, it should continue in power. Through distortion and lies, Stalin had his way.

The Big Three met soon after in Yalta, Crimea, on February 4–11, 1945. The agreement struck there proved a devastating blow to the Poles. Churchill and Roosevelt gave Poland's eastern frontier along the Curzon Line to the Soviets. Stalin gained vast timber forests, oil fields, and Lviv. While the agreement annexed some German territory for Poland, Stalin's gain of the kresy grossly reduced the landmass of interwar Poland. Even worse from the Poles' perspective, in Yalta Roosevelt and Churchill recognized the Provisional Government of National Unity (TRJN) as Poland's rightful governing body—even though the Polish population did not support it.[18]

Although the Yalta agreement called for an immediate reorganization of the Polish Provisional Government of National Unity by bringing in noncommunists, it gave little direction and had few tools to measure compliance. And while it did charge the governing body to hold "free and unfettered elections as soon as possible on the basis of universal suffrage and secret ballot,"[19] it did not specify the practicalities of voting supervision. The later July 1945 Potsdam meeting solidified these Soviet wins.[20] The Poles, who had fought courageously alongside the Allies, and who were the first invaded population to form a formidable and complex resistance network against Nazi onslaught, were betrayed by the West. They were sacrificed in exchange for peace with Soviet Russia.

Securing Immediate Postwar Communist Rule

Though World War II came to an end on September 2, 1945, the war did not cease for the Poles. As Stanisław Mikołajczyk writes in his book *The Rape of Poland*, "[n]ow the banners of the enemy had changed, but the fight for freedom

---

17 Lane, *I Saw Poland Betrayed: An American Ambassador Reports to the American People*, 48–49.
18 Statura, *Poland 1918–1945: An Interpretive and Documentary History of the Second Republic*, 169.
19 Polonsky, *The Jews in Poland and Russia*, 3:596.
20 Ibid.

and independence continued."[21] The Soviets emerged as the primary enemy. The eleven-thousand-strong Soviet security service, known as the NKVD, which had been sent to Poland in 1943 on a pacification campaign, had arrested nearly seventeen thousand Home Army fighters and activists by the end of 1944.[22] Additionally, the Soviets had interned thousands more AK fighters whom they had captured during the Warsaw Uprising. They deported them to the far corners of the USSR.[23] Upon liberation, PPR propaganda posters proclaimed the Polish Home Army a "spittle-bespattered dwarf of reactionary forces".[24] AK veterans had to hide their wartime underground ties or risk arrest, internment, censure, or humiliation.[25] The Soviet-led governing body labeled AK soldiers "collaborators."

Poles aided this Soviet takeover. By the end of 1944, the Polish communist security apparatus employed roughly several thousand people, most of whom had been in the underground Polish communist military, the People's Army. As WWII edged toward its conclusion in May 1945, the Ministry of Public Security (MBP) amounted to some eleven thousand employees. Within five months there were twenty-eight thousand agents and informers monitoring and infiltrating Poland's functioning political parties, church groups, and other associations.[26]

The security apparatus had tremendous power in enforcing new laws, such as the August 1944 decrees regarding the "dissolution of secret organizations" and the punishment of war criminals and "traitors to the Polish nation"—which now included the military and civilian wings of the Polish underground state, the Home Army, and Delegatura respectively.[27] By December 1945, despite the Home Army's dissolution, roughly two hundred thousand armed fighters continued an underground anticommunist campaign, making some six thousand attacks on the new communist government's institutions. The situation neared

---

21 Stanisław Mikołajczyk, *The Rape of Poland: Pattern of Soviet Aggression* (New York: Whillesey House, 1948), 2.
22 Paczkowski, *The Spring Will Be Ours: Poland and the Poles from Occupation to Freedom*, 130.
23 Ibid., 130.
24 Jan Gross, *Fear: Antisemitism in Poland after Auschwitz* (Princeton: Princeton University Press, 2006), 7.
25 Ibid., 7.
26 Paczkowski, *The Spring Will Be Ours: Poland and the Poles from Occupation to Freedom*, 161–2. See Jerzy Andrzejewski's *Ashes & Diamonds*, trans. D. J. Welsch (Evanston: Northwestern University Press, 1997), specifically his character of Maciek Chelmicki, for a thoughtful portrayal of the transient nature of political allegiance during the early postwar years.
27 Paczkowski, *The Spring Will Be Ours: Poland and the Poles from Occupation to Freedom*, 131.

civil war, with Poles in the underground felling roughly seven thousand Polish supporters of the new Soviet puppet government.[28]

The clash between Soviet forces and the Polish Home Army was mirrored in political discourse. When government-in-exile Prime Minister Stanisław Mikołajczyk returned to postwar Poland in 1945, most Poles held him in exceptionally high esteem (even though they blamed the Warsaw Uprising catastrophe on the government-in-exile). Mikołajczyk aimed to lead the newly created Polish Peasant Party (PSL),[29] in its battle for representation and free national elections—which all parties, including the Soviets, had agreed to at Yalta. Indeed, by 1946 the PSL had amassed six hundred thousand members. Despite the communist Polish Workers' Party (PPR) pressure on laborers to officially join its card carrying ranks, the PPR numbered only about eight hundred thousand, just a bit stronger than the PSL.[30] The PSL's popularity lay in its audacious public statements that freedom extend not only to the individual but also to social, economic, and cultural institutions.[31]

In response to the PSL's growing popularity, Stalin approved the communist PPR's heightened intimidation tactics. Not only did it limit allocation of materials to print newspapers, but it also carried out censorship, propaganda, mass arrests, and assassinations.[32] Prior to the PSL's first congress, held in January 1946, the communists physically attacked Polish Peasant Party leaders

---

28 Polonsky, *The Jews in Poland and Russia*, 3:597.
29 The PPR had created fake political parties with the names of prewar parties, hoping people who associated with the former would join the latter and be swayed by intense propaganda to accept communist rule. Thus, a fake Peasant Party attracted old adherents of the original organization. After Mikołajczyk conferred with old friends who had misguidedly joined the fake Peasant Party, they decided to merge the two parties into one, renaming it the Polish Peasant Party (PSL). See Mikołajczyk, *The Rape of Poland: Pattern of Soviet Aggression*, 146.
30 Ibid., 152.
31 The PSL called for the nationalization of basic industry while allowing for private enterprise. It argued for equal educational rights for all people and positive relations with both the West and the Soviet Union. See ibid., 147–48.
32 The Soviets deployed such tactics against other anticommunist activists. Concurrently, the Soviet approach to win over the Polish people also included positive measures that helped the individual Pole move forward after the immense destruction wrought by World War II. The Soviets confiscated land from the relatively well-off Polish gentry and redistributed it to impoverished peasants who had little to no land of their own prior to the war. Additionally, the Soviets rehired workers and teachers to their previous jobs held before the war. They also reactivated prewar Polish political groups and prewar Polish professional and cultural organizations, which gave the superficial impression of a democratic society. Paczkowski, *The Spring Will Be Ours: Poland and the Poles from Occupation to Freedom*, 132–136.

and members. The Ministry of Public Security acted as the party's political police.

The fall and winter of 1945 was violent: three hundred PSL members were arrested in Kępno and taken from their homes. While most were released, at least forty-eight never returned. (Their graves were later discovered on the grounds of the Kępno Security Police station.) Soon thereafter, on November 14, the communists arrested some five hundred PSL members in the Tarnobrzeg district for holding a meeting in memory of the late party leader, Wincenty Witos. The communist authorities arrested PSL executive committee members in the Wrocław region, torturing some. Earlier in Bochnia, on September 8, 1945, the security police station commander Bartkowicz murdered several Polish Peasant Party leaders himself.[33] According to Mikołajczyk, Bartkowicz also ordered the torture of the PSL local executive committee member Józef Szydłowski. Only after his tongue was cut out, his fingernails ripped off, and his eyes seared with a hot poker was he shot and killed.[34] After the January 1946 PSL congress, the Soviets applied even more terror tactics, including burning some 333 farms in a single day in Wąwolnica, near Puławy.[35]

Soviet-driven intimidation continued up until the day of a referendum, which Stalin viewed as a plebiscite on the Poles' view of Communist Party rule. To coerce the population into voting for the PPR agenda, Moscow and the PPR surrounded voting buildings with armed men. After counting the votes themselves, the PPR decided to falsify the results, given that only 27% voted for communist rule. Despite PSL protests, the falsified election results stood.[36]

Not only did Stalin manipulate the referendum, but he also engineered the actual "free and unfettered" vote held later on January 19, 1947, after which he proclaimed that 80.1% of the population preferred communist rule to a Polish Peasant Party-led government. The PPR determined these "results" prior to the vote itself. To generate the desired figures, the communist-run security

---

33 Those killed included Mayor Józef Kołodziej of Bogucice, Wojcieh Kaczmarczyk, chairman of the PSL youth movement Wici, and Stanisław Mariasz, a PSL executive.
34 Mikołajczyk, *The Rape of Poland: Pattern of Soviet Aggression*, 149–50.
35 Ibid., 158; Kersten, *The Establishment of Communist Rule in Poland, 1943–1948*, 194–195.
36 Regarding the first question, about whether to abolish the Senate, the PPR contended that 67% of Poles agreed, and obviously opposed the PSL mandate of an independent Polish state. To the second question, about approving the agrarian reform and nationalization of industry while allowing small-scale private production, the PPR held that 78% of Poles voted "yes." And to the third question, about whether they supported the new western border for Poland established at Potsdam, the PPR professed that 92% of Poles voted "yes." Paczkowski, *The Spring Will Be Ours: Poland and the Poles from Occupation to Freedom*, 183.

apparatus arrested sixteen well-known PSL leaders, conducted mass arrests of PSL activists, removed people from electoral rolls, and intimidated voters on election day by making them pass soldiers, police, security officials, and armed "protection-propaganda brigades" on their way to cast ballots. Knowing that their democratic bloc could receive no more than 28–35% of the real vote, Stalin ordered his stewards to falsify ballots. A popular statement among the people was that "some people voted, but other people counted."[37] Thus, through intimidation, coercion, and fraud, Polish communists secured four-fifths of the vote. Eventually, the people acquiesced to the so-called results.

By February 1947. the Polish people had been worn down into accepting communism. Exhausted from years of fighting, forced migration, poverty, hunger, homelessness, and intimidation, this last "vote" and the West's lack of any meaningful response to its falsification only further paralyzed the people.[38] Party purges and a reign of terror directed the rhetoric; as in other Soviet-controlled Eastern European states, the Soviet-styled security apparatus ensured that the country as a whole transitioned to Stalin's grim version of communism. At the same time, some Poles voluntarily jumped on board in the hope of opportunities. However, most who eventually joined the PPR were filled with dread. Communist Poland would be ruled by a mix of careerists, people bent on survival, and a smattering of die-hard idealists.

Polish Communists

Poles who joined the communist cause in the 1920s and '30s did so for ideological reasons. Their intellectual leaders gathered around the tables of Warsaw's Café Ziemańska, crafting arguments for workers' economic, social, and political equality. Among this dominant literary clique, known as the Skamander group, were avant-garde writers of Jewish origin: Julian Tuwim, Antoni Słonimski, Bruno Jasieński, Alexander Wat, and Tadeusz Peiper. With their Polish colleagues they leapt into communism and accepted a new role in society.[39] No longer were they willing to reflect life in their art. Instead, they wished to turn

---

37 Ibid., 185–186.
38 Ibid., 187–188.
39 In Marci Shore's *Caviar and Ashes: A Warsaw Generation's Life and Death in Marxism* (New Haven: Yale University Press, 2009), the author presents a tremendous accounting of the political, interwoven, and complex lives of the Skamander and Futurist poets, their journey from Marxism to Stalinism, and their reflections on their choices.

their compositions into hammers and chisels with which to forcefully shape people and society. While they viewed their role as patriotic creators of a necessary revolution, others might well call their work propaganda. They stood on the fringe of society, beckoning others to join.

All who chose communism learned to accept the overarching power of the party, and the requisite that the individual submit to it. To bring History to its ideal state, an individual had to relinquish their identity to the masses and work for the party. It was only through self-negation that one could come to communism.[40] The future lay not in the individual's dreams, but rather in those of the people as a whole. Thus, to make the future, one had to sublimate one's individual needs to the party's central authority, to Stalin. Adhering to Stalin's will, party leaders learned to atone for sins through self-criticism and accept any punishment deemed necessary.[41]

S. L. Shneiderman, an American Jewish journalist born and raised in Kazimierz Dolny, Poland, travelled back to Poland at the war's end. He met with several acquaintances from his youth, including Moshe Reisman, who spoke about crossing into the USSR. This prewar Polish communist, like many in his cohort, suffered terribly at Stalin's behest.[42] Stalin could not accept one's ability to be both a Polish patriot and a loyal communist. Thus, Polish communists experienced communism as pain, judgement, and often arrest. What they encountered in Soviet Lviv was not idealism, but rather Marxism in power. How reality differed from the dream! A young Polish Jewish prose writer, Adolf Rudnicki, described Soviet Lviv as a place where "even the most thick-skinned felt how difficult it was to live without one's mother."[43] Fear soaked through their once unshakable trust in ideology. Shneiderman recalls his astonishment that despite intense suffering, Reisman remained a stalwart communist: "just as his father became more pious the greater his poverty, so he, the son, embraced communism more fervently the more blatant its failures."[44] Such cognitive dissonance would play a large role for both Jews and Poles. The more facts emerged that

---

40   Ibid., 369.
41   Ibid., 369, 371.
42   When in 1939 the Soviets invaded eastern Poland, they deported roughly four hundred thousand inhabitants to the bitter Soviet interior, of which two-thirds were Poles and one-fifth were Jews. Included in those groups were Polish communists living in that territory. They had been charged with Polish nationalism. Paczkowski, *The Spring Will Be Ours: Poland and the Poles from Occupation to Freedom*, 48.
43   Shore, *Caviar and Ashes: A Warsaw Generation's Life and Death in Marxism*, 155.
44   S. L. Shneiderman, *The River Remembers* (New York: Horizon Press, 1978), 12–13.

contradicted communist propaganda, the more Communist Party members doubled down to insist they were right all along.

Oddly, through self-criticism and self-flagellation, punishment strengthened many Polish communists' desires to demonstrate their loyalty to the cause. Most Polish communists readily accepted Stalin's preemptive rehabilitation of them prior to Germany's June 1941 invasion. Though Stalin still did not trust Polish communists, he now needed them. This relationship would prove to be an ever-changing system of protection and abandonment, welcome and rejection.

Ideologically, communism opposed religion and its control of the people. In an ironic twist, however, the people found in Stalin's aggressive atheism a quasi-religion. People looked to Stalin, the leader of party, as a god. What this god demanded, one did... in the name of party... in the name of History. In time, they lost themselves to their god and did Stalin's bidding, whether it be through violence, making false confessions, or completely upending their moral code. Most lost the ability to think for themselves and, instead, thought only for and about the good of the party.

Adam Ważyk's August 1955 "A Poem for Adults" ("Poemat dla dorosłych") attests to this phenomenon:

> I returned home
> like one who had gone out for medicine
> and returned after twenty years. [...]
>
> Fourier, the dreamer, charmingly foretold
> that the sea would flow with lemonade.
> And does it not?
>
> They drink seawater,
> and cry out—
> lemonade!
> They return home furtively
> to vomit.
> to vomit.[45]

---

45 Quoted in Shore, *Caviar and Ashes: A Warsaw Generation's Life and Death in Marxism*, 306–307.

After publication in *Nowa Kultura* (for which the editor was summarily dismissed), Ważyk often repeated to himself, "I've been in an insane asylum."[46]

Żydokomuna

Most Poles who saw the communists as the enemy had also been schooled in Żydokomuna, the conspiracy theory which teaches that Jews created communism to take over the world, Jews led the communist assault on Poland, and Jews manipulated the power arrangements within the Polish communist regime. As we saw earlier, after World War I Żydokomuna roused fear among large numbers of Europeans, including Poles. Two decades later, during the Second World War, the Soviets struck Poland with ferocious aggression. For many Poles, it seemed that their worst fears had come to fruition. Jews—who until this time had lacked broad political power—were now in positions of authority. Given that Poles had rarely seen Jews in such important roles, the Jews' rise was difficult to accept.

In the postwar years when Poles recognized Jewish-*sounding* surnames among communist authorities, it allowed them to ignore the majority of people working for the party with Polish-*sounding* surnames. By disregarding the non-Jewish Polish role in formulating, generating, and expanding communism, non-Jewish Poles could sidestep any national shame over facilitating and managing the communist takeover of Poland.

Żydokomuna is a myth. Communism is not a Jewish system. Communism is not based on Jewish theology or ideology. The majority of its leaders, activists, and members in Poland were non-Jews. As the communist state opposed and dismantled Jewish traditional religion and culture, most Jews remained traditional. They did not support this anti-religious system, which also repressed capitalists, including shopkeepers, middlemen, and peddlers—roles in which Jews were highly represented. By clinging to Żydokomuna, Poles distracted themselves from any responsibility communists of Polish-Catholic origin had in foisting this system on the country against the people's will. However, like most myths, there is a kernel of truth embedded within it.

---

46   Quoted in ibid., 309.

Jews' Early Leadership in Russian Communism

Jews searching for a way out of their traditional lives gravitated to Bolshevik messianism, which toyed with traditional Jewish language: "The proletariat is the chosen people which will fulfill its mission and complete history."[47] For Jews, revolutionary socialism promised a bulwark against antisemitism, a path to social integration, and a way out of poverty. In the early history of Soviet Russia and communist Poland, there is no denying that people of Jewish origin held prominent leadership positions.

At first, this new ideology appealed to those who had been denied previous social access. Jews who had been accepted into the intelligentsia, be it Russian or Polish, like their colleagues, felt an intense attraction to communism. Jewish students who yearned for this elite intellectual identity also followed suit.[48] With post-World War I urbanization and improved secular educational opportunities, a large number of Jews in the new Soviet Union assimilated linguistically and culturally, finding upward mobility. When the postrevolutionary exodus left a leadership vacuum, secularly educated Jews helped to fill it. Indeed, in the early years of the Soviet Union, people with Jewish parentage held prominent posts. These leaders included Yakov Sverdlov, Lenin's first head of state, Leon Trotsky, war commissar and founder of the Red Army, Lev Kamenev, leader of the powerful Leningrad Communist Party, and G. Zinoviev, first president of the Comintern. Five of the seven supreme leaders of the ruling Politburo were of Jewish origin.[49]

It is normal for individuals, and no less large national or ethnic populations, to resist negative truths about the past. This is as true for Jews as it is for Poles. Some Soviet leaders of Jewish origin had a terrorizing impact on Poles. Indeed, Israel Leplevskii, Lev Raikhman, and Boris Berman, all born to Jewish families, had major roles in the 1937–38 Great Terror in Soviet Ukraine and Belarus—the Polish Operation. They helped to falsely blame the Poles for the failures of collectivization, including the Soviet policies of deliberate starvation by famine,

---

47 Antony Polonsky, "Jews and Communism in the Soviet Union and Poland," in *Jews and Leftist Politics: Judaism, Israel, Antisemitism, and Gender*, ed. Jack Jacobs (Cambridge: Cambridge University Press, 2017), 165–166.
48 Ibid., 149.
49 Paul Lendvai, *Antisemitism without Jews: Communist Eastern Europe* (Garden City: Doubleday & Company, Inc., 1971), 53.

which killed millions in 1933.⁵⁰ Portraying the Poles as a new enemy, the Soviet authorities charged the Soviet Secret Police (NKVD) with the "total liquidation of the networks of spies of the Polish Military Organization,"⁵¹ which had supposedly infiltrated the Soviet Union. No such Polish organization existed, however, except in Stalin's and his advisor's imaginations. At this point, Poles who had crossed into the USSR aligned with communism. But the Soviets designated all Polish people, including Polish communists, as enemies of the state.⁵² Without formal oversight, the NKVD arrested, deported, or killed members of the Polish minority in the USSR. Poles living in the Soviet Union numbered roughly six hundred thousand. During the extremely bloody Polish Operation, the Soviets arrested 143,810 people accused of espionage for Poland. Of the 111,091 executed, most were Poles.⁵³

In 1937, about one third of all high-ranking NKVD officers were of Jewish origin. However, due to his heightened paranoia Stalin replaced most communists of national minority ethnicity with Russians. With remarkable speed Stalin erased Jews from his ranks, with only 4% remaining in Soviet Russia's NKVD by November 1939. One possible reason for this purge was Stalin's secret preparation to collaborate with Hitler in dividing Poland.⁵⁴ Still, the reality remains that communists of Jewish origin collaborated in Stalin's earlier terror against the Poles.⁵⁵

Jews' Presence in Polish Communism

In interwar Poland, relatively few Jews gravitated to communism. Out of roughly three million Jews in Poland, only some five thousand affiliated with communism. Left-wing radicalism and its call for social justice attracted those Jews who craved an escape from their impoverished, closed, traditional communities. Like their fellow non-Jewish ideological travelers, they had been swallowed up by

---

50   Snyder, *Bloodlands: Europe Between Hitler and Stalin*, 89, 92, 102. The USSR also made a similar charge against the Ukrainians and implemented the so-called "kulak action," executing 386,798 Soviet citizens of Ukrainian ethnicity by the end of 1938.
51   Ibid., 94–95.
52   Ibid., 94–95, 81.
53   Ibid., 103.
54   Antony Polonsky, "Jews and Communism in the Soviet Union and Poland," 155.
55   Snyder, *Bloodlands: Europe Between Hitler and Stalin*, 108.

talk of History and party. However, those who became revolutionaries to fight injustice soon turned into instruments of oppression.

Though small in actual number, the fact that Jews made up 25% of the prewar Polish Communist Party, and that many of them aided the Soviet system, signified to Poles the Jews' important role in crushing Poland's dreams of postwar independence. Polish nationalists had not only experienced the Soviet wrath from 1939–1941, but had also witnessed local Communist Party allies of Jewish parentage ascend into mid-level administrative positions and implement Moscow's orders. Coupled with some Jews' arrogant and even terrorizing behavior toward the Poles, this Jewish success underscored for many the so-called truth of the Jew-communist conspiracy theory.

In addition, Stalin's power play on the banks of the Vistula left Polish Home Army forces abandoned by their supposed Soviet ally. Standing alone to combat the Nazi forces in Warsaw, and cut off from Allied support, the AK was defeated. Moscow followed this Polish loss with an intense pacification campaign. Who should the Poles blame? During WWII, the Germans plastered Polish walls with posters of Leon Trotsky's caricature, insinuating that Jews were the Poles' real enemy. It mattered little that already in 1937 Stalin had purged most Jews from leadership and administrative posts in the USSR. Poles needed only to look at the communist leadership in various Soviet client states and in their own backyard to believe they could see the reach of Jewish-communist power.[56]

When the Soviets manipulated their way to power in postwar Poland through politics, terror, and intimidation, most Poles opposed communism. That communists of Jewish origin played a role in Poland's loss of sovereignty allowed Poles to distort their own role. Poles cast not only specific Jews by heritage as responsible for their sociopolitical crisis, but ergo also the entire Jewish people. Żydokomuna furnished Poles with a convenient, albeit unrealistic, means to retain their "primal" memory of Polish heroism.

At this point in time, only about 10% of Polish Jewry had survived Hitler's death camps and Stalin's deportations. Estimates of postwar numbers vary due to many Jews choosing not to affiliate publicly as Jews. At least two hundred thousand Jewish survivors had returned to Poland by the beginning of

---

56 Hungary had Mátyás Rakosi (née Rosenfeld, 1892–1971), the Czechoslovakia had Rudolf Slánský (1901–1952), Romania had Ana Pauker (née Rabinsohn, 1893–1960), and the Polish People's Republic had Jakub Berman (1901–1984) and Hilary Minc (1905–1974). Throughout the Eastern bloc a renewed hatred grew for the Jews, as a representation of communism and sovietization. See Lendvai, *Antisemitism without Jews: Communist Eastern Europe*, 55.

July 1946. (This includes those 130,000 repatriated after internment in the Soviet Union.) About one hundred thousand Jews fled Poland between June 1946 and September 1946 because of the July 4, 1946, Kielce pogrom and others that followed.[57] By January 1952, seventy to eighty thousand Jews remained in the Polish People's Republic. Thus, Poles who believed Żydokomuna, accepted these weakened Holocaust survivors as the penultimate enemy. By focusing on high profile officials of Jewish origin in the security apparatus, the Ministry of Foreign Affairs and Ministry of Foreign Trade, as well as the press and radio, Poles believed the Jews were assaulting Poland.

This response mirrors the conservative reaction to the Enlightenment. When the French Revolution opened the ghetto gates Jews became more successful in French society. Perceiving the Jew as the greatest beneficiary of European social turmoil and revolutions people blamed Jews for staging it.

In the prewar era, Polish nationalists and the Church had identified the Jews as Poland's enemy. Now they could point to some Jews who actually held political office. By extension they imagined all Jews as the devil incarnate. They argued that the Jew threatened Poles' religious, economic, and social fabric—indeed, even Poland's very existence. It did not matter that the Jews, who had once stood at 10% of Poland's population, now comprised only 0.1%.

Jews in High-Ranking Polish Communist Posts

Jews cannot ignore the fact that between 1944 and 1956, numerous Communist Party members of Jewish origin, many of whom spent the war years in the USSR or abroad, returned to Poland and filled high official positions. According to Andrzej Paczkowski, nearly 30% of communist Poland's top officials were of Jewish origin. Of course, that still leaves 70% non-Jews. Hilary Minc, Jakub Berman, and Roman Zambrowski (1909–1977) were just a few of the many Jews who survived the war in the Soviet Union and attained leadership positions. These three were elected members of the Politburo and the Central Committee of the PPR. As minister of industry (1944–1949) and head of Polish state planning, Minc instituted economic policies for peasant collectivization and fast-paced industrialization. Both failed miserably and caused emotional and economic turmoil. Zambrowski held the deputy chairmanship of the Polish

---

57 Polonsky, *The Jews in Poland and Russia*, 3:646. CKŻP records of registered Jews show that Poland's Jewish population fell from 240,489 in June 1946 to 88,257 in 1948. An additional 30,000 emigrated between 1949 and 1951, leaving Poland with 58,000 to 70,000 Jews.

parliament (1947–1952). Berman worked as undersecretary in the Ministry of Foreign Affairs (1945–1952). In that government department alone, out of eight directors five were Jews of origin; to fill open deputy director posts, only four people were nominated, of whom three were Jews; of twenty-eight division managers, eighteen were Jews.[58]

As a top advisor to Bolesław Bierut (1892–1956, an ethnic Pole and president of Poland from 1947 to his death in 1956), Jakub Berman dictated cultural policy during the harshest years of socialist realism. In cultivating relationships with writers, he ably mandated a strict black-and-white representation of society: good versus evil, progress versus reaction. Writers depicted Soviet policy as the hero in this tale, and its enemies as revolting.[59] Berman also supervised the dreaded Ministry of Public Security (Ministerstwo Bezpieczeństwa Publicznego—MBP), also known as Bezpieka, or UB. This ministry broke the Polish people's will to resist communism and Sovietization. through repression, undercover agents, informers, terror, and murder. Other functionaries of Jewish origin filled the MBP ranks far beyond the proportion of Jews in the Polish population.[60] From 1944–1954, Jews of origin filled between 30 and 37% of the highest-ranking positions in the MBP.

However, in no way does their overrepresentation in high-power positions mean that Polish communism was "Jewish communism," or Żydokomuna. The data indicates that between 63 and 70% of high-ranking MBP security officials were largely Polish Catholics. Additionally, Jewish representation dropped significantly at the local security apparatus level: district bosses and deputies with Jewish backgrounds stood at 13.7%, while their participation dropped to low single digits at the provincial level.[61]

Numerous Jews returning from Hitler's hell and who wished to remain in Poland recognized communism's antipathy to antisemitism as a life raft. Communist ideology supported the Jews at a time when antisemitism was deepening. The 1945 May Day celebration in Wałbrzych serves to illustrate

---

58 Krajewski, *Poland and the Jews: Reflections of a Polish Polish Jew*, 119–120; 127.
59 Shore, *Caviar and Ashes: A Warsaw Generation's Life and Death in Marxism*, 267–268, 279.
60 Antoni Alster, Leon Andrzejewski, Julia Brystygier, Józef Czaplicki, Anatol Fejein, Adam Humer, Mieczysław Mietkowski, Roman Romkowski, Józef Światło, and Konrad Świetlik are just some of the individuals with Jewish ancestry who contributed to the Stalinist repression apparatus in the Polish People's Republic from 1944–1954. See Jerzy Eisler, "1968: Jews, Antisemitism, Emigration," in *1968: Forty Years After*, eds. Leszek W. Głuchowski and Antony Polonsky, Polin: Studies in Polish Jewry, vol. 21 (Oxford: The Littman Library of Jewish Civilization, 2009), 41.
61 Ibid., 41–42.

the widening chasm between postwar Poles and Jews. According to Zofia Machejkowa's account of that day,

> something happened which badly affected people's moods. Jews manifested on a mass scale, the Bund, *"szorzy"* [members of the *Zionist* organization Hashomer Hatzair][62] in special uniforms, and the Jewish committee. All had banners in Polish and Yiddish: "Long Live Comrade Stalin" [. . .] No one else apart from them were heard chanting slogans of that sort.'[63]

Poles watched Jews link themselves to the PPR, if only to be on outward good terms with those who would determine how difficult the road to a Jewish future would be. A dangerous cycle emerged as the decades-old false narrative of Żydokomuna gained influence among Poles, people who had fought and suffered for Poland's independence and who now stood on the precipice of losing it. Poles viewed the emerging communist authorities as instituting another partition of Poland—and those Jews assisting it and welcoming it as the enemy.

Polish thought leader Jerzy Andrzejewski responded to this dangerous moment when he addressed both Jews and Poles:

> Jews should understand that Majdanek and Treblinka in no way redeem those Jewish individuals whose actions deserve condemnation. . . . And Poles must once again understand that the flaws or crimes of Jewish individuals cannot incriminate Jews in general, nor can they serve as testimony to some imagined "Jewish spirit."[64]

For Andrzejewski, Żydokomuna was a fabrication. But many believed it.

---

62 Bożena Szaynok added this explanation of *szorzy*. I changed her spelling.
63 Quoted in Bożena Szaynok, "Poles and Jews from July 1944 to July 1946," in *Reflections on the Kielce Pogrom*, ed. Łukasz Kamiński and Jan Żaryn (Warsaw: Institute of national Remembrance, 2006), 25.
64 Jerzy Andrzejewski, "The Problem of Polish Anti-Semitism," in *Against Anti-Semitism: An Anthology of Twentieth-Century Polish Writings*, ed. Adam Michnik and Agnieszka Marczyk (Oxford: Oxford University Press, 2018), 110.

The Immediate Postwar Polish Street and Context

As with WWI, the war left Poland in a state of violent chaos. People robbed, injured, and killed others at will. Combined with this barbarity was the anxiety of a nation at war with itself over Poland's future course. Poles killed one another in the name of the Communist Party or the Polish Home Army, edging ever closer to a full-blown civil war, and leaving more than twenty thousand fighters dead.[65]

Postwar violence also targeted Jews. Here, "violence" refers to inflicting damage not only on Jewish property, including homes, shops, institutions, and synagogues, but also the harassment, assault, and murder of Jews. Because Poles tended to stereotype Jews as part of the collective communist enemy which forcefully sought to subjugate the Polish people, violence against any Jew could be twisted into resisting the communist enemy, as national self-defense.[66]

Historians disagree on the number of Jews that Poles murdered in the immediate postwar years, in part due to the context of anarchy and near-civil war. While some, like David Engel, offer a conservative estimate of five hundred to six hundred Jews killed in this period, others, including Jan Gross, estimate is as closer to fifteen hundred.[67]

When Jewish survivors began returning from the camps, the majority of Poles did not respond with sympathy. According to historian Bożena Szaynok: "Indifference was likewise a reaction to the enormity of a crime that could not be prevented, and a defense mechanism in a situation that could not be changed."[68] At the same time, much of Polish society had been desensitized to the Jews' suffering.[69] When Jewish returnees were greeted with violence, most Poles were ambivalent. The leading postwar Polish sociologist Stanisław Ossowski wrote

---

65 Gross, *Fear: Anti-Semitism in Poland after Auschwitz*, 28.
66 Joanna Michlic-Coren, "Anti-Jewish Violence in Poland, 1918–1939 and 1945–1947," in *Focusing on the Holocaust and Its Aftermath*, ed. Antony Polonsky, Polin: Studies in Polish-Jewry, vol. 13 (London: The Littman Library of Jewish Civilization, 2000), 34, 49.
67 Gross, *Fear: Anti-Semitism in Poland after Auschwitz*, 28.
68 Bożena Szaynok, "The Role of Antisemitism in Postwar Polish-Jewish Relations," in *Antisemitism and Its Opponents in Modern Poland*, ed. Robert Blobaum (Ithaca: Cornell University Press, 2005), 267.
69 American society experienced a similar phenomenon during the second Iraq war. Initially, people listened attentively to every report of American soldiers' deaths. Yet once it reached the two thousand mark the population's surprise and anger dulled. Similarly, in the fight against ISIS, the 2014 kidnappings and beheadings of American journalists James Foley and Daniel Pearl kept the United States breathless. Yet subsequent victims did not receive the same intense media coverage and public response. The American public grew somewhat

in his famous 1946 essay "With Kielce in the Background" ("Na tle wydarzeń kieleckich"): "People condemn the crime out of a sense of duty but they do not actively try to oppose it. This lack of distress in the face of crime is largely an effect of wartime practice: murdering Jews ceased to be extraordinary."[70]

Poles' desensitization to the Jews' pain had been seeded by prewar Polish nationalism and divisive German policies. The Nazis not only separated the two populations by interning the Jews in ghettos, but also pumped extreme antisemitic propaganda through loudspeakers to manipulate the Polish populace. In Warsaw, the Nazis had reinforced Catholic Church teachings about the blood libel. By distributing hundreds of thousands of leaflets with a painting of four bearded Jews stabbing a Christian child, the Nazis reminded Poles to fear Jews.[71] This image warning Poles against seeing Jews as human beings in need of compassion and aid retained its strength even after the Nazis' defeat. Thus, when Poles met Jews on the postwar Polish street, they did not only observe Holocaust survivors, broken people. They feared a physical threat to Christian children.

Poles also equated the Jewish survivor with Jew-communists, who the Nazi propaganda machine had blamed for the Katyń massacre. Just prior to the final mass deportations from the Warsaw Ghetto, German propaganda ascribed Katyń's horrors to the Jews: "[i]n the show windows of the most crowded streets were exhibited photographs of the murdered Poles with captions explaining that their assassins were Jews."[72] The Germans reported their findings to the Poles years later in April 1943, manipulating Katyń as an explanation for the Nazi destruction of the Warsaw Ghetto.[73] The *Stroop Report*, which contains the German account of the destruction of the Warsaw Ghetto, corroborates this misrepresentation of Katyń. The Germans portrayed themselves as helping the Poles by avenging their pain. The Germans hoped Poles would return the favor by pointing out escapees from the burning ghetto. Blaming Katyń on the Jew

---

numb to the wretched violence as it became the new normal. To remain in a constant state of despair, grief, and fear would be to set course to insanity.

70 Stanisław Ossowski, "With Kielce in the Background," in Michnik and Marczyk, *Against Anti-Semitism: An Anthology of Twentieth-Century Polish Writings*, 120.
71 S. L. Shneiderman, *Between Fear and Hope* (New York: Arco Publishing Co., 1947), 117.
72 Ibid., 80.
73 In his proclamation to the Poles, Governor Hans Frank raised "the mass graves found in Katyń; at the same time . . . [Poles] were asked to assist us in our fight against Communist agents and Jews." SS-Brigade Leader Jürgen Stroop, *The Stroop Report: The German Account of the Destruction of the Warsaw Ghetto in German and English*, trans. Arthur Kemp (London: Ostara Publications, 2014), 34.

and the Jew-communist, Nazi propaganda convinced Poles of the veracity of the prewar Endek contention that the Jew was Poland's constantly threatening Other. Such beliefs lasted well past the war.

Nazi propaganda validated Poles' indifference to the Jewish tragedy, which in turn aided Poles' physical and emotional survival. It staved off Poles' guilt over activity or lack thereof regarding the Jews.[74] Writers, such as Stanisław Ossowski, questioned the impact this moral corruption had on the Polish psyche:

> compassion is not the only imaginable response to misfortune suffered by other people. [...] We could be reminded that if one person's disaster benefits somebody else, an urge appears to persuade oneself and others that that disaster was morally justified, and it could be pointed out that this is exactly the situation of today's proprietors of formerly Jewish shops, or those who felt previously threatened by Jewish competition.[75]

Given that three million Polish Jews died, *at least* tens of thousands of ethnic Poles gained materially from their murders, be it through plundering household items after ghetto Aktions or Jew hunts, or through the appropriation of Jewish homes and businesses permitted by the Nazi administration and the postwar Polish communist authority. As in other Eastern bloc countries, Poles—through cognitive dissonance and violence—grasped onto such arguments to justify their possession of Jewish property and resist any rising residual guilt.[76] Thus, by recognizing *the Jew* as the new powerful enemy subjugating the Polish people under the communist regime, some Poles responded to any wartime guilt with violence targeting the Jew-communist. Although a fabrication, Żydokomuna molded reality. As we shall see, the blood libel, another anti-Jewish fabrication deeply ingrained in the Polish mindscape, also informed postwar Polish-Jewish relations.

---

74 Steinlauf, *Bondage to the Dead: Poland and the Memory of the Holocaust*, 54; Szaynok, "The Role of Antisemitism in Postwar Polish-Jewish Relations," 267–268.
75 Quoted in Gross, *Fear: Anti-Semitism in Poland after Auschwitz*, 131.
76 In Kyiv, groups of Ukrainian Jews returning to reclaim their prewar property experienced antisemitic violence. Lithuania, while not as brutal, also recorded assaults on individual Jews. But because Poland had been home to the largest prewar Jewish community, the situation was more intense there and the Jewish world's attention gravitated to it. Polonsky, *The Jews in Poland and Russia*, 3:608.

Poles and Jews on the Postwar Polish Streets

In 1946, the number of returning Jews peaked between two hundred fifty thousand and three hundred thousand.[77] It has been estimated that between fifty to one hundred twenty thousand Jews survived the Holocaust while in Nazi occupied territory, whether in hiding or with false Aryan identities, fighting with the partisans or in the camps. Some 138,000 additional Jews survived having been forcefully deported for hard labor to the interior of the Soviet Union. When the Soviets permitted repatriation in early 1946, these Jews returned to Poland along with prewar Christian Polish citizens who had also survived Stalin's cruel deportations.

Many Poles perceived these returning Jews as communist enemy implants who would contribute to the Soviet seizure of power in Poland.[78] (A similar fear took hold with the Litvak migrations in the late nineteenth and early twentieth centuries.) Poles experienced Jews returning from the USSR in 1946 as an invasion. Poles had gained job opportunities due to the Jews' "disappearance." Now they feared that their economic elevation would prove only temporary, especially given the deeply held belief that Jews occupied the best government posts and controlled all policy.

For these reasons, Jewish survivors felt rejected by the large number of Poles who seemed unhappy with their return. Jews' loneliness heightened when many discovered they were the lone family survivor or, at times, even the sole living community member. Alone. Terrified. Poor. And sick. About one-third lacked the ability to work due to tuberculosis, which necessitated a long period of rest and intensive treatment.[79] It was this weakened and crushed Jewish population which stepped back onto Poland's streets.

---

77 According to records from the Central Committee of Jews in Poland (Centralny Komitet Żydów w Polsce, CKŻP), which had been established in the fall of 1944, the postwar Jewish population in Poland reached its peak of two hundred forty thousand in the summer of 1946. However, because many assimilationists chose not to register and some 10–20% of Jews who self-identified as such were simply missing from the registry, historians often recognize this number as two hundred fifty thousand to three hundred thousand. Bożena Szaynok, "The Impact of the Holocaust on Jewish Attitudes in Postwar Poland," in *Contested Memories: Poles and Jews During The Holocaust And Its Aftermath*, ed. Joshua D. Zimmerman (New Brunswick: Rutgers University Press, 2003), 243; Natalia Aleksiun, "Jewish Responses to Antisemitism," in Zimmerman, *Contested Memories: Poles and Jews During The Holocaust And Its Aftermath*, 248–249.
78 Gross, *Fear: Anti-Semitism in Poland after Auschwitz*, 125; Szaynok, "The Role of Antisemitism in Postwar Polish-Jewish Relations," 271.
79 Szaynok, "The Impact of the Holocaust on Jewish Attitudes in Postwar Poland," 239.

Jewish survivors who returned to their villages or towns, typically, found their homes either destroyed or occupied. If the latter, the Polish person living in a formerly Jewish house often responded to their arrival by exclaiming, "What! Still alive?!"[80] In most cases, they were unhappy to see the returnee, as the Polish individual's claim to the structure now came into question.

For the Pole, who had moved into a better home, or whose prewar home had been destroyed by war, or who had been forced to migrate to a completely foreign area, the Jew's reappearance was destabilizing. Immediate postwar Poland saw the forced migration of peasants from villages to larger towns. Often such peasants, who had lost their own homes, now occupied Jews' homes in the traditional Jewish quarter surrounding the town marketplace.[81] Traumatized by their own wartime experiences, Poles sought security in Jews' homes. Though the peasant's advance was not premeditated, "the return of the former owners was perceived as harmful."[82] A Jew's return challenged a Poles' vision of a better future for their family and led to hostility.

While a small number of Jews were able to create some semblance of a new life in their hometowns or villages, most felt rejected by the majority of Poles and extremely isolated given that they were often the sole survivor. Many felt a need to move away from the prewar homes of murdered relatives. Others moved only after being warned by neighbors to leave for their safety. They relocated to the cities, where they could be near other Jews, feel safer, and perhaps lose themselves in the anonymity of urban life.

Despite the Jews' weakened bodies, tortured minds, and economic impoverishment, Poles believed they were rich. Jews returning from concentration camps received monetary subsidies from three groups: the government, the UNRRA, and JOINT (the American Jewish Joint Distribution Committee).[83] Rumors abounded concerning the amount. Jews also obtained "new" clothing, which stood out against Poles' ragged garb. Additionally, at a time when food supplies were low, Jews received packages of food; Poles, on the other hand, were hungry. Poles' resentment of Jews intensified. Thus, this depleted and diminished Jewish population was a great source of angst for many Poles. During the Communist

---

80 Monika Rice, *"What! Still Alive?!": Jewish Survivors in Poland and Israel Remember Homecoming* ed. Henry Feingold, Modern Jewish History (Syracuse: Syracuse University Press, 2017).
81 Steinlauf, *Bondage to the Dead: Poland and the Memory of the Holocaust*, 59.
82 Szaynok, "The Role of Antisemitism in Postwar Polish-Jewish Relations," 269.
83 Joanna Tokarska-Bakir, *Pogrom Cries—Essays on Polish-Jewish History, 1939–1946* (Frankfurt am Main: Peter Lang, 2017), 251.

Party's consolidation of power in immediate postwar Poland, 1944–1947, antisemitism burned across much of the country.

Violence as a Polish Response to Jewish Returnees

Catholic Church anti-Jewish teachings, prewar Polish political antisemitism, Żydokomuna, and Nazi propaganda comingled with the fear that returning Jews would reclaim their prewar Jewish property. Poles responded with an intensifying wave of antisemitism. It crashed into villages and towns, with Poles threatening, robbing, beating, and harassing those few Jews who had survived Hitler's death machine and Stalin's hard labor deportations.

According to the Polish writer Irena Chmieleńska's December 9, 1945 essay "Wartime Children" published in the political literary weekly *Kuźnica*, the Polish youth played a large role in this postwar violence because it accepted Żydokomuna and had been demoralized by the war. She argues that exposure to the black market, propaganda and antisemitic behavior, violence and destruction led to the disintegration of Polish youths' moral compass:

> The Germans accustomed our children and us grown-ups as well to concepts of differentiating between human beings and people who were less than human. A Jew belonged to a different category from a human being.[. . .] I cannot forecast the future moral development of children who during their formative years, when moral and ethical notions crystallize, were taught that it is all right to kill a few million people.[84]

Added to this learned differentiation of human worth, some youth emerged from the war with a ruthless selfishness, taking advantage of every material gain without consideration for other people's welfare.[85] The acclaimed postwar Polish novelist Jerzy Andrzejewski portrays this disheartening reality in his 1948 book *Ashes & Diamonds* (*Popioł i Daiment*): the protagonist, Juliusz Szretter, who himself killed a friend with little to no regret, not only involved his followers in such bloodguilt but insisted they resist remorse.[86]

---

84 Quoted in Gross, *Fear: Anti-Semitism in Poland after Auschwitz*, 72.
85 Ibid., 71.
86 Jerzy Andrzewjewski, *Ashes & Diamonds*, trans. D. J. Welsh, introduction by Heinrich Böll, and foreword by Barbara Niemczyk (Evanston: Northwestern University Press, 1991).

Postwar anti-Jewish violence occurred more often against individuals or small groups. In December 1945, Poles shot and killed three Jews in Tarnów, one a nine-month-old baby. In an April 1946 CKŻP report, Poles murdered one Jewish repatriate in Tarnów and five in Nowy Targ. On April 30, near Czorsztyn, Poles executed seven Jews, including a fourteen-year-old boy.[87] Attacks also took place on large groups of Jews at Jewish orphanages, senior citizens' facilities, summer camps, and buildings housing Jewish returnees.[88] Contemporary Polish authorities insisted attacks against Jews were politically motivated (in that such Jews must have been communists). But this excuse is quite thin. For even if some of the Jewish victims affiliated with communism, too often ritual murder stood as the pretext for attacks. Surely communists could not be blamed for a crime that the Church claimed traditional Jews committed.

Pogroms coursed across Poland in 1945 and 1946. The first occurred in Chełm in late March and early April 1945, followed by riots in Rzeszów on June 14–15, 1945. Two months later, Poles murdered five Jews and maimed dozens during the Kraków pogrom, when assailants also plundered the synagogue, Jewish apartments, and stores.[89] These and other pogroms were driven by the nationalist version of the blood libel charge. The traditional blood libel warned that Jews needed the blood of Christian children for ritual purposes, such as the baking of matzah for Passover. In the nationalist version, the blood libel warned that Jews killed specifically *Polish* children for their blood. Here the Jews represented an enemy invasion which targeted the Polish nation's future ... its children.[90] Poles who chose to lash out against the returning Jew could do so believing they were protecting their children from danger. They did not need proof. The disinformation campaign had started long ago. Over centuries, generations had not only heard such falsehoods from trusted Church leaders, teachers, and parents, but also passed it on to the next generations, transforming them into accepted "fact."

Despite no evidence that Jews performed this fictitious ritual, people insisted on it. One letter originating in Kraków falsely states:

---

87 Szaynok, "Poles and Jews from July 1944 to July 1946," 17.
88 Jan Gross, "Stereotypes of Polish-Jewish Relations after the War: The Special Commission of the Central Committee of Polish Jews," in Polonsky, *Focusing on the Holocaust and Its Aftermath*, 200.
89 Gross, *Fear: Anti-Semitism in Poland after Auschwitz*, 82.
90 Tokarska-Bakir, *Pogrom Cries—Essays on Polish-Jewish History, 1939–1946*, 177–178.

> In our town, there are skirmishes with Jews [a reference to the Kraków pogrom], 'cause, can you imagine, the Jews have gone so far as to kill Polish children to get blood from them. [...] The militia found a few corpses in the synagogue cellar. This instantly spread across the town, and the Poles, wherever they came across a Jew they beat him and smashed their stalls at the second-hand market.[91]

Another letter writer charged that "we've got news here i.e. in Kraków—the Jews have murdered a dozen-or-so Polish children. Barrels of blood have been found."[92] People added to this nationalist fantasy the belief that "the Jews catch little children and draw blood from them for the Jews returning from camps."[93] In other words, it was rumored that Jews drank blood as medicine. Associated with the new medical procedure of blood transfusion, this spin gave the blood libel further validity in postwar Poland.

How could twentieth-century Poles actually believe in the blood libel? Some scholars, including Jan Tomasz Gross, hold that Poles did not believe it but simply employed it to further their agenda against the Jews.[94] In her book *Pogrom Cries*, Joanna Tokarska-Bakir challenges this common position. While agreeing with Gross that the ritual murder legend has functioned as a justification to release economic or political anger onto Jewish communities, Tokarska-Bakir demonstrates that there was a deep-seated belief in the blood libel among various sectors of Poles—be they laborers, government officials or Church leaders. In their minds, it was true.

The Polish intelligentsia responded to this violence in horror. So far removed from the pulse of the people, it had no inkling that Poles still held such beliefs nor that they would unleash violence against Jews. Following the Kraków pogrom, Wincenty Bednarczuk published an article in *Odrodzenie*, one of the period's most important political-literary weeklies:

> No longer an economic issue, it is no longer a political issue either. It is a moral problem pure and simple. Today is not a question of saving the Jews from misery and death, it is a problem of saving the Poles from moral misery and spiritual death.[95]

---

91 Ibid., 183.
92 Ibid.
93 Ibid.
94 Ibid., 245–246.
95 Quoted in ibid., 29.

Despite such outcries, blood libel charges rang out in Polish streets, rousing people against the Jews in Kraków, Kielce, Bytom, Białystok, Szczecin, Bielawa, Otwock, Przemyśl and Legnica.[96]

The main question facing Jewish survivors was whether to remain in Poland or to emigrate. Interestingly, until July 1946, postwar antisemitism had not prompted Jews to leave Poland: brutality affected all people in the postwar Polish streets. Rather, Jews chose to leave because of the constant reminder that they had survived when their relatives and friends had not. Moshe Maltz, a survivor from Sokal, Galicia, wrote in his diary, "I have begun to venture out a little, but never very far from my house because I still don't feel strong enough to see the homes of my relatives and friends who are gone."[97] David Meller, a Jewish activist in postwar Poland, understood this situation when he wrote: "Everybody wanted to be as far as possible from the places with the ashes of the murdered, the dearest ones; everybody wanted to escape the memories, to be like other people, and have his own nook, his Homeland."[98]

The CKŻP explained in a memorandum to the British-American Commission the necessity many felt to leave Poland: "The basic reason for the emigration trend is the fact that many Jews . . . cannot live in the places that are the cemeteries of their families, relatives, and friends . . . For the remnants of savagely murdered families it is hard to decide to go on living where they had lost their dearest ones."[99] Thus, tens of thousands emigrated. Some stole into Palestine through Bricha, the illegal underground movement smuggling Polish Jews into the Holy Land. Many other Polish Jews migrated to countries in which they had relatives. This desire to escape Poland took on greater urgency after the Kielce pogrom.

Kielce, July 4, 1946

On July 1, 1946, eight-year-old Henryk Błaszczyk left his hometown of Kielce without telling anyone. He missed his old village and his friends, and wanted to pick the summer cherries he remembered from prior years. He got a ride from

---

96 Gross, "Stereotypes of Polish-Jewish Relations after the War: The Special Commission of the Central Committee of Polish Jews," 201. According to Szaynok, until spring 1946, the majority of violent anti-Jewish events and attempts at pogroms took place in central and eastern parts of Poland, including Rzeszów, Tarnów, Kalisz, Lublin, Parczewo, and Kolbuszowa. Bożena Szaynok, "Poles and Jews From July 1944 To July 1946," 17.
97 Quoted in Aleksium, "Jewish Responses to Antisemitism in Poland, 1944–1947," 249.
98 Quoted in Szaynok, "The Impact of the Holocaust on Jewish Attitudes in Postwar Poland," 242.
99 Quoted in ibid., 241.

Jan Bartosiński, father of Henryk's village friends (Józek and Czesiek), and travelled twenty-five kilometers to the Bartosiński's farm.[100] As stated in testimony given in the 1990s, when the boy returned on July 3, neighbors suggested that he had been taken by Jews.[101]

According to S. L. Shneiderman's interview with Henryk Błaszczyk on July 5, 1946, Jan Bartosiński ordered Henryk to blame his disappearance on having been kidnapped by Jews. It would have looked terribly irresponsible of Bartosiński to have taken the boy on a days-long trip without first asking permission from his parents. Bartosiński directed Henryk to say that he had been kept in the cellar of the building occupied by Jews at 7 Planty Street. This building housed various Jewish organizations as well as some 180 Jewish survivors, most of whom had recently been repatriated from the Soviet Union.[102] Upon his return, Henryk claimed that he had been starved and maltreated, and that he had seen the bodies of murdered Christian children in the cellar.[103] Henryk's father, Walenty Błaszczyk, informed the police of Henryk's kidnapping. With some prodding that same morning, the boy pointed out an older Jewish man wearing a green hat walking on the street near 7 Planty. Kalman Singer, Henryk charged, was his assailant.[104]

Kielce's inhabitants first learned about the alleged local ritual murders from five plainclothesmen, who worked for the Ministry of Public Security (known as UB or MBP), and nine uniformed policemen (Milicja Obywatelska, Citizens' Militia, MO—also under the MBP, but which had a number of Home Army members in it).[105] On their way to 7 Planty to investigate the matter, Kielce residents followed them. News of the supposed murders spread quickly and more people gathered in front of the building. The postwar clash between Polish nationalists and Polish communists converged there: when the UB told the crowd that the blood libel charges were merely a provocation and untrue, the

---

100 Gross, *Fear: Anti-Semitism in Poland after Auschwitz*, 281, notes 5 and 6.
101 One of the two neighbors listening to his conversation with the returned boy was Antoni Pasowski, the Błaszczyk's landlord, who also owned two Kielce houses which belonged to Jews in the prewar era. Purported to be a UB officer, Pasowski feared he would lose his property with the Jews' return. See Joanna Tokarska-Bakir, *Pogrom Cries—Essays on Polish-Jewish History, 1939–1946*, 253n32.
102 Shneiderman, *Between Fear and Hope*, 88.
103 Ibid., 88, 94.
104 Gross, *Fear: Anti-Semitism in Poland after Auschwitz*, 84.
105 Ibid., 231, 233–234.

mob turned on them. They shouted: "Down with the Russian security that protects the Jews."[106] The UB requested reinforcement from the army.

Both the army and MO were passive when confronted with the mob's rage, however. Most likely due to their own antisemitism and emboldened by the mob's chants, members from both the army and MO entered the building. Civilians followed suit. It did not matter that 7 Planty had neither a basement nor corpses of children in it. The killing of Jews by members of the police and army ensued. Those sent to protect the Jews from the mob had turned against their wards. In fact, they played a large role in starting the pogrom. Once the uniformed officers began thrusting Jews out of the building and into the crowd, the mob fell on them.[107] When the Security Service commander Władysław Sobczyński arrived on the scene, he took no steps to stop the massacre. This was the same Sobczyński who was responsible for the wartime murders of Jewish refugees by the communist partisan unit Świt.

Top secret reports written by members of the Central Committee of the PPR—people who investigated the social tensions in Kielce and other urban areas—and which were declassified only at the end of the twentieth century, state: "It must be stressed that the police took part in the pogrom. The police and army were the first to enter the Jewish house. Policemen dragged the Jewish victims out of the building and exposed them to the crowd."[108] The crowd beat the Jews with heavy blunt objects, killing many and critically injuring others. Despite the fact that several high-ranking officers were near the scene, not one took decisive action to control the crowd. Newly arriving authorities finally dispersed the mob around noon.[109]

But the pogrom did not end. A second phase began when workers from the Ludwików steelworks foundry arrived en masse, entered the building, and murdered and maimed more Jews. In the end, Poles brutally beat and killed forty-two Jews in Kielce, including two pregnant women, one of whom was stabbed in the belly.[110]

The murder of Jews was not confined to the Jewish Committee's building or to the town. Assaults and murders of Jews traveling by trains, which stopped at or near Kielce, also took place, leaving thirty more Jews dead. That same

---

106 Tokarska-Bakir, *Pogrom Cries—Essays on Polish-Jewish History, 1939–1946*, 256–257.
107 Gross, *Fear: Anti-Semitism in Poland after Auschwitz*, 87.
108 Quoted in Joanna Michlic-Coren, "Polish Jews during and after the Kielce Pogrom: Reports from the Communist Archives," in Polonsky, *Focusing on the Holocaust and Its Aftermath*, 263.
109 Gross, *Fear: Anti-Semitism in Poland after Auschwitz*, 90.
110 Ibid., 91.

declassified report cited above notes that "[r]ailway workers have been responsible to a great extent for the anti-Jewish atmosphere [...]. It must be said that the railway guards from the Kielce Częstochowa line help the perpetrators to find the Jews by pointing at them and encouraging the perpetrators to beat up the Jews."[111]

Unlike the authorities in Kielce, those in Kalisz and Częstochowa (together with respected citizens) prevented violence from erupting after rumors of ritual murder circulated amongst an assembled mob. In Częstochowa, Bishop Teodor Kubina, together with city and county officials, issued an immediate and emphatic statement against the murder of Jews, the Kielce pogrom, and the medieval lie which prompted it: "We declare: all statements about ritual murder are lies. [...] We do not know of a single case of a Christian child abducted by Jews. [...] We appeal to all ... to combat with all your strength all the attempts to organize anti-Jewish excesses."[112] The city of Sopot (Zoppott) went further than making official statements. It set up lectures to demonstrate to the public that the belief in ritual murder was based on lies.[113] Thus, while the population held antisemitic views, and they could be easily swayed by antisemitic tales, their anger could also be quelled by proactive local authorities.

Post-Kielce: Jews and Poles

Kielce proved a turning point for returning Jews ... and for Poles. Jews feared for their safety and their future in Poland. Poles too feared for their safety and their future in the country. This point is too often ignored. Both Jews and Poles had been victimized; and both had been victimizers. And while some Jews and Poles believed fully in the need to live once again in the same land together, more Jews and Poles concluded that each population needed its own land.

Right-wing nationalists applauded the post-Kielce uptick in emigration when some one hundred thousand Jews fled to safety. Crushed at seeing communism take the country, they linked all Jews to the imposed power structure. The postwar Endek underground press proposed forcing Jews out of Poland, albeit in a "humane" fashion:

---

111 Quoted in Michlic-Coren, "Polish Jews during and after the Kielce Pogrom: Reports from the Communist Archives," 264.
112 Quoted in Gross, *Fear: Anti-Semitism in Poland after Auschwitz*, 149–150.
113 Ibid., 152n*.

> As all Poles consider Jews as a needless and a highly harmful factor in a national organism [...] Poles will get rid of them. It will be done in a human way, without fierceness and racial hatred [...] Poles do not intend to murder Jews on a mass scale or to starve them to death—they will simply make them leave the country.[114]

In other words, the Endeks advocated a "civilized" form of ethnic cleansing.[115] The belief that targeting Jews in a "humane way" was *not* racially motivated formed a Polish nationalist mantra, which lasted for generations.

As both Jews and Poles agitated for the former's emigration, they each did so out of fear of the Other. The Polish historian Krystyna Kersten highlights the underground press view of Jews as a threat to Polish society—a threat against which the people could fight and release their anger:

> It is characteristic that Jews—as real people and as a cliché-concept—appear in the underground materials solely as an element of threat; aggression intensified by the sense of helplessness—the reaction to the postwar situation in the country—not having any outlet in the form of openly pointing out the real perpetrators of the Polish defeat, turned against a surrogate enemy—Jews.[116]

By blaming the Jews for the imposed communist regime and its system of terror, Poles could relinquish their own responsibility.

Yet for Poles to have reached this somewhat whitewashing conclusion, they first had to have *an inclination* to see Jews as a threat. Only with this foundation could Poles perceive communists of Jewish parentage as *Jews* in the first place. Since the early twentieth century, Dmowski's political antisemitic rhetoric had been married to the Church's historical Jew-hatred, increasing the number of Poles who embraced the enemy-Jew position.

---

114 Quoted in Szaynok, "Poles and Jews from July 1944 to July 1946," 20.
115 *Ethnic cleansing* is an emotionally charged term that readers typically associate with genocide. However, it refers to the forced removal of an ethnic group from a territory by a stronger ethnic group through various methods, including intimidation, violence, or genocide. See Michlic, *Poland's Threatening Other: The Image of the Jew from 1880 to the Present*, 217.
116 Quoted in Szaynok, "Poles and Jews from July 1944 to July 1946," 20.

The historian Joanna Beata Michlic's research shows that this postwar presentation of Jews as a grave threat to the Polish nation was grounded in Roman Dmowski's interwar rhetoric. The same vilifying language with which nationalists targeted interwar Poland's Jews filled postwar nationalist diatribes. Descriptions of the Jews as a "menace," a "curse," and "a tribe of parasites" were penned and voiced during the interwar period. In the immediate postwar period, the Endek rhetoric of the Jew as the threatening Other united Polish nationalists in their struggle for the country and provided a simple explanation for social problems and failures, just as it had in the late interwar years.[117] The difference being that now, after the Second World War and the communist takeover, Poles had not only been defeated but saw the feared Jew-communist in power.

Post-Kielce: The Communist Authorities and Workers

Through a top secret investigation into the pogrom, the PPR gained insight into workers' relations with the Jews. Communist leaders had expected its base to follow party ideology, as it had in prewar Poland. Workers' groups refusal to sign prepared statements against the Kielce massacre surprised officials. The workers held onto their own specific baggage, their negative perceptions of Jews (and Germans) as prewar bosses and factory owners. Workers were unhappy that Jewish returnees appeared to lead a more privileged existence. They did not have to work, but instead collected aid from international Jewish organizations, such as the JOINT, as well as the government. Some Jews had reclaimed "Polish" shops, and some even received managerial positions in factories.[118]

Polish workers had rebuilt the factories; they had believed that the communists would eventually hand management over to them. But that did not happen. The state encroached on the workers' rights to factory leadership positions. Workers lost their patience, organized, and mounted strikes.[119] The post-Kielce

---

117 Michlic-Coren, "Anti-Jewish Violence in Poland, 1918–1939 and 1945–1947," 41.
118 Padriac Kenney, "Whose Nation, Whose State? Working-Class Nationalism and Antisemitism in Poland, 1945–1947," in Antony Polonsky, *Focusing on the Holocaust and Its Aftermath*, 227, 230–231. What Poles did not see was that by 1947 46% of Jewish wage earners worked in mining and industry. More than 18% of working Jews held posts in the state administration and 12% in commerce. See Polonsky, *The Jews in Poland and Russia*, 3:625.
119 Kenney, "Whose Nation, Whose State? Working-Class Nationalism and Antisemitism in Poland, 1945–1947," 227.

legal trials became a lightning rod for workers' dissatisfaction when the system displayed a paucity of due process, and sentenced nine pogromists to death after a quick two-day trial. The people's anger flared.

The Kielce pogrom and the communists' swift convictions allowed people to conflate two separate anti-Jewish orientations: the Church's blood libel and the politicians' Żydokomuna charge. During an emergency meeting of Dęblin railway workers, the fifteen hundred attendees shouted at the Polish Workers' Party (PPR) representatives who had convened there: "Get rid of the Jews! It's a disgrace that they [the PPR representatives] came to defend the Jews! . . . The Jews murdered thirteen Polish children and they . . . are defending them!"[120] At the same time, workers spewed resentment of the Jews' supposed military imposition of communism. They were convinced that Poles were suffering directly due to Jews' actions: "In Poland the Soviets drive tanks and terrorize us with their rifles! Is this freedom?!!! Why are so many Poles held in prisons and why are the military barracks full of those arrested?!"[121] They answered these questions themselves, stating: "The Jews are the heads of Public Security!!"[122] By 1947, the Jew as powerful communist replaced the prewar image of the Jew as powerful capitalist.

The workers' uproar surprised PPR Central Committee representatives. They expected the workers to align with the PPR's support for the Jewish pogrom victims. Instead, Polish workers viewed those Poles sentenced to death at the first Kielce trial as the real victims. The PPR had organized mass meetings at factories so that workers would sign condemnations of the anti-Jewish pogroms. Instead, workers refused, expressed their anger, and went on strike. Clearly, the PPR did not have the Poles' approval. The party would have to change tactics to generate greater support among the workers. Just a year prior, the PPR offered financial compensation to victims of the Kraków pogrom. After Kielce, the PPR took the workers' lead. Muting its position on the pogromists, it turned against the Jews, blaming the pogrom on their so-called unproductiveness.[123]

---

120 Quoted in Michlic-Coren, "Polish Jews and the Kielce Pogrom," 261.
121 Quoted in ibid..
122 Quoted in ibid.
123 Gross, *Fear: Anti-Semitism in Poland after Auschwitz*, 127–128.

Post-Kielce: Church Leadership

Most Polish Catholic clergy, who identified with the Polish war victim and Polish victim of communism, were reluctant to express too much support for the Jews. When Czesław Olejniczak and his fellow investigators visited Kalisz July 10–12, 1946, they met with the parish priest of Saint Nicholas Parish. They requested that the Reverend Martuzalski sign an appeal for harmony and encourage the clergy to offer calming sermons. Though Martuzalski condemned the Kielce pogrom, he also "stated that the loathsome Jews were not needed, that these vile rats headed by Minc and Borejsza had taken over our lives."[124] As the heads of the economy, the press, and publishing, these two communist chiefs of Jewish heritage were a symbol of Jews ruling Poland. Martuzalski suggested that "we should follow Czechoslovakia in its policy to get rid of Jews."[125]

Some Church leaders, such as Bishop Teodor Kubina of Częstochowa, opposed this type of argument. As we have seen, he immediately stepped in to counter the ritual murder lie and to quell the rising fury of his parishioners. Father Henryk Weryński of Kraków also took this more liberal Catholic stance:

> the Kielce pogrom cannot be viewed as an isolated event in our republic . . . I appeal to parents, to teachers in both secular and religious schools, to do everything in their power to prevent a repetition of this situation. The words of Sienkiewicz: "Hatred not only poisons those who indulge in it, it also degrades them," are still true. Let us see to it that our nation is not degraded by hatred.[126]

But some of Poland's high-ranking Church clergy actually believed in the blood libel.

As the auxiliary bishop of Upper Silesia, Bishop Juliusz Bienik shared his opinion on the subject with Victor Cavendish-Bentinck, the British ambassador to Poland. The latter wrote of a shocking conversation held one and a half months after Kielce:

---

124 Quoted in Michlic-Coren, "Polish Jews and the Kielce Pogrom," 260.
125 Quoted in ibid.
126 Quoted in Shneiderman, *Between Fear and Hope*, 115–116.

> Bishop Bienik ... astonished me yesterday by stating that there was some proof that the child [Henryk Błaszczyk] whose alleged maltreatment by Jews had provoked the Kielce pogrom had in fact been maltreated and that the Jews had taken blood from his arm. If a bishop is prepared to believe this, it is not surprising that uneducated Poles do so too.[127]

Not only did a bishop accept the blood libel, so too did the Vatican. Arieh Kochavi demonstrates that "there was little or no difference between Vatican Antisemitism and that of the Polish bishops."[128] He cites a Vatican memorandum which notes that "'the influx of Jews [from the USSR] into Poland coincided with the mysterious vanishing of Christian children.'"[129] The Vatican accepted that the child in Kielce had been kidnapped for his blood, and only expressed doubts concerning the number of Jewish victims in the pogrom. The Catholic Church not only generated this false charge, but also continued it.

When speaking with foreign journalists about the Kielce pogrom, Poland's primate Cardinal August Hlond deflected the idea that the Church's blood libel accusation had sparked the Kielce conflagration. To maintain the clergy's standing and deny that antisemitism led to the murders, Hlond argued that the pogrom "violence did not occur for racial reasons."[130] Rather, he submitted that Poles killed Jews in Kielce because "Jews occupy the leading positions in Poland's government and endeavor to introduce a governmental structure which the majority of people do not desire."[131] Hlond willingly swapped an anti-Jewish fantasy for an antisemitic one.

Lublin's Bishop Wyszyński concurred with this more dominant view that Poles hated Jews because Jews supposedly drove the communist takeover of Poland. Speaking with foreign journalists about the Kielce pogrom, he stressed that "[i]n Poland, Jews are not the only ones being murdered; Poles too suffer that fate."[132] Herein lies one of the central problems we must confront: Poles' suffering during the war had been overshadowed by Jews' suffering. And now, in this postwar hell, Poles' suffering had once again been hijacked by the Jews.

---

127 Quoted in Michlic, *Poland's Threatening Other: The Image of the Jew from 1880 to the Present*, 219–220.
128 Arieh Kochavi, *Post-Holocaust Politics: Britain, the United States & Jewish Refugees, 1945–1948* (Chapel Hill: University of North Carolina Press, 2001), 181.
129 Ibid.
130 Quoted in Shneiderman, *Between Fear and Hope*, 112–113.
131 Quoted in ibid.
132 Quoted in Gross, *Fear: Anti-Semitism in Poland after Auschwitz*, 148–149.

Thousands upon thousands of Poles were murdered in the immediate postwar years. For Poles, this reality overshadowed the much smaller number of Jews killed in the same period. Poles were unconcerned about anti-Jewish violence while they endured their own crisis. Kielce represents the Poles' inability to see beyond their own agony and empathize with the Jews' particular misery. Kielce represents a gulf so wide that one must wonder how it can ever be bridged.

Post-Kielce: Polish Intellectuals

Not all Poles resented the Jews' victimhood. Poland's intellectuals were horrified by the people's continued antisemitism in the post-Holocaust world. One year before Kielce, the Polish poet Mieczysław Jastruń[133] commiserated over wartime and postwar Polish-Jewish relations. He wrote the following in "The Power of Ignorance" ("Potęga clemnoty"), published June 17, 1945 in the cultural weekly *Odrodzenie* (Rebirth):

> Antisemitism, which was already deeply rooted in Poland before this war, has not weakened—despite the murder of over three million [Polish] Jews, and people designated as Jews by the Nazi inquisition. In the realm of morality, this fact is no less horrible than that of the mass-scale Nazi crime.[134]

To express their sense of tragedy, Polish intellectuals wrote articles, signed dramatic protest letters, and made public appeals.[135] Stanislaw Lec even argued: "We do not need articles or short stories. What is needed is a new law that would protect the lives of our citizens."[136]

Jerzy Andrzejewski, a prewar Endek turned supporter of Jews, agreed with other leading intellectuals that antisemitism had become ingrained in the Polish people: "Polish antisemitism did not burn itself out in the rubble and the smoldering ruins of the ghettos." In his essay "The Question of Polish Antisemitism"

---

133 Mieczysław Jastruń was born into a Jewish family, published in the interwar monthly Skamander, and later joined the Polish Communist Party (PZPR).
134 Mieczysław Jastruń, "The Power of Ignorance," in Michnik and Marczyk, *Against Anti-Semitism: An Anthology of Twentieth-Century Polish Writings*, 86.
135 Polish intellectuals grieved over the Jews' particular tragedy in the Holocaust. See Władysław Broniewski's poem "To Polish Jews," Czesław Miłosz's "Giordano Bruno," several of Jerzy Zagórski's stanzas, as well as plays by Stefan Otwinowski and Flora Bieńkowska.
136 Quoted in Shneiderman, *Between Fear and Hope*, 120.

(written before Kielce, but published in *Odrodzenie*, July 7, 1946, immediately after the tragedy), he acknowledged that

> for six years, in the most cruel of all battles in the history of the world, humanity—let us use this grand word—fought for freedom, justice, and human dignity; and woe to the nations unable to draw the right conclusions from this experience. Hatred, contempt, and racial prejudice are certainly not the right conclusions.[137]

Having lived close to the Warsaw Ghetto during the war, Andrzejewski was greatly impacted by the ghetto liquidation:

> Those days and nights, filled with the sounds of gunshot salvos and spurts of machine gunfire, were the most difficult moments of the entire occupation. Only the following Easter, and the Warsaw Uprising, surpassed them in bitterness, shameful helplessness, and loss of faith in the meaning of Poland and Poles.
>
> For all honest Poles, the fate of the perishing Jews must have been exceptionally painful. Innocent people were dying, and our nation did not have the right to look them in the eye with a clear conscience.[138]

Andrzejewski concludes:

> How I wish I could honestly answer: "Yes! Antisemitism is dying out in Poland, the Polish nation has learned what it needed to learn." Unfortunately [...] I cannot reach any conclusion other than that the Polish nation—with all its strata and in its entire intellectual cross-section—had, and after the war continues to have, an antisemitic orientation.[139]

Andrzejewski suggests that the Polish-Jewish conflict is central to Poland's cultural landscape— just as in the United States, where for centuries racism has

---

137 Jerzy Andrzejewski, "The Problem of Polish Anti-Semitism," in Michnik and Marczyk, *Against Anti-Semitism: An Anthology of Twentieth-Century Polish Writings*, 95.
138 Ibid., 98.
139 Ibid., 99–100.

caused major social, political, and economic problems. In the baggage Poles carry and pass on to the next generation, the Polish-Jewish conflict is ever-present, even when Jews are barely visible. Like racism in the United States, it often exists just under the surface. The question Andrzejewski asks is: Which leader will people align with when tensions erupt into violence again? Bishop Teodor Kubina or Cardinal August Hlond?

Andrzejewski fought against this plague:

> [l]iving at a turning point and laying down the very first foundations for tomorrow, we have to be vigilant so we do not fill new social forms with the content of old habits. The shaping of our own minds and hearts seems to be just as momentous and pressing as the formation of the socio-economic order.[140]

The Polish leadership did not heed his words as Polish intellectuals neither represented nor influenced the Polish majority. Kielce spotlighted the enormous chasm between the intellectual elites and the masses.

Memory Making

The weak response to Kielce by most Polish authorities merged with the Soviet agenda of ingratiating the communist regime to Eastern bloc populations. By highlighting—and thereby empathizing with—the people's wartime horrors, the Communist Party attempted to gain the people's trust and the party's own legitimization within the various Soviet client states. As such, Polish communist officials underscored the Polish people's tragedy during WWII, while silencing recognition of the separate Jewish catastrophe. Influenced by the Kremlin's own swift movement toward the suppression of knowledge about specifically Jewish tragedies, the Poles, like communists in other East European countries, conflated the two wartime horrors into one.[141] Students would not learn that Hitler

---

140 Ibid., 105.
141 See John-Paul Himka and Joanna Beata Michlic, introduction to *Bringing the Dark Past to Light: The Reception of the Holocaust in Postcommunist Europe*, ed. John-Paul Himka and Joanna Beata Michlic (Lincoln: University of Nebraska Press, 2013); Polonsky, *The Jews in Poland and Russia*, 3:614–615. Stalin transitioned from demonstrating some respect for the particular Jewish experience during WWII after growing paranoid over Soviet Jews' response to Israel's 1948 declaration of statehood. Fearing Jewish nationalism, he quashed references to the Holocaust.

had killed three million non-Jewish Poles and three million Polish Jews. Instead, Polish students would learn that Hitler had killed six million Poles through gas chambers, mass shootings, starvation, and slave labor.

To be clear, since the very beginning of the Polish People's Republic, not only did the authorities bury the Jews' particular experience during the Holocaust, but the Jews' experience in general as part of the Polish past. This effort fortified the construction of the official party discourse which centered communist Poland as the direct heir to Poland's Piast tradition. In their struggle for legitimization, the communist authorities embraced this early period of Poland's existence as their own. To create this convoluted correspondence between the Piast dynasty and the Polish People's Republic, the authorities actively erased any notion of the Jagiellonian multi-ethnic tradition.[142] Fitting to the new postwar borders that had shifted westward to the smaller Piast territory, this false narrative also secured the image of Poles' constant friendship with a benevolent yet stronger Russia. As such, the regime ignored that Poland had once swallowed up and controlled part of the land now under Soviet rule. And in so doing it also edited out of national memory the significant ethnic populations that filled that land and formed its multiethnic past. Thus, school curriculums made no mention of Roma, Germans, Belarussians, Ukrainians, and Jews as part of Poland's past. During the existence of the Polish People's Republic, the country would be viewed through this homogenizing lens. Indeed, "[o]ne of the results of this policy was the almost total elimination of the Jews from official Polish history."[143] The Jews had disappeared. That is, except for the "Jews" charged with controlling the government. (Such colliding messages did not concern the authorities. Regime propaganda simply ignored any logical contradictions.)[144]

The 1964 unveiling of the monument at the Treblinka death camp (the second largest extermination camp after Auschwitz) is a good example of this revisionist history. In his dedication, Prime Minister Cyrankiewicz referred to the victims as "800,000 citizens of European nations."[145] Although Polish leaders knew that Jews made up the vast majority of the martyred at Treblinka, the official narrative stressed, "the resistance and martyrdom of Poles and citizens of

---

142 Jan Kubik, *The Power of Symbols against the Symbols of Power: The Rise of Solidarity and the Fall of State Socialism in Poland* (University Park: The Pennsylvania State University Press, 1994), 65.
143 Ibid.
144 Ibid., 42–49.
145 Polonsky, *The Jews in Poland and Russia*, 3:697.

other nationalities."¹⁴⁶ Poles concerned themselves with their national narrative, and the Jewish tragedy could only undermine it. Thus, the Communist Party in Poland, and elsewhere in the Soviet bloc, rewrote the past.

We see this alternative reality presented in the 1966 edition of the *Great Universal Encyclopedia* (*Wielka encyclopedia powszechna*). In volume 8, the original article "Nazi Concentration Camps" drew a distinction between two types of camps: *annihilation* camps, which were designated almost entirely for Jews most of whom were killed immediately upon arrival, and *concentration* camps, which imprisoned various nationalities, including a high number of Poles. To the editors' demise, this recognition that Jews and Poles both suffered but to different degrees was not acceptable to the Polish communists (who were now also Polish nationalists and known as the Partisans). The authorities fired the editor (of Jewish origin), dismissed the article, and ordered a new version.¹⁴⁷ Such was the shaping of memory.

Myth Reconstruction

With the 1989–1991 transition from the Polish People's Republic to the Third Polish Republic, the possibility arrived for individuals to share their memories in public without fear of harassment (though old fears die hard). However, even today, it does not feel acceptable to utter the word "Żydokomuna." Poles avoid it, many knowing that it indicates a past acceptance of deep Polish antisemitism. At the same time, American Jews resist any truths contained in this stereotype. As we have already seen, while some Poles have engaged this problem for decades, American Jews have been slow to recognize it, let alone teach about it outside of college classrooms.

Some courageous Poles have argued for the communal need to wrestle with the Żydokomuna narrative. Poles have resisted acknowledging that communism was *not* a specifically Jewish political ideology. It was not an attempt to help people of the Jewish faith. Jews who did participate in its installation in Poland were secular idealists searching for a way out of traditional Judaism and poverty. When the communists conquered a territory, they did not insist that the Jewish religion be held in higher regard than any other faith. They excoriated all religion, including Judaism. Communism appealed to minorities because it promised all people equal treatment as human beings, with a particular emphasis on

---

146 Ibid.
147 Ibid.

the proletariat, which had been trampled for so long. Communism promised a better future for Polish Jews and Polish non-Jews alike.

It is through this lens that Kielce resident Bogdan Bialek researches the taboos of the Kielce pogrom and the blood ritual fiction. The acclaimed 2016 documentary film *The Last Pogrom: Bogdan's Journey* about the 1946 pogrom is an attempt to address this social tragedy. The film opens with the disclaimer: "First, I'm a Christian and a Pole. That's a big obligation for me. Everything good in me comes from my faith."[148] Bialek's compassionate approach to Kielce is measured: "[e]ach of us has a tough moment in our past. Either we were harmed, or we harmed someone. Until we name it, we drag the past behind us. All the time. The past ends when we end it. We end it when we learn to talk about it normally."[149]

Together with Kielce's United Methodist Church minister Janusz Daszuta, Bogdan Bialek has wrestled for decades with the forced and the selective amnesia that settled on Kielce, and the country, during the forty years of communist repression. Nobody wanted to talk about it: not the communists, not the Church, and not the people. "There was fear, shame, a sense of guilt."[150] According to the historian Marek Maciągowski, "removing the pogrom from collective memory was the Communist's success."[151]

In the year 2000, Bogdan Bialek and Janusz Daszuta led their first "March of Memory and Prayer." Without pressuring people to participate, and without protesting the past, they took action to show respect to the victims of Kielce and their families. "We would simply come and say what happened, where it happened, who was killed."[152] Dressed in black, they walked to the Jewish cemetery where the Kielce victims are buried. There, they also said the mourner's kaddish and blew the shofar (respectively: the prayer Jews recite when in mourning or observing the anniversary of a close relative's death and a ram's horn Jews blow during the High Holy Days). Over the years, this march has grown in size. Citizens throughout Poland travel to join Kielce's residents in the healing process. Bialek has also set up an educational program through which he engages Poland's youth. To face the horrors of one's past actions is to open the door to healing. It is a necessary step in leading a country away from national egoism and towards a positive future.

---

148 *The Last Pogrom: Bogdan's Journey*, dir. Michał Jaskulski and Lawrence Loewinger (Metro Films and Two Point Films, 2016), 00:39.
149 Ibid., 1:19–1:45.
150 Ibid., 4:00.
151 Ibid., 4:13.
152 Ibid., 6:00.

Just as Polish Christians have been facing up to their dark past, so too have Polish Jews been trying to think about their own bad actors. Having embraced and learned to merge his Polish and Jewish identities, Stanisław Krajewski discusses the taboo topic of Żydokomuna through the lens of Jewish victimization in his book *Poland and the Jews: Reflections of a Polish Polish Jew*. He argues that Jews' victimization has taken too central a role: it has almost entirely identified Jewishness with the Holocaust: "The museums replace the synagogues and houses of study, Auschwitz replaces Sinai."[153] Krajewski warns that this victim narrative can lead to a black-and-white picture: "we Jews are the victims, the innocent good people; the others are the bad guys, the enemy, the guilty. While this makes sense in relation to the Shoah, it does not do justice to all later situations."[154] One such situation would be the imposition of communism on Polish society.

Krajewski supports his argument with Andrzej Paczkowski's statistics, discussed earlier,[155] which demonstrate that communists of Jewish origin had important roles during the early years of People's Poland. Most Jews in the US have excused, ignored, or not heard of these statistics. While Krajewski demonstrates that communism was not a Jewish system, he also acknowledges that just as its doctrines attracted individual Poles, they also appealed to individual Jews. He posits that Jews fail to recognize that Poles of Jewish origin not only played significant parts in communist groups in interwar Poland, but that they also participated in the forced communist takeover of the Polish people: "The number of Jewish communists, and their role, was so important that other Jews must not ignore it."[156] As we have noted, communists of Jewish origin were at the heart of the hated security apparatus of the new regime.[157]

The historian Andrzej Paczkowski affirms that "Jews were over-represented, occupied higher rather than lower positions and that the higher the level, the greater their proportion."[158] Indeed, despite Stalin's oppression of Jews in the Soviet Union, which included purging them from powerful positions, destroying the Soviet Yiddish cultural establishment, and eradicating "Jewish cosmopolitans," the Soviets kept Jews in powerful posts in the Polish People's Republic. Antony Polonsky contends that the Kremlin tolerated Jews because it mistrusted

---

153 Krajewski, *Poland and the Jews: Reflections of a Polish Polish Jew*, 26.
154 Ibid.
155 Polonsky, "Jews and Communism in the Soviet Union and Poland," 161.
156 Krajewski, *Poland and the Jews: Reflections of a Polish Polish Jew*, 125.
157 Polonsky, "Jews and Communism in the Soviet Union and Poland," 160.
158 Ibid., 161

Polish nationalism much more than *Jewish* nationalism: "The retention of Jews in these positions in Poland was clearly intended by Stalin to be a temporary expedient until a larger group of reliable local communists could be trained."[159]

As we have seen, Polish society in 1946 was not ready to heal. After World War II, Poles continued battling over the future shape of their country. Communism had entrenched itself in the country through international diplomacy, military trickery, and national violence. Polish nationalists blamed communists of Jewish origin for the Soviet infiltration and takeover of Poland. Early on, communists of Jewish origin held an outsized proportion of high-level government posts. Especially when Jewish survivors of the Holocaust and Soviet internment returned to Poland, Poles succumbed to the potent antisemitic and anti-Jewish conspiracy theories of Żydokomuna and ritual murder. In acts of heinous violence, Poles attacked Jews. They blamed Jews for communism. In this way, they could unleash their outrage without facing up to the unappetizing reality that Poles of Christian origin were a prime cause of this national calamity. Intellectuals wrote scathing articles about Polish violence and condemned antisemitism. But, clearly, they did not have the ear of the people. While some clergy acted promptly to stop further violence, too many clerics asserted the Jews' enemy status, thus in part supporting the people's anger. Although the Communist Party first attempted to mitigate anti-Jewish violence, they ultimately permitted it, meeting the people where they stood in order to secure legitimacy.

---

159 Ibid., 165.

CHAPTER 16

Party Strife and Anti-*Zionism*

After July 1946, roughly one hundred thousand Jews fled Poland. Yet some seventy to eighty thousand remained. Why would Jews choose to live in Poland after Kielce? Physically weak, emotionally frail, many could not envision moving to a foreign land, learning a new language, and finding a viable job. Still others did not leave because they did not have relatives or friends in other countries. They could not imagine starting anew without some sense of support.

Other people of Jewish descent chose to stay after Kielce 1946 because they identified themselves as Poles and considered Poland their motherland. Assimilated, and often intermarried, many had survived the war by living in the open under the cover of false documents. With a deep connection to Poland, and fearing the ongoing stigma of their Jewish heritage, often these Poles of Jewish origin maintained their wartime "Aryan" identities.[1] They would find, however, that they could not completely repress their true identities. They may have felt authentically Polish; but society soon chose to designate them first as Jews. The changing political climate transformed Poles of Jewish ancestry into what Paul Lendvai has aptly termed "Jews by force."[2]

Other Jews who stayed did so believing that the new Polish People's Republic (Polska Rzeczpospolita Ludowa—PRL) would eliminate antisemitism and allow Jews to recreate communal life in Poland. Indeed, the PRL sanctioned funding from the American-based JOINT for the Jewish Social and Cultural Association (TSKŻ). However, unbeknownst to Jews in their post-Kielce deliberations, by 1949 the Polish United Workers' Party (PZPR) would ban foreign Jewish organizations from the Polish People's Republic and completely seal the borders due to the Cold War. Stalinism opposed any Western influence over the PRL's Jewish population. Additionally, once communists established a monopoly of power in 1947, the Kremlin encouraged the Polish authorities not only to

---

1 Szaynok, "The Impact of the Holocaust on Jewish Attitudes in Postwar Poland," 243.
2 Lendvai, *Antisemitism without Jews: Communist Eastern Europe*, 3.

surveil, but also to control all Jewish groups—social and religious. Effectively, the government took over the TSKŻ, Jewish schools, Jewish papers, and Jewish theatre.[3] By the time these Jews might have chosen to leave, the borders were sealed.

In this chapter, we will explore Polish-Jewish relations in terms of Communist Party dynamics and its anti-*Zionist* policies. As we have seen, in the past Poles had varying views of Jews. The Communist Party in Poland was no different.

Communist Party In-Fighting

As World War II neared its end, Polish communists who had spent years in Moscow (aka., Muscovites) returned to Poland to take political control. Crossing into the country, they faced off with those Polish communists who had remained underground and fought the German occupation. Stalin had confidence in the Muscovites, a large segment of which was of Jewish origin. He believed their tendency toward higher education made them more capable than Poles of functioning in high bureaucratic positions. Stalin also favored communists of Jewish extraction over Polish communist leaders due to his belief and fear that the latter would prioritize nationalist loyalty to Poland over the communist internationalist agenda. The returning Muscovites of Jewish background, who had few or no living family members, tended toward party loyalty, to a fault.

The Communist Party provided a sense of mission and meaning, and Muscovites responded with unconditional zeal. Thus, when Moscow ordered Roman Zambrowski, a Muscovite of Jewish descent, to issue an arrest warrant for Władysław Gomułka, an ethnic Pole who had headed the Communist Party in Poland, Zambrowski—a Moscow loyalist, Politburo member, and secretary of the Central Committee—complied. Due to Gomułka's activism in wartime Poland, Moscow conveniently labeled him a nationalist traitor, who deviated from communism's internationalist agenda. After Gomułka's 1948 imprisonment, Bolesław Bierut rose to power in the new Polish People's Republic.[4] At this time, Moscow also smeared other Polish communist chiefs as right-wing nationalist deviants, including Mieczysław Moczar. Though not imprisoned, Moczar was dismissed from his position as head of the Łodz Ministry of Public Security, (UB).[5]

---

3   Polonsky, *The Jews in Poland and Russia*, 3:646.
4   Lendvai, *Antisemitism without Jews: Communist Eastern Europe*, 78–79.
5   Michlic, *Poland's Threatening Other: The Image of the Jew from 1880 to the Present*, 240.

In December 1953, Józef Światło, defected to the West. A former deputy in the infamous Tenth Department of the Ministry of Public Security, Światło was of Jewish origin.[6] His 1955 broadcast on Radio Free Europe described not only a harsh, repressive terror system and the bestial Secret Police, but also the hypocritical economic disparity between Party leaders and the public.[7] The Polish People's Republic had been humiliated on the world stage. To disclaim Światło's accusations, communist Poland followed the USSR lead set by Nikita Khrushchev's de-Stalinization efforts and initiated a political thaw. Several interrogators from the Ministry of State Security were put on trial. Additionally, the thaw addressed broader economic and religious concerns: it halted the failing peasant collectivization policies, thus returning land to the people who farmed it; it sought a modus vivendi with the Catholic Church;[8] and it very quietly released several political prisoners, including Gomułka.

Władysław Gomułka Returns to a Fractured Party

While the Polish people welcomed Gomułka's rehabilitation and trusted him implicitly to lead their society along "Poland's path to socialism," they greatly misunderstood his loyalties and motivations. The public viewed him as a Polish martyr jailed by the malevolent Soviets. But like good communists of his time, Gomułka accepted his punishment without straying from his Party convictions. Instead of embracing the people's understanding of him as a more liberal person, who would carry forward the "Polish October," Gomułka remained a stalwart supporter of hardline Soviet communism.[9]

Upon his return to the political sphere, Gomułka met a fractured Polish Communist Party, consisting of the Puławska and Natolin groups. Named after the street in Warsaw where several members lived, the Puławska faction sought to push the thaw to its economic and cultural limits. With an internally diverse membership of ethnic Polish communists and those of Jewish origin (many of whom were Muscovites), Puławska was known as a reform-oriented group. While some members chose it out of ideological disillusionment with the old system and repented for their role in it, others did so out of political convenience and opportunism. Having the backing of the PZPR's intelligentsia, the Puławska

---

6   Polonsky, *The Jews in Poland and Russia*, 3:647.
7   Lendvai, *Antisemitism without Jews: Communist Eastern Europe*, 217–218.
8   Ibid., 218.
9   Polonsky, *The Jews in Poland and Russia*, 3:677.

faction was not anti-Soviet—but it did press for greater internal sovereignty, as well as liberalization and political democratization.[10]

The opposing Natolin faction, named after the small palace in a Warsaw neighborhood where members often gathered, consisted of ethnic Polish nationalists. Natolin was not only pro-Soviet, but also had strong anti-intelligentsia and anti-semitic proclivities. It attracted people who had been raised on Endecja's national chauvinism. The Natolin group sought to replace the old cadre of Stalinist chiefs with its own members, while retaining the same dogma and authoritarian rule.[11] It categorized any disapproved person as a Jew. Hoping to discredit their rival, Natolin referred to Puławska members as *Żydy* (Yids or kikes—the pejorative of *Żydi*, Jews); Puławska could be heard labelling Natolin members as *chamy* (boors, peasants).[12]

In his bid for power, Gomułka made a strategic pact with the Puławska group, the very people who had sent him to prison years earlier. On October 21, 1956, Gomułka was chosen to lead the Polish United Workers' Party (PZPR). He launched a political thaw, permitting many freedoms earlier denied. Within this framework, he readmitted the Jewish Joint Distribution Committee into the PRL. Due to this influx of American Jewish monetary and organizational support, the TSKŻ (the Jewish Social and Cultural Association) developed broad community programming for its 7,000–7,500 registered members, of whom about 25% were seniors. (Of course, those persons of Jewish origin who retained their wartime non-Jewish surnames did not register as part of Poland's postwar Jewish community.)

This was a time of devastating economic hardship. JOINT's funding allowed its Jewish recipients a slightly easier lot than the average Polish citizen. This distinction did not go unnoticed by some Poles, despite the existence of charitable organizations that dispensed aid to Poles in general, since they received much less per capita than the Jews. In conjunction with ORT, JOINT also provided TSKŻ members vocational training, as well as jobs in two factories that employed roughly two thousand Jews. JOINT supported the expansion of Yiddish culture by creating a publishing house, Jewish schools, Jewish summer camps, and sponsoring Jewish youth groups, such as the Warsaw Babel group.

---

10   Michlic, *Poland's Threatening Other: The Image of the Jew from 1880 to the Present*, 236.
11   Ibid., 235.
12   Ibid., 236; Polonsky, *The Jews in Poland and Russia*, 3:676, 683, 688.

The TSKŻ also established a dynamic Jewish theatre which honored and often featured Polish Jewish actress Ida Kamińska.[13]

Mieczysław Moczar's Return

General Mieczysław Moczar, who earlier had been victimized by Zambrowski's accusation of "nationalist deviation," was part of Gomułka's inner circle. A prewar ethno-nationalist who aligned with the Soviet Union during the war, Moczar formulated a new dogma that would lead the country down its particular Polish path to socialism: Endo-communism. Moczar tapped into latent beliefs, held by a large portion of the populace but suppressed by the authorities. He heard the people's silent clamor for an exclusivist vision of Polish national identity that had been "shaped, and deformed, by the war years and two decades of Communist rule."[14] Church-driven antisemitism, political nationalism, and fear of the Other—the Jew—had relatively lain dormant since those late interwar years. All that was needed to release the hurricane was good leadership.

Under Gomułka's tutelage, Moczar rose to deputy minister of the interior. He helped to rebuild its weakened security apparatus, soon transforming it into his own personal power base.[15] Creating a network of informers, he compiled a system of index card files on everyone who held power. In 1964, Moczar was promoted to minister. His rise was not only due to his controlling the police apparatus, but also due to his controlling the country's memory.

Moczar took on the presidency of the Polish veteran's group, the Union of Fighters for Freedom and Democracy (Związek Bojowników o Wolność i Demokrację— ZBOWiD). Under Moczar, the ZBOWiD served both communist partisans and rehabilitated noncommunist Home Army fighters and veterans who had fought abroad with the Polish army. He was the first communist leader to show a modicum of respect for the Home Army. Former policy had labeled all AK soldiers as traitors. Thus, Moczar's policy shift afforded tens of thousands of veterans greater societal belonging and official recognition. He

---

13 Polonsky, *The Jews in Poland and Russia*, 3:685-686.
    Another Jewish organization also existed: The Jewish Religious Union (Związek Religijny Wyznania Mojżeszowego, ZRWM) had roughly 7,500 members and its activities were restricted to serving its members' religious ritual needs.
14 Steinlauf, *Bondage to the Dead: Poland and the Memory of the Holocaust*, 78.
15 Ibid.

"transformed them from outcasts into freedom fighters."[16] He redefined them as essential members of the ZBOWiD, "the guardian of patriotism, love, and service to one's homeland."[17] Both groups, but especially AK veterans, were grateful to him for his attention and respect, as well as for giving them privileges.

In uniting rival underground veterans, Moczar secured "popular legitimization to appropriate the entire heritage of anti-Nazi resistance."[18] He also secured the veterans' undying allegiance. They became a mouthpiece for Moczar's specific brand of national memory, marked by ethno-nationalism, authoritarian and anti-elitist ideals, and tinged by antisemitism.[19] Moczar directed the ZBOWiD's rise to power. Due to its expanding branch representation throughout the country and climbing membership, which by 1968 had reached 250,000, the ZBOWiD gained tremendous political leverage.[20] By bridging prewar communists and nationalists, Moczar established Endo-communism and its antisemitism as official doctrine and policy.

1956

A primitive populist and antisemite, who had been burned by the "Yid" Zambrowski, Moczar aided the Natolin group's 1956 drive to seize power. Native communists had grown increasingly agitated by the disproportionate Jewish presence in high office, believing they blocked Poles from upward mobility. In need of a smokescreen to screen its pro-Soviet stance, Natolin channeled the public's hatred for communism onto its allegedly Jewish leadership. Despite both the Natolin and Puławska groups' numerous non-Jewish officials who had taken part in the Stalin-era terror, the former emphasized that the culpability for Stalinism lay solely with the PZPR's Jewish leadership. For Natolin, responsibility for the terrible economic conditions also lay at the Jews' feet. The terrified, angry, and hungry people should blame "Jewish Stalinists."[21]

For his part, Moczar initiated a whispering campaign together with PAX (Stowarzyszenie—PAX), a government-sponsored right-wing Catholic

---

16   Ibid., 79.
17   Quoted in Michlic, *Poland's Threatening Other: The Image of the Jew from 1880 to the Present*, 241.
18   Steinlauf, *Bondage to the Dead: Poland and the Memory of the Holocaust*, 79.
19   Polonsky, *The Jews in Poland and Russia*, 3:695.
20   Włodzimierz Rozenbaum, "The March Events: Targeting the Jews," in Głuchowski and Polonsky, *1968: Forty Years After*, 64–65.
21   Lendvai, *Antisemitism without Jews: Communist Eastern Europe*, 220.

association. A counterbalance to both the Roman Catholic Church and the progressive Catholic intelligentsia, PAX peddled antisemitism. Prewar and wartime right-wing fascist political leader Bolesław Piasecki[22] was behind PAX's campaign targeting high-level bureaucrats, mainly of Jewish heritage.

By the end of 1956, antisemitism had spread into many pockets of both the bureaucracy and public. Moczar had led Poles to recognize the enemy Jew as both a Stalinist enforcer and a Polish martyrdom denier. For Polish nationalists, Polish martyrdom and resistance defined their self-worth. The world ignored their country's pain, they felt, and since Kielce it had been branded a victimizer.[23] The Poles blamed Jews in the West for this new image, which challenged the heroic self-image Poles held.

Historians have tended to downplay the consequences resulting from the 1956–57 antisemitic campaign. Though they recognize the hatred against Jews passed down by Moscow and the Polish authorities, they believe it barely trickled down to the population. Pawel Machewicz's research, however, reveals a climate responsive to the combination of the whispering campaign and the political thaw. As Jakub Berman was gradually sidelined, people gained unspoken permission to articulate once repressed antisemitic attitudes.[24] Although the press itself warned the population of the societal dangers of antisemitism, now newspapers also published anonymous readers' antisemitic responses to articles.[25]

People felt free to express antisemitic views during the thaw. Even authority figures, including Zenon Nowak—a key figure under Bierut—made similar pronouncements. In Nowak's speech at the seventh plenary session of the Polish

---

22 Paczkowski, *The Spring Will Be Ours: Poland and the Poles from Occupation to Freedom*, 168, 254. Piasecki led the fascist ONR-Falanga group. During the war he headed the extreme ethno-nationalist political group, the National Confederation, which often published antisemitic material in its underground press. He turned Soviet agent after postwar imprisonment in the USSR. PAX promoted a communist-Catholic perspective to counter the anticommunist views of the Catholic Church. See Michlic, *Poland's Threatening Other: The Image of the Jew from 1880 to the Present*, 241.

23 Despite a speech in which Gomułka condemned discrimination, hate continued to be directed towards people with Jewish backgrounds. A purge of officials of Jewish origin began, focused mainly on the security apparatus. See Lendvai, *Antisemitism without Jews: Communist Eastern Europe*, 220–221; Polonsky, *The Jews in Poland and Russia*, 3:649.

24 Paweł Machewicz, "Antisemitism in Poland in 1956," in *Jews, Poles, Socialists: The Failure of an Ideal*, ed. Antony Polonsky, Israel Bartal, Gershon Hundert, Magdalena Opalski, and Jerzy Tomaszewski, Polin: Studies in Polish Jewry, vol. 9 (Oxford: The Littman Library of Jewish Civilization, 2008), 172; Shore, *Caviar and Ashes: A Warsaw Generation's Life and Death in Marxism, 1918–1968*, 305.

25 Quoted in Machewicz, "Antisemitism in Poland in 1956," 175.

Communist Party Central Committee, he rebranded the party's image by blaming Stalinist era policy solely on communists of Jewish parentage. He made false allegations, charging that "the entire leadership of the army" and "all Department Heads in the Security Service" were "comrades of Jewish origin."[26] Natolin's 1956 antisemitic campaign "reflected and gave voice to the thoughts and resentments present in broad circles of society."[27]

By 1957, Gomułka began a low-key assault on Puławska officials of Jewish origin by gradually dismissing them from important positions in the party apparatus and government administration. He also eliminated several members of Jewish origin from the Central Committee of the PZPR due to so-called "revisionism"—code for "Jew."[28] Thus, between 1956 and 1960 when the Polish border re-opened as part of the political thaw (it had closed in 1951), roughly fifty-one thousand people of Jewish origin who had been demoted, dismissed, harassed, or frightened because of antisemitism emigrated from the Polish People's Republic.[29] By the early 1960s, some thirty to thirty-five thousand people of Jewish origin remained in Poland. Most did not affiliate with Jewish institutions.[30]

In 1956–57, Gomułka and Moczar portrayed "Jewish" communists as fully responsible for the Stalinist era. This positioned ethnic Polish communist officials who had participated in the early state apparatus as bearing no responsibility for it.[31] But this effort was limited in its effectiveness. Outspoken liberal Catholic Poles, officials of Jewish origin, and the foreign media dubbed it an antisemitic campaign, which harmed the PRL's international reputation.

Moczar's Partisans

The Partisans (Partyzanci), a new faction within the party, also had problems with the campaign. For them, it proved too ineffective. The Partisans drew together an increasing yet disparate collective of both disaffected second-tier functionaries and Gomułka's communist wartime subordinates. (Natolin's

---

26 Quoted in Polonsky, *The Jews in Poland and Russia*, 3:677.
27 Machewicz, "Antisemitism in Poland in 1956," 176.
28 Włodzimierz Rozenbaum, "The March Events: Targeting the Jews," in Głuchowski and Polonsky, *1968: Forty Years After*, 62.
29 This number included 13,000 of the 18,000 Jews repatriated in 1956 from their Soviet wartime deportation, who had returned with some 249,000 Poles. (A first wave of 130,000 Jews had been repatriated already in 1946.)
30 Polonsky, *The Jews in Poland and Russia*: 3:684.
31 Machewicz, "Antisemitism in Poland in 1956," 171.

roster overlapped to a degree with that of the Partisans.) Most Partisans bonded over their communist armed resistance against the German occupation and their loathing for the Muscovites' seizure of power. The Partisans called for more authoritarian policies vis-à-vis the Church and intellectuals. Seeking to replace officials of Jewish descent with hardline Stalinists in the early 1960s, the Partisans took Moczar for their leader. To gain popular support, the Partisans underscored their local roots and patriotism as ethnic Polish nationalists. Theirs was a drive for greater political and economic power.[32] Aligned in their dissatisfaction with Gomułka's policies and prevailing economic stagnation, by June1964 the Partisans had become a significant force in the party.[33]

Power had eluded most members of the Partisans. Despite the minor purges in 1951–52 and later in 1956, only a small number of Partisans had benefitted. With relatively few opened job positions, the Partisans had not profited economically as much as they had hoped. This new middle class yearned for enough future job vacancies to help thousands of ethnic Poles rise in the bureaucracy. A vacancy in one high-level job allowed a dozen or more functionaries to get ahead.[34] Upward mobility brought not only a larger salary, but also perks including foreign made cars and travel abroad. Additionally, they would gain access to better apartments which the dismissed would be forced to vacate (either because the flats belonged to the party or because they could no longer afford them).[35] Like jobs, one apartment vacancy allowed many families to improve their living situations. Greater changes would develop as Moczar availed himself of his high position in the Ministry of the Interior.

June 1967: Anti-*Zionism*

In June 1967, Gomułka and Moczar returned to employing Jews as a scapegoat to steer public anger away from the system: the country and people had long been exploited by the Soviet Union, as had every Eastern bloc member. Next to Romania, Poland may have suffered most from such colonial abuse: Moscow's exploitation of the Polish coal industry had led to losses in exports reaching close

---

32 Dariusz Stola, "The Hate Campaign of March 1968: How Did It Become Anti-Jewish?," in Głuchowski and Polonsky *1968: Forty Years After*, 19; Michlic, *Poland's Threatening Other: The Image of the Jew from 1880 to the Present*, 240.
33 Polonsky, *The Jews in Poland and Russia*: 695.
34 Lendvai, *Antisemitism without Jews: Communist Eastern Europe*, 170.
35 Ibid., 169–170.

to half a billion dollars.³⁶ The Polish people had been whittled down by not only scarcity, but also ceaseless delays and inefficiency wrought by the ever-expanding state bureaucracy: "The labyrinthine difficulties of obtaining anything from consumer goods to medicines to apartments were one of the most oppressive aspects of the system."³⁷ But in 1967, substantial increases in meat prices, broader food shortages, and a doubling of transportation cost shocked the people.³⁸ The government worried that workers would strike as they had in 1956.

Moczar solved this problem by locating the system's fatal flaws in the State of Israel. Israel's remarkable June 1967 victory against a coalition of Arab states not only shocked the world, but also embarrassed the Soviet Union, which had backed the Arab assault. In a mere six days (June 5–10, 1967), Israel defeated an alliance of Egypt and Syria that had more than double Israel's troop size and three times its available weaponry; the Jewish state also gained a huge swath of land, including the Sinai Peninsula, the Golan Heights, the West Bank, and the Gaza Strip. In People's Poland, Jews responded with relief and joy. Prominent lay Catholics expressed pro-Israeli sentiments. The Israeli embassy in Warsaw received numerous congratulatory and sympathetic telegrams from Poles. Even Poles on the street could be heard acclaiming Israel's victory.³⁹

Yet, Eastern bloc leaders were humiliated by the Jewish state's military victory, given that it was the USSR which had supplied weapons and training to the defeated Arab countries.⁴⁰ Following the Soviet lead, and despite the Arab states having initiated the conflict,⁴¹ the Polish People's Republic cast Israel as the aggressor. The tainted party's news coverage of Israel's swift and successful military "aggression" caused Party, army, and public morale to plummet.

With the Ministry of Internal Affairs under his control, Moczar transformed the negative emotions and optics of a strong and violent Israeli army into an adversary the Polish people could see and fear. Within the context of the Six Day War, Moczar's propaganda barrage unleashed decades worth of pent-up

---

36 Ibid., 217.
37 Steinlauf, *Bondage to the Dead: Poland and the Memory of the Holocaust*, 64.
38 Rozenbaum, "The March Events: Targeting the Jews," 77.
39 Ibid., 68–72.
40 Polonsky, *The Jews in Poland and Russia*: 656. Stalin supported Israel's bid for statehood in 1948 in the hope that he would gain leverage in the region. When in 1956 it became clear this plan had failed, Israel took on more of an enemy status and the USSR sought out relations with the surrounding Arab states.
41 Paczkowski, *The Spring Will Be Ours: Poland and the Poles from Occupation to Freedom*, 316–317.

political and social tension.⁴² He ordered another purge of "Jewish" officials in high and mid-tier Party and government posts. By manipulating the Arab-Israeli conflict he quashed members of Puławska while simultaneously addressing the Partisans' needs for upward mobility.⁴³ In a June 27 speech, Gomułka made it quite clear that the time was ripe "to speak against the seeds of a fifth column."⁴⁴

Gomułka formally inaugurated the anti-*Zionist* campaign on June 19, 1967, during his speech to the Sixth Trade Union Congress:

> Since the Israeli aggression on the Arab countries was met with applause in *Zionist* circles of Jews—Polish citizens *who even on this occasion celebrated with drinking parties . . .* We maintain that every Polish citizen should have only one fatherland—People's Poland. (Applause) *. . . we do not want a fifth column to be created in our country.* (Applause) We cannot remain indifferent towards people who in the face of a threat to world peace, and thus also to the security of Poland and the peaceful work of our Polish nation, come out in favour of the aggressor, the wreckers of peace, and imperialism.⁴⁵

The antisemitic italicized text was deleted from the following day's published text due to two Politburo members' insistence; at the same time the following italicized words were added to the same text, which appeared in the party organ *Trybuna Ludu* on June 20, 1967: "*This view is shared by the overwhelming majority of Polish citizens of Jewish nationality, who faithfully serve our country. The state authorities treat all citizens the same irrespective of their nationality. Every citizen of our country has the same rights, but also the same citizen's responsibilities towards People's Poland.*"⁴⁶ However, such textual manipulation could not change the speech in real time and therefore could not hide its underlying antisemitic intent.

Those listening to his original June 19 speech in person, on the radio, or on television heard Gomułka's reference to Jews as a fifth column. Poles knew this dangerous terminology. The expression "fifth column" recalled those traitors living within Poland who had collaborated with Nazi Germany. It implied that

---

42   Jerzy Eisler, "1968: Jews, Antisemitism, Emigration," in Głuchowski and Polonsky *1968: Forty Years After*, 44.
43   Rozenbaum, "The March Events: Targeting the Jews," 69.
44   Quoted in ibid., 70.
45   Quoted in ibid.
46   Ibid.

an internal enemy lay in wait with the intention of causing harm to the PRL. This reference to a fifth column also resembled Endecja's prewar core ethno-nationalist slogan: "the Jew as the Fourth Partition."[47] In his June 19 speech, Gomułka stated: "we must take steps with regard to people who have two souls and two fatherlands."[48]

The PZPR presented a complex explanation for *Zionism's* threat to Poland. This enemy was both physical and abstract. On the one hand, the PZPR propagated the view that Israel schemed to take over the world. This analysis is averse to Zionism's true political ideology, which affirms that a Jewish state has the right to existence, development, and security in what is now the State of Israel. As such, I am following Dariusz Stola's lead and placing the terms *Zionist* and *Zionism* in italics when referring to the PZPR's dystopian exploitation of it. According to Moczar's office, *Zionists* were people primarily of Jewish nationality who supported Israel's supposed aim for world domination. To this end, *Zionists* spread across the globe, gained the confidence of their host countries, and eventually spied for the Israeli enemy state, providing it with important intelligence. Moczar had simply modernized the age-old conspiracy theory against the Jews professed in the *Protocols of the Elders of Zion* and folded it into his anti-*Zionist* campaign.

Memory and *Zionism*

The second and more abstract PZPR explanation of *Zionism* related to memory. According to Moczar, *Zionists*, that is, Jews in Poland and in the West, challenged Polish memory with their claims of antisemitic oppression. Jews lambasted the Poles for violent anti-Jewish acts during the German occupation. American Jews listening to family members' horrific experiences at the hands of some Poles made generalizations from what they heard. Thus, we have such claims as, "Poles suckle antisemitism with their mothers' milk."[49] These kinds of anti-Polish charges landed when Poles yearned for international compassion and respect.

---

47 Michlic, *Poland's Threatening Other: The Image of the Jew from 1880 to the Present*, 247.
48 Quoted in Rozenbaum, "The March Events: Targeting the Jews," 70.
49 Such sentiments have been expressed by a number of Israeli politicians, including Prime Minister Yitzhak Shamir in 1989 and more recently Acting Foreign Minister Israel Katz in 2019. See "Shamir's Remarks About Poland Held Up Diplomatic Relations," *Jewish Telegraphic Agency*, December 8, 1989, https://www.jta.org/archive/shamirs-remarks-about-poland-held-up-diplomatic-relations; Cnaan Liphshitz/JTA, "Polish Holocaust Survivor Xalls

It was heartbreaking for Poles that even in their own country, overrun as it was by communism, their own physical and emotional struggle for sovereignty was not respected. No monument was raised to honor Poland. The Jews' struggle, on the other hand, received a monument. Indeed, the Warsaw Ghetto Uprising was acclaimed forty years before the Poles' own Warsaw Uprising. In 1948, "[N]athan Rapoport's creation stood alone in a vast field of rubble, easily read by Poles as a symbol of the new government's decision to honor the Jews, while consigning the Polish national struggle to the dustbin of history."[50] Polish nationalists envied the respect shown to the ghetto fighters.

Moczar saw Rapoport's massive monument. Moczar had experienced the first years of People's Poland when PZPR school textbooks not only gave credence to Polish antisemitism by explaining it as "Polish reactionaries [who] supported [Hitler's] barbaric racist policies,"[51] but also attested to the supposed "collaboration of the AK leadership with the Germans."[52] Moczar and the Partisans retaliated against this state memory by crafting their own conspiracy theory in which the West Germans and *Zionists* collaborated in a worldwide conspiracy against Poland. "Their weapons are revanchism and historical revisionism, their goals the mutilation of the nation's borders and memory, its body and soul."[53] That the State of Israel had established working relations with West Germany and accepted wartime reparations from that country fueled Moczar's conspiracy. He combined a fear of German revanchism—that the Germans would demand the return of that Western part of Poland taken from the defeated nation at the end of WWII—with anger towards the Jews, i.e., the *Zionists*, for casting the Poles as antisemitic. Moczar instead offered the people an entirely different narrative from that which dominated the early years of the Polish People's Republic.

Nationalists—worn down by occupation, the authoritarian systems of Others, violence, and the loss of power—wished to live in a sovereign and proud Poland. Jewish and Western claims of antisemitism challenged these Polish dreams. Using a Soviet tactic, Moczar denied and deflected, pointing to the *Zionists* as the true enemy of Poland. It takes a strong, confident person, let

---

Israel Katz a 'stupid idiot,'" *Jerusalem Post*, May 22, 2019, https://www.jpost.com/diaspora/nj-holocaust-survivor-calls-israel-katz-a-stupid-idiot-588556.
50 Steinlauf, *Bondage to the Dead: Poland and the Memory of the Holocaust*, 49.
51 Quoted in Anna Radziwiłł, "The Teaching of the History of the Jews in Secondary Schools in the Polish People's Republic, 1949–1988," in *Poles and Jews: Perceptions and Misperceptions*, ed. Władysław Bartoszewski, Polin: Studies in Polish Jewry, vol. 4 (Liverpool: The Littman Library of Jewish Civilization, 2004), 413–414.
52 Quoted in ibid.
53 Steinlauf, *Bondage to the Dead: Poland and the Memory of the Holocaust*, 85.

alone a nation, to hear derogatory and incriminating statements, recognize some truth in them, and set upon a healthier course. People's Poland was not confident. Instead, Moczar's Endo-communism offered Poles complete deniability of all ugly accusations.[54]

Inaugurated by Gomułka, and crafted by Moczar, the anti-*Zionist* campaign saturated Polish discourse. Waves of anti-*Zionist* media coverage inundated the public; rallies everywhere sought to teach people that the true enemy of Poland was *Zionism*. According to Moczar's own June 28, 1967 definition, the Jews were infected with dangerous *Zionism*. He painted the struggle against *Zionism* as the first priority for the security of the PRL.[55]

The propaganda seemed to work. Polish soldiers demanded the removal of all people of Jewish nationality from state and administrative posts. One report expressed the soldiers' conviction "that Polish citizens of Jewish descent . . . may at a proper moment become the proverbial fifth column" [underlined in original].[56] The military did not latch onto Gomułka's division of the Jews into three categories and insistence that the majority were loyal Polish patriots. Rather, like so many others, soldiers gravitated to the Partisans' message that *all* Jews, due to being born of Jewish lineage, were a security risk for the Polish People's Republic. The military purged itself of "undesirables." By the end of 1967, there remained no more than fifty officers of Jewish origin within the Polish military. Between 1967 and 1969, roughly 180 officers of Jewish descent had been dismissed from military service. Some one hundred left Poland.[57]

Ostensibly to unmask and capture these threatening *Zionists*, who were portrayed as anti-Polish informers or spies, Moczar completed his surveillance project begun several years prior when he had collected data on people of Jewish origin in important posts. The people investigated also included individuals who had previously converted to Catholicism, Poles openly sympathetic to Israel, and even those merely suspected of such sympathies. In addition, research provided detailed information on their spouses, children, parents, and in-laws.[58] The Ministry of Interior's security apparatus (MSW) generated exhaustive lists along with incriminating material. Whether true or fabricated, these stories gave the press, government offices, civic organizations, and industrial enterprises justifications for party expulsions as

---

54   Rozenbaum, "The March Events: Targeting the Jews," 75.
55   Stola, "The Hate Campaign of March 1968: How Did It Become Anti-Jewish?," 24.
56   Quoted in Rozenbaum, "The March Events: Targeting the Jews," 74.
57   Tadeusz Pióro, "Purges in the Polish Army, 1967–1968," in Głuchowski and Polonsky *1968: Forty Years After*, 298, 305.
58   Michlic, *Poland's Threatening Other: The Image of the Jew from 1880 to the Present*, 239.

well as job demotions and dismissals. Moczar also oversaw close surveillance of ordinary individual Jews, people who had visited the Israeli embassy, and Jewish clubs, which were the supposed portals for *Zionists* to infiltrate communist Poland.[59]

Those targeted met grave consequences. People of Jewish origin were harassed with threatening phone calls and letters. They were dismissed from jobs, with no hope of making a horizontal move. Spouses of Jews were also fired. Children were harassed at school. For Poles of Jewish descent, who were highly assimilated, went to church, celebrated Christmas, and had no connection to their Jewish roots, this discrimination proved especially devastating. It was often at school that children learned for the first time that they were Jews . . . "Jews by force."[60]

PZPR Anti-*Zionis*m against Students

This anti-*Zionist* campaign grew exponentially in March 1968. Students and the intelligentsia had been vocal in their condemnation of Gomułka's retreat from the liberalizing promise of the "Polish October." As Gomułka turned more autocratic, cultural repression increased. Students, writers, and academics (of both Catholic and Jewish origins) experienced recriminations for critical thinking. They countered by criticizing this resurgence of government sponsored Stalinist-era tactics, such as the invasive reach of the secret police. One example is the short-lived Inter-School Discussion Club (also known as the Club of Contradiction Seekers), headed by the young free-thinking communists Adam Michnik, Jan Gross, and Jan Koffman. After a year of open discussions, which included taboo subjects such as the Katyń massacres, the Molotov-Ribbentrop Pact, and PZPR factions,

---

59   Eisler, "1968: Jews, Antisemitism, Emigration," 44–47. In August 1967 the PZPR Central Committee permitted the development of secret teams for the "verification of people in executive positions." Relying on material supplied by the MSW, these squads were tasked with listing the remaining *Zionists* and "revisionists" to be removed from the party and their posts. Such secret teams could be found in every government workplace within the Polish People's Republic. On the evidence of a special report by the MSW's First Department, it appears that the political leadership believed that foreign Jewish organizations and Israel carried out well-run intelligence operations in Poland, which the Jewish community supported. See Rozenbaum, "The March Events: Targeting the Jews," 77–78.
60   Pióro, "Purges in the Polish Army, 1967–1968," 305.

the authorities shut it down.⁶¹ With Czechoslovakia's reformers in mind, slogans rang out: "Poland is waiting for its Dubcek" ("Polska czeka na swego Dubceka").⁶²

Doubling down, in late January 1968 Gomułka shut down the play *Dziady*. Written by the nineteenth-century Polish national cultural icon Adam Mickiewicz, *Dziady* expresses anti-Russian sentiment through a nineteenth-century lens. Referencing the partitions and Russian rule over Poland, contemporary Poles related to its message of Polish patriotism. Though previously it had never been banned in the Polish People's Republic, Gomułka prohibited it to generate a "crisis."⁶³

He achieved his goal. Students protested this cultural repression after the show's last performance on January 30, 1968. Detained by the militia, students were interrogated about their ethnic and religious identity. When the authorities asked students Natan Tanenbaum and Ewa Morawska if they were Jewish, the two were shocked: communists were supposed to be uninterested in religion and ethnicity. Tanenbaum recalled thinking about his interrogator: "you son-of-a-bitch, if I informed the party control commission what you are interested in, you would be sacked ... from both the party and your job." He added, "That is basically how little I knew about what was in the making."⁶⁴ Morawska's situation demonstrates the depth of the research that had gone into finding students of Jewish background: Morawska's father, a philosophy professor at the University of Warsaw, hailed from a long-time assimilated family and her mother was a well-known Catholic writer.⁶⁵ Morawska did not consider herself Jewish. But the PZPR did. Ewa Morawska was now a "Jew by force."

Adam Michnik and fellow student Henryk Szlajfer informed *Le Monde* journalists about the protests. They in turn were suspended from the University of Warsaw. The Warsaw chapter of the Writers' Union held an extraordinary meeting on February 29, 1968 in which it criticized the government not only for closing *Dziady*, but also for its disproportionate response to the student protests and for the increasing antisemitism. On March 4, 1968, the minister of higher education expelled Michnik and Szlajfer from the university. Four days later, hundreds of students at the university protested.

On March 8, events exploded. At the end of what had been a peaceful student demonstration against the expulsion of Michnik and Szlajfer, plainclothesmen in

---

61 Rozenbaum, "The March Events: Targeting the Jews," 65.
62 Polonsky, *The Jews in Poland and Russia*, 3:699.
63 Rozenbaum, "The March Events: Targeting the Jews," 78.
64 Quoted in Eisler, "1968: Jews, Antisemitism, Emigration," 49.
65 Ibid.

attendance attacked participants with clubs. Motorized militia units surrounded the university and beat students and passers-by.[66] Students were arrested on trumped-up charges of *"Zionist* conspiracy" against People's Poland. The only so-called evidence against them was the students' Jewish ancestry.[67] Expulsions from the university followed these brutal and unprovoked attacks and arrests.

Thousands of students reacted to the government's excessive tactics and repressive policy by demonstrating in over one hundred localities throughout the country.[68] In Warsaw alone, officers arrested twelve hundred students on the first day and convicted 207 in summary trials. As of April 8, 1968, the prime minister reported to the Sejm that 2,739 individuals had been arrested, 1,952 released within twenty-four hours, and 132 sentenced to prison terms.[69] What he did not reveal was that the authorities conscripted roughly six hundred students into the army, separated them from their fellows, and sent them to military penal garrisons far away.[70] Many more students were beaten, blacklisted by the secret police, harassed, and expelled from their universities.

1968: The PZPR Anti-*Zionist* Campaign

Only three days after the initial student protest at Warsaw University, on March 11 Józef Kępa (Warsaw PZPR committee propaganda secretary) gave the keynote address to the conference of the Warsaw Party activists. In his speech, he singled out Jews as the primary leaders of the demonstrations. Equating the students with *Zionists*, he implored his audience to understand that *"Zionists* in Poland want to turn the intellectuals and the youth against their primary responsibility to People's Poland . . . *Zionist* circles in Israel and West German revanchists have combined to inspire Polish *Zionist* circles to sow trouble in Poland" (emphasis mine).[71] Knowing the West would label these acts "antisemitic," he asserted that such a claim of antisemitism was *Zionist* propagation intended to make the regime look bad. He ended the speech: "We will not be frightened; We will destroy *Zionists* wherever they are. No sentiments. We have already

---

66 Stola, "The Hate Campaign of March 1968: How Did It Become Anti-Jewish?," 17; Rozenbaum, "The March Events: Targeting the Jews," 79.
67 Stola, "The Hate Campaign of March 1968: How Did It Become Anti-Jewish?," 19.
68 Ibid., 17.
69 Rozenbaum, "The March Events: Targeting the Jews," 80.
70 Stola, "The Hate Campaign of March 1968: How Did It Become Anti-Jewish?," 17.
71 Quoted in Lendvai, *Antisemitism without Jews: Communist Eastern Europe*, 112.

prepared all media for this task" (emphasis mine).[72] Indeed, the Partisans led by Moczar and supported by Gomułka had been preparing for this "crisis" since the early 1960s when the former began his anti-Jewish data collection project. The party organ *Trybuna Luda* published Kępa's message on March 12, 1968.

On March 11, the same day as Kępa's speech linking demonstration organizers to *Zionists*, two newspaper articles covering the crisis came to similar conclusions but using different language. *Trybuna Ludu* alluded to the student leaders' fathers as Jews by calling them "bankrupt politicians," an expression which had become synonymous with "Jews." It continued by listing the fathers' names and posts. Some of the students singled out in *Trybuna Ludu* were the same as those mentioned in the anonymous article published in the right-wing PAX daily *Słowo Powszechne*.

As Dariusz Stola aptly argues, although no one took responsibility for writing the PAX article, given the totalitarian system, it was certainly Gomułka-approved. The PAX piece directly linked the students to their parents' participation in the Stalinist system of terror, repression, and poverty. As such, it combined collective responsibility with the accepted myth of Żydokomuna. It claimed that the parents, "bankrupt politicians" (i.e., Jews), had directed their children to organize students to riot and undermine the political order. The article further asserted that the students agreed because they were upset by Gomułka's policy against Israel after the Six Day War. It named ten organizers of the demonstrations and their fathers, "Antoni Zambrowski, son of Roman Zambrowski; Katarzyna Werfel, daughter of Roman Werfel; ... Henryk Szlajfer, son of a censor from the Office of Press Control; Adam Michnik, son of a senior editor in the *Książka i Wiedza* party publishing house."[73] In case it was not clear that these people should be understood as Jews, the writer affirmed that they used to meet at the Babel Club, a youth group connected with the Social and Cultural Association of Jews—the TSKŻ.[74]

On the same day that the two articles appeared and Kępa gave his keynote address, a leaflet titled *Whom Are You Supporting?* circulated on the Warsaw

---

72 Quoted in Rozenbaum, "The March Events: Targeting the Jews," 80.
73 Quoted in Stola, "The Hate Campaign of March 1968: How Did It Become Anti-Jewish?," 20. The following students were named in the *Trybuna Ludu* article: Antoni Zambrowski, Katarzyna Werfel, Maria Petrusewicz, Henryk Szlajfer, Adam Michnik, Irena Grudzińska, Alster, Blumsztajn, Rubinstein, and Dojczgewant. The students listed in the *Słowo Powszechne* article include Aleksander Smolar, Wiktor Górecki, Józef Dojczgewant, Irena Lasota, Henryk Szlajfer, Ewa Zarzycka, Katarzyna Werfel, and Adam Michnik. See Stola, "The Hate Campaign of March 1968: How Did It Become Anti-Jewish?," 20–21.
74 Lendvai, *Antisemitism without Jews: Communist Eastern Europe*, 112.

University campus. Its message mirrored the articles. It emphasized the students' Jewish origins by printing their parents' presumed Yiddish first names. For example, after one student's name, it read: "the son of Fajga and Szlomo." The leaflet also described the students' families as wealthy, and that they inherently disdained the working class and peasantry.[75] It painted the students as collectively responsible for their parents' wrongdoings during the Stalinist era and the parents' as responsible for their children's warped views and harmful actions. This three-pronged messaging signaled the unleashing of a clear anti-*Zionist* campaign. A propaganda deluge flooded Polish public discourse in the following days, weeks, and months, alerting Poles to be wary and fearful of Jews in their midst.

The Communist Party controlled most newspapers, as well as those belonging to satellite organizations, which amounted to a government daily press totaling close to eight million copies. These papers joined the anti-*Zionist* campaign, and in the first ten days together printed 250 suitable articles in central and regional papers. A significant portion of the articles contained antisemitic content. If, to be conservative, we allow that only half of these pieces attacked *Zionists* and then multiply the number of texts by the size of the print runs, "we see that Poland was literally showered with millions, and in times tens of millions, of anti-*Zionist* messages."[76]

People's Poland was awash with *anti-Zionist* propaganda. Thousands of public meetings and mass rallies occurred nationwide. Several were enormous in size, with crowds that crested one hundred thousand. However, most involved smaller groups. They often occurred in workplaces, as well as in youth groups, women's organizations, and trade unions. In Warsaw alone there were more than nineteen hundred POP meetings (basic party organizations—Podstawowa Organizacja Partyjna), the majority of which included non-party members in attendance. In the same period, nearly four hundred rallies, approximately seven hundred meetings of party activists and six hundred meetings of Communist Party groups also took place in the capital. In addition, the army took part in leading forty-two thousand meetings throughout the country, which attracted a reported 3.7 million people to hear the anti-*Zionist* message.[77] It did not take long for this anti-*Zionist* campaign to transition into a witch hunt for officials of Jewish origin.

---

75 Stola, "The Hate Campaign of March 1968: How Did It Become Anti-Jewish?," 21. The students named in the leaflet are the following: Adam Michnik, Aleksander Smolar, Henryk Szlajfer, Irena Grudzińska, Ewa Zarzycka, Toruńczyk, Józef Dajczgewant, Krystyna Flato, Krzysztof Topolski, and Krystyna Winawer.
76 Ibid., 28, emphasis mine.
77 Ibid., 29.

The Anti-*Zionist* Campaign's Results

As early as March 12, the party led an assault on seven writers and several scholars of Jewish origin, as well as non-Jewish moderates. It accused them of being "enemies of People's Poland" who belonged "to circles devoted to Israeli and West German propaganda."[78] On March 21, this second phase solidified around what the party deemed the epicenter of the crisis—Warsaw University. Party leaders dismissed the lauded dissident professors Baczko, Bauman, Brus, Morawski, Kołakowski, and Hirszowicz (four out of the six were of Jewish origin). "This was the first time in Polish history that senior faculty members with tenure were sacked."[79] Thousands of students and friends rallied to support them, with slogans: "There can be no studies without freedom!"; "There can be no Polish economics without Brus—no Polish philosophy without Kołakowski!" The PZPR responded by closing several university departments and divisions, effectively blocking 1,616 students at Warsaw University from their studies. Measuring 8.6% of Warsaw University's student body, these students had to apply for readmission with no guarantees of acceptance.[80]

On March 13, the POP convened a quick meeting and abruptly, without evidence, removed from the party the former Politburo member, senior-level PZPR official, and Communist Party member of forty years, Roman Zambrowski. Though absent from the meeting, and unable to defend himself, the POP dismissed this one-time powerful secretary of the central committee in an instant. Press coverage of Zambrowski's fall signaled that anyone could be expelled from the party and dismissed from a post on charges of *Zionism*.[81]

On March 19, Gomułka gave his first public speech since the student protest on March 8. This proved a seminal moment in the anti-*Zionist* campaign, not so much for Gomułka's message, but rather for the spectacle within the venue. It also marked a pivotal shift in the PZPR's molding of public perception: it began exploiting the popular new medium of television for one of its hate campaigns. Reaching into the public's living rooms, Gomułka presented a calm and relatively moderate explanation for the anti-*Zionist* campaign. In balanced language, he said that while some Jews in People's Poland were aligned with Israel to promote *Zionism*, most Jews were loyal to the PRL. His message of relative moderation got lost, however, as television cameras focused on his audience

---

78   Quoted in Lendvai, *Antisemitism without Jews: Communist Eastern Europe*, 114.
79   Ibid., 136.
80   Rozenbaum, "The March Events: Targeting the Jews," 80.
81   Stola, "The Hate Campaign of March 1968: How Did It Become Anti-Jewish?," 30.

of three thousand party activists. Home television screens filled with banners: "Everyone Has Only One Fatherland," "We Demand a Complete Unmasking and Punishment of the Political Instigators," and "Down with the Agents of Imperialism and Reactionary *Zionism*!"[82] When the first secretary referred to emigration, the audience cried out, "Now, today." Indeed, one viewer recalled in a memoir:

> I will never forget this TV broadcast. Watching the screen I saw faces marked with thirst for blood and cruelty. [. . .] [M]others who were connected with the condemned people reacted to the broadcast in the same way: they locked the door out of fear of a pogrom.[83]

By April 3, 1968, the Foreign Service had dismissed forty diplomats, as well as other Jews of origin who held important posts. That same month, employees of Jewish heritage had been fired from the Scientific Publishing House. The goal became clear—life would be so difficult that "unmasked" Jews would leave the country. The precise number of people who were dismissed from their jobs on charges of *Zionism* is unknown. We do know that they were not solely from the elite. The anti-*Zionist* campaign affected not only top government officials, editors in chief of newspapers, university professors, doctors, and lawyers, but also bookkeepers in cooperatives, teachers, factory foremen, and factory workers.[84] Unable to find new jobs, most often those dismissed ran out of funds. This hunt for Jews took its most extreme form in the city of Łódz. The city's prewar Jewish population of some two hundred thousand Jews measured one third of the entire urban population. Some 3,500 to 4,000 Jews settled there after the war. Łódz became Judenrein after this anti-*Zionist* campaign and witch hunt.[85]

The exact number of émigrés is also unknown. According to Jerzy Eisler, between 1967 and 1971 at least fifteen thousand people emigrated, 25% of whom settled in Israel. Of that number, 1,823 held university diplomas and 944 were university students.[86] Of the more than fifteen thousand émigrés, several hundred had worked as part of the Stalinist repressive apparatus. These hundreds "committed various shameful deeds, even crimes, but avoided legal responsibility by

---

82 Ibid., 30–31.
83 Quoted in ibid., 32.
84 Ibid., 30
85 Lendvai, *Antisemitism without Jews: Communist Eastern Europe*, 154–159.
86 Eisler, "1968: Jews, Antisemitism, Emigration," 55.

emigrating."[87] At the same time, more than fourteen thousand additional Jews of origin were exiled due to Polish antisemitism.

The exodus marked a tragedy. People had to sell their apartments and belongings at ridiculously low prices, as it had become a buyers' market. The authorities also charged Jews for permission to leave. Devices for expropriation, flight taxes, and fees to reimburse the state for children's education amounted to more than fifteen thousand zlotys per person, an exorbitant figure that was higher than most people's yearly income.[88] But more important were the human costs. Marriages fell apart and friendships ended. Families broke up, with some family members remaining in the PRL during the Cold War. To leave, people had to renounce their Polish citizenship, and could not return. The stress was so pervasive and severe that many people had nervous breakdowns and at least forty individuals committed suicide.[89]

Myth Reconstruction

Party leadership spread its message through the media, meetings, and mammoth rallies. Banners made the main points plain: "*Zionists* to Dayan!" "Antisemitism—No! Anti-*Zionism*—Yes!"[90] According to the PZPR, the country was under siege by *Zionist* spies and those who could be turned into spies at any given moment. All Poles of Jewish origin became suspect despite Gomułka's March 19, 1968, televised insistence that the Polish People's Republic "will oppose with complete firmness every manifestation of antisemitism ... the sole criterion for evaluating a citizen of our nation is his attitude towards socialism and towards the interests of our state and its people."[91] And yet, people with ties neither to Judaism (except by way of heritage) nor to Israel were blacklisted as *Zionists*. And those who identified in some part as Jews, but who were loyal to People's Poland and loved Polish culture, became outcasts. The party's play with semantics won the day, twisting the minds of many people. And though some resisted the propaganda, they rarely resisted publicly lest they too be targeted.

---

87   Ibid., 56.
88   Lendvai, *Antisemitism without Jews: Communist Eastern Europe*, 178.
89   Eisler, "1968: Jews, Antisemitism, Emigration," 57–58; Lendvai, *Antisemitism without Jews: Communist Eastern Europe*, 176.
90   Quoted in Stola, "The Hate Campaign of March 1968: How Did It Become Anti-Jewish?," 29.
91   Quoted in ibid., 31.

Party heads received thousands of letters from individuals and POP meeting representatives responding to the anti-*Zionist* campaign. Workers from the Baildon steel works, for example, demanded "a purge of *Zionist* elements from party ranks, removal from their positions, and the refusal to permit their children to continue further university studies."[92] Workers from the Polfer factories wrote: "We will not permit revisionist and *Zionist* rioters to accuse us of antisemitism."[93] Together, Moczar and Gomułka carried the people to their desired location vis-à-vis the Jews.

By focusing the problems of society on the "Jews" in 1956 and on the *Zionists* in 1967, Polish politicians stressed that "true Poles" would not behave this way. This horrific branding prevented the people from joining the youth protests and transformed them into a vehicle for general anger over the dire economic situation.[94] Jews and *Zionists* were the regime's smokescreen for the real causes of society's problems.

In 2007, I spoke with one middle-aged Polish man who remembered 1968 as a child. I suggested that People's Poland promoted antisemitism. He was outraged. To this university graduate and engineer, antisemitism was the extreme act of killing—the domain of the Nazis. He contended that any acts against Jews were strictly related to economics, not antisemitism. Hours later, however, he quietly affirmed, "But there was Kielce." And after some silence, he also recalled 1968, with a sad, soft tone, as the year his sister's friend was forced to leave Poland together with her family and thousands of other Jews. The banners and slogans, headlines and printed articles . . . the teaching . . . had stayed with him. Only now is he free to question it.

Since marking World War I's end with the controversial Minorities Treaty, American Jewry has accused Poles of antisemitism, with varying proportions of both acumen and ignorance. Piłsudski embraced Polish Jewry, thus modeling for the people to do the same. Dmowski rejected Polish Jews, directing Poles to nurture a hatred for them. That same split attitude toward Polish Jews continued in postwar People's Poland. Much of the intelligentsia accepted Jews as citizens with equal rights. But for a large segment of the population, Church-fed antisemitic ideas combined with old right-wing Polish nationalist antisemitism and Żydokomuna. Hatred for the Jews persisted. Thus Kielce. Thus March 1968. "The Jew" did not represent one evil, but many; he was the ultimate bogeyman,

---

92 Quotes of letters found in ibid., 29.
93 Ibid.
94 Ibid., 34.

which allowed Poles to blame an Other for their loss of sovereignty, the scarcity of good jobs, failed economy, and lack of international respect.

As we have seen, Polish nationalists vied for power within the Communist Party in People's Poland. After being released from prison and restored to leadership posts, Gomułka and Moczar elevated the Partisans at the so-called Jews' expense. By portraying the 1967 Israeli victory as part of a *Zionist* drive for world domination, which would include German revanchism, Moczar described all communists of Jewish origin as future or current enemies to the PZPR. Though dubbed an anti-*Zionist* campaign, politicians had made it clear that in fact it was an anti-Jewish campaign. In the late 1940s, Poles had learned to repress any negative images of Jews to live in a communist state that initially welcomed Jews. The political opposition tapped into those tamped down antisemitic attitudes in 1956, and completely released them in 1967 and 1968. The opposition harnessed the corrosive and combined hatred for the Jews and Germany to drive the people's tacit acceptance of a purge of Jews from officialdom. The anti-*Zionist* campaign reached its peak during student protests over rescinded cultural freedoms. In the end, the Polish communist policy forced some fifteen thousand Poles of Jewish origin from their homeland, many in economic despair and emotional distress. Off-loading their woes onto Jews, ethnic Poles could free themselves from any responsibility for the country's desperate circumstances.

CHAPTER 17

Solidarity and the Church

When Westerners think of Solidarity's origins, many imagine a robust mustachioed man standing atop a platform at the Lenin Shipyard in Gdańsk, beckoning his fellow workers to strike. Lech Wałęsa is the face of Solidarity in the West. But what birthed Solidarity in the hot August of 1980 was the presence of people from multiple social strata willing to work together. Historically, Polish workers distrusted the intelligentsia, who in turn disrespected the workers. And while many workers found solace in the Church, the secular intelligentsia dismissed the priest's Sunday sermon. Divided by ideology and preconceptions, these three social spheres bridged their divisions to work in concert toward some form of freedom and transparency. Pushing aside what separated them, they nurtured their shared experiences: political brutality and cultural repression mixed with economic decay. They had two things in common: love for Poland and hatred of its totalitarian communist regime.[1]

December 1970: Strikes and Murder

On December 13, 1970, the Gomułka regime attempted to quietly breathe new life into the republic's shriveled economy by raising staple food prices for the first time in decades. Just two weeks before Christmas, as people prepared for

---

1   In his "The Dilemma," Adam Michnik notes that though both the Church and intellectuals opposed the communist regime they did so for vastly different reasons. The Church resented communism's doctrine of atheism, which denies the Church's "truth." The intellectuals resisted communism's totalitarian system, which denied through force and lies any truth other than that held by party. See Adam Michnik, "The Dilemma," in *Letters from Freedom: Post-Cold War Realities and Perspectives*, ed. Irena Grudzińska Gross, foreword by Ken Jowitt, trans. Jane Cave (Berkeley: University of California Press, 1998), 75.

the festivities, food costs soared from 13 to 30%, with meat going up by 17%.² On Monday, December 14, distressed workers at the Gdańsk Lenin Shipyard went on strike (more than fifteen thousand workers operated one of the socialist regime's most successful enterprises). They demanded the elimination of the new food prices. By late afternoon, several thousand had gathered in the center of Gdańsk. Armed units sent to maintain order turned brutal. Hundreds of people were beaten and detained. The strikers retaliated, setting automobiles and newsstands on fire.³

On Tuesday, December 15, more workers in the region of Gdańsk, Gdynia, and Sopot joined the strike and fury filled the streets.⁴ They set the regional Party office ablaze. Gomułka authorized the use of bullets against the strikers.⁵ Shots were fired. Buildings went up in flames. Workers at the Lenin Shipyard proclaimed a sit-in; police and army units blockaded the shipyard and the docks.

A massacre took place on Wednesday, December 16 as troops opened fire at Gate Two of the shipyard, killing nine workers. On Thursday, workers arriving at the Gdynia shipyard encountered a blockade. Troops fired, killing seventeen people. Shipyard workers in Szczecin now went on strike. There, government troops felled fifteen workers. In all, the authorities killed at least forty-one people. During the strike, government forces injured more than one thousand people, of whom four hundred were admitted to hospitals; they detained roughly thirty-two hundred people, most of whom were beaten brutally while in custody.⁶

Work stoppages and rallies ensued in roughly one hundred factories in seven provinces, including Warsaw. A common demand was for the creation of independent trade unions—free from Party influence—which would truly represent the workers' interests.⁷ They also demanded transparency in their dealings with the authorities.

---

2   At the same time compensatory wage increases were directed only to very large families, and that did not exceed 5–10% of one's monthly income. See Paczkowski, *The Spring Will Be Ours: Poland and the Poles from Occupation to Freedom*, 346.
3   Ibid., 347.
4   Enterprises joining the strike included the port of Gdańsk, the Refitting Shipyard, the Railroad Rolling-Stock Repair Yard, the Paris Commune Shipyard in Gdynia, and the Zamech plant in Elbląg. See ibid.
5   Ibid.
6   Ibid., 348.
7   Additional demands included the rescinding of food cost increases, punishment of those responsible for the massacre and brutality, and workers' access to the mass media to give their own account of events. See ibid., 348, 351.

As part of its response, the Politburo replaced Gomułka with Edward Gierek—a former coal miner. Using this tried-and-true method in an attempt to reset relations with the people, the new leadership blamed their predecessors for the economic and social problems facing the country. Gierek also distanced himself from his predecessor through the image he cultivated. Gomułka's image suggested an old, badly dressed, emotional, authoritative, and inaccessible leader. Gierek, on the other hand, presented himself as a young, vigorous, well-dressed, modest, authoritative, yet straightforward and informal leader.[8] Meeting several times with workers, he manipulated his image to successfully persuade striking workers back into the factories.[9]

Just as former regimes had dealt with criticism and crises, Gierek employed strict censorship to suppress memory of the strikes and the December massacre. But those who had been present at the Lenin Shipyard, who had lost friends and colleagues, had the events at Gate Two seared into their hearts and minds. The lead keeper of that memory was Lech Wałęsa, who organized unauthorized and therefore illegal anniversary memorials. At first, the public hardly noticed these ceremonies, since PZPR officials quickly removed any memorial items that workers had placed on the spot where their fellow strikers had been killed. Yet every year, with flowers, candles, and prayers, Wałęsa and his supporters continued this effort to bring dignity to those killed.

Secular Intellectuals and Poland's Workers

In the last chapter, we saw that in 1968, students and the intelligentsia erupted in protests. Two years later, workers also voiced their objections to the regime. In both instances, this nascent political opposition had little support outside of its own population segment. Workers did not aid students in March 1968, nor did weakened student and dissident groups aid workers in December 1970. This dynamic of division and isolation changed after June 24, 1976, however, when

---

8   Kubik, *The Power of Symbols against the Symbols of Power: The Rise of Solidarity and the Fall of State Socialism in Poland*, 33.
9   In recalling his past as a worker, and listening to the workers' complaints after hours, Gierek asked them to help him solve the problems besetting the nation: "So what do you say? Will you help?" Workers in Warsaw, Gdańsk, and Szczecin answered: "*Pomożemy!*" "We will help you!" Among them was Lech Wałęsa. See Timothy Garton Ash, *The Polish Revolution: Solidarity*, third edition (New Haven: Yale University Press, 2002), 15.

the Gierek government raised food prices to distract the populace from its failing economic policies. The conventional social divide was crossed.

The Geirek government introduced what it euphemistically referred to as "reforms." They increased prices on anything from thirty to 100%; the cost of meat rose by as much as 70%.[10] Workers in Radom and Ursus went on strike on June 25, 1976, prompting workers in other towns to follow suit. Though the police did not respond with fire power, several thousand factory workers were sacked or suffered a marked reduction in wages. Some 2,500 striking workers were detained in police custody and more than 350 were sentenced to steep fines and severe sentences, many serving from four to ten years in prison.[11]

On September 23, 1976, a group of secular intellectuals, led by the novelist Jerzy Andrzejewski and former student activists Adam Michnik and Jacek Kuroń, formed the Workers' Defense Committee (Komitet Obrony Robotników, KOR). KOR's mission was to defend those workers persecuted after the June 25, 1976, strikes and to publicize cases in which the authorities broke international law. Thus began the alliance between intellectuals and workers.

KOR supported the creation of the illegal Gdańsk Free Trade Unions, which, in fact, included some KOR activists. The Gdańsk Free Trade Unions organized commemorations marking the 1970 shipyard massacre. In 1977, with several hundred small announcements placed on walls throughout the town, eight hundred to one thousand people stood at Gate Two to pay homage to the Lenin Shipyard's fallen workers. In 1978, despite the government arresting and detaining organizers, two to five thousand people gathered to pay tribute to the memory. On December 18, 1979, despite even more preventative police measures, five to seven thousand people took part.[12] As in previous commemorations, people laid flowers and lit candles, listened to workers' speeches and prayed with Reverend Bronisław Sroka, who brought an air of dignity and compassion to the event.[13] Wałęsa and his fellow activists refused to forget the massacre, taking on the PZPR memory apparatus. Facing down the regime's brutality, the workers' cohesion grew exponentially.[14] At the same time, both KOR's and the Church's relationship with the workers strengthened and that between KOR and the Church grew.

---

10   Paczkowski, *The Spring Will Be Ours: Poland and the Poles from Occupation to Freedom*, 358.
11   Workers had gone on strike in Radom, Ursus, Gdańsk, Grudziądz, Łódź, Warsaw, Starachowice, Nowy Targ and Płock. See ibid., 379.
12   Kubik, *The Power of Symbols against the Symbols of Power: The Rise of Solidarity and the Fall of State Socialism in Poland*, 164.
13   Ibid., 168.
14   Ash, *The Polish Revolution: Solidarity*, 13–14.

What set KOR apart from other opposition groups were its foundational principles. KOR's battle was internal, as individuals and as a collective. Members were mindful of their actions, insistent that they did not give credence to the government's repression by imbibing characteristics of it. As such, not only did KOR align with the idea of nonviolence, which was daunting in and of itself, but also encouraged members to have autonomy of action, trust in one another (which was counterintuitive in a time of government infiltration into civil organizations), and speak only truths based on facts. Indeed, the "simple" act of speaking the truth was perceived as an act of sabotage against communist society.

Another precept that KOR highlighted was that its membership only engage in "legal" actions. The 1975 Helsinki Act, to which People's Poland was a signatory, acted as its legal model.[15] KOR hoped it would garner international support in this way. While the Helsinki agreement drew Poland's Western border along the Oder and confirmed the Soviet Union's incorporation of the kresy, it also stated that all parties to the agreement would follow international human rights laws.

KOR's publication of its declaration of purpose reflected its defining policies: members not only signed their names to the text, but in doing so they also exposed their addresses and phone numbers. Such openness was unheard of in communist Poland.[16] The government responded by targeting KOR activists. They searched apartments and handed out beatings. On March 21, 1979, a band of a dozen or so men attacked the Kuroń's apartment in Żoliborz. They beat Kuroń's wife, Grazyna, and son along with their visitors, Adam Michnik and another friend, Wujec.[17] Government harassment against KOR activists also included damage to automobiles, fines, confiscation of property, firing from work, denial of passports, and detention (often in harsh conditions, although it was short-term due to the regime's desire to keep easing Cold War tensions). Despite being targeted by the regime, KOR members doggedly pursued what they described as "social work"—work to benefit factory workers that was deemed legal by international agreements which Poland had signed.[18]

Most of the intelligentsia did not rise to such courageous acts. In his book *A Warsaw Diary 1978–1981*, the blacklisted writer Kazimierz Brandys laments the intelligentsia's complicity for decades in this system of lies and facades: "in

---

15 Czesław Miłosz, foreword to Adam Michnik to *Letters from Prison and Other Essays,*, trans. Maya Latynski (Berkeley: University of California Press, 1985), xiii.
16 Jonathan Schell, introduction to Michnik, *Letters from Prison and Other Essays*, xxviii.
17 Kazimierz Brandys, *A Warsaw Diary 1978–1981*, trans. Richard Lourie (New York: Random House, 1983), 57.
18 Schell, introduction, xxvii.

exchange for the chance to publish poetry, we give up on stating the values that that poetry conceals, from which it arose, and to which it makes reference."[19] Like so many in the nomenklatura (people appointed to influential posts in government or industry), they had been reticent to take a stand, knowing the heavy price they would be forced to pay: "salary, apartments, children getting into university, trips, daily life. That's enough to make people afraid."[20] Adam Michnik refers to this capitulation by intellectuals as the "first betrayal."[21] In 1976, Brandys joined the revolt against "this system of shams," in which "everything conceals the corpses hidden under the floor."[22]

Brandys cooperated with other courageous underground writers and publishers to fill a deep void in the Poles' knowledge. They understood that a "society in captivity must produce an illegal literature because it must know the truth about itself, see an unfalsified picture of itself, hear its own genuine voice."[23] By running illegal printing presses, the group mounted an attack on the PZPR education and censorship system. They stripped away government lies, offering greater clarity of past and present to those who both read and passed along their samizdat texts.[24] In sum, underground opposition groups published several dozen different periodicals, beginning with KOR's series of *Communiqués (Komunikaty)* and its *Information Bulletin (Biuletyn Informacyjny)*. With a nominal imprint of forty thousand copies, each one passed from hand to hand among scores of people.[25]

Independent (i.e., illegal) publishing houses played a critical role in this "battle over consciousness." The most effective and longest lasting, the Independent Publishing House (NOWA), published more than a hundred titles over the years. Of the uncensored books it put out, a great many were reprints of émigré history books, as well as works by foreign authors translated into Polish for the first time. These books included George Orwell's *Animal Farm* and *1984*. The underground organizations also published many original works, including Kazimierz Brandys'

---

19 Brandys, *A Warsaw Diary 1978–1981*, 43.
20 Ibid., 59.
21 Michnik, "The Dilemma," 69.
22 Brandys, *A Warsaw Diary 1978–1981*, 42.
23 Adam Michnik, "Shadows of Forgotten Ancestors," in Michnik, *Letters from Prison and Other Essays*, 207.
24 Brandys, *A Warsaw Diary 1978–1981*, 44.
25 These included Brandys' *Zapis* (Record), as well as *Opinia* (Opinion), *Głos* (The Voice) and *Krytyka* (the latter two expressing opposing trends within KOR). See Norman Davies, *God's Playground: A History of Poland*: 472; Kazimierz Brandys discusses his 1976 founding of *Zapis* in *A Warsaw Diary 1978–1981*, 42–44.

memoir *A Warsaw Diary*, novels such as Jerzy Andrzejewski's *Pulp* (1979) and Julian Styjkowski's *The Big Fear* (1980), as well as political books and pamphlets, of which Adam Michnik's *The Church and the Left* (1977) is best known.[26]

In this clarion call for facts, members of the intelligentsia established the Flying University, a twentieth-century iteration of the late nineteenth-century secret learning society by the same name.[27] Similar to its predecessor, the Flying University met weekly in different apartments to avoid the authorities' detection. In each major city it held secret study classes.[28] Within this forum, activists uncovered Poland's authentic past, which the censor and education apparatuses had masked. They discussed taboo topics, including Soviet-Polish relations during occupation, the Soviet massacre of Polish officers at Katyń, and the Soviet sabotage of the Warsaw Uprising.[29] Given that Jews were an important part of Poland's history, the opposition's investigation into the Polish past necessarily revealed Jews' roles within and outside of Polish society. For a population that had witnessed most of Poland's few remaining Jews exiled in 1968, granting Jews a place in Poland's history was an act of power against the authorities.

People entered these learning sessions at great physical risk, as the government would send gangs from officially sanctioned student organizations to disrupt them. At one lecture held at a housing development in Ursyn, a squad of twenty-year-olds blocked the building entrance, while another group stood guard inside by the stairs. The PZPR's goal was to provoke a physical clash. By eliciting violence from KOR members, the authorities could brand them as dangerous hooligans and justify arresting them. Adam Michnik, the designated lecturer that night, was permitted to pass through, but was attacked on the stairs. "They dragged him upstairs to an apartment, pushed him against the glass doors in the foyer, breaking the glass, and then roughed him up, throwing him to the floor, picking him up, then throwing him back down again."[30]

---

26 Paczkowski, *The Spring Will Be Ours: Poland and the Poles from Occupation to Freedom*, 384.
27 The original Flying University was founded in 1882–1883 by Jadwiga Szczawińska (1863–1910).
28 Davies, *God's Playground: A History of Poland*: 472.
29 Paczkowski, *The Spring Will Be Ours: Poland and the Poles from Occupation to Freedom*, 401.
30 KOR members also risked bringing these heretofore taboo topics to workers who attended worker lectures. Brandys, *A Warsaw Diary 1978–1981*, 56.

The Polish Catholic Church Stands Its Ground

From its inception, the Polish People's Republic waged a war against Church power and influence over the people. The regime restricted or eliminated many Church privileges: it nationalized most Church land and hospitals, censored Church publications, halted its radio broadcasts, suspended religious instruction in schools, and removed chaplains from hospitals, prisons, and the army.[31] To retain peace, the Church chose not to react with hostility. But when the state demanded that it take over the right to make and revoke ecclesiastical appointments, the bishops responded with strongly worded opposition. During Warsaw's June 4, 1953 Corpus Christi procession, Cardinal Wyszyński (1901–1981) stated: "We teach that one must give to Caesar what is Caesar's and to God what is God's. And if Caesar sits down on the altar, we must say simply: *That is not allowed!*"[32] In reaction, the authorities arrested Wyszyński and jailed him for three years. Standing up to the Goliath state secured for him the people's respect.

This contest between state and Church for the public's allegiance would persist until the collapse of the Polish People's Republic. That the Church had been permitted any type of agency led Jan Kubik to refer to "the schizophrenic dualism pervading public life in Poland."[33] An example of this dynamic can be seen in the Great Novena of the Millennium. As Polish statehood approached its millennium—966–1966—the still imprisoned Cardinal Wyszyński developed a nine-year program of spiritual preparatory celebrations to ready Poles to honor what the Church and tradition refer to as the "Polish baptism." Wyszyński asserted the "Polish nation was to renew itself spiritually and ask God, through Mary, for the victory of faith and freedom of the Church."[34]

To begin this magnificent effort, Cardinal Wyszyński proposed that the Polish people make a pilgrimage to Jasna Góra, where in Polish tradition God, through Mary, rescued Poland from the 1655 Swedish invasion. This national myth presents a Swedish army that virtually swept away all opposing Polish battalions,

---

31   Kubik, *The Power of Symbols against the Symbols of Power: The Rise of Solidarity and the Fall of State Socialism in Poland*, 105.
32   Ibid., 107.
33   Ibid., 104.
34   Andrzej Micewski, *Cardinal Wyszyński: A Biography*, trans. William R. Brand and Katarzyna Mrockowska-Brand (San Diego: Harcourt, Brace, Jovanovich, 1984), 157.

thereby forcing Poles to recognize the Swedes' rule. Only a miracle could save Poland. And one did. At the Jasna Góra monastery in Częstochowa, Polish soldiers unexpectedly repelled the enemy. They did not do it on their own. They staved off the Swedish army by carrying into battle the holy icon housed in the monastery. Known as the *Black Madonna*, this icon is claimed to have been painted by Saint Luke on a cypress board taken from a table belonging to the Holy Family. Tradition holds that it was the *Black Madonna* which forced the Swedes' retreat. After regaining his throne, King Jan Kazimierz venerated the Blessed Virgin as the "Queen of the Crown of Poland."[35] Ever since, people of all estates—kings, nobility, burghers, and peasantry—acknowledged the spiritual presence and control of the *Black Madonna* over their lives. Pilgrimages to Jasna Góra were signs of this connection to God through Mary.

Thus, while the communist authorities fed the people secularism and atheism, Cardinal Wyszyński prepared for a pilgrimage to Jasna Góra for Poles to reassert their trust in God. On August 26, 1956, close to a million pilgrims attended the opening mass of the Great Novena held in Częstochowa.[36] The imagery was compelling and affirming: while not the sole "sanctuary of the nation," at Jasna Góra Poles saw how to regain their political independence.

The Great Novena was for the Church also a type of pilgrimage *to* the people. In affirming the Church's respect for every individual, its representatives escorted the *Black Madonna* to parishes throughout the country and offered Poles the honor of hosting the icon in their homes. The *Black Madonna* was seen by most Polish Catholics. This intimate experience steadily drew more people back to the Church.[37]

The power play between Church and state continued. Gomułka recognized the significance of the Church for Poles. He hoped that by repealing earlier restrictions against it and restoring Cardinal Wyszyński to his post, Gomułka would gain support and legitimacy from the people. But his political thaw did not last and the relationship between the state and the Church soon deteriorated.[38] The struggle for the Polish soul continued. One authority against an Other.

---

35 Kubik, *The Power of Symbols against the Symbols of Power: The Rise of Solidarity and the Fall of State Socialism in Poland*, 109.
36 Ibid., 108–111.
37 Ibid., 112.
38 Ibid., 107.

Secular Intellectuals and the Polish Catholic Church

Given that in the Polish People's Republic, Church "pastoral letters and sermons constituted the only free ideological thus, like it or not, also political, public life,"[39] the Church soon came to represent the only way to express oneself outside of the official censored discourse. As such, the Church gained new adherents. According to the noted émigré Polish poet, Czesław Miłosz, the Church had changed because of the people who needed it and gravitated to it: "It ceased to be the Church of the peasants, and attracted more and more young people of high intellectual caliber into its ranks as clergy and parishioners."[40] By 1970 the Church had welcomed a new breed of Church philosopher—one who not only expressed a need for government liberalization, but also demonstrated greater concern for the people's particular oppression.

Some Church publications, including the Catholic weekly *Tygodnik Powszechny*, became more liberal by opening their pages to intellectuals. Indeed, Antoni Słonimski—an atheist of Jewish origin—contributed regularly to it. In the past, such a strong demonstration of support for secularists would have raised the ire of Church leaders. Now this vocal support was welcomed by Cardinal Karol Wojtyła of Kraków, who had close ties with *Tygodnik Powszechny* (and who would later be named Pope John Paul II).[41] This link can also be seen in some parish priests' willingness to pass on samizdat material to inquiring parishioners.[42] However, most Church leaders retained traditional conservative views, including an intolerance for Others' religious truths.

Perceived by the people as the strongest opposition to communism in Poland, the Church came under increased government surveillance. The authorities hired more people to watch the clergy and evaluate their sermons.[43] In a January 1974 sermon, Cardinal Wyszyński incorporated support for freedom of the press, public opinion, publishing, discussion, and scientific inquiry.[44] After the 1976 strikes and harsh government reprisals, the episcopate's language in official letters and statements became even more forceful. Leaning toward militancy,

---

39   Ibid., 119.
40   Miłosz, foreword to *Letters from Prison and Other Essays*, x-xi.
41   Paczkowski, *The Spring Will Be Ours: Poland and the Poles from Occupation to Freedom*, 378.
42   Ash, *The Polish Revolution: Solidarity*, 28.
43   Paczkowski, *The Spring Will Be Ours: Poland and the Poles from Occupation to Freedom*, 392.
44   In addition, the secular opposition responded to the proposed constitutional clause with a statement signed by fifty-nine intellectuals, later known as "the letter of the fifty-nine." See ibid., 390.

they addressed the broader social and political problems facing the Polish people. They spoke of "the meaning of humanity; the dignity of the human person."[45]

In a 1979 publication, Adam Michnik underscored the essential role of the Church in enabling the opposition to move forward:

> It is obvious that independent [i.e., illegal] institutions could not function at all if it were not for the existence of a middle ground between the open opposition and the institutions of coercion—between, for example the Workers' Defense Committee (KOR) and the Politburo of the Central Committee of the PUWP.[46]

The Church provided the opposition the space, symbols, and rituals by which to express its resistance to communist policies and actions.

For example, in the Polish People's Republic it was taboo to celebrate November 11, 1918 as the date of Polish independence if one did not follow the state script that linked independence with the Bolshevik Revolution. The state censors had also wiped out the name of Józef Piłsudski, who had led the fight for independence. By the late 1970s, opposition groups actively embraced this date as their own and would gather in church sanctuaries to celebrate Poland's short-lived freedom (1918–1939). On November 10, 1978, opposition groups unveiled a plaque honoring Marshal Józef Piłsudski in Saint Alexander's Church in Warsaw.[47]

The following day illegal celebrations took place throughout the country in various churches. In Warsaw, Saint John's Cathedral hosted opposition groups, including KOR and ROPCiO. The leaflet advertising this illegal gathering read, in part:

> Although the Republic fell in 1939 under the blows of the Hitler's Reich and the Stalinist Soviet Union and the Yalta dictate sanctioned the satellite-like dependence of our Motherland on the Soviet Union—Poland did not die. She lives in us and will live forever . . . That is why the celebrations of the sixtieth anniversary of the Rebirth of the Republic should become the

---

45 Jan Kubik, *The Power of Symbols against the Symbols of Power: The Rise of Solidarity and the Fall of State Socialism in Poland*, 121.
46 Adam Michnik and Jan Józef Lipski, "Some Remarks on the Opposition and the General Situation in Poland 1979," in Michnik, *Letters from Prison and Other Essays*, 150.
47 Jan Kubik, *The Power of Symbols against the Symbols of Power: The Rise of Solidarity and the Fall of State Socialism in Poland*, 171.

huge manifestation of the will of the whole society to regain FREEDOM AND SOVEREIGNTY.[48]

Joining in a solemn Holy mass, some twenty thousand people affirmed a desire for their own national freedom. The nation and Church intermingled as one— and secular intellectuals grew closer to the Church.

The Pope's Visit to People's Poland

The Church's influence on the opposition expanded when in October 1978 Cardinal Karol Wojtyła was named Pope John Paul II. A Polish pope! For the majority, which for generations had been Catholic, the ascension of a Polish pope was nothing short of a miracle. Poles had suffered under Hitler and Stalin. Though they had resisted occupation, Yalta had brought them dishonor. Only now—through the Church—did dignity grace the Polish people.

June 2–10, 1979 marked Pope John Paul II's first pilgrimage back to his homeland. He planned it to coincide with the celebration of Saint Stanisław. As legend has it, on April 11, 1069, Kraków's Bishop Stanisław Szczepanowski was murdered on orders from King Bolesław the Bold. The bishop had excommunicated the king due to the latter's serious maltreatment of his knights and their wives. Purportedly, the outraged king retaliated by sentencing the bishop to dismemberment, without a trial. In 1253, Pope Innocent IV canonized Stanisław. Ever since, Saint Stanisław has been an accepted symbol of justified resistance against the excesses of any government.[49] By marking the nine-hundredth anniversary of the Saint's martyrdom, Pope John Paul II reminded the people that rebellion is acceptable against tyranny.

Despite the PZPR's postponement of the visit and the regime's attempted censoring of the pope's message, Pope John Paul II spoke to the people and transformed them. Poles flocked to his Masses. While about one million Poles attended the first Warsaw mass, the last pontifical mass attracted 2.5 to 3 million people. Young people dominated the crowd. In the end, some eight to ten million people celebrated the pope's presence, publicly demonstrating their love of the Church and their hope in the pope. His visit came to be known as "the second baptism of Poland." In his poignant book, Jan Kubik underscores that not only did the pope confirm "the unbreakable link between the Polish nation

---

48   Ibid., 170.
49   The pope, himself, had filled Stanisław's post in Kraków. Ibid., 130.

and Catholicism, challenging the official *secular* definition of Polish statehood,"[50] but in doing so he offered the people something more—the dissolution of the party's monopoly on public discourse in Poland:

> Millions of people, organized not by the state agencies, but by volunteers directed by Catholic activists, came together in an orderly fashion to celebrate "their" pope. They realized that civil organization of the society outside the state was possible. This led to a considerable lowering of the barrier of fear vis-à-vis the state and the development of the consciousness of "we" crystallized in the towering personality of the pope, popularly perceived as the only genuine moral, religious, and even political authority.[51]

Speaking from the pulpit of his old Kraków cathedral, the Polish pope extolled that "The future of Poland [. . .] will depend on how many people are mature enough to be nonconformists."[52] His message of human rights and dignity, coupled with the people's own disciplined, nonviolent behavior, elevated the Poles' state of mind. As one observer noted: "In bowing before the Holy Father, Poland got up off its knees."[53]

The pope solidified the workers' connection with the Church. He also attracted intellectuals to the Church. Nurtured since 1976 by Adam Michnik's *The Church and the Left* (a work perceived by many liberals as the Left's bible), liberal intellectuals proposed a rational embrace of the Polish Catholic Church, not as a political ally (for they believed in the strict separation of Church and state), but rather as a social, moral ally.[54] Michnik himself was wary of this course of action, given the Church's long established practice of traditionalism and intolerance. However, he believed that the rise of a relatively more liberal leadership within the Church, as evidenced by the then-cardinal Wojtyła, provided an opening into what could be a meaningful and respect-driven relationship between the two sides. Michnik hoped that the creation of true dialogue—"a readiness to understand the validity

---

50   Ibid., 142.
51   Ibid., 145.
52   Quoted in Ash, *The Polish Revolution: Solidarity*, 31–32.
53   Quoted in Paczkowski, *The Spring Will Be Ours: Poland and the Poles from Occupation to Freedom*, 395.
54   Adam Michnik, *The Church and the Left*, ed. and trans. David Ost (Chicago: The University of Chicago Press, 1993), xii.

of someone else's position... a method by which an ideologically diverse society can learn to live together"[55]—could take shape between the Church and secular intellectuals. He pursued a dialogue that would solidify the sanctity of personal justice and freedom while holding intolerance at bay. In effect, he hoped to promote the evolution of the liberal variant he witnessed within the Church and thus to realign (i.e., decrease) the Church's influence in society.[56] Conservatives, however, found his approach audacious.

Solidarity: More Than a Response to Economic Collapse

Gierek's Great Leap Forward of 1971–1975 was a devastating failure. To launch economic reform by repairing and expanding Poland's industrial infrastructure, he took out Western loans. At first, Poles experienced monetary growth and a sense of cultural liberalization. Gierek opened up to the West, enjoying personal meetings with heads of state, allowing Western products to be sold in the Polish People's Republic, and encouraging Western investment in the country. Rural youth moved to urban centers to work in new factories. The public mood grew optimistic. More people joined the PZPR, believing it had changed and that their lives would be better for that affiliation.[57] However, in the end, People's Poland could meet neither the necessary projected industrial and agricultural output, nor reap the necessary export revenue to pay back its debt. Thus, Gierek's government entered a downward spiral, taking out new loans to pay previous ones. The country's debt rose from 8.4 billion in 1975 to 23.8 billion in 1979.[58]

By 1980 Gierek could see no way out, aside from strict austerity. Every available product had to be sold overseas, leaving Polish stores and markets to sell what little was left at soaring prices.[59] By the harsh winter of 1978–1979, when snow and below zero temperatures toppled Warsaw, and the scarcity of coal left people freezing in hospitals and apartments, medicines could not be had.

---

55   Quoted in David Ost, introduction to Michnik, *The Church and the Left*, 5.
56   Michnik, *The Church and the Left*, xi–xvi; also see Ost, introduction to Michnik, *The Church and the Left*, 9.
57   Indeed, the nomenklatura—those administrative bureaucratic posts reserved for party members, and access to which was controlled by the PZPR—grew to some five hundred thousand. More people wanted access to those jobs, for such posts carried many lifestyle benefits for the worker and his or her family. See Ash, *The Polish Revolution: Solidarity*, 9.
58   Paczkowski, *The Spring Will Be Ours: Poland and the Poles from Occupation to Freedom*, 357.
59   Davies, *God's Playground*: 472.

People stormed the stores to buy up the last reserves of potatoes.[60] Long lines for staple goods consumed daily life: "The line at the fish store stretched down Wąski Dunaj Street. Some herring was supposed to have been delivered... The store opened at eleven o'clock. I learned that the people at the head of the line had been there since two o'clock in the morning."[61] During the summer of 1980, Brandys noted in *A Warsaw Diary* that

> as I was crossing Monte Cassino Street, I heard shouts and an uproar from the other side of the street. A commotion had suddenly erupted in a long line in front of the meat store. People shouted, squeezed together, pressing up against the door. I saw red faces, open mouths, bulging eyes. I thought something had collapsed or exploded. No. The line had spotted a van pulling up. Meat was being delivered.[62]

Dire escalating social discontent followed the dramatic breakdown of Gierek's economic façade. "A silence heavy with menace holds sway in the lines in the Old City."[63]

In response to the debilitating economic conditions, workers went on strike in the summer of 1980. This strike wave ebbed and flowed, like that of 1976 before it, until it reached the Gdańsk Lenin Shipyard on August 14, 1980. Gdańsk became the strike's focal point. For a decade, this site where more than fifteen thousand people worked had been a center of opposition, whether in the form of ceremonies, strikes, or education. Due to particular individual leadership, various opposition groups successfully cooperated in harmony. The city was second only to Warsaw in its political opposition to the PZPR. It was here that ceremonies were organized with the greatest frequency and attracted the largest numbers of people.[64] The workers at the shipyard had trained for this moment in 1980 and members of the still independent, that is, illegal Free Trade Union, organized their strike.

The Lenin Shipyard workers called for the reinstatement of two former employees—Lech Wałęsa and Anna Walentynowicz—who had been sacked due to their activism. The workers sought a pay raise as well as a guarantee of

---

60   Brandys, *A Warsaw Diary 1978–1981*, 35–38.
61   Ibid., 32.
62   Ibid., 156.
63   Ibid., 158.
64   Kubik, *The Power of Symbols against the Symbols of Power: The Rise of Solidarity and the Fall of State Socialism in Poland*, 182.

no reprisals. They also demanded that a monument be built to those massacred by the authorities in 1970.[65] They wanted the facts known, and their coworkers remembered and respected. This last demand grew in importance, and came to symbolize the workers' call for human dignity.

When the authorities met the Gdańsk Lenin Shipyard's specific demands, the strikers turned back to work. But Wałęsa changed course. The leaders of strikes in much smaller industrial facilities urged him to continue the Lenin Shipyard strike lest their own lack of leverage would leave their particular demands unmet. Wałęsa took a risk and urged his colleagues in Gdańsk to reframe the moment as a national "solidarity" strike. The workers, who for a decade had been involved in the growing resistance movement, had the wherewithal to take this large risk with him. Forming an Interfactory Strike Committee (Międzyzakładowy Komitet Strajkowy—MKS), the strike leaders created their famous List of Twenty-One Demands.[66]

Symbols and ceremonies that workers and secular intellectuals had embraced over the decade filled the strike zone at Gate Two. Flowers filled the space. Brought by supporters, they represented KOR's long call for nonviolent and dignified resistance. At the spot where the workers had been killed, they planted a large wooden cross, symbolizing defiance against the communist state, as well as national martyrdom. Later, people adorned it with flowers, a picture of the *Black Madonna*, a red and white ribbon signifying independent Poland, and a drawing of the intended monument to the murdered workers.[67] These symbols represented the cooperation among the Church, intellectuals, and workers that had led to this auspicious moment.

Daily, strikers and their supporters (sometimes in the thousands) celebrated mass. Interestingly, the two Church figures who often led mass at Gate Two differed greatly from one another. Father Henryk Jankowski from Wałęsa's Saint Brigid Church was a staunch fundamentalist, who later would be denounced for his antisemitic statements, as well as for his unwillingness to recognize Poles' participation in the Jedwabne pogrom.[68] Father Józef Tischner (1931–2000),

---

65 Paczkowski, *The Spring Will Be Ours: Poland and the Poles from Occupation to Freedom*, 405.
66 Kubik, *The Power of Symbols against the Symbols of Power: The Rise of Solidarity and the Fall of State Socialism in Poland*, 186–187.
67 Ibid., 186
68 In 1997 the Polish Catholic Church suspended Father Jankowski for one year for making antisemitic remarks. In 1999, the Gdańsk archbishop ordered him to stop selling antisemitic literature at his parish church—so he moved the book stand to his apartment. Numerous Church representatives publicly criticized his position. See "Priest in Poland under Fire for Selling Anti-semitic Books," *JTA*, January 13, 1999, https://www.jta.org/archive/

known as a great philosopher and priest of exceptional openness, not only "proclaimed the Good News" to preschool children, workers, and highlanders, but also engaged in meaningful and respectful dialogue with intellectuals, nonbelievers, and those questioning God.[69] Tischner became known as the unofficial chaplain of Solidarity.[70] Importantly, though, Jankowski retained a prominent place on the podium. These two figures pointed to a conflict Solidarity and the country would eventually face.

By August 20, the illegal Gdańsk Free Trade Union had come to represent workers at more than three hundred factories. Despite arrests and news blackouts, the strikes persisted[71] due to the determination of Jacek Kuroń and other KOR members. They gathered and publicized information in their underground paper *Robotnik*, as well as transmitted it to strikers throughout Poland over Radio Free Europe and Voice of America.[72] By this time, the workers' demands had transformed from purely economic concerns over rising food costs to those encompassing better working conditions, social security benefits, health care, better organization of work, a reform of the existing unions, as well as free and fair local elections. In those places where KOR and other oppositional groups had formed a relationship with the workers, the demands also included the formation of new trade unions, independent of the party and state.[73]

On August 31, the crisis ended: the deputy premier of the Polish People's Republic, Mieczysław Jagielski, and the chairman of the Interfactory Strike Committee (MKS), Lech Wałęsa, signed an agreement on the grounds of the Lenin Shipyard. It included the establishment of a free and independent trade union.[74] Solidarność—Solidarity—had been born. "For the first time organized

---

priest-in-poland-under-fire-for-selling-anti-semitic-books-2. Regarding Jankowski's far-right position on Jedwabne, see "Poland and the Holocaust: It Wasn't just Germans," *Economist*, April 28, 2001, https://www.economist.com/europe/2001/04/26/it-wasnt-just-germans. In later years activists charged Jankowski with child molestation. See Tamara Evdokimova, "Polish Activists Topple Statue of Iconic Priest as Vatican Summit on Sex Abuse Begins," *Slate*, February 21, 2019, https://slate.com/news-and-politics/2019/02/poland-priest-henryk-jankowski-statue-clergy-sex-abuse.html.

69 Krzysztof Wieczorek, "Tischner as a Metapolitican," *Studies in East European*, 71, no. 4 (2019): 349.
70 Kubik, *The Power of Symbols against the Symbols of Power: The Rise of Solidarity and the Fall of State Socialism in Poland*, 197.
71 Paczkowski, *The Spring Will Be Ours: Poland and the Poles from Occupation to Freedom*, 407.
72 Kubik, *The Power of Symbols against the Symbols of Power: The Rise of Solidarity and the Fall of State Socialism in Poland*, 184.
73 Ibid.
74 Polonsky, *The Jews in Poland and Russia*: 3:738; Michnik, "A Year Has Passed 1981," 124.

authority was signing an accord with an organized society,"[75] which stood at ten million strong.[76]

Solidarity was a spontaneously growing independent and self-governing labor union. From Adam Michnik's perspective, the union answered the people's broad demands:

> a labor union that defends the rights of the working people in their places of employment; an office that prosecutes lawbreakers in the power apparatus; a defender of political prisoners, law and order, and an independent culture—a true representative of the people in dealings with the authorities. But one thing it has not been: a political party aiming to take over power, even though it has been accused of precisely this.[77]

Solidarity signaled the end of socialism in its classic Soviet European form.[78]

The Regime's Reaction against Solidarity

Greatly troubled by his perceived failure in assenting to Solidarity, the Politburo requested the resignation of Gierek and other holders of high office. Gierek's replacement, Stanisław Kania, stonewalled during fourteen months of negotiations, attempting to defeat Solidarity or at least to minimize its reach and influence. The government focused on further dividing the factions within the enormous Solidarity leadership, pitting radicals against moderates. Due to strikes, an attempt in the courts to change the wording of Solidarity's statute failed. At the same time, the government's information blackout failed to weaken the nationwide strike given Jacek Kuroń's mobilization and distribution of incoming reports about additional strikes. Government obstruction of the actual registration process for trade unions also failed. There were even attempts to coopt some aspects of Solidarity into the party. These too failed.[79]

---

75 Ibid.
76 Paczkowski, *The Spring Will Be Ours: Poland and the Poles from Occupation to Freedom*, 419.
77 Michnik, "A Year Has Passed 1981," 129.
78 Paczkowski, *The Spring Will Be Ours: Poland and the Poles from Occupation to Freedom*, 410.
79 For details on the government attempts to shut Solidarity down, see ibid., 414, and 419–420, and Michnik, "A Year Has Passed 1981," 125–128.

Among its varied efforts to mask Solidarity's collective outcry and massive force, the authorities painted the independent trade union as another so-called *Zionist* conspiracy. Given that some of its leaders were the same activists of Jewish origin who had stood up against the government in '67 and '68, the authorities called it a *Zionist* plot to takeover People's Poland.[80] But this distraction did not work as it had over a decade prior. By 1980, those who came of age during the second half of the 1970s had broken with their parents' belief that the socialist concept of history would vindicate the repressive methods employed by the PZPR. However, unlike opposition groups in East Germany, which only had to look beyond the wall into West Germany to find a model for their hopes and dreams, Poles had nowhere to turn but backwards, into their own past. But the last time there was a genuine Poland, it was a Poland with Jews. "So, in a paradox of Polish nationalism, having Jews gave a stamp of authenticity to Poland."[81]

It then followed that if one opposed the oppressive system—which purged a great number of Jews from the party in its early stage and forced many from Poland through its 1968 antisemitic campaign—then one would emphasize that particular part of the Polish past which Jews inhabited. This time, the roughly ten million members of Solidarity acted against the government's propaganda and stood their ground against the undermining ethno-nationalist subculture.[82]

In mid-December the government attempted yet again to deflect blame for its failings onto the Jews, claiming that Solidarity had been taken over by the children of Jewish Stalinists. It launched a series of radio lectures, in which government spokespeople asserted that "The Soviet camp, whatever we may think about their system, is a barrier to Jewish chauvinism in its plans to dominate the world."[83] This approach was quickly abandoned, however, perhaps due to General Wojciech Jaruzelski, who replaced Kania as first secretary of People's Poland and expressed sensitivity toward the Jews' experience in 1968.[84]

Finally, after months of government delay tactics, the two sides held a twelve-hour meeting. Neither the government nor Solidarity felt progress had been

---

80 Polonsky, *The Jews in Poland and Russia*: 738.
81 Author's interview with Konstanty Gebert, December 2007.
82 Michnik, "Shadows of Forgotten Ancestors," 204.
83 Wojciech Jaruzelski, "A Painful and Complex Subject," in Głuchowski and Polonsky, *1968: Forty Years After*, 314.
84 General Jaruzelski wrote years later: "In the land where the Nazis carried out the terrible crime of the Holocaust, not only sensitivity but hypersensitivity is necessary towards everything that might strike at that memory, feelings, and pain. It is in this respect that I look with deep self-critical sorrow at the situation which developed particularly in the last years of the sixties." See ibid.

made. Each desired action that would demonstrate strength. Solidarity planned a twenty-four-hour strike and a December 17 protest rally in Warsaw's Victory Square (coinciding with the anniversary of the 1970 massacre in Gdynia).[85] General Jaruzelski's reaction was seismic. On December 13, 1981 he imposed martial law.[86] All trade unions which had been authorized were now suspended; the right to assembly and protest was severely restricted; and nearly six thousand people were arrested, including the entire Solidarity leadership.[87] Some three hundred top Solidarity leaders remained in prison (until 1986 when Jaruzelski capitulated to Western sanctions and negotiated an amnesty). Solidarity was hit hard and contained.

By the mid-'80s it was clear that the Jaruzelski regime would not be able to reverse its sharp economic decline by coopting Solidarity. General Jaruzelski's insistence on austerity measures led to price increases during the summer of 1988, which in turn resulted in yet another wave of strikes. By February 1989 General Jaruzelski's government entered into two months of Round Table discussions with a broad spectrum of Solidarity opposition leaders. These talks, were mediated in part by the Church. Through these negotiations Solidarity gained legalization and a senate was established. Free and fair elections would determine its members.[88] In elections to the lower house, 65% of seats would be retained for party members; the remaining 35% would be elected through open voting. Surprising most onlookers, Solidarity won a landslide victory, with 161 contested seats in the Sejm and ninety-nine out of one hundred seats in the Senate. All power-sharing arrangements were now untenable. A coalition government headed by Tadeusz Mazowiecki—a liberal Catholic opposition politician—took charge in August 1989.[89]

Myth Reconstruction

To understand and respect the power of this moment, one must be willing to understand and respect its symbols. I am an outsider. As a Jew raised in the United States, the Cross proves somewhat problematic. I see it everywhere:

---

85 Paczkowski, *The Spring Will Be Ours: Poland and the Poles from Occupation to Freedom*, 442–443.
86 Ibid., 445.
87 Polonsky, *The Jews in Poland and Russia*, 3:739.
88 Ibid., 740.
89 Ibid.

piercing the sky atop church spires, hanging on walls in homes and hospitals, looming out of enormous highway billboards, on television shows, and decorating people's necks. As a Jew, I experience this Cross as an imposition much of the time, as a reminder of institutionalized Christian power and influence not only in this place and time, but throughout the world and reaching back centuries. It reminds me that I am a minority—different, excluded, and often misunderstood. It recalls for me those eras in which the Church used the so-called "enemy Jew" to unite Christians. It triggers personal memories of being blamed for Jesus's murder. But I have also grown to understand that the Cross is much more than these offenses. For those who embrace it, the Cross means love. For me, it took stepping outside of my red brick walled education to find a path past my negative reactions to it.

During graduate school, curiosity led me across Broadway's wide expanse and into the Union Theological Seminary. Engaging with young future Protestant Church leaders about the theology of Paul Tillich, I studied the powerful symbol of Jesus on the Cross and gained a true understanding of how it succeeds in pointing to God.[90] Through open dialogue, I came to respect Christian theology and its images. However, sometimes it is difficult to reconcile a theological ideal with the ways in which people interpret it in order to assert power over Others.

For many Jews and Muslims, the Cross stands for the Crusades and the institutionalized intolerance of Other's truths. But for Christians, it stands for love, compassion, and community. As one who remains outside of the Church—as one whose people have been both harmed and helped by the Church—my personal thinking about the Cross is that it represents both the sin of power and the grace of God.

Having researched the important role played by Pope John Paul II, as well as many Polish bishops and local priests, I respect the Church for supporting and empowering the Polish people during those tumultuous years of violence, arrests, and martial law. The Church reminded Poland of its worth as a nation and its people's inner strength. By once again establishing the Church's importance, the Catholic leadership provided the people with a sense of national belonging, confidence, and safety. The Church offered space and a sense of freedom to those actively struggling against the totalitarian state. At the same time, however, I know that its own foundation is built on a similar apparatus of intolerance.

In the early 1980s cracks appeared in the previously unheard-of union between intellectuals and the Church. Upon Archbishop Wyszyński's death in May 1981,

---

90 I searched for a Jewish symbol that could be as powerful. That which comes closest is the burning bush. But Jews rarely reference it and so such a symbol eludes us.

the Church filled his seat with Cardinal Józef Glemp. Archbishop Glemp's steadfast focus on directing society's moral code through Church-petitioned political policy opened those cracks. He promoted a resurgence of Church fundamentalism, which left little room for meaningful dialogue with the secular intelligentsia.[91] For the archbishop, "Jews, Freemasons and Trotskyists" remained negative influences on society. In addition, he supported the controversial beatification of Maksymilian Kolbe, the Franciscan monk who sacrificed his life for another's in Auschwitz. Prior to the war, however, Kolbe was the managing editor of the antisemitic paper *Mały Dziennik*. Supporting his arguments against the Jews with the *Protocols of the Elders of Zion*, Kolbe wrote an article in 1926 directed to masons who had recently gathered for a conference in Bucharest that the Jews "secretly govern you ... consider you to be like cattle, herded into Masonic lodges to achieve goals that you do not even expect."[92] For Glemp, the Jew remained the enemy who, together with liberals, held the Church under siege in order to manipulate it and dominate Polish society. Lech Wałęsa and his fellow workers, who mostly had been raised in the Church, felt at home in this old and comfortable fundamentalist-nationalism.[93]

Interestingly, while the Church did not accept liberals under Archbishop Glemp, many liberals embraced the Church. Some saw in it their only refuge. During martial law, many feared Solidarity was dead. They believed the Church was the only sanctuary in which to continue their oppositional activity against the totalitarian state. Other intellectuals came to the Church in a true quest for God, and others still sought to access legitimacy and power through it. Michnik refers to the latter as Polish intellectuals' "second betrayal,"[94] the first being their willing submission to communist totalitarianism.

Two opposing truths often exist in one place at one time. The Catholic Church is no exception. Although for centuries it has maintained a fundamentalist rigidity in its teaching and practice, the Polish Catholic Church made room for a wave of more tolerant thinking. While it portrays itself as a single, cohesive institution, within this behemoth there developed in the 1970s and 1980s an oppositional approach to its traditional role in society. More tolerant of difference, it accepted the ideal Church as *one* influence on society, not the *only* influence.

This movement away from fundamentalism might well have been influenced by the Second Ecumenical Council of the Vatican, commonly known as Vatican

---

91 Ost, introduction, 19.
92 Polonsky, *The Jews in Poland and Russia*: 3:83, 819.
93 Ost, introduction, 15, 24.
94 Michnik, "The Dilemma," 69.

II. Convened by Pope John XXIII between 1962 and 1965, its final documents circle the theme of reconciliation. Among other changes demanded by Vatican II, the Church now allowed Catholics to pray with other Christian denominations and encouraged friendship with non-Christian faiths.[95] After eighteen centuries, Pope John XXIII opened the fortress, allowing Catholics to regard Other religions "as different, distinctive and also honorable ways to God."[96]

That encyclical concerning Catholic relations with non-Christian religions is known as *Nostra Aetate*. One section formulates a way into Catholic-Jewish dialogue, with the goal of mutual respect: "Since the spiritual patrimony common to Christians and Jews is thus so great, this sacred synod wants to foster and recommend that mutual understanding and respect which is the fruit, above all, of biblical and theological studies as well as of fraternal dialogues."[97]

The encyclical goes on to denounce its centuries-long propaganda that the Jews are damned by God for causing Jesus's death on the Cross:

> True, the Jewish authorities and those who followed their lead pressed for the death of Christ; still, what happened in His passion cannot be charged against all the Jews, without distinction, then alive, nor against the Jews of today. Although the Church is the new people of God, the Jews should not be presented as rejected or accursed by God, as if this followed from the Holy Scriptures.[98]

Additionally, through *Nostra Aetate* Pope John XXIII implored the Catholic world to reject political rhetoric and reject all forms of antisemitism:

> Furthermore, in her rejection of every persecution against any man, the Church, mindful of the patrimony she shares with the Jews and moved not by political reasons but by the Gospel's spiritual love, decries hatred, persecutions, displays of antisemitism, directed against Jews at any time and by anyone.[99]

---

95 Jordan G. Teicher, "Why Is Vatican II so Important?," npr.org, October 10, 2012, https://www.npr.org/2012/10/10/162573716/why-is-vatican-ii-so-important.
96 Author's interview with Stanisław Obirek, Warsaw, April 2019.
97 Pope Paul IV, *Nostra Aetate* (October 28, 1965), https://www.vatican.va/archive/hist_councils//ii_vatican_council/documents/vat-ii_decl_19651028_nostra-aetate_en.html.
98 Ibid.
99 Ibid.

Vatican II opened doors for respectful dialogue with people who are outside the Catholic fold. With regard to the Jews in particular, it attempted to reform the almost innate negative views it had promulgated for centuries. For Stanisław Obirek, a former Jesuit Father, Vatican II was nothing less than a Copernican revolution.[100]

Yet not everyone chose to be part of this revolution. Indeed, many in the Catholic hierarchy in both Europe and the United States tried to dampen it through reinterpretation.[101] In the Polish People's Republic, fundamentalists guarded against this revolutionary overture. Though some important Polish Catholic figureheads had opened Church doors to provide a supportive space for the intellectual opposition, most of whom were secular, many clergy refused them equal respect. Nonbelievers remained the Other—as secularists who threatened the Church's status and influence. While some in the Church were influenced by Pope John Paul II to become activists on behalf of tolerance, most Polish Church leaders would remain intolerant to and fearful of Enlightenment ideals and the secularists who touted them. In Poland, most practicing Catholics who advocate tolerance belong to what is called the "Open Church" and the traditional conservatives belong to the "Closed Church."

It is vital that Jews recognize this evolution within Polish Catholicism and the internal tensions it causes. From the Open Church have come "the most outspoken critics of the traditional forms of religiosity represented by the Closed Church"[102] and resistance to the rejection of other Christian and non-Christian religions. Additionally, Open Church adherents have "frequently condemned the core national orientation of the Closed Church as a deformation of Christian principles and defined it as a formation of 'the besieged fortress.'"[103] Open Church representatives have also accused the Closed Church of "representing anti-Catholic/anti-Christian values"[104] when dealing specifically with Jewish topics. Stanisław Obirek, once part of the Open Church, maintains a very critical view of the Closed Church. He describes the institution as "immature, very

---

100 Author's interview with Stanisław Obirek, Warsaw, April 2019.
101 Christopher Lamb, "Francis Affirms No Place in Church for Those Who Reject Vatican II," ChicagoCatholic.com, February 3, 2021, https://www.chicagocatholic.com/vatican/-/article/2021/02/03/vatican-city-pope-francis-announced-the-establishment-of-a-world-day-of-grandparents-and-the-elderly-as-a-reminder-of-the-important-role-they-play-as-.
102 Joanna Michlic, "'The Open Church' and 'the Closed Church' and the Discourse on Jews in Poland between 1989 and 2000," *Communist and Post-Communist Studies*, 37, no. 4 (December 2004): 467.
103 Ibid.
104 Ibid.

authoritarian, and is not able to be part of the democratic society."¹⁰⁵ He does not recognize official Catholicism as a partner in democratic Poland, but rather as something that threatens the country.¹⁰⁶

In public, the Closed Church tends to ignore the Open Church: it presents the entire Church as united around its fundamentalist structure and makes little mention of the Open Church within its expansive media outlets.¹⁰⁷ However, given that it identifies itself as the true defender of both the Catholic faith and Polishness, when it does mention the Open Church it calls it "an internal enemy that [has] betrayed Catholic principles and that is run by left-wing Catholic groups, the Jews and masons and their servants."¹⁰⁸ For Adam Michnik, who long ago moved away from his cooperation with the Church because of its suffocation of liberal elements, the Closed Church represents righteousness, xenophobia, and rigid dogma.¹⁰⁹

One example of the Closed Church stamping out tolerance is its relationship with the Jesuit Father Stanisław Musiał. In 1986, several Open Church leaders¹¹⁰ launched the Episcopate Sub-Commission for Dialogue with Judaism, which later became known as the Episcopate Committee for Dialogue with Judaism. Its main objectives are "to re-shape approaches of Catholics to Jews and Judaism, including the elimination of anti-Jewish prejudices."¹¹¹ Jesuit Father Stanisław Musiał dedicated himself to this pioneering work in Catholic-Jewish dialogue and Polish-Jewish reconciliation. Through his leadership in Catholic-Jewish dialogue, he cultivated self-reflection, communication, and tolerance.

According to Stanisław Obirek, Father Musiał's former Jesuit colleague who shared Musiał's passion for dialogue with Jews, the Polish Catholic Church demonstrated tremendous disrespect for Musiał's contributions to Catholic-Jewish dialogue. Obirek noted,

---

105 Author's interview with Stanisław Obirek, Warsaw, April 2019.
106 Ibid.
107 Michlic, "'The Open Church' and 'the Closed Church'": 467.
108 Ibid.
109 Ost, introduction, 10.
110 The Open Church has revolved around the lay Catholic intelligentsia and an association of upper and lower clergy. Some of its best-known proponents have been the former prime minister Tadeusz Mazowiecki (1927–2013—the ex-secretary of the Polish episcopate), Bishop Tadeusz Pieronek (1934–2018), Archbishop Henryk Muszyński, Archbishop Józef Życiński (1948–2011), and Archbishop Stanisław Gądecki. They advocated for a tolerant Church, which would reflect on its past attitudes, behavior, and negative influence on Poles vis-à-vis the Jews. See Michlic, "'The Open Church' and 'the Closed Church'": 470.
111 Ibid.: 471.

> I was surprised that our enthusiasm was not shared by the majority. It (Catholic-Jewish dialogue) was often declared anarchy. It was perceived more or less as . . . marginal and not so relevant because we had to deal mainly with our own Christian-Catholic questions. And perhaps, more even, it was perceived as disturbing.[112]

In retaliation against Musiał's leadership in Catholic-Jewish dialogue, the Church persecuted him through quiet and constant ostracism. He himself was marginalized.[113] Suffocated. After Obirek's own participation in Catholic-Jewish dialogue grew more intense, he too suffered the Church's rejection.[114] Obirek left the Jesuit order and the priesthood in 2005.

We have seen that Poles rediscovered their collective power and national memory. By building bridges between estranged groups, Polish opposition activists secured the downfall of a tyrannical regime. Indeed, when tolerance of the Other forms among once disparate groups, mountains can be moved. The leadership and symbols of the Church played a huge role in supporting the Poles' elevation of communal consciousness. This connection between the Church and secular activists waned when more traditionalist Church leadership rose to power.

Despite its islands of openness, most of the Polish Catholic Church's hierarchy and clergy have chosen to remain in a closed fundamentalist fortress. In the 1980s, Adam Michnik, as an outsider, desired too much from the Church. He asked that it remain separate from the political realm. The Church's leadership was too invested in maintaining and growing its institutional power to commit to such democratic ideals. And politicians, who themselves desired Church support in order to win the traditional vote, provided the Church with privileges that circumscribe democratic conventions. For Obirek, "this is why democracy in Poland is weak, fragile, and the future is uncertain."[115] True, some in the Church have aligned with Vatican II and its ideals formulated in *Nostra Aetate*, but the majority of the Church's leadership have ignored the encyclical. Pope Francis' ascension has refocused the Church on accepting the principles

---

112 Author's interview with Stanisław Obirek, Warsaw, April 2019.
113 Ibid.
114 Ibid.
115 Ibid.

of Vatican II. The question remains whether the Polish Catholic Church will follow his lead.[116]

At the same time, some Poles who discovered their own Jewish heritage have been investigating paths into Judaism.

---

116 Lamb, "Francis Affirms No Place in Church for Those Who Reject Vatican II."

CHAPTER 18

Jewish Self-Discovery and Community Building

Poles of Jewish origin stood with the opposition against the totalitarian regime. However, especially since the PZPR's 1968 anti-*Zionist* campaign, Poles aware of having Jewish lineage kept this heritage hidden. After the expulsion of roughly fifteen thousand Jews, there remained a combined total of some five thousand members in the two government-sanctioned Jewish organizations—the TSKŻ and the Jewish Religious Union (Związek Religijny).[1] Those still gathering to pray at Warsaw's Nożyk Synagogue were a dying breed of elderly Jews. Small groups remained dispersed across several cities. But overall, one's Jewish identity was a taboo topic. Most Jews did not talk of their roots. They had learned to bury their heritage either out of ideology or Self-protection.

Some Poles of Jewish origin who identified as communists survived the war by finding haven in the USSR. Alec Matuszewski's paternal grandmother left her Jewish family's home in eastern Poland (now Ukraine) during the 1930s to study in Lviv. After joining the Communist Party, she broke all contacts with her family, as her internationalist ideology required. In Lviv, she met her future husband who, as a former priest and member of the prewar Polish Socialist Party (PPS), had no qualms regarding her ethnic origins. During the war they fled eastward, finding security as Soviet citizens and making a living as teachers. When she returned to Warsaw, she worked as part of the nomenklatura—that influential group of card-carrying communists in high-ranking posts. She raised her children as atheists, never speaking of her past Jewish identity. She had evaded forced emigration in 1968. When her son asked her in the 1970s what happened to her family during the war, she responded: "They were all killed in the Holocaust."[2] She did not lie. But she did not say more.

---

1 Polonsky, *The Jews in Poland and Russia*: 3:741.
2 Author's interview with Alec Matuszewski, Warsaw, November 2007.

Most Holocaust survivors who identified with their Jewish heritage left Communist Poland after the war. Those who had survived on the Aryan side tended already to have assimilated to Polish culture prior to the war. Those who survived the war in the USSR and remained in Poland afterwards often felt either connected to Poland and its culture or hoped to be part of a new Poland. Many clung to communism as the answer for humanity. And though some told their children of their roots, the vast majority did not school them in Jewish history or Jewish culture. Their future was communism. That is, until communism disavowed them and other "hidden" Jews in the various *Zionist* purges. It was clear to those who remained in Poland after 1968 that, despite their parents' belief that there would be a utopian equilibrium created amongst all people, reality singled out people with Jewish roots as an ultimate enemy. Thus, to stay safe, one cocooned one's family in layers of obfuscation and even deceit.

In this chapter we will examine the period during which young Poles discovered their Jewish heritage. Embracing their identity was an act of rebellion against the communist regime. Though supported by non-Jewish Polish friends, Polish Jews also encountered various forms of antisemitism. Some of it drew on prewar messaging, other antisemitic rhetoric came as reaction to contemporary Polish-Jewish conflicts.

Opposition and Awakening

A pivotal Jewish moment occurred in the summer of 1979, when about 120 opposition activists attended a workshop organized by the American humanist psychologist Carl Rogers (1902–1987). Rogers suggested the participants divide into groups—such as artists, divorcees, and parents with young children—and reflect on specific problems. Somebody proposed they add a "Jewish" group. Konstanty Gebert, who grew up in Warsaw's Polonized Jewish milieu, still remembers the nervous giggles throughout the room: "You can discuss sex as much as you want, but Jews, that wasn't safe."[3] When he walked into the designated room set aside for the "Jewish" group, Gebert was astonished: "That's when I discovered that most of my friends were Jewish! And that's when most of my friends discovered that I am Jewish!"[4] Until that day, no one had spoken openly about their heritage.

---

3   Author's interview with Konstanty Gebert, Warsaw, December 2007.
4   Ibid.

In this group therapy, people felt safe, for the first time, to confess to one another the difficulties each had experienced due to his or her secret Jewish identity. There was a monumental sense of liberation, and their bonds to one another grew even deeper. Two evenings at the workshop could not make up for years of neglecting their Jewish identities, of course. They needed to speak, listen, and feel. Having decided to continue meeting as a group, they added content layers to the gatherings, including an educational exploration of Judaism. The Jewish Flying University (Żydowski Uniwersytet Latający, ŻUL, which translates to hoodlum) was modelled after the Flying University devised by the democratic opposition. Over the next two years—until the imposition of martial law—it gathered fortnightly on Saturday evenings in various private apartments. The makeup of the group fluctuated. Friends would tell friends, who would tell their friends, about the group. But a consistent core membership emerged, including both Jews and non-Jews (the non-Jews being friends, boyfriends, girlfriends, husbands, and wives).

Individuals' new interest in their Jewish heritage was stimulated not by religious beliefs, nor a need for Jewish continuity, but rather by the sense that Jewish identity stood in opposition to the communist regime. By embracing their Jewish roots, they would help to shape a more open, multicultural Polish identity with which they could identify.[5] One participant told me that "the Jewish Flying University was a show of courage: because even though the regime might have known that these informal meetings were being held, people still [got together because they] believed it was their right to do so."[6]

For classical musician Marek Jeżowski this period marked "a renaissance of rediscovery of what Jewish life may mean among university and graduate students." Having emigrated from the Polish People's Republic to the United States with his family in 1971 at age fourteen, Marek returned in 1977 to pursue a degree in music.[7] His plan to return to the United States stalled, however, when the excitement in Poland took him by surprise. "There was so much worth straining for in order to create something viable in the future."[8] Activists Konstanty Gebert and Stanisław Krajewski got his attention: "They were trying to create something, to

---

5 Antony Polonsky, foreword to Barry Cohen, *Opening the Drawer: The Hidden Identities of Polish Jews* (London: Vallentine Mitchell, 2018), xv.
6 Author's interview with Marek Jeżowski, Warsaw, November 2007.
7 Although the authorities revoked Polish citizenship from people who had held high positions, not every family emigrating after March '68 experienced it. Marek retained his own citizenship, thus enabling him to return to Poland in 1976. See ibid.
8 Ibid.

discover something, experience something. They had weathered those first terrible years and reasserted their identities here [in the Jewish Flying University]."[9]

Gebert remembers one evening meeting particularly well. The theme for that night's discussion was antisemitism. He recalls standing and looking at those gathered. To his surprise they had neatly and subconsciously sorted themselves into clusters of Jews and non-Jews. "I immediately understood why. I was sick and tired of explaining to non-Jews what I'm afraid of, and hearing that I'm paranoid, and that I exaggerate. They got sick and tired of hearing that there are things to be afraid of."[10]

Though the two groups were similar in culture, politics, and lifestyle, this bifurcation would occur again and again. The one thing that set them apart was antisemitism—one group's experience of it, the other's lack of understanding of it. Gebert found that the difference in experience simply could not be bridged. "Until '89 I had furious arguments with my non-Jewish friends, who genuinely said that I'm paranoid, and they genuinely believed it. And they had a right to, because their experience simply did not include that. Mine did."[11]

The Jewish Flying University disbanded with martial law. However, after several years, martial law loosened, and people started to gather again . . . this time to celebrate Jewish holidays. In 1987 they decided to observe Rosh Hashanah (the Jewish New Year) as a group. Some seventy people crammed into the Gebert's living room, with still more calling days later to ask why they were not invited. "So, while '79–'81 was group therapy and education, '87 was Rosh Hashanah and Sedarim (Passover Seders)."[12] For the group's core members who had remained in Poland, the issue of Jewish identity became so important that they were willing to change their lives for it. Because they were so limited in ways to express their Jewish identity, including the fact that a meaningful secular Jewish community did not exist, most took the observant religious route.

Building Jewish Life in Postcommunist Poland

With the dissolution of communism, a Jewish awakening erupted among people who had previously either no knowledge of their heritage or simply were afraid to express it. During the first several years of the Third Polish Republic—decade, even—people made constant new discoveries of familial Jewish roots. The

---

9   Ibid.
10 Author's interview with Konstanty Gebert, December 2007.
11 Ibid.
12 Ibid.

Jewish Historical Institute in Warsaw, which had opened in 1947 and remained in some form of perfunctory service during the communist reign, experienced a deluge of requests to search records. Researchers often heard stories about ailing elderly family members who for the first time shared with their children that they are Jewish.

Recognizing that people's fears of "coming out" were still deep, Jewish leaders set up an anonymous telephone hotline through which to enter the conversation.[13] It offered "hidden, insecure Jews an opportunity to talk about their problems related to their Jewishness."[14] Jewish activists created support groups, in the hope that among the thousands discovering their Jewish ancestry, some would begin "the uneasy journey into Jewishness."[15]

The now Chief Rabbi of Poland, Michael Schudrich, who had served the Polish Jewish community from 1990 through 1998 with the Ronald S. Lauder Foundation, recalls the countless people calling his office to discuss their newfound Jewish roots.[16] Among them were Jewish children who had been orphaned by the war, rescued by Polish families or convents, then raised as Catholics. Most did not learn of their Jewish roots until much later in life. The 1993 creation of the Association of Children of the Holocaust helped a supportive Jewish community to form, of which most members were Catholics.[17]

Konstanty Gebert and Stanisław Krajewski were among those leaders of the Jewish Flying University who moved toward a ritual and educational embrace of their Jewish roots. They began from the place of tradition, and thus started their inquiry within the orthodox Nożyk Synagogue at 6 Twarda Street. Like Rabbi Schudrich, they were inundated with calls for help and guidance in this personal, yet collective, journey. "What happened is that we genuinely had a Jewish boom in the early 1990s. People were crawling out of the woodwork in the hundreds, by the thousands... When people were finally feeling free to get in touch with Jews, they'd come to the [Nożyk] Synagogue."[18] Today Gebert recognizes

---

13 Author's interview with Chief Rabbi Michael Schudrich, December 2007.
14 Krajewski, *Poland and the Jews: Reflections of a Polish Polish Jew*, 27–28.
15 Ibid., 28.
16 Author's interview with Rabbi Michael Schudrich, December 2007.
17 Barry Cohen, *Opening the Drawer: The Hidden Identities of Polish Jews*, 3.
18 Author's interview with Konstanty Gebert, December 2007. However, according to Krzysztof Izdebski, not all older Jews divulged their long-hidden Jewish identity to their families. In 2007, he said "Many in the older generation still have not told their children or grandchildren. They're still so much afraid of telling anyone [...]. It's very sad [...]. There are still so many people like this." See author's interview with Krzysztof Izdebski, Warsaw, November 2007.

that even though they were perceived as the leaders, they were still very much at the preliminary stages of defining and organizing themselves into a functioning community. In a reflective tone he told me: "We were still sorting ourselves out. We really had nothing to offer to the people who came looking. By the time we got our act together, the boom was over."[19] Their own personal understanding was still being formed, their collective identity only just taking shape.

For many Jews who were just coming out into the open, the Nożyk Synagogue appeared ominous, foreign, and inaccessible. This was due to a multiplicity of factors. One, religious services were conducted in what, for the emerging Jews, was an unknown language: Hebrew. Because they knew little, or nothing about Jewish tradition, the newcomers felt extremely self-conscious and judged for their lack of knowledge. With the encouragement and financial support of Severyn Ashkenazy, a Polish Jewish Holocaust survivor, who had emigrated to the United States after the war, an alternative to the Nożyk Synagogue emerged in 1999.

Ashkenazy returned to independent Poland to do business. There, he organized a loose group of like-minded Jews who traveled to Poland for business and Poles who were starting to explore their Judaism through a non-traditional lens. By word of mouth, this monthly Friday evening Shabbat gathering in one family's apartment expanded rapidly. The group eventually located its home at 113 Wiertnicza Street on the outskirts of Warsaw. A two-story white stucco house set far back from the street, Beit Warszawa—which affiliates with the World Union of Progressive Judaism—attracts families, individuals, and young university students investigating their Jewish roots. In 2006 it was not unusual to have more than one hundred people coming together for a lecture on Polish Jewish history or culture, followed by Shabbat evening services and a communal dinner, which Ashkenazy sponsored. In a 2007 interview, the then program director at Beit Warszawa, Gosia Szymańska, explained, "They come here because they have a spiritual need to connect with Judaism, with the community."[20]

In 2007 many people still hid their personal search for their Jewish identities. Tadeusz Woleński, then a young Jewish activist said, "They don't talk about their Jewish heritage and many simply don't know yet about their Jewish roots."[21] Of those who as young teenagers had known about their Jewish origins, the great majority grew up in families that did not observe any Jewish holidays and traditions. Woleński added that in such an environment "it's hard to *see* what

---

19 Author's interview with Konstanty Gebert, December 2007.
20 Author's interview with Malgorzata Szymańska, December 2007.
21 Author's interview with Tadeusz Woleński, Warsaw, November 2007.

it means to be Jewish."²² In response, in March 2007 Woleński and Krzysztof Izdebski helped to reorganize the Polish Union of Jewish Students into the All-Poland Jewish Youth Organization (Żydowska Ogólnopolska Organizacja Młodzieżowa). Known by its acronym ZOOM, the organization is a secular Jewish association with chapters throughout Poland. It provides a place for young adults to examine their newfound Jewish identity.²³ In its early inception, ZOOM members recognized Beit Warszawa as a destination for further Jewish exploration. Zymańska understood the need to provide programming for them "so that they can come here and feel comfortable . . . so they can be who they want to be. So that they can learn and grow and develop."²⁴

Miles from the Nożyk Synagogue, Beit Warszawa's location outside of central Warsaw symbolizes its initial outsider status. In its infancy, Beit Warszawa struggled to attach itself to the official Warsaw Jewish community (the gemeinde). This kehillah was the one institutional representation of Warsaw's Jews which the Polish government recognized. Several cities have a gemeinde, which provides a Jewish voice in that area. Together, these groups create a nationwide gemeinde or kehillah. In Warsaw, the gemeinde organizes much of Jewish life. It creates programs for both Orthodox and secular Jews, including members of ZOOM. Any Polish Jew is welcomed to join.

Who Is a Jew?

Traditional Jewish law—halakhah (as stated in the Torah's commandments and later expounded upon in the Talmud)—views Jewish identity as passed down by blood through the mother. If maternal Jewish identity cannot be established, three options remain regarding the child's Jewish identity: the mother may undergo an Orthodox conversion before her child's birth, thereby rendering that child Jewish by Orthodox standards; the mother may choose not to convert, but the child itself may convert through the Orthodox system; and finally, neither the mother nor the child converts through Orthodox procedures and the child therefore is not considered Jewish. Given that for many Poles their Jewish roots are paternal, Orthodoxy would require conversion before being able to be counted in a minyan, which in traditional Judaism constitutes a quorum of

---

22 Ibid.
23 Beit Warszawa had become a destination for some ZOOM participants.
24 Author's interview with Malgorzata Szymańska, Warsaw, November 2007.

ten *men* necessary to say certain prayers and to read from the Torah.[25] In 2007, Stanisław Krajewski spoke about the Warsaw Orthodox synagogue's relatively bold approach of welcoming people with any Jewish ancestry as Jews, whether maternal or paternal, with a specifying indicator of "halakhic Jew" and "non-halakhic Jew." In Poland all are considered to be Jews who have Jewish roots, "but some people have full rights of participation in the synagogue liturgy and others do not. Of course, this does create tension."[26]

A tension also arises because the gemeinde does not recognize the conversions carried out by Beit Warszawa's rabbi or any other Reform or Progressive rabbi. At the same time, as opposed to Orthodox communities in the West, it did accept conversions carried out by Conservative rabbis. The Orthodox community does not recognize the Jewish legal authority of Progressive Judaism because the latter opposes Jewish law's defining role in traditional Judaism. Thus, one Jewish leader in Beit Warszawa—whose father is Jewish, but mother is not, and who did not undergo Orthodox or Conservative conversion—is not regarded by the Nożyk community as a Jew with full rights. It is not how one expresses connection to Judaism that is most at issue in Poland, but how one ritually moves into Judaism.

When we spoke, Krzysztof Izdebski was secular. While this secular-observant distinction might cause consternation for some Orthodox Jews in the United States, Izdebski has gained automatic respect within the Warsaw Orthodox community because his mother is Jewish. He is a "halakhic Jew." This issue of who is a Jew has gotten even more complicated in the last several years as the Nożyk Synagogue, which in the past had accepted Conservative rabbis' conversions as halakhic, has shifted policy to only accept Orthodox conversions. A question then arises for those who went through Conservative rabbinic conversions as to their current halakhic status within the kehillah. This debate has caused some long-time members of the Nożyk Synagogue to leave and to join either Beit Warszawa or Ec Chaim, a gemeinde-run progressive synagogue.[27]

This problem is not unique to Poland. In fact, the issue of Jewish authority and the question of who is a Jew appear in most Jewish communities. In our

---

25 Though many Jewish men and women were willing to accept Orthodox Judaism's non-egalitarian status in order to connect with their authentic Jewish heritage, this same concept kept some from entering the Nożyk Synagogue. However, it might be that in Poland, which is so familiar with patriarchal Catholicism, this issue was not as big a problem as it has been in the United States.

26 Author's interview with Stanisław Krajewski, Warsaw, November 2007.

27 Ibid.

conversation, Izdebski stressed that "in every small community there is a place for sectarianism. It is quite normal. Of course, everyone wants to change it so that it will be better, but it is very complicated."[28] Gosia Szymańska acknowledged that "it's a shame it didn't work out for Beit Warszawa to become a part of the kehillah—a Reform congregation in the Warsaw kehillah. Politics, personalities ... Jewish world." When I pushed her in 2007 on whether she believed that the two sides could resolve their issues, Szymańska replied, "I wish, but realistically I don't think so. There is a little bit of bad blood between the two communities. Not between the people. But on the institutional level, which is a shame. Such a shame."[29]

That the board of the gemeinde incorporates non-Orthodox Jews is important when considering the various needs of segments within the broad Jewish community. In 2010, the Warsaw gemeinde created a Reform synagogue, Ec Chaim (Etz Chaim—Tree of Life), for a group which had broken from Beit Warszawa in 2006. Hired by the gemeinde, the Reform rabbi Stas Wojciechowicz leads Ec Chaim. Born and raised outside of Poland, Wojciechowicz learned Polish quickly. While Russian is his mother tongue, he also speaks Hebrew and English. According to Józefina Wardanga (née Jeżowska), Ec Chaim's office manager and assistant to the rabbi since 2014, the Reform synagogue provides weekly Friday night and Saturday morning Shabbat services, as well as holiday services and celebrations. It runs a Shabbat school for children. The synagogue also hosts communal seders for some 120–130 people for Passover and celebratory meals for Rosh Hashanah.[30]

Bridging Chasms

Though the tension over who is a Jew has proven an obstacle to communal cohesion, the younger generation—known as the third generation of postwar Jews—has been able to bridge chasms the older, second generation created or got stuck in. It might be that it is these younger "halakhic Jews" who do the bridge building by virtue of inhabiting several communal identities at once. Emil Jeżowski is a prime example.

While his father, Marek, discovered in his teens that his parents were Jewish, Emil's mother, Ludmiła, grew up in an irreligious, non-Jewish household. After

---

28 Author's interview with Krzysztof Izdebski, Warsaw, November 2007.
29 Author's interview with Malgorzata Szymańska, Warsaw, November 2007.
30 Author's interview with Józefina Wardanga, Warsaw, April 2019.

the couple had children, Marek and Ludmiła searched for an existing community to help them transmit their values to their children. When they did not find one, Marek engaged in building their community at Beit Warszawa. Together, he and Ludmiła raised their children as Jews. And it was not long before the children's desire to see their friends at synagogue compelled the parents to deepen their own involvement: "Suddenly I found myself not only teaching them, but also being pulled by them. It was a joint venture."[31] After years of integrating Jewish identity into their family experience, in 2005 Ludmiła and four of their children underwent the in-depth process of halakhic conversion.[32]

Now in his thirties, Emil Jeżowski is a leader within this third generation of postwar Polish Jews. Having celebrated his bar-mitzvah at Beit Warszawa in 2007 at age seventeen, where his father was synagogue president, Emil later worked for Poland's Chief Rabbi Schudrich at the Nożyk Synagogue and then for three years as an assistant to the Israeli ambassador to Poland. A fixture in the Warsaw Jewish community, Emil has focused on several Jewish communal projects, including cooperating with Krzysztof Izdebski on a post-Birthright (*Taglit*) Jewish leadership program, which engages young Polish Jews who visited Israel through the financial sponsorship of Taglit. In the past, upon return to Poland, Taglit attendees would have been ignored, left on their own to figure out how to get involved in Jewish communal life. Now, by providing a Polish Jewish counselor for each cohort that travels to Israel, and who also maintains connection with program participants upon return to Poland, the Jewish community ensures that young people exploring their Jewish identities are welcomed. The counselor invites former Taglit participants to join in discussions regarding the Polish Jewish community, including its flaws, with the goal of creating new programming that speaks to their needs and interests. Through this process, two Taglit participants saw a need for a Jewish sports organization. In response, they resurrected Makabi Warszawa, a well-respected interwar Jewish organization sports club.[33]

Emil is passionate about his role in reviving Hashomer Hatzair (Young Guard), another interwar *Zionist* youth movement.[34] A little like the Scouts, it

---

31   Author's interview with Marek Jeżowski, Warsaw, April 2019.
32   The Conservative conversion was done by Rabbi Harry Levin, a New York rabbi who was connected with Beit Warszawa. See Barry Cohen, *Opening the Drawer: The Hidden Identities of Polish Jews*, 233–236, and author's interview with Marek Jeżowski, Warsaw, November 2007.
33   Author's interview with Emil Jeżowski, Warsaw, March 2019.
34   Founded in Poland, many Hashomer Hatzair leaders went on to establish the State of Israel. Additionally, Mordechai Anielewicz, one of the leaders of the Warsaw Ghetto Uprising, was also a leader of his prewar group.

fills a void in contemporary Poland, as before there had not been any other such Jewish youth group. Unique in that it is teen-led, it is a "place where Jewish children can create friendships and develop their Jewish identities, while engaging in civil society and social awareness."[35] Hashomer Hatzair has had an integrating effect within the broader Jewish community as secular, Progressive, Reform, and Orthodox parents trust the group with their children.[36]

Many from the second generation of postwar Polish Jews have been tarnished by the communal divisions resulting from Beit Warszawa's fight for independence from the gemeinde and its formation of an autonomous countrywide Jewish progressive community, Beit Polska. In contrast, Emil is comfortable spending Shabbat with any of Warsaw's various Jewish communities, whether at Beit Warszawa, the Nożyk Synagogue, or Ec Chaim, where his sister manages the office. Marek Jeżowski takes comfort knowing that his children and their generation "feel comfortable with their Jewishness in the world and society that they live in."[37] He also recognizes that their connections with Poland's small yet diverse Jewish population points to something bigger than themselves: "This generation is finding bridges and creating bridges across the divide that seemed insurmountable for our generation."[38] His cohort of "self-starters and activists," who upon Polish independence in 1989 had "to rediscover and put back in place some of the structures that were not there,"[39] is learning from their children. "We are overcoming our limitations . . . In that sense I feel hopeful."[40]

The Lauder-Morasha School is another institution that has demonstrated how to bridge different Jewish identities. Having opened in 1994, by 2020 the school had grown to accommodate 230 students from kindergarten through eighth grade. While some of the children come from the Orthodox Nożyk Jewish community, others associate with Beit Warszawa, Ec Chaim, or remain unaffiliated. Thus, this younger generation is learning to respect and create bonds with Jews who have entered Judaism through different avenues.

Lauder-Morasha's curriculum follows the Polish state's core requirements while also providing courses on Jewish subjects, including Hebrew and Jewish history, religion, and culture. As with its affiliate in Wrocław, the day school is

---

35 Author's interview with Emil Jeżowski, Warsaw, March 2019.
36 Ibid.
37 Ibid.
38 Ibid.
39 Ibid.
40 Ibid.

open to non-Jewish students too. Interestingly, close to half of its students do not identify outwardly as Jewish. Yet by sending their children there, families agree that their children will participate in all of the Jewish aspects of the school. Additionally, between one-third to one-half of Lauder-Morasha's teachers are non-Jewish.[41] In September 2020 it opened the Zuzanna Ginczka High School. Named after an interwar Polish Jewish poet, it the first Jewish high school in Poland since 1968.

Józefina Wardanga made the decision with her husband Adam to send their four children to Lauder-Morasha when her eldest was about to go into fifth grade. While their children were in public school, Wardanga experienced the personal discomfort and, at times, ostracism that resulted from opting out of the state-sponsored compulsory religion class. Marek Jeżowski, Józefina's father, underscores how awkward it is that "the democratic government succumbed to the Catholic Church and allowed it into the [public] schools."[42] Noting that this is similar to the arrangement during the interwar years (and even during part of communism's reign), he adds that "It's not a democratic step because you're saying that Poles equal Catholics, which is not true."[43] Józefina accepts the hour-long commute to the school, knowing her children will learn tolerance of all nationalities, religions, and cultures.

Antisemitism in Postcommunist Poland

The antisemitism about which the young emerging Jews had spoken in the 1980s, but which their non-Jewish friends could neither see nor understand, became more apparent to the broader society with the negotiated end of communism. Various hardline nationalist groups, including the Grunwald Association, promoted antisemitic ideology and linked themselves to Dmowski's prewar Endecja. Some sold antisemitic leaflets and books, such as the *Protocols of the Elders of Zion*, supported by several circles within the Polish Catholic Church

---

41 Author's interview with Anna Szytz, Warsaw, November 2007; author's interview with Józefina Wardanga, Warsaw, March 2019.
42 Author's interview with Marek Jeżowski, Warsaw, April 2019.
43 This perception, held by right-wing Poles, that one must be Catholic to identify as Polish, grew stronger during partition. Author's interview with Marek Jeżowski, Warsaw, April 2019.

(including Lech Wałęsa's priest Henryk Jankowski, as well as the group operating out of the church on Zagorna Street).[44]

According to the Polish historians Jolanta Ambrosewicz-Jacobs and Annamaria Orla-Bukowska, international "expectations ran high that the dusk of absolute tyranny would be quickly followed by the dawn of absolute tolerance."[45] As reality throughout Central and Eastern Europe proved this premise incorrect, the world's disappointment developed, and its impatience grew. Amrosewicz-Jacobs and Orla-Bukowska detail the development of stereotypes and the difficulty in ridding a population of them: "What has once entered the cultural subconsciousness cannot easily be removed . . . Once created, stereotypes are rather unalterable and permanent; hence they do not require continual intergroup contact in order to continue to exist."[46] Thus, despite the enormous decrease in Poland's Jewish population, prewar stereotypes about Jews persist. At the same time, new stereotypes have emerged. Because contemporary Jews living in postwar Poland no longer wore the traditional Jewish garb and had become irrecognizable, Polish nationalists spoke of "hidden" Jews—secret agents in plain clothes and with changed surnames.

At the same time, the less one could recognize Jews, the more they became an abstract term for "the enemy." We saw that by 1968 the term *Jew* served as an amalgam of different, often conflicting images that had combined from various historical periods. By 1968, the "Jew" was viewed at one and the same time as a traditional blood-sucker, a bourgeois cosmopolitan, a communist, and a nationalist war-mongering anti-Christ. A metaphorical monster, the "Jew" threatened Poles' stability. The term *Jew* took on a negative connotation not only in politics, but in any situation. As decades passed, "[a]lmost no one knew what a Jew was, but everyone knew that to be called one was bad."[47] Sebastian Rejak, a one-time Catholic theology student, remembers as a boy being called "Jude" by a peer, and shrinking back knowing it was bad.[48] When Gosia Szymańska's father disclosed to her at age twelve or thirteen that he was Jewish, "[m]y jaw dropped. I was in a state of shock . . . I knew the word 'Jew' was not a nice one."[49] Politicians

---

44 Konstanty Gebert, "Antisemitism in the 1990 Polish Presidential Election," *Social Research* 58, no. 4 (1991): 724.
45 Jolanta Ambrosewicz-Jacobs, Annamaria Orla-Bukowska, "After the Fall: Attitudes Towards Jews in Post-1989 Poland," *Nationalities Papers* 26, no. 2 (1998): 265.
46 Ibid.: 270.
47 Ibid.
48 Author's interview with Sebastian Rejak, Warsaw, March 2019.
49 Author's interview with Malgorzata Szymańska, Warsaw, November 2007.

adapted the word "Jew" to refer to a political opponent, whether or not that person actually had Jewish roots.[50]

The 1990 presidential election emerged as a shocking expression of latent Polish antisemitism. Lech Wałęsa's campaign embraced Primate Glemp's fundamentalist Church and its corresponding Polish nationalism. Wałęsa's opponent, Tadeusz Mazowiecki, the prime minister and a devout Catholic, was believed by many in Solidarity to be a secret Jew.[51] Some Wałęsa supporters shouted vitriolic antisemitic slurs at Mazowiecki and those campaigning for him: "Jewish flunkey! Mazowiecki may rule in the synagogue, but not in Poland! We vote Wałęsa, that's a true Pole and Catholic!"[52] Antisemitic rhetoric also ignited during many of Wałęsa's campaign rallies, when attendees had the opportunity to ask the candidate questions like "When is he going to throw the Jews out of government?" or simply scream "Gas the Jews!"[53] Most problematic was Wałęsa's stunning answer: silence.

Though Jewish intellectuals, such as Adam Michnik, who knew Wałęsa well, understood that he was not antisemitic, his silence enabled antisemitism to spread in independent Poland. That Wałęsa permitted it to fester in his campaign demonstrated his willingness to tolerate antisemitism because it appealed to part of the Polish electorate. When he did finally respond, he denied emphatically that he was an antisemite. At the same time, however, he permitted a person's Jewish origin to play an important role in a political debate. Underscoring that Jews "conceal their origins," Wałęsa repeatedly declared that he was a "hundred percent Pole," a Pole "for generations untold" and with "documents to prove it."[54] Though a few important Polish leaders, such as the WWII hero Jan Karski and Father Michał Czajkowski, a priest involved with Christian-Jewish dialogue in Poland, wrote articles protesting rising antisemitism, most political voices and Church leaders remained silent or took part in the antisemitic rhetoric.[55]

By the 1990 elections, ideological divisions within Solidarity had fractured the movement. Opposition leaders, who had believed that negotiations with the

---

50 Adam Michnik, "My Vote against Wałęsa," in *Letters from Freedom: Post-Cold War Realities and Perspectives*, ed. Irena Grudzinska Gross, trans. Jane Cave (Berkeley: University of California Press, 1998), 158.
51 This accusation was later dismissed by Bishop Orszulik based on baptismal certificates depicting Mazowiecki's genealogical tree up to the fifteenth century. See Konstanty Gebert, "Antisemitism in the 1990 Polish Presidential Election": 746.
52 Ibid.: 742.
53 Ibid.: 740.
54 Ibid.
55 Ibid.: 743–4, 748–9.

government required compromise, had been willing to set aside judgment of the post-1956 PZPR in order to enter a new era. But opposition leaders, who believed that one could not leave discussions without explicitly condemning the communist system, judged PZPR members as traitors. The split took on the appearance of "liberal" versus "national" aspirations; a division between those who would willingly work with former communists, without necessitating consequential punishment, and those who believed Polish pride necessitated cutting former communists out of future political participation. Adam Michnik, a formidable presence at the 1989 Round Table discussions between opposition and government leaders, took the former path, as did the moderate presidential candidate Tadeusz Mazowiecki; Lech Wałęsa led the latter more radical, anticommunist charge. Though Michnik's approach won at the Round Table—known also as the Velvet Restoration because it secured a bloodless end to communism—it was Wałęsa's illiberalism which won the presidential election.[56]

This divide grew wider with time. By 1995, those on the nationalist spectrum believed that the Round Table Agreement had enabled former communist revisionists to rise to new political leadership positions within the Third Polish Republic. Additionally, nationalists incorporated and promoted the belief that so-called former communist revisionists were also of Jewish origin. Why would such a characterization matter for voters in the new Poland? Despite the now scant number of Jews in the country, people who sat in fundamentalist church pews, who could not see communist anti-*Zionist* rhetoric as mere propaganda, and who remembered the terror unleashed by Stalinists of Jewish origin, believed Jewish roots signified a negative liberal "foreigner" harmful to the emerging Polish democracy. The 2001 Sejm elections entrenched this age-old theory: Adam Michnik's Jewish origins became a stain on both him and liberals in general.[57]

Shoah and the Carmelite Convent

To understand in some part the rise of political antisemitism in postwar Poland, one needs to address its social-historical context. In 1985, the French director Claude Lanzmann released his film *Shoah*. Described by Lanzmann himself as

---

56 Ost, introduction, 24.
57 Polonsky, *The Jews in Poland and Russia*, 3:810–811. Polish scholar Elżbieta Janicka emphasizes that Poles maintain the concept of Żydokomuna today and employ it to rationalize violent antisemitism.

completely historically accurate, the nine-and-one-half-hour film is the culmination of more than three hundred hours of filmed interviews. The result is a meaningful presentation of Jewish experience during the Holocaust. But as Władysław Bartoszewski points out, "[t]he greatest of Lanzmann's sins are those of omission."[58] The arduously long film does not include descriptions of Jews who survived due to Polish help. It also virtually ignores the Jewish resistance. Instead, Lanzmann's epic—shown throughout the world—presents as truth "the idea that Jews went to their death because the Poles were totally indifferent" to their plight.[59]

Jews and Poles throughout the world responded differently from one another to the film. Many Jews committed to the anti-Polish perspective, which reflected the West's already existing negative stereotype of Poles. The film presented Jews as having been abandoned to their fate by bystanders. As a consequence, Jews came to see "the Gentiles in general and Poles in particular [. . .] as partially responsible for, or even guilty of, the extermination of the Jews."[60] Poland was slandered. Poles reacted with strong criticisms of the film, and there were even some demonstrations in the West. Indeed, as we shall see in a later chapter, Lanzmann's film created an enemy around which the opposition and the communist authorities could unite. Both sides felt a need to defend the country's wartime reputation.

At about the same time, a few Discalced Carmelite nuns gained rights to establish a convent at Auschwitz. They built a Catholic shrine in a building that preexisted the Nazis, but which the Nazis had used as a warehouse for Jewish belongings. Although the convent site sat just outside a fence thought to be the Auschwitz border, in actuality the building was within the UNESCO World Heritage Site. Over a span of nearly two years the Nazis created a sprawling camp complex, including a concentration camp opened in May 1940, known as Auschwitz I, and a death camp about two miles away near the Polish village Brzezinka. People refer to the death camp by its German name, Birkenau, or Auschwitz-Birkenau. While the first transports of Jews were gassed in Crematorium I at Auschwitz I, by spring 1942 most Jews were sent directly to Auschwitz II, that is, Auschwitz-Birkenau, where the gassing took place.[61]

---

58 Władysław T. Bartoszewski, *The Convent at Auschwitz* (New York: George Braziller, 1991), 24–25.
59 Ibid., 24–25.
60 Ibid., 27.
61 The United States Holocaust Memorial Museum, "Auschwitz," last modified March 16, 2023, https://encyclopedia.ushmm.org/content/en/article/auschwitz. The labor camp Auschwitz III was located near Monowice, and thus called by its German name Monowitz.

Jews worldwide do not distinguish between the Auschwitz I and Auschwitz II. For Jews, the name "Auschwitz" not only symbolizes Auschwitz-Birkenau, where 90% of victims were Jews, but, because of the enormity of the number of Jews killed there, also the Holocaust tragedy in its entirety. For Poles, "Auschwitz" signifies their own horrific fate: roughly 150,000 Poles were deported to Auschwitz I, where for some twenty-one months, Poles constituted the vast majority of its inhabitants. At least seventy-five thousand non-Jewish Poles were killed at Auschwitz I.[62] Additionally, because of the communist description of Polish Jews who died in the Holocaust as part of the "six million Poles" murdered by the Nazis, Poles understood themselves as the ultimate victim. In 1985 "Auschwitz" symbolized only their Polish national suffering. As both groups contested who could claim the camp as their own, neither side could see the Other's perspective.

The convent brought several important questions to the forefront, including that of comparative suffering. As one Belgian Jewish leader explained, "we want to keep Auschwitz as an eternal memorial to the Holocaust of the Jews."[63] Yet most Poles saw this response as a Jewish attempt "to monopolize Auschwitz as a Jewish cemetery, despite the fact that the majority of inmates at Auschwitz I, as opposed to Birkenau, were not Jewish."[64]

Jews outside of Poland vehemently rejected the presence of a Christian religious sect on what they viewed as hallowed Jewish ground. The detailed language in the convent's mission statement caused controversy because it stressed that the convent "will become a spiritual fortress and a guarantee of the conversion of strayed brothers from our countries."[65] Jews understood these words as a declaration of "war," as the text suggested that the nuns would not only pray for the conversion of the Jews, but also "convert" the Jewish victims of Auschwitz-Birkenau. Despite the convent denying this interpretation, Jews continued to loudly oppose the convent's location, eventually forcing a meeting to solve the problem.

A 1987, Catholic-Jewish agreement signed in Geneva stated that the convent would relocate within two years. When this arrangement was not upheld in July 1989, various Jewish groups from abroad protested on the convent's site.

---

62 Ibid. Bartoszewski provides a higher estimate of some 270,000 non-Jewish Poles killed at Auschwitz I. See Bartoszewski, *The Convent at Auschwitz*, 10.
63 Stated by Markus Pardes, president of the Coordinating Committee of Jewish Organizations in Belgium. Quoted in ibid., 8.
64 Ibid., 74.
65 Quoted in ibid., 7.

The already tense argument worsened when Rabbi Avi Weiss from the Orthodox Hebrew Institute of Riverdale, New York, traveled to Poland to lead a small but effective demonstration. He contended that the Catholic Church wanted to "remove the Jewish character of the *Shoah* and give it a Christian character."[66] The March 1989 placement of a twenty-three-foot-high cross in front of the convent furthered this belief for Jews, who perceive the Cross as a symbol of oppression. Dressed in striped outfits reminiscent of the Jewish prisoners' garb when interned in Auschwitz-Birkenau, the group jumped over the convent fence when their knocking at the gate remained unanswered. (The protesters' demand to speak with the nuns disclosed the former's insensitivity to the nuns' cloistered life.) The group spent hours in the courtyard, praying and ignoring construction workers' instructions to leave. After several hours, the workmen employed at the convent dragged Rabbi Weiss and his cohort away "in a fairly brutal fashion."[67]

While the violent Polish response on the site enraged Jews, the Jews' own insensitivity also escalated the Polish public debate. Although Jerzy Turowicz, the editor of the liberal Catholic weekly *Tygodnik Powszechny*, attempted to explain Jewish sensitivities and Jewish Polish leader Stanisław Krajewski tried to explain the Poles' right to pray for their victims, neither Poles nor Jews were reassured.[68] Poles remained incensed that "international Jewry" believed it had the right to interject itself into Polish affairs. Some Poles saw in the Jews' reaction to the convent a real-time display of the antisemitic stereotypes they harbored. "Jews have too much power in Poland," they claimed; there is a "Jewish world conspiracy."

At a time when the communist system had only just been disassembled, such stereotypes perhaps expressed Poles' fears that they would never really gain true freedom. They feared the enemy was hiding and waiting to reassert repressive measures.[69] For many Poles, the Jews' fight over the Carmelite convent not only showed the Jews' continued outsized influence in Poland, but also an example of the power of this ever-present enemy.[70] Antisemitism expanded as antisemitic

---

66 Ibid. 87.
67 Ibid., 86.
68 Other leading Polish figures responded, including Jacek Kuroń, a government minister in the Solidarity-led system, who expressed his shame as a Pole about the incident. Some moderate voices from the Church, Monsignor Muszyński and Father Musiał, tried to explain to a Polish audience differences between Judaism and Catholicism in matters of death. See ibid., 89.
69 Ambrosewicz-Jacobs and Orla-Bukowska, "After the Fall: Attitudes Towards Jews in Post-1989 Poland."
70 Alina Cała, "Antisemitism without Jews and without Antisemites," *Jewish Studies at the Central European University 200–2003* (2003): 19, accessed August 21, 2023, https://archive.jpr.org.uk/download?id=5953.

parties conflated this perceived Jewish aggression with existing Polish fears that Jews and Germans would reclaim their prewar property now inhabited by Poles. Politicians who were not obvious antisemites, but who tolerated antisemitism for their political gain, gave it room to grow. Consequently, antisemitism found greater expression in both Church homilies and street incidents.[71]

Jedwabne

A key moment in the evolution of Polish-Jewish relations occurred a year prior to the 2001 elections, when the Princeton University professor Jan T. Gross (part of the student opposition in 1968 People's Poland) published his research on the massacre of close to one thousand Jewish residents in the town of Jedwabne.[72] In July 1941, Poles forced Jewish men, women, and children of all ages into resident Bolesław Śleszyński's barn. The Poles locked the doors and set the barn on fire. As we have discussed, what shocked Gross's Polish audience was the documentation and eyewitness accounts which testified to the truth that Poles, *not* Nazis, committed this heinous crime. According to the ethnologist Alina Cała, "[t]his knowledge was not easily absorbed by Polish society."[73] Cała explains that because Poles typically believed they were the main victims of Nazi occupation, "[i]t was not easy to accept the fact that Poles [. . .] had committed the war crime."[74]

Courageously, Poles broke into public debate with an avalanche of articles appearing in various press outlets, focused on the crime as well as on its social and national implications. Those who accepted the facts and acknowledged criminal Polish behavior recognized that national contrition was imperative. They asked the country to face up to the implications of Jedwabne. They asked: Does this heinous crime committed by dozens of Poles, but watched by hundreds more, characterize the Polish nation and its people? Does Jedwabne forever break the myth of Polish honor and victimhood?

---

71 Konstanty Gebert, "Antisemitism in the 1990 Polish Presidential Election": 728.
72 As noted in chapter 13n100, historians differ regarding the number of Jewish victims burned in the barn. Gross based his reporting on the memorial stone which read sixteen hundred victims. Polish historian Dariusz Stola suggests the number of Jews murdered in the Jedwabne barn is closer to six hundred. The IPN report assessed the number of dead to have been closer to one thousand.
73 Alina Cała, "Antisemitism without Jews and without Antisemites": 19.
74 Quoted in ibid. For a listing of publishing companies that specialize in antisemitic literature, see ibid.

In a 2007 interview, Stanisław Krajewski praised Poland's initial public debate over *Neighbors*:

> The Jedwabne debate has shown how advanced Poland is compared to other countries. Look at Lithuania, Belarussia, Ukraine, Slovakia, Romania, even Hungary: The discussion has not really reached that level at all. In Romania they have barely begun to speak of the fact of the Holocaust. In Lithuania, to speak about massacres of Jews by Lithuanians is still something you don't do. So, it's really to the credit of Poland, despite the fact that it was painful, and it was divisive. The debate has changed the atmosphere, and also the reality in this way that now when you talk about the history of Jews in Poland, basically there's no taboo anymore. And the taboos were very strong before.... It's a remarkable achievement.[75]

That a large cross section of Polish society grappled with the painful reverberations of Jedwabne's past, and acknowledged the event as a shameful secret, signals major collective progress.

In 2001, the then president of Poland, Aleksander Kwaśniewski, acknowledged Polish responsibility in the crime:

> We know with certainty that among the persecutors and perpetrators there were Poles. We cannot have any doubt that here in Jedwabne, citizens of the Polish Republic perished at the hands of other citizens of the Republic ... We are here to perform a collective examination of conscience ... Today's Poland has the courage to look in the eye the truth about the nightmare that darkened one of the chapters of her history. We have come to realize that we are responsible for our attitude toward the black pages of history.[76]

---

75 Author's interview with Stanisław Krajewski, Warsaw, November 2007.
76 Aleksander Kwaśniewski, "Address by President of Poland Aleksander Kwaśniewski at the Ceremonies in Jedwabne Marking the Sixtieth Anniversary of the Jedwabne Tragedy on 10 July 2001," in *The Neighbors Respond: The Controversy Over the Jedwabne Massacre in Poland*, ed. Antony Polonsky and Joanna B. Michlic (Princeton: Princeton University Press, 2004), 130–131.

In a similar vein, the Institute of National Remembrance opened an investigation into the Jedwabne murders. Its fifteen-hundred-page report, published in 2002, corroborated Gross's thesis and detailed similar Polish pogroms in the same part of the country in 1941.[77]

The Jedwabne debate also included people who denied, directly or indirectly, Polish responsibility for the event. Some refuted the evidence and continued to blame the Nazis for burning Jews inside the barn. Others placed the massacre in the context of the war, asserting that the Jews had been punished for welcoming the Soviets in 1941, taking Polish jobs, and helping the Soviets exile Poles to inner Russia.[78] As I have argued, some Jews did take part in the Soviet occupation. Most, however, did not. Yet the charge of Żydokomuna, that the communist takeover of Poland was a Jewish-led conspiracy, gained even greater significance in postcommunist Poland.[79] Many right-wing politicians, historians, and Church leaders, including Marek J. Chodakiewicz, Piotr Gontarczyk, Bogdan Musiał, and Tomasz Strzembosz, suggested that Gross's central aim was to promote hostility toward Poland and Poles through "insinuations calculated to blacken the image of the nation."[80] The expanding antisemitic press charged that the purpose of any negative portrayal of Poles was to discredit Poland's image on the world stage. The old technique of deny and deflect found a modern audience with the claim that Jews sought to ruin Poland's good name.[81]

The 2001 Sejm elections provided an arena in which to start a nationalist backlash against the so-called liberal and Jewish campaign against Poland's reputation. Right-wing candidates branded their liberal opponents as Jewish communists. They equated the State of Israel with Nazi Germany and the Stalinist Soviet state. The extremist right-wing media network, run by a charismatic priest, Tadeusz Rydzyk, also broadcast the "image of the Jew as the greatest perpetrator of violence in world history, who cannot stop himself from committing monstrous crimes against Christians both in the past and at the present."[82]

---

77 Paweł Machcewicz and Krzysztof Persak, *Wokół Jedwabnego* (Warsaw: n.p., 2002).
78 Cała, "Antisemitism without Jews and without Antisemites": 18
79 Joanna B. Michlic, "Antisemitism in Contemporary Poland: Does It Matter? And for Whom Does It Matter?" in Cherry and Orla-Bukovska, *Rethinking Poland and Jews*, 163.
80 Cała, "Antisemitism without Jews and without Antisemites": 16.
81 For a listing of publishing companies that specialize in antisemitic literature, see ibid.: 19.
82 Michlic, "Antisemitism in Contemporary Poland," 163–164.

Radio Maryja

In 1994, Rydzyk set up Radio Maryja in the medieval walled city of Toruń. It is the only Roman Catholic airwave media with nationwide coverage.[83] Although its hosts have tended to avoid direct antisemitic opinion, they have frequently raised their listeners' fears of Jews through veiled antisemitic slurs. One example will suffice: "In Poland there is a fifth column stemming from *the* national minority." Here "national minority" is code for Jews.[84] Often the sole source of information for older rural listeners, Radio Maryja feeds its audience a daily diet of stories about a Godless world where gay people trample Polish values and the Roman Catholic Church is under siege.[85] By focusing on those who felt left behind during Poland's transition to capitalism—the rural elderly—Rydzyk built a deeply loyal base. In 2007, twenty-nine out of thirty of my interviewees referred to Radio Maryja as a station that only "old grannies" listened to, and which would lose power as the older generation died off. But by 2019 this right-wing media network had grown into a powerful giant. Rydzyk is one of the most influential unelected people in today's Poland.

Since 1998 the right-wing network has also published a daily *Nasz Dziennik*, which claims to have a Catholic mission. It has a print circulation of two hundred fifty thousand to three hundred thousand.[86] Its title and ideology allude to *Mały Dziennik*, the antisemitic paper established by the Polish episcopate and printed from 1934 to 1939. *Nasz Dziennik*'s columns often express openly antisemitic sentiments.[87] In 2003, Rydzyk's network expanded to include the television station *Trwam*. Rydzyk has funded a university, museum, and church through the fifty-five million dollars in subsidies given by ruling ministers in the Law and Justice Party to his many businesses—including a cellphone network provider and a geothermal plant. The money is a sign of appreciation for securing millions of votes in the 2015 election from people like Kazimierz Bujnowski, a sixty-one-year-old retired transport worker who is concerned that Polish

---

83 Ambrosewicz-Jacobs and Orla-Bukowska, "After the Fall: Attitudes Towards Jews in Post-1989 Poland": 271.
84 Stanislaw Krajewski, "The Evolution of Catholic-Jewish Relations in Poland after 1989," in Cherry and Orla-Bukowska, *Rethinking Poles and Jews*, 147.
85 Marc Santora and Joanna Berendt, "Mixing Politics and Piety, A Conservative Priest Seeks to Shape Poland's Future," *New York Times*, September 21, 2019
86 *Nasz Dziennik*'s current circulation has dwindled to ten to twenty-five thousand. This might reflect an audience that accesses the paper online rather than in print. See 4international media & newspapers, accessed 23 August, 2023, https://www.4imn.com/reviews/1171.htm.
87 Cała, "Antisemitism without Jews and without Antisemites": 10.

patriotism is being replaced by a toxic multiculturalism. Bujnowski "fears that Poles are being made to feel ashamed to be Polish."[88]

A divisive figure in Poland, Rydzyk, with his xenophobia, homophobia, antisemitism, and Euroscepticism, has many critics. The Open Church which aligns more with Pope John Paul II's liberal position on Jews, opposes Rydzyk, while the Closed Church supports him. One representative of the Open Church, the late Jesuit Father Stanisław Musiał, acknowledged that "both the Polish State and the Catholic Church in Poland are joined in a sorrowful confraternity of guilt against Jews—in Jedwabne as well as over the entire extent of our history."[89] The Closed Church, which Cardinal Archbishop Józef Glemp represents (and to a much greater extreme Father Rydzyk represents), has made no such claim.

It is noteworthy that in 2001 Primate Glemp recognized the need for a genuine and meaningful apology to God and to people on behalf of "everyone who suffered and to do so on behalf of those Polish citizens who committed evil acts against citizens of the Mosaic faith."[90] Yet, he would not acknowledge prewar Church antisemitism and its implications for Polish-Jewish relations. Instead, Glemp cast Jewish-Polish relations only within economic and political contexts:

> Jews were cleverer, and they knew how to take advantage of Poles. That, in any case, was the perception. Another cause of dislike for Jews was their pro-Bolshevik attitude. [...] In Poland before the war, matters of religion did not play any significant role as far as dislike for Jews was concerned.[91]

As I have already discussed, the great majority of prewar Poland's three million Jews did not accept Bolshevism. Also, as has been demonstrated, Church-propagated antisemitism—including the blood libel and perceptions of world Jewry's hunger for international power—greatly affected Polish-Jewish relations, especially during the second half of the 1930s. Surely these negative stereotypes of Jews promulgated in part by the Church, and held by many Poles,

---

88 Santora and Berendt, "Mixing Politics and Piety, A Conservative Priest Seeks to Shape Poland's Future."
89 Rev. Stanisław Musiał, "We Ask You to Help Us Be Better," *Gazeta Wyborcza*, 23 May 2001, in Polonsky and Michlic, *The Neighbors Respond: The Controversy Over the Jedwabne Massacre in Poland*, 173.
90 The Catholic Information Agency, "Interview with the Primate of Poland, Cardinal Jozef Glemp, on the Murder of Jews in Jedwabne, 15 May 2001," in ibid., 167.
91 Ibid.

did not disappear with Germany's invasion. Instead, they influenced Poles' continued perception of Jews as an enemy during World War II and the Holocaust.

Myth Reconstruction

Just as the answer to "Who is a Jew?" is different in Poland than elsewhere, so too is the understanding of antisemitism. Both definitions are rather blurry and difficult to pin down with exactness. Each has a particularly Polish aspect to it, given the context of place and time. With this said, it is crucial to point out that most Polish Jews do not see Poland as a particularly antisemitic country—for Poland does not stand out from other states in this category. During a 2007 interview, the then University of Wrocław student and third generation Jewish activist Jan Kirschenbaum explained, "there are countries much more antisemitic than Poland. But people hold onto the stereotype of Polish antisemitism because the Holocaust happened in Poland."[92] At the same time, he acknowledged that there are Poles who express antisemitic views. He also noted that the Jewish youth club at the university did not advertise at the time: "We're protective. We're afraid of antisemitism. It is not [the fear of] something that we are experiencing; rather the fear of what could be."[93] From his standpoint, "You cannot really measure antisemitism in Poland." He added: "I don't really care if they are antisemitic. I don't change who I am."[94]

In 2019 most of my Jewish interviewees still held that Poland's antisemitism was nothing extraordinary. They noted that political rhetoric constituted the vast majority of it, while violence remained peripheral. Some even pointed out that Radio Maryja's own antisemitic rhetoric had decreased lately.[95] As a dangerous nationalist wave has swept the globe—including Europe, the United States, and Israel—they are struck by Poland's lack of extreme violence.

At the same time, for Stanisław Krajewski it is important to recognize that in its own particular way contemporary Poland is a very antisemitic country. It "is in the background and it can resurface at any time."[96] Only a few days prior to my interview with Krajewski, the Polish internet lit up with a video capturing residents in Poland's southeastern town of Pruchnik resurrecting an old Easter

---

92 Author's interview with Jan Kirschenbaum, Wrocław, November 2007.
93 Ibid.
94 Ibid.
95 Author's interviews with Emil Jeżowski and Stanisław Krajewski, Warsaw, April 2019.
96 Author's interview with Stanisław Krajewski, Warsaw, April 2019.

ritual once practiced throughout the Balkans. On Good Friday, they staged the trial of an enormous effigy of Judas—the disciple of Jesus who in the Christian Bible betrayed Jesus to the Roman authorities. The 2019 trial ended, according to tradition, with the condemnation of Judas to death. The townspeople beat the effigy and then dragged it down the street, hanged it from a massive makeshift gallows, and set fire to it. What was disturbing for outsiders was that this tradition characterizes Judas as a stereotypical Hasidic prewar shtetl Jew, with *peyot* (side curls), a *shtreimel* (traditional black-brimmed hat), and a grotesquely large nose. What was even more disturbing for people living in Poland, both Christians and Jews, was not only the violence directed at the "Judas," but that many children joined the adults in kicking and beating it.

A good number of people link this revival of an abandoned (and Church-condemned) ritual to the recent, and fiery, international debate over Poland's controversial Amendment to the Act on the Institute of National Remembrance in 2018. Commonly referred to as the "Holocaust Law," it is the Law and Justice Party's (PiS) attempt to halt the oft-mistaken attribution of the Nazi death camps on Polish territory as "*Polish* death camps." The right-wing PiS government led by Jaroslaw Kaczynski instituted this law that fines and/or jails, for up to three years, anyone who states Poland or Poles were complicit in the Holocaust. After an immediate international outcry, led by Israel and followed by the US, the Polish government removed the criminal penalty of jail time, leaving it a civil matter penalized monetarily.[97] Some hold that it was the perception that international Jewry could "once again" step on Polish sovereignty and change Polish law that unleashed this particularly shocking display of primitive antisemitism in Pruchnik.

For Stanisław Krajewski and other Jews aware of such practices, the ritual became personal when at the end of the beating one adult shouted, "add five more for the reparations!"[98] No longer could people regard it as merely an old ritual, just theatrical violence performed on an abstract figure Poles would only recognize from outdated books and could not possibly meet on the streets. With the order to beat the Judas because of Jews' legal battles over property restitution, this ritual was quickly read as asserting the modern Jew as an enemy of Poland. It connected Judas's ancient disloyalty to Jesus to Jews' supposed contemporary

---

97 Harriet Sherwood, "Anger as Poland Plans Law That Will Stop Jews Reclaiming Wartime Homes," *Guardian*, August 2, 2021, https://www.theguardian.com/world/2021/aug/01/anger-as-poland-plans-law-that-will-stop-jews-reclaiming-wartime-homes.
98 Author's interview with Sebastian Rejak, Warsaw, April 2019.

economic threat to Poland. This Judas "was a link to real Jews and that is why it was so problematic and tough for us."[99]

Since the fall of communism, Jewish survivors or heirs to Jews killed in the Holocaust have petitioned for the return of their families' property initially stolen by the Nazis, then taken by the communists. Poland remains the only EU country that has not legislated on property restitution, making the process cumbersome and often decades long.[100] As prewar Poland was home to some 3.2 million Jews, many of today's politicians hold that restitution would devastate Poland economically.[101] This argument of economic demise through Jewish manipulation is an old one that strikes a chord with Polish right-wing nationalists. Roman Dmowski used it in interwar Poland; Polish politicians used it in election debates ahead of the EU vote and later parliamentary elections.[102] The issue has been complicated by the fact that after the dismantling of communism, the government sold some of the nationalized property originally seized by the Nazis. Thus, private individuals or companies who purchased the property are in fear of losing their investments. In early May 2019, just after the Pruchnik Judas burning, thousands of Polish nationalists took to Warsaw's streets to rally against property restitution. It has been described as one of the largest anti-Jewish street demonstrations in recent times.[103]

What brought the Judas ritual back to Pruchnik is the same force that has compelled hate speech and hate crimes to escalate in the United States and around the globe. People feel under siege by Others who they perceive challenge their value system and core memory of Self and nation. Nationalist politicians seize on this anxiety to strengthen their base.

Poles responded in disgust to the Pruchnik Judas effigy. Some posted photos online of the same ritual occurring in Germany prior to World War II, suggesting that teaching children hate can lead directly to destruction. The day following the ritual, the Polish episcopate voiced its condemnation of the event; Interior Minister Joachim Brudzinski referred to it as "idiotic" and the perpetrators as

---

99 Author's interview with Stanisław Krajewski, Warsaw, April 2019.
100 Joanna Plucinska, Dan Fastenberg, "75 years on, Holocaust Survivors Struggle to Recover Property in Poland," Reuters, January 20, 2020, https://www.reuters.com/article/us-holocaust-memorial-auschwitz-restitut/75-years-on-holocaust-survivors-struggle-to-recover-property-in-poland-idUSKBN1ZJ0Y8.
101 Ibid.
102 "Polish Prime Minister: Paying Holocaust Property Restitution Would Be 'victory for Hitler,'" *Times of Israel*, May 20, 2019, https://www.timesofisrael.com/polish-pm-paying-holocaust-property-restitution-would-be-victory-for-hitler/.
103 Ibid.

"Satans."[104] On Facebook, Pruchnik's mayor wrote that he opposed the tradition and that the city had not organized it. The Polish response to the scandal shows the other side of Poland that most outsiders do not see, even when right in front of them. For Krajewski, "there is a whole beautiful face of Poland, which to me is at least as important as the antisemitic face of Poland. And it's here. And it's important. I see and feel it all the time."[105]

In this chapter I have shown that just as Catholic-born Poles found their way back to the Church during the last two decades of the Polish People's Republic, so too did Poles of Jewish origin discover their own specific pathway into Judaism. In an act of rebellion against the totalitarian state, Polish Jews revealed, discussed, and embraced their once taboo identities. Since the birth of the Third Polish Republic, the Jewish community has grown as more people reclaim connection to it. As with any living Jewish community, its landscape is patchy, dotted with deep chasms and precarious bridges. At the same time, the Jewish Polish community is distinct and has its own challenges having confronted specific communist government-sanctioned antisemitic stereotypes and policies. Perhaps still harder to navigate is the painful knowledge of intimate Polish anti-Jewish violence during and after World War II. In addition, Jewish Poles have had to contend with Western Jews judging their very presence in Poland. Because Poland was the epicenter for the Holocaust, many American Jews, me included, have thought badly of Polish Jews for adapting and creating new life so near to where *our* people were beaten and burned. We have had the gall to judge them. I hope that now we have the understanding to admire and respect them.

---

104 "Polish church condemns beating of Jewish effigy in Poland," apnews, accessed April 5, 2020, https://apnews.com.
105 Author's interview with Stanisław Krajewski, Warsaw, April 2019.

CHAPTER 19

Myth and Its Reconstruction

This journey into Polish-Jewish relations began with an understanding that national myths play a critical role in how the collective perceives its Self in relationship to Others. Those concepts which a nation's leaders choose to emphasize become embedded in that national myth . . . that national self-depiction, self-understanding. A wealth of scholarly research has investigated the curation of such myths as collective memory. Unlike historical consciousness, memory has "no sense of the passage of time; it denies the "pastness" of its objects and insists on their continuing presence."[1] The historian Peter Novick explains:

> "Typically, a collective memory, at least a significant collective memory is understood to express some eternal or essential truth about the group—usually tragic. A memory, once established, comes to define that eternal truth, and along with it, an eternal identity for the members of the group."[2]

Opposed to what one might naturally view as the process of memorialization, it is not the actual occurrence of the moment remembered that makes it meaningful. Rather, the meaning is derived from present concerns. Thus, it is the present which determines what from the past we remember and how we remember it.[3] When current concerns markedly change, leaders often respond through manipulating collective memory—repressing some memories and elevating others.

Here, collective memories (which when stitched together form a group's myth) are defined not only by a set of beliefs held by a given community "about its past, about people and events that inhabited it,"[4] but also by the way the community commemorates the past and educates its members about it. Such

---

1 Peter Novick, *The Holocaust in American Life* (Boston: Mariner Books, 2000), 4.
2 Ibid.
3 Ibid., 3.
4 Ibid., 13.

knowledge—gleaned from the classroom, press, historians, documentaries, movies, television, as well as official holidays, memorials, and ceremonies—becomes the "obligatory equipment of each member of this community."[5] A fascinating yet problematic characteristic of collective memory is that it does not necessarily correlate with facts and the historical truth. As one researcher notes, "images of past events and persons are valued by collective memory more than historical knowledge reproduced and provided by historians."[6] All collectives participate in some form of memory making, or as I refer to it, *mythmaking and myth reconstruction*. To challenge that collective memory is to challenge what that memory represents: the identity of the nation, the group, one's family, one's Self.

In this chapter I will explore how American Jews and Polish Christians have curated and challenged their myths concerning Polish-Jewish relations. Both groups elevate the Other's enemy status to attract adherents. It is worth noting that the Poles are well ahead of American Jews in the myth reconstruction process. That said, they are currently experiencing a strong backlash against these new perspectives.

American Jews' Mythmaking

In his book *The Holocaust in American Life*, Peter Novick recounts that in the 1940s rivalry defined American Jewry: the old divisions continued on American shores between German Jews and Polish Jews, the Reform and Orthodox; and all religious camps saw Jewish secularists as a curse.[7] Physical geographic separation among American Jewish communities only further nurtured these old resentments and generated disrespect.

During World War II, and in the decades that followed, most American Jews, like Americans in general, veered away from discussing the complexity of the Holocaust. Victimhood was viewed negatively in American society and, in turn, within the separate Jewish communities in the country. Americans became interested in the Holocaust only in the late 1970s. Novick argues that when the shame once generally associated with victimhood was replaced by an embrace of "victim communities," American Jews gained the confidence to reexamine their ultimate victim experience—the Holocaust.[8] According to Novick, they

---

5   Quoting Barbara Szacka in Piotr Forecki, *Reconstructing Memory: The Holocaust in Polish Public Debate* (Frankfurt am Main: Peter Lang, 2013), 13.
6   Quoting Bronisław Baczko in ibid., 14.
7   Novick, *The Holocaust in American Life*, 31.
8   Ibid., 8, 34, 276–277.

wanted to be respected, and in the 1980s and 1990s such respect would come from demonstrating that *they* too had endured tragedy and that *they* had survived to create a new and prosperous community.⁹

Sebastian Rejak adds to this thesis in his book *American Judaism: Adventure in Modernity*, which focuses on American Jews' growing secularism. Why did the Holocaust take on the overwhelming importance it plays in contemporary American Jewry? Rejak argues that the Holocaust provided the expanding Jewish secularist sector the centering and unifying narrative it lacked. If secularizing American Jews no longer coalesce around a generalized unifying path to God (some discarding God entirely from their understanding of the world), what makes this new Jew special? Rejak answers with a quote from Leonard Fein:

> Along comes the Holocaust and makes us special. It's not the kind of special we'd have chosen, but there it is, ours by right, and awesomely substantial. If you have the Holocaust, what more do you need? . . . And if the Holocaust becomes a definition, then you don't have to hunt for other answers, other ways of defining yourself.¹⁰

Not only did the secularists locate a new quasi-deity in the Shoah, but most American Jews came to view the Holocaust as a bridge to one another—a way to Jewish unity.

Emil Fackenheim named this so-called deity the "Commanding Voice of Auschwitz." For Fackenheim, while Auschwitz represents the horrors of the Shoah, it also provides a great opportunity for self-reflection and community solidarity. Buried beneath the tragedy booms the "Commanding Voice of Auschwitz." Rejak contends,

> the "Commanding Voice of Auschwitz" is a moral-religious imperative that compels authentic Jews to oppose Hitler's plan of extermination. That is why those who can hear the voice cannot cease being Jewish; they must not quit Judaism lest Hitler be given a posthumous victory. [. . .] Auschwitz [had become] a rationale for remaining Jewish.¹¹

---

9   Ibid., 8.
10 Quoted in Sebastian Rejak, *Jewish Identities in Poland and America: The Impact of the Shoah on Religion and Ethnicity* (London: Vallentine Mitchell, 2011), 66.
11 Ibid., 71.

Fackenheim did not just hear this resounding voice; he gave deep religious meaning to it by affirming that remembering the Shoah is a commandment of such import that it should be viewed as the 614th commandment in the Torah. (Traditionally, the Torah includes 613 commandments.) Indeed, a radical concept, it appealed to an ever-expanding number of American Jews. The Shoah commanded religious and secularist Jews alike to unify as an identifiable Jewish collective.

Alongside this particular American Jewish embrace of Jewish victimhood, Jewish identity, and Jewish unity through Holocaust memory, there has been a wave of American and Jewish American Holocaust memorial building. Simultaneously, there has been a surge in Holocaust-related university classes and academic research. Together with Holocaust-themed novels and memoirs, documentaries and movie productions, what some critics call a Holocaust Industry has emerged.[12]

Plenty of American Jewish intellectuals have chastised this often uncritical fixation on the Holocaust as problematic and dangerous for the American Jewish community.[13] However, there is a disconnect between elite intellectuals and the general populace, with the laity firmly holding onto its Holocaust-centrism. Thus, a type of civil religion has materialized around the Holocaust. It is replete with "sacred texts"—memoir literature and films such as *Shoah* and *Schindler's List*. It has places of worship: Nazi death camps located in Poland, academic centers for Holocaust and genocide studies, local Holocaust memorials, the US Holocaust Memorial Museum in Washington, D.C. and Israel's Yad Vashem. It has rituals: annual memorial ceremonies (including the March of the Living), scholarly conferences, and art exhibitions. It has saints: the survivors, and well-known victims, such as Anne Frank. And it has the faithful: people for whom the Holocaust constitutes the core of their Jewish identity.[14]

American Jewry's Guilt

One can argue that the current attention given to the Shoah has grown in part out of American Jewry's desire for repentance. As discussed earlier, critics have contended that the American Jewish leadership did not do enough to save

---

12 In 2000 Norman Finkelstein's *The Holocaust Industry: Reflections on the Exploitation of Jewish Suffering* garnered international attention except in the United States. The once-esteemed legal scholar Alan Dershowitz called for his removal from the DePaul University faculty, politicizing Finkelstein's work in the United States.
13 See Novick, *The Holocaust in American Life*.
14 Rejak, *Jewish Identities in Poland and America: The Impact of the Shoah on Religion and Ethnicity*, 72.

their fellow Jews in Europe during World War II. This was for several reasons: American Jews in general and Rabbi Stephen Wise in particular—who had the ear of President Roosevelt—were so enthralled by FDR that they were unwilling to confront his administration with bold demands for rescue;[15] the American Jewish leadership feared that agitating for rescue would exacerbate the rising domestic antisemitism of the early 1940s; they also believed that they did not have the strength to fight for their two most pressing needs—an end to the Holocaust and the establishment of a Jewish homeland. In an address to a conference of the *Zionist* Organization of America, American *Zionist* leader Nahum Goldman lamented his generation's tragic position: "One half of the generation is being slaughtered before our eyes, and the other half has to sit down and cannot prevent this catastrophe."[16] He urged his audience "not to despair but instead to work for a Jewish state that would make future tragedies impossible."[17] Over time there emerged a commonly held view that American Jews had been "unforgivingly delinquent in not continually and energetically pressing for rescue."[18] As such, they repent.

The Yiddish writer Kadya Molodovsky confronts this truth in her book *A Jewish Refugee in New York: Rivke Zilberg's Journal*. Initially published as a serialized novel, the first installment debuted on May 30, 1941 in the New York Yiddish newspaper *Morgn-zhurnal* (Morning journal).[19] A young Jewish émigré to the United States herself, Molodovsky addresses the question of American Jewish action on behalf of European Jewry. Her protagonist Rivke Zilberg is a young, lonely, frightened refugee from Poland who struggles to assimilate into New York City Jewish culture while her beloved family is hiding from the Nazis. Rivke recognizes that her concerns are frivolous compared to her family's in Poland. And yet, predictably in one so young, her immediate daily worries take precedence over her concern for her family back in Lublin. Rivke reflects on this moral conflict as one that plagues not only herself but the whole refugee community—those who established themselves in America well before Rivke's arrival, as well as their children who grew up in the *goldene medina* (the Yiddish term for America as the land of opportunity).

---

15 Novick, *The Holocaust in American Life*, 42.
16 Ibid., 43–44.
17 Ibid.
18 Ibid., 39.
19 Anita Norich, introduction to Kadya Molodovsky, *A Jewish Refugee in New York: Rivke Zilberg's Journal*, trans. Anita Norich (Bloomington: Indiana University Press, 2019), vii.

In a letter she receives in March 1940, Rivke reads that her father and brother are homeless, living in the family cowshed. Rivke cries uncontrollably. After sharing the terrible news with the few who are close to her, and expressing a deep irrational desire to walk all the way back to Lublin, she asks: "But how long can a person cry? And what about me? I needed to find a roof over my head too."[20] One sentence later she asks again, "But, really, how long can a person cry? I put on my new stockings and shoes and went downstairs [...] I went to chase away my gloom."[21] When Rivke shows the letter to her future husband, Red, who grew up in America and never learned Yiddish, he responds: "'You're here, not there.' [...] I could see in his face that he wasn't the least bit concerned."[22]

In her journal entry dated May 25, 1940, Rivke recalls having attended a meeting of the Lublin Ladies' Society with her aunt: "at the meeting I learned that hundreds of young people were taken from Lublin to work as slaves. Where is Mikl [Rivke's brother]? And what is happening with my father if Mikl has been taken away?"[23] Immediately following the meeting, however, Rivke finds Eddie—a tragic love interest—waiting for her. The rest of the day's entry is about her relationship with him.

Molodovsky continues this juxtaposition between Old World destruction and New World constructions by describing American Jewry's responses to the former and their materialism. Rivke's fashionable cousin, Selma, and the travails around her upcoming wedding represent American Jews' fixation on wealth and status. Rivke's uncle refers to the wedding as a "conflagration" because it will burn up all of their funds. After reading two pages filled with obsessive details of this costly event one finds a refugee friend's revelation that "Łodz no longer exists."[24] Molodovsky laments American Jews' exhaustive misprioritization on their own materialism and their inability to focus steadily on the real conflagration burning up their loved ones overseas.

Molodovsky, however, also acknowledges contemporary Jewry's grass-roots efforts to aid their European brethren. The Lublin Ladies' Society's fundraising event, a gala ball, is an example. American Jews fundraised . . . but while eating, drinking, and dancing. American Jewry went on living. By juxtaposing one American Jewish community's responses to the European conflagration with the concerns that consumed them, Molodovsky assesses her subjects in

---

20   Molodovsky, *A Jewish Refugee in New York: Rivke Zilberg's Journal*, 48.
21   Ibid.
22   Ibid., 50.
23   Ibid., 117.
24   Ibid., 113.

real time. Could greater American Jewish uproar have changed the trajectory for European Jewry? Probably not. But at the same time, Molodovsky's reflections underscore the guilt some of the American Jewish community wrestled with and the guilt she believed other Jews should feel.

Jewish Youth Pilgrimages Perceive Polish Danger

While Poland was still under communist rule, American Jewry incorporated the Holocaust into its collective memory as central to its identity. After the Poles' transition away from communism 1989, American Jewish educators (and Israeli educators) clung onto youth pilgrimages to Poland as an assured path to Jewish identity construction. American Jews have sent their youth to the land of their forbears to find their Jewish essence, that is, the ever-present specter of Jewish destruction. They travel with different Jewish groups, including summer camps, youth groups, and private Jewish high schools. The Jewish American ethnographer Jack Kugelmass describes Poland as a stage for American Jewry to perform a sacred ritual of belonging.[25] On these pilgrimages, Jewish teens take in destruction in order to be reborn. Auschwitz-Birkenau, Treblinka, Majdanek, Sobibór, Chełmno, Bełżec, Gross-Rosen, Stullhoff. Jewish youth walk the same desolate land, feel the same biting wind, and step into the same horrifying buildings as their twentieth-century ancestors. Yet *these* youth come out the other side. Trembling with responsibility, they commit to securing the Jewish future. They recognize that it is their responsibility to ensure that six million Jews did not die in vain. After a week of painful empathy with Holocaust victims, most board planes bound for Israel. They will experience new life there . . . Jewish life. They will understand the absolute necessity for the Jewish state's continued existence.

There is no question that these programs have important value in connecting American Jewish youth with their Jewish identity. But for decades they have done so at Poland's expense. Students connect Poland with Jewish death: intentional Jewish destruction. In 2014, a group of twelfth graders studying at a Jewish high school in Atlanta, Georgia reflected on their recent school trip to Poland, which was followed by several months in Israel. They spoke of a constant barrage of sadness while in Poland. Like most such trips to Poland, they spent eight days visiting ghettos, empty synagogues, cemeteries, mass graves,

---

25 Jack Kugelmass, "The Rites of the Tribe: The Meaning of Poland for American Jewish Tourists," in *YIVO Annual 21: Going Home*, ed. Jack Kugelmass (Evanston: Northwestern University and the YIVO Institute of Jewish Research, 1993).

and death camps. After visiting Auschwitz and Birkenau, Sam told me, "I felt my body emptying of my soul—my life force. You felt hollow. Poland felt like a husk of a country. You felt like a husk of a person."[26]

Andrzej Folwarczny, founder of Forum for Dialogue among the Nations, notes that "[i]f you see only death camps and cemeteries you can be pretty sure that you think Poland is the worst place ever."[27] Though they had glimpses of contemporary Jewish life at both the Kraków and Warsaw Jewish Community Centers (JCC), they felt the weight of a "death shroud around the trip [...] we were in the past; we didn't live in any sort of present."[28] This was Sam's biggest regret from the trip. He had come with the expectation of also seeing contemporary Poland. He was left only with its difficult past. Folwarczny proposes bringing groups of Jewish youth and Polish youth together to meet, to talk, to break down mythic barriers ... and thereby to teach tolerance.

Since its inception in 1988, the March of the Living (MOL) has brought more than 260,000 Jewish youth from fifty-two countries on an annual pilgrimage marking International Holocaust Memorial Day to walk the three kilometers from Auschwitz to Birkenau. In MOL, a central role is played by Holocaust survivors, who testify to the horrors that they endured. Like the pilgrimages to Poland made by some forty thousand Israeli teens annually, the goal is for those who listen to the witnesses to become witnesses themselves. MOL has been quite successful at harnessing the Shoah to energize the Jewish people's continuation. With a razor-sharp focus on Jewish destruction and Polish antisemitism, MOL—like other Jewish pilgrimages to Poland—set no time aside to meet with Poles.

At a 2010 MOL orientation, the leader answered a question about visiting strictly Polish historical sites by explaining that the trip was too short to include such detours. When asked if the young people would have free time to shop, the leader responded that it would be best to save their money for Israel.[29] What participants understand is, we have no time for Poland; we do not want to financially support Poland.

Folwarczny says, "When you don't have opportunities for dialogue you learn about the other side from the media."[30] In contemporary Poland there are several media voices, in print, radio, and television that spew antisemitic rhetoric. In the

---

26   Author's interview with Sam Durham and Daniela Friedman, Atlanta, Georgia, May 2014.
27   Author's interview with Andrzej Folwarczny, Warsaw, November 2007.
28   Author's interview with Sam Durham and Daniela Friedman, Atlanta, Georgia, May 2014.
29   Author's interview with Rabbi David Steinhardt, Boca Raton, Florida, December 28, 2010.
30   Author's interview with Andrzej Folwarczny, Warsaw, November 2007.

American Jewish community, books such as the important graphic novel *Maus*, which tells the story of author Art Spiegelman's father's survival during the Holocaust, paints a relatively black-and-white image of Polish-Jewish relations. In fact, Poles are depicted as pigs. A metaphor for unkosher food, the Polish pig symbolizes that which Jews should avoid. Movies including Lanzmann's *Shoah*, which educators continue to show in class, also paint a black-and-white image of Polish-Jewish relations in its neglect of the Polish Righteous.

Over the years, much change has taken place within the March of the Living toward encountering contemporary Poles and Poland. However, the driving force behind a youth delegation's experience, and the opportunities it offered, will be determined by its adult leader—just as Polish history teachers continue to influence how their students will read Poland's past. According to Rabbi David Steinhardt of B'nai Torah Congregation in Boca Raton, Florida, and leader of two groups participating in MOL pilgrimages, it is fair to say that whatever agenda, preconceptions, and misconceptions a leader brings with him or her, their perspective will shape the group experience and understanding of Poland. What one leader chooses to raise with their bus of visitors will likely be different from what another bus leader underscores. The theological lessons taught by Orthodox rabbis are different from those relayed by Conservative, Reform, and Reconstructionist rabbis. The life lessons explored by a person who knows Polish history and views Poland through a wide-angle lens will be fundamentally different from those lessons shared by one who knows very little, if anything, about Poland outside of it being ground zero for the Shoah.[31]

The time in Poland on these trips is short, with little opportunity to interact with Polish people. Rabbi Steinhardt recounted March of the Living buses arriving at a small town in 2008. "On the day when the March of the Living comes to this little town you don't see a single person. It's as if it's a ghost town. Everyone boards themselves up in their houses."[32] During this visit, an elderly woman walked out from her front door to her garbage cans. As the kids were walking by "she screamed 'Żyd!' at the girl in front of me and spat at her. It was horrible. It was ugly. Really ugly."[33] A similar scenario took place on his first trip in 2003, when his group was walking along a Warsaw street. A shopkeeper spat at them and called out "Żyd!" He reflected that those types of incidents reinforce stereotypes Jews have of Poles. At the same time, Jewish isolation during these trips reinforce old Polish stereotypes of a Jewish invasion and Jewish

---

31 Author's interview with Rabbi David Steinhardt, Boca Raton, Florida, December 28, 2010.
32 Ibid.
33 Ibid.

attempt only to depict Poland and Poles as beasts. Had the MOL leader offered a nuanced history of Polish-Jewish relations, it would have been easier to discuss such incidents and the reasons why some older Poles are prone to antisemitic views. It would not have erased the pain felt by the Jewish visitors. But to have learned the context for such vitriol would have helped these American Jewish students understand why some Poles viewed them so menacingly. To have learned that numerous Poles felt their tragedy had been completely overshadowed by the Jews' own experience, and that so many had been schooled not only in the Church's blood libel but also in Żydokomuna, would at least have helped American Jewish students grasp the complex dynamics of the past that have produced those in the present.

Jewish Youth Pilgrimages at Poles' Expense

Regarding visitors to Poland, the anthropologist and Jewish memory activist Jonathan Webber argues that "You find what you are looking for."[34] In an interview with the Neshoma Project, Webber explains the origins of this understanding. When with an Israeli group in Poland he heard a tourist ask the Israeli tour guide if he ever experienced antisemitism in Poland. The guide responded: "No ... But you can feel it in the air." This phrase struck Webber. He would later ask visiting groups he met with: "What do you feel in the air?" Responses differed depending on people's religious affiliations. Whereas Orthodox and Hasidim feel the sanctity (because "this is a country that produced great Jewish culture and the greatest rabbis and the greatest mystics"), the secular and assimilated Jews feel the antisemitism.[35]

Webber's theory suggests that the Jewish high school students I interviewed experienced Poland negatively on their 2014 pilgrimage due to the anti-Polish stereotypes the students and their teachers brought with them. Indeed, prior to their trip, adult leaders advised them not to wear Jewish symbols, whether on clothing or jewelry, while in Poland. When students asked why, the adults revealed that Poland was still an antisemitic country. An argument could easily be made that the same might be said of the United States, where in the twenty-first-century Jews have been killed while praying in their synagogues and harassed and beaten while walking in their neighborhoods. And yet Jewish educators do

---

34 See Leora Tec's interview with Jonathan Webber, neshomaproject.org, video, 1:29:12, accessed August 31, 2023, https://neshomaproject.org/video-blog/2019/4/4/jonathan-webber.
35 Ibid.

not make a point of advising students to hide their Jewish symbols while in the United States. Nonetheless, the decision to conceal markers of Jewish identity in Poland was viewed as a preventative measure to ensure the students' protection.

Though these Atlanta travelers saw no signs of antisemitism in 2014, the students felt physically unsafe, as if pulled back to the late 1930s. Secular American and Israeli Jews coalesce around feeling the danger on Poland's land in order to cultivate Jewish peoplehood. According to the former Polish ambassador to Israel, Maciej Kozłowski, the American Jews focus on preserving their community identity. Religion is no longer a useful instrument, as so many Jews are unaffiliated with a religious institution. For Kozłowski, the only way, then, to preserve identity is to find a "common enemy." The Germans no longer serve this role, as they have taken exhaustive measures to demonstrate contrition for the Holocaust. The Soviets no longer serve this role due to the crumbling of the Soviet Union and the release of all refuseniks.[36] Like Sebastian Rejak, Ambassador Kozłowski holds that opposition to Poland's difficult history with antisemitism serves to unify American Jews.[37]

The Jewish youth pilgrimage to Poland is a powerful ritual that many Jewish Americans recognize as having been essential to their formation of a strong Jewish identity.[38] But I would argue that it is also a harmful ritual if treated uncritically. For as Ambassador Kozłowski suggests, one way that American Jews have developed a sense of belonging has been by labeling Poles and Poland as not only the place of Jewish destruction, but also as the enemy incarnate. As the Forum for Dialogue has demonstrated, left to their own biases many Jewish students maintain deeply rooted anti-Polish stereotypes. Most trips have been orchestrated to avoid much contact with contemporary Poles. It is only the past—the Jewish destruction on Polish land—that seems to matter.

Such tunnel vision is the fatal flaw of these trips. Jewish pilgrimage leaders tend to reduce Jewish history and Jewish identity to a horrendous, yet relatively brief, moment in time—Jews' terrifying victimization by the Nazis, and by Poles. In so doing, they ignore the possibility of building a different future, one in which lines between groups are crossed, and connection and understanding

---

36 *Refusenik* is a term for a Soviet Russian citizen of Jewish origin who applied for permission to immigrate to Israel but who was refused by the Soviet state. Consequences of applying for an exit visa to Israel included job loss, KGB surveillance, and public harassment.
37 Author's interview with Ambassador Maciej Kozłowski, Warsaw, November 2007.
38 For an exploration of Israeli teens' pilgrimages to Poland see Jackie Feldman, *Above the Death Pits, Beneath the Flag: Youth Voyages to Poland and Performance of Israeli National Identity* (New York: Berghahn Books, 2010).

take root. What message do American Jews send to Poles by regarding them as aliens and projecting Jewish American antipolonism onto them? During these sacred pilgrimages, Jewish youth unite. But at what cost?

For Christian Poles who watch bus after bus filled with visiting American Jewish youth gazing at them from behind windows, they know that their reputation is being sullied. Many grow angry that tens of thousands of Jewish teens invade their nation, wading in its ruins, many carrying assumptions of a general Polish complicity in the Holocaust. As they do so, their own antisemitic stereotypes rise to the surface.

For Jewish Poles the relationship with MOL has been vexed. During its first decade, MOL ignored the presence of Polish Jews. That Polish Jews called Poland their home was problematic for the MOL message. However, having insisted that they be heard, Polish Jews now meet with some visiting groups in Jewish spaces.[39] They know that they too are being judged for living in a "Jewish cemetery." Krzysztof Izdebski, a young secular Jewish leader in the Warsaw gemeinde, resents that Israeli and American Jews typically first ask, "Why do you live here?" It puts him on the defensive: "You have to say 'sorry' that you live here and explain [why] with a strong argument."[40]

Stanisław Krajewski clarifies,

> [i]t's a very simple thing if you think about it. We live normal lives in a place where tragedy took place. I'm not surprised that the Jewish visitors are somehow unhappy or uneasy with that, but I'm angry they try to impose their feelings upon us, [intimating] we have the wrong feelings or the wrong way. It's not that we forget, or that we don't think, of course we do. But we want to lead our normal lives. [. . .] Poland as the place of the mass murder of Jews and consequently a Jewish cemetery is an image that has a good grounding in reality. I understand it has somehow dominated their perceptions. [. . .] But Poland is more than just a cemetery, not just for Poles in general, but also for us, Polish Jews.

---

39 Author's interview with Sebastian Rejak, via Zoom, February 8, 2022.
40 Author's interview with Krzysztof Izdebski, Warsaw, November 2007.

Krajewski then asks:

> What is the ultimate consequence of this approach that Poland is the cemetery of the Jewish people? It would be that there should be no Jews in Poland. Would it be better somehow for the world, for Jews, for Jewish history to have Poland completely without Jews? It would be perhaps a neater picture. I don't think it would be better. I think it would be much worse.[41]

I hold that for these emotionally weighted youth trips to reach their positive potential, they must include *meaningful* exchanges with Catholic Poles and Jewish Poles.

American Jewish Myth Reconstruction: Youth Pilgrimages

Concerning Polish-Jewish relations, myth reconstruction is in its beginning stages in the United States. It faces tremendous resistance from Jews who find comfort in branding Poles as *our* enemies. Like any group which resists change, Jews have difficulty accepting that Poland and Poles can exist outside the old stereotypes. Part of what makes this process so complicated is our physical distance from the Other. American Jews do not confront this problematic stereotyping because we do not encounter it in our daily living. We rarely meet challenges to our antipolonism at school, in the playground, at the movies, or around the dinner table. Although the United States has the largest Polish diaspora, we do not purposefully meet Poles and engage with them to challenge our myth. It is in-person and meaningful dialogue that best shocks the senses into acknowledging truths that counter and dismantle our stereotypes.

The March of the Living has evolved from an event weighed down by antipolonism into one slowly opening to positive encounters with contemporary Poland.[42] For more than ten years some groups from MOL have been willing to enter into discussion with Polish Christian youth with the help of the Forum for Dialogue among the Nations. The Forum for Dialogue (as it has been known since 2013), in partnership with the American Jewish Committee,

---

41 Author's interview with Stanisław Krajewski, Warsaw, November 2007.
42 Carolyn Slutsky, "March of the Living: Confronting Anti-Polish Stereotypes," in Cherry and Orla-Bukowska, *Rethinking Poles and Jews*, 189–196.

developed a book to facilitate open debate between visiting Jewish youth and their Polish contemporaries—*Difficult Questions in Polish-Jewish Dialogue*. One thousand Polish Christian high school students, American Jewish students, and Israeli students submitted questions they would not ask the Other in fear that they cause offensive or hurt feelings. "You can see that these kids bring their stereotypes from the older generation. And these questions are really shocking. They reflect existing stereotypes. And if you ask me, I would say these are as important as the answers."[43] The editors selected fifty of the most crucial questions and had experts respond to them. Folwarczny explains that some questions are asked several times in different ways and answered by scholars in the field of Polish-Jewish relations somewhat differently each time: "Our goal was not to give *the* answer. Our goal was to show that even if we differ in details, we should look for answers in difficult matters."[44]

Folwarczny underscores that for Polish youth such an opportunity for Polish-Jewish dialogue,

> is very important because very often this is the only time, they can meet Jewish people. This is the chance for them to confront their stereotypes of reality ... For Jewish students I think this is the only chance for them to learn something about contemporary Poland ... and to show how much they have in common.[45]

He adds that "very often we hear that these meetings with Polish and Jewish students were the highlight of the program."[46]

The Jewish teen pilgrimage to Poland is the most fruitful starting point for the development of purposeful engagement with the Other. I suggest adding to these groups a two-part program of education and humanization. By permitting students heretofore absent opportunities to encounter the Other's history in depth, Jewish students will think about how Poland's experiences have shaped its people. They will learn about the commonwealth, partition, interwar independence, World War II, communist Poland, and contemporary Poland. At the same time, Polish students will learn about the variety of Jewish cultures in Poland, as well as the breadth of attitudes Poles have had of Jews—for example, Church antisemitism, Polish right-wing nationalist rhetoric, and actions taken by both against Jews.

---

43 Author's interview with Andrzej Folwarczny, Warsaw, November 2007.
44 Ibid.
45 Ibid.
46 Ibid.

Clearly, for students to meet and digest such information they will require teachers who themselves understand it and are able to convey it in a respectful manner.

As of 2012, the Forum for Dialogue has collaborated with Facing History and Ourselves, a US educational organization dedicated to fighting xenophobia, antisemitism, and racism. Many Holocaust educators use its curriculum. This cooperative program brings American educators who teach a variety of subjects dealing with Polish Jews (the Holocaust, Yiddish culture and literature, and Polish-Jewish relations) to Poland for a week-long study tour. For many, it is their first time in the country. Forum exposes these American teachers to the nuances of Polish history, introduces them to Polish activists and Polish teachers dedicated to protecting Jewish memory, and addresses the difficult past as well as the challenging present. Teachers return to the classroom having addressed the stereotypes of Poland and Poles they had previously espoused and thereby add depth and humanity to their lessons.

It is this profound connecting experience that was missing from my own children's Holocaust classes, the teacher of which herself used material from Facing History and Ourselves. When she and I spoke, she portrayed Poland as a land filled only with Jewish death. Had she taken part in Forum for Dialogue's intensive study tour she would have had a broader view of Poles and their country. This would have influenced her students, some of whom later traveled to Poland with their Jewish high school and were interviewed for this book. I propose that had they acquired a more complete overview of Polish-Jewish relations in their eighth and twelfth grade curriculums, the students would have more likely encountered the present with greater depth.

Teachers who are more knowledgeable will also be more likely to welcome the opportunity to help their students humanize the Other during their lessons and trip. Video conferencing offers new ways to meet the Other. Jewish pilgrimage groups can now meet their Polish contemporaries several times on screen prior to meeting with them in Poland. Breaking the ice on screen could allow for more robust and purpose-driven gatherings in Poland.

American Jewish Myth Reconstruction: Reaching Adults

Along with American Jewish educators who teach Polish Jewish history and the Holocaust, it is also vital to take American Jewish community and spiritual leaders to Poland to fully explore the past and present. Since 2006, the American Jewish Committee has collaborated with Forum for Dialogue in a leadership exchange. A delegation of emerging Polish leaders visits the United States to investigate issues of concern in Polish-American and Polish-Jewish relations. At the same time, an American Jewish group visits Poland for intensive meetings with experts on Polish-Jewish history and contemporary issues. This exchange allows adults to face the difficult past and challenging present while broadening their understanding of Poland and its people.[47]

Another program that brings visitors into meaningful encounters with the past and present is Bridge To Poland. Its founder Leora Tec has organized trips to introduce visitors to the variety of both Jewish life in Poland and Polish-Jewish relations. Tec grew up knowing that Poles rescued her mother during the war, and that thousands of other Poles acted with similar bravery. Her mother, Nechama Tec (1931–1923), a well-regarded sociologist and Holocaust scholar, conducted research on Polish Christians who aided Jews during the Holocaust and collected hundreds of examples of such courage for her book *When Light Pierced the Darkness*. Unlike most of us, Leora Tec started from a place of knowledge, accepting truths outside of the standard antipolonism that grounds American Jews' perceptions of Polish-Jewish relations. Still, she had much to learn concerning contemporary Poles in the newly born Third Republic of Poland.

In 2005, Tec traveled for the first time to Lublin, the city where generations of her mother's family were born. What surprised her most about the Polish people she met with was their involvement in Jewish memory keeping. In Poland, non-Jewish Poles were playing primary roles as memory keepers for centuries of Jewish life in Poland. It amazed her that non-Jewish Poles cared so deeply about the Jewish past and made such tremendous efforts to preserve it in the Polish national narrative. Through numerous personal trips back to Poland, Tec built relationships and friendships with many whom she refers to as "Rescuers of Memory." These Poles "see Jewish history as their history and, when confronted with empty space or absence where Jews used to belong, feel an overwhelming urge to fill those spaces with Jewish memory."[48]

One of Tec's first encounters with Rescuers of Memory occurred when she met Tomasz Pietrasiewicz, founder and director of the Grodzka Gate-NN Theatre Centre in Lublin. Only when Pietrasiewicz first sought to establish his

---

47 "AJC Polish-Jewish Leadership Exchange Program to Poland," ajc.org, accessed August 31, 2023, https://www.ajc.org/exchangeprograms/polish-jewish-leadership.
48 Jolanta Ambrosewicz-Jacobs and Leora Tec, "An Inclusive Model of Memory Work in Poland: Bridge To Poland as a Case Study," *Politeja* 1, no. 70 (2021): 230.

theatre company in the building surrounding Grodzka Gate—also known as the Jewish Gate that had been a passage connecting the Christian and Jewish parts of Lublin—did he learn about Jewish life on the "other side of the Gate." He told Tec, "I felt there was something deeply not right about this situation, that an adult man living in this city doesn't know anything about the Jews."[49] The Grodzka Gate-NN Theatre Centre has taken on the mission of remembering Lublin's Jews. Pietrasiewicz has organized his large cohort of activists (today reaching some sixty non-Jewish Poles) to collect photographs and documents and interview inhabitants who remember when Jews lived in Lublin.

Tec was so moved by meeting Pietrasiewicz that she formed Bridge To Poland so that other American Jews could meet him and the many Rescuers of Memory who commemorate Jewish life in Poland through education, theater, visual art, music, cemetery restoration, and so forth. On her small group study tours of Poland, she "seeks to challenge old stories, blank space—the undiscovered or unknown—and fossilized representations about Poland, 'the Poles' and Polish-Jewish history."[50] Grzegorz Jędrek, who worked with the Grodzka Gate-NN Theatre Centre, and who has met with people Tec brings to Poland, explains, "Thanks to her trips, people realize that Poland is not only a cemetery, but actually there are people living on this cemetery who also lost their identity because they lost their neighbors."[51]

Tec also curates an online video library of Polish Rescuers of Memory. The Neshoma Project educates Jews about the efforts non-Jewish Poles have made to remember the Jewish community, its former cultures, and specific individual Jews.

Importantly, Bridge To Poland states that one "cannot tell the story of Jewish Poland without telling the non-Jewish story as well."[52] This story includes Polish suffering. As we have discussed, however, American Jews too often get mired in a game of comparative suffering. By bringing the devastating Polish experience under Nazi and Soviet occupation to Western Jews, Tec helps Jews to develop compassion for Poles, and to question our tired assumptions.

---

49   Ibid.: 232.
50   "About Leora Tec," BridgetoPoland, accessed August 23, 2023, https://bridgetopoland.com/about-leora.
51   Ambrosewicz-Jacobs and Tec, "An Inclusive Model of Memory Work in Poland: Bridge To Poland as a Case Study": 234–235.
52   Ibid.: 233.

Polish Memory: Elementary Myth Reconstruction

Many Poles who grew up under KOR and Solidarity engaged that legacy of transparency in their own post-1989 work. Beata Maliszkiewicz[53] opposed the communist manipulation of the collective. She derided its ability to prevent the people from asking questions and seeking answers. In early 1990, immediately after the collapse of the regime, Maliszkiewicz opened an alternative grammar school in Opole. Angered and frustrated by decades of hearing "No!" from an oppressive regime, Maliszkiewicz and her team named their school TAK, which means "Yes." The concept from its inception was to nurture an environment of freedom, openness, and tolerance.

Early on, TAK worked with the Opole University psychologist Barbara Weigl on a research project assessing youth attitudes towards minority groups. Given the school's doctrine of tolerance, the results shocked researchers and teachers alike. TAK students tested as highly prejudiced against ethnic, national, and religious minority groups. In response, Maliszkiewicz and Weigl created a two-year project to break those stereotypes.

They began where their own personal education under communism had failed:

> "Poland's history was presented in a way that could promote the ideal of a monocultural society, ethnically pure, uniform in every regard. Traces of other cultures were eliminated from social consciousness, from curricula, and from the official images of cities and regions. Jewish cemeteries, synagogues and other preserved relics were marginalized and forgotten."[54]

Forever on a quest for legitimacy, communist heads again and again purged not only Poles of Jewish origin, but also the memory of their presence. Nationalist party leaders understood the need to unite their population by cultivating a collective memory—a myth—that emphasized unity by romanticizing victimhood

---

53   Having written her dissertation on the famed Yiddish writer Isaac Bashevis Singer, Maliszkiewicz brought sensitivity to both Hasidism and secular Yiddish culture. Author's interview with Beata Maliszkiewicz, Warsaw, November 2007.
54   Zdzisław Mach, "The Memory of the Holocaust and Education for Europe," in *Why Should We Teach about the Holocaust?*, ed. Jolanta Ambrosewicz-Jacobs and Leszek Hońdo, trans. Michael Jacobs, 2nd ed. (Cracow: The Jagiellonian University Institute of European Studies, 2005), 24.

and heroism. They insisted that the country forget that which countered the officially accepted memory.[55] The Polish People's Republic formally excised any mention of minorities, including Jews, from education. Maliszkiewicz and Weigl began to fill in those gaping holes. They fought stereotypes with truth.

Maliszkiewicz and Weigl incorporated lessons on Jews, Roma, Belarussians, Germans, Ukrainians, Lithuanians, and Silesians into the school's Polish language and literature programs. However, realizing that knowledge alone is not enough to counter prejudice, they also introduced art activities into cultural lessons. Because art can trigger empathy, creative projects gave students the opportunity to *feel*, and thus better understand, the Other. Grounded in an appreciation for the impact of theater in educational development, TAK organized joint theater projects with students and representatives from the minority under study. Meeting real people through a collaborative venture allowed for dialogue and the natural dissolution of social barriers.

Upon the students' completion of only the first two sections—on the Jews and the Roma—Weigl re-interviewed students who had answered the original questionnaire. The data from the empirical study revealed that children's attitudes toward *all* minorities shifted markedly after participating in the program, despite having learned only about two of the six groups. Their 1997 book documents their research.[56]

To understand the essence of history, in 2006 all TAK students participated in a year-long project entitled "The History of My Street" ("Głosy z ulicy Barlickiego"). Among other things, they discovered that the former German city of Opole had once been home to a vibrant Jewish community. Its members included Max Friedlaender, the brewery owner and city leader. The students also discovered Reform Rabbi Leo Baeck, who served in the New Synagogue which opened in 1897. With a six-hundred-seat capacity sanctuary, the Moorish revival building stood on the ground across from the future TAK school. Students learned that the Nazis destroyed the New Synagogue on November 9–10, 1938. On that evening, known as *Kristallnacht*, the "Night of Broken Glass," Nazis burned and vandalized Jewish shops and synagogues in Opole and the rest of Germany, beating, arresting, and murdering Jews.

---

55 Forecki, *Reconstructing Memory: The Holocaust in Polish Public Debate*, 21–22.
56 Barbara Weigl i Beata Maliszkiewicz, *Inni To Także My: Mniejszości narodowe w Polsce: Białorusini, Cyganie, Litwini, Niemcy, Ukraińcy, Żydzi. Program Edukacji Wielokulturowej w Szkole Podstawowej* (Sopot: Gdańskie Wydawnictwo Psychologiczne, 1997).

The students assembled this broader knowledge of their hometown's history into an outdoor festival, held in the town center. Included in the students' artistic presentations of Opole's history were seven realistic life-size black-and-white cutout portraits of historical figures. Among them was Rabbi Leo Baeck and Max Friedlaender. On each of the seven figures' black-clothed torso was the individual's short biography in white type. Enlarged photographs showed the once beautiful New Synagogue; a theater group included a Jewish wedding scene, replete with chuppah (wedding canopy) and the bride circling the groom seven times. A book on this project, by the same title, was published in 2007.[57]

In 2009, Beata Maliszkiewicz's dedication to building tolerance was recognized when she won the Irena Sendler " Repairing the World" award. In recognition, TAK school changed its name to the Irena Sendlerowa school. In a 2007 interview, Maliszkiewicz expressed surprise that more Polish educators had not adopted the programs that she and Weigl, together with TAK educators, had formulated. Though many people said they were interested in it, few teachers and school directors followed through. At the time, Maliszkiewicz attributed this lack of action to an overwhelming number of problems facing the country in the immediate postcommunist period. But now? The following chapter will examine this question.

Polish Memory: Secondary Myth Reconstruction

Although most Polish educators have not embraced Maliszkiewicz and Weigl's pioneering work, the Forum for Dialogue employs a similar approach in its School of Dialogue program, which reaches some fifty schools each year. In towns that once buzzed with Jewish cultural and economic activity, Forum opens up the Jewish past to local students. They get acquainted with the history of Jews in Poland, as well as with the Jews' contribution to the social, cultural, and economic fabric of the country in general, and to their own towns in particular.

When teaching the Holocaust, Forum for Dialogue facilitators communicate the historical facts and put a face on the past by studying the lives of individuals. By learning about a child who likely shared a school bench with a contemporary

---

57 Głosy z ulicy Barlickiego. ed. Beata Maliszkiewicz i Joanna Biskup (Opole: Wydawca, 2007).

student's grandparents, students sense the loss of a neighbor. Feeling the void this absence creates is a transformative experience.[58]

Participants explore their often forgotten local Jewish history and culture by conducting interviews, researching archives, and talking to local Jewish memory activists. Like activists themselves, the students present the Jewish past to local residents. This may include guiding a walking tour of the town's Jewish past, making films, websites, and brochures, or undertaking the cleanup and maintenance of the town's Jewish cemetery. Students have stepped into the public sphere to educate officials on issues connected with neglected Jewish heritage sites or a lack of commemoration. As of 2021, the Forum for Dialogue has engaged 9,775 students in 391 secondary schools.[59]

Such important efforts cannot veil the fact that most Polish public school curriculums neglect the Jewish past in Polish history and have been slow to teach the Jews' specific experience during World War II, that is, the Holocaust. While communism did not permit open discussion of minorities, it also created a taboo around speaking about the Holocaust. Piotr Forecki writes:

> [f]orgetting the Holocaust was [...] a state-organized element of the official historical policy on the war memory. To claim, however, that the process of forgetting resulted only from the state policy and the nature of the system would be a simplification and a limitation of the cognitive perspective. [...] Official memory of the Holocaust in Poland responded to the need of the common memory to repress the difficult past.[60]

Communist Poland had championed the Polish nationalist vision of World War II.

Education is a key instrument in the production and reproduction of nationalism, as well in our ability to break free from it. Until 1989, Poles learned that six million Polish citizens were murdered in the war. (Polish studies conducted since the birth of the Third Polish Republic have lowered the number of Polish Christians killed by the Germans during World War II from between 1.5 to 2.77 million. These same studies have put the number of Polish Jews murdered at roughly three million.)[61] The communist regime's number ignores that half the

---

58 See Forum for Dialogue, accessed August 23, 2023, https://www.dialog.org.pl.
59 Ibid.
60 Forecki, *Reconstructing Memory: The Holocaust in Polish Public Debate*, 25–26.
61 Snyder, *Bloodlands: Europe between Hitler and Stalin*, 406.

"Polish" victims were of Jewish origin; it thus covers over the specific plight of Poland's Jewish population. Timothy Snyder has shown that Jakub Berman, the eminence grise of the post-1944 communist regime, desired an equivalence of Polish and Jewish suffering and thereby invented the number of six million Polish deaths after he understood that the Germans murdered close to three million Polish Jews.[62] Indeed, communist Poland's memorial at the Auschwitz-Birkenau State Museum emphasized to visitors that those who died in the camps were Poles and prisoners "of many different nationalities." It listed in alphabetical order the other nations affected. Jews—*Żydow*—were put at the very bottom of the plaque. Communist Polish historiography further memorialized Auschwitz-Birkenau as a site of mainly Polish national martyrdom.[63]

As a young student in communist Warsaw, Robert Szuchta "searched in vain in the history textbooks for information on how the Polish Jews lived and how they perished."[64] Today, Szuchta is a leading youth educator about Polish Jewish life and the Holocaust. For Szuchta, teaching Polish history without its multicultural dimension is pointless and unfair to students. He reminds his students, who are all from Warsaw, that seventy years ago one third of Warsaw's population was Jewish.[65] A passion for truth led Szuchta and Piotr Trojański to challenge Polish collective memory by writing the first Holocaust curriculum for Polish students. Published for middle schoolers in 2000, they followed it with the first Polish Holocaust textbook in 2003.[66]

Several other Holocaust-oriented educational initiatives to train teachers in Poland have developed. The organizations involved include the Ministry of Education, Yad Vashem, the International Center of Education about Auschwitz and the Holocaust, the Center for Citizenship Education (CCE), and the Foundation for the Preservation of Jewish Heritage in Poland (FODŻ). The

---

62   Ibid.
63   Jolanta Ambrosewicz-Jacobs, "The Holocaust and Coming to Terms with the Past in Post-Communist Poland," Ina Levine Annual Lecture, United States Holocaust Memorial Museum, April 25, 2012, 5.
64   Robert Szuchta, "Against Silence and Indifference: Why I Teach about the Holocaust—Reflections of a Teacher," in Ambrosewicz-Jacobs and Hońdo, *Why Should We Teach about the Holocaust?*, 55.
65   Author's interview with Robert Szuchta, Warsaw, November 2007.
66   Note: a 2008 educational reform changed the Holocaust curriculum to begin with high school students. Robert Szuchta and Piotr Trojański, *Holocaust. Program nauczania o historii i zagładzie Żydów na lekcjach przedmiotów humanistyczny w szkołach ponadpodstawowych* Warsaw: n.p., 2000; Robert Szuchta and Piotr Trojański, *Holokaust. Zrozumieć dlaczego* (Warsaw: Bellona, 2003).

POLIN Museum has also worked with the US embassy to hold conferences that support educators throughout Poland who teach the Holocaust. But it is not enough.

Holocaust teachers are few in number in Poland, as interest in the subject often necessitates a prior educational foundation, which as we have seen is often withheld from primary and secondary school curriculums. According to a well-established Polish Holocaust educator, the biggest barriers to Holocaust education in Poland are a teacher's lack of knowledge of past Jewish life and culture in Poland. For most teachers, Jewish culture and the Holocaust are two irrelevant subjects. Most contemporary Poles have never seen a Jewish person, let alone spoken with one (given the small number of Holocaust survivors, postwar Jewish migrations from Poland, and hidden Jewish identities under communism).[67] Though more teachers may be interested in studying the Holocaust, the barriers, including a lack of professional and material support for Holocaust educators, as well as negative community responses, prevent most from reaching this goal.

Like most people, Poles prefer the comfort of their national myth rather than facts about the horrors of the past. Indeed, some Holocaust teachers in Poland have experienced great resistance from peers and parents. Some have received hate mail containing comments like "How are your Jews today?" and "No more Jewing up the curriculum."[68] In one small town near Warsaw, a middle school teacher encountered daily chanting from her colleagues upon entering the school: "None of those Jews today! *Zadnych Żydow dzisiaj!*"[69]

The Forum for Dialogue has responded to the loneliness many local activists feel when confronted by Polish opponents of their work. They have created a platform for activists and teachers to share experiences, exchange best practices, and develop a network of support. An annual nationwide spring conference draws together fellow activists working throughout the country. They learn from experts and share their own achievements and setbacks.[70]

---

67 Magdalena H. Gross, "No Longer Estranged: Learning to Teach the Holocaust in Poland," *Holocaust Studies* 24, no. 2 (2018): 138.
68 Ibid.: 131–132.
69 Ibid.
70 See Forum for Dialogue.

Polish Memory: Advanced Myth Reconstruction

Though the majority of the population and even most middle school and high school history teachers avoid dealing with the Holocaust, leading Polish academics have taken it upon themselves to make meaningful inroads into the field. In 1996, Professor Zdzisław Mach established the small Research Group for Holocaust Studies at the Center for European Studies at Jagiellonian University. In 2008, the Center for Holocaust Studies opened in Kraków, as an independent unit within the Faculty of International and Political Studies at Jagiellonian University. Its sole purpose is to conduct research on the Holocaust, to educate about it, and to commemorate it. The sociologist Jolanta Ambrosewicz-Jacobs served as its director and published numerous works focusing on Holocaust education in Poland and solving the challenges of integrating the difficult past into the history curriculum.[71]

A great deal of new courageous scholarship has also been undertaken at the Polish Center for Holocaust Research (Centrum Badań nad Zagładą Żydów), which opened in 2003 as a division of the Institute of Philosophy and Sociology at the Polish Academy of Sciences. Under Professor Barbara Engelking's stewardship, researchers have revived part of the dark, repressed Polish past to reconstruct Polish collective memory. "Erasure of memory can be caused by a number of traumatic events: witnessing mass murder, witnessing family members or friends killing Jewish neighbors, or even involvement in the crime."[72] Poles refrained from facing the Holocaust because they feared accusations of collaboration or stealing Jewish homes. They felt the shame of a nation that witnessed some of its own people commit barbarous deeds. Instead of grappling with the ramifications, Poles suppressed the memory.[73] They turned away from it in order to let live a more palatable image of Poland.

Defensiveness is common in Poland. One response to the work carried out by the historian Jan Grabowski at the Polish Center for Holocaust Research on people who aided the Nazis in their hunts for Jews has been to point to the Jews' own behavior during the war: "Look, they killed themselves." Katarzyna Person conceded that part of her motivation in writing her book on the Warsaw Ghetto Jewish Order Service was seeing the prevalence of antisemitic literature on the

---

71 Joanna Beata Michlic, "'At the Crossroads': Jedwabne and Polish Historiography of the Holocaust," *Dapim: Studies on the Holocaust* 31, no. 3 (2017): 299.
72 Ambrosewicz-Jacobs, "The Holocaust and Coming to Terms with the Past in Post-Communist Poland," 4.
73 Ibid.

subject in some Polish schools. Person recognized a need for "an objective book that will give you facts, rather than antisemitic stereotypes, which is really the only way it is present in Polish schools."[74]

The Polish Center for Holocaust Research attempts to make thoroughly documented information available to a population polarized over how to approach the Holocaust and Poles' relationship with it. Its publications have revealed "that some individuals and groups of ethnic Poles collaborated with Germans in carrying out the Holocaust."[75] Although Jan Gross's 2000 work on the Jedwabne massacre demonstrated some Polish complicity, Poles remain divided over how to incorporate such knowledge into their personal views of the past and, therefore, into present Polish identity.

For Robert Szuchta the attitude of Poles toward Jews is very important. A taboo for decades, Poles rarely even talked amongst themselves about wartime attitudes toward Jews, let alone with outsiders. In 2007, Szuchta believed that educational efforts had begun to break this taboo, allowing the younger generation to face the past with honesty. At that time, he felt that students had become more open to hearing viewpoints and facts that contradicted the national stereotype of the Polish hero.[76]

Some Poles responded to this in-depth debate over Jewish life and death in Poland by focusing their academic careers on Jewish studies. Writing in 2011, Marcin Wodziński holds that "[f]rom being close to non-existent, to the impressive institutional, teaching, research, and publishing developments, Polish-Jewish studies have changed beyond all recognition in the past three decades."[77] Jagiellonian University in Kraków founded the Institute of Jewish Studies. Jerzy Tomaszewski (1930–2014) established the Mordechai Anielewicz Centre for the Study and Teaching of the History and Culture of the Jews of Poland at the University of Warsaw, which also hosts the Department of Hebrew Studies. Jerzy Woronczak began what has become the Department of Jewish Studies at the University of Wrocław. The Maria Curie-Skłodowska University in Lublin also launched the Department of Jewish Studies, with the leadership of Monika Adamczyk-Garbowska. This interest in Jewish Studies includes a resurgence of

---

74 Author's interview with Katarzyna Person, Warsaw, April 2019.
75 Jolanta Ambrosewicz-Jacobs and Robert Szuchta, "The Intricacies of Education about The Holocaust in Poland. Ten Years after The Jedwabne Debate, What Can Polish School Students Learn about the Holocaust in History Classes?," *Intercultural Education* 25, no. 4 (2014): 288.
76 Author's interview with Robert Szuchta, Warsaw, November 2007.
77 Marcin Wodziński, "Jewish Studies in Poland," *Journal of Modern Jewish Studies* 10, no. 1 (March 2011).

Yiddish in Poland.[78] Taught in the most important universities in the country, non-Jewish scholars, students, artists, musicians, tour guides, and political activists learn the language. As a result of these programs and initiatives, thousands of undergraduates have explored Poland's past relationship with its once large Jewish population.

Stanisław Obirek understands the importance of these educational efforts and is optimistic about the educational process. It profoundly impacted his own life. Obirek is from Tomaszow Lubelski in southeast Poland. For eighteen years he grew up not knowing that his town had once been a typical shtetl with a Jewish population reaching 50%. Nearby lay the remains of Bełżec, a Nazi death camp where between 430,000 and 500,000 Jews were murdered. Yet during his youth, Obirek viewed Bełżec as a place where the Germans had killed *Poles* and members of other nationalities. Even the Jewish cemetery near his high school did not connect him to the very real presence of Jews in his town's past. It was only as a university student that he learned of the Jewish underpinnings of his hometown and of the great tragedy that occurred so close to him. For Obirek, "coming out of this forgetting of the Jewish past is a liberating experience."[79]

Still, it took Obirek many years to understand the unintentional consequences of his amnesia... that his forgetting about the Jewish past would be exceedingly painful to Jews who once walked his town's streets. In 2000, during an exchange with Milosz Lehrman, a Jew who had lived in Obirek's hometown prior to the war, Obirek had the epiphany that his amnesia had rendered him an "anonymous antisemite."[80]

This revelatory moment guides Obirek. A theologian turned cultural anthropologist, he teaches at the University of Warsaw. There, he meets students like his former self—students who are unaware of the Jewish life that once permeated Poland. Obirek finds great joy helping his students through this process of reconciling the past with the present. As a final class presentation, he often asks them to examine what happened during the Holocaust to the Jewish communities in their respective hometowns. This exercise allows them to move past intellectualizing the Jewish past and to make the Jewish past personal. Having gone through the process himself, and guiding others through it, he feels optimistic that education can effect tremendous change in the way Poles think about the Jewish past.

---

78 In a Taube Center lecture on October 20, 2021, Dr. Karolina Szymaniak discussed Yiddish in Poland.
79 Author's interview with Stanisław Obirek, Warsaw, April 2019.
80 Ibid.

Yet one must ask if younger people are interested enough in the field to become Poland's next educators. Yes. Hundreds of graduate students have poured their energy into researching Poland's former Jewish communities and bringing their discoveries to future students. While they enter the field for a variety of reasons, the majority speak of a personal need to discover a way into Polishness that opposes the xenophobic nationalism that has reasserted its presence in contemporary Poland. Referring to his students in Wrocław, Wodziński recognizes that they are searching for whether

> another version of Polishness is or, historically speaking, was possible. What other national culture could have developed in Polish lands? Is this possible even today and if so, how to achieve it... they refer to knowledge about Jews in order to verify knowledge about themselves and to question some elements of their own past.[81]

He believes that this search for a relatable Polish past is "the most important mission of Jewish studies in Poland."[82]

Myth Reconstruction: The POLIN Museum of the History of Polish Jews

During my 2007 research trip to Poland, I met with Jacek Olejnik, a young Polish Christian man who worked an assistant at the Israeli embassy in Warsaw. One afternoon we met in an office alive with people and productivity. When I asked about the work, Jacek handed me a thick forest-green folder. Inside it I found material describing a future museum dedicated to Polish Jewry. Surely, this museum indicates that Poles in high office are engaging in myth reconstruction. The POLIN Museum opened in 2014 with support of the Association of the Jewish Historical Institute of Poland, the Polish Ministry of Culture, and the city of Warsaw. As such, it is the result of the cooperation of private and public entities, the first of this kind in Poland.[83] Naturally, conflicts among the agencies have arisen concerning the general approach toward the past. While the

---

81 Wodziński, "Jewish Studies in Poland," 109.
82 Ibid.
83 Konrad Matyjaszek, "'You need to speak Polish': Antony Polonsky Interviewed by Konrad Matyjaszek," *Studia Litteraria et Historica* 6 (2017): 3.

museum's historians have argued for a critical approach, many contemporary right-wing state representatives demand apologetics.

It is not news that governments have a difficult time challenging accepted national myths. Poland is no exception. Polish government officials have pressured museum historians, especially concerning the accounts of Polish antisemitism, communism, postwar violence, and the 1968 expulsion of Jews. Government advocates have argued for a more Polish-friendly narrative, one that ignores any Polish misdeeds and focuses squarely on Others' culpability. As POLIN's chief historian Antony Polonsky acknowledges, "it was possible to block these pressures then, which would be much more difficult at present"[84] due to the strength of the current PiS government.

According to current director Zygmunt Stępiński, the museum's mission is to narrate a millennium[85] of Jewish life in Poland through the perspective of the Jews who lived it.[86] It is a testament to the Israeli Polish historian Jacob Goldberg's statement that we have no Polish history without Jewish history, and we have no Jewish history without Polish history. Polish and Polish-Jewish history are an integrated whole.[87] Having won several prizes for its core exhibition, the museum offers Poles an opportunity to learn what the communist authorities barred from the school curriculum: the experience over centuries of the Jewish minority, the Jews' separate and specific victimhood in the Holocaust, and their struggles in the postwar years and limited role under communist rule.

Visitors to the POLIN Museum's core exhibit embark on an experiential journey through Poland's varied Jewish past. One walks beneath the ceiling of the nineteenth-century Gwoździec wooden synagogue and steps onto its bimah—the platform from which one reads the Torah aloud to the congregation. Extremely different from American Jewish architecture, every inch is brightly painted with Jewish texts, images of animals and fish, and gorgeous floral designs. Along the way, visitors sit at individual wooden desks to view Hebrew and Yiddish texts in a Jewish library, and then stroll through a typical shtetl market. After entering a city, one wanders along a cobblestoned street in an interwar Jewish

---

84 Ibid.: 5.
85 This notion that Jews have resided on Polish territory for a millennium has been countered by historians who have noted that while singular Jews have been present since the tenth century, actual settled Jewish communities have been present on Polish lands since the late twelfth century. This nuance questions the museum's subtitle: 1000 Year History of Polish Jews. See ibid., 10n23.
86 Author's interview with Zygmunt Stępiński, Warsaw, April 2019.
87 Adam Teller, "Polish-Jewish Relations: Historical Research and Social Significance. On the Legacy of Jacob Goldberg," *Studia Judaica* 15, nos. 1–2 (2012): 27–47.

neighborhood, explores a railroad station that provided new opportunities for travel, and crosses a bridge in the Warsaw Ghetto. The museum galleries provoke questions. The borders of these galleries are themselves the borders of Polish history, expressing the symbiotic relationship between Polish and Jewish history.[88] One encounters the construction and reconstruction of Jewish identities and sectarian clashes and interactions—good and bad—between Poles and Jews.

Critics have argued that the museum misses the mark by perpetuating "a performance about a millennium of Polish tolerance, pluralism and multiculturality."[89] People have criticized the core exhibition for a lack of readily visible material on Polish antisemitism. For example, one is hard-pressed to find *Rola*, the late nineteenth-century conservative weekly that aligned with the Church and painted Jews as the enemy of both the Poles and Church. Additionally, little mention is made of Roman Dmowski, who employed antisemitism as a Polish nationalist political weapon. The chief historian of the museum Antony Polonsky acknowledges that one must look high and low for an explanation of *Rola*, and that "maybe more could have been said about Dmowski."[90] But he also argues that the audio guides do a very good job at leading the visitor to that which is not easily found, and provide more information than is visible. Additionally, Polonsky stresses that temporary exhibitions fill in educational gaps and continue to challenge stereotypes. In the end, for Polonsky, "the fact that the museum came into being is a miracle in a sense."[91]

That almost all Jewish teen pilgrimages to Poland now include a visit to this museum allows American Jewish twelfth graders the ability to reflect on Jewish life in Poland, not only on Jewish death. It affords Christian Poles the opportunity to "meet" Jews and to break down their misconceptions. And it provides Polish Jews a voice. Often chastised by their Western brethren for living in a "Jewish cemetery," they can point to the past; and those judging them can learn that for close to a thousand years Poland has been an important home for Jews. Like any other Polish citizen, Jewish Poles are connected to the country. It is their home, and they belong to it.

Every year, some four hundred thousand people visit the museum. This includes roughly eighty thousand Polish school children, who not only visit the core exhibition but also take part in museum-led educational programming. For

---

88   Author's interview with Artur Markowski, Warsaw, April 2019.
89   Konrad Matyjaszek and Joanna Tokarska-Bakir, "History's History: Polish-Jewish Studies," *Studia Litteraria et Historica* 6 (2017): 2.
90   Konrad Matyjaszek, "'You need to speak Polish'": 7.
91   Ibid.: 1.

those who live too far to travel to Warsaw, POLIN has created a "Museum on Wheels," a fifty-square-meter space that travels to twenty towns a year. It focuses on visiting the eastern lands that were the prewar homes of the majority of traditional Jews. Through cooperation with local teachers and activists, the museum experience includes learning about the specific Jewish community that once inhabited and thrived in each of these small towns.[92]

As we have seen, American Jews and Polish Christians are involved in the laborious process of myth reconstruction. Each group began with a negative perception of the Other. American Jews have long held onto the "good Jew, bad Pole" narrative in order not only to unite Jewish secularists but also to expunge any hint of guilt from our past weak attempts to save Jewish lives during the Holocaust. After 1946, Polish communists silenced Jews' Holocaust suffering to elevate Polish suffering during World War II. The authorities complimented the erasure of this painful Jewish memory with the suppression of close to eight hundred years of the minority's presence in and contributions to Poland. It is against this silence that activists continue to fight, be it through independent commemorative projects, Polish-Jewish dialogue, school curriculums, museums, or academic research. While a few notable American Jewish organizations have contributed to this work, Jewish teen pilgrimage programs tend to exploit the status of the negative other that Poles hold in the American Jewish imagination.

Myth reconstruction began in earnest in Poland with the crumbling of the communist system. It was palpable during my 2005 and 2007 visits. But time and politics have not stood still. Polish activists haunted by Jan Gross's research on Jedwabne have continued to investigate Polish–Christian and Polish–Jewish relations during the Holocaust. However, many Poles have had difficulty reconciling the Polish myth of wartime heroism with the growing evidence of Polish betrayals of and violence against Jews searching for refuge during the Holocaust's last stage. Poles have grown tired of being assailed for past misdeeds. In response, some political actors have encouraged a backlash bursting with denial and deflection.

---

92 Author's interview with Zygmunt Stępiński, Warsaw, April 2019.

CHAPTER 20

Myth Reconstruction and the Backlash in Poland

During Solidarity, the opposition began the challenging task of national myth reconstruction. As part of that awakening, it opened up and peered into the history of Polish Jews. Some investigated specifically Jewish victimization during the Holocaust and even challenged the Polish response to the Jews' ghettoization and murder by the Germans. After the state transitioned from a communist imposed society to a democratic system of governance, interest in uncovering Poland's former Jewish life spread.

Although the opposition had carried out a bloodless negotiated revolution, unity was elusive. What had made this resistance successful was its comingling of disparate groups willing to look past former conflicts and ideological impasses to meet current needs. The inherent internal division further splintered over defining the future Polish state. Conflicts peaked when, for the sake of a nonviolent end to communism, the liberal opposition leaders' plan prevailed allowing former communist leaders from People's Poland to recast themselves into a social democratic party, the Democratic Left Union (Sojusz Lewicy Demokratycznej, SLD). Fissures deepened and spread to destabilize the fragile union between liberals and conservatives in the post-Solidarity camp.

In 1989 the opposition's objective was to move towards the West. The difficulty lay in agreeing not only to the participants, but also to the parameters. Opposition factions contended over which of the two authentically Polish models to replicate: the closed, traditional Catholic Piast State or the more open, multicultural and tolerant Polish-Lithuanian Commonwealth. In March 1999 Poland joined NATO. In April 2003 some 77% of Polish voters assented to enter the liberal European Union, which took effect May 2004.[1] It seemed the commonwealth model had won.

---

1   Peter S. Green, "Poles Vote Yes to Joining European Union," *New York Times*, June 9, 2003.

Since Poland's alignment with Brussels, however, right-wing conservative leaders have steadily focused public debate on the supposed loss of sovereignty in meeting EU membership conditions known as the "Copenhagen criteria." These include a stable democracy whose institutions guarantee the rule of law, human rights, respect for and protection of minorities, as well as a functioning market economy and acceptance of all EU legislation. The concept of following the dictates of the EU—an outside political behemoth—disturbs many Poles (as "outsiders" have always disturbed many Poles) who have just regained national independence. It is in this context of a Piast-Commonwealth tug-of-war that we should understand the current rise of Polish national populism.

In this chapter we will explore the rise of PiS, its nationalist populist message, and the tremendous backlash to the myth reconstruction work the Poles had been engaged with since the 1980s. Coupling rhetoric with ritual and topographical symbolism to bring its national narrative to the forefront, PiS has challenged documented Polish complicity in the Holocaust by refocusing the conversation onto the Polish Righteous. We will discover the social repercussions of these initiatives as well as Polish Holocaust researchers' battle with it.

The Rise of Polish National Populism

Prior to 2005, and despite the plethora of political party births, divisions, and deaths, voters consistently elected two central groups to power. The post-Solidarity camp first held power from 1989 to 1993 and again between 1997 and 2001, while the postcommunist SLD emerged in control from 1993 to 1997 and between September 2001 to 2005.

At the start, the identical twin brothers Lech and Jarosław Kaczyński, who had been aligned with Lech Wałęsa in Solidarity (but who fell out with him beginning in 1993), took government positions in the Third Republic of Poland.[2] In 2001, the Kaczyński brothers founded the Law and Justice Party (Prawo i Sprawiedliwość—PiS). Serving up Polish nationalism and xenophobia, PiS attracted disenchanted Poles who had suffered in the successful transition of Poland to a market economy. PiS spoke through a populist bullhorn in broad sweeping terms, offering oversimplified and demagogic solutions.[3] Not fitting into a neat political category, PiS took an aggressive, critical, and at times hostile

---

2   Britannica, s.v. "Lech Kaczyński," accessed February 24, 2022, https://www.britannica.com/biography/Lech-Kaczynski.
3   Antony Polonsky, "What Went Wrong?": 2 (forthcoming).

stand regarding EU policies and Poland's historical enemies: Germany and Russia. PiS railed against domestic corruption and advocated for strong central government while promoting populist policies such as tax cuts and a strong economic safety net.[4] PiS rhetoric pitted "the people" against "the liberal elite," arguing that the latter did not understand the common Pole's love of nation and Roman Catholic traditional "family values," and hindered conservative Poles' expression. Traditional and economically disenchanted Poles also fed off the political conspiracy theories and dramatic anti-immigration sentiments served up by the Kaczyński brothers.

In October 2005 voters elected a coalition containing PiS and two more openly right-radical groups, the League of Polish Families (LPR) and Self-Defense (Samoabrona). However, this national populist coalition was short-lived. Its erratic character and highly demagogic foreign policy antagonized both Russia and Germany—Poland's NATO and EU ally. In 2007 voters replaced it with a new centrist government, guided by Donald Tusk's Civic Platform Party (Platforma Obywatelska—PO).[5]

Established in 2001, PO soon emerged as Poland's main liberal organization. Its activists believed that they had dealt a death blow to the populist challenge in 2007. This false sense of security grew when voters elected PO candidate Bronisław Komorowski to the presidency in 2010. Despite the national sorrow surrounding the shocking 2010 airplane crash over Smolensk that killed the then president Lech Kaczyński, who had been running for a second term as the PiS candidate, the PO party prevailed.[6] Though PO won that contest, over time PiS won the crusade.

Lech Kaczyński's surviving twin brother, Jarosław, cultivated a mythology of martyrdom and aggrieved Polish nationalism around his sibling's death. Despite two independent inquiries blaming the crash on bad weather and human error, Jarosław Kaczyński has consistently presented the tragedy as a malicious political act.[7] PiS has claimed that Russian sabotage brought down the plane carrying Polish government officials to a Katyń memorial ceremony, and that the PO government deliberately covered it up. Though baseless, these accusations

---

4   Britannica, s.v. "Lech Kaczyński."
5   Polonsky, "What Went Wrong?": 2.
6   Ibid.: 4.
7   Marc Santora, "After a President's Shocking Death, a Suspicious Twin Reshapes a Nation," *New York Times*, June 16, 2018, https://www.nytimes.com/2018/06/16/world/europe/poland-kaczynski-smolensk.html.

gained a huge following and undermined the PO government.⁸ Amplifying his message for years, Jarosław Kaczyński gained national prestige not only for PiS, but also for his own more right-wing tendencies. In 2015, PiS candidate Andrzej Duda recaptured the presidency.

To sow anxiety among the populace, Jarosław Kaczyński attached his conspiratorial theory about Smolensk as a physical attack against Poland to the already existing negativity surrounding Poland's EU membership. Calling it a moral attack on the nation, PiS claimed that one sign that EU liberalism had overrun the country was the growing nation-wide acceptance of LGBTQ rights. Outraged, PiS asserted that LGBTQ individuals threatened "Polish family values" as they called into question traditional Church definitions of family. Thus, from a PiS perspective, to protest LGBTQ communities in Poland symbolizes a battle against the big bad European Union over traditional Polish values and national sovereignty. In October 2015, PiS won a decided majority in the Sejm and formed the first single-party government since the fall of communism. The October 2019 election secured the party a parliamentary majority and the people re-elected Duda as president in June 2020.

PiS and the Holocaust

For PiS, another symbol of the EU's stranglehold on Poland is its insistence on highlighting the Jewish Holocaust. During the country's initial return to the West, Poles discovered the immense role the Holocaust and unique Jewish suffering have played in Western memory: indeed, in a text formally adopted by the European Parliament one reads that "the Holocaust has been seared on the consciousness of Europe."⁹ This collective European governing body not only admonishes "European citizens to remember and condemn the enormous horror and tragedy of the Holocaust" but also encourages member states to acknowledge "the disturbing rise in anti-semitism, and especially anti-semitic incidents in Europe."¹⁰

Prior to PiS's ascent, the Polish classroom had opened up to teach the Holocaust and Jedwabne, aligning not only with EU policy on history, but also

---

8   Polonsky, "What Went Wrong?": 4.
9   *European Parliament resolution on remembrance of the Holocaust, antisemitism, and racism*, 27 January 2005, https://www.europarl.europa.eu/doceo/document/TA-6-2005-0018_EN.html.
10 Ibid.

with Polish liberal ideology that called for a reckoning with the troubling parts of the national past. Polish liberals welcomed this myth reconstruction process as necessary for building a pluralistic, outward looking, and tolerant polity.[11] For several years Poles placed Jedwabne at the heart of the historical discourse, allowing passersby not only to see it, but also to observe the nation's changing identity. To the Poles' credit, a large portion of the population took part in the Jedwabne debate and confronted the dark past. Indeed, the debate over Jedwabne proved the most serious, protracted, and profound national discussion on Polish-Jewish relations since the war.[12]

Yet for those Poles who align with the national populist surge and who were taught anticommunist history (which included Żydokomuna and the erasure of the Jewish-Polish past), this global embrace of Jews' unparalleled victimhood challenged their own collective identity. Poles for whom the depiction as the most victimized nation—as the Christ of all nations—is paramount, resent the constant reminders of the Jewish Holocaust. They fear it relativizes their own suffering and will lead to the loss of their own specific stories, memories, and identity.

National populist resistance to the EU's Holocaust policies only increased when scholars carefully unearthed facts that challenged the memory of Polish heroics and honor during World War II. It was not by chance that the Kaczyńskis founded PiS following the Jedwabne revelation. The party's first success, in 2005, came just after the Institute of National Remembrance (Instytut Pamięci Narodowej—IPN) 2003 assertion that Jedwabne was not an anomaly, but rather a pattern of regional Polish wartime brutalization discovered in numerous locales. PiS won by a landslide in 2015 after Polish scholars uncovered Poles' complicity in Nazi Jew hunts. Publications, including Jan Grabowski's 2013 *The Hunt for the Jews*, set the stage for PiS to counter Poles' burning shame and intensified international scrutiny. Discoveries by Polish historians crushed the people's morale. Even people who at first accepted the evidence of Gross, Grabowski, Engelking, and others soon grew tired of the constant international judgment. Katarzyna Person notes that during purely domestic debates concerning Jedwabne, Poles were still able to hold onto wartime stories of their own suffering. But when the debate entered the international arena, the stakes grew enormous. The issue of national shame grossly overshadowed any sense of Polish suffering during the war.[13]

---

11 Polonsky, "What Went Wrong?": 5.
12 Ibid.: 7.
13 Author's interview with Katarzyna Person, Warsaw, April 2019.

Polish national populists both fed and feasted on the agonizing identity crisis that split the populace. People grew defensive and national populists raced to publicly maintain Polish honor.[14] They did so by radically shifting the understanding of history away from the concept that "[h]istory is the study of change over time, and it covers all aspects of human society."[15] For PiS, history stands still. It is "the biography of the national community and the source of the traditions and values that hold everything together."[16] For PiS, history is not the process of studying the past to reveal new insights. Rather, it is the unchanging foundation of national pride. Thus, ironically, for PiS Jedwabne and the debate surrounding it was, in fact, an attack on the country. The Law and Justice Party took power in part due to the national populist backlash against this "liberal" myth reconstruction.

Once in power, PiS sought to halt the memory bleed. In a defensive posture, PiS closed off the classroom to discussion of Polish pogroms and Poles aiding the Nazis in Jew hunts. Early on, the radical right-wing coalition introduced a so-called historical policy (polityka historyczna), which condemns critical patriotism and pedagogy of shame as unpatriotic. Twisting the past through the well-worn conspiracy theory of Żydokomuna, PiS promoted right-wing Polish historians who worked within anticommunist intellectual frameworks. These writers contend that though Poles murdered Jews in Jedwabne and elsewhere, they did so to protect the nation from the hidden enemy, the "Jew-Bolshevik." Anna Zawadzka argues that through this anticommunist outlook, which defines any Polish citizen engaged in communism as "non-Polish," right-wing Polish historians, such as Marek Jan Chodakiewicz and Sebastian Bojemski, have fashioned generally accepted beliefs into so-called facts.[17] Right-wing historians accept and have popularized the stereotype that Jews gravitated en masse to communism due to their disloyal DNA. Thus, Jews in general threatened Poland, and Poles rightly defended themselves against the Jewish collective.

It is one thing to understand that people acted against Jews because they believed the ingrained Żydokomuna stereotype running rampant at the time; it is another thing entirely for historians to assign truth to that very stereotype.

---

14 Ibid.
15 See "What Is History?," Valdosta State University, accessed August 22, 2023, https://www.valdosta.edu/history/documents/what-is-history.pdf.
16 Brian Porter-Szűcs, "Meritocracy and Community in Twenty-First-Century Poland," *Shofar: An Interdisciplinary Journal of Jewish Studies* 37, no. 1 (Spring 2019): 87.
17 Anna Zawadzka, "Żydokomuna: The Construction of the Insult," in *World War II and Two Occupations: Dilemmas of Polish Memory*, ed. Anna Wolff-Powęska and Piotr Forecki (Frankfurt am Main: Peter Lang, 2016), 250.

In positing that Polish antisemitic behavior reacted to the supposed real threat that "Commie Jews" posed to Polish sovereignty, right-wing Polish historiography contends that those Poles who murdered Jews did so in the name of state survival and not due to Polish antisemitism. Thus, in assessing Jedwabne, anticommunist historians shift blame to the victims for their own demise.[18]

PiS's return to power in 2015 allowed President Andrzej Duda and the PiS-dominated Sejm to enforce this historical policy with full force, countering evidence-based critical analysis of Polish society during the Holocaust. It has promoted nationalists to lead institutions like the IPN, which in 2003 verified Jan Gross's findings and discovered a regional pattern of brutality against Jews. Once again under PiS control, in 2016 the IPN redefined the goal of historical study as follows:

> Historical policy refers to the interpretation of facts, lives, and events and is assessed according to the interests of the society and the nation, as an element that has a long-range character and constitutes the foundation of state policies. Historical policy is a type of history that serves to shape the historical consciousness of society, including economic and territorial consciousness, as well as to strengthen public discourse about the past in the direction of nurturing national bonds regardless of the momentary policies of the state.[19]

Historical policy is a theory of history: what we learn from the past must secure the national collective bond.

PiS and Holocaust Education

Despite some exemplary primary and secondary education efforts to introduce Poles to the large Jewish population that once inhabited the same land, the national public school curriculum resists teaching about the Jewish past. It discards any discussion of Polish-Jewish relations that might mention antisemitism in its economic, educational, religious, political, and violent iterations. It remains an uphill struggle to change the nation-wide curriculum to include programs on minorities in Poland, their histories and cultures. The social anthropologist and

---

18 Ibid., 258.
19 Quoted in Porter-Szücs, "Meritocracy and Community in Twenty-First-Century Poland": 87.

POLIN Museum Temporary Exhibition Manager Joanna Fikus explained to me that most teaching about minorities in Polish classrooms was phased out by 2019.[20] The work proven to dispel children's stereotyping of minorities has been put aside by most Polish educators.

Andrzej Folwarczny, the Forum for Dialogue founder, explained that the problems stem from not only a lack of teacher interest in Poland's multicultural past, but also its absence from public school curriculums. Thus, a vicious cycle ensues, with most Polish history teachers understanding their subject through a nationalist prism. Researchers have discovered that

> [m]ost define history in nationalist terms and regard nationalist representations of the past as natural and taken for granted. Teachers tend to reproduce the dominant structures of collective memory by using history lessons to nurture their pupils' attachment to the Polish nation and nation state. [. . .] teachers see their role primarily in terms of imposing the dominant structures of collective memory on the pupils.[21]

Indeed, the current PiS-directed Ministry of Education focuses the core history curriculum on the development of students' understanding of national identity and loyalty to the nation. Were the curriculum to provide students with a multicultural education to begin with, their generation would later produce history teachers interested not only in Polish suffering, but also in minority victimhood. However, given the current belief that students need more education in "patriotism"—a popular Polish and American euphemism for nationalism—it follows that teachers see less need to mention, let alone study, the histories of minorities.[22]

In an interview about his new school curriculum, and its turn away from European history, Przemysław Czarnek, the Polish minister of education stated: "If Poles do not know their past, are not tied to their identity, Poland will not develop naturally."[23] He added that Poles should learn more about Poland than

---

20 Author's interview with Joanna Fikus, Warsaw, April 2019.
21 Krzysztof Jaskulowski, Piotr Majewski, and Adrianna Surmak, "Teaching the Nation. History and Nationalism in Polish School History Education," *British Journal of Sociology of Education* 39 (2017): 2.
22 Ibid.: 9.
23 Derek Scally, "Poland's New History Syllabus to Frame EU as an 'Unlawful Entity': Ruling Party Accused of Pushing Nationalist Identity Politics with 'New Deal' Programme," *Irish Times*, May 2020, 2021, https://www.irishtimes.com/news/world/europe/poland-s-new-history-syllabus-to-frame-eu-as-an-unlawful-entity-1.4570798.

Europe in general, "so that we can feel pride that we are Poles."[24] This drive to develop pride in Polish identity also undergirds the commission Czarnek has established to set out guidelines for teaching the Holocaust in schools. It features apologist and populist scholars, such as Jan Żaryn and Maciej Korjuć, and excludes critical scholars from the Polish Center for Holocaust Research.[25]

PiS and Polish Righteousness

In its battle for Poland's identity and honor, the PiS-led government has also buried Poles' complicity in the destruction of Polish Jews (as we have seen in Jedwabne and the Jew hunt), by inundating society with images of the victimized and heroic Pole. Its actions have included foregrounding the "disavowed soldiers" (Żołnierze wyklęci—Polish anticommunist military units repudiated by the regime from 1945 to 1963),[26] branding Polish Righteousness as normative behavior vis-à-vis Jews, and coopting former Jewish physical space for the Polish nationalist conservative narrative.

PiS has masked the troubling aspects of Polish-Jewish relations during the Holocaust by focusing on Poles who saved Jews. In this way, the government deflects attention from evidence that offers alternative views: numerous *szmalcowniks*—blackmailers—betrayed those very same Righteous Poles, leading them and their Jewish charges to their deaths. We see this tactic in the new museum dedicated to the Ulma family. It is not a question of worthiness. Józef and Wiktoria Ulma, who lived on the outskirts of Markowa, deserve great praise: they risked their lives and those of their six young children when they provided long-term shelter to eight Jewish members of the Szall and Goldman families. After a Polish policeman denounced the Ulma family to the Nazis, Józef, his pregnant wife, their six children, and the hidden Jews were killed.

In implementing historical policy, PiS magnifies the Polish Righteous and ignores the Polish traitor. PiS has mythologized the Righteous into normative Polish actions during the Holocaust. Critics charge that the museum's narrative pays disproportionate attention to examples of rescue while obfuscating the fact that most Poles were bystanders and many cooperated with the occupiers. Michał Bilewicz, the director of the Center for Research on Prejudice at the

---

24 Ibid.
25 Author's email correspondence with Antony Polonsky, January 12, 2022.
26 Michlic, "'At the Crossroads': Jedwabne and Polish Historiography of the Holocaust": 299–301.

University of Warsaw, holds that the museum has been commandeered for political purposes—to contest the image of the complicit Pole found in Jedwabne and the Jew hunt. He argues there is "a reason all the guests of the Ministry of Foreign Affairs are now sent to Markowa."[27]

At the same time, it is significant that the number of Righteous recognized by Yad Vashem (Israel's Holocaust Museum) does not reflect the full extent of help given by non-Jewish Poles to Jews during the Holocaust. Rather, the number reflects only those for whom a rescued Jew has provided Yad Vashem with documentary proof of worthiness. Such documentation includes photos, diaries, or letters that establish that the Polish individual(s) rescued Jews, without necessitating material benefit or sexual payment. Emil Jeżowski, who worked for the Israeli embassy in Poland, organized the ceremonies honoring the Polish Righteous recognized by Yad Vashem.[28] For Jeżowski, "this medal is for the Righteous of the righteous. It does not mean what other Poles did to save Jews was not honorable. But they don't merit the medal that says they are heroes."[29] Jeżowski empathizes with the difficulty some Polish families have in establishing their status with Yad Vashem: "These are hard issues that are frustrating for the families."[30] But without Jewish testimony, it is unclear what the relationship between the rescuer and the rescued "really looked like."[31]

The number of Righteous has also been limited because requests must come from Jewish survivors. Some survivors could not "overcome the difficulty of grappling with the painful past and didn't come forward."[32] Others were not aware of the program or could not apply due to living behind the Iron Curtain. Some survivors were children and have no recall of required details. Still others died before they could proceed with the request.[33] Some Poles attempted to save Jews, but both parties were killed in the war and no documentation of their heroism remains. Jeżowski notes that some Polish families who have been

---

27 Judy Maltz, "Why People Are Boycotting a Museum Dedicated to Poles Who Saved Jews," *Haaretz*, May 8, 2018, https://www.haaretz.com/world-news/europe/.premium.MAGAZINE-why-people-are-boycotting-a-museum-dedicated-to-poles-who-saved-jews-1.6070200.
28 In 2017, Yad Vashem bestowed forty-three medals. In 2018, almost thirty were bestowed, and as of May 2019 about twenty. Most of these medals were given to relatives of the Righteous because most have died. See author's interview with Emil Jeżowski, Warsaw, March 2019.
29 Ibid.
30 Ibid.
31 Ibid.
32 Ibid.
33 See https://yadvashem.org.

recognized by the Polish government "will never be able to be recognized by Yad Vashem . . . [yet] should be."³⁴ Thus, the argument advanced by the nationalist camp that more Poles should be counted among the Righteous has much merit.

Yet Jeżowski wrestles with the surge in government propaganda concerning the "Polish Righteous" since PiS took office in 2015. While in the past the Polish government gave its own medal to recipients of the Yad Vashem Righteous among the Nations award, today it bestows the designation of "Polish Righteous" to people who did not receive that title from Yad Vashem. While "the Polish government has all the right to recognize their own Righteous, [. . .] sometimes it has a political context."³⁵ For example, the topic of the Polish Righteous gets tremendous coverage in the government-run media. Michał Bilewicz's argues that the average Pole believes that 49% of Poles alive during the war rescued Jews.³⁶ This fantasy means that millions were Righteous.

To further shift memory towards the "Righteous Pole" and away from Jedwabne and Polish collaboration in Jew hunts, the nationalist Right has opened a new museum, the Chapel of Memory of Rescuers in Toruń. Headed by Radio Maryja's Father Rydzyk, the museum normalizes righteousness to the point where people lose sight of the traumatic context that brought Yad Vashem to honor as Righteous among the Nations the more than 6,992 Poles who aided Jews. The museum's website is telling. It opens with a short paragraph describing Nazi anti-Jewish policies—armbands, ghettoization, the confiscation of property, labor camps, and extermination. Immediately following this quick synopsis, we read that "the Government of the Republic of Poland in exile as well as the Polish Underground State took intensive measures to save the endangered Jewish community."³⁷ Certainly, I do not deny this statement. As we have already seen, a number of actors in both institutions worked for the benefit of the Jews. However, this quick presentation exaggerates Polish help. This short text suggests (through what is left unsaid) that it was Polish institutions in their entirety, and not simply a small number of people within them, that actively worked to rescue the Jews.

It is clear by reading the introduction to its website that the intention behind the museum is to project to the world an image of Poles very different from the one in

---

34   Author's interview with Emil Jeżowski, Warsaw, March 2019.
35   Ibid.
36   Maltz, "Why People Are Boycotting a Museum Dedicated to Poles Who Saved Jews."
37   See "The Chapel of Remembrance," accessed August 31, 2023, https://www.kaplica-pamieci.pl.

Jan Gross's *Neighbors*.[38] The museum's website responds to Gross and other historians without naming them when it states that the "many false accusations against the Polish nation—allegedly partly responsible for the tragedy of the Holocaust—can be refuted by showing the facts."[39] What are these facts that counter the claim of Polish complicity? The website cites Yad Vashem's own data. The fact that Poland's share of the Righteous among the Nations constitutes 25% of the twenty-six thousand individuals designated as such supposedly proves not only the Polish nation's righteousness, but also the impossibility of Gross's and others' assertions that numerous Poles dealt brutally with Jews seeking safety from the Nazis.

It is obvious to me, however, that the high percentage of Poles among the Righteous does not exclude the possibility of collaboration and barbarism. In one nation, there exist simultaneously those who seek to help and those who seek to harm. Not only does a nation contain both types of individuals, but so too does every individual exhibit both good and bad impulses, particularly during times of war.

PiS and Polish right-wing historians argue that any Poles who killed Jews stood on the fringes of society, while those who aided and saved Jews were the norm. In "proving" that Poles were Righteous, nationalist right-wing ideologues ignore, and thereby forget, that history is complex. Critics have argued that Polish government bodies have elevated people to heroic heights without documentary proof and witness testimony, and, as result, have not given a thought to people's motives. Did Poles aid Jews out of a sense of moral obligation? Or did they help in exchange for money or sex? Were some Polish saviors also abusers or even killers?[40] These questions remain important for an honest and critical assessment of the Polish Righteous.

PiS and the Pilecki Institute

Controversy has swirled around the appointment of Magdalena Gawin—known for her extreme ethno-nationalist views—as the director of the government-funded Pilecki Institute. Since Gawin's appointment, the Pilecki Institute, which

---

38 Once PiS came into power in 2005, the IPN embraced the party's historical policy and began work on a project entitled "Poles Saving Jews." This project led to building the Chapel of Memory of Rescuers.
39 See "The Chapel of Remembrance."
40 Michlic, "'At the Crossroads': Jedwabne and Polish Historiography of the Holocaust": 301–304.

researches the consequences of the Nazi and Soviet regimes on Poles, has grown more politicized and has started to peddle an apologist agenda. We see this shift in the program titled "Called by Name," which launched in 2019. Its purpose is to recover stories of Poles who were killed while trying to save Jews during the Holocaust. It is extremely commendable to remember people who risked themselves and their loved ones to help Jews. And it is important to retrieve stories that have been lost over the decades (many because the heroes kept their heads down due to the political climate). The project has placed small boulders in public squares, each of which bear a commemorative plaque inscribed with the name of a hero. According to the institute's website, each boulder is "a permanent sign of remembrance of the heroes in the public space where tragic events took place."[41] The program also aims to make sure that "a broad information campaign serves to introduce the fate of the 'Called by Name' to the collective memory in Poland and around the world."[42]

The project's beguiling and subtle neglect of historical context troubles many Polish historians, including Jan Grabowski and Adam Leszczyński. The recent ceremony honoring Jan Maletka in the village of Treblinka illustrates this problem. According to researchers, in 1942 the Nazis murdered a twenty-one-year-old Polish railroad worker for giving water to a Jew who was dying of thirst while locked in a cattle car just outside the Treblinka death camp. The controversy lies in what is presented for public consumption and what is suppressed. While "the project highlights the realities of the ruthless German occupation policy in Poland, which destroyed all ties of solidarity between Poles and Jews and punished the slightest human gesture of compassion with death,"[43] important contextual information is withheld because only the Germans are blamed for poor relations. There is no admission that criminal acts were perpetrated by Poles against Jews.

Magdalena Gawin, the then Polish deputy minister of culture and national heritage, presided over the Jan Maletka ceremony. Although she highlighted Maletka's courage, compassion, and strength of character in the face of Nazi anti-Jewish brutality, Gawin overlooked aspects of the context that actually accentuate his heroism. Individuals who risked their lives and acted according to their moral convictions should be honored. It is likely that many contemplated helping Jews, but did nothing out of fear of getting caught. In fact, they were

---

41 "Called by Name," Instytut Pileckiego, accessed February 25, 2022, https://instytutpileckiego.pl/en/zawolani-po-imieniu.
42 Ibid.
43 Ibid.

frightened not only because Nazi laws banned helping Jews, but also because of the Polish reaction to such actions. As discussed in earlier chapters, prewar Polish antisemitism encouraged by Endecja painted Jews as Poland's main enemy. The Żydokomuna conspiracy theory—that Jews were traitors responsible for the Soviet occupation—added oxygen to this perception during the war, in part due to the already broad acceptance of Endecja in the east. A troubling number of Poles denounced both fleeing Jews and fellow Poles who aided them in order to gain personal material profit. And some Poles who helped did so only in exchange for payment.

We see this dangerous contextual backdrop in Maletka's own situation. Jewish survivor testimony from Treblinka

> recalled groups of Polish railway workers and Polish youths who stood close to the cattle cars ready to hand over water—in exchange for gold or cash. In their oral histories and written accounts, survivors described how they were met not with compassion, but with greed. [. . .] Abram Jakub Krzepicki remembered that people in the wagon were dying of thirst. He described terrible scenes of Jews pleading with the workers, handing over fistfuls of money for a mere half cup of water.[44]

It is this very context that makes Maletka's quiet act of bravery an extraordinary one. It is the juxtaposition of his exceptional behavior with the crowd's base tendencies that brings understanding of Maletka's heroic act.

In a written response to critics who charged that the project misrepresents the nuances involved in Polish aid to Jews, Wojciech Kozłowski defended the program's lack of context:

> the "Called by Name" project does not seek to address matters concerning the scale of Polish assistance to Jews; it is devoted exclusively to those individuals who gave aid and who died. This is the fundamental difference.
>
> It is impossible to understand how the existence of criminal elements, who profit[ed] from the tragedy faced by the Jewish population, might cause the "Called by Name" project to be associated with the falsification of history via a restoration of the

---

44 Jan Grabowski, "The New Wave of Holocaust Revisionism," *New York Times*, January 29, 2022, 2, https://www.nytimes.com/2022/01/29/opinion/holocaust-poland-europe.html.

memory of local heroes—residents of small towns and villages—about whom very few people knew anything until now.

If the iniquity of a few precluded respect for the heroism of others, then there could be no commemoration of Home Army soldiers in Warsaw, because Gestapo agents also existed; there would be no commemoration of activists of the democratic opposition in the Polish People's Republic, because there were agents of the Ministry of Public Security working parallel to them.[45]

This rationale is misleading. For it is the very juxtaposition of opposition with complicity that allows for a greater understanding of the heroism involved in taking the physically dangerous moral stand to act against the occupier's agenda. Based on this flawed argument, it follows that the project managers excluded this information simply because they deemed it muddied the waters. They wished to communicate the simple message that individual honorable deeds bear witness to Polish national heroism.

The Polish Nationalist Imprint on Jewish Space: Under Communism

The commemorative boulders placed by the "Called by Name" project are the more recent attempts to cement a memory within the Polish public sphere. In this land which has undergone extreme political changes, including war and occupation, symbolic topography plays a crucial role in the contest for memory. This battle to direct the narrative has played out in key public spaces that had been central Jewish locations during World War II. An iconic location within the boundaries of the extinguished Warsaw Ghetto, the courtyard outside of the POLIN Museum of the History of Polish Jews has long been such a battleground.

Since the end of the war, Jews have recognized and marked this location as symbolic of Jewish wartime martyrdom and heroism. In 1946, the Central Committee of Polish Jews commemorated the Jewish Fighting Organization that led the Warsaw Ghetto Uprising by placing a subtle sandstone relief at a central

---

45 Wojciech Kozłowski, "Jan Maletka Deserves Commemoration. A Response to Adam Leszczyński," The Pilecki Institute, accessed February 25, 2022, https://instytutpileckiego.pl/en/zawolani-po-imieniu.

location of the former ghetto. (This space would later be turned into a public square.) The tribute looks like the entrance to a bunker or sewer, where most of the Jewish insurgents died. Two years later, at the nearby corner of Zamenhoff and Gesia Streets (the latter renamed M. Anielewicz Street), the Warsaw Jewish Committee placed Nathan Rapoport's mammoth free-standing stone wall in the Warsaw Ghetto rubble. The monument resembles not only an enormous tombstone and the ghetto wall that divided Christian Poles from Jewish Poles, but also the Western Wall in Jerusalem.[46] With this edifice, Rapoport depicts a two-part simplified version of the Jews' wartime experience. On one side, from right to left trudge deported and wretched diaspora Jews. On the other side, strong, defiant, and heroic figures rise from swirling ghetto flames.[47]

Since its placement, the monument has elicited both reverence and resentment. Polish and non-Polish Jews, as well as Polish Christians, gather there formally or spontaneously in prayer; they lay flowers and stones and find inspiration. Without their own monument to Polish heroism during the war, Solidarity leaders saw in Rapoport's figures a universal symbol of resistance to the communist government. At the same time, when Christian Poles looked at this massive memorial to Jewish heroism, many felt a deep bitterness.[48] Indeed, only in 1989 did the government unveil a monument to the 1944 Polish Warsaw Uprising.

As Solidarity gathered around the Ghetto Fighters' Monument in the 1980s the communist regime fought back. Its leadership sought to break Solidarity's link with the monument's universal message of resistance. James E. Young notes that "the government seems to recognize, the memorial space, if left vacant, will be filled by someone else's meaning, some memory other than theirs."[49] Thus, the square encircling the Ghetto Fighters' Monument became "both a dangerous and necessary memorial space for the state."[50]

But the two opposing sides ended up cooperating, ironically, in an effort to counter the negative international attention on Poland after the 1985 cinematic release of Claude Lanzman's *Shoah*. Reacting to the horrifying portrayal of Poles as antisemitic collaborators in Hitler's destruction of Polish Jewry, they created the Memorial Route of Jewish Martyrdom and Struggle. The twenty stones that bear inscriptions in Polish and Hebrew mark Jewish individuals and important

---

46 Young, "The Biography of a Memorial Icon: Nathan Rapoport's Warsaw Ghetto Monument," 85.
47 Ibid., 90.
48 Ibid.
49 Ibid., 93.
50 Ibid.

cultural places. Concurrently, to recast Polish-Jewish relations during the war within a more positive light, "they emphasize the theme of Polish aid to the Jews and provide information suggesting that the myth of the Polish-Jewish brotherhood of arms was a reality."[51]

Four of these large markers surround the Ghetto Fighters' Monument. One stone block commemorates Emmanuel Ringelblum, the founder of the underground Warsaw Ghetto Oyneg Shabbos Archive (Oneg Shabbat). It highlights that Poles hid him from the beginning of 1943 and were eventually killed with him on March 10, 1944.[52] Next to another large stone block (now by the entrance to the POLIN Museum) is a large oak tree. The inscription on the stone reads "Tree of Common Memory: [dedicated] to the Polish Jews murdered in 1939–1945 by the German invaders and the Poles who died rescuing the Jews."[53] As I have argued already, the Polish aid offered to these Jewish martyrs and heroes should be recognized. The problem here, however, is the lack of nuance—the neglect of the unusual nature of such expressions of unity.

The Polish Nationalist Imprint on Jewish Space: Under Twenty-First-Century Democracy

Attempts to present Polish-Jewish relations in a positive light have continued into the twenty-first century as Poles memorialize past Polish heroism and victimization. Because many of these markers have been placed in formerly Jewish spaces where important events in the Holocaust occurred, some critics contend that they aim to uplift Poles at the expense of Jewish memory and presence. The Polish cultural anthropologist Elżbieta Janicka proposes that through topographic symbolism the Polish government has filled what was once a Jewish public square with a Polish nationalist narrative of extreme Polish Righteousness and victimhood. Though many examples exist, due to limited space we will look in detail at only two of these spaces.

The first space is the Rapoport Ghetto Fighters' Monument, which was erected in what is now the courtyard for the POLIN Museum of the History of Polish Jews. The museum's core exhibition has itself been criticized for a lack of

---

51 Elżbieta Janicka, "The Square of Polish Innocence: POLIN Museum of the History of Polish Jews in Warsaw and Its Symbolic Topography," *East European Jewish Affairs* 45, nos. 2–3 (2015): 201.
52 Ibid.: 202.
53 Ibid.: 203.

easily accessible information about interwar Polish antisemitism. The courtyard deepens that silence. Studding it with even more monuments and markers to daring Poles who risked their lives to save Jews during the Holocaust, the government has continued to impose a narrative of general Polish wartime support for the Jews and opposition to the Final Solution. Yet because the courtyard is just outside the museum and shares space with the Rapoport monument, visitors may easily assume this message is part of a Jewish narrative.

After announcing the decision to build the POLIN Museum, the Polish government built new memorials to preemptively clarify the Polish narrative in what would become an even more well-known Jewish space. In its posturing, the Polish government chose to cement in popular memory that moment in 1970 when the visiting West German chancellor Willy Brandt stood before the Ghetto Fighters' Monument and knelt before it in a show of German responsibility and remorse for the Holocaust. The Willy Brandt Monument reminds the world that the Nazis organized the destruction of European Jewry. For Poles, it also symbolizes the country's absolute innocence of any complicity. It is telling that only after it knew the museum would be built did the government feel a need to assert this innocence.[54] The marker works, then, to suppress the Jewish narrative.

At the grand opening of the museum, government representatives dedicated a pathway leading from a parking lot to the museum entrance to Irena Sendler, a Righteous among the Nations. An incredibly courageous Polish Christian woman, Sendler rescued 2,500 children from the Warsaw Ghetto. I do not question embracing Sendler's heroism. I question the timing of it and the failure to place her act in context. Certainly, Jews around the world should know about her bravery. However, it is odd that hers is the first name that visitors to a museum dedicated to the history of Jews in Poland see. Would it not be more appropriate at this moment and in this Jewish space for the government to commemorate a Polish Jew?

I suggest the need for more nuanced commemorative action. To recognize in a lasting monument sorrow over Poles who betrayed Jews seeking aid and Poles who were strong enough to provide it; the monument would give the context necessary to enrich knowledge about the Polish Righteous. Without context, visitors to the museum's courtyard understand

> Polish solidarity with the Jews as a fact, and [that] it stood the test of terror and death brought by the Germans. Such a version of events is drastically different from the actual facts (although it

---

54 Ibid..

does not undermine the veracity of the few and isolated exceptions). This is a narrative pattern characteristic of the dominant Polish narrative.[55]

Janicka argues that this narrative pattern has been in place since 1963 and has secured its continuing role in Polish education and the politics of memory within the independent Third Republic of Poland.

The Polish Nationalist Imprint on Jewish Space: Muranowski Square

A second example of the Polish suppression of the Jewish narrative by the Polish nationalist narrative is found in the placement of the Monument to the Fallen and Murdered in the East. This important memorial to the roughly three hundred thousand Poles who suffered through Soviet deportation rests at that location in the Warsaw Ghetto where Nalewki Street joined Muranowski Square. During the Warsaw Ghetto Uprising, Muranowski Square was one of three major points of determined Jewish resistance. Although a small plexiglass plaque—transparent and hard to locate—marks the Jews' heroism, it is easily overlooked. In a case of arbitrary assignment, and commemorating events unrelated to the place, the imposing Monument to the Fallen and Murdered in the East dominates the iconic Jewish square.

The dramatic structure, telling the important story of Polish victimization at the hands of the Soviets, includes railroad ties each inscribed with names of Polish deportation and execution sites. Katyń's inscription rests among them. A mound lies at the end of the ominous track. Raised on top stands a railroad car overflowing with large crosses, crammed together, spilling up and out from the car's confines. If one looks closely on the opposite side of the railway car, one can find a few other religious symbols, including some Orthodox crosses, a Tatar Muslim symbol with a five-armed star and half-moon, and a Jewish tombstone. However, "in the common consciousness [...] the monument functions as a car of crosses and is called the Golgotha of the East. This notion is given on postcards, tourist guides, websites, and children's drawings."[56] This monument pays tribute to the accepted motif of Poland as the Christ of all nations.

---

55 Ibid.: 210.
56 Elżbieta Janicka, "Memory and Identity in the Former Warsaw Ghetto Area" (trans, J. Dziubińska), *Herito* 13 (2013): 71.

Poles gather here annually to mark the Katyń massacre. Dressed in long wartime winter wool coats designating officer status, men line up next to each other in between the railroad ties, facing the cattle car with hands bound behind their backs. Church and government leaders preside over the Catholic ceremony as onlookers stand nearby dressed in 1940s clothing. That between 438 and seven hundred Jewish officers serving in the Polish army were also murdered in Katyń remains ignored in the Polish consciousness.

Interestingly, Poles recognize the anniversary of Katyń as the day they *learned* about the carnage, that is, April 13, 1943, rather than the date the massacre actually took place in 1940. The Germans chose to inform Poles about Katyń in 1943 to widen the chasm between Poles and Warsaw's walled-in Jews. With propaganda posters depicting the Soviets as fat menacing Jews with grotesque large noses, the Germans blamed the "Bolshevik-Jews" for carrying out this gruesome massacre. Encouraging hatred of the Jews, the Nazis prepared Poles to accept the final liquidation of the Warsaw Ghetto, which the Germans would begin the following week, April 19, 1943. Indeed, blaming "Bolshevik-Jews" for the deaths of thousands of Poles "provided rationalization and created a moral alibi for the crimes against Jews."[57]

Critics argue that through the 2007 PiS government's acceptance of April 13, 1943 as the Katyń anniversary, and by staging the Katyń memorialization within the Warsaw Ghetto boundaries, Poles have set themselves up to appropriate Jewish time and space. The date also reinvigorates the German spread of Żydokomuna, that Bolshevik-Jews were responsible for Poles' terror and heartache. Additionally, some find it troubling that this monument is situated on the same street as the Umschlagplatz Memorial, where some 350,000 Jews boarded trains that carried them to their deaths. They have argued that by choosing this arbitrary site, the Polish leadership has established an equality between the Nazis' crimes against the Jews and the Soviet crimes against the Poles. A double genocide theory emerges through this symbolic topography and the equation of the two totalitarian regimes.[58] It is a symptom of the victimization contest in which so many on both sides participate.

Through its historical policy and physical memorialization programs, PiS has undermined the Jews' victimhood and the Jedwabne humiliation with a reenergized return to Polish suffering and a resurgence of Polish righteousness. Jan Grabowski recognizes in it

---

57 Ibid.: 78.
58 Ibid.: 73.

a dangerous new threat that is spreading rapidly today in Eastern Europe: Holocaust distortion. A false equivalence of victimization is but one hallmark of the new Polish historical revisionism. Another hallmark is a state-sponsored effort that downplays antisemitic terror at the hands of the Poles, though such incidents are well documented in the historical record.[59]

Historical memory has become ground zero in Poland's internal debate over its identity and honor.

POLIN Challenges the Nationalist Narrative

While Polish nationalist messaging has taken over the public square, within its building POLIN has waged a defiant battle to give voice to the Polish Jewish experience. POLIN's temporary exhibitions play a crucial role in expanding the discourse on the subject. Its 2017 exhibit entitled "Blood: Unifying and Dividing" examined the meaning of blood as a religious identifier in both Judaism and Christianity, the blood libel accusation as a Church weapon in the guise of protection, and the horrific twentieth-century consequences of blood as a central factor of belonging. It ended by asking visitors to question the concept of identity on both a global and personal level: What creates my identity if it is not blood?[60]

The temporary exhibit "March 1968 and Its Aftermath" opened on the fiftieth anniversary of the brutal and aggressive antisemitic campaign in the Polish People's Republic. In 2018 visitors were challenged to understand "March '68" through the experience of Poland's Jews. The Polish communist government fired thousands of Poles of Jewish origin from their posts and expelled roughly fifteen thousand on the grounds that they were *Zionists*, who had supposedly been colluding with the enemy Israeli state. Its curators recounted not only the facts but also the experienced emotions felt by those "Jews by force" who left, as well as those who remained behind. It exposed the government's hate speech and the often ignored role of the million or so Poles who embraced it.

The museum asked, "What is the role of language in society?" Delving into that question, the exhibition juxtaposed antisemitic quotes from Roman Dmowski's prewar nationalist Endecja and Gomułka's and Moczar's 1968 antisemitic

---

59   Grabowski, "The New Wave of Holocaust Revisionism," 1.
60   Author's interview with Joanna Fikus, Warsaw, April 2019.

nationalist-communist rhetoric with quotes from nationalist right-wing political leaders in the 2018 Third Polish Republic. This juxtaposition made clear that current rhetoric mirrors antisemitic speech from both the 1930s and March '68. The exhibit asked its viewers: Is language relevant to society's direction? Is the language I choose important?[61]

Joanna Fikus, POLIN's temporary exhibition manager, recalls that "it made many people furious." The ruling Law and Justice Party led by President Andrzej Duda and Prime Minister Mateusz Morawiecki responded angrily to the museum's suggestion that current PiS political speech could lead to dangerous social consequences if left unchecked. It also took issue with the museum's specific categorization of participants. "It was not Poles who expelled [the Jews]," Piotr Gliński, the minister of culture, told the then deputy director of the POLIN Museum Zygmunt Stępiński. In a clear expression of the anticommunist historical paradigm, Gliński asserted, "They were Communists! Poles would never act like this!"[62]

The Warsaw University historian Artur Markowski understands this argument: one defines the perpetrators in such a way as to create "history" to suit one's needs. Given that there were thousands of victims seen by the world, and they were Jews, one cannot claim that the 1968 anti-*Zionist* expulsion did not happen. But to save face, one can change the narrative by insisting on a different perpetrator. Who were the people who developed and implemented that terrible policy? The document-based POLIN Museum exhibition points to *Polish* communists. The ideological argument of the PiS government points to *communists*.

POLIN and the "Holocaust Law"

Just six weeks prior to the "March 1968" exhibition opening, the right-wing PiS government passed the Amendment to the Act on the Institute of National Remembrance. Outside of Poland, it has come to be known as the "Holocaust Law." The controversial law criminalizes any implication of Polish guilt in Nazi atrocities. The harshest penalty of up to three years in prison has been reserved for those who refer to Nazi-built extermination and concentration camps as *Polish* death camps. The Irena Sendlerowa Award recipient Beata Maliszkiewicz explained to me, with a heavy sigh, "I think it is a really big problem ... People in

---

61 Ibid.
62 Author's interview with Zygmunt Stępiński, Warsaw, April 2019.

Poland are sick of hearing people (visiting Jews or foreign politicians) say *Polish* camps. They are sick of it. And of course, some of those people are antisemitic."[63]

But not all of them. In our conversation, Maliszkiewicz asked, "how is it possible for people who have family stories from the Second World War to hear now about *Polish* camps?!"[64] News anchors broadcast when this gross mistake is made. "And it happens all of the time."[65] She added, "I am afraid... because people are more aggressive because of it."[66] When some Poles with little knowledge of Jewish culture and history hear Jews, who are visiting Poland, mention *Polish* camps their hackles rise. Some respond with verbal assaults, to defend themselves and the Polish national ethos. Maliszkiewicz stated that "it is not simple." She thinks people fear that history is being rewritten to paint Poles as complicit in *planning* the Holocaust.[67]

Maliszkiewicz recognizes that during the war some Poles perpetrated horrific acts against Jews. But in her opinion, because Poles as a people have been blamed, over and over again, for crimes they did not commit, it is difficult for some Poles to enter into a dialogue regarding those wrongs that did take place. For some Poles, it feels as though accepting responsibility for one crime necessarily leads to accepting responsibility for another. Those raised under communism understandably become defensive. Under the dictatorship, they learned about anti-Nazi Polish heroism; but now people are telling them that that Poles collaborated with the Nazis in the Final Solution. It is easy for them to dismiss this development as "fake news."

The so-called "Holocaust Law" has become an explosive topic. Polish historians who study World War II and the Holocaust responded to the law with great anxiety. Although the law states that academics and artists are free to continue their work, many remained alarmed.[68] In a 2019 interview, Stępiński told me that the Polish government clearly stands against the truth. He noted that President Duda, the prime minister, and right-wing commentators have publicly attacked the Polish Center for Holocaust Research and its researchers. They have called the center's work "lies," despite that "it is fully based on documents. Polish documents. Jewish documents. German documents."[69] There is a crisis in public

---

63 Author's interview with Beata Maliszkiewicz, Warsaw, April 2019.
64 Ibid.
65 Ibid.
66 Ibid.
67 Ibid.
68 Tara John, "Poland's Holocaust Law: What You Need to Know," *Time Magazine*, February 1, 2018, https://time.com/5128341/poland-holocaust-law/.
69 Author's interview with Zygmunt Stępiński, Warsaw, April 2019.

discourse, then. How should the Polish people define truth? Is it document-based or driven by ideology?

Stępiński explained that the question of Polish guilt or innocence is not simple: "You know the Poles were not only the heroes fighting back the Germans, but in some way, some part of Poles also took part in the Holocaust . . . they were helping Germans to kill Jews."[70] Yehuda Bauer, an internationally recognized Israeli Holocaust scholar states, "Everyone knows there were Poles who took part in the murder of Jews."[71] Bauer continues: "[t]o claim otherwise is a denial of the research that has already proved these things, and in my opinion is also Holocaust denial."[72] For Stępiński this problem extends well beyond Poland's internal understanding of itself: "if you want to present [to the international community] a picture of Poles . . . as a country which is ready to face the tragic history, to understand it and finally to accept it . . . you have to take responsibility for [your response to] it."[73]

In February 2018 Zygmunt Stępiński was the deputy director of the POLIN Museum, when museum leaders organized an emergency meeting concerning "those scholars who are so courageous to write against the official propaganda."[74] Not only did they fill the five-hundred-seat auditorium, but some two hundred more people stood outside the meeting room, watching it live stream on large screens. They encouraged one another to remain strong and to stand up for the truth . . . for full transparency. It is within this context that the then POLIN museum director Dariusz Stola decided to follow through with the "March '68" temporary exhibition, which drew attention to parallels between the communist regime's anti-*Zionist* campaign of 1968 and the antisemitic rhetoric and policy of Poland's PiS government.[75]

The museum paid a heavy price for bringing truth to its audience and for fully supporting its colleagues in the field. The Ministry of Culture refused the museum all grants for which it had applied to cover future expenses. Even more devastating was the government's refusal to renew the contract for Professor Stola, whose advice, knowledge, and very strong personality have been very

---

70 Ibid.
71 Ibid.
72 Don Snyder, "Poland Is Poised to Put 'Bad' Historians of the Holocaust in Prison," Forward, September 2, 2016, https://forward.com/news/world/349179/poland-is-poised-to-put-bad-historians-of-the-holocaust-in-prison/.
73 Author's interview with Zygmunt Stępiński, Warsaw, April 2019.
74 Ibid.
75 Ibid.

important and necessary for the museum's success.⁷⁶ Although Stola had won a second term as museum director in May 2018, the culture minister Piotr Glinski refused to reappoint him. This left Stępiński as interim acting director; and in February 2019 he became the museum's director.

The Courts and the "Holocaust Law"

By passing the "Holocaust Law," the PiS government opened the door for right-wing litigation against Polish Holocaust scholars. The founder of the heavily government-subsidized NGO Polish Anti-Defamation League, Maciej Świrski, coordinated an attack against Holocaust scholars Barbara Engelking and Jan Grabowski. For several years the two faced libel charges based on a footnote in their co-edited *Night Without End: The Fate of Jews in Selected Counties of Occupied Poland* (2018). *Gazeta Wyborcza* journalist Wojciech Czuchnowski writes: "Once the book had been published, Mr. Świrski began a meticulous examination of the facts it contained. He was supported by the Institute of National Remembrance, which set up a special team to discredit the book, carefully examining every single detail of the thousands of accounts it referenced."⁷⁷ Świrski persuaded eighty-year-old Filomena Leszczyńska to file a lawsuit against the scholars regarding their description of her uncle, Edward Malinowski. Świrski arranged payment of her lawyers' fees and actively participated in the lawsuit process.⁷⁸

A wartime village elder in Malinowo, Edward Malinowski was known for having saved a Jew. While a Jewish survivor's immediate postwar testimony supported Malinowski when he faced a postwar trial, that same person's testimony some twenty-five years later contradicted the initial testimony and accused him of crimes against Jews. In *Night Without End*, Engelking argues that the witness's earlier testimony was given at a time when survivors were forced to whitewash their oppressors.⁷⁹ She includes both testimonies in the book, then, but suggests that the latter statement is more reliable. The lawyers for Malinowski's niece, Filomena Leszczyńska, sought to defend not only his reputation as a "hero who

---

76 Ibid.
77 Wojciech Czuchnowski, "Holocaust Scholars Engelking and Grabowski Ordered to Apologize in Libel Case," Gazetta Wyborcza, February 12, 2021, 10, https://wyborcza.pl/7, 173236,26783046,holocaust-scholars-engelking-and-grabowski-ordered-to-apologize.html.
78 Ibid., 19.
79 Ibid.

saved Jews" but also the "right to national identity and pride."⁸⁰ They demanded monetary compensation and an apology which would assert that Engelking and Grabowski published inaccurate information about Malinowski's betrayal of Jews to the Germans. The plaintiff also requested that the two scholars write a statement explaining that they had intentionally filled their book with falsehoods to demonstrate the Poles' complicity in the Nazis' mass murder of the Jews.⁸¹

The district court in Warsaw found the two academicians guilty. Judge Ewa Jończyk stated:

> We can assume that ascribing to Poles the crimes of the Holocaust committed by the Third Reich can be construed as harmful and detrimental to the sense of identity and of national pride. [...] Attributing to the Polish nation the responsibility for the Holocaust, for the killing of Jews during World War II and for the confiscation of their property touches upon the sphere of the national heritage and, consequently, as completely untrue and harmful, can significantly impact one's feeling of own national dignity, destroying the justified—based on facts—belief that Poland was the victim of war operations initiated and conducted by the Germans.⁸²

Jończyk was unwilling to accept the ability of people—that is, of Poles—to have different responses to the same tragic situation. She thereby ignored the fact that, although Poles were victimized by the Nazis, they were also victimizers: many confiscated Jewish property, betrayed Jews to the Nazis, or killed them. In its ruling the court ordered Engelking and Grabowski to post the first apology to the website of the Polish Center for Holocaust Research. However, it discarded the other plaintiff's requests. (It is necessary to note that the day after the historians' initial February sentencing, a rotary near the POLIN Museum was named for the Polish Righteous.)⁸³

---

80   Ibid., 5.
81   Ibid.,19.
82   Grabowski, "The New Wave of Holocaust Revisionism," 4.
83   On February 11, 2021, two days after the first court verdicts against the two scholars, the councilors of the Śródmieście [Downtown] district adopted the project of naming the roundabout for the Righteous. On March 18, 2021, the council of the city of Warsaw approved the decision to name the roundabout after the Righteous Among the Nations. See "Przez Rondo Sprawiedliwych do Muzeum POLIN?," Jewish.pl, February 12, 2021, https://jewish.pl/pl/2021/02/12/przez-rondo-sprawiedliwych-do-muzeum-polin/.

Engelking and Grabowski appealed the verdict. They contended that the idea that one has a right to national pride "is an ambiguous and legally undefined sentiment that effectively means any member of the Polish nation has the right to sue historians whose findings offend them."[84] In August 2021, a Warsaw appellate court dismissed the libel case in its entirety, stating that "it is not the task of a court to interfere in academic research."[85] Reflecting on their experience, Grabowski writes,

> It seemed to me that the real objective of the lawsuit was not to rescue a man's name or alter his reputation, but to frighten scholars of the Holocaust, to instill Poland's pervasive atmosphere of fear into an entire discipline and to make students and educators think twice before choosing topics that would challenge the government-sponsored version of history.[86]

Given Filomena Leszczyńska's subsequent death, the case cannot advance up to the Supreme Court.

A Call for Myth Reconstruction

It is nuance, categorization, and definition which are at the heart of memory making in contemporary Poland. Solidarity's drive toward transparency, once so vital, has been eroded. Though it showed itself during the nationwide

---

84 Grabowski, "The New Wave of Holocaust Revisionism," 4–5. Indeed, additional attacks on historians and journalists have since taken place. A government-funded organization called Verba Veritatis (The Word of Truth) launched a complaint against journalist Katarzyna Markusz over her October 2020 article in which she stated that "Polish participation in the Holocaust is a historical fact." The Warsaw police investigated, but found no crime of slandering Poland. Markusz, who is not Jewish, stated: "This whole investigation was meant to scare me and other journalists and historians from writing the truth about Polish involvement in the Holocaust." See Ofer Aderet, "Poland Drops Case against journalist Who Wrote That Poles Participated in the Holocaust," *Haaretz*, February 23, 2021, https://www.haaretz.com/world-news/europe/.premium-poland-drops-case-against-journalist-who-wrote-that-poles-participated-in-the-holoca-1.9563081.
85 Wojciech Czuchnowski, "Appeals Court Dismisses Libel Case against Holocaust Scholars Grabowski and Engelking," Gazetta Wyborcza, August 17, 2021, 5, https://wyborcza.pl/7,173236,27463746,appeals-court-dismisses-libel-case-against-holocaust-scholars.html.
86 Grabowski, "The New Wave of Holocaust Revisionism," 4–5.

Jedwabne debate—when Poland went through a period of introspection, and later in 2011when the Polish government formally apologized for the killing of Jews by Poles—it has since retreated into fear . . . fear of losing Poland's strong, valiant identity.[87] This fear means high school students are no longer taught about Jedwabne. Already in a 2011 survey, Antoni Sułek discovered that 41% of fifteen- to nineteen-year-olds had not heard of Jedwabne. This number even includes students who had been exposed to the Holocaust in the classroom.[88] If Jedwabne and the harsh truth that some Poles murdered innocent Jews during the Holocaust is not discussed in the classroom, and families have long grown tired of speaking about it, and the media ignores it, then later generations will never learn of it.

Despite this setback, Artur Markowski remains optimistic: "I am sure that we will come back as a society. We as a society know more now. [. . .] I'm sure we know more. It is not possible to throw out this information."[89] Understanding that dialogue, when open and honest, creates connection, Markowski adds, "I hope we will find the moment when we can sit and talk normally and say, 'I am sorry for this history. It was a bad and dark moment of *our* history.'"[90]

Myth reconstruction is a long and arduous process fraught with pitfalls. Though many Poles have succeeded in recognizing the place of Jewish culture, and its destruction, in Poland's history, the general population has struggled to do so. Equally, while many American academics recognize Poland's suffering and national trauma, as well as the positive Polish impact on Jewish culture and history, the vast majority of American Jews have paid little attention (or no attention at all) to it. Both populations have internalized and acted on the idea that "communities of memory cultivate memories of their own suffering and are impregnable against the suffering of other communities."[91] Each nation—Polish and Jewish—has been traumatized over the centuries. "Traumatized nations and societies have a particular tendency to look towards the past to find comfort or confirmation of their identity."[92] As such, each doubles down when confronted with proof that their group was not only victimized but also the victimizer. Each

---

87 Snyder, "Poland Is Poised to Put 'Bad' Historians of the Holocaust in Prison."
88 Jolanta Ambrosewicz-Jacobs and Robert Szuchta, "The Intricacies of Education about the Holocaust in Poland: Ten Years after the Jedwabne Debate, What Can Polish School Students Learn about the Holocaust in History Classes?," *Intercultural Education* 25, no. 4 (2014): 287.
89 Author's interview with Artur Markowski, Warsaw, April 2019.
90 Ibid.
91 Piotr Forecki, *Reconstructing Memory: The Holocaust in Polish Public Debates*, 34.
92 Ibid., 19.

tries to close its eyes to the pain of the Other lest it leads to the dulling of its own pain. Each forgets.

For Poles to face their past with honesty, the Jewish past need find its rightful place in the curriculum for Polish history. Jews were so great a part of the Polish cultural landscape, explains Markowski, that after the Holocaust, when most of the survivors had emigrated, "Poland felt like a very strange place. Why? Because Jews had been here since medieval times. And now we had our arms and legs cut off."[93] At the same time, to understand Polish history clearly also requires that Poles accept into their description of Polish history the proven presence and impact of antisemitism within their society—that is, some Poles' active role in pogroms and some Poles' cooperation in the Nazi's planned destruction of the Jews during the Holocaust.

American Hebrew day and afternoon schools need to include a broader and more nuanced understanding of Poland in their school curriculums too. Speaking as an American Jew, raised with a strong Jewish identity, it is my belief that for American Jews to arrive at a fuller understanding of our Selves it helps first to understand that many of our ancestors immigrated to the United States from Poland. Prior to World War II, Poland had the largest Jewish population in the world—3.3 million Jews. It is estimated that 70% of today's Jews—more than nine million people—descend from this territory (some of which lies within the borders of current Belarus and Ukraine).[94] Thus, to know our true Selves is to know about our ancestors' lives in Poland. And it is absolutely necessary to see the Jews' nearly one thousand year presence in Poland as much more than a straight path towards almost total victimization and destruction. The fact that Jewish culture thrived and developed in Poland speaks to the relatively tolerant nature of the country and its people. Jewish life included varying kinds of discrimination and numerous freedoms. To know Poland is to understand that while antisemitism is part of Poland's relationship with its Jewish population, it in no way defines that complex relationship. If we can put less emphasis on victimization, we will create room within collective memory—our national myth—for more categories of Jewish experience in Poland.

Reevaluating and reconstructing this myth allow Jews the opportunity also to meet Poles and their multicultural past. It is to understand the centrality of the land itself, the various strata of society including the crown, nobility, peasantry,

---

93 Author's interview with Artur Markowski, Warsaw, April 2019.
94 Barbara Kirschenblatt-Gimblett, "Theater of History," *Polin: 1000 Year History of Polish Jews*, ed. Barbara Kirschenblatt-Gimblett and Antony Polonsky, 2nd ed. (Warsaw: Museum of the History of Polish Jews, 2015), 19.

and the Catholic Church. It is to recognize the pain of partition, the collaboration between Jew and Pole, as well as divisions over belonging. It is to lament the agony of a German-planned Polish genocide while knowing that numerous communists of Jewish origin arrested and harassed Poles. It is to feel the defeat when Stalin claimed Poland for himself with the West's silent blessing. It is to recognize the communist regime's manipulation of Polish national memory. It is to connect to the hardships under communism and to glory at the courage exhibited by workers, students, intellectuals, and the Church to join together to secure a better future. It is to understand that in the Third Polish Republic, while the Church has huge political influence, liberalism also has a strong voice. It is to glory in the continued Jewish presence in Poland, Polish Jews' drive for community, and the numerous non-Jewish Poles who support it.

If American Jews will permit a Polish perspective to inform our own, we will gain a greater understanding of Poles' perceptions of Jews. Understanding breeds a willingness to engage in dialogue. If Christian Poles will view the past through the prism of Polish Jews who lived it, they will generate understanding of why most Jews in Poland retained their social separation and refused assimilation, and why some Jews were attracted to socialism, communism, and Jewish nationalism. Today's Poles and American Jews could gain insight into the Other, as well as the Self's own misperceptions.

As each side, Polish Christian and American Jew, discards the closed nationalist definitions of the Self, a fuller image of the past and of Polish-Jewish relations during it will emerge. Filled with the endless spectrum of grays, and dotted with illuminating splashes of color, this new image will make collective connection possible. Furthermore, to recognize that one's people were not only saints but also sinners brings reality to the surface. Christian Poles and Jewish Poles have hurt one another at different historical junctures—through economics, politics, violence. Additionally, American Jews have been quick to unthinkingly label Poles in negative ways. To appreciate the injuries and consequential pain on each side, as well as one's possible ancestral role in causing that pain, could heal wounds. It does not lessen a people's suffering; but it does build a bridge to the Other which, perhaps, then helps us to live *with* the Other—who, after all, is an important part of one's Self.

CHAPTER 21

Shifting Perspectives

In 2007 I travelled to Poland to interview Jews and non-Jews involved in the Polish Jewish communal revival. The optimism I found then contrasted starkly with the tension I discerned when I returned in 2019. What had changed? Once "hidden" Jews still explored their relationships with Judaism. Numerous Polish Christians remained stalwart activists in the country's inquiry into its relationship with Polish Jews. Indeed, the enormous success of the POLIN Museum testifies to both groups' continued relevance in Polish society. What had changed was the political context, both domestic and global.

In 2015 Poland moved in the direction of so many other countries—away from a liberal, open, and tolerant society, towards an illiberal, closed, and conservative one. As I have demonstrated throughout this book, both political positions have roots in the Polish past. When in the 1990s Poles looked for answers in the West's democratic, tolerant, and secular societies, they connected to that part of their own national myth encompassing the Polish-Lithuanian Commonwealth's multicultural state, the Polish Enlightenment, and the rise of positivism. When Poles reassessed and elevated political leaders who supported a Church-driven, closed, traditional society, they clung to the mythic self-image that "to be a Pole is to be Catholic."

By 2015 this latter isolationist myth had attracted more Polish citizens, allowing the Law and Justice Party to sail to political victory amid a backdrop of fear-inducing and destabilizing global developments. These shifts included Russia's 2014 invasion of Ukraine and the UK's debate about leaving the EU (which many believed would result in a significantly weakened union). One issue fueling the Brexit debate was the EU's demand that member states accept a specified number of Syrian refugees fleeing the Syrian Civil War. Numerous EU countries claimed that they were being overwhelmed by Syrians seeking asylum, and Britain was not alone in its resistance. Central Eastern European countries expressed little empathy for the Syrian refugees, matching the Poles' own racist anti-Muslim response. Simultaneously, nationalism was sweeping numerous continents. From Recep Erdogan in Ankara to Viktor Orbán in Budapest,[1] more leaders bowed to nationalist trends. Nigel Farage realized his dream of getting Britain out of the EU; Marine Le Pen's far-right National Front expanded into a major political force in France.

Fear mobilizes society to change its course. Indeed, in a 2016 interview with Bob Woodward and Robert Costa, presidential candidate Donald Trump acknowledged: "Real power is—I don't even want to use the word—fear."[2] In their campaigns to usurp political control, nationalists have branded themselves the true representatives and saviors of their respective national ethos ... those who will quell fear and restore national glory. And voters from the UK, France, Israel, Poland, and the United States have bought into it.

Nationalism: MAGA and PiS

Shockwaves sailed throughout the United States and the world when Donald Trump won the 2016 presidential election on a campaign to "Make America Great Again." He set out to build a wall along the border with Mexico, ban Muslim's from traveling to the US, bully the free press, manipulate the judiciary, upset relations with European allies, and severely restrict America's international role. This America appeared disconnected from that country I knew. And yet it had existed from the beginning, as Peter Schrag demonstrates in his work on nativism and immigration restrictionism.[3] What has caused the reemergence of this ugly nationalism in contemporary US society?

The American author and journalist Thomas Friedman explains this wave of American intolerance and traditionalism as a workers' response to decades of liberalism and change that has threatened traditionalists' understanding of Self, society, and the world. Basic age-old social norms dealing with sexual identity were upended by the legalization of gay marriage and the growing liberal social acceptance of gender fluidity and transgender people. On the economic front, President Clinton's North American Free Trade Agreement (NAFTA) allowed the Midwest auto industry and other manufacturers to move their factories to

---

1 As I write these words, Hungary has shut down its parliament under the guise of the Coronavirus global pandemic and declared autocratic rule.
2 Bob Woodward, *Fear: Trump in the White House* (New York: Simon & Schuster, 2018), quote prior to "Note to Readers."
3 Peter Schrag, *Not Fit for Our Society: Immigration and Nativism in America* (Berkeley: University of California Press, 2010).

other countries where they could pay meager wages. That gutted the American working-class economically. As the US shifted from a manufacturing-based economy to a service-based one, nothing replaced these lost jobs and the health insurance and retirement benefits that accompanied them. Additionally, robots have since replaced human workers in remaining US factories, further threatening people's livelihoods.

Fear only deepened when white Christian Americans felt that their cultural beliefs and privileges were under threat by the mass migration of Brown people, including millions of Muslims fleeing war and violence in Syria and Central America. By reasserting American intolerance of the Other, Trump spoke directly to this panicked portion of the electorate, which feared the changes already occurring in their backyards. To secure his ascent, Trump welcomed the American conservative Evangelical Church to his movement. In effect, Trump's wall came to represent not only the prevention of illegal migration, but also— and more importantly—a metaphorical barrier against the winds of change.[4]

In 2015, Poland's President Andrzej Duda (PiS) accomplished a similar feat. The Western tide that washed over Poland with communism's fall, had run into problems and elicited a backlash. The country's embrace of secularism, multiculturalism, and social liberalism had threatened traditional groups and institutions, including the Catholic Church. Needing a tangible enemy around which to unite, the Church replaced the enemy Jew with the enemy LGBTQ community. This new enemy served the Church by diverting attention away from its pedophilia crisis, thus pointing to an Other as the real threat to Polish family values.

Additional problems arose from Poland's new liberal policies associated with belonging to the European Union when the EU demanded that its Central Eastern European member states accept a quota of Syrian refugees—read Brown and Muslim, therefore alien and unrelatable. A large segment of the Polish populace erupted in protest. It feared that the (quite low) number of seven thousand incoming Muslims would alter the Catholic identity of Poland, which according to a Vatican City 2016 report stood at 97.6% of the population, or 36,607,000 people.[5] Traditionalists clung to the PiS promise of restoring and guarding not only illiberal Polish Catholic culture, but also the Polish nation's sense of sovereignty.

To comprehend this inward turn, it is helpful to place it within the context of a global trend. Insularity is not intrinsically Polish any more than it is intrinsically

---

4 Thomas Friedman speaking on *Morning Joe*, MSNBC, December 19, 2019.
5 See Press office of the Holy See, The Holy See, accessed 29 August, 2023, https://www.press.vatican.va.

American. As we have seen in both countries, multiculturalism and tolerance have fueled each society at different times. It is within this perspective that I address Polish-Jewish relations.

Perspective: Unrealistic Expectations

When Central and Eastern Europe broke free from communism, the West applauded. Professors Jolanta Ambrosewicz-Jacobs and Annamaria Orla-Bukowska point out that "expectations ran high that the dusk of absolute tyranny would be quickly followed by the dawn of absolute tolerance [. . .] the newly liberated nations were expected to open not only their borders, but also their attitudes."[6] Onlookers expected Poland, which they had viewed as especially antisemitic since Kielce and March '68, to demonstrate exacting openness and tolerance, not only to the small Jewish community just emerging in democratic Poland but also to the past which Poles and Jews shared.

After just eleven years of transitioning into democracy, Jan Gross publicly compelled Poland to strip off four decades of communist-scrubbed national memory. His book *Neighbors* and Poland's own subsequent IPN investigation forced a nationwide debate over the Polish national myth of most victimized and heroic people. Not only did it educate Poles on the murder of some six million Jews during the Holocaust (which communist Poland had ignored), it also focused attention on the problematic decisions made by Poles regarding Jews and the violence Poles enacted against Jews during the Nazi murder campaign. In essence, the investigation turned the Polish national myth on its head, bringing Jews' victimhood to the fore and questioning the heroic character of the Polish people vis-à-vis the Jews.

The then Polish government—led by the moderate right-of-center Civic Platform Party (PO)—digested this new information. But the more conservative nationalist elements refused its veracity. Instead, they took on a defensive posture. They blamed liberalism for this "politics of shame" which they asserted undermined Poland's good name. Americans on both sides of the aisle have been appalled by the steady rise of ethno-nationalism in Poland and Poles' unwillingness to accept the country's difficult past. However, if we pay closer attention to our own backyard, we will not be so shocked by the Poles' increasing resistance

---

6 Ambrosewicz-Jacobs and Orla-Bukowska, "After the Fall: Attitudes Towards Jews in Post-1989 Poland."

to facing and accepting the very difficult and tragic past relations between Poles and Jews.

In the United States, we find a similarly energetic attempt to dismiss responsibility for our own difficult and tragic past (and present) race relations. Liberal Americans have accused the police of systemic racism. Some academics have linked contemporary racial disparities to systemic racism rooted in slavery and Jim Crow. They argue that deeply embedded stereotyping makes academic, professional, and economic advancement much more difficult for Black and Brown people than for the average white person. To deflect this potent argument and deny any white responsibility to make amends, right-wing extremists, such as Alex Jones and Republican legislators such as Georgia's Marjorie Taylor Green, have twisted established academic methodology into the latest threat to American culture. They have attacked Critical Race Theory (CRT), which is "a decades-old academic framework that scholars use to interrogate how legal systems—as well as other elements of society—perpetuate racism and exclusion."[7] They have made an academic theory a political bogeyman. In essence, American right-wing extremists find themselves fighting the same fight as their Polish contemporaries: they dismiss any critique of the national past as simply an attempt to make the country look bad, rather than view it for what it is—an attempt to face a complex past.

Legions of Americans have jumped onto this bandwagon. At least twenty-five US states have since proposed, or acted, to restrict how teachers discuss America's problems with racism and oppression (including, of course, sexism).[8] Numerous far-right lawmakers believe it their right and responsibility to protect white students' positive self-perception. Therefore, asserting that CRT connects "responsibility, blame or guilt" to race or sex, Texas lawmakers banned CRT from being taught in K-12 public schools. Yet no one has found a Texas high school class that teaches the theory.[9] In Florida, Governor Ron DeSantis' conservative administration has gone beyond the core curriculum to ban a voluntary new Advanced Placement (AP) class on African American studies from Florida

---

7   Olivia B. Waxman, "Critical Race Theory Is Simply the Latest Bogeyman: Inside the Fight over What Kids Learn about America's History " *TIME*, June 24, 2021, https://time.com/magazine/us/6075407/july-5th-2021-vol-198-no-1-u-s/.
8   Ibid.
9   Michael Powell, "In Texas, a Battle over What Can Be Taught, and What Books Can Be Read," *New York Times*, December 10, 2021, https://www.nytimes.com/2021/12/10/us/ texas-critical-race-theory-ban-books.html.

high schools.¹⁰ What does this administration fear by exposing teenagers to a thoughtful and critical investigation into the Black American experience? These campaigns corroborate a recent nationwide study on Americans' perceptions of history. In it, 84% of Republicans surveyed said that history should celebrate our nation's past, whereas 70% of Democrats said that history should question it.¹¹

To further the battle, across the United States members of local school boards and state legislatures have engaged in book banning campaigns. While culture wars typically raise demands for books to be taken off library shelves, this battle became fierce in 2021, with a 67% increase in officially proposed bans from just one year prior.¹² One Texas state legislature compiled a list of 850 books it wanted pulled from shelves because, it claimed, they might "make students feel discomfort, guilt, anguish" due to race or sex.¹³ Books on the Holocaust and Judaism have been caught up in the purges. In the state of Missouri, a new law threatens educators with jail time if they do not remove books deemed to provide "explicit sexual material" to students. *Maus*, the Pulitzer Prize-winning graphic novel depicting the Holocaust, was removed from shelves in Missouri and Tennessee because it contains "inappropriate curse words and a depiction of a naked character."¹⁴

---

10   Andrew Atterbury, "DeSantis Defends Banning African American Studies Course as Black Leaders Call for Action," Politico, January 24, 2023, https://www.politico.com/news/2023/01/23/desantis-banning-african-american-studies-00079027.
11   Pete Burkholder and Dana Schaffer, "A Snapshot of the Public's Views on History: National Poll Offers Valuable Insights for Historians and Advocates," American Historical Association, August 20 2021, https://www.historians.org/publications-and-directories/perspectives-on-history/september-2021/a-snapshot-of-the-publics-views-on-history-national-poll-offers-valuable-insights-for-historians-and-advocates.
12   Brooke Migdon, "Oklahoma Lawmaker Introduces Book-Banning Bill with $10,000-a-Day Penalty," The Hill, December 28, 2021, https://thehill.com/changing-america/respect/diversity-inclusion/587517-oklahoma-lawmaker-introduces-book-banning-bill; Nomin Ujiyediin, "There's New Pressure to Ban Books at schools," npr.org, December 6, 2021, https://www.npr.org/2021/12/06/1061727091/pressure-grows-to-ban-books-at-schools.
13   In Williamson County, Tennessee, Moms for Liberty has called for the ban of numerous books, including two about Ruby Bridges, an icon of desegregation. At age six Ruby Bridges faced a mob in New Orleans when as a new student she entered the all-white school. The group did not approve of the book because it showed images of the angry mob that was ready to kill her. By keeping the book off of library shelves the group hoped to retain the sanitized version of American exceptionalism it prefers. See Powell, "In Texas, a Battle over What Can Be Taught, and What Books Can Be Read."
14   Andrew Lapin, "Not Just 'Maus': A Missouri School District Removed Several Holocaust History Books, Too," Jewish Telegraphic Agency, November 16, 2022, https://www.jta.org/2022/11/16/united-states/several-holocaust-books-including-maus-have-been-yanked-from-some-missouri-schools-amid-state-law. See also, Jenny Gross, "School Board in Tennessee

Some libraries in stalwart conservative districts removed hundreds of books which deal with race, gender, and sexuality for review, even before there was a vote on the law.¹⁵ Clearly, just as traditionalist Polish lawmakers have done, these American conservatives are blocking access to knowledge that challenges myths of white Christian heterosexual superiority.

At the same time, many Jewish Americans unrealistically expect Poland to find a quick path back to tolerance. The United States well knows the challenges of a sovereign nation showing vulnerability before international spectators. In her book *A Problem from Hell*, the former US ambassador to the United Nations, Samantha Power, examines the US's response to the UN General Assembly's December 1948 passage of the Genocide Convention. This legal document defines genocide and permits the international enforcement of a genocide ban. While the necessary US Senate ratification initially appeared a mere formality, it actually took forty years to achieve. Some senators opposed ratification because they feared it would license critics of the United States to investigate the government's intentional eradication of native American tribes in the nineteenth century. Some senators, particularly those from the South, feared that lawyers might use it to argue that segregation in the South was a form of genocide.¹⁶

> American opposition was rooted in a traditional hostility toward any infringement on U.S. sovereignty. [. . .] If the United States ratified the pact, senators worried they would thus authorize outsiders to poke around in the internal affairs of the United States. [. . .] It was hard to see how it was in the U.S. interest to make a state's treatment of its own citizens the legitimate object of international scrutiny.¹⁷

Despite the Genocide Convention having already dealt with and safeguarded against these possibilities of international and domestic scrutiny, the United States upended the vote. In effect, the United States successfully blocked the same kind of scrutiny which the young Polish democracy faced during and after the Jedwabne debate—the judgment of outsiders.

Bans Teaching of Holocaust Novel 'Maus,'" *New York Times*, January 27, 2022, https://www.nytimes.com/2022/01/27/us/maus-banned-holocaust-tennessee.html.
15   Powell, "In Texas, a Battle over What Can Be Taught, and What Books Can Be Read."
16   Power, *A Problem From Hell: America and the Age of Genocide*, 67.
17   Ibid., 69.

Anxiety over outside judgment generates leadership paralysis, and even a doubling down resistance to openness, which in turn affects society at large. When leadership refuses to recognize and address social inequities and mistreatment, one cannot expect the average citizen to denounce them. We see this situation clearly in the United States. In 1955 two white men in rural Mississippi's Tallahatchie County abducted and brutally murdered fourteen-year-old Emmett Till on grounds that he had abrogated social norms. He was accused of insulting a white woman. He was lynched. Mamie Bradley, Till's mother, courageously held an open casket funeral for her battered son so that the world would see what the white, male murderers had done to him. It caused international outrage and damaged America's international reputation and even foreign policy.[18] Traveling anywhere and everywhere to speak about the case, Bradley generated a huge protest movement that gave rise to the American civil rights movement.[19] But the murderers were never held accountable for their crime, despite the January 24, 1956 publication of their confessions in *Look* magazine. Those who held power in the courts and in the government were not ready to change the social dynamic.

In the United States we are familiar with the sociopolitical backlash that results from publicly naming past social misdeeds. We have experienced the length of time it takes for the general citizenry to embrace meaningful social reform. It took fifty years after the acquittal of Till's murderers for Tallahatchie County to apologize for the miscarriage of justice. Yet, even in 2008 when the county's newly launched Emmett Till Memorial Commission erected a highway memorial sign a vandal scrawled "KKK" across it. According to Patrick Weems, the executive director of the commission, "since that time, our signs have been shot at, thrown in the river. Someone threw acid on one of them. And so it's been this constant struggle."[20] The fourth sign to mark the place where Till's broken body was pulled from the river is five hundred pounds, made of one-inch-thick steel and supposedly bulletproof.[21] That is a good thing. The last sign had more than forty bullet holes fired through it. In 2021, just days after the

---

18 Timothy B. Tyson, *The Blood of Emmett Till* (New York: Simon & Schuster Paperbacks, 2017), 5.
19 Ibid.
20 Scott Simon, Weekend Edition, "Emmett Till Memorial Dedicated for 4th Time after Vandalism," npr.org, October 19, 2019, https://www.npr.org/2019/10/19/771518825/emmett-till-memorial-dedicated-for-4th-time-after-vandalism.
21 Aimee Ortiz, "Emmett Till Memorial Has a New Sign. This Time, It's Bulletproof," *New York Times*, October 20, 2019, https://www.nytimes.com/2019/10/20/us/emmett-till-bulletproof-sign.html.

sixty-sixth anniversary of Till's murder, someone drove a car into the sign that marked the storefront where Till spoke to Carolyn Bryant.[22] A large swath of white people in the US still take great offense to the reminder of white ancestral racial injustices. By policing curriculums and pulling knowledge and ideas down from library shelves, white Americans attempt to hold onto the powerful myth of white Christian American (male) exceptionalism.

Poles have been taught to hitch their individual dignity to Polish exceptionalism, to the national myth of Polish heroism and martyrdom. However, it is near impossible to hold onto that image when critically investigating the rise of Polish antisemitism and concurrent violence against Jews. What should Polish traditionalists do when confronting not only the Polish hero and Polish victim, but also the Polish victimizer? The threat of losing national honor, which in part sustained Poles for centuries—throughout partition, occupation, and communism—left many feeling untethered and besieged. After more than a decade of Poland publicly acknowledging Jedwabne, PiS secured power in 2015, with a campaign promising to restore the nation's traditional sense of its heroic and victimized Self. The party would restore honor by covering Poland's shame. As Polish Jewish activist Stanisław Krajewski noted, by re-engaging and accentuating the simple myth of a brave and martyred people, PiS promised to "Make Poland Proud Again."[23]

It is naïve to expect any country, let alone a newly independent one, to resist a sociopolitical backlash after facing assaults to its reputation. The question is: How destructive will the backwards slide be before a return to equilibrium?

Perspective: Donald Trump's Rise to Power

Words are powerful. They shape our perceptions of the world. They ignite emotions and provoke action. Too often lately politicians have used language to corrosive effect. The United States is one of numerous countries seeing a rise in hate speech and hate crimes. The Brookings Institute has demonstrated that Donald Trump's racist rhetoric not only benefitted him politically, but also led to an increase in hate crimes throughout the nation. FBI data shows that since Trump's election there has been a spike in hate crimes in counties where Trump

---

22 Zoe Christen Jones, "Emmett till Memorial Sign Missing Days after 66th Anniversary of His Death," CBS News, September 3, 2021, https://www.cbsnews.com/news/emmett-till-marker-missing-mississippi-66th-anniverary/.
23 Author's interview with Stanisław Krajewski, Warsaw, April 2019.

won by larger margins. A study by the Anti-Defamation League shows that counties that hosted a Trump campaign rally in 2016 saw hate crime rates more than double compared to similar counties that did not host a rally. Since Trump's 2016 victory, the US has experienced the second-largest uptick in hate crimes in the twenty-five years for which data is available. His induced hate is second only to the spike seen after September 11, 2001.[24]

That August following President Trump's inauguration, Americans watched throngs of torch-wielding neo-Nazis and white supremacists march at a "Unite the Right" rally in Charlottesville, Virginia. They had converged from all corners of the country to protest the city's decision to remove the statue of the Confederate general Robert E. Lee from a public park.[25] By this time, a large section of the populace had finally come to understand such bronze and stone tributes to the Confederacy as an early twentieth-century organized defense of the South's heritage, that is, white power. General Lee's monument was stony, silent aggression directed at the nation's Black citizens.

Like all countries, the United States wrestles over how much truth and vulnerability to allow into its historical narrative. Our society has long taught that Blackness is a dangerous foreign element that physically threatens white society. Conservative white society fears Black Americans will rise up like the Israelites and become "more and mightier than we,"[26] thereby overtaking us. Traditional white society fears losing its power, control, and prestige. Though we fought over this issue in the civil war, confronted it with the carnage of Reconstruction, and marched against it a century later during the civil rights era, we are still fighting those who resist racial tolerance and social change. Although the nation has made great strides with educational reforms and desegregation, we keep returning to dance the same dance and fight the same fight.

Back in 1965, television cameras recorded the violence against Black marchers crossing the Edmond Pettus Bridge in Selma, Alabama in protest against voter suppression. Viewers saw peaceful Black citizens being bludgeoned to near death by the white authorities. Today, courageous individuals who film American inequity on their smartphones force us to confront the same dark elements. On May 25, 2020, the American public could not turn away from the images of unarmed George Floyd (1973–2020) splayed on the ground with a

---

24 Vanessa Williamson and Isabella Gelfand, "Trump and Racism: What Do the Data Say?," Brookings, August 14, 2019, https://www.brookings.edu.
25 Debbie Lord, "What Happened at Charlottesville: Looking Back on the Rally That Ended in Death," *Atlanta Journal Constitution*, April 10, 2018.
26 Exodus 1:9.

policeman's knee to his neck. In front of our eyes, Mr. Floyd gasped for air for nine minutes and twenty-nine seconds, cried for his mother, and died.[27] The Black Lives Matter movement (which began as a hashtag in response to the murder of another unarmed African American man, Trayvon Martin) gained a tremendous following at this defining moment. It demands that we confront and change the nation's systemic racism. Denying such racism exists, many white Americans do everything they can to keep it in place.

Charlottesville represents one inflection point in this domestic battle over our national memory and national myth. Various extremist right-wing groups gathered that weekend to create a single force of hatred. Hoisting flaming tiki torches as they circled Lee's imposing bronze figure astride his horse, these fascists shouted the Nazi slogan "Blood and Soil!"[28] They confirmed their anti-semitism when chanting "You will not replace us. Jews will not replace us!"[29] They declared their racism by crying "White Lives Matter!"[30] They marched out of fear of being forgotten, their narrative of heroism dismantled by a more transparent liberal educational policy. They rejected being told by Others that they were wrong. The following day before the rally could take place a bloody melee broke out between white power advocates and counter-demonstrators. When a driver ploughed his car into a group of anti-racist activists, he sent bodies flying into the air, wounding many and killing thirty-two-year-old Heather Heyer.

President Trump attempted to calm the nation by condemning "in the strongest possible terms this egregious display of hatred, bigotry and violence."[31] But then he equivocated: the hatred, bigotry, and violence he deplored was "on many sides."[32] He added: "I think there is blame on both sides."[33] He explained: "You had a group on one side that was bad. You had a group on the other side that was

---

27 "How George Floyd Died, and What Happened Next," *New York Times*, November 1, 2021, https://www.nytimes.com/article/george-floyd.html.
28 Matt Pearce, Robert Armengol, and David S. Cloud, "Three Dead, Dozens Hurt after Virginia White Nationalist Rally Is Dispersed; Trump Blames 'Many Sides,'" *Los Angeles Times*, August 12, 2017.
29 This popular white supremacist slogan alludes to the conspiracy theory that Jews (with George Soros as their leader) are promoting the extinction of the white race, and thereby white American Christians, by bringing in millions of non-white refugees into the country. This position has gained much traction in the United States and in Europe due to Syrian and South American refugees seeking asylum.
30 Pearce, Armengol, and Cloud, "Three Dead, Dozens Hurt after Virginia White Nationalist Rally Is Dispersed; Trump Blames 'Many Sides.'"
31 Ibid.
32 Ibid.
33 Lord, "What happened at Charlottesville: Looking Back on the Rally That Ended in Death."

also very violent."³⁴ The American public was in shock: it had just heard the president of the United States propose an equivalence between racist, homophobic, and antisemitic white supremacists, on the one hand, and counter-protestors standing for tolerance of ethnic and racial difference, on the other.

In that moment, the president further protected white supremacy in his refusal to utter the words "Black lives matter." During the country's debate over whether to define the US as systemically racist, with civil war statues and police brutality at the heart of the matter, the president refused to acknowledge the specific pain suffered by people of color in this country. That he blamed protestors "on both sides" for the mayhem in Charlottesville only furthered the conflict over our national self-identity.

Trump's diehard base knows that the slogan "Make America Great Again" is a dog whistle for "Make it acceptable again for Americans to be racist, antisemitic, xenophobic, homophobic, nativist, and restrictionist again." Indeed, his response to Charlottesville solidified the radical right's love of Trump. Even before he won the White House, Rachel Pendergraft, a national organizer for the Knights Party, which succeeded David Duke's Knights of the Ku Klux Klan, stated that Trump's campaign "just proves that our views resonate with millions."³⁵

Since Trump took office these far-right fringe elements have broadened their reach and created a wave of extreme violence against minority ethnic, racial, and religious groups, which have included but are not limited to Black and Brown people, Asians, immigrants, migrant workers, LGTBQ people, Muslims, Sikhs, and Jews. Given the purview of this work, I will now briefly describe some recent and horrific examples of violence against Jews in the United States. In 2018, Fox News consistently blamed the "invasion" of illegal immigrants into the US on George Soros. A Hungarian Holocaust survivor who immigrated to the US, Soros became an American businessman and billionaire. Through his Open Society Foundations, he supports liberal democratic causes. For decades the far right has personified him as the "Jewish mastermind pulling the strings" in a conspiracy theory to replace white people with immigrants.³⁶ This construct is a twenty-first-century iteration of the *Protocols of the Elders of Zion*. On

---

34 Ibid.
35 German Lopez, "Actual White Supremacist: Trump Success 'proves that our views resonate with millions,'" Vox.com, October 14, 2016, https://www.vox.com/policy-and-politics/2016/10/14/13287532/trump-white-supremacists-racists.
36 "Why Is Billionaire George Soros a Bogeyman for the Hard Right?," BBC News, September 7, 2019, https://www.bbc.com/news/stories-49584157.

October 27, 2018, a white man obsessed with this caricature of Soros entered Pittsburgh's Tree of Life Congregation during a Shabbat morning service armed with an automatic rifle and three handguns.[37] He murdered eleven Jews and terrorized the whole community. "Soros" remains an antisemitic dog whistle used in the US and abroad.

While the Pittsburgh massacre was the worst act of antisemitic violence in recent American history, the amount of violence against Jews has risen exponentially in the US.[38] Shootings and stabbings, murder, and maiming. The Anti-Defamation League keeps a record of hate crimes, as well as specific antisemitic crimes. Almost daily, there is at least one antisemitic crime or example of hate speech—less extreme than murder, yet effective in worrying its recipients. These incidents include the desecration of tombstones, swastikas painted on synagogues, protests on college campuses inciting violence against the state of Israel and Jews in general through the chant "from the river to the sea, Palestine will be free," and Jewish Zoom meetings hacked by people who message "Heil Hitler" or "Gas the Jews."[39]

A national myth provides an identity, a general understanding of the collective past, which in turn impacts decision-making in the present. Because it includes several components incorporated over time, a country's national myth waxes and wanes. Politicians stress some elements over others, depending on political and social contexts. Today we are witnessing traditionalists respond to their fear that liberal education and policies will culturally and economically displace them. In Poland, historians have caused panic by challenging the long-standing perception of the nation's honor, bravery, and martyrdom by researching 1941

---

37 Ibid.; Campbell Robertson, Christopher Mele, and Sabrina Travernise, "11 Killed in Synagogue Massacre; Suspect Charged With 29 Counts," *New York Times*, October 27, 2018.

38 A separate gunman killed a Jewish woman in California's Chabad Poway synagogue and injured three more community members. See Andrew Marantz, "The Poway Synagogue Shooting Follows an Unsettling Script," *New Yorker*, April 29, 2019.

39 See https://www.ADL.org.
Antisemitic incidences have mushroomed in the United States with the October 7, 2023 Hamas massacre of more than 1200 Israelis and taking of some 240 hostages, including toddlers and senior citizens. There appears an inability by the vocal extreme left to recognize the slaughter of Israeli civilians as inhumane. Many see it as justified in the political reckoning of the Palestinian cause. College campuses have erupted with violent protests against Israel's response to the Hamas massacre. Israelis, read Jews, are the bogeyman yet again. The lack of interest in nuance in the conflict and the irresponsible role Hamas has played in subjecting the Palestinians to its control are ignored.

Polish pogroms and Poles' participation in Nazi Jew hunts. In the United States, the discussion of race relations causes tremendous fear for white conservatives; they do not want their children to lose their political, economic, and social advantages. Nationalist leaders have responded. In Poland, PiS passed so-called the "Holocaust Law" and used Żydokomuna to quiet revelations about Jedwabne and Jew hunts. In the United States Republicans craft anti-CRT laws, ban books, and bar classes that challenge the traditional pretty version of the past. An extreme traditionalist backlash swept through the Polish parliament, dividing the populace. Similar to America's current nationalist turn, though I dare say Poland's divide is not as violent as that in the United States.

Hatred of the Other is present, to one degree or another, in most societies. The question is whether a leader will tamp it down or surrender to it and thus allow it to fester. According to the *ADL Global 100: An Index of Antisemitism*, antisemitic attitudes increased in 2019 throughout Eastern and Central European countries. Of those, Poland has seen an 11% increase in antisemitic attitudes since the last survey in 2015: "In Poland, where restitution of Holocaust-era Jewish property and a controversial law on Holocaust speech were widely debated in recent years, antisemitic attitudes rose to 48% of the population, up from 37% in 2015."[40] As in the United States, such hatred of the Other will not burn out and die.

---

40 Knowing that President Trump responded to the global Covid-19 pandemic through a political lens, undermining scientists' assessments and public health policy to gain votes, it is not so surprising that to maintain its own base, Poland's government defends a refusal to responsibly deal with the issue of property restitution. See "ADL Global Survey of 18 Countries Finds Hardcore Anti-Semitic Attitudes Remain Pervasive," ADL, November 15, 2019, https://www.adl.org/resources/press-release/adl-global-survey-18-countries-finds-hardcore-anti-semitic-attitudes-remain.

Conclusion

The Opposition

Having lived under the Trump administration I now have a greater understanding of nationalism and the fear-filled rhetoric that directs it. When I look at what is occurring in my own country, I am not as shocked by Poland's Pruchnik effigy. Having heard President Trump tell lie after lie to veil his misdeeds, I am not surprised that leaders in other countries, such as Poland, also attempt to suppress the truth. After President Trump filled judicial vacancies with ill-experienced ideologues, seven of whom have been confirmed for lifetime appointments, and who the nonpartisan American Bar Association has rated as "not qualified,"[1] I recognize the politicization of the judiciary, which Poland's PiS government has mirrored. I am not looking to relativize Poland's bad actors. I am putting such cases in a global context.

I used to judge people living under nationalist regimes. Why did they allow such people to get into power? As part of the resistance that is trying to educate people and counter Trumpism I have gained an appreciation for *the opposition*, especially for those activists who face(d) brutality and imprisonment as a consequence of fighting a government. I think particularly of those Polish intellectuals and workers who banded together against the oppressive communist regime. To actively side with the opposition is dangerous, frustrating, and completely exhausting. For many, strain and disillusion eventually make continuing near impossible. I appreciate resignation as I myself have felt it.

I also have come to relate to the opposition's need for recognition by outsiders. When I travelled to Europe in 2017, I felt a great need to communicate my rejection of Trump and his latest version of American nativism. I wanted people to know I do not agree with his hateful rhetoric or hurtful policies. I did not want

---

1 According to Dianne Feinstein, then ranking member of the Senate Judiciary Committee, Trump has elevated people deemed incompetent to sit as judges due to "the extreme views of the nominees and their troubling records on issues like voting rights, health care, women's reproductive rights, LGBT rights, gun safety and executive power." Dianne Feinstein, "Republicans Keep Confirming Unqualified Judicial Nominees," Law360, June 24, 2020, https://www.law360.com/articles/1285914.

people to judge my character based on my nationality and my country's political leader. This deep need to distance myself from my government has helped me relate to the multiplicity of opposing political voices in Poland, present and past.

The Necessity of Meeting

I have learned the importance of meeting the Other. The relationship between American Jews and Polish Christians will only mature and deepen when *the people* meet one another, to talk and listen with respect. It is the face-to-face encounter that opens opportunity for discovery and relationship building. When I traveled to Poland in 2007 for my initial round of interviews, I gave a talk about Rabbi Leo Baeck at the "TAK" school in Opole. It was a unique opportunity for students to see and talk with a Jewish person. There, I met Danuta Reinert, a golden-haired teenager who asked if I might be willing to visit her family. She knew that her eighty-five-year-old grandmother, Martha Péch, who often spoke fondly of her childhood Jewish friends in the prewar town of Dobrodzień, would want to meet me. I jumped at this opportunity to meet the Reinerts. When I entered their dining room, I found a feast-laden table. At the middle of the table sat Martha, bright long silver strands crowning her head. Martha's sparkling eyes greeted me as she said, "Gut morgen." I did not understand then what she was trying to communicate. Only now, after having taken Yiddish courses, do I recognize those words and Martha's connection to them.

As I was speaking with Martha about her youth (with Danuta translating), tears welled in her soft eyes. She recalled her dear Jewish childhood friend Erica, and how they often used to play together. Martha spoke about tolerance: she never divided people by religion or nationality: they were either stupid or wise. Her daughter, Ewa, underscored that Martha's example taught her to teach her own children *not* to divide people by nationality and religion. At the end of a lovely evening, Danuta and her father drove me to see a project. When we arrived in the dark of night, the car's headlights lit up the old Jewish cemetery of Dobrodzień. Surprisingly, it was in wonderful condition. All the gravestones stood upright, it had been recently weeded, and a new fence encircled it. Danuta had been part of the Polish-German-Israeli team of youths which had repaired it. By being open to meeting Danuta and her family, I also had the opportunity to see this marvelous site.

I have learned about the Other and my Self through meeting Polish Christians in their country. When I first visited Poland, I was weighed down with baggage: ignorance learned as an American Jew who grew up in the Holocaust-centric

1970s and 1980s, coupled with an implicit anti-Polish bias. Our young Polish Catholic friends had arranged our time in Poland based on what we wanted to see. Our list included only Jewish sites. We had no interest in Polish sites, as we had no interest in Polish history or Polish culture. We only wanted to see *Ourselves*. We had no desire to see *Them*.

During that 2005 visit, we spent one day in Kraków with our friends Beata and Przemek. They had arranged a guided tour of the Kazimierz district, which had been home to Kraków's large prewar Jewish community. Throughout the long day, I assumed our young tour guide was Jewish. Why else would she care enough to dedicate her time and energy to learning the history of Kazimierz's Jews? I was wrong. When asked about her family's experience during the war, she answered that the Nazis had captured her grandmother and forced her onto a truck bound for Auschwitz. Luckily, she found the wherewithal to jump off and escaped with her life. That was the first time I remember hearing of non-Jewish Poles being sent to Auschwitz . . . *Our* place of agony. True, I might have learned about it briefly in the past, but I did not hold onto that knowledge for the present. When that same tour guide told us that she was a university student in the Jewish Studies department, I was even more shocked. I could not understand her drive to study someone else's history. Only now, after eighteen years, do I understand that the history of Jewish life in Poland is *her* history as well.

Contemporary Polish Jewry

To understand Jews who live in Poland today is to accept that most identify first as Poles. Most grew up with little to no Jewish identity, let alone affiliation. Those who have a connection to Judaism have nurtured it out of their own desires. They did not enter the synagogue or sit at a Shabbat dinner table with any understanding of ritual and language, unlike many American Jews who have had some exposure to the Jewish community since birth. Polish Jews have been raised within an overwhelmingly Catholic country. Many were baptized in a parental effort to demonstrate belonging to the prevalent culture. They entered Judaism as foreigners.

In 2005, and without understanding this difference, I equated the American and Polish Jewish communities—the first of many early mistakes I made. I also knew very little of Polish Jews' history. I knew only what I had been taught by Jewish educators in the United States and Israel, several of whom held strong biases against Poland and Poles. Thus, to begin to know Polish Jews is to understand their history as they have lived it, not as *we* have perceived it.

At the exact same time, Polish Jews are like any other Jews in the world in that they are evolving individuals. To expect them to remain glued to the same understanding they voiced during a brief encounter is to make another mistake. I met Jan Kirschenbaum in 2007 as a young university student. Having kept his Jewish identity concealed from friends since learning of it at age thirteen, he fully expressed it he became a Jewish activist at the university. In our conversation, Jan voiced his understanding that outsiders want to peer into the Polish Jewish community and grab a snapshot of it. My interview with him proves his point, as it was just one of many. But he said emphatically, "This is not a zoo!" Indeed, visitors may treat it as such, staring at Polish Jews as if they are an exhibition. But unlike caged animals which lack the freedom to change, Polish Jews are individuals like you and me; we all evolve in response to time, education, and societal factors.

Jan's own experience bears out this truth. Believing that Polish Jews felt more united in traditional synagogues, Jan went through an Orthodox conversion in 2007. "The reason I'm choosing to be religious is because I want to be part of this people."[2] While thankful for the structure that Orthodox Jewish life provided by teaching him traditions and culture, Jan's Jewish self-expression evolved. No longer religiously observant, in 2014 he co-founded Cukunft, which runs out of the Wrocław Jewish Community Center. Cukunft (Yiddish for "future") takes its name from the youth organization of the General Jewish Workers' Alliance (Bund). It attracts younger people who want to identify culturally as Jews.[3]

Jan is but one example of Jews in Poland who are searching for meaningful ways to define and access the Jewish community while cultivating sustainability. The Polish Jewish community is made up of all types of Jews: those who affiliate with the Orthodox and those who connect with Progressive Judaism; those who unite on a Jewish cultural level and those who desire a Jewish secular identity. And then there are plenty who recognize their Jewish roots, but who remain disconnected from the Jewish people. In this way, Polish Jews resemble most other Jewish populations.

One main difference, however, between the two Jewish populations is that American Jews often take their Judaism for granted. Ironic as it may be, most American Jews stop actively learning about their heritage when they become a bar or bat mitzvah, which is typically age thirteen. Too often they take little

---

2   Author's interview with Jan Kirschenbaum, Wrocław, November 2007.
3   Jan Kirschenbaum, in Barry Cohen, *Opening the Drawer: The Hidden Identities of Polish Jews*, 205.

personal responsibility after this milestone for understanding Judaism's depths and varied forms of expression. When left on its own, without any additional nurturing, watering, or weeding, their understanding of Judaism and the Jewish community easily lingers in its childish, preadolescent state. By contrast, most contemporary Polish Jews only begin to investigate their heritage as young adults. As such, those who take on the challenge are often able to bring maturity and inquisitiveness to the task.

Jews worry about sustainability. Jan Kirschenbaum's grandfather, a Holocaust survivor, once believed his would be the last generation of Polish Jews. He has derived much joy and pride knowing that Jan and his twin brother, Mati, have moved beyond his own son's "lost generation" to embrace Judaism.[4] The issue of sustainability pokes and prods at the small Polish Jewish community. Are there enough Jews in Poland to create meaningful demographic, spiritual, and communal growth? If there are enough, are the current community institutions doing all that they can to support a continued flow of interest in those who know about their Jewish roots? And are those same institutions and their members welcoming of the newcomer who feels uneasy about opening *the* Jewish door?

American Jewish leaders often fret about survey numbers which demonstrate not only high intermarriage rates, but also the general trend away from synagogue affiliation and communal participation. In this regard, Polish Jewish leaders and the communities they guide have achieved "normalcy." Yet the dysfunction within the institutions is normal too. It is extraordinary that the younger generation has succeeded in building some bridges to ameliorate this dysfunction. What is striking about Poland's twenty-first-century Jewish community is that the individuals participating in it have not only had to actively search out their identity through probing questions, but also to create meaningful expressions of it. They do so not in isolation but, as I have discussed, in cooperation with Polish Christians who endeavor to understand, respect, and secure Polish Jewish life.

Poles and Jews: Identities Forged in Victimization and Villainization

In this book I have tried to demonstrate that to support each group's unity, both Poles and Jews have majorities which place victimization at the center of the respective myth with which they identify. Polish Christian and American Jewish

---

4   Ibid., 204.

responses to the Holocaust, World War II, and communism, and the ignorance both groups have had—and typically still have—about the Other's past suffering has produced an instinctive competition between the two for the title of "most victimized."

Poles had been invaded, partitioned, and culturally abused. Subjugated to international political whims and humiliated by the Minorities Treaty (which Jewish leaders in France, England, and the United States influenced), Poland was split apart and occupied by the Soviets and Nazis. Its civilian leaders were murdered outright and its citizens killed off through forced labor. Although the Poles proved an important partner in the Allied struggle against Hitler, in the end the Allies gave Poland to Stalin at Yalta. Consequentially, for more than four decades Poland suffered under an imposed political system that trampled individual rights and restricted access to goods and services, while cutting people off from facts known in the West but deemed dangerous by the USSR.

Fundamental to the Jewish ritual calendar is the theme of Jewish victimization: Passover seders commemorate freedom from four hundred years of forced labor under Egyptian rule; Purim's groggers (noise makers) drown out the name of the Persian king's advisor, Haman, who attempted to murder the Jews in his region; the Hanukkah menorah recounts the Greek ruler Antiochus's prohibition against Jewish religious practice; on Tisha B'Av Jews sit on the floor, as mourners, grieving over the Roman destruction of the Second Temple, the Jews' forced exile from the Land of Israel, and the subsequent restructuring of Jewish religious practice.

In addition, Jews recall the medieval Church-led Crusades and Spanish Inquisition. Treated by their Christian (and at times Muslim) "hosts" as the Other, Jewish communities in Europe, Africa, and Asia suffered ghettoization, inequality, violence, and expulsion. With the rise and spread of political antisemitism, Jews were rejected, blamed, and attacked. Hitler took antisemitism to its extreme when he ghettoized and starved, shot and gassed millions of Jews. Despite the Holocaust, governments and groups continued to threaten Jewish communal life. Postwar Jews in the Soviet Union were harassed, fired from their jobs, and ostracized. Anti-Israel sentiment, often laced with antisemitism, leads to hateful rhetoric and policies, and even guns and bombs. The barbarous October 7, 2023 Hamas attacks on Israeli civilians launched a full-scale war, in which Israel, and Jews in general, have been portrayed as vicious genocidal actors. With Palestinian deaths reaching past 30,000, and Gaza's infrastructure demolished, some activists seek vengence on Jews collectively. While sincee 2015 we have seen a resurgence of violence and murder targeting Jews in Europe and the United States, since the start of the war in Gaza, Jews (especially on college campuses) have met a violent explosion of antisemitism.[5] Recently, a resurgence of violence and murder targeting Jews in Europe and the United States has increased Jews' insecurity.[6]

This book has focused mainly on the false ideas Catholic Poles living in Poland have of Jews, including American Jews, and the distorted beliefs American Jews have of Poland's Catholic populations. Beginning in the 1980s, intellectuals on both sides have challenged popular misunderstandings each group has of the Other. Despite academic work, the larger populace clings to its prejudices, especially during political and social upheaval. Time and again, each community emphasizes its victimhood while suppressing its victimizers.

Both Jews and Poles, always frightened of losing touch with their central, painful narratives, resist full acknowledgement of the Other's experience, as well as their hurtful role in it. Jewish leaders refuse to use the word *genocide* to refer to the Nazi horrors inflicted on Poles. Rarely do American Jews speak of the involvement of Jews in the Soviet displacement of Poles (and Jews) from eastern Poland, Jews' part in the communist takeover of Poland, and Jews' role in the horrific Stalinist era. At the same time, the vast majority of Polish middle school and high school curriculums remain silent about the important interrelationship Jews and Poles shared over centuries. If students learn about antisemitism in Poland they do so only through an economic lens. They learn that the Jews barred Poles from accessing the middle class and that an economic protest against the Jews therefore makes sense. They do not learn that Polish antisemitism was grounded by Church policy and the false narratives of the "Elders of Zion" and the "Jew-communist," and the enormous impact each had on creating the ultimate enemy out of the Jews. And still today most Polish students do not learn about the Jews' Holocaust suffering. Only teachers who are highly motivated to locate the necessary material and training while withstanding some likely colleagues' disapproval teach these difficult subjects. Most students do not learn about Jedwabne and Jew hunts, unless through the lies of the Żydokomuna narrative. In its drive to reestablish Poles' heroic self-perception and good name, PiS has broadened efforts to magnify only Polish Righteousness. Concurrently, the government has attempted to stifle challenging research conducted by

---

5 "American Jewish Committee Condemns Anti-Jewiish Violence at UC Berkeley," and "What It's Like to Be Jewish at Harvard Among Antisemites and Hamas Supporters," See https://www.ajc.org, February 29, 2024.
6 Noah Raymanm, "Kosher Grocery Assault Confirms Worst Fears of French Jews," *TIME*, January 9, 2015, https://time.com/3661697/paris-terror-attack-kosher-grocery-jewish/#:~:text=The%20assault%20on%20the%20Kosher,according%20to%20the%20Associated%20Press.

Polish academics through the so-called "Holocaust Law." People on each side resist learning about the Other to safeguard their own sense of Self.

There is an argument I often hear from Jewish community members against affirming such historical nuances out loud. People worry that antisemites will grasp onto ugly truths from the Jewish past and convert them into antisemitic fodder. They contend that we should not talk about the Judenräte, the Jewish police, the Jewish criminal underworld, and communists of Jewish origin. It muddies the self-image we present to the world and our Selves.

Jews also worry about the possibility that the uniqueness of the Jewish experience in World War II will be diminished if we acknowledge other forms of genocide as equally horrific. Jews wish to maintain their ownership of the term *holocaust*. American Jews tend to view the Holocaust as *our* tragedy. We worry that to recognize an Other's tragedy that was contemporary with *ours* will lead down the slippery slope of forgetting the scope of *our* victimization. This is despite that there is now a well-known alternative to the word *holocaust*—the Hebrew term *Shoah*. As an American Jew, in the past I, myself, have shuddered at what I perceived as Others co-opting "holocaust." Why? I was afraid that if Others employed the word for *their* genocide it would signify that *the Jews'* genocide was less significant.

What an unenviable position: the need to establish my uniqueness by not recognizing the genocidal horrors another group faced. Throughout history genocide has been part of humanity's experience. The Holocaust was but one more genocide. Some Jewish scholars stress that the suffering of the victims of this genocide was in no sense greater than the suffering of victims of other genocides—there is no gradation of suffering. Thus, the fate of Roma victims at Auschwitz was exactly parallel to that of the Jewish victims.[7]

Equally, scholars have argued that some aspects of the Holocaust *thus far* have been unique in the extreme form and reach they took. In *Rethinking the Holocaust*, the Israeli Holocaust scholar Yehuda Bauer proposes that there were several unique components to the Holocaust: its ideological rootedness in the myth of the Jewish Satan, its crossing of national boundaries, and its intended totality of destruction.[8] However, Bauer emphasizes that *"the horror of the Holocaust is not that it deviated from human norms; the horror is that it didn't"* (italics in original).[9] Thus, while up until now the Holocaust has

---

7   Yehuda Bauer, *Rethinking the Holocaust* (New Haven: Yale University Press, 2002), 50.
8   Ibid., 48–49.
9   Ibid., 42.

within it elements that are unique, those elements may be repeated "by anyone toward anyone."[10]

The term *Holocaust* (with a capital H) refers to the specific genocide against the Jewish people by the Nazi regime. There is a danger that because it is an "extreme form of genocide" and the one most widely known—through television, literature, and museums—that it is the standard by which all other genocides are judged. But genocide does not have to reach the extremes of the Holocaust to be understood as the human tragedy that is genocide. As such, I hold there is no need to use the term *Holocaust* for another genocide. What is necessary is the recognition of that genocide by world leaders. Some, however, argue that "holocaust" (with a lower-case h) elevates recognition of the trauma. With respect to the Poles, I have shown that genocidal acts perpetrated against the Poles by the Nazis in the beginning of World War II may not have been completed, but that they were nevertheless genocidal in intent and practice.

While presenting the Holocaust as an "extreme form of genocide" it is incumbent upon us to simultaneously name as genocides the merciless and unyielding persecution, enslavement, and murder of millions more people which occurred along with, and at different historic junctures from, the Holocaust. In recognizing these concurrent genocides, I do not seek to compare them, but to respect them. Thus, to address American Jews' misperceptions of Poles I believe we must educate our youth regarding the Nazi-directed genocide against Poles during World War II. Despite our fear of losing status as most victimized, we must educate ourselves about the Poles' victimization with respect, humility, and compassion.

Education about the Other Begins with Questioning the Self: American Jews

In this book I have wrestled with respective narratives of the past with honesty—and I call for others to do the same. It is my firm opinion that we—Jew and Pole—must run toward the truth, not from it.

To face Poles with honest reflection, American Jews can start by checking our possibly hypocritical positions. Groups often view the world through their very specific communal lens: How does this situation affect *us*? It would be somewhat easy, then, even natural, for American Jews who ignore(d) Donald Trump's

---

10 Ibid.

explicit racism and sexism to support him—because of his economic, Middle East, and/or social policies—to be infuriated with Poland's own brand of bigotry. I hope that this section of American Jewry finds the courage to recognize the moral inconsistency of its anger, even rage, against PiS's specific impact on Holocaust education and the Jewish narrative. Indeed, today any American Jew who continues to support the current hard-right MAGA Republican Party has no rational argument against Poland's PiS Party. Ethno-nationalism is ethno-nationalism. One is either for it or against it.

In evaluating our education, American Jews can ask: What are we ignoring? By acknowledging that there is more to the past than we have been taught, we open the door to greater understanding of Polish-Jewish relations. By looking beyond our stereotype of the Polish antisemite, we gain understanding of Poles as a multifaceted people. We accept the centuries of Polish-Jewish relations as layered and complex. We find Polish kings who welcomed Jews when Germany persecuted and killed them as scapegoats for the fourteenth-century Black Plague and when Spain expelled Jews at the close of the fifteenth century. In return for the economic aid given by influxes of Jewish merchants and moneylenders, the crown provided the Jewish community with privileges and rights. Certainly, some sectors, specifically the Church and the burghers (Christian townsmen involved in trade and moneylending) opposed the inroads Jews made, with some arguing against Jewish settlement. However, throughout the Polish-Lithuanian Commonwealth, Jewish economic, intellectual, communal, and religious life flourished.

Unlike the Jews' situation in other lands, the Jews in the Polish-Lithuanian Commonwealth were trusted to participate in Arenda, thus managing the magnates' estates while also becoming indispensable craftsmen in the rural economy. Jewish communal life also flourished. Under the Council of Four Lands (Va'ad Arba Aratsot), Jews in the commonwealth enjoyed their unique autonomy to structure their communities according to Jewish law. The commonwealth's Talmudic higher educational institutions transformed into the best yeshivot in Europe. And though at odds one with the other, Hasidism and the Haskalah took root and developed broadly over time, establishing new Jewish viewpoints and opponents.

A fuller view of Polish-Jewish relations reveals the impact of partition. Poles and Jews lived amongst groups vying to attain, keep, and regain power. Polish-Jewish relations became dependent on how each population's subgroups reacted separately to new rulers and their new laws and how they understood one another within new, often changing contexts. To try to understand Polish-Jewish relations is to make room for Polish responses to their oppressors. Both the Freemasons and positivists saw Jews as possible allies and made room for them in their opposition to the tight grip of the Church and Russia. During uprisings (1830–31 and 1863–64), some Poles felt entitled to the Jews' support. While some Jews joined wholeheartedly, especially in the latter rebellion, most just hoped to keep their families safe by aligning with the governing power.

Part of delving into the past is to wrestle with our own behavior and ideas near the end of World War I and during the interwar years. American Jews organized aid for endangered Jews across the Atlantic. Influenced by the long-accepted caricature of Poles present in American culture (as well as among British and French Jews), they misunderstood Poland's post-World War I attacks on Jews and spiraled into hateful verbal assaults on the country. That they lobbied for some form of a Minorities Treaty in an independent Polish state is understandable. But that they did so in a patronizing fashion without grasping both the true political affinities of the majority Polish Jewish population, and actual Polish pogroms vis-à-vis other nations' assaults on Jews, remains problematic.

As in the United States today, Poland's inter-war citizenry was divided over whether their state should be multiethnic or relatively homogeneous. To see the strength of this cultural divide one need study not only the antisemitic policies of Roman Dmowski and his Endecja, but also be willing to look beyond him to the federalist multicultural dreams of Marshal Józef Piłsudski, who led the country from 1926–35. In the country that American Jews have pegged as the Jews' hateful enemy, there existed not only throngs of philosemitic allies, but also more opportunities for Jewish cultural, religious, and political development than anywhere else in the world at the time. Yiddishists, Hebraists, *Zionists*, Bundists, secularists, Hasidim, neo-Orthodox, and communists, vied for influence. There remained an active Polish opposition to Polish right-wing antisemitic policies until Nazi Germany—the common enemy—was on the verge of attack. Only then did liberal Poles ignore their grievances with the antisemitic Right to ward off this larger enemy.

When American Jews open the door to better understand Polish-Jewish relations during WWII, we need to explore both the Jews' experiences and the Poles'. It is important to learn about Nazi genocidal tactics against Poles and Soviet abuse of Poles during the war. When we engage with issues surrounding WWII, it is of utmost importance that we pay tribute to the incredible valor of Poles who distanced themselves from the growing ethno-nationalism and abhorrent antisemitic propaganda to recognize the humanity within the Jew. Thousands of individual Poles rescued Jews through extreme, daring, and drawn-out acts of courage. Even more attempted isolated acts of kindness and compassion. Yet, despite twenty acts of Polish kindness shown to one Jew in hiding, one Pole's denouncement could destroy other Poles' heroic efforts. At the same time, let neither Pole nor Jew be misled by the current nationalist false narrative that the majority of Poles saved Jews. For indeed, most Poles ignored the Jews' victimization. Furthermore, reflecting on the bloody civil war that began the forty-plus years of communist rule is crucial to better understand Poles and their relations with Jews. To gain access to the Poles we need to pay attention not only to what they went through as a collective, but also to what they were taught.

Education about the Other Begins with Questioning the Self: Poles

To face Jews honestly, Poles have begun wrestling with some of their heroes.[11] A towering 16.5-foot bronze statue of Roman Dmowski meets Poles in Warsaw on Na Rozdroźu Square at the intersection of Szuch and Ujazdów Avenues. For some a hero who stood up for Poland, Dmowski's ethno-nationalism also fiercely divided the country. His divisive rhetoric and policy against Poland's Jews prepped some Poles to walk that "narrow bridge" erected by Nazi propagandists. Some Poles have already begun questioning this monument's presence. Given that it took almost one hundred years to remove American Confederate iconography from the public square, I do not expect Poland to move this statue any time soon. But I do hope there will be a continued public wrestling with Dmowski's antisemitic laden nationalism.

Poles have also been contemplating the country's acceptance of the cult of the "disavowed soldiers." Once vilified for continuing to fight after WWII to oust the communists, the "disavowed soldiers" have been resurrected with honor. Along with the 1989 transition from communism to democracy, Poland understandably reassessed its heroes, removing some while elevating former villains to that glorified seat. Through educational efforts and governmental action, however,

---

11 A segment of the population did protest the 2006 installation of Roman Dmowski's statue, but to no avail. Politicians argued that his contributions to the nation far outweighed the hurt he caused through his antisemitic statements and writings. See August Grabski, "The Jews and the "Disavowed Soldiers" (trans. Gunnar Paulsson), in *New Directions in the History of the Jews in the Polish Lands*, ed. Antony Polonsky, Hanna Węgrzynek, and Andrzej Żbikowski (Boston: Academic Studies Press and POLIN Museum of the History of Polish Jews, 2018), 471.

the once "disavowed soldiers" have not only been rehabilitated but also transformed into a cult.

At first glance, a new admiration for this group seems in order. The problem arises, however, in its orientation and tactics. Even the anticommunist Polish Peasant Party (Polskie Stronnictwo Ludowe, PSL) condemned the political extremism of this small radical group of between thirteen to seventeen thousand.[12] Documentation abounds which testifies to its members' extreme nationalism and murder of more than five thousand civilian members of ethnic minorities, including Ukrainians, Belarussians, and Jews (among them 187 children fourteen-years-old or younger).[13] Their written propaganda displays broad hatred for Jews. Indeed, they argue that "Commie-Jews" and only "a few Communist Poles" were to blame for the communist takeover of Polish lands.[14] Rafal Wnuk's study found that the longest lasting rebel organization, named Freedom and Independence (WiN—1945–1952), portrayed Jews in a negative light in 10% of its newspapers and 40% of its leaflets.[15] WiN rhetoric described Jews as not only "the declared parasite and traitor" but also those "whom imperialist Russia has hired for its expansionist purposes."[16]

Given that Żydokomuna played a role in WiN's propaganda, it is no surprise that Polish anticommunist soldiers killed Jewish survivors in postwar Poland. The problem now is that under PiS the country has established a cult around them in a dramatic effort to make amends and to thank these "heroes" for defending the country when most other Poles acquiesced to communist rule. Unfortunately, despite individuals within the "disavowed soldiers" having killed numerous Jews and other minority civilians, they have retained their heroic status. Although the taboo of raising postwar antisemitic violence had been broken by the collective debate over Jedwabne, PiS is reestablished that taboo by ousting Jedwabne and the Holocaust from the classroom, by insisting that an enormous number of Poles helped Jews during the war, and by instituting the so-called "Holocaust Law."

Despite these setbacks, I hope that Poles will continue to question their heroes and institutions, including the Catholic Church. A beacon of hope and source of heroism during communist rule, the Catholic Church has had more than a millennium of influence over Poles. As such, the Church has had a range of opinions about the Jews. While some pontiffs negated the malicious blood

---

12   Ibid., 456.
13   Ibid., 457.
14   Cited in ibid., 465.
15   Ibid., 462.
16   Cited in ibid.

libel, others leaned into it. While some, like Pope John Paul II, argued that the Jews are not enemies of Christianity, others such as Pope Pius XI, who waged war against liberalism, the Freemasons, and communism, did paint the Jews as Poland's enemy. Thus, at various junctures, the Church has either hindered or promoted positive Polish-Jewish relations.

Throughout this book I have called for an honest critical re-evaluation of our respective myths regarding the Self and Other. Polish Christians and American Jews will understand the Self and the Other more fully, by embracing curiosity, compassion, and critical thinking. To seek to know the Other is not only to investigate their shame, but to explore their heroism. To seek to know the Self is not only to question our heroism but also to explore our shame. To understand more fully is to face one's identity with courage and vulnerability.

It is my firm hope that this analysis will help readers shift away from a simple black-and-white perception of Polish-Jewish relations to one that is marked by nuance. Messy, difficult, and at times painful, the Polish-Jewish past is anything but simple. Neither side is easy to describe; neither has a simple agenda. Rather, each has a myriad understandings of Self, which wax and wane depending on the era's local and global challenges. I hope that this work engages clergy, educators, and lay people in the myth reconstruction process. May we all have patience for its ebb and flow while remaining part of the conversation.

***

I have tried to demonstrate that there is not one single truth, but rather several that exist simultaneously, in time, in space, within individuals and within a nation. As I write this conclusion, the Polish people have opened their borders, homes, and hearts to Ukrainian refugees fleeing Vladimir Putin's insane and devastating bombardment. In 2022, the Poles have demonstrated to the world how one nation can help to save another nation. This tolerance and enormous aid do not negate Poles' unwillingness to host Syrian refugees. Nor do they mask many Poles' antisemitic actions during the last century and in the twenty-first. What Poles are demonstrating in 2022–23 is that a nation can be its best Self even after having shown its worst Self. Additionally, the 2023 victory of the Center-Left opposition over the Law and Justice party demonstrates Poles' desire to move away from PiS policies of intolerance. We wait to see where the United States 2024 election lands on this broad scale denoting closed and open societies. Today the Polish people represent the world's hope. What will the Americans represent?

Bibliography

Abramsky, Chimen, Maciej Jachimczyk, and Antony Polonsky, eds. *The Jews in Poland*. Oxford: Basil Blackwell, 1986.

Abramson, Henry. *A Prayer for the Government: Ukrainians and Jews in Revolutionary Times, 1917–1920*. Harvard Series in Ukrainian Studies. Boston: Ukrainian Research Institute of Harvard University, 1999.

Aderet, Ofer. "Poland Drops Case against Journalist Who Wrote That Poles Participated in the Holocaust," *Haaretz*, February 23, 2021. https://www.haaretz.com/world-news/europe/.premium-poland-drops-case-against-journalist-who-wrote-that-poles-participated-in-the-holoca-1.9563081.

ADL. ADL Tracker of Anti-Semitic Incidents. Accessed April 18, 2020. https://www.ADL.org.

Aleksiun, Natalia. "Jewish Responses to Antisemitism." In *Contested Memories: Poles and Jews during the Holocaust and Its Aftermath*, edited by Joshua D. Zimmerman, 247–261. New Brunswick: Rutgers University Press, 2003.

Almog, Shmuel. *Nationalism & Antisemitism in Modern Europe 1815–1945*. New York: Pergamon Press, 1990.

Ambrosewicz-Jacobs, Jolanta. "The Holocaust and Coming to Terms with the Past in Post-Communist Poland." Ina Levine Annual Lecture, United States Holocaust Memorial Museum, April 25, 2012.

Ambrosewicz-Jacobs, Jolanta, and Annamaria Orla-Bukowska. "After the Fall: Attitudes Towards Jews in Post-1989 Poland." *Nationalities Papers* 26, no. 2 (1998): 265–282.

Ambrosewicz-Jacobs, Jolanta, and Leora Tec. "An Inclusive Model of Memory Work in Poland: Bridge To Poland as a Case Study." *Politeja* 18, no. 1 (2021): 227–38.

Ambrosewicz-Jacobs, Jolanta, and Robert Szuchta. "The intricacies of education about the Holocaust in Poland. Ten years after the Jedwabne debate, what can Polish school students learn about the Holocaust in history classes?" *Intercultural Education* 25 no. 4 (2014): 283–299.

American Israelite. "The Polish Pogroms." January 9, 1919.

Andrzejewski, Jerzy. "The Problem of Polish Anti-Semitism." In *Against Anti-Semitism: An Anthology of Twentieth-Century Polish Writings*, edited by Adam Michnik and Agnieszka Marczyk, 93–112. Oxford: Oxford University Press, 2018.

Andrzejewski, Jerzy. *Ashes & Diamonds*. Translated by D. J. Welsch. Evanston: Northwestern University Press, 1997.

Applebaum, Anne. *Twilight of Democracy: The Seductive Lure of Authoritarianism*. New York: Doubleday, 2020.

Arad, Yitzhak, Yisrael Gutman, and Abraham Margaliot, eds. *Documents on the Holocaust: Selected Sources on the Destruction of the Jews of Germany and Austria, Poland, and the Soviet Union*. Jerusalem: Yad Vashem, in cooperation with the Anti-Defamation League and Ktav Publishing House, 1981.

Aronson, I. Michael. "The Anti-Jewish Pogroms in Russia in 1881." In *Pogroms: Anti-Jewish Violence in Modern Russian History*, edited by John D. Klier and Shlomo Lambroza, 44–61. Cambridge: Cambridge University Press, 1992.

Asch, Sholem. *Three Cities: A Trilogy*. Translated by Willa and Edwin Muir. New York: G. P. Putnam's Sons, 1943.

Ash, Timothy Garton. *The Polish Revolution: Solidarity*. 3rd ed. New Haven: Yale University Press, 2002.

Assmann, Jan. "Collective Memory and Cultural Identity." Translated by John Czaplicka. *New German Critique* 65 (1995): 125–133.

Astashkevich, Irina. "Gendered Violence: Jewish Women in the Pogroms of 1917 to 1921." PhD diss., Brandeis University, 2013.

Bacon, Gershon. "Messianists, Pragmatists, and Patriots: Orthodox Jews and the Modern Polish State (Some Preliminary Observations)." In *Netiot Ledavid: Jubilee Volume for David Weiss Halivni*, edited by Yaakov Elman, Ephraim Bezalel Halivni, and Zvi Ari Steinfeld. Jerusalem: Orhot, 2004.

Baron, Salo W. *The Russian Jew Under Tsars and Soviets*. 2nd ed. New York: Schocken Books, 1987.

Bartal, Israel. *The Jews of Eastern Europe, 1772–1881*. Translated by Chaya Naor. Jewish Culture and Contexts. Philadelphia: University of Pennsylvania Press, 2005.

Bartoszewski, Władysław T. *The Convent at Auschwitz*. New York: George Braziller, 1991.

———. "Polish-Jewish Relations in Occupied Poland, 1939–1945." In *The Jews in Poland*, edited by Chimen Abramsky, Maciej Jachimczyk, and Antony Polonsky, 147–160. Oxford: Basil Blackwell, 1986.

———. "Some Thoughts on Polish-Jewish Relations." In *Poles and Jews: Renewing the Dialogue*, edited by Antony Polonsky, 278–287. Polin: Studies in Polish Jewry, vol. 1. Oxford: The Littmann Library of Jewish Civilization, 2004.

Bartoszewski, Władysław T., and Zofia Lewin. *The Samaritans: Heroes of the Holocaust*. Edited by Alexander T. Jordan. New York: Twayme Publishers, 1970.

Bauer, Yehuda. *Rethinking the Holocaust*. New Haven: Yale University Press, 2002.

Bentley-Edwards, Keisha L., Malik Chaka Edwards, Cynthia Neal Spence, William A. Darity Jr., Darrick Hamilton, and Jasson Perez. "How Does It Feel to Be a Problem? The Missing Kerner Commission Report." *RSF: The Russell Sage Foundation Journal of the Social Sciences* 4, no. 6 (2018).

Best, Gary Dean. *To Free a People: American Jewish Leaders and the Jewish Problem in Eastern Europe, 1890–1914*. Westport: Greenwood Press, 1982.

Bialik, Chaim Nachman. "In the City of Slaughter." Translated by Jeffrey Burghauser. Orlando: Argus Huber, 2021.

Biskupski, M. B. B. *The History of Poland*. The Greenwood Histories of the Modern Nation. Santa Barbara: ABC-Clio, 2000.

———. *Hollywood's War with Poland, 1939–1945*. Lexington: The University Press of Kentucky, 2010.

Biskupski, M. B. B., and Antony Polonsky. Introduction to *Polish-Jewish Relations in North America*, edited by Mieczysław B. Biskupski and Antony Polonsky, 3–53. Polin: Studies in Polish Jewry, vol. 19. Oxford: The Littman Library of Jewish Civilization, 2007.

Blejwas, Stanislaus A. "Polish Positivism and the Jews." *Jewish Social Studies* 46, no. 1 (1984): 21–36.

Blobaum, Robert. "Criminalizing the 'Other.'" In *Antisemitism and Its Opponents in Modern Poland*, edited by Robert Blobaum, 81–102. Ithaca: Cornell University Press, 2005.

Bloom, Harold. Foreword to Yosef Yerushalmi, *Zakhor: Jewish History and Jewish Memory*. Seattle: University of Washington Press, 1996.

Bonacich, Edna. "A Theory of Middleman Minorities." *American Sociological Review* 38 (1973): 583–594.

Boyce, Travis D., and Winsome M. Chunnu. "Toward a Post-Racial Society, or a 'Rebirth' of a Nation? White Anxiety and Fear of Black Equality in the United States." In *Historicizing Fear: Ignorance, Vilification, and Othering*, edited by Travis D. Boyce and Winsome M. Chunnu, 122–156. Louisville: University Press of Colorado, 2019.

Brandys, Kazimierz. *A Warsaw Diary 1978–1981*. Translated by Richard Lourie. New York: Random House, 1983.

Bronsztejn, Szyja. "Polish-Jewish Relations in Memoirs." In *Jews in Independent Poland, 1918–1939*, edited by Antony Polonsky, Ezra Mendelsohn, and Jerzy Tomaszewski, 66–88. Polin: Studies in Polish Jewry, vol. 8. Oxford: The Littman Library of Jewish Civilization, 2004.

Brooks, David. "What Happened to American Conservatism?" *Atlantic*, December 8, 2021.

Brownstein, Ronald. "The Democrats' New Voting Rights Obstacle." *Atlantic*, July 8, 2021.

Budnitskii, Oleg. *Russian Jews between the Reds and the Whites, 1917–1920*. Translated by Timothy J. Portice. Philadelphia: University of Pennsylvania, 2012.

Bukowczyk, John J. *A History of the Polish Americans*. New Brunswick: Transaction Publishers, 2009.

Burkholder, Pete, and Dana Schaffer, "A Snapshot of the Public's Views on History: National Poll Offers Valuable Insights for Historians and Advocates." Perspectives on History, August 20 2021. https://www.historians.org/publications-and-directories/perspectives-on-history/september-2021/a-snapshot-of-the-publics-views-on-history-national-poll-offers-valuable-insights-for-historians-and-advocates.

Butterwick-Pawlikowski, Richard. "Jews in the Discourses of the Polish Enlightenment." In *Jews in the Kingodm of Poland, 1815–1918*, edited by Glenn Dynner, Antony Polonsky, and Marcin Wodziński, 45–62. Polin: Studies in Polish Jewry, vol. 27. Oxford: The Littman Library of Jewish Civilization, 2015.

Cała, Alina. *Jew. The Eternal Enemy?: The History of Antisemitism in Poland*. Translated by Jan Burzynski and edited by Mikołaj Gołubiewski. Polish Studies—Transdisciplinary Perspectives, vol. 22. Berlin: Peter Lang, 2018.

The Catholic Information Agency. "Interview with the Primate of Poland, Cardinal Jozef Glemp, on the Murder of Jews in Jedwabne, 15 May 2001." In *The Neighbors Respond: The Controversy over the Jedwabne Massacre in Poland*, edited by Antony Polonsky and Joanna B. Michlic, 166–172. Princeton: Princeton University Press, 2004.

Cherry, Robert. "Measuring Anti-Polish Biases among Holocaust Teachers." In *Rethinking Poles and Jews: Troubled Past, Brighter Future*, edited by Robert Cherry and Annamaria Orla-Bukowska, 69–82. Lanham: Rowman & Littlefield Publishers, Inc., 2007.

Cherry, Robert, and Annamaria Orla-Bukowska, eds. *Rethinking Poles and Jews: Troubled Past, Brighter Future*. Lanham: Rowman & Littlefield Publishers, Inc., 2007.

Chojnowski, Andrzej. "The Jewish Question in the Work of the *Instytut Badań Spraw Narodowościowych* in Warsaw." In *Poles and Jews: Perceptions and Misperceptions*, edited by Władysław T. Bartoszewski, 159–168. Polin: Studies in Polish Jewry, vol. 4. Oxford: The Littman Library of Jewish Civilization, 2004.

Ciechanowiecki, Andrzej. "A Footnote to the History of the Integration of Converts into the Ranks of the Szlachta in the Polish-Lithuanian Commonwealth." In *The Jews in Poland*, edited by Chimen Abramsky, Maciej Jachimczyk, and Antony Polonsky, 64–69. Oxford: Basil Blackwell, 1986.

Cobas, José A. "Six Problems in the Sociology of the Ethnic Economy." *Sociological Perspectives* 32 (1989): 201–214.

Cohen, Barry. *Opening the Drawer: The Hidden Identities of Polish Jews*. London: Vallentine Mitchell, 2018.

Cohen, Naomi W. *Not Free to Desist: The American Jewish Committee 1906–1966*. Philadelphia: The Jewish Publication Society of America, 1972.

Cohn, Norman. *Warrant for Genocide: The Myth of the Jewish World Conspiracy and the Protocols of the Elders of Zion*. London: Serif, 2005.

Connelly, John. *Captive University: The Sovietization of East German, Czech, and Polish Higher Education 1945–1956*. Chapel Hill: The University of North Carolina Press, 2000.

Corrsin, Stephen D. "Aspects of Population Change and of Acculturation in Jewish Warsaw at the End of the Nineteenth Century: The Censuses of 1882 and 1897." In *The Jews in Warsaw*, edited by Władysław T. Bartoszewski and Antony Polonsky, 212–231. Oxford: Basil Blackwell, 1990.

Cox, John. *To Kill a People: Genocide in the Twentieth Century*. Oxford: Oxford University Press, 2017.

Czerniakow, Adam. *The Warsaw Diary of Adam Czerniakow*. Edited by Raul Hilberg, Stanislaw Staron, and Josef Kermisz and translated by Stanislaw Staron and the Staff of Yad Vashem. Chicago: Elephant Paperback in association with the United States Holocaust Memorial Museum, 1999.

Czuchnowski, Wojciech. "Appeals Court Dismisses Libel Case Against Holocaust Scholars Grabowski and Engelking." *Gazetta Wyborcza*, August 17, 2021. https://wyborcza.pl/7,173236,27463746,appeals-court-dismisses-libel-case-against-holocaust-scholars.html.

———. "Holocaust Scholars Engelking and Grabowski Ordered to Apologize in Libel Case." *Gazetta Wyborcza*, February 12, 2021. https://wyborcza.pl/7,173236,26783046,holocaust-scholars-engelking-and-grabowski-ordered-to-apologize.html.

Dąbrowska, Maria. "Annual Shame." In *Against Anti-Semitism: An Anthology of Twentieth-Century Polish Writings*, edited by Adam Michnik and Agnieszka Marczyk, 45–54. New York: Oxford University Press, 2018.

Davies, Norman. "Ethnic Diversity in Twentieth Century Poland." In *Poles and Jews: Perceptions and Misperceptions*, edited by Władysław T. Bartoszewski, 143–158. Polin: Studies in Polish Jewry, vol. 4. Oxford: The Littman Library of Jewish Civilization, 2004.

———. *God's Playground: A History of Poland, 1795 to the Present*. 2 vols. Rev. ed. New York: Columbia University Press, 2005.

———. *White Eagle, Red Star: The Polish-Soviet War 1919–1929 and the Miracle on the Vistula*. London: Pimlico, 2003.

Dawidowicz, Lucy. *The War against the Jews*. Middlesex: Penguin Books, 1979.

Dinnerstein, Leonard. *Antisemitism in America*. Oxford: Oxford University Press, 1994.

Dray, Philip. *At the Hands of Persons Unknown: The Lynching of Black America*. New York: The Modern Library, 2003.

Dubnow, Simon M. *History of the Jews in Russia and Poland: From the Earliest Times until the Present Day*. Vol. 3, *From the Accession of Nicholas II until the Present Day with Bibliography and Index*. Translated by I. Friedlaender. Philadelphia: The Jewish Publication Society of America, 1920.

Dynner, Glenn. *Men of Silk: The Hasidic Conquest of Polish Jewish Society*. Oxford: Oxford University Press, 2006.

———. *Yankel's Tavern: Jews, Liquor, & Life in the Kingdom of Poland*. Oxford: Oxford University Press, 2014.

Dynner, Glenn, and Marcin Wodziński. "The Kingdom of Poland and Her Jews: An Introduction." In *Jews in the Kingdom of Poland: 1915–1918*, edited by Glenn Dynner, Antony Polonsky, and Marcin Wodziński, 3–44. Polin: Studies in Polish Jewry, vol. 27. Oxford: The Littman Library of Jewish Civilization, 2015.

Eisen, Norman, Aaron Klein, Mario Picon, Robin J. Lewis, Lilly Blumenthal, Scott Johnston, and Charlie Loudon. Brookings Sanctions Tracker, March 22, 2022. https://www.brookings.edu/research/the-brookings-sanctions-tracker/.

Eisler, Jerzy. "1968: Jews, Antisemitism, Emigration." In *1968 Forty Years After*, edited by Leszek W. Głuchowski and Antony Polonsky, 37–61. Polin: Studies in Polish Jewry, vol. 21. Oxford: The Littman Library of Jewish Civilization, 2009.

Eisenbach, Artur. *The Emancipation of the Jews in Poland, 1780–1870*. Edited by Antony Polonsky and translated by Janina Dorosz. Jewish Society and Culture. Cambridge: Basil Blackwell, 1991.

Elliott, Philip. "The Big Lie Has Been Proven False. Republicans Can't Shake It." *TIME*, November 1, 2021. https://time.com/6112488/trump-2020-election-republicans/.

Encyclopedia Judaica. s.v. "Chmielnicki, Bogdan." 16 vols. 2nd ed. Farmingham Hills: Macmillan, 2007.

Engel, David. "An Early Account of Polish Jewry under Nazi and Soviet Occupation Presented to the Polish Government-In-Exile, February 1940." *Jewish Social Studies* 45, no. 1 (1983): 1–16.

———. *Facing A Holocaust: The Polish Government-in-Exile and the Jews, 1943–1945*. Chapel Hill: The University of North Carolina Press, 1993.

———. *In the Shadow of Auschwitz: The Polish Government-in-Exile and the Jews, 1939–1942*. Chapel Hill: The University of North Carolina Press, 1987.

———. "Lwów, 1918: The Transmutation of a Symbol and Its Legacy in the Holocaust," *Contested Memories: Poles and Jews during the Holocaust and Its Aftermath*, edited by Joshua Zimmerman 33–44, New Brunswick: Rutgers University Press, 2003.

———. "On the Bowdlerization of a Holocaust Testimony: The Wartime Journal of Calek Perechodnik." In *Focusing on Galicia: Jews, Poles, and Ukrainians*, edited by Israel Bartal and Antony Polonsky, 316–329. Polin: Studies in Polish Jewry, vol. 12. Oxford: The Littman Library of Jewish Civilization, 1999.

Engelking, Barbara. *Such a Beautiful Sunny Day . . . Jews Seeking Refuge in the Polish Countryside, 1942–1945*. Jerusalem: Yad Vashem Publications, 2016.

Engelking-Boni, Barbara. "Psychological Distance between Poles and Jews in Nazi-Occupied Warsaw." In *Contested Memories: Poles and Jews During the Holocaust and Its Aftermath*, edited by Joshua Zimmerman, 47–53. New Brunswick: Rutgers University Press, 2003.

Etkes, Emmanuel. "Haskalah." In *Yivo Encyclopedia*. Accessed March 13, 2019. www.yivoencyclopedia.org/article.aspx/Haskalah.

Ettinger, Shmuel. Foreword to *Nationalism and Antisemitism from 1815–1945*, by Shmuel Almog, xi–xxv. Edited by Yehuda Bauer. Studies in Antisemitism. Oxford: Pergamon Press, 1990.

Evdokimova, Tamara. "Polish Activists Topple Statue of Iconic Priest as Vatican Summit on See Abuse Begins." *Slate*, February 21, 2019. https://slate.com/news-and-politics/2019/02/poland-priest-henryk-jankowski-statue-clergy-sex-abuse.html.

Feinstein, Dianne. "Republicans Keep Confirming Unqualified Judicial Nominees." Law360.com, June 24, 2020. https://www.law360.com/employment-authority/articles/1285914/republicans-keep-confirming-unqualified-judicial-nominees-.

Feldman, Jackie. *Above the Death Pits, Beneath the Flag: Youth Voyages to Poland and Performance of Israeli National Identity*. New York: Berghahn Books, 2010.

Fishman, David. *The Rise of Modern Yiddish Culture*. Pittsburgh: University of Pittsburgh Press, 2010.

Fleming, Michael. *Auschwitz, the Allies and Censorship of the Holocaust*. Cambridge: Cambridge University Press, 2014.

———. Review of *Wobec "niespotykanego w dziejach mordu": Rząd RP na uchodźstwie, Delegatura Rządu RP na Kraj, AK a eksterminacja ludności żydowskiej od "wielkiej acji" do powstania w getcie warszawskim*, by Adam Puławski. American Association for Polish-Jewish Studies. Accessed March 3, 2022. http://www.aapjstudies.org/index.php?id=262.

Forecki, Piotr. *Reconstructing Memory: The Holocaust in Polish Public Debate*. Frankfurt am Main: Peter Lang, 2013.

Friedman, Thomas. Interview on *Morning Joe*. MSNBC, December 19, 2019.

Frydel, Tomasz. "*Judenjagd*: Reassessing the Role of Ordinary Poles as Perpetrators in the Holocaust." In *Perpetrators and Perpetration of Mass Violence: Action, Motivations and Dynamics*, edited by Timothy Williams and Susanne Buckley-Zistel, 187–203. London: Routledge, 2018.

Furber, David, and Wendy Lower. "Colonialism and Genocide in Nazi-Occupied Poland and Ukraine." In *Empire, Colony, Genocide: Conquest, Occupation, and Subaltern Resistance in World History*, edited by A. Dirk Moses, 372–402. New York: Berghahn Books, 2008.

Gąsowski, Tomasz. "The Second Republic and Its Jewish Citizens." In *The Jews in Poland*, vol. 2, edited by Sławomir Kapralski, 125–136. Kraków: Jagiellonian University Printing House, 1999.

Gebert, Konstanty. "Anti-Semitism in the 1990 Polish Presidential Election." *Social Research* 58, no. 4 (1991): 723–55.

Gieysztor, Aleksander. "Beginnings of Jewish Settlement in Poland." In *The Jews in Poland*, edited by Chimen Abramsky, Maciej Jachimczyk, and Antony Polonsky, 15–21. Oxford: Basil Blackwell, 1986.

Gilman, Neil. *Sacred Fragments: Recovering Theology for the Modern Jew*. Philadelphia: The Jewish Publication Society, 1990.

Ginzburg, Ralph. *100 Years of Lynchings*. Baltimore: Black Classic Press, 1988.

Gladsky, Thomas S. *Princes, Peasants and Other Polish Selves: Ethnicity in American Literature*. Amherst: The University of Massachusetts Press, 1992.

Goldberg, Jacob. "The Privileges Granted to Jewish Communities of the Polish Commonwealth as a Stabilizing Factor in Jewish Support." In *The Jews in Poland*, edited by Chimen Abramsky, Maciej Jachimczyk, and Antony Polonsky, 31–54. Oxford: Basil Blackwell, 1986.

Gordon, Linda. *Cossack Rebellions: Social Turmoil in the Sixteenth-Century Ukraine*. Albany: State University of New York Press, 1983.

Goska, Danusha. *Bieganski: The Brute Polak Stereotype in Polish-Jewish Relations and American Popular Culture*. Boston: Academic Studies Press, 2010.

———. "The Necesssity of 'Bieganski.'" In *Polish-Jewish Relations in North America*, edited by Mieczysław B. Biskupski and Antony Polonsky, 205–228. Polin: Studies in Polish Jewry, vol. 19. Oxford: The Littman Library of Jewish Civilization, 2007.

Grabowski, Jan. *Hunt for the Jews: Betrayal and Murder in German-Occupied Poland*. Bloomington: Indiana University Press, 2013.

———. "The New Wave of Holocaust Revisionism." *New York Times*, January 29, 2022. https://www.nytimes.com/2022/01/29/opinion/holocaust-poland-europe.html.

Grabowski, Jan, and Barbara Engelking, eds. *Night without End: The Fate of Jews in German-Occupied Poland*. Bloomington: Indiana University Press, 2022.

Grabski, August. "The Jews and the 'Disavowed Soldiers.'" [Translated by Gunnar Paulsson] In *New Directions in the History of the Jews in the Polish Lands*, edited by Antony Polonsky, Hanna Węgrzynek and Andrzej Żbikowski. 452–471. Boston: Academic Studies Press and POLIN Museum of the History of Polish Jews, 2018.

Grade, Chaim. *My Mother's Sabbath Days: A Memoir*. Translated by Channa Kleinman Goldstein and Inna Hecker Grade. Lanham: Rowman & Littlefield Publishers, Inc., 2004.

Green, Peter S. "Poles Vote Yes to Joining European Union." *New York Times*, June 9, 2003. https://www.nytimes.com/2003/06/09/world/poles-vote-yes-to-joining-european-union.html.

Greenstone, Julius H. "House of Israel: More Pogroms Reported in Poland and Galicia." *Jewish Exponent*, May 30, 1919.

Gross, Jan T. *Fear: Anti-Semitism in Poland After Auschwitz*. Princeton: Princeton University Press, 2006.

———. *Neighbors: The Destruction of the Jewish Community in Jedwabne, Poland*. 2nd ed. New York: Penguin Books, 2002.

———. "Stereotypes of Polish-Jewish Relations after the War: The Special Commission of the Central Committee of Polish Jews." In *Focusing on the Holocaust and its Aftermath*, edited by Antony Polonsky, 194–205. Polin: Studies in Polish Jewry, vol. 13. Oxford: The Littman Library of Jewish Civilization, 2000.

Gross, Jenny. "School Board in Tennessee Bans Teaching of Holocaust Novel 'Maus.'" *New York Times*, January 27, 2022. https://www.nytimes.com/2022/01/27/us/maus-banned-holocaust-tennessee.html.

Gross, Magdalena H. "No Longer Estranged: Learning to Teach the Holocaust in Poland." *Holocaust Studies* 24, no. 2 (2019): 131–149.

Grossman, Lt. Col. Dave. *On Killing: The Psychological Cost of Learning to Kill in War and Society*. rev. ed. New York: Back Bay Books/Little Brown and Company, 2009.

Grundzińska-Gross, Irena. Introduction to *Pogrom Cries—Essays on Polish-Jewish History, 1939–1946*, by Joanna Tokarska-Bakir, 9–12. Frankfurt am Main: Peter Lang, 2017.

Grynberg, Henryk. *Drohobycz, Drohobycz and Other Stories: True Tales from the Holocaust and Life After*. Translated by Alicia Nitecki and edited by Theodosia Robertson. New York: Penguin Books, 2002.

Guesnet, Francois. "Migration and Stereotype: The Case of Russian Jews in the Polish Kingdom at the End of the Nineteenth Century." *Cahiers du monde russe Russie Empire russe Union soviétique États indépendants* 41, no. 4 (2000): 505–518.

Gutterman, Alexander. "The Origins of the Great Synagogue in Warsaw on Tłomackie Street." In *The Jews of Warsaw*, edited by Władysław T. Bartoszewski and Antony Polonsky, 181–211. Oxford: Basil Blackwell in association with the Institute for Polish-Jewish Studies, 1991.

Gutman, Yisrael, and Shmuel Krakowski. *Unequal Victims: Poles and Jews during World War II*. Translated by Ted Gorelick and Witold Jedlicki. New York: Holocaust Library, 1986.

Hagen, William W. "The Moral Economy of Popular Violence: The Pogrom in Lwów, November 1918." In *Antisemitism and Its Opponents in Modern Poland*, edited by Robert Blobaum, 124–147. Ithaca: Cornell University Press, 2005.

———. *Anti-Jewish Violence in Poland, 1914–1920*. Cambridge: Cambridge University Press, 2018.

Halasz, Nicholas. Introduction to *Five Years of My Life: The Diary of Captain Alfred Dreyfus*, by Alfred Dreyfus. New York: Peebles Press, 1977.

Heifetz, Elias. *The Slaughter of the Jews in the Ukraine in 1919*. New York: Thomas Seltzer, Inc., 1921.

Heller, Celia S. *On the Edge of Destruction Jews of Poland between the Two World Wars*. Detroit: Wayne State University Press, 1994.

Hendrix, Steve. "As Israel's Longest-Serving Leader, Netanyahu Transformed His Country—and Left It More Divided Than Ever." *Washington Post*, June 21, 2021. https://www.washingtonpost.com/world/middle_east/israel-prime-minister-benjamin-netanyahu-legacy/2021/06/13/aa9b2d7e-c9e8-11eb-8708-64991f2acf28_story.html.

Hilberg, Raul, and Stanislaw Staron. Introduction to *The Warsaw Diary of Adam Czerniakow: Prelude to Doom*, by Adam Czerniadow, edited by Raul Hilberg, Stanislaw Staron, and Josef Kermisz, and translated by Stanislaw Staron and the Staff of Yad Vashem, 25–72. Chicago: Elephant Paperback in association with the United States Holocaust Memorial Museum, 1999.

Himka, John-Paul. "Dimensions of a Triangle: Polish-Ukrainian-Jewish Relationship in Austrian Galicia." In *Focusing on Galicia: Jews, Poles, and Ukrainians, 1772–1918*, edited by Israel Bartal and Antony Polonsky, 25–48, Polin: Studies in Polish Jewry, vol. 12. London: The Littman Library of Jewish Civilization, 1999.

Himka, John-Paul, and Joanna Beata Michlic. Introduction to *Bringing the Dark Past to Light: The Reception of the Holocaust in Postcommunist Europe*, edited by John-Paul Himka and Joanna Beata Michlic, 1–24. Lincoln: University of Nebraska Press, 2013.

Hoffman, Ewa. *Shtetl: The Life and Death of a Small Town and the World of Polish Jews*. New York: Public Affairs, 2007.

Hundert, Gershon. *Jews in Poland-Lithuania in the Eighteenth Century: A Genealogy of Modernity*. Berkeley: University of California Press, 2004.

Ives, Mike. "Beyond Tulsa, Overlooked Race Massacres Draw New Focus." *New York Times*, June 29, 2021. https://www.nytimes.com/2021/06/29/us/elaine-massacre-history-lessons.html.

Janicka, Elżbieta. "Memory and Identity in the Former Warsaw Ghetto Area." [Translated by J. Dziubińska] *Herito* 13, no. 4 (2013): 66–81.

———. "The Square of Polish Innocence: POLIN Museum of the History of Polish Jews in Warsaw and Its Symbolic Topography." *East European Jewish Affairs* 45, nos. 2–3 (2015): 200–214.

Janowsky, Oscar I. Foreword, to *The Jews and Minority Rights: 1898–1919*, by Julian Mack. New York: Columbia University Press, 1933.

Jaruzelski, Wojciech. "A Painful and Complex Subject." In *1968: Forty Years After*, edited by Leszek W. Gluchowski and Antony Polonsky, 310–314. Polin: Studies in Polish Jewry, vol. 21. Oxford: The Littman Library of Jewish Civilization, 2009.

Jaskulowski, Krzysztof, Piotr Majewski, and Adrianna Surmak. "Teaching the Nation: History and Nationalism in the Polish School History Education." *British Journal of Sociology of Education* 39 (2018): 77–91.

Jastruń, Mieczysław. "The Power of Ignorance." In *Against Anti-Semitism: An Anthology of Twentieth-Century Polish Writings*, edited by Adam Michnik and Agnieszka Marczyk, 85–92. Oxford: Oxford University Press, 2018.

"Jews The Only Victims of Polish Pogroms." *Jewish Advocate*, December 12, 1918, 3.

"Jewish Ill Treatment Denied by Lubomirski." *Jewish Exponent*, July 30, 1920.

John, Tara. "Poland's Holocaust Law: What You Need to Know." *TIME*, February 1, 2018. https://time.com/5128341/poland-holocaust-law/.

Jones, Adam. *Genocide: A Comprehensive Introduction*. 3rd ed. London: Routledge, 2017.

Jones, Zoe Christen, "Emmett Till Memorial Sign Missing Days after 66th Anniversary of His Death." CBS News, September 3, 2021. https://www.cbsnews.com/news/emmett-till-marker-missing-mississippi-66th-anniversary/.

Kapiszewski, Andrzej. *Conflicts across the Atlantic: Essays on Polish-Jewish Relations in the United States During World War I and the Interwar Years*. Kraków: Księgarnia Akademicka, 2004.

Kapralski, Sławomir. "The Holocaust: Commemorated but Not Remembered? Post-Colonial and Post-Traumatic Perspectives on the Reception of the Holocaust Memory Discourse in Poland." *Journal of Historical Sociology* 31 (2017): 48–65. https://doi.org/10.1111/johs.12165.

Kassow, Samuel D. Introduction to *Who Will Write Our History?: Rediscovering A Hidden Archive from the Warsaw Ghetto*, by Emanuel Ringleblum, 1–16. New York: Vintage Books, 2007.

Katz, Jacob. *Jews and Freemasons in Europe, 1723–1939*. Cambridge, MA: Harvard University Press, 1970.

Kenez, Peter. "Pogroms and White Ideology in the Russian Civil War." In *Pogroms: Anti-Jewish Violence in Modern Russian History*, edited by John D. Klier and Shlomo Lambroza, 293–313. Cambridge: Cambridge University Press, 1992.

Kenney, Padriac. "Whose Nation, Whose State? Working-Class Nationalism and Antisemitism in Poland, 1945–1947." In *Focusing on the Holocaust and its Aftermath*, edited by Antony Polonsky, 224–235. Polin: Studies in Polish Jewry, vol. 13. Oxford: The Littman Library of Jewish Civilization, 2000.

Kermisz, Joseph. Introduction to *The Warsaw Diary of Adam Czerniakow: Prelude to Doom*, edited by Raul Hilberg, Stanislaw Staron, and Josef Kermisz, translated by Stanislaw Staron and the Staff of Yad Vashem, 1–24. Chicago: Elephant Paperback in association with the United States Holocaust Memorial Museum, 1999.

Kersten, Krystyna. *The Establishment of Communist Rule in Poland, 1943–1948*. Translated by John Micgiel and Michael H. Bernhard. Berkeley: University of California Press, 1991.

Kertzer, David. *The Popes against the Jews: The Vatican's Role in the Rise of Modern Antisemitism*. New York: Vintage Books, 2002.

Kieniewicz, Stefan. "Assimilated Jews in Nineteenth-Century Warsaw." In *The Jews in Warsaw*, edited by Wladyslaw T. Bartoszewski and Antony Polonsky, 171–180. Oxford: Basil Blackwell in association with the Institute for Polish-Jewish Studies, 1991.

———. "The Jews of Warsaw, Polish Society and Partitioning Powers 1795–1861." In *The Jews of Warsaw*, edited by Władysław T. Bartoszewski and Antony Polonsky, 151–170. Oxford: Basil Blackwell in association with the Institute for Polish-Jewish Studies, 1991.

———. "Polish Society and the Jewish Problem in the Nineteenth Century." In *The Jews in Poland*, edited by Chimen Abramsky, Maciej Jachimczyk, and Antony Polonsky, 70–77. Oxford: Basil Blackwell, 1986.

Kirschenblatt-Gimblett, Barbara. "Theater of History." In *Polin: 1000 Year History of Polish Jews*, edited by Barbara Kirschenblatt-Gimblett and Antony Polonsky, 19–36. 2nd ed. Warsaw: Museum of the History of Polish Jews, 2015.

Klein, Charlotte. "Damascus to Kiev: *Civiltà Cattolica* on Ritual Murder." In *The Blood Libel Legend: A Casebook in Anti-Semitic Folklore*, edited by Alan Dundes, 180–196. Madison: The University of Wisconsin Press, 1991.

Klier, John D. "The Pogrom Paradigm in Russian History." In *Pogroms: Anti-Jewish Violence in Modern Russian History*, edited by John D. Klier and Shlomo Lambroza, 13–38. Cambridge: Cambridge University Press, 1992.

Klier, John D., and Shlomo Lambroza. "The Pogroms of 1881–1884." In *Pogroms Anti-Jewish Violence in Modern Russian History*, edited by John D. Klier and Shlomo Lambroza, 39–43. Cambridge: Cambridge University Press, 1992.

Kochavi, Arieh. *Post-Holocaust Politics: Britain, the United States & Jewish Refugees, 1945–1948*. Chapel Hill: University of North Carolina Press, 2001.

Kohut, Zenon E. "The Khmelnytsky Uprising, the Image of Jews, and the Shaping of Ukrainian Historical Memory." *Jewish History* 17 (2003): 141–163.

Kopstein, Jeffrey S., and Jason Wittenberg. *Intimate Violence: Anti-Jewish Pogroms on the Eve of the Holocaust*. Ithaca: Cornell University Press, 2018.

Kossak, Zofia. "'Protest!'"—a Proclamation of the Underground Front for the Revival of Poland. Warsaw, August 19, 1942." In *"Żegota": The Council for Aid to Jews 1942–1945. Selected Documents*, edited by Andrzej Krzystof Kunert. Warsaw: Rada Ochrony Pamięci Walk I Męczeństwa, 2002. 77–79.

Kozłowski, Maciej. *The Emissary: The Story of Jan Karski*. Translated by Johanna Maria Kwiatowska. Warsaw: The Ministry of Foreign Affairs, 2007.

———. "Jan Maletka Deserves Commemoration. A Response to Adam Leszczyński." The Pilecki Institute. Accessed February 25, 2022. https://instytutpileckiego.pl/en/zawolani-po-imieniu.

Krajewski, Stanisław. "The Evolution of Catholic-Jewish Relations in Poland after 1989." In *Rethinking Poles and Jews: Troubled Past, Brighter Future*, edited by Robert Cherry and Annamaria Orla-Bukowska, 141–154. Lanham: Rowman & Littlefield Publishers, Inc., 2007.

———. *Poland and the Jews: Reflections of a Polish Polish Jew*. Kraków: Wydawnictwo Austeria, 2005.

Krakowski, Shmuel. "The Polish Underground and the Extermination of the Jews." In *Jews, Poles, Socialists: The Failure of an Ideal*, edited by Antony Polonsky, Israel Bartal, Gershon Hundert, Magdalena Opalski, and Jerzy Tomaszewski, 161–170. Polin: Studies in Polish Jewry, vol. 9. Oxford: The Littman Library of Jewish Civilization, 1996.

Krzemiński, Ireneusz. "In Light of Later History." In *Why We Should Teach About the Holocaust*, edited by Jolanta Ambrosewicz-Jacobs and Leszek Hońdo, translated by Michael Jacobs, 26–32. Kraków: The Jagiellonian University Institute of European Studies, 2005.

Krzywiec, Grzegorz. *Chauvenism, Polish Style: The Case of Roman Dmowski (Beginnings: 1886–1905)*. Translated by Jarosław Garliński. Frankfurt am Main: Peter Lang, 2016.

Kubik, Jan. *The Power of Symbols against the Symbols of Power: The Rise of Solidarity and the Fall of State Socialism in Poland*. University Park: The Pennsylvania State University Press, 1994.

Kugelmass, Jack. "The Rites of the Tribe: The Meaning of Poland for American Jewish Tourists." *Going Home: YIVO Annual 21*, edited by Deborah Dash Moore and Jack Kugelmass. Evanston: Northwestern University, 1993.

Kunert, Andrzej Krzysztof, ed. *"Żegota": The Council for Aid to Jews 1942–1945, Selected documents*. Warsaw: Rada Ochrony Pamięci Walk I Męczeństwa, 2002.

Kuznitz, Cecile Esther. *YIVO and the Making of Modern Jewish Culture: Scholarship for the Yiddish Nation*. Cambridge: Cambridge University Press, 2014.

Kwaśniewski, Aleksander. "Address by President of Poland Aleksander Kwaśniewski at the Ceremonies in Jedwabne Marking the Sixtieth Anniversary of the Jedwabne Tragedy on 10 July 2001." In *The Neighbors Respond: The Controversy Over the Jedwabne Massacre in Poland*, edited by Antony Polonsky and Joanna B. Michlic, 130–132. Princeton: Princeton University Press, 2004.

Lamb, Christopher. "Francis Affirms No Place in Church for Those Who Reject Vatican II." ChicagoCatholic.com, February 3, 2021. https://www.chicagocatholic.com/vatican/-/article/2021/02/03/vatican-city-pope-francis-announced-the-establishment-of-a-world-day-of-grandparents-and-the-elderly-as-a-reminder-of-the-important-role-they-play-as-.

Lambroza, Shlomo. "The Pogroms of 1903–1906." In *Pogroms: Anti-Jewish Violence in Modern Russian History*, edited by John D. Klier and Shlomo Lambroza, 195–246. Cambridge: Cambridge University Press, 1992.

Landau, Jacob M. "Ritual Murder Accusations in Nineteenth-Century Egypt." In *The Blood Libel Legend: A Casebook in Anti-Semitic Folklore*, edited by Aland Dundes, 197–232. Madison: The University of Wisconsin Press, 1991.

Landau-Czajka, Anna. "The Image of the Jew in the Catholic Press during the Second Republic." In *Jews in Independent Poland, 1918–1939*, edited by Antony Polonsky, Ezra Mendelsohn, and Jerzy Tomaszewski, 146–175. Polin: Studies in Polish Jewry, vol. 8. Oxford: The Littman Library of Jewish Civilization, 2004.

Lane, Arthur Bliss. *I Saw Poland Betrayed: An American Ambassador Reports to The American People*. Indianapolis: The Bobb-Merrill company, 1948.

Lapin, Andrew. "Not Just 'Maus': A Missouri School District Removed Several Holocaust History Books, Too." Jewish Telegraphic Agency, November 16, 2022. https://www.jta.org/2022/11/16/united-states/several-holocaust-books-including-maus-have-been-yanked-from-some-missouri-schools-amid-state-law.

Lawson, Tom. *Debates on the Holocaust*. Manchester: Manchester University Press, 2010.

Lehmann, Rosa. *Symbiosis and Ambivalence: Poles and Jews in a Small Galician Town*. New York: Berghan Books, 2001.

Lemkin, Raphael. *Axis Rule in Occupied Europe: Laws of Occupation, Analysis of Government, Proposals for Redress*. Foundations of the Laws of War. 2nd ed. Clark: The Lawbook Exchange, Ltd., 2008

Lendvai, Paul. *Anti-Semitism without Jews: Communist Eastern Europe*. Garden City: Doubleday & Company, Inc., 1971.

Lerski, George J. "Dmowski, Paderewski and American Jews, (A Documentary Compilation)." In *Jews and the Emerging Polish State*, edited by Antony Polonsky, 95–116. Polin: Studies in Polish Jewry, vol. 2. Liverpool: The Littman Library of Jewish Civilization, 2008.

Leslie, R. F. *Polish Politics and the Revolution of November 1830*. University of London Historical Studies, vol. 3 Westport: Greenwood Press Publishers, 1969.

———. *Reform and Insurrection in Russian Poland 1856–1863*. University of London Historical Studies, vol. 7. London: University of London and The Athlone Press, 1963.

Levene, Mark. *War, Jews, and the New Europe: The Diplomacy of Lucien Wolf 1914–1919*. Rev. ed. Liverpool: The Littman Library of Jewish Civilization in association with Liverpool University Press, 2009.

Lewandowski, Józef. "History and Myth: Pińsk, April 1919." In *Jews and the Emerging Polish State*, edited by Antony Polonsky, 50–72. Polin: Studies in Polish Jewry, vol. 2. Oxford: The Littman Library of Jewish Civilization, 2008.

Liekis, Sarunas. *"A State within a State?": Jewish Autonomy in Lithuania 1918–1925*. Edited by Edvardas Tuskenis. Vilnius: Versus Aureus Publishers, 2003.

Lindemann, Albert S. *Esau's Tears: Modern Anti-Semitism and the Rise of the Jews*. Cambridge: Cambridge University Press, 1997.

———. *The Jew Accused. Three Anti-Semitic Affairs: Dreyfus, Beilis, Frank, 1894–1915*. Cambridge: Cambridge University Press, 1991.

Little, Becky. "How Boarding Schools Tried to 'Kill the Indian' Through Assimilation." History, July 11, 2023. https://www.history.com/news/how-boarding-schools-tried-to-kill-the-indian-through-assimilation.

Lopez, German. "Actual White Supremacist: Trump Success 'Proves That Our Views Resonate with Millions.'" Vox.com, October 14, 2016, https://www.vox.com/policy-and-politics/2016/10/14/13287532/trump-white-supremacists-racists.

Lord, Debbie. "What Happened at Charlottesville: Looking Back on the Rally That Ended in Death." *Atlanta Journal Constitution*, April 10, 2018. https://www.ajc.com/news/national/what-happened-charlottesville-looking-back-the-anniversary-the-deadly-rally/fPpnLrbAtbxSwNI9BEy93K/.

Lukas, Richard C. *Forgotten Holocaust: The Poles under German Occupation 1939–1944*. Rev. ed. New York: Hippocrene Books, 2005.

Mach, Zdzisław. "The Memory of the Holocaust and Education for Europe." In *Why We Should Teach About the Holocaust*, edited by Jolanta Ambrosewicz-Jacobs and Leszek Hońdo, translated by Michael Jacobs, 22–25. Kraków: The Jagiellonian University Institute of European Studies, 2005.

Machewicz, Paweł. "Antisemitism in Poland in 1956." In *Jews, Poles, Socialists: The Failure of an Ideal*, edited by Antony Polonsky, Israel Bartal, Gershon Hundert, Magdalena Opalski, and Jerzy Tomaszewski, 170–186. Polin: Studies in Polish Jewry, vol. 9. Oxford: The Littman Library of Jewish Civilization, 1996.

Madison, James H. *A Lynching in the Heartland: Race and Memory in America*. New York: Palgrave MacMillan, 2003.

Maliszkiewicz, Beata and Joanna Biskup. eds. *Głosy z ulicy Barlickiego*. Opole: Wydawca, 2007.

Maltz, Judy. "Why People Are Boycotting a Museum Dedicated to Poles Who Saved Jews." *Haaretz*, May 8, 2018. https://www.haaretz.com/world-news/europe/.premium.MAGAZINE-why-people-are-boycotting-a-museum-dedicated-to-poles-who-saved-jews-1.6070200.

Marantz, Andrew. "The Poway Synagogue Shooting Follows an Unsettling Script." *New Yorker*, April 29, 2019.

Marcus, Sheldon. *Father Coughlin: The Tumultuous Life of the Priest of the Little Flower*. Boston: Little, Brown and Company, 1973.

Markowski, Artur. "Anti-Jewish Pogroms in the Kingdom of Poland." In *Jews in the Kingdom of Poland, 1815–1918*, edited by Glenn Dynner, Antony Polonsky, and Marcin Wodziński, 219–256. Polin: Studies in Polish Jewry, vol. 27. Oxford: The Littman Library of Jewish Civilization, 2015.

Matyjaszek, Konrad, and Joanna Tokarska-Bakir. "History's History: Polish-Jewish Studies." *Studia Litteraria et Historica* 6 (2017).

Matyjaszek, Konrad. "You need to speak Polish": Antony Polonsky Interviewed by Konrad Matyjaszek." *Studia Litteraria et Historica* 6 (2017). https://www.academia.edu/38545860/_You_need_to_speak_Polish_Antony_Polonsky_interviewed_by_Konrad_Matyjaszek.

McBride, Jared. "Peasants into Perpetrators: The OUN-UPA and the Ethnic Cleansing of Volhynia, 1943–1944." *Slavic Review* 75 (2016): 630–654.

Mendelsohn, Ezra. "Jewish Historiography on Polish Jewry." In *Jews in Independent Poland, 1918–1939*, edited by Antony Polonsky, Ezra Mendelsohn, Jerzy Tomaszewski, 3–13. Polin: Studies in Polish Jewry, vol. 8. Oxford: The Littman Library of Jewish Civilization, 2004.

———. *The Jews of East Central Europe Between the World Wars*. Bloomington: Indiana University Press, 1987.

———. *Zionism in Poland: The Formative Years, 1915–1926*. New Haven: Yale University Press, 1981.

Mendes-Flohr, Paul, and Yehuda Reinharz, eds. *The Jew in the Modern World*. 2nd ed. Oxford: Oxford University Press, 1995.

Meyer, Michael A. *Response to Modernity: A History of the Reform Movement in Judaism*. Detroit: Wayne State University Press, 1988.

Micewski, Andrzej. *Cardinal Wyszyński: A Biography*. Translated by William R. Brand and Katarzyna Mrockowska-Brand. San Diego: Harcourt, Brace, Jovanovich, 1984.

Michlic, Joanna. "Antisemitism in Contemporary Poland: Does It Matter? And for Whom Does It Matter?" In *Rethinking Poland and Jews*, edited by Robert Cherry and Annamaria Orla-Bukovska, 155–168. Lanham: Rowman & Littlefield Publishers, Inc., 2007.

———. "'At the Crossroads': Jedwabne and Polish Historiography of the Holocaust," *Dapim: Studies on the Holocaust* 31, no. 3 (2017): 296–306.

———. "'The Open Church' and 'the Closed Church' and the Discourse on Jews in Poland between 1989 and 2000." In *Communist and Post-Communist Studies* 37, no. 4 (2004): 461–479.

———. *Poland's Threatening Other: The Image of the Jew from 1880 to the Present*. Lincoln: University of Nebraska Press, 2006.

Michlic-Coren, Joanna. "Anti-Jewish Violence in Poland, 1918–1939 and 1945–1947." In *Focusing on the Holocaust and Its Aftermath*, edited by Antony Polonsky, 34–61. Polin: Studies in Polish Jewry, vol. 13. Oxford: The Littman Library of Jewish Civilization, 2000.

———. "Polish Jews during and after the Kielce Pogrom: Reports from the Communist Archives." In *Focusing on the Holocaust and Its Aftermath*, edited by Antony Polonsky, 253–267. Polin: Studies in Polish Jewry, vol. 13. Oxford: The Littman Library of Jewish Civilization, 2000.

Michlic, Joanna B., and Antony Polonsky. Letter to the Editor. *History* 93, no. 1 (January 2008): 154–158.

Michnik, Adam. *The Church and the Left*, edited and translated by David Ost. Chicago: The University of Chicago Press, 1993.

———. "The Dilemma." In *Letters from Freedom: Post-Cold War Realities and Perspectives*, edited by Irena Grudzińska Gross, translated by Jane Cave, 68–95. Berkeley: University of California Press, 1998.

———. "My Vote against Wałęsa." In *Letters from Freedom: Post-Cold War Realities and Perspectives*, edited by Irena Grudzinska Gross, translated by Jane Cave, 156–168. Berkeley: University of California Press, 1998.

———. "Poles and the Jews: How Deep the Guilt?" In *The Neighbors Respond: The Controversy over the Jedwabne Massacre in Poland*, edited by Antony Polonsky and Joanna B. Michlic, 434–439. Princeton: Princeton University Press, 2004.

———. "Reply of Adam Michnik." In *The Neighbors Respond: The Controversy over the Jedwabne Massacre in Poland*, edited by Antony Polonsky and Joanna B. Michlic, 442–446. Princeton: Princeton University Press, 2004.

———. "Shadows of Forgotten Ancestors." In *Letters from Prison and Other Essays*, translated by Maya Latynski, 202–222. Berkeley, University of California Press, 1985.

———. "A Year Has Passed 1981." In *Letters from Prison and Other Essays*, translated by Maya Latynski, 124–132. Berkeley, University of California Press, 1985.

Michnik, Adam, and Jan Józef Lipski. "Some Remarks on the Opposition and the General Situation in Poland 1979." In *Letters from Prison and Other Essays*, translated by Maya Latynski, 149–154. Berkeley, University of California Press, 1985.

Mickiewicz, Adam. *Pan Tadeusz*. Translated by George Rapall Noyes. London: J. M. Dent & Sons, Ltd., 1917.

Migdon, Brooke. "Oklahoma Lawmaker Introduces Book-Banning Bill with $10,000-a-Day Penalty." *The Hill*, December 28, 2021. https://thehill.com/changing-america/respect/diversity-inclusion/587517-oklahoma-lawmaker-introduces-book-banning-bill.

Mikołajczyk, Stanisław. *The Rape of Poland: Pattern of Soviet Aggression*. New York: Whillesey House, 1948.

Miller, Jacob. "Soviet Theory on the Jews." In *The Jews in Soviet Russia since 1917*, edited by Lionel Kochan, 46–63. 3rd ed. Oxford: Oxford University Press, 1978.

Miłosz, Czesław. Foreword to *Letters from Prison and Other Essays*, by Adam Michnik, translated by Maya Latynski, ix-xvi. Berkeley: University of California Press, 1985.

Mincer, Laura Quercioli. "Ida Kamińska." Jewish Women's Archive. Accessed July 19, 2021. https://jwa.org/encyclopedia/article/kaminska-esther-rachel-and-ida-kaminska.

Modras, Ronald. *The Catholic Church and Antisemitism: Poland, 1933–1939*. Studies in Antisemitism, vol. 1. London: Routledge, 1994.

Molodovsky, Kadya. *A Jewish Refugee in New York: Rivke Zilberg's Journal*. Translated by Anita Norich. Bloomington: Indiana University Press, 2019.

Morawska, Ewa. "Polish-Jewish Relations in America, 1880–1940: Old Elements, New Configurations." In *Polish-Jewish Relations in North America*, edited by Mieczysław B. Biskupski and Antony Polonsky 71–86. Polin: Studies in Polish Jewry, vol. 19. Oxford: The Littman Library of Jewish Civilization, 2007.

Moses, Dirk. "Empire, Colony, Genocide: Keywords and the Philosophy of History." In *Empire, Colony, Genocide: Conquest, Occupation, and Subaltern Resistance in World History*, edited by A. Dirk Moses, 3–54. New York: Berghahn Books, 2008.

Moyers, Bill D. "What a Real President Was Like." *Washington Post*, November 13, 1988. https://www.washingtonpost.com/archive/opinions/1988/11/13/what-a-real-president-was-like/d483c1be-d0da-43b7-bde6-04e10106ff6c/.

Musiał, Bogdan. "The Pogrom in Jedwabne: Critical Remarks about Jan T. Gross's Neighbors." In *The Neighbors Respond: The Controversy over the Jedwabne Massacre in Poland*, edited by Antony Polonsky and Joanna B. Michlic, 304–343. Princeton and Oxford: Princeton University Press, 2004.

Musiał, Rev. Stanisław. "We Ask You to Help Us Be Better." In *The Neighbors Respond: The Controversy over the Jedwabne Massacre in Poland*, edited by Antony Polonsky and Joanna B. Michlic, 173–180. Princeton: Princeton University Press, 2004.

Nathans, Benjamin. *Beyond the Pale: The Jewish Encounter with Late Imperial Russia*. Berkeley: University of California Press, 2002.

New York Times "Fixes Blame for Polish Pogroms." January 19, 1920.

———. "How George Floyd Died, and What Happened Next." November 1, 2021. https://www.nytimes.com/article/george-floyd.html.

———. "Lemberg Pogroms Were Not by Poles." June 2, 1919.

———. "Paderewski Asks American Inquiry." June 2, 1919.

Norich, Anita. Introduction to *A Jewish Refugee in New York: Rivke Zilberg's Journal*, by Kadya Molodovsky. Translated by Anita Norich, vii-xxiii. Bloomington: Indiana University Press, 2019.

Novick, Peter. *The Holocaust in American Life*. Boston: Mariner Books, 2000.

Ochs, Michael. "Tsarist Officialdom and Anti-Jewish Pogroms in Poland." In *Pogroms: Anti-Jewish Violence in Modern Russian History*, edited by John D. Klier and Shlomo Lambroza, 164–190. Cambridge: Cambridge University Press, 1992.

Oniszczuk, Aleksandra. "The Jews in the Duchy of Warsaw: The Question of Equal Rights." In *Jews in the Kingdom of Poland, 1815–1918*, edited by Glenn Dynner, Antony Polonsky, and Marcin Wodziński, 63–88. Polin: Studies in Polish Jewry, vol. 27. Oxford: The Littman Library of Jewish Civilization, 2015.

Opalski, Magdalena, and Israel Bartal. *Poles and Jews: A Failed Brotherhood*. Hanover: Brandeis University Press and University Press of New England, 1992.

Ortiz, Aimee. "Emmett Till Memorial Has a New Sign. This Time, It's Bulletproof." *New York Times*, October 20, 2019. https://www.nytimes.com/2019/10/20/us/emmett-till-bulletproof-sign.html.

Ossowski, Stanisław. "With Kielce in the Background." In *Against Anti-Semitism: An Anthology of Twentieth-Century Polish Writings*, edited by Adam Michnik and Agnieszka Marczyk, 113–126. Oxford: Oxford University Press, 2018.

Ost, David. Introduction to *The Church and the Left*, by Adam Michnik. Edited and translated by David Ost, 1–29. Chicago: The University of Chicago Press, 1993.

Paczkowski, Andrzej. "The Jewish Press in the Political Life of the Second Republic." In *Jews in Independent Poland, 1918–1939*, edited by Antony Polonsky, Ezra Mendelsohn, and Jerzy Tomaszewski, 176–193. Polin: Studies in Polish Jewry, vol. 8. Oxford: The Littman Library of Jewish Civilization, 2004.

———. *The Spring Will Be Ours: Poland and the Poles from Occupation to Freedom*. Translated by Jane Cave. University Park: The Pennsylvania State University Press, 2003.

Pearce, Matt, Robert Armengol, and David S. Cloud. "Three Dead, Dozens Hurt after Virginia White Nationalist Rally Is Dispersed; Trump Blames 'Many Sides.'" *Los Angeles Times*, August 12, 2017. https://www.latimes.com/nation/nationnow/la-na-charlottesville-white-nationalists-rally-20170812-story.html.

Pease, Neal. *Rome's Most Faithful Daughter: The Catholic Church and Independent Poland, 1914–1939*. Athens: Ohio University Press, 2009.

Perechodnik, Calel. *Am I a Murderer? Testament of a Jewish Ghetto Policeman*. Edited and translated by Frank Fox. Boulder: WestviewPress, 1996.

Persak, Krzysztof. "Not Only Jedwabne." [Translated by David M. Dastych] *Tygodnik Powsechny*, November 10. 2002; "IPN (Institute of National Remembrance) Presents the Results of the Inquiry into the Crimes in Bialystok Region." The Canadian Foundation of Polish-Jewish Heritage, Montreal Chapter. Accessed July 30, 2007. http://www.polish-jewish-heritiage.org/eng/grudzien_not_only_jedwabne.htm.

Penn, Shana. "American Press Coverage of Poland's Role in the Holocaust." In *Rethinking Poles and Jews: Troubled Past, Brighter Future*, edited by Robert Cherry and Annamaria Orla-Bukowska, 55–68. Lanham: Rowman & Littlefield Publishers, Inc., 2007.

Person, Katarzyna. *Assimilated Jews in the Warsaw Ghetto, 1940–1943*. Syracuse: Syracuse University Press, 2014.

———. *Warsaw Ghetto Police: The Jewish Order Service during the Nazi Occupation*. Translated by Zygmunt Nowak-Soliński. Ithaca and London: Cornell University Press in association with the United States Holocaust Memorial Museum, 2021.

Petrovsky-Shtern, Yohanan. *The Golden Age Shtetl: A New History of Jewish Life in East Europe*. Princeton: Princeton University Press, 2014.

———. *Jews in the Russian Army, 1827–1917: Drafted into Modernity*. Cambridge: Cambridge University Press, 2009.

———. Seforimchatter, February 27, 2022. Podcast, 45:01. https://seforimchatter.buzzsprout.com/1218638/10149479.

Petrovsky-Shtern, Yochanan, and Antony Polonsky. Introduction to *Galicia: Jews, Poles, and Ukrainians (1772–1918)*, edited by Yochanan Petrovsky-Shtern and Antony Polonsky, 3–24. Polin: Studies in Polish Jewry, vol. 12. Oxford: The Littman Library of Jewish Civilization, 2014.

———. Introduction to *Jews and Ukrainians*, edited by Yochanan Petrovsky-Shtern and Antony Polonsky. Polin: Studies in Polish Jewry, vol. 26. Oxford: The Littman Library of Jewish Civilization, 2014.

Pinchuk, Ben-Cion. *Shtetl Jews under Soviet Rule: Eastern Poland on the Eve of the Holocaust*. Oxford: Basil Blackwell, 1990.

Pinsker, Leon. "Auto-Emancipation." Jewish Virtual Library. Accessed July 15, 2021. https://www.jewishvirtuallibrary.org/quot-auto-emancipation-quot-leon-pinsker.

Pióro, Tadeusz. "Purges in the Polish Army, 1967–1968." In *1968: Forty Years*, edited by Leszek W. Głuchowski and Antony Polonsky, 290–309. Polin: Studies in Polish Jewry, vol. 21. Oxford: Littman Library of Jewish Civilization, 2009.

Piotrowski, Tadeusz. *Poland's Holocaust: Ethnic Strife, Collaboration with Occupying Forces and Genocide in the Second Republic, 1918–1947*. Jefferson: McFarland & Company, Inc., Publishers, 1998.

Pires, Fernanda. "Poland's Welcome of Ukrainian Refugees Comes with Challenges." University of Michigan News, March 14, 2022. https://global.umich.edu/newsroom/polands-welcome-of-ukrainian-refugees-comes-with-challenges/.

Plucinska, Joanna, and Dan Fastenberg. "75 Years on, Holocaust Survivors Struggle to Recover Property in Poland." Reuters, January 20, 2020. https://www.reuters.com/article/

us-holocaust-memorial-auschwitz-restitut/75-years-on-holocaust-survivors-struggle-to-recover-property-in-poland-idUSKBN1ZJ0Y8.

Polonsky, Antony. "The Dreyfus Affair and Polish-Jewish Interaction, 1890–1914." In *Jewish History* 11, no. 2 (Fall 1997): 21–40.

———. Foreword to *Opening the Drawer: The Hidden Identities of Polish Jews*, by Barry Cohen, viii–xviii. London: Vallentine Mitchell, 2018.

———. Introduction to *Focusing on Jews in the Polish Borderlands*, edited by Antony Polonsky, 3–18. Polin: Studies in Polish Jewry, vol. 14: Oxford: The Littman Library of Jewish Civilization, 2001.

———. "Jews and Communism in the Soviet Union and Poland." In *Jews and Leftist Politics: Judaism, Israel, Antisemitism, and Gender*, edited by Jack Jacobs, 147–168. Cambridge: Cambridge University Press, 2017.

———. *The Jews in Poland and Russia*. Vol. 1, *1350 to 1881*. Oxford: Littman Library of Jewish Civilization, 2009.

———. *The Jews in Poland and Russia*. Vol. 2, *1881 to 1914*. Oxford: Littman Library of Jewish Civilization, 2010.

———. *The Jews in Poland and Russia*. Vol. 3, *1914 to Present*. Oxford: Littman Library of Jewish Civilization, 2012.

———. "What Went Wrong?" Unpublished.

Polonsky, Antony, and Joanna B. Michlic, eds. *The Neighbors Respond: The Controversy over the Jedwabne Massacre in Poland*. Princeton: Princeton University Press, 2004.

Porter, Brian. *When Nationalism Began to Hate: Imagining Modern Politics in Nineteenth-Century Poland*. Oxford: Oxford University Press, 2000.

Porter-Szűcs, Brian. *Faith and Fatherland: Catholicism, Modernity, and Poland*. Oxford: Oxford University Press, 2011.

———. "Meritocracy and Community in Twenty-First-Century Poland." *Shofar: An Interdisciplinary Journal of Jewish Studies* 37, no. 1 (Spring 2019): 72–95. https://www.researchgate.net/publication/331828464_Meritocracy_and_Community_in_Twenty-First-Century_Poland.

———. *Poland in the Modern World: Beyond Martyrdom*. Malden: Wiley Blackwell, 2014.

Powell, Michael. "In Texas, a Battle over What Can Be Taught, and What Books Can Be Read." *New York Times*, December 14, 2021. https://www.nytimes.com/2021/12/10/us/texas-critical-race-theory-ban-books.html.

Power, Samantha. *"A Problem from Hell": America and the Age of Genocide*. New York: Harper Collins, 2007.

Prusin, Alexander Victor. *Nationalizing a Borderland: War, Ethnicity, and Anti-Jewish Violence in East Galicia, 1914–1920*. Birmingham: University of Alabama Press, 2016.

Pruszyński, Franciszek Ksawery. "The Przytyk Market Stands." In *Against Anti-Semitism: An Anthology of Twentieth-Century Polish Writings*, edited by Adam Michnik and Agnieszka Marczyk, 33–44. Oxford: Oxford University Press, 2018.

Quint, Alyssa. *The Rise of the Modern Yiddish Theater*. Bloomington: Indiana University Press, 2019.

Rabon, Israel. *The Street*. New York: Four Walls Eight Windows, 1990.

Radziwiłł, Anna. "The Teaching of the History of the Jews in Secondary Schools in the Polish People's Republic, 1948–1988." In *Poles and Jews: Perceptions and Misperceptions*, edited by Władysław T. Bartoszewski, 402–424. Polin: Studies in Polish Jewry, vol. 4. Oxford: Littman Library of Jewish Civilization, 2004.

Raper, Arthur F. *The Tragedy of Lynching*. New York: Dover Publications, 1933.
Rayman, Noah. "Kosher Grocery Assault Confirms Worst Fears of French Jews." *TIME*, January 9, 2015. https://www.adl.org/news/adl-in-the-news/kosher-grocery-assault-confirms-worst-fears-of-french-jews.
Rejak, Sebastian. *Jewish Identities in Poland and America: The Impact of the Shoah on Religion and Ethnicity*. London: Vallentine Mitchell, 2011.
Remarque, Erich Maria. *All Quiet on the Western Front*. Translated by A. W. Wheen. New York: Random House, 2013.
Riasanovsky, Nicholas V. *A History of Russia*. 5th ed. New York: Oxford University Press, 1993.
Rice, Monika. *"What! Still Alive?!": Jewish Survivors in Poland and Israel Remember Homecoming*. Edited by Henry Feingold. Modern Jewish History. Syracuse: Syracuse University Press, 2017.
Ringelblum, Emmanuel. *Notes from the Warsaw Ghetto: The Journal of Emmanuel Ringelblum*. Edited and translated by Jacob Sloan. New York: Schocken Books, 1984.
———. *Polish-Jewish Relations during the Second World War*. Edited by Joseph Kermish and Shmuel Krakowski, translated by Dafna Allon, Danuta Dabrowska, and Dana Keren. Evanston: Northwestern University Press, 1992.
Rogger, Hans. *Jewish Policies and Right-Wing Politics in Imperial Russia*. Oxford: MacMillan in association with St. Antony's College, 1986.
Rosman, M. J. *The Lords' Jews: Magnate-Jewish Relations in the Polish-Lithuanian Commonwealth during the 18th Century*. Cambridge, MA: Harvard University Press, 1990.
Robertson, Campbell, Christopher Mele, and Sabrina Travernise. "11 Killed in Synagogue Massacre; Suspect Charged With 29 Counts." *New York Times*, October 27, 2018. https://www.nytimes.com/2018/10/27/us/active-shooter-pittsburgh-synagogue-shooting.html.
Rosenfarb, Chava. *The Tree of Life: A Trilogy of Life in the Łódz Ghetto*. Book One, *On the Brink of the Precipice, 1939*. Translated by Chava Rosenfarb and Goldie Morgentaler. Madison: The University of Wisconsin Press, Terrace Books, 1985.
Roskies, David G. Introduction to *The Dybbuk and Other Writings*, by S. Ansky. Edited by David G. Roskies, translated by Golda Werman. New Haven: Yale University Press, 2002.
Rothberg, Michael. *Multidirectional Memory: Remembering the Holocaust in the Age of Decolonization*. Stanford: Stanford University Press, 2009.
Rothschild, Joseph. *East Central Europe between the Two World Wars*. A History of East Central Europe, vol. 9. Seattle: University of Washington Press, 1992.
Rozenbaum, Włodzimierz. "The March Events: Targeting the Jews." In *1968 Forty Years After*, edited by Leszek W. Głuchowski and Antony Polonsky, 62–92. Polin: Studies in Polish Jewry, vol. 21. Oxford: The Littman Library of Jewish Civilization, 2009.
Rozett, Robert. "Distorting the Holocaust and Whitewashing History: Toward a Typology." *Israel Journal of Foreign Affairs* 13 (2019): 23–36.
Rudnicki, Szymon. "Anti-Jewish Legislation in Interwar Poland." In *Antisemitism and Its Opponents in Modern Poland*, edited by Robert Blobaum, 148–170. Ithaca: Cornell University Press, 2005.
———. "From 'Numerus Clausus' To 'Numerus Nullus.'" In *Jews and the Emerging Polish State*, edited by Antony Polonsky, 246–268. Polin: Studies in Polish Jewry, vol. 2. Oxford: The Littman Library of Jewish Civilization, 2008.
———. "The Jews' Battle in the Sejm for Equal Rights." In *The Jews in Poland*, vol. 2, edited by Sławomir Kapralski, 147–163. Kraków: The Jagiellonian University Printing House, 1999.

Rürup, Miriam. "Demographics and Social Structure." Institut für die Geschichte der deutschen Juden, September 22, 2016. https://jewish-history-online.net/topic/demographics-and-social-structure.

Russell, Nicolas. "Collective Memory before and after Halbwachs." *French Review* 79 (2006): 792–804.

Rutherford, Phillip T. *Prelude to the Final Solution: The Nazi Program for Deporting Ethnic Poles, 1939–1941*. Lawrence: University Press of Kansas, 2007.

Sachar, Howard M. *Dreamland: Europeans and Jews in the Aftermath of the Great War*. New York: Vintage Books, 2002.

Sainati, Tatiana E. "Toward a Comparative Approach to the Crime of Genocide." *Duke Law Journal* 62, no. 1 (October 2012): 161–202.

Santora, Marc. "After a President's Shocking Death, a Suspicious Twin Reshapes a Nation." *New York Times*, June 16, 2018. https://www.nytimes.com/2018/06/16/world/europe/poland-kaczynski-smolensk.html.

Santora, Marc, and Joanna Berendt. "Mixing Politics and Piety, A Conservative Priest Seeks to Shape Poland's Future." *New York Times*, September 21, 2019. https://www.nytimes.com/2019/09/21/world/europe/poland-elections-tadeusz-rydzyk.html.

Scally, Derek. "Poland's New History Syllabus to Frame EU as an 'Unlawful Entity': Ruling Party Accused of Pushing Nationalist Identity Politics with 'New Deal' Programme." *Irish Times*, https://www.irishtimes.com/news/world/europe/poland-s-new-history-syllabus-to-frame-eu-as-an-unlawful-entity-1.4570798.

Schapiro, Leonard. Introduction to *The Jews in Soviet Russia Since 1917*, edited by Lionel Kochan, 1–14. 3rd ed. Oxford: Oxford University Press, 1978.

Scharf, Raphael. "Janusz Korczak and His Time." In *Poland, What Have I to Do with Thee . . . : Essays without Prejudice*. London: Vallentine Mitchell, 1998.

Schell, Jonathan. Introduction to *Letters from Prison and Other Essays*, by Adam Michnik. Translated by Maya Latynski, xvii-xlii. Berkeley: University of California Press, 1985.

Schrag, Peter. *Not Fit for Our Society: Immigration and Nativism in America*. Berkeley: University of California Press, 2010.

Schwartz, Barry, et al. "The Recovery of Masada: A Study in Collective Memory" *Sociological Quarterly* 27 (1986): 147–164.

Segel, Binjamin W. *A Lie and A Libel: The History of the Protocols of the Elders of Zion*. Edited and translated by Richard S. Levy. Lincoln: University of Nebraska Press, 1996.

Shaw, Martin. *What Is Genocide?* 2nd ed. Cambridge: Polity Press, 2015.

Sherwood, Harriet. "Anger as Poland Plans Law That Will Stop Jews Reclaiming Wartime Homes." *Guardian*, August 2, 2021. https://www.theguardian.com/world/2021/aug/01/anger-as-poland-plans-law-that-will-stop-jews-reclaiming-wartime-homes.

Shneiderman, S. L. *Between Fear and Hope*. New York: Arco Publishing Co., 1947.

———. *The River Remembers*. New York: Horizon Press, 1978.

Shore, Marci. *Caviar and Ashes: A Warsaw Generation's Life and Death in Marxism*. New Haven: Yale University Press, 2009.

Simon, Scott. "Emmett Till Memorial Dedicated For 4th Time After Vandalism." npr.org, October 19, 2019. https://www.npr.org/2019/10/19/771518825/emmett-till-memorial-dedicated-for-4th-time-after-vandalism.

Singer, I. J. *The Brothers Ashkenazi*. Translated by Joseph Singer. New York: Other Press, 2010.

———. *Steel and Iron*. Translated by Joseph Singer. New York: Funk & Wagnalls, 1969.
———. *Yoshe Kalb*. Translated by Maurice Samuel. New York: The Vanguard Press, Inc., 1961.
Slezkine, Yuri. *The Jewish Century*. Princeton: Princeton University Press, 2004.
Slutsky, Carolyn. "March of the Living: Confronting Anti-Polish Stereotypes" In *Rethinking Poles and Jews: Troubled Past, Brighter Future*, edited by Robert Cherry and Annamaria Orla-Bukowska, 189–196. Lanham: Rowman & Littlefield Publishers, Inc., 2007.
Smith, R. E. F., and David Christian. *Bread and Salt: A Social and Economic History of Food and Drink in Russia*. Cambridge: Cambridge University Press, 1984.
Snyder, Don. "Poland Is Poised to Put 'Bad' Historians of the Holocaust in Prison." Forward, September 2, 2016. https://forward.com/news/world/349179/poland-is-poised-to-put-bad-historians-of-the-holocaust-in-prison/.
Snyder, Timothy. *Bloodlands: Europe between Hitler and Stalin*. New York: Basic Books, 2012.
Sorkin, David. "The Impact of Emancipation on German Jewry: A Reconsideration." In *Assimilation and Community: The Jews in Nineteenth-Century Europe*, edited by Jonathan Frankel and Steven J. Zipperstein, 177–198. Cambridge: Cambridge University Press, 1992.
Stachura, Peter D. *Poland 1918–1945: An Interpretive and Documentary History of the Second Republic*. London: Routledge Taylor & Francis, 2004.
Stampfer, Shaul. "What Actually Happened to the Jews of Ukraine in 1648?" *Jewish History* 17 (2003): 207–227.
Stanislawski, Michael. *Tsar Nicholas I and the Jews: The Transformation of Jewish Society in Russia 1825–1855*. Philadelphia: The Jewish Publication Society of America, 1983.
Stauter-Halsted, Keely. *The Nation in the Village: The Genesis of Peasant National Identity in Austrian Poland, 1848–1914*. Ithaca: Cornell University Press, 2001.
Steinlauf, Michael. *Bondage to the Dead: Poland and the Memory of the Holocaust*. Syracuse: Syracuse University Press, 1997.
Steinsaltz, Adin. *The Essential Talmud*. Translated by Chaya Galai. New York: Basic Books, 1976.
Stelter, Brian. *Hoax: Donald Trump, Fox News, and the Dangerous Distortion of Truth*. New York: One Signal Publishers, 2020.
Stevenson, Bryan, and Equal Justice Initiative. *Lynching in America: Confronting the Legacy of Racial Terror*. Montgomery: Equal Justice Initiative, 2017.
Stolberg, Sheryl Gay, and Nicholas Fandos. "McConnell Faces Pressure from Republicans to Stop Avoiding Shutdown Fight." *New York Times*, January 3, 2019. https://www.nytimes.com/2019/01/03/us/politics/mcconell-setate-republican-shutdown.html.
Stola, Dariusz. "The Hate Campaign of March 1968: How Did It Become Anti-Jewish?" In *1968: Forty Years After*, edited by Leszek W. Głuchowski and Antony Polonsky, 16–36. Polin: Studies in Polish Jewry, vol. 21. Oxford: The Littman Library of Jewish Civilization, 2009.
Stroop, Jürgen. *The Stroop Report: The German Account of the Destruction of the Warsaw Ghetto in German and English*. Translated by Arthur Kemp. London: Ostara Publications, 2014.
Szaynok, Bożena. "The Impact of the Holocaust on Jewish Attitudes in Postwar Poland." In *Contested Memories: Poles and Jews During the Holocaust and Its Aftermath*, edited by Joshua D. Zimmerman, 239–246. New Brunswick: Rutgers University Press, 2003.
———. "Poles and Jews from July 1944 to July 1946." In *Reflections on the Kielce Pogrom*, edited by Łukasz Kamiński and Jan Żaryn, 118–137. Warsaw: Institute of National Remembrance, 2006.
———. "The Role of Antisemitism in Postwar Polish-Jewish Relations." In *Antisemitism and Its Opponents in Modern Poland*, edited by Robert Blobaum, 265–283. Ithaca: Cornell University Press, 2005.

Szuchta, Robert. "Against Silence and Indifference: Why I Teach about the Holocaust—Reflections of a Teacher." In *Why Should We Teach About the Holocaust?*, edited by Jolanta Ambrosewicz-Jacobs and Leszek Hońdo, translated by Michael Jacobs, 55–59. 2nd ed. Kraków: The Jagiellonian University Institute of European Studies, 2005.

———. *Holokaust. Zrozumieć dlaczego*. Warsaw: Bellona, 2003.

Szuchta, Robert, and Piotr Trojański. *Holocaust. Program nauczania o historii i zagładzie Żydów na lekcjach przedmiotów humanistyczny w szkołach ponadpodstawowych*. Warsaw: Bellona, 2000.

Tazbir, Janusz. "Images of the Jew in the Polish Commonwealth." In *Poles and Jews: Perceptions and Misperceptions*, edited by Wladyslaw T. Bartoszewski, 18–30. Polin: Studies in Polish Jewry, vol. 4. Oxford: The Littman Library of Jewish Civilization, 1989.

Tec, Nechama. *When Light Pierced the Darkness: Christian Rescue of Jews in Nazi-Occupied Poland*. New York: Oxford University Press, 1986.

Teicher, Jordan G. "Why Is Vatican II so Important?" npr.org, October 10, 2012. https://www.npr.org/2012/10/10/162573716/why-is-vatican-ii-so-important.

Teller, Adam. "Polish-Jewish Relations: Historical Research and Social Significance. On the Legacy of Jacob Goldberg." *Studia Judaica* 15, nos. 1–2 (2012): 27–47.

Thompson, Maury. "Charles Evans Hughes Was a Consistent Voice against Racial Inequality." *Post Star*, July 11, 2020. https://poststar.com/charles-evans-hughes-was-a-consistent-voice-against-racial-inequality-copy/article_59b63fad-c1da-5fcf-b1b2-7192f7cf42b7.html.

Times of Israel. "Polish Prime Minister: Paying Holocaust Property Restitution Would Be 'Victory for Hitler.'" May 20, 2019. https://www.timesofisrael.com/polish-pm-paying-holocaust-property-restitution-would-be-victory-for-hitler/.

Tobin, Diane Daufman, Gary A. Tobin, and Scott Rubin. Foreword to *In Every Tongue: The Racial & Ethnic Diversity of the Jewish People*, by Lewis Gordon. San Francisco: Institute for Jewish and Community Research, 2005.

Tokarska-Bakir, Joanna. *Pogrom Cries—Essays on Polish-Jewish History, 1939–1946*. Frankfurt am Main: Peter Lang, 2017.

Tomaszewski, Jerzy. "The Civil Rights of Jews 1918–1939," In *Jews in Independent Poland, 1918–1939*, edited by Antony Polonsky, Ezra Mendelsohn, Jerzy Tomaszewski, 115–128. Polin: Studies in Polish Jewry, vol. 8. Oxford; Portland, Oregon: The Littman Library of Jewish Civilization, 2004.

———. "Pinsk, 5 April 1919." In *Poles and Jews: Renewing the Dialogue*, edited by Antony Polonsky, 227–251. Polin: Studies in Polish Jewry, vol. 1. Oxford: The Littman Library of Jewish Civilization, 2004.

Trachtenberg, Joshua. *The Devil and The Jews: The Medieval Conception of the Jew and Its Relation to Modern Antisemitism*. Cleveland: Meridian Books and The Jewish Publication Society of America, 1961.

Trunk, Isaiah. *Judenrat: The Jewish Councils in Eastern Europe under Nazi Occupation*. New York: Macmillan, 1972.

Tyson, Timothy B. *The Blood of Emmett Till*. New York: Simon & Schuster Paperbacks, 2017.

Ujiyediin, Nomin. "There's New Pressure to Ban Books at Schools." npr.org, December 6, 2021. https://www.npr.org/2021/12/06/1061727091/pressure-grows-to-ban-books-at-schools.

Walicki, Andrzej. *Philosophy and Romantic Nationalism: The Case of Poland*. Oxford: Clarendon Press, 1982.

Wandycz, Piotr S. *The Lands of Partitioned Poland, 1795–1918*. A History of East Central Europe, vol. 7. Seattle: University of Washington Press, 1984.

Waxman, Olivia B. "Critical Race Theory Is Simply the Latest Bogeyman: Inside the Fight over What Kids Learn about America's History." *TIME*, July 16, 2021, https://time.com/magazine/us/6075407/july-5th-2021-vol-198-no-1-u-s/.

Webber, Jonathan. "Personal Reflections on Auschwitz Today." In *Auschwitz: A History in Photographs*, compiled and edited by Teresa Świebocka. English edition prepared by Jonathan Webber and Connie Wilsack, 281–291. Oświęcim: The Auschwitz-Birkenau State Museum, 2004.

Weeks, Theodore R. *Nation and State in Late Imperial Russia: Nationalism and Russification on the Western Frontier, 1863–1914*. Dekalb: Northern Illinois University Press, 2008.

———. "Assimilationism, Nationalism, Modernization, Anti-Semitism: Notes on Polish-Jewish Relations, 1855–1905." In *Antisemitism and Its Opponents in Modern Poland*, edited by Robert Blobaum, 20–38. Ithaca: Cornell University Press, 2005.

_____. *From Assimilation to Antisemitism: The "Jewish Question" in Poland, 1850–1914*. DeKalb: Northern Illinois University Press, 2005.

Weigl, Barbara i Beata Maliszkiewicz. *Inni To Także My: Mniejszości narodowe w Polsce: Białorusini, Cyganie, Litwini, Niemcy, Ukraińcy, Żydzi. Program Edukacji Wielokulturowej w Szkole Podstawowej*. Sopot: Gdańskie Wydawnictwo Psychologiczne, 1997.

Weinryb, Bernard D. *The Jews of Poland: A Social and Economic History of the Jewish Community in Poland from 1100–1800*. Philadelphia: The Jewish Publication Society of America, 1972.

Wieczorek, Krzysztof. "Tischner as a Metapolitican." *Studies in East European Thought* 71, no. 4 (2019): 345–360.

Wiesel, Elie. "Eichmann's Victims and the Unheard Testimony." *Commentary* 32, no. 6 (1961): 510–515.

Wieseltier, Leon. "Washington Diarist: Righteous." In *The Neighbors Respond: The Controversy Over the Jedwabne Massacre in Poland*, edited by Antony Polonsky and Joanna B. Michlic, 440–450. Princeton and Oxford: Princeton University Press, 2004.

Weisman, Jonathan. *(((Semitism))): Being Jewish in America in the Age of Trump*. New York: St. Martin's Press, 2018.

Wilkerson, Isabelle. *The Warmth of Other Suns: The Epic Story of America's Great Migration*. New York: Vintage Books, 2011.

Williams, Pete, and Nicole Via y Rada, "Trump's Election Fight Includes over 50 Lawsuits. It's Not Going Well." nbcnews.com, November 23, 2020. https://www.nbcnews.com/politics/2020-election/trump-s-election-fight-includes-over-30-lawsuits-it-s-n1248289.

Williamson, Vanessa, and Isabella Gelfand. "Trump and Racism: What Do the Data Say?" Brookings, August 14, 2019. https://www.brookings.edu/articles/trump-and-racism-what-do-the-data-say/.

Wodziński, Marcin. *Haskalah and Hasidism in the Kingdom of Poland: A History of Conflict*. Translated by Sarah Cozens. Oxford: The Littman Library of Jewish Civilization, 2005.

———. "'Civil Christians': Debates on the Reform of the Jews in Poland, 1789–1830." [Translated by Claire Rosenson] In *Culture Front: Representing Jews in Eastern Europe*, edited by Benjamin Nathans and Gabriella Safra, 46–78. Jewish Culture and Contexts. Philadelphia: University of Pennsylvania Press, 2008.

———. "Jewish Studies in Poland." *Journal of Modern Jewish Studies* 10, no. 1, March 2011, 101–118.

———. "Reform and Exclusion: Conceptions of the Reform of the Jewish Community during the Declining Years of the Polish Enlightenment." In *Jews and Their Neighbors in Eastern Europe Since 1750*, edited by Israel Bartal, Antony Polonsky and Scott Ury, 31–48. Polin: Studies in Polish Jewry, vol. 24. Oxford: The Littman Library of Jewish Civilization, 2012.

———. *Hasidism and Politics: The Kingdom of Poland, 1815–1864*. Oxford: The Littman Library of Jewish Civilization, 2013.

Wojdowski, Bogdan. *Bread for the Departed*. Translated by Madeline G. Levine and Henryk Grynberg. Evanston: Northwestern University Press, 1997.

Woodward, Bob. *Fear: Trump and the White House*. New York: Simon & Schuster, 2018.

Wróbel, Piotr. "Jewish Warsaw before the First World War." In *The Jews in Warsaw*, edited by Władysław Bartoszewski and Antony Polonsky, 246–277. Cambridge, MA: Blackwell in association with the Institute for Polish-Jewish Studies, 1991.

———. "The 'Judenrate' Controversy: Some Polish Aspects." *Polish Review* 42, no. 2 (1997): 225–232.

———. "Polish-Jewish Relations and *Neighbors* by Jan T. Gross: Politics, Public Opinion, and Historical Methodology." In *Lessons and Legacies*. Vol. 7, *The Holocaust in International Perspective*, edited by Dagmar Herzog, 387–399. Evanston: Northwestern University Press, 2006.

Wyman, David S. *The Abandonment of the Jews: America and the Holocaust 1941–1945*. New York: Pantheon Books, 1984.

Wynot, Edward D. Jr. *Polish Politics in Transition: The Camp of National Unity and the Struggle for Power 1935–1939*. Athens: University of Georgia Press, 1974.

Yerushalmi, Yosef Hayim. *Zakhor: Jewish History and Jewish Memory*. Seattle: University of Washington Press, 1996.

Young, James E. "The Biography of a Memorial Icon: Nathan Rapoport's Warsaw Ghetto Monument." *Representations* 26 (Spring 1989): 66–106.

Zawadzka, Anna. "Żydokomuna: The Construction of the Insult." In *World War II and Two Occupations: Dilemmas of Polish Memory*, edited by Anna Wolff-Powęska and Piotr Forecki, 249–280. Frankfurt am Main: Peter Lang, 2016.

Żbikowski, Andrzej. "Polish Jews under Soviet Occupation." In *Contested Memories: Poles and Jews During the Holocaust and Its Aftermath*, edited by Joshua D. Zimmerman, 54–60. New Brunswick: Rutgers University Press, 2003.

———. "Why Did Jews Welcome the Soviet Armies?" In *Focusing on the Holocaust and Its Aftermath*, edited by Antony Polonsky, 62–72. Polin: Studies in Polish Jewry, vol. 13. Oxford: The Littman Library of Jewish Civilization, 2000.

Zelichowski, Ryszard. "Pilate's Gesture." In *My Brother's Keeper: Recent Polish Debates on the Holocaust*, edited by Antony Polonsky, 150–154. Oxford: Routledge, 1990.

Zimmerman, Joshua D. *Poles, Jews, and the Politics of Nationality: The Bund and the Polish Socialist Party in Late Tsarist Russia, 1892–1914*. Madison: University of Wisconsin Press, 2004.

Zipperstein, Steven J. *Pogrom: Kishinev and the Tilt of History*. New York: Liveright Publishing Corporation, 2018.

Żukowski, Tomasz. "'This Is My Homeland...'" By Władysław Bartoszewski and Zofia Lewinówna (1966): A Critical Reading." Edited by Mateusz Szepaniak. Polin Museum of the History of Polish Jews. Accessed January 7, 2023. https://sprawiedliwi.org.pl/en/o-sprawiedliwych/kim-sa-sprawiedliwi/ten-jest-z-ojczyzny-mojej-lektura-krytycna.

Maps

Polish-Lithuanian Commonwealth, 1619 (compared with today's borders)

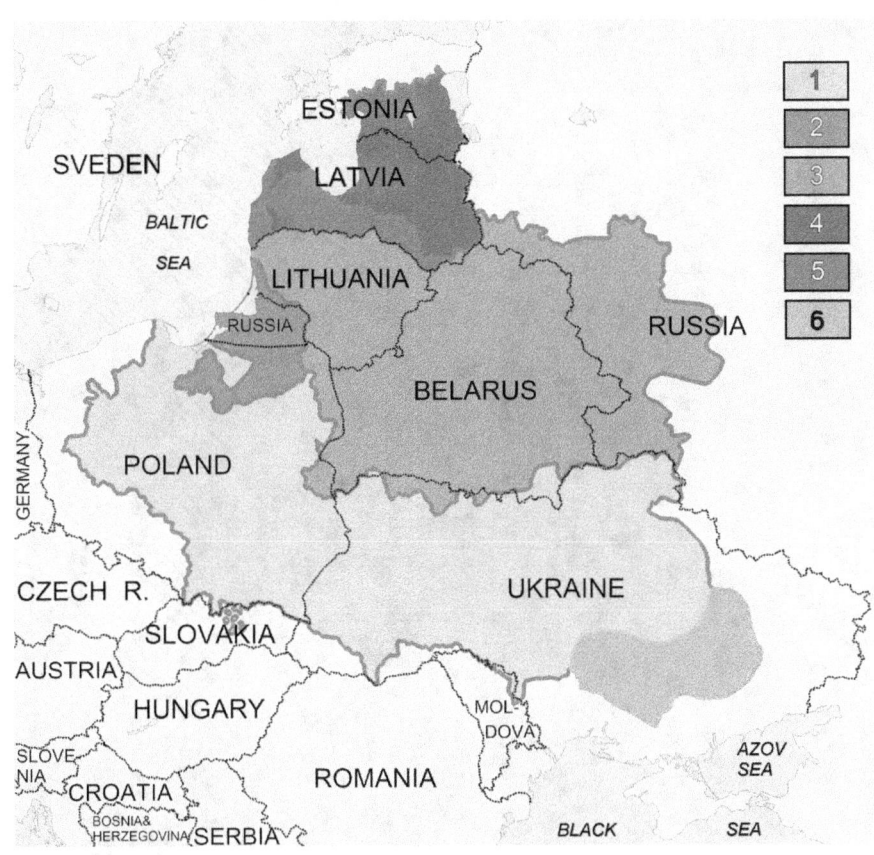

Legend
1 - The Crown (Kingdom of Poland),
2 - Duchy of Prussia - Polish fief,
3 - Grand Duchy of Lithuania,
4 - Livonia,
5 - Duchy of Courland - Livonian fief,
6 - "Wild lands" of the Zaporozhian cossacks.

Source: Creative Commons, https://commons.wikimedia.org/wiki/File:Polish%E2%80%93Lithuanian_Commonwealth_1619.png

Partitions of the Polish-Lithuanian Commonwealth in 1772, 1793, and 1795, Overlaid with the Borders of the Second Polish Republic, 1918–1939, with the Volhynian Voivodeship (1921–1939)

Source: Creative Commons, https://commons.wikimedia.org/wiki/Category:Maps_of_partitions_of_Poland#/media/File:Partitioned_Poland_&_the_2nd_Republic_(1772-1939).png

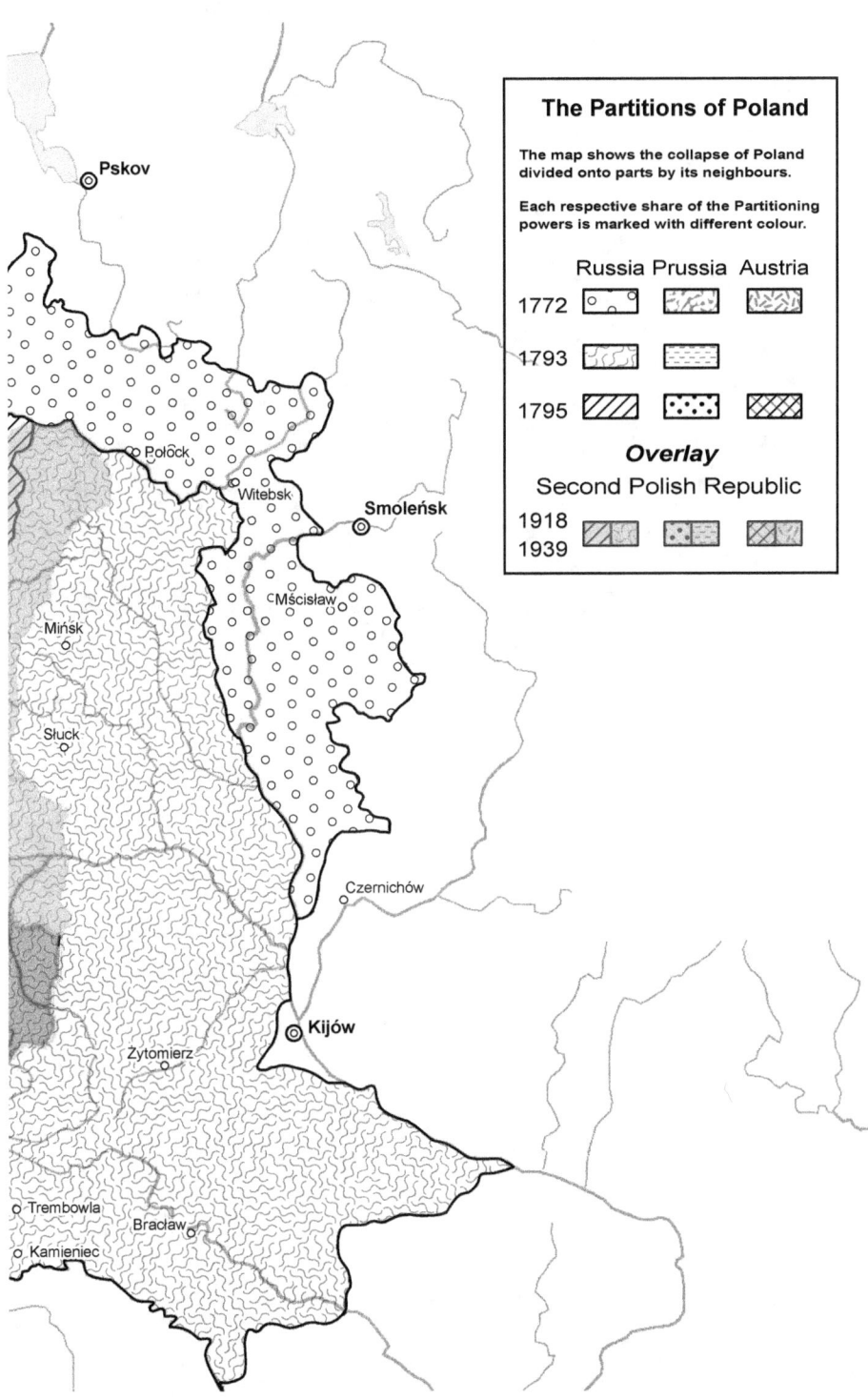

Territorial changes of Poland, 1815: Congress Poland

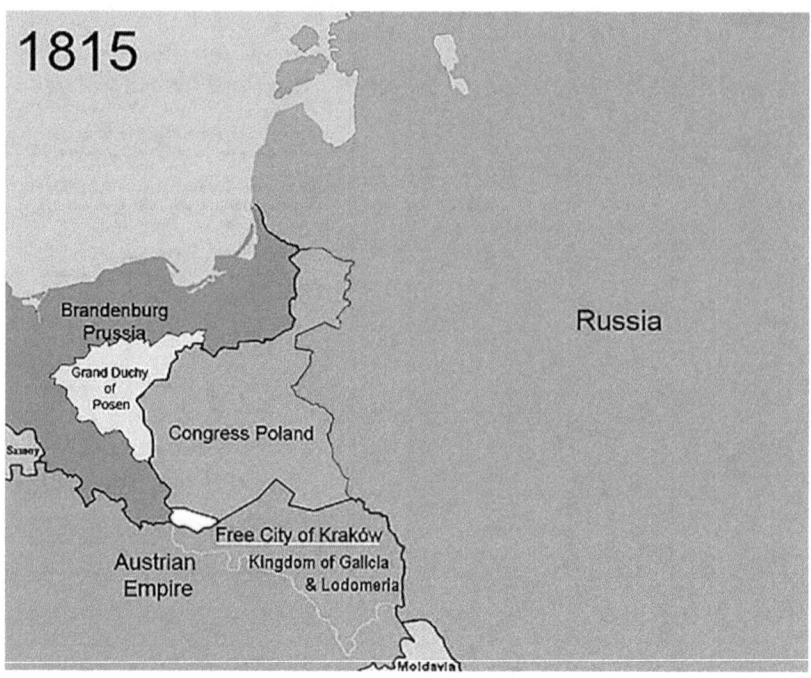

Source: Public domain, https://commons.wikimedia.org/wiki/File:Territorial_changes_of_Poland_1815.jpg

Maps

Territories of Poland Annexed by the Third Reich and the Soviet Union
(Lines of Partition from 10.21.1939 to 6.22.1941)

Source: Creative Commons, https://en.m.wikipedia.org/wiki/File:Occupation_of_Poland_1939.png#/media/File%3AOccupation_of_Poland_1939_(b%26w).png

The Interwar Poland and Surrounding States

https://commons.wikimedia.org/wiki/File:Rzeczpospolita_1923.png#metadata
Source: Wikimedia Commons,

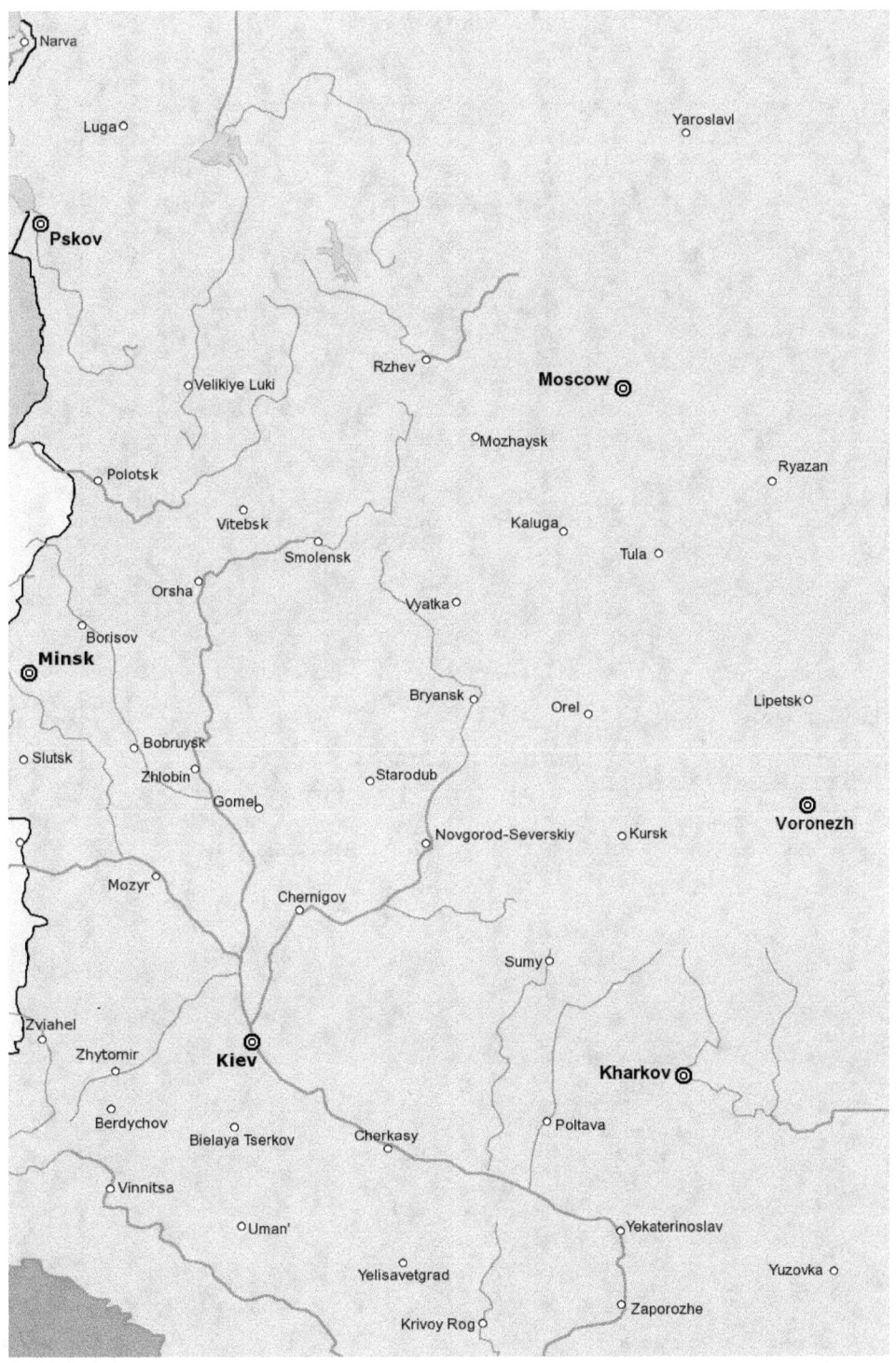

Poland in 1945

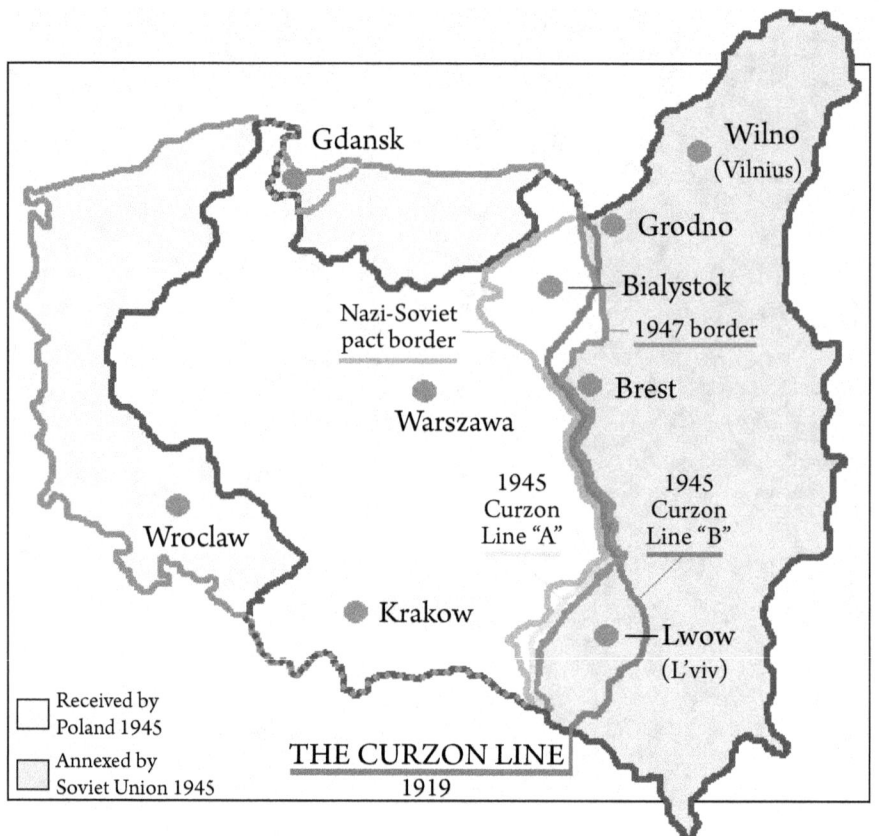

Source: Public domain, https://commons.wikimedia.org/wiki/File:Map_of_Poland_(1945).png

Contemporary Poland

Map Sources: UNGIS, ESRI.
The boundaries and names shown and the designations used on this map do not imply official endorsement or acceptance by the United Nations. Map created in Sep 2019.

Source: Creative Commons, https://commons.wikimedia.org/wiki/File:Poland_-_Location_Map_(2019)_-_POL_-_UNOCHA.svg

Index

Academy of Sciences, 500
Adamczyk-Garbowska, Monika, 501
Africa, xxv, 54n25, 556
Agricultural Society, 99
Agudat Yisrael, 244, 250, 331n69
Aid Funds Center, 315n1
AJC. *See* American Jewish Committee
AK (Armia Krajowa). *See* Polish Home Army
AL (Armia Ludowa). *See* Polish People's Army
Alabama, 546
Aleichem, Sholem, 248
Alexander I, tsar of Russia, 68–69, 72, 78, 82, 85
Alexander II, tsar of Russia, 98–99, 104–6, 109–11, 142–43, 172
Alexander III, tsar of Russia, 138, 143
Aleynhilf, group, 338
Alliance Israélite Universelle, 123
Allies (Allied governments), 16, 183–85, 193, 195, 198, 205, 209n48, 211, 213, 215–16, 254, 272n3, 327, 330–31, 340, 356–57, 358n8, 359–60, 370, 556
All-Polish Anti-Racist League (Ogólnopolska Liga do Walki z Rasizmem), 16
All-Poland Jewish Youth Organization (ZOOM), 456
All-Polish Youth (MWP), organization, 258
Almog, Shmuel, 253
Alster, Antoni, 372n60, 416n73
Alter, Isaac Meir, rebbe of Ger (Góra Kalwaria), 89, 120

AMAD (acr). *See* Dik, Ayzik Meir
Amazon, company, 5n9, 177n36
Ambrosewicz-Jacobs, Jolanta, 462, 500, 534n88, 540
America, xxii–xxiii, xxviii, xxix, 4, 7–9, 21, 39, 125, 144, 195, 221, 268, 270, 331n69, 439, 481–82, 538–39, 548. *See also* USA
American Bar Association, 551
American Civil War, 215, 546, 548
American Communist Party, 10
American Emergency Committee for Zionist Affairs, 331n69. *See also* JEC
American Jewish Committee (AJC), viii, 22, 199–200, 207, 208n37, 331n69, 489, 491. *See also* Jewish Committee
American Jewish Congress, 208, 331
American Jewish Joint Distribution Committee (JOINT), 19, 378, 387, 399, 402
American Peace Commission, 208n44
American revolution, 50
American World Congress of Jews, 19
Andrzejewski, Jerzy, 361n26, 373, 379, 391–93, 426, 429
Andrzejewski, Leon, 372n60
Angers, 326n43
Anielewicz, Mordechai, 459n34, 522
Anielewicz Centre, 501
Ankara, 538
Ansky, S. Y., 179n42, 248
Antall, József, Sr., 325
Anti-Defamation League, 177n36, 322n33, 531, 546, 549
Antiochus Epiphanes, 134n97, 556

Anti-*Zionist* campaign in March 1968, xxviii, 19, 254, 413–22, 425, 429, 441, 450–51, 504, 527–28, 530, 540
Applebaum, Anne, 257n6
Arab-Israeli conflict, 408–9, 416. *See also* Six Day War
Arendt, Hannah, 335n81
Arkansas, 220n95
Armenian genocide, 216n78, 274
Asch, Sholem, 178, 186, 248
Ashkenazim, religious group, xxvii, xxix, xxxv, xxxvii, 77, 170
Ashkenazy, Severyn, 455
Asia, 556
Assmann, Jan, xxxi, xxxvi
Association of Children of the Holocaust, 454
Association of Doctors, 262
Association of the Jewish Historical Institute of Poland, 503
Atlanta, x, xv–xvii, 483, 487
Atlantic ocean, 156, 287, 297, 561
Atlantic Charter, 357
Auerswald, Heinz, 337
Auschwitz, xvii–xviii, 1, 16, 281, 310, 321n25, 322, 328n55, 340, 394, 397, 444, 465–67, 479, 483–84, 498, 553, 558
Auschwitz II Birkenau, 465–67, 483–84, 498
Auschwitz III Monowitz, 465–66n61
Austria, 54n25, 62, 68, 88, 114, 121–22, 192
Austro–Hungarian Empire, xxvii, 62, 127, 198, 222

Ba'al Shem Tov (acr. Besht), 75–76
Babel Club, group, 402, 416. *See also* TSKŻ
Baczko, Bronisław, dissident, 418, 478n6
Baeck, Leo, rabbi, viii, 495–96, 552
Baildon steel works, 421

Balfour Declaration, 177
Baliński, count, 329
Balkans, 474
Balta, 206
Balwierzyszki, 139n121
Baranowicze, 342
Barnett, Bernice M., xxxiii
Barney Medintz, camp, xv, xx
Barrès, Maurice, 122–23
Bartal, Israel, 67n17, 113n74
Bartel, Kazimierz, 261
Bartkowicz, commander, 363
Bartosiński, Czesiek, 383
Bartosiński, Jan, 383
Bartosiński, Józek, 383
Bartoszewski, Władysław T., 18–19, 321, 465, 466n62
Bauer, Yehuda, 430, 558
Bauman, dissident, 418
BBC, 329
Bednarczuk, Wincenty, 381
Bedzin, 89
Beilis, Menachem Mendel, 235
Beit Polska, 460
Beit Warszawa, xviii, 455–60
Belarus, xxv, 9, 32, 184, 195, 368, 469, 535
Belgium, 86, 89, 225, 466n63
Belvedere camp, 197
Belvedere Palace, 86
Bełżec, 483, 502
Ben-Yehudah, Eliezer (Perlmann), 149
Berkowicz, Joseph, 88
Berman, Boris, 368
Berman, Jakub, 16–17, 370n56, 371–72, 405, 498
Bermuda Refugee Conference, 332
Bernstein-Kogan, Jacob, 173
Besht (acr). *See* Ba'al Shem Tov
Bezpieka (Ministerstwo Bezpieczeństwa Publicznego). *See* Ministry of Public Security

Beys Yankev schools, 250
Bialek, Bogdan, 396
Bialik, Hayim Nahman, 174
Białystok, 266, 295, 312, 382
Biden, Joe, president, 234n49
Biegański stereotype, 5, 9
Bielawa, 382
Bielski brothers, 335n80
Bienik, Juliusz, bishop of Upper Silesia, 389–90
Bieńkowska, Flora, 391n135
Bierut, Bolesław, 372, 400, 405
Bilbo, Theodore, 20
Bilewicz, Michał, 515, 517
Billauer, Guy, viii
Birkenau, 465–67, 483–84, 498. See also Auschwitz
Berlin, 67n16, 337
Birnbaum, Nathan, 245n104
Biskupski, Mieczysław B., 9, 183
Black Hundreds, groups, 174–76, 178
Black Lives Matter, movement, 547–48
Błaszczyk, Henryk, 382–83, 390
Błaszczyk, Walenty, 383
Bloc of National Minorities, 229
Blue Police, xxi, 302, 306, 314, 346
Blum, Léon, 122n38
Blumenthal, Jeff, vi, x, xv, xvii
Blumenthal, Lilly, xxivn9
Blumsztajn, student, 416n73
B'nai B'rith, 331n69
B'nai Torah Congregation, 485
Boas, Franz, 6
Bobruisk, 104
Boca Raton, 484–85
Bochnia, 363
Bodzianowski, Feliks, priest, 235–36
Bogucice, 363n33
Bojemski, Sebastian, 512
Bolesław the Bold, king, 434
Bolesław the Pious, duke, 27

Bolshevik Party (Bolsheviks faction), xxviii, xxxiii, 169, 176–80, 184, 186, 190, 193, 195–96, 200–1, 203n19, 206–7, 222–23, 233, 236–38, 255, 257, 265–66, 270, 285, 288–91, 368, 433, 472, 512, 526
Bolshevik Revolution, 184, 190n86, 433. See also Russian Revolution
Bonacich, Edna, 30–31, 52, 70, 164
Book of Esther, 14
Book of Judges, 14
Book of Revelation, 132n89
Borejsza, Jerzy, 389
Borensztajn, Chudesa, 345
Bór-Komorowski, Tadeusz, general, 359
Boston, 21
Boy-Żeliński, Tadeusz, 236n54
Brandeis University, xix
Brandt, Willy, chancellor, 524
Brandys, Kazimierz, 427–29, 437
Braude, schools, 250n125
Bradley, Mamie, 544
Breditschew, 202
Breslau, 107. See also Wrocław
Brest, 39–40
Bricha, movement, 382
Bridges, Ruby, 542n13
Bridge To Poland, program, 492–93
Britain. See Great Britain
Broniewski, Władysław, 391n135
Bronshtein, Lev Davidovich. See Trotsky, Leon
Bronsztejn, Szyja, 238
Brookings Institution, 545
Brudzinski, Joachim, 475
Brus, Włodzimierz, 418
Brussels, 508
Bryant, Carolyn, 545
Brystygier, Julia, 372n60
Brzezinka. See Birkenau
Bucharest, 444
Buchner, Ignatz, 340

Budapest, 538
Bujnowski, Kazimierz, 471–72
Bulgaria, xxiii
Bund (Bundists). *See* General Jewish Workers' Alliance
Bunge, Nikolai, 174n23
Bureau of Information and Propaganda, 321n25, 321n27, 328n52
Bush, David, viii
Bush, Marylou, viii
Butrymowicz, Mateusz, 55n17, 68n22
Bytom, 382
Byzantium, 27n7

Cabot Lodge, Henry, 200, 269
Cairo, 136
Cała, Alina, 468
California, 214n68, 549n38
Camp of Great Poland (OWP), 241
Camp of National Unity (OZN), 267
Capuchins, order of, 136n107
Carmelite, nuns, 464–65, 467
Carthage, 274
Casimir III the Great, 27
Caspi, Yuval, ix
Center for Citizenship Education (CCE), 498
Center for European Studies, 500
Center for Holocaust Research (Centrum Badań nad Zagładą Żydów), xxi–xxii, 500–1, 515, 529, 532
Center for Research on Prejudice, 515
Center of Education about Auschwitz and the Holocaust, 498
Central America, 539
Central Committee of Jews in Poland (CKŻP), 371n57, 377n77, 380, 382, 521
Central Europe, 84, 143, 185, 197, 199, 208, 209n48, 330, 356, 462, 540, 550

Central Yiddish School Organization (TSYSHO), 249–50
Chanukah (Hanukkah), 14, 556
Chabad Poway synagogue, 549n38
Chapel of Memory of Rescuers, 517, 518n38
Charleston, 219
Charlottesville, 546–48
Charney, Israel, 279
Chełm, 189, 380
Chelmicki, Maciek, 361n26
Chełmno, 328, 342, 483
Cherikover, Elias, 191
Cherkasy, 191
Cherry, Robert, 12
Chicago, xiii, 219
China, 213n68
Chișinău, 173. *See also* Kishinev
Chłopicki, Józef, 87–88
Chmieleńska, Irena, 379
Chmielnicki, Bogdan. *See* Khmelnytsky, Boghdan
Chodakiewicz, Marek Jan, 470, 512
Chodnicki, Marian, 302
Christian Democrats, party, 243, 257
Christian Front, movement, 270
Christmas, 137, 413, 423
Churchill, Winston, 271, 357, 360
Ciechanów, 108
Cincinnati, 202
Citizens' Committee for the Care of Polish Refugees, 325
Citizens' Guard, 294
Citizens' Militia (MO), 201, 383–84
Civic Platform, party (PO), xxv, 509–10, 540
CKŻP (Centralny Komitet Żydów w Polsce). *See* Central Committee of Jews in Poland
Clement VI, pope, 135
Cleveland, 21
Clinton, Bill, president, 538

Club of Contradiction Seekers, 413
Cold War, 16–17, 23, 226n12, 399, 420, 427
Comintern, 368
Committee for the Amelioration of the Jews, 52
Committee for the Defense of Students' Honor (Komitet Obrony Honoru Akademika), 260
Committee of Jewish Delegations, 208–9, 211
Committee on Immigration and Naturalization, 269
Committee on New States and for the Protection of Minorities, 209
Communist Life (Życie), student group, 260
Communist Party in Poland (later PZPR), xxvi, xxviii, 3–4, 16–18, 254, 285–86, 288, 290, 298–99, 311, 358, 361, 363–67, 369–71, 374, 376, 378–79, 383, 387, 391n133, 393, 395, 400–1, 406, 417–18, 420, 422, 436, 450, 506, 527–28. *See also* Polish United Workers' Party (PZPR)
Confederation of Polish Electrical Engineers, 262
Confederation of Warsaw, 47
Congregation of Marian Fathers, 239
Congress of Jews in America, 19
Congress Kingdom of Poland, 68, 95, 112–13, 131n81, 141, 146, 149, 155, 157, 169, 232n41
Congress of Vienna, 68, 85
Connelly, John, 261
Conservative Jews, xiii, 457, 459n32
Constantine, grand duke, 84, 86
Constantinople, 39
Constitutional Assembly, 179
Cooper, Eli, 219
Copenhagen, 508

Copernicus, Nicolaus, 446
Costa, Robert, 538
Coughlin, Charles E., priest, 270
Council of Four Lands (Va'ad Arba Aratsot), 28, 59, 560
Council of Jewish Elders. *See* Judenrat
Council for Aid to Jews. *See* Żegota
Counter-Reformation, 39, 48, 129
Courts of Honor, 353
Crémiux, Isaac Adolphe, 136
Crete, 135
Crimea, 360
Cromwell, Oliver, 4
CRT (Critical Race Theory), 541, 550
Crusades, 443, 556
Cukierman, Yitzhak, 322n22
Cukunft, Community Center, 554
Curie-Skłodowska, Maria, 501
Curzon Line, 272, 356, 360
Cyrankiewicz, Józef, 394
Czacki, Taduesz, 52, 68n22
Czajkowski, Michał, priest, 463
Czaplicki, Józef, 372n60
Czarnek, Przemysław, 514–15
Czartoryski, Adam, 103
Czechoslovakia, 370n56, 389, 414
Czerniaków, Adam, 337, 340–41, 344, 346, 350
Czernovitz, 245, 246n106
Częstochowa, 129, 139n121, 385, 389, 431
Czorsztyn, 380
Czuchnowski, Wojciech, 531

Dąbrowa council, 340
Dąbrowa Tarnowska, 301–2
Dąbrowska, Kamila, ix
Dąbrowska, Maria, 259–60, 262
Dajczgewant, Józef, 417n75
Dale, village, 300
Damascus, 135–36, 139
Danzig-Westpreussen, 273, 280

Darwin, Charles, 159, 181
Daszuta, Janusz, 396
Daum, Menachem, 307
Davitt, Michael, 173
Dawidowicz, Lucy, 252–53
Dęblin, 388
Decembrists' rebellion, 85
Delegatura, organization, 361
Democratic Left Union (SLD), 507–8
Democratic Party in the USA, 20, 53n20, 234n49, 542
Democritus, 134n97
Denikin, Anton, general, 190
Denmark, xv
DePaul University, 480n12
DeSantis, Ron, 541
Dershowitz, Alan, 480n12
Detroit, 21
Devil's Island, 146n27
Diamant, Ita, 318
Dik, Ayzik Meir (acr. AMAD), 113n74
Dillingham, William P., 8
Dmitrow, Edmund, 294n103
Dmowski, Roman, 158–66, 169, 180–86, 189, 198–99, 201, 203, 206–7, 209–12, 217, 221, 223, 228–31, 235, 241, 243, 244n97, 257, 263, 266–67, 270, 317, 386–87, 421, 461, 475, 505, 527, 561–62
Doboszyński, Adam, 265
Dobrodzień, 552
Dojczgewant, Józef, 416n73
Don, river, 191n93
Donat, Alexander, 316
Ignacy oevsky, Fyodor, 248
Dowbór-Muśnicki, Józef, general, 195
Dreyfus, Alfred, captain, 146–48, 162, 167–68
Drumont, Édouard, 122, 123n42, 147
Drymmer, Wiktor Tomir, 197
Dubček, Alexander, 414

Dubnow, Simon M., 150, 244, 250
Duchy of Warsaw, 62–63, 65–66, 68–69, 84, 90, 100
Duda, Andrzej, president, 510, 513, 528–29, 539
Duke, David, 548
Durham, Sam, ix, 484
Durkheim, Emile, xxx
Dynner, Glenn, ix, 88, 108

East Germany, 441
East St. Louis, 219–20
Easter, 173, 392, 473
Eastern (Soviet) bloc, countries of, xxiii, 17, 22–23, 357, 364, 370n56, 376, 393, 395, 407–8
Eastern Europe, xxxv, 4–5, 8, 14–15, 20, 77, 197, 199, 206–8, 209n48, 212, 214, 245n105, 251, 307, 325, 364, 462, 527, 537, 539–40, 550
Ec Chaim, synagogue, 457–58, 460
Ecumenical Council. *See* Vatican II
Edelman, Marek, 352
Egypt, 14, 135, 408, 556
Eichmann, Adolf, xivn1
Einsatzgruppen, 279–80, 294, 336. *See also* SS
Eisenberg, Hersh, 343n114
Eisler, Jerzy, 419
Ejzenberg, Israel, 108
EKOPO (Jewish Committee for the Aid of War Victims), 191
Elaine, 220n95
Elbląg, 424n4
Elijah, rabbi, gaon of Vilna, 76n52
Elisavetgrad, 143
Ellis Island, 269
Endecja, party (Endeks/National Democrats). *See* National Democratic Party
Engel, David, 308, 309n167, 310, 326–28, 330, 350n149, 374

Engelking, Barbara (née Boni), xxii, 299–301, 312n179, 315, 353n161, 500, 511, 531–33
England, xxvi, 28, 116, 130n78, 131n80, 134, 136, 269, 556. *See also* Great Britain
Entente, 16, 186, 198, 205, 215–16, 223
Episcopate Committee for Dialogue with Judaism, 447
Erdogan, Recep Tayyip, president, 538
Esther, biblical figure, 14
Etz Chaim. *See* Ec Chaim
European Parliament, 510
European Union (EU), xxii–xxiii, xxv, 475, 507–11, 537–39

Facebook, 476
Facing History and Ourselves, organization, 491
Fackenheim, Emil, 479–80
Falanga group, 405n22. *See also* ONR
Farage, Nigel, 538
FBI (Federal Bureau of Investigation), 545
Fejein, Anatol, 372n60
Fein, Leonard, 479
Feinstein, Dianne, 551n1
Fikus, Joanna, ix, 514, 528
Finkelstein, Norman, 480n12
First Republic of Poland, 32. *See also* Polish-Lithuanian Commonwealth
Fishman, David, 245, 246n108
Flato, Krystyna, 417n75
Fleming, Michael, 327–29
Florida, 485, 541
Floyd, George, 546–47
Flying University (ŻUL), 429, 452–54
Foley, James, 374n69
Folkspartei, party, 244
Folwarczny, Andrzej, ix, 484, 490, 514
FOP (Front for the Rebirth of Poland/Front Odrodzenia Polski), 323

Ford, Henry, 268–69, 271n76
Forecki, Piotr, 497
Foreign Service. *See* Ministry of Foreign Affairs
Forum for Dialogue among the Nations, 484, 487, 489, 491, 496–97, 499, 514
Foundation for the Preservation of Jewish Heritage in Poland (FODŻ), 498
Fourth Universal, 190n86
Fox News, 548
France, 28, 50, 61–62, 94, 114, 116, 121–23, 136, 146–48, 167–68, 193, 195–96, 225–26, 230, 326n43, 538, 556
Francis, pope, 448
Franciscans, order of, 132n87, 239, 444
Franco-Prussian War, 62
Frank, Anne, 480
Frank, Hans, 273, 280, 283, 306, 317, 322, 337n91, 375n73
Frank, Jacob, 76n50
Frankists, religious group, 76
Franklin, Benjamin, 269
Frederick August, king of Saxony, 63
Freedom and Independence Association (WiN), organization, 563
Free Trade Union, 424, 426, 437, 439
Freemasonry, 84, 130–33, 175, 177, 228–29, 235–38, 444, 447, 561, 564
French Guiana, 146n27
French Revolution, xxvii, xxxvi, 50, 231, 371
French Third Republic, 123n41
Friedlander, Israel, 43
Friedlaender, Max, 495–96
Friedman, Daniela, ix
Friedman, Thomas, 538, 539n4
Frydel, Tomasz, 299, 304–6
Furber, David, 283

Gąbin, 139n121
Gądecki, Stanisław, archbishop, 447n110
Galicia, 54n25, 62, 69n23, 73n42, 127–28, 156, 157n66, 186, 189, 192, 203n19, 204, 232, 234, 301n133, 304, 356, 382
Gambetta, Léon, 123n41
Gancwajch, Abraham, 345–46
Ganganelli, Lorenzo, cardinal, 135n106. *See also* Clement VI, pope
Ganszyniec, Ryszard, 260
Gawin, Magdalena, 518–19
Gaza Strip, 408, 556
Gdańsk, viii, xvii, 224, 423–24, 425n9, 426, 437–39
Gdynia, 424, 442
Gebert, Jan, viii
Gebert, Konstanty, viii, 12, 451–54
General Government, 273, 280, 282–83, 312, 316–17, 324–25, 336
General Jewish Workers' Alliance (Bund), 157–59, 161, 165, 183, 232n41, 244, 249, 252, 264, 328–29, 338, 373, 554, 561
Geneva, 466
Genoa (Genova), 107n44
Gentiles, 16, 31n23, 49, 55–58, 121, 145, 172, 174, 305, 325, 465
Georgia, ix–x, xv–xvi, 219, 483, 541
Ger, 89, 120
Gergel, Nakhum, 190n87
Germany, xiv, 10, 12n28, 13, 16, 20, 22, 28, 46, 68n20, 72n38, 94, 116, 118–19, 121–22, 144, 146–47, 159, 169, 182n53, 183n56, 185, 198, 213, 216, 230n37, 236, 270, 272–73, 280–85, 308, 316–17, 327, 330, 353, 357n3, 366, 409, 411, 422, 441, 470, 473, 475, 495, 509, 560–61
Gestapo, 282, 317–18, 343, 345–46, 521
Ghetto Fighters' Monument, 522–24
Gierek, Edward, 425–26, 436–37, 440

Gilbert, Martin, 328n55
Gilman, Neil, rabbi, xxxv, 2
Ginczka, Zuzanna, 461
Ginczka High School, 461
Glemp, Józef, cardinal, archbishop, 444, 463, 472
Gliński, Piotr, 528, 531
Goddard, Henry H., 269
Goebbels, Joseph, 357
Goedsche, Hermann, 171
Golan Heights, 408
Goldberg, Jacob, 504
Goldfaden, Avrom, 248
Goldman, Bernard, 107
Goldman, Isaac, 108
Goldman, Nahum, 481
Goldman, family, 515
Goldstein, Israel, rabbi, 332
Gomułka, Władysław, 400–3, 405n23, 406–7, 409–10, 412–14, 416, 418, 420–25, 431, 527
Gontarczyk, Piotr, 470
Góra Kalwaria. *See* Ger
Górecki, Wiktor, 416n73
Gorbachev, Mikhail, president, 317n10
Gordin, Jacob, 248
Gordon, Linda, 43
Gorodishche, 191
Górski, Konrad, 261
Goska, Danusha V., 22
Gozhanski, Shmuel, 151–52
Goose Creek, 219
Grabowski, Jan, xxii, 299, 301, 313, 353n161, 500, 511, 519, 526, 531–33
Grabski, Władysław, 234
Grade, Chaim, 178, 180, 247
Grand Duchy of Lithuania, 32, 50, 95, 141. *See also* Lithuania
Grant, Madison, 5–6
Great Britain, xxii, 21, 177, 179n45, 180n45, 193, 211, 326, 329, 331–32, 356, 537–38. *See also* UK

Great Depression, 20n43, 121, 137, 226–27, 243, 257, 270
Great Novena of the Millennium, 430–31
Great War. *See* World War I
Greater Poland (Wielkopolska), 27, 32
Greece, 14, 556
Greenstone, Julius H., 203n19
Gregory X, pope, 134n101
Grimm, Jacob and Wilhelm, 72n38
Grodno, 149, 320
Gross, Jan Tomasz, xx, 292–93, 374, 381, 413, 468, 470, 501, 506, 511, 513, 518, 540
Grossman, Dave, lieutenant colonel, 187
Gross-Rosen, 483
Grudziądz, 426n11
Grudzińska, Irena, 416n73, 417n75
Grünbaum, Yitzhak, 149–50, 155, 229
Grunwald Association, 461
Grzegorzówka, 307
Gujarat, 30
Gwoździec, 504

Ha'am, Ahad, 246
Habsburg monarchy, 50, 234
Hadle Szklarskie, 306
Halbwachs, Maurice, xxx–xxxi
Haller, Józef, general, 195–96
Haman, biblical figure, 13, 556
Hamas, xxxiii, 549n39, 556
Handelsman, Marceli, 259
Hanukkah (Chanukah), 14, 556
Harper, Janice, ix
Harvard University, 208n38, 269
Harzfeld, Jacob, captain, 180n45
Hashomer Hatzair (Young Guard), youth movement, 252, 373, 459–60. *See also* Zionist party
Hasidim, religious group, 66, 75–78, 89, 108, 119–21, 139–40, 248, 474, 486, 494n53, 560–61

Haskalah, movement, 14, 66–68, 72–75, 97, 118–19, 246, 560
Hebrew Institute of Riverdale, 467
Heilpern, Maksymilian, 154
Heller, Celia S., 254
Helsinki Act, 427
Henry, Patrick, 335n80
Herzl, Theodore, 149
Hetnal, Adam, priest, 239
Heydrich, Reinhard, 279, 312, 335–37
Heyer, Heather, 547
Ḥibat Tsiyon (Love of Zion), organization, 149, 168, 244. *See also* Zionist party
High Holy Days, 78, 396
Hilberg, Raul, 335n81
Himmler, Heinrich, 279, 281
Hirszowicz, dissident, 418
Hitler, Adolf, xvi, xxxii, 6, 14, 16, 19, 259, 267, 270–71, 273, 274n7, 278–79, 282, 284, 298–99, 308–11, 321–22, 331–33, 369–70, 372, 379, 393–94, 411, 433–34, 479, 522, 549, 556
Hlond, August, cardinal, 265, 390, 393
Hoffman, Eva, 23, 58
Hollywood, 9–10, 19
Holocaust Law, xxii, 474, 528–29, 531, 550, 558, 563
Holocaust Memorial Day, 484
Holocaust Memorial Museum in Washington, 480
Holocaust Museum in Israel. *See* Yad Vashem
Holy Cross Church, 137
Holy Land, 382
Holy Family, 431
Holy See, 133, 435, 539n5
Home Army *See* Polish Home Army
Hoover, Herbert, president, 6, 20
Horev schools, 250
Horowitz, Maks, 157
Houston, 219
Hudson, Manley O., 209n48

Hughes, Charles Evan, 204–5
Hugo, Victor, 248
Humer, Adam, 372n60
Hundert, Gershon, 75n48
Hungary, xxiv, 10, 135, 144, 325, 370n56, 469, 538n1
Hurvitsch, Tsivia, 155n62
Hyżne, 306

Iberian Peninsula, xxxv
Ignatiev, Nikolay P., 143
Illinois, 219
Iłowa, 139n121
Independent Publishing House (NOWA), 428
Innocent IV, pope, 134n101, 135n106, 434
Inquisition. 556
Instytut Badań Spraw Narodowościowych, 242
Institute of Jewish Studies, 501
Institute of National Remembrance (IPN), 293–95, 312n179, 313, 468n72, 470, 474, 511, 513, 518n38, 528, 531, 540
Institute of Philosophy and Sociology, 500
Interfactory Strike Committee (MKS), 438–39
International Center of Education about Auschwitz and the Holocaust, 498
Inter-School Discussion Club, 413
IPN (Instytut Pamięci Narodowej). *See* Institute of National Remembrance
Iraq war, 374n69
Iron Curtain, xxxiv, 23, 313, 516
Isaac Meir Alter, rebbe of Ger (Góra Kalwaria), 89, 120
ISIS, 374n69
Islamic Caliphate, 27n7
Israel, xivn1, xxii, xxix, xxxii–xxxiii, 12–14, 18, 21, 22n49, 77, 105, 135n106, 208n39, 235, 252, 312, 335n80, 354, 393n141, 408–12, 413n59, 415–16, 418–20, 422, 459, 470, 473–74, 480, 483–84, 487, 516, 527, 538, 549, 553, 556
Israel ben Eliezer. *See* Ba'al Shem Tov
Italy, 114, 131, 193, 353
Izdebski, Krzysztof, viii, 454n18, 456–59, 488

Jabotinsky, Vladimir (Ze'ev), 311n174
Jackan, Samuel Jacob, 150
Jadwiga, queen, 32
Jagiełło, Eugeniusz, 162
Jagiellonians, dynasty, 32, 394
Jagiellonian University in Kraków, 44, 257, 500–1
Jagielski, Mieczysław, 439
Jan Kazimierz (John II Casimir Vasa), king, 431
Janicka, Elżbieta, 464n57, 523, 525
Jankowski, Henryk, priest, 438–39, 462
January Uprising (1863), 15, 70n29, 98, 107, 111–12, 115, 117, 120n28, 125, 138, 152, 182, 292, 561
Japan, 175n25, 193, 213n68
Jaruzelski, Wojciech, general, 441–42
Jasieński, Bruno, 364
Jasinowski, Israel, 149
Jasna Góra, 430–31
Jasto, 307
Jastrow, Marcus Mordechai, rabbi, 68n20, 102–4, 112, 120
Jastruń, Mieczysław, 391
JEC (Joint Emergency Committee on European Jewish Affairs), 331–32
Jędrek, Grzegorz, 493
Jedwabne, xx, xxii, 292–96, 297n116, 313, 438, 439n68, 468–70, 472, 501, 506, 510–13, 515–17, 526, 533–34, 543, 545, 550, 557, 563
Jeleński, Jan, 124, 160

Jerusalem, xxxii, 13, 79, 134n97, 174, 177, 522
Jesuit Order, 48, 133, 446–48, 472
Jesus Christ, 39, 49, 80, 83–84, 117, 128, 130, 132n87, 132n89, 174, 176, 235, 238, 443, 445, 474, 511, 525
Jew hunts (Judenjagd), 302–6, 313, 326, 352–53, 376, 419, 500, 511–12, 515–17, 550, 557
Jewish Civil Guard, 89
Jewish Committee (KŻ), 158, 191, 384, 522. See also American Jewish Committee
Jewish Committee for the Aid of War Victims (EKOPO), 191
Jewish Community Centers (JCC), 484, 554
Jewish Council (kahal), 27–28, 58, 74, 201, 242, 244, 334–40, 342, 346, 349
Jewish Council of Elders. See Judenrat
Jewish Educational Committee, 211
Jewish Electoral Committee, 160–61
Jewish Enlightenment. See Haskalah movement
Jewish Fighting Organization, 521
Jewish Flying University (ŻUL), 429, 452–54
Jewish Ghetto Police, 346–51, 353
Jewish Historical Institute (ŻIH), 287n77, 454, 503
Jewish Labor Committee, 331n69
Jewish National Council, 19
Jewish Order Service, 346–50, 352–53, 355, 500
Jewish Religious Union (ZRWM), 403n13, 450
Jewish Social and Cultural Association (TSKŻ), 399–400, 402–3, 416, 450
Jewish Social Democratic Group (Vilna Group), 151–58, 165, 168
Jewish Studies, xiii, 501, 503, 553

Jewish Syndicate, organization, 123, 147
Jewish Theological Seminary, xix
Jeżowska, Ludmiła, viii, 458–59
Jeżowski, Emil, viii, 458–60, 516–17
Jeżowski, Marek, viii, 452, 460–61
Jim Crow Laws, 205n24, 214–15, 218, 223, 541. See also US South
Jogaila, grand duke. See Władysław II Jageiłło
John Paul II, pope (Wojtyła), 432, 434–35, 443, 446, 472, 564
John XXIII, pope, 445
Johnson, Albert, 269
Johnson-Reed Act, 269
JOINT (American Jewish Joint Distribution Committee), 19, 378, 387, 399, 402
Joly, Maurice, 171
Jończyk, Ewa, 532
Jones, Alex, 541
Jordan River, West Bank of, 408
Joselewicz, Berek, 62, 88
Judas Iscariot, biblical figure, 474–75
Judenrat (Council of Jewish Elders), 305, 335–43, 346, 348–50, 353–54, 355, 558
Judenjagd. See Jew hunts

Kaczmarczyk, Wojcieh, 363n33
Kaczyński, Jarosław, 474, 508–11
Kaczyński, Lech, president, 508–9, 511
Kądziolka, Władysław, 302
Kahan, Anna, 189n82
Kahana, Abraham Isaac, rabbi, 108
Kalisz, 27, 67n18, 139n121, 382n96, 385, 389
Kamenev, Lev, 178, 368
Kamińska, Ester Rachel, 248
Kamińska, Ida, 248, 403
Kamińska, Maria, 222
Kamiński, Aleksander, 321–22
Kania, Stanisław, 440–41

Kansas, 325
Kapralski, Sławomir, xxxiv, xxxvii
Karlip, Joshua, 149n38, 244n97, 245n105
Karski, Jan, 288–89, 290n86, 316, 326n43–44, 328, 331–32, 463
Katyń, 317, 375, 413, 429, 509, 525–26
Katz, Israel, 410–11n49
Katz, Sandra (née Stark), 335n82
Kazimierz, district, xvii, 189, 553. *See also* Kraków
Kazimierz III the Great (Casimir III the Great), king, 27
Kazimierz Dolny, 365
Kępa, Józef, 415–16
Kępno, 363
Kersten, Krystyna, 309n167, 386
KGB, 487n36
Khazaria, 27
Kherson Province, 143
Khmelnytsky, Boghdan, 41–44, 48–49
Khrushchev, Nikita, 401
Kielce, 4, 11, 266, 303, 371, 375, 382–85, 387–93, 396, 399, 405, 421, 540
Kieniewicz, Stefan, 88
Kinderfraind, Abraham, 96
Kingdom of Poland, xxviii, 28, 50, 64, 66–78, 82–86, 89–90, 92, 94–98, 100, 107, 109–10, 112–15, 119, 123–25, 131, 138–39, 141, 144–50, 152–53, 155, 157, 160–61, 166–68, 170, 233. *See also* Polish-Lithuanian Commonwealth
Kirschenbaum, Jan, viii, 473, 554–55
Kirschenbaum, Mati, 555
Kishinev, 172–74. *See also* Chişinău
KKK (Ku Klux Klan), 215, 218, 544, 548
Knights Party, 548
Knights of the Ku Klux Klan, 548
Knox, Alfred, general, 180n45
Knoxville, 219
Kock (Kotzk), 89
Kohut, Zenon E., 43

Koffman, Jan, 413
Kołakowski, Leszek, 418
Kolbe, Maksymilian, Franciscan monk, 444
Kolbuszowa, 382n96
Kołłątaj, Hugo, 52
Kołodziej, Józef, mayor, 363n33
Komorowski, Bronisław, 509
Kopelzon, Tsemakh, 151
Kopstein, Jeffrey, 295–96
KOR (Komitet Obrony Robotników). *See* Workers' Defense Committee
Korjuć, Maciej, 515
Kossak-Szczucka, Zofia, 322–24
Kościuszko, Tadeusz, 61–63, 102, 387n6
Kot, Stanisław, 237n55
Kotarbiński, Tadeusz, 260
Kotula, Franciszek, 306
Kotzk (Kock), 89
Kovno, 339
Kozłowski, Maciej, ix, 487
Kozłowski, Wojciech, 520
Krahelska-Filipowicz, Wanda, 324
Krajewski, Stanisław, viii, xxxvi, 397, 452, 454, 457, 467, 469, 473–74, 476, 488–89, 545
Kraków, xx, 34, 150, 189, 229, 247n113, 257, 265, 273, 280, 303, 320, 380–82, 388–89, 432, 434–35, 484, 500–1, 553
Kramsztyk, Izaak, rabbi, 68n20, 102, 104
Kraszewski, Józef Ignacy, 101, 112
Kremer, Arkadi, 154, 165
Kremlin, 393, 397, 399
Kristallnacht, 495
KRN (Krajowa Rada Narodowa). *See* National Council of the Homeland
Kronenberg, Samuel, 100
Kronenberg, Leopold, 100–1, 107
Kroszyński, Leib, 108
Krupska-Wysocka, Krystyna, ix
Krushevan, Pavel, 171–72, 174

Krzepicki, Abram Jakub, 520
Krzywicki, Ludwik, 238
Kuban, 191n93
Kubik, Jan, 430, 434
Kubina, Teodor, bishop of Częstochowa, 385, 389, 393
Kucharzewski, Jan, 161–62
Kugelmass, Jack, 483
Kuhn, Fritz, 271n76
Kulczyński, Stanisław, 260
Kultur-Lige, 248
Kuroń, Grazyna, 427
Kuroń, Jacek, 426–27, 439–40, 467n68
Kwaśniewski, Aleksander, president, 469
Kyiv, xiii, 376n76
KŻ (Komitet Żydowski). *See* Jewish Committee

Labor Party (SP), centrist party, 257
Landy, Michał, 105
Lane, Arthur Bliss, 359
Lanota, Anna, viii–ix
Lanzmann, Claude, 464–65, 485
Laqueur, Walter, 328n55
Lasota, Irena, 416n73
Latvia, 184
Lauder Foundation, 454
Lauder-Morasha School, 460–61
Laughlin, Harry, 269
Law and Justice (PiS), party, xxv, xxxv, 11, 471, 474, 504, 508–15, 517–18, 526, 528, 530–31, 537–39, 545, 550–51, 557, 560, 563–64
Lawson, Tom, 311
League for the Attainment of Full Rights for the Jewish People of Russia, 160–61
League for the Defense of Human and Civil Rights (Liga Obrony Praw Człowieka i Obywatela), 236n53, 433

League of Nations, 330
League of Polish Families (LPR), right-radical group, 509
League of Polish Lawyers, 262
Lec, Stanisław, 391
Lee, Robert E., general, 546–47
Legge, Jerry, ix
Legion Młodych (Youth Legion), faction, 236, 260
Legnica, 382
Lehrman, Milosz, 502
Lelewel, Joachim, 90
Lemberg. *See* Lviv
Lemkin, Raphael, 274–76
Lendvai, Paul, 399
Lenin, Vladimir, 178–79, 368
Lenin Shipyard in Gdańsk, 423–26, 437–39
Leningrad Communist Party, 368
Leo XIII, pope, 132, 135
Le Pen, Marine, 538
Leplevskii, Israel, 368
Leska, Szolem, 264–65
Lesser Poland (Małopolska), 301, 303–5, 320
Leszczyńska, Filomena, 531, 533
Leszczyński, Adam, 519
Levanda, Lev, 113n74
Levin, Harry, rabbi, 459n32
Lewin (Lewinówna), Zofia, 18–19
LGBT, 551n1
LGBTQ, 510, 539
Lilienblum, Moses Leib, 144, 149
Lindbergh, Charles, 271
Lindemann, Albert S., 100n9
Lipniszki, 286
Lipstadt, Deborah, viii
Listowski, Antoni, general, 196–97
Lithuania, xiii, 9, 38–39, 67n16, 158, 161, 184, 376n76, 469. *See also* Grand Duchy of Lithuania
Litva. *See* Lithuania

Litvaks (Russian Jews), 141–43, 145–46, 148–50, 154, 155n62, 157–58, 164, 167–68, 233, 237n61, 238, 241, 377
Łodz, 91, 126, 142, 149, 167, 266, 339, 341, 342n110, 400, 419, 482
Łomza District, 295
London, 165, 171, 173, 322n33, 326–31, 359–60
Longchamps, Roman, rector, 260
Long Depression. *See* Great Depression
Lorenc, Michał, ix
Los Angeles, 21
Love of Zion (Ḥibat Tsiyon), organization, 149, 168, 244
Lower, Wendy, 283
Lubelski, Abram, 108
Lubiński, Jurek, ix
Lublin, 32, 34, 46, 273, 322, 358, 359n11, 382n96, 390, 481–82, 492–93, 501
Lublin Ladies' Society, 482
Lubliner, Ludwik, 106
Lubomirski, Kazimierz, prince, 206–7
Łuczak, Czesław, 309n167
Ludwików, 384
Łukasiński, Walerian, 52n17
Łuków, 303
Lutsk, 287
Lutyk, Leon, 237n55
Luxemburg, 278
Luxemburg, Rosa, 153
Lviv (Lwów, Lemberg), 18, 192–95, 200, 203, 232, 242, 247n113, 257, 260–61, 320, 340, 360, 365, 450

Maccabees, biblical rebel warriors, 174
Mach, Zdzisław, 500
Machejkowa, Zofia, 373
Machewicz, Pawel, 405
Maciągowski, Marek, 396
Mack, Julian, 208, 209n47, 216
Madrid, 274n11

MAGA, movement, 538, 548, 560. *See also* Republican Party in the USA
Magdeburg Castle, 184
Maimon, Salomon, 67n16
Maj, Tadeusz, 299
Majdanek, 304n144, 373, 483
Makabi Warszawa, organization, 459
Maletka, Jan, 519–20
Malinowo, 531
Malinowski, Edward, 531–32
Maliszkiewicz, Beata, viii–ix, 494–96, 528–29
Maliszkiewicz, Julia, viii–ix, xv–xix
Maliszkiewicz, Kaja, viii–ix, xv, xvii–xix
Maliszkiewicz, Przemysław, viii–ix, xviii–xix, xxvi, xxx, 166, 553
Małopolska (Lesser Poland), 301, 303–5, 320
Maltz, Moshe, 382
Manchuria, 175n25
Mann, Thomas, 331n68
March 1968, anti-Zionist campaign, xxviii, 19, 254, 413–22, 425, 429, 441, 450–51, 504, 527–28, 530, 540
March of the Living (MOL), 480, 484–86, 488–89
Marchand, W. E., 187n75
Marcus, Sheldon, 270n73, 271n76
Mariasz, Stanisław, 363n33
Markowa, 515–16
Markowski, Artur, ix, 528, 534–35
Markusz, Katarzyna, 533n94
Markuszowa, 307
Marr, Wihelm, 121
Marshall, Louis, 199–200, 207–10, 216
Marshall Plan, 23
Martin V, pope, 134n101
Martin, Trayvon, 547
Martov, Julius, 178
Martuzalski, Reverend, 389

Maskilim, religious group, 65–67, 68n20, 72–73, 75, 78, 81, 97, 112–13, 120, 142, 145. *See also* Progressive Jews
Massachusetts, 21, 269
Materski, Wojciech, 309n167
Matuszewski, Alec, ix, 450
Mauthausen-Gusen, 325
Mazowiecki, Tadeusz, 442, 447n110, 463–64
Mazur, Leon and Sarah, ix
MBP (Ministerstwo Bezpieczeństwa Publicznego). *See* Ministry of Public Security
McConnell, Mitch, 53n20
Medeazza, Juliusz von, 337n91
Mehemet Ali, 136
Mehmet Talaat, 274n10
Meisels, Dov Berush, chief rabbi, 102, 104, 108, 112
Meller, David, 382
Menahem Mendel of Kotzk (Kock), 89
Mendelsohn, Ezra, 252
Mendelsohn, Moses, 66
Mendelson, Stanisław, 152
Mendes-Flohr, Paul R., 177n35
Mensheviks, faction, 178. *See also* Social Democratic Workers' Party in Russia
Messiah, 49, 76, 148, 290
Mexico, 538
Michlic, Joanna Beata, xxxvii, 293, 387
Michnik, Adam, 296, 297n116, 413–14, 416, 417n75, 423n1, 426–29, 433, 435, 440, 444, 447–48, 463–64
Mickiewicz, Adam, 83, 101, 104, 414
Mickiewicz, Władysław, 104
Middle East, xxv, 560
Miechów County, 300
Mielec County, 302
Mietkowski, Mieczysław, 372n60
Miklaszewski, Bolesław, 257
Mikołajczyk, Stanisław, 358–60, 362–63
Miliutin, Nicholas, 109

Mill, John (Yoysef Shloyme), 151, 153, 155
Miller, David Hunter, 208n44, 209n48
Miłosz, Czesław, 317, 391n135, 427n15, 432
Milówka, 189
Minc, Hilary, 370n56, 371, 389
Ministry of Culture, 503, 530
Ministry of Education, 498, 514
Ministry of Foreign Affairs, 194, 330n63, 371–72, 419, 516
Ministry of Foreign Trade, 371
Ministry of Information, 329
Ministry of Internal Affairs / of the Interior and Administration, (MSW), 384, 406–7, 408, 412, 413n59
Ministry of Public Security/ of State Security (MBP/SB/UB), 361, 363, 372, 383–84, 388, 400–1, 521. *See also* Secret Police
Ministry of Security Matters (MSW). *See* Ministry of the Interior and Administration/ Internal Affairs
Minkowski, family, 264–65
Minneapolis, 21
Minorities Treaty, 209n48, 210–13, 216–17, 220, 223, 231, 233, 235, 241, 254–55, 421, 556, 561
Mississippi, 20, 544
Missouri, 562
Mitnaggedim, religious group, 76–78, 89, 140
Mizrachi, party, 244, 250n125. *See also* Zionist party
MKS (Międzyzakładowy Komitet Strajkowy). *See* Interfactory Strike Committee
młoda prasa, group, 115–16, 118
Młodożeniec, Stanisław, 236n55
Młodzianowski, Kazimierz, 241
MO (Milicja Obywatelska). *See* Citizens' Militia

Moczar, Mieczysław, general, 400, 403–13, 416, 421–22, 527
Mohammad Ali of Egypt. *See* Mehemet Ali
MOL. *See* March of the Living
Moldova, xxiv, 173
Molière, 248
Molodovsky, Kadya, 247, 481–83
Molotov, Vyacheslav, 272
Molotov-Ribbentrop Pact, 272, 283, 357n4, 413
Monowitz (Monowice), 465–66n61. *See also* Auschwitz
Montana, 20
Montefiore, Moses, sir, 136
Monument to the Fallen and Murdered in the East, 525
Morawiecki, Mateusz, 528
Morawska, Ewa, 414
Morawski, Kazimierz M., 237, 418
Morgenthau, Henry, Sr., 216–18, 223
Mosaic faith, 79–81, 90, 247, 472
Moscow, 39, 125, 143n11, 202, 236, 272, 358–59, 363, 370, 400, 405, 407
Moses, biblical figure, 75, 79–80
Moses, A. Dirk, 276
Móscicki, Ignacy, 256
Mothers, organization, 20
Mozdzyński, Adam, ix
MSW (Ministerstwo Spraw Wewnętrznych). *See* Ministry of the Interior and Administration/Internal Affairs
Mumbai, 30
Muscovite wars, 43
Musiał, Bogdan, 293, 470
Musiał, Stanisław, priest, 447–48, 467n68, 472
Muszyński, E., 236
Muszyński, Henryk, archbishop, 447n110, 467n68

MWP (Młodzież Wszechpolska), organization, 258
Myślenice, 265

NAFTA (North American Free Trade Agreement), 538
Nalewajko's Rebellion, 40n66
Napoleon, emperor, 62–66, 68–69, 84–85, 88
Narodnaya Volya (People's Will), terrorist group, 143
Narodowa Demokracja (National Democracy), party. *See* National Democratic Party
Narutowicz, Gabriel, 229–30
National Armed Forces (NSZ), organization, 298
National Guard, 86–89
National Concentration, party, 161–62
National Confederation, group, 405n22
National Council of the Homeland (KRN), 357
National Democratic Party (Endecja), xxxvii, 147, 158–63, 165–66, 180–82, 189, 193, 199, 217, 221, 228–29, 232, 241–42, 244n97, 253, 257–59, 261, 263, 265–67, 299, 317, 376, 385–87, 391, 402, 410, 461, 520, 527, 561
National Radical Camp (ONR), 257, 317, 405n22
National Workers' Party, 243, 257
National Workers' Union (NZR), 159
NATO, xxiv, 507, 509
Natolin faction, 401–2, 404, 406–7
Nazi-Soviet Pact. *See* Molotov-Ribbentrop Pact
Nebraska, 219
Neisse, river, 356
Neshoma Project, 486, 493
Netanyahu, Benjamin (Bibi), xxii, 22
Netherlands, 278

Neufeld, Daniel, 120
New Orleans, 542n13
New Synagogue, 495–96
New York, viii, 20, 199, 203–4, 206, 209–10, 216, 270, 459n32, 467, 481
Nicholas I, tsar of Russia, 82, 85–87, 89, 91–95, 98
Nicholas II, tsar of Russia, 160, 175, 176n31
Nicholas V, pope, 134n101
Niemcewicz, Julian Ursyn, 100–1
Niepokalanów, 132
Nissenbaum, Yitzhak, 155
NKVD (Soviet Security Service/ Secret Police), 361, 369, 401
Nocznicki, Tomasz, 237n55
Nora, Pierre, xxx
North Africa, xxv
North America, xxii, xxix, 39, 144, 195–96, 538
Norway, 278
Norwich, 134
NOWA (Niezależna Oficyna Wydawnicza), Independent Publishing House, 428
November Uprising (1830), 4, 15, 82, 86–87, 89–92, 94n59, 96–97, 101, 108, 182, 292, 561
Novick, Peter, 477–78
Nowak, Zenon, 405
Nowy Targ, 380, 426n11
Nożyk Synagogue, xviii, 450, 454–57, 459–60
NPR (Narodowa Partia Robotnicza), party. *See* National Workers' Party
NSZ (Narodowe Siły Zbrojne), organization, 298
Nuremberg, 271
Nuremberg Laws, 259, 285
NZR (Narodowy Związek Robotniczy), union. *See* National Workers' Union

Obirek, Stanisław, ix, 446–48, 502
Ocmulgee, 219
Oder, river, 356, 357n3, 427
Odessa, 195, 206–7
Office of Press Control, 416
Ogólnopolska Liga do Walki z Rasizmem, 16
Oklahoma, 220
Olejniczak, Czesław, 389
Olejnik, Jacek, viii–ix, 503
Olczak, Bartek, ix
Olczak, Maria Eleonora, viii–ix
Olczak–Lipska, Magda, viii–ix, xv, xviiin3, xix
Omaha, 219
O'Neill, Eugene, 248
Oyneg Shabbos (Oneg Shabbat), group, 287, 315n1, 338, 523
ONR (Obóz Narodowo-Radykalny). *See* National Radical Camp
Opalski, Magdalena, 113n74
Open Society Foundations, 548
Operation Barbarossa, 280n29
Operation Reinhardt, 312
Operation Tannenberg, 279
Operation Tempest, 358
Opole, viii, 494–96, 552
Opole University, 494
Opportunists, 123n41, 401
Orbán, Viktor, 538
Oreglia, Giuseppe, priest, 135n105
Organizacja Bojowa, 182. *See also* PPS
Orla-Bukowska, Annamaria, ix, 44, 462, 540
ORT (Organization for Rehabilitation through Training/Obshestvo Remeslennogo i zemledelcheskogo Truda), 402
Orthodox Jews, xiii, 247, 331n69, 457, 460, 467, 478, 485–86, 554
Orwell, George, 428
Orzeszkowa, Eliza, 116–18, 137

Orszulik, Alojzy, bishop, 463n51
Ossowski, Stanisław, 374, 376
Ostrowski, Antoni, 88
Oświęcim. *See* Auschwitz
Ottoman Empire, 30, 216
Otwinowski, Stefan, 391n135
Otwock, 302, 350–51, 382
Oxford, xxvi
OWP (Obóz Wielkiej Polski), 241
OZN (Obóz Zjednoczenia Narodowego). *See* Camp of National Unity

Paczkowski, Andrzej, 371, 397
Paderewski, Ignacy, 199, 203, 206–7, 210–11, 216, 231
Pale of Settlement, 62, 73–74n42, 95, 141–44, 146, 148–49, 155, 158, 172n10, 244, 246, 287
Palestine, xxii, 21, 130, 144, 150, 208n39, 235n51, 246, 311n174, 335n80, 382, 549, 556
Papal States, 131
Pardes, Markus, 466n63
Paris, 86, 89, 147, 171, 208, 209n47
Paris Commune Shipyard, 424n4
Paris Peace Conference, 184, 198, 200, 205, 207–8, 211–12, 216, 223
Parnas, Joseph, 340
Parczewo, 382n96
Partisans (Partyzanci), 297–98, 395, 406–9, 411–12, 416, 422
Paskevich, Ivan, 91
Pasowski, Antoni, 383n101
Passover, 14, 58, 134, 380, 453, 458, 556
Patek, Stanisław, 183n59
Patriotic Society, 86. *See also* Union of Polish Patriots
Pauker, Ana (née Rabinsohn), 370n56
Pawlak, Maciej, rabbi, viii
Pawlikowski, Józef, 68n22
PAX, association, 404–5, 416
Pearl, Daniel, 374n69

Peasant Party (SL), 257, 260, 266, 358, 362n29. *See also* Polish Peasant Party (PSL)
Pech, Martha, ix, 552
Peiper, Tadeusz, 364
Pelley, William Dudley, 271n76
Peltyn, Samuel, 137
Pendergraft, Rachel, 548
PEN International, organization, 248
Pennsylvania, 21, 269
People's Will (Narodnaya Volya), terrorist group, 143
Perechodnik, Calek, 350–51
Peretz, Isaac Leib, 244n97, 245, 246n106, 248
Perl, Felix, 155
Perlmann, Eliezer (later Ben-Yehudah), 149
Persak, Krzysztof, 294–95, 312n179
Persia, 556
Person, Katarzyna, 347, 349–50, 500–1, 511
Person, Krystyna, ix
Petlyura, Symon, 191, 202, 206
Petrovsky-Shtern, Yochanan (Yohanan), xxiii, 35, 95
Petrusewicz, Maria, 416n73
Piasecki, Bolesław, 405
Piast, dynasty, 185, 394, 507–8
Piast Polish Peasant Party (PSL "Piast"), 243. *See also* PSL
Pieronek, Tadeusz, bishop, 447n110
Pietrasiewicz, Tomasz, 492–93
Pilecki Institute, 518
Piłsudski, Józef, 152–53, 156–58, 165, 168–69, 181–86, 196–98, 203, 222, 227–30, 234, 239–43, 253, 255–56, 258, 261, 267, 315, 421, 433, 561
Pińsk, 195–97, 203–4, 206, 208
Pinsker, Leon, 148
PiS (Prawo i Sprawiedliwość), party. *See* Law and Justice, party

Pittsburgh, 549
Pius IX, pope, 131, 132n89
Pius XI, pope, 237, 564
PKWN (Polski Komitet Wyzwolenia Narodowego). *See* Polish Committee of National Liberation
Plehve, Vyacheslav Konstantinovich, 173
Plessy v. Fergusson case, 214
Płock, 67n18, 426n11
PO (Platforma Obywatelska), party. *See* Civic Platform
Po'alei Zion, party, 244, 315n1. *See also* Zionist party
Podgajek, 264
Podlasie, 139n121
Polesie Division, 196
POLIN museum, viii, xix, 499, 503–4, 506, 514, 521, 523–24, 527–28, 530, 532, 537
Polish Civil War, 362, 562
Polish Committee of National Liberation (PKWN), 358
Polish Ethical Society (Polskie Stowarzyszenie Etyczne), 236n53
Polish government-in-exile, 10, 291, 311n174, 318, 324–30, 332–33, 357–59, 362
Polish Free Thought Union (Polski Związek Wolnej Myśli), 236n53
Polish Home Army (AK), xxi, 11, 18, 297–98, 313, 321, 358–59, 361–62, 370, 374, 383, 403–4, 411, 521
Polish-Lithuanian Commonwealth (First Republic of Poland), xxvii, 9, 15, 28, 32, 38–39, 42, 46–47, 50, 56, 59, 62, 69, 78, 153, 180, 182, 185, 230, 507, 537, 560. *See also* Kingdom of Poland
Polish National Committee, 183, 199
Polish National Council, 329–30
Polish Peasant Party (PSL), 362–64, 563
Polish People's Army (AL), 298–99, 361

Polish People's Republic (PRL), xxviiin16, 16–17, 22, 310, 370n56, 371, 372n60, 394–95, 397, 399–402, 406, 408, 410–12, 414, 418, 420, 430, 432–33, 436, 439, 446, 452, 476, 495, 521, 527
Polish Progressive Party, 183n59
Polish Security Service / Office. *See* Ministry of Public Security
Polish Socialist Party (PPS), 152–61, 165, 168, 181–82, 231n39, 240, 257, 264, 267, 303, 324–25, 359, 450
Polish-Soviet War, 186, 190
Polish Underground State, 328, 361, 517
Polish Union of Jewish Students, 456
Polish United Workers' Party (PZPR), 391n133, 398–402, 404, 406, 410–11, 413–15, 417–18, 420, 422, 425–26, 428–29, 433–34, 436–37, 441, 450, 464. *See also* Communist Party in Poland
Polish Uprising. *See* November Uprising
Polish Workers' Party (PPR), 358, 361–64, 371, 373, 384, 387–88
Politburo, 368, 371, 400, 409, 418, 425, 433, 440
Polonsky, Antony, ix, xxin6, xxvi, 43, 190n87, 293, 308n165, 397, 504–5
POP (Podstawowa Organizacja Partyjna), 417–18, 421. *See also* PZPR
Porter-Szűcs, Brian, 83
Posesorski, Leon, 302
Poswol (Pasvalys), xiii
Potocki, Stanisław, 63
Potsdam, 360, 363n36
Power, Samantha, 274n7, 274n10, 275n14, 543
POWs, 192, 302, 306
Poznań, 34, 62
PPS (Polska Partia Socjalistyczna). *See* Polish Socialist Party

PPS Left (Young Faction), 158–59, 161
PPR (Polska Partia Robotnicza).
    See Polish Workers' Party
Praga, district of Warsaw, 62
Preny, 139n121
Princeton University, 468
Privislinskiy Krai. See Vistula Land
PRL (Polska Rzeczpospolita Ludowa).
    See Polish People's Republic
Progressive Alliance, 161
Progressive Democratic Union (Związek
    Postępowo-Demokratyczny),
    160–61
Progressive Jews, 65–68, 72–73, 75, 78, 81,
    97, 100, 102, 106, 112–13, 120–21,
    142, 144–45, 455, 457, 460, 554
Pronin, Georgi, 174
Provisional Government of National
    Unity (TRJN), 358, 360. See also
    Russian Provisional Government
Pruchnik, 473–76, 551
Prus, Bolesław, 116–17, 123
Prussian Empire, xxvii, 4, 50, 62, 66, 68,
    114, 198, 210
Pruszyński, Franciszek Ksawery, 263
Przemyśl, 285, 382
Przytyk, 264
PSL (Polskie Stronnictwo Ludowe).
    See Polish Peasant Party
Puławska faction, 401–2, 404, 406, 409
Puławski, Adam, 328
Puławy, 363
Pulitzer Prize, 542
Purim, 13, 556
Putin, Vladimir, xxiii–xxv, xxxiv–xxxv,
    564
PUWP. See Polish United Workers' Party
    (PZPR)
Pużak, Kazimierz, 359
PZPR (Polska Zjednoczona Partia
    Robotnicza). See Polish United
    Workers' Party

Quint, Alyssa, 248

Rabon, Israel, 186–88
Rachkovsky, Pyotr, 171
Racławice Commune, 300
Raczyński, Edward, 330
Rada Pomocy Żydom "Żegota".
    See Żegota
Radio Free Europe, 401, 439
Radio Maryja, 471, 473, 517
Radom, 264, 319, 426
Radziłow, 294
Raikhman, Lev, 368
Rakosi, Mátyás (née Rosenfeld), 370n56
Rapoport, Nathan, 411, 522–24
Rappaport, Yitzhak, rabbi, viii
Rauschning, Hermann, 278n23
Reconstruction in US, 214, 234n49, 546
Reconstructionist Jews, xxxii, 485
Red Army, 16, 179, 184, 190, 198n3, 222,
    272, 286, 288, 291, 317, 326n43,
    359–60, 368
Red Cross, 191, 325n25
Reform Jews, xiii, 117, 331, 457–58, 460,
    478, 485, 495
Reform Synagogue in Warsaw, 68, 100,
    458
Refusenik, 487
Reiner, Rózia, 300–1
Reinert, Ewa, viii–ix, 552
Reinert, Danuta, viii–ix, 552
Reinert, Henryk, vii–ix, 552
Reinharz, Yehuda, 177n35
Reisman, Moshe, 365
Rejak, Sebastian, ix, 462, 479, 487
Rek, Tadeusz, 237n55
Remarque, Erich Maria, 188
Republican Party in the USA, 20, 53n20,
    234n49, 538, 541–43, 548, 560
Rescuers of Memory, movement, 492–93
Ribbentrop, Joachim von, 272. See also
    Molotov-Ribbentrop Pact

Riga, 226n12, 237
Righteous Among the Nations, title of, 18, 517–18, 524, 532n83
Ringelblum, Emmanuel, 287n77, 315, 320–21, 338, 345, 523
Riverdale, 467
Roberts, Kenneth, 6–7
Rogers, Carl, 451
Rogger, Hans, 173n18
Romania, xxiii–xxiv, 204, 370n56, 407, 469
Romanov, dynasty, xxviii, 82, 85, 87, 92n46, 104–5, 108, 111, 120, 142n5, 143n11, 178
Rome, 39, 104, 131, 145, 274
Romkowski, Roman, 372n60
ROPCiO (Ruch Obrony Praw Człowieka i Obywatela), 433
Roper poll, 271
Rosewood, 220
Rosenfarb, Chava, 341n109
Rosh Hashanah, 453, 458
Rothschild, house of, 136, 175n25
Roosevelt, Theodore, president, 5, 10, 20, 270–71, 331, 357, 360, 481
Round Table Agreement, 442, 464
Rubinstein, student, 416n73
Rucki, Michał, viii
Ruda, Malka, 345
Rudavsky, Oren, 308n164
Rudnicki, Adolf, 365
Rudnicki, Szymon, 235n44
Ruhr, 225
Rumkowski, Chaim, 341–42
Russell, Nicolas, xxxi
Russian Civil War, 169, 179, 190–91, 201, 233
Russian Empire, xiii, xxvii–xxviii, 4, 15, 50, 64, 67n19, 68–69, 83, 91, 92n46, 93, 109, 116, 125, 142, 152, 155, 160, 175n25, 176, 226n12, 232n41
Russian Provisional Government, 179–80, 190. *See also* TRJN

Russian Revolution, 151, 153, 160, 169, 171, 177, 179n45. *See also* Bolshevik Revolution
Russian State Duma, 160–61, 210, 243
Russo-Japanese War, 159, 175n25
Rutherford, Phillip T., 280n30, 284
Rydz-Śmigły, Edward, general, 256
Rydzyk, Tadeusz, priest, 470–72, 517
Rzeszów, 306, 380, 382n96

SA (Sturmabteilung), 271n76
Sachs, Feliks, 158
Sachsenhausen, 280
Saint Alexander's Church, 433
Saint Brigid Church, 438
Saint John's Cathedral, 433
Saint Luke, 431
Saint Nicholas Parish, 389
Saint Petersburg, 91, 109, 125, 143n11, 150, 174
Saint Stanisław, 434
Samet, Michał, viii
Sanacja, movement, 240, 256–58, 262, 264, 266–67, 299
Santo Stefano, 135n105
Saratov, 104
Sapieha, bishop of Kraków, 229
Saxony, 63–64
SB (Służba Bezpieczeństwa). *See* Ministry of Public Security
Schenirer, Sara, 250
Schiff, Jacob, 175n25, 204
Schorr, Moses, 264
Schrag, Peter, 268, 538
Schudrich, Michael, chief rabbi, viii, 454, 459
Schuster, Sandra, x
Schwartz, Barry, xxxiii
Schwarzbart, Ignacy, 329
Schweitzer, Pinhas, 89
Scouts, organization, 459
Screen Writers' Guild, 10

SD (Sicherheitsdienst), intelligence agency of the SS, 335n83
SDKP (Socjaldemokracja Królestwa Polskiego), party. *See* Social Democracy of the Kingdom of Poland
SDKPiL (Social Democrats of the Kingdom of Poland and Lithuania), party, 161
Second Republic of Poland, 3, 17, 127n62, 180, 185, 197, 224–26, 230–31, 233, 244, 246, 247n110, 252, 267
Second World War. *See* World War II
Second Temple, 79, 174, 556
Sejm, 25–26, 47, 50–53, 56, 61, 67, 69, 78–79, 91, 113, 197, 227, 228n22, 231, 233, 240, 242, 252, 264–65, 363n36, 415, 442, 464, 470, 510, 513
Sejm Education Committee, 242
Self-Defense (Samobrona), right-radical group, 509
Selma, 546
Sendlerowa (Sendler), Irena, 324–25, 496, 524, 528
Sendlerowa Award, 496, 528
Sephardi Jews, religious group, xxxv
Shabbatai Zevi, 76n50
Shafran, Rubin, ix
Shakespeare, William, 248
Shamir, Yitzhak, 410n49
Shaw, Martin, 310
Shneiderman, S. L., 365, 383
Shoah, 308, 397, 464, 467, 479–80, 484–85, 522, 558
Shore, Marci, 364n39
Shul-Kult schools, 250n125
Shuman, Burt, rabbi, viii
Shushan, biblical figure, 13
Siberia, 89, 104, 108
Sigismund II Augustus, king, 40

Siedlce, 342n114
Siedliska, 303
Sienkiewicz, Henryk, 389
Sikorski, Władysław, general, 196–97, 358
Silver Shirts, organization, 20, 271n76
Sinai, mount, 14, 79, 397
Sinai, peninsula, 408
Singer, Isaac Bashevis, 247, 494n53
Singer, I. J., 170, 178, 247
Singer, Kalman, 383
Siudak, brothers, 303
Six Day War, 408, 416. *See also* Arab-Israeli conflict
Skamander group, 364, 391n133
Slánský, Rudolf, 370n57
Sławek, Walery, colonel, 256
Sławik, Henryk, 325
Sławoj-Składkowski, Felicjan, 242, 265
SLD (Sojusz Lewicy Demokratycznej). *See* Democratic Left Union
Slezkine, Yuri, 29, 114
Śleszyński, Bolesław, 293, 468
Słomka, J., 225
Slonim, 285
Słonimski, Antoni, 364, 432
Slovakia, xxiv, 469
Smith, Bert, 219
Smoczyński, Joe, viii
Smolar, Aleksander, 416n73, 417n75
Smolensk, 509–10
Smolenskin, Perets, 149
Snyder, Timothy, 16, 309n167, 498
Sobański, Antoni, 261
Sobczyński, Władysław, 298–99, 384
Sobibór, 483
Social Democracy of the Kingdom of Poland (SDKP), party, 153n56
Social Democratic Workers' Party in Russia, 178
Socialist Federation, 153
Socialist Party. *See* Polish Socialist Party (PPS)

Society for the Defense of Freedom and Conscience in Poland (Stowarzyszenie Obrony Wolności i Sumienia w Polsce), 236n53
Society for the Promotion of Birth Control (Towarzystwo Krzewlenia Świadomego Macierzyńsłwa), 236n54
Society for Trades and Agricultural Labour. *See* ORT
Society of Friends of Learning (Towarzystwo Przyjaciół Nauk), 72n38
Sokal, 382
Solarz, Ignacy, 237n55
Solidarity (Solidarność), union and movement, xxix, 423, 439–42, 444, 463, 467n68, 494, 507–8, 522, 533
Sopot, 385, 424
Soros, George, 547n29, 548–49
South America, xxiii, 547n29
South Carolina, 219
Southern Europe, 4
Southern United States, 22n49, 214–15, 218–19, 223, 296, 543, 546. *See also* Jim Crow Laws
Soviet (Eastern) bloc, countries of, xxiii, 17, 22–23, 357, 364, 370n56, 376, 393, 395, 407–8
Soviet-Polish Pact, 334
Soviet Security Service/ Secret Police (NKVD), 361, 369, 401
Soviet Union, xxvii, 10, 22, 180, 198, 246–47, 249, 272n3, 283, 287, 317, 333, 357, 362n31, 368–69, 371, 377, 383, 397, 403, 407–8, 427, 433, 487, 556. *See also* USSR
SP (Stronnictwo Pracy), centrist party, 257
Spain, xxxv, 50, 560
Spiegelman, Art, 485
Sroka, Bronisław, priest, 426

SS (Schutzstaffel), 271n76, 280–81, 283, 319, 335n83, 340, 375n73. *See also* Einsatzgruppen
Stalin, Joseph, 17, 287, 333, 357–60, 362–66, 369–70, 373, 377, 379, 393n141, 397–98, 400, 404, 408n40, 434, 536, 556
Stalingrad, 284
Stampfer, Shaul, 42n70
Stańczyk, Jan, 327n47, 333
Starachowice, 426n11
Stark, Andrea, x
Stark, Arthur, x, 335n82
Staszic, Stanisław, priest, 55, 79, 80, 123–24
Steinhardt, David, rabbi, ix, 485
Stępiński, Zygmunt, ix, 504, 528–31
Stern, Abraham, 72n38
Stola, Dariusz, xxviii, 293n100, 410, 416, 468n72, 530–31
Storm Troopers. *See* SA
Stowarzyszenie Obrony Wolności i Sumienia w Polsce (Society for the Defense of Freedom and Conscience in Poland), 236n53
Strauss, Nathan, 204
Streicher, Julius, 271
Stroop, Jürgen, 375n73
Strzembosz, Tomasz, 470
Stullhoff, 483
Styjkowski, Julian, 429
Sułek, Antoni, 534
Supreme Court, 199, 204, 214–15, 234, 533
Sutzkever, Avrom, 247
Suwałki, 294
Sverdlov, Yakov, 178, 368
Swank, R. L., 187n75
Swartz, Sarah, ix
Swedish wars, 43, 430–31
Światło, Józef, 372n60, 401
Świetlik, Konrad, 372n60

Świętochowski, Aleksander, 116–17, 160
Świętostowski, Wojciech, 261
Świrski, Maciej, 531
Świt combat unit, 298–99, 384
Switzerland, 208n41
Synagogue Council of America, 331n69, 332. *See also* Warsaw Synagogue Council
Syria, xxiii, xxv, 136n107, 408, 537, 539, 547n29, 564
Syrian Civil War, 537
Szacka, Barbara, 478n5
Szall, family, 515
Szapiro, Paweł, 350
Szarota, Tomasz, 309n167
Szaynok, Bożena, 373n62, 374, 377n77, 382n96
Szczawińska, Jadwiga, 439n27
Szczecin, 382, 424, 425n9
Szczepanowski, Stanisław, bishop of Kraków, 434
Szeryński, Józef, colonel, 346
Szic, Adam, viii
Szic, Anna, ix
Szlajfer, Henryk, 414, 416, 417n75
Szmalcowniks, 317–18, 325, 515
Szpilman, Władysław
Szreckenbach, Bruno, 281
Sztarkman, Urełe (Aron), 298
Sztrumpf, Cylka, 303
Sztrumpf, Słupska, 303
Sztrumpf, Szymon, 303
Szuchta, Robert, ix, 498, 501
Szuza, Wojciech, 236n55
Szydłowski, Józef, 363
Szygielbojm, Szmul, 329
Szyldyner, Gershon, 108
Szymaniak, Karolina, 502n78
Szymanóvek, district, viii
Szymańska, Gosia, vii, 455, 458, 462
Szytz, Anna, 461n41

Taglit, program, 459
TAK Skole (school), viii, xii, 494–96, 552
Talaat Pasha, 274n10
Tallahatchie County, 544
Tanenbaum, Natan, 414
Tarbut, school system, 250
Tarnobrzeg, 363
Tarnów, 133n93, 380, 382n96
Taube Center, 502n78
Taylor Green, Marjorie, 541
Tec, Leora, ix, xxvii, 492–93
Tec, Nechama, 320n22, 335n80, 492
Tehran, 357, 358n8
Temple, 134n97, 174
Tennessee, 219, 542
Texas, 219, 541–42
Third Polish Republic, xx, 395, 453, 464, 476, 492, 497, 508, 525, 528, 536
"Thirteen", group, 345–46
Thorkelson, Jacob, 20
Thugutt, Stanisław, 237n55
Till, Emmett, 544–45
Tillich, Paul, 443
Tischner, Józef, priest, 438–39
Tisha B'Av, 556
Tisza-Eszlar, 135
Tokarska-Bakir, Johanna, 297–98, 303–4, 381
Tolstoy, Aleksey, 331n68
Tomaso, priest, Capuchin friar, 136n107
Tomaszewski, Jerzy, ix, xxvi, 18, 110n62, 210n53, 501
Tomaszow Lubelski, 502
Topolski, Krzysztof, 417n75
Torah, xxxii, 14, 59, 75, 77, 79–80, 149, 456–57, 480, 485, 504
Toruń, 471, 517
Toruńczyk, student, 417n75
Towarzystwo Krzewienia Świadomego Macierzyństwa (Society for the Promotion of Birth Control), 236n54

Trade Union Congress, 409
Treblinka, 320–21, 373, 394, 483, 519–20
Tree of Life Congregation, 549. *See also* Ec Chaim
Trepov, D. F., general, 176n31
TRJN ((Tymczasowy Rząd Jedności Narodowej). *See* Provisional Government of National Unity
Trojański, Piotr, 498
Trotsky, Leon, 179, 222, 368, 370
Truman, Harry S., president, 21
Trump, Donald, president, xxii, 234n49, 538–39, 545–48, 550n40, 551, 559
Trunk, Isaiah, 335n81, 350
Trzeciak, Stanisław, priest, 239
Tsarstvo Pol'skoe, 109n53
Tsifranovich, inspector, 191
TSKŻ (Towarzystwo Społeczno-Kulturalne Żydów w Polsce). *See* Jewish Social and Cultural Association
TSYSHO (Tsentrale Yidishe Shul-Organizatsye), 249–50
Tugenhold, Jakob, 73, 91, 96
Tukhachevsky, Mikhail, 198n3
Tulchin, 44n75
Tulsa, 220
Turkey, 274n10, 538
Turowicz, Jerzy, 467
Tusk, Donald, xxv, 509
Tuwim, Julian, 364
Tyszowice, 349

UB (Urząd Bezpieczeństwa). *See* Ministry of Public Security
UK, xxii, 330, 537–38. *See also* England
Ukraine, xiii, xxiii–xxv, xxxv, 9, 32, 39, 41–42, 44, 75, 95, 184, 189, 190n86, 192, 195, 204, 206, 368, 450, 469, 535, 537
Ukrainian People's Army, 189–91
Ukrainian Rada, 190n86
Ulma, Józef, 515
Ulma, Wiktoria, 515
UNESCO, 465
Union of Brest, 39–40
Union of Fighters for Freedom and Democracy (ZBOWiD), 403–4
Union of Independent Socialist Youth (Związek Niezależnej Młodzieży Socjalistycznej), 260
Union of Lublin, 32, 46
Union of Orthodox Rabbis, 331n69
Union of Polish Patriots, 359n11. *See also* Patriotic Society
Union of Russian People, right wing movement, 175n27
Union of Village Youth (Związek Młodzieży Wiejskiej), youth movement, 236n55
Union of Young Polish Democrats (Związek Polskiej Młodzieży Demokratycznej), 260
Union Theological Seminary, 443
United Nations (UN), xxiii, 275–76, 309–10, 330n63, 543
University in Kraków, 44, 257, 500–1
University in Lublin, 501
University in Lviv, 257–58, 260
University of Vilna, 72, 258
University of Warsaw, 72, 92b46, 109, 258–59, 414–18, 501–2, 516, 528
University of Wrocław, 473, 501
Upper Silesia, 195, 340, 389, 495
Ursus, 426
Ursyn, 429
USA, xxiii, xxvi–xxviii, xxxvii, 4–5, 7–10, 13, 19–21, 22n49, 53n20, 72n38, 127, 145, 154, 157n66, 173, 183, 187, 193, 195, 198–200, 203, 205–8, 210n51, 212–16, 218–21, 223, 226, 230, 234n49, 235, 260, 268, 270–71, 274n11, 278, 296–97, 313, 329n59,

331–33, 356, 359, 374n69, 392–93, 397, 442, 446, 452, 455, 457, 473–75, 480–81, 486–87, 489–91, 499, 535, 538–39, 541–50, 553, 556–57, 561, 564. *See also* America
US Congress, 8, 20–22, 199, 215, 220
US National Conference on Lynching, 205n24
US Senate, 53n20, 543, 551n1
US South, 22n49, 214–15, 218–19, 223, 296, 543, 546. *See also* Jim Crow Laws
US War Refugee Board, 20
USSR, 272–73, 287, 291, 333–34, 357n4, 361, 365, 369–71, 377, 390, 401, 405n22, 408, 450–51, 556. *See also* Soviet Union

Va'ad Arba Aratsot (Council of Four Lands), 28, 59, 560
Vac, 325
Vatican, 131, 133–34, 390, 444, 539
Vatican II (Second Ecumenical Council of the Vatican), 444–46, 448–49
Velvet Restoration, 464
Verba, Rudolf, 328n55
Verba Veritatis, organization, 533n84
Versailles, 205, 209, 211–12, 215–16, 220, 231, 272n3
Vienna, 68, 85, 88
Vilna, 72, 76n52, 151, 155n62, 156, 158, 238, 248–49. *See also* Vilnius
Vilna Group (Jewish Social Democratic Group), 151–58, 165, 168
Vilnius, 195, 232, 238, 251, 261, 272. *See also* Wilno
Virginia, 546
Virgin Mary, 39, 430–31
Virgin Mary of Częstochowa, 129
Vistula, river, 359, 370
Vistula Land (Privislinsky Krai), 109, 112
Voice of America, 439
Volhynia, xxv, 42n72

Wałbrzych, 372
Wałęga, Leon, bishop of Tarnów, 133n93
Walentynowicz, Anna, 437
Wałęsa, Lech, president, 423, 425–26, 437–39, 444, 462–64, 508
Wallace, Bonnie, ix
Wallenberg, Raoul, 325
Wardanga, Adam, vii, 461
Wardanga, Józefina (née Jeżowska), vii, 458, 461
Wannsee, 321
Warsaw Citadel, 104
Warsaw Ghetto, viii–ix, xvii, xxi, 11, 19, 287, 315, 318, 321–23, 328, 330, 338–40, 343–52, 375, 392, 411, 459n34, 500, 505, 521–26
Warsaw Ghetto Archive, 287n77. *See also* Ringelblum, Emmanuel
Warsaw Ghetto Uprising (1943), 411, 459n34, 521, 525
Warsaw Main School (Szkoła Główna), 109, 115
Warsaw Orthodox synagogue, 457
Warsaw Synagogue Council, 90. *See also* Synagogue Council of America
Warsaw Uprising (1944), 359, 361–62, 392, 411, 429, 522
Wartheland, 273, 280
Washington, D.C., 219, 480
Wasilewski, Leon, 157
Wat, Alexander, 364
Wąwolnica, 363
Ważyk, Adam, 366–67
We, organization, 20
Webber, Jonathan, 486
Webster, Noah, 72n38
Weeks, Theodore R., ix, 65n11, 99n7, 109n53
Weems, Patrick, 544
Weigl, Barbara (Basia), viii–ix, 494–96
Weinberg, Adolf, 340
Weisman, Jonathan, 268

Weiss, Abraham, 339
Weiss, Avi, rabbi, 467
Weiss, Bernard, ix
Werfel, Katarzyna, 416
Werfel, Roman, 416
Weryński, Henryk, priest, 389
West America, 213n68
West Bank (of Jordan River), 408
West Germany, 22, 411, 415, 418, 441, 524
West Point, 187
West Ukrainian Republic, 192
Western Europe, 23, 27–28, 46, 50, 67, 94, 116, 184–85, 207, 330
Western Ukraine, xxv
Western Wall, 522
Wetzler, Alfred, 328n55
White Army, 177, 179, 184, 190, 195, 201, 299
White House, xxii, 22, 209n47, 548
Wiązowna, 302
Wici, youth movement, 260, 363n33
Wielkopolska (Greater Poland), 27, 32
Wielopolski, Aleksander, marquis, 98–99, 105–7, 125
Wiesel, Elie, 22
Wieseltier, Leon, 296, 297n116
Wieśniak, Stanisław, 264
Wiesztort, Bolesław, 302
Wilhelm (William) II, german kaiser and king, 205n24
Wilno, 195, 258. See also Vilna
Wilkerson, Isabelle, 214
Williamson County, 542n13
Wilson, Woodrow, president, 5, 198, 200, 208–9, 213–16, 220
WiN (Wolność i Niezawisłość), organization. See Freedom and Independence Assocoation
Winawer, Krystyna, 417n75
Wise, Stephen, rabbi, 20, 331, 481
Wiślicz, Eugeniusz, 299

Witelson, Tadeusz, 347
Witte, Sergei Yulyevich, count, 176n31
Wittenberg, Jason, 295–96
Witos, Wincenty, 363
Wiżna, 294
Władysław II Jagiełło (Jogaila), king and grand duke, 32
Wnuk, Rafal, 563
Wodziński, Marcin, ix, 63–64, 67n19, 501, 503
Wohl, Henryk, 107
Wojciechowicz, Stanisław, rabbi, 231n39, 458
Wojdowski, Bogdan, 344
Wojtowicz, Andrzej, 307
Wojtyła, Karol, cardinal of Kraków, 432, 434–35. See also John Paul II, pope
Woleński, Tadeusz, vii, 455–56
Wolf, Lucien, 209n48, 210–11
Wolfke, Mieczysław, 260
Women's Civil Service Union (Związek Pracy Obywatelskiej Kobiet), 236
Woodruff, Elizabeth, nun, 220n95
Woodward, Bob, 538
Workers' Defense Committee (KOR), 426–29, 433, 438–39, 494
World War I, xxviii, 3, 123, 169, 176–77, 179–80, 183–88, 191, 195, 196n113, 198, 203, 216, 220, 226, 243–44, 252, 268–69, 270n73, 285, 311, 317, 367–68, 421, 561
World War II, vii, xiv, xvi, xix, xx, xxii–xxvi, xxviii, 3, 9–11, 15–19, 59, 187n75, 273–75, 279, 299, 310–11, 313, 326, 334, 350n149, 354, 356, 360–61, 362n32, 367, 370, 387, 393, 398, 400, 411, 463, 473, 475–76, 478, 481, 490, 497, 506, 511, 521, 529, 535, 556, 558–59, 561–62
World Union of Progressive Judaism, 455
Woronczak, Jerzy, 501
Writers' Union, 414

Wróbel, Piotr, 293n97
Wrocław, viii, 107, 363, 460, 473, 501, 503, 554
Wujec, Henryk, 427
Wyszyński, Stefan, bishop of Lublin, archbishop, cardinal, 390, 430–33

Yad Vashem, Holocaust museum, 18, 350n149, 480, 498, 516–18
Yalta, 16, 360, 362, 433–34, 556
Yavne, school, 250n125
Yerushalmi, Yosef Haim, xxx–xxxii
YIVO (Yiddish Scientific Institute/ Yidisher Visnshaftlekher Institut), 250–51
Yishuv, 335n80
Young, James E., 522
Young Guard (Hashomer Hatzair), youth movement, 252, 373, 459–60
Young press (młoda prasa), group, 115–16, 118
Youth Legion (Legion Młodych), faction, 236, 260

Zachęta, 264
Zagórski, Jerzy, 391n135
Zaleski, August, 183n59
Zambrowski, Roman, 371, 400, 403–4, 418
Zambrowski, Antoni, 404, 416n73
Zamech plant in Elblag, 424n4
Zamość, 67n18
Zamoyski, Andrzej, 99n4
Zapusty, 303
Żaryn, Jan, 515
Zarzycka, Ewa, 416n73, 417n75
Zawadzka, Anna, 512
Zawiercie, 340
Żbikowski, Andrzej, xxi
ZBOWiD (Związek Bojowników o Wolność i Demokrację). *See* Union of Fighters for Freedom and Democracy

Żegota (Council for Aid to Jews), 18–19, 318, 321, 324–25
Zelenskiy, Volodymyr, xxiv
Zerubavel, Yael, xxxiii
Zevi, Shabbatai, 76n50
Żeligowski, Lucjan, general, 195
Żemiński, Stanisław, 303, 304n144
ŻIH (Żydowski Instytut Historyczny), 287n77, 454, 503
Zhitlovsky, Chaim, 245n104, 246n106
Zhytomyr, 203n19
Zieliński, Henry, 18
Zimmerer, Jürgen, 273
Zinoviev, Grigori, 178, 368
Zionist Conference, 149, 481
Zionist Congress, 149, 177n35. *See also* American World Congress of Jews
Zionist Hashomer Hatzair (Young Guard), youth movement, 252, 373, 459–60
Zionist organization Love of Zion (Ḥibat Tsiyon), 149, 168, 244
Zionist party, 155, 250n125, 252
Zionist party Mizrachi, 244, 250n125
Zionist Workers Party (Po'alei Zion), 244, 315n1
Zipperstein, Steven, 171
Zola, Émile, 147
Żoliborz, 427
ZOOM (Żydowska Ogólnopolska Organizacja Młodzieżowa). *See* All-Poland Jewish Youth Organization
Zoppott. *See* Sopot
ŻUL (Żydowski Uniwersytet Latający). *See* Jewish Flying University
Związek Bojowników o Wolność i Demokrację (ZBOWiD, Union of Fighters for Freedom and Democracy), 403–4
Związek Młodzieży Wiejskiej (Union of Village Youth), 236n55

Związek Niezależnej Młodzieży Socjalistycznej (Union of Independent Socialist Youth), 260

Związek Polskiej Młodzieży Demokratycznej (Union of Young Polish Democrats), 260

Związek Postępowo-Demokratyczny (Progressive Democratic Union), 160

Związek Pracy Obywatelskiej Kobiet (Women's Civil Service Union), 236

Związek Religijny Wyznania Mojżeszowego (ZRWM). *See* Jewish Religious Union

Związek Wolnej Myśli (Polish Free Thought Union), 236n53

Życie (Communist Life), student group, 260

Życiński, Józef, archbishop, 447n110

Żyndul, Jolanta, 265–66